MANAGING SERVICES

Marketing, Operations, and Human Resources

CHRISTOPHER H. LOVELOCK

PRENTICE HALL, *Englewood Cliffs, New Jersey 07632*

Library of Congress Cataloging-in-Publication Data

Managing services : marketing, operations, and human resources
  [compiled by] Christopher H. Lovelock.
      p.   cm.
   Bibliography: p.
   ISBN 0-13-547514-7
   1. Service industries--Management.   I. Lovelock, Christopher H.
HD9980.5.M345 1988
   658--dc19   87-32784
                                                              CIP

Editorial/production supervision: Eleanor Perz
Cover design: Wanda Lubelska Design
Manufacturing buyer: Barbara Kittle

© 1988 by Christopher H. Lovelock

Printed in the United States of America
10   9   8   7   6   5   4   3   2

ISBN 0-13-547514-7 01

Prentice-Hall International (UK) Limited, *London*
Prentice-Hall of Australia Pty. Limited, *Sydney*
Prentice-Hall Canada Inc., *Toronto*
Prentice-Hall Hispanoamericana, S.A., *Mexico*
Prentice-Hall of India Private Limited, *New Delhi*
Prentice-Hall of Japan, Inc., *Tokyo*
Simon & Schuster Asia Pte. Ltd., *Singapore*
Editora Prentice-Hall do Brasil, Ltda., *Rio de Janeiro*

To the memory of
Daryl Wyckoff

CONTENTS

II UNDERSTANDING SERVICES: BREAKING FREE FROM INDUSTRY TUNNEL VISION

III DESIGNING AND DELIVERING SERVICES

IV MANAGING CAPACITY AND MANAGING DEMAND

V THE SEARCH FOR SERVICE QUALITY

VI CUSTOMER SERVICE

VII THE HUMAN DIMENSION IN SERVICES MANAGEMENT

PREFACE

By definition, a book of readings and cases is a collaborative effort. I'm very appreciative of the contributions made by each of the authors and co-authors of the materials in this book—obviously, I think highly of their work! Their names and affiliations will be found in the following section, "About the Contributors." I'm also grateful to the copyright holders for granting permission to reproduce previously published articles and cases, and to my former secretary at Harvard, Beverly Outram, who typed many of my own materials prior to their first publication.

The value added by a book of readings and cases lies not only in bringing together an array of materials previously published over several years in a variety of locations, but also in grouping them in meaningful clusters and in structuring the sequence in which they appear. The framework of this book reflects my experience in teaching courses in service management at the Harvard Business School and, more recently, at Harvard University Extension. Many people helped me in this work, especially James L. Heskett, Theodore Levitt, David H. Maister, Christopher W. L. Hart, and W. Earl Sasser. I learned much, too, from my own students.

My thinking has also been influenced in useful ways by the Marketing Science Institute and the American Marketing Association. MSI, under the leadership of Alden Clayton and Diane Schmalensee, and AMA, under the presidencies of Stephen Brown and Leonard Berry, have played key roles in bringing together academics and managers from different fields to discuss how marketing management in service businesses can be better integrated with other management functions.

Thanks are also due to three reviewers, Professors Jeffrey S. Conant, Texas A&M University, Raymond P. Fisk, Oklahoma State University, and Nancy L. Hansen, University of New Hampshire, who provided valuable suggestions for enhancing this book. I'm grateful, too, to Whitney Blake, Eleanor Perz, and Allison DeFren at Prentice-Hall for their assistance in bringing the volume to publication.

Finally, I would like to pay special tribute to the late D. Daryl Wyckoff, a friend and colleague at the Harvard Business School, who died in 1985 at the age of 47. Daryl, who held the James J. Hill Chair of Transportation, was one of several Harvard faculty members who helped to pioneer the application of production and operations management techniques to service businesses. Having earlier taught Management of Service Operations at Harvard, Daryl was scheduled to take over the Service Management course from me in January 1985. My last memory of him is at a meeting we had in his office the previous December to discuss his plans for the course.

No one who had ever been in Daryl's office at Harvard could easily forget it. It epitomized his zest for life—which he knew might be cut short early—and his enthusiasm for his field. Glowering at the visitor from the opposite wall was a gold-framed oil portrait of James J. Hill, founder of the Great Northern Railroad. Decorative Chinese artifacts in red and gold, souvenirs of his visits to the Far East, hung from the high ceiling. A large poster advertised the Twentieth Century Limited as it was in the heyday of U.S. rail travel. There were model trains and model aircraft, two of the latter bearing the colors of Midway Airlines, of which he was a director. Linking his interests in both railroading and restaurants was a collection of British railway memorabilia, presumably acquired through his association with the Victoria Station restaurant chain, whose board he also served on.

Although visibly ailing on this occasion, Daryl spoke with enthusiasm about some innovations he planned for the course, including several sessions on service quality based on his own work in this field. His article "New Tools for Service Quality" (reproduced in Part V of this book) had just been published, and the two of us had used some of the concepts and tools it presented when teaching together in a corporate seminar some months earlier. Sadly, health problems prevented Daryl from teaching the course, and less than two months later he died. Had he lived, he would surely have had a major impact on how managers approach the task of improving service quality. This book is dedicated to his memory.

CHRISTOPHER H. LOVELOCK

About the Contributors

Author and Editor

• **Christopher H. Lovelock** is principal of Christopher Lovelock & Associates. Based in Cambridge, Massachusetts, he specializes in consulting and executive education for large service businesses. From 1973 to 1984, Dr. Lovelock was on the faculty of the Harvard Business School, where he developed courses in Marketing of Services and Service Management. He has also taught at Stanford and the University of California at Berkeley. A native of Great Britain, he graduated with a B.Com. and an M.A. in economics from Edinburgh University, later obtaining his M.B.A. from Harvard and Ph.D. from Stanford. He has written or co-authored twelve books and numerous articles and cases—including six of the readings and nine of the cases reproduced in *Managing Services: Marketing, Operations, and Human Resources.*

Authors of the Readings

- **John E.G. Bateson** is senior lecturer in marketing at the London Business School and has taught at Stanford. His research and consulting emphasize marketing of services.
- **Leonard L. Berry** is Foley's/Federated Professor of Retailing and Marketing Studies at Texas A&M University. He has done extensive research in the area of service quality. His books include *Marketing Financial Services: A Strategic Vision* (Dow Jones-Irwin, 1985).
- **Richard B. Chase** is professor of decision systems and director of the Center for Operations Management, Education and Research at the University of Southern California. He has written widely on service operations management.
- **William H. Davidow** is a general partner of Mohr, Davidow Ventures, a high technology venture capital firm. He has spent more than 25 years working in high technology industries and is author of *Marketing High Technology: An Insider's View* (The Free Press, 1986).
- **Thomas A. DeCotiis** is a partner in the consulting firm of DeCotiis Erhard, and Associates.
- **Pierre Eiglier** is on the faculty of the Institut d'Administration des Affaires, Universite d'Aix-Marseille, France. He is also active as a consultant with the Service Management Group in Paris.
- **Jack Falvey** is a business consultant and writer based in Londonderry, New Hampshire.
- **Kevin Farrell** writes for *Venture* magazine.
- **Mortimer R. Feinberg** is chairman of the board, BFS Psychological Associates, New York.
- **Christopher E. Gagnon** is a member of the M.B.A. Class of 1988 at the Amos Tuck School of Business Administration, Dartmouth College.
- **James L. Heskett** is 1907 Foundation Professor of Logistics at the Harvard Business School and the author of *Managing in the Service Economy* (Harvard Business School Press, 1986).
- **Casey Jones** is president of Gamma Vision, Inc., a professional firm that has developed a guest relations video test now used by many hospitality companies to select personnel.
- **Stephen Koepp** writes for *Time* magazine.
- **Eric Langeard** has served on the faculty of the Institut d'Administration des Entreprises, Universite d'Aix-Marseille, France. He has also taught at the University of Texas and the University of California and is active as a consultant with the Service Management Group in Paris.

- The late **Aaron Levenstein** was professor emeritus of management, Baruch College.
- **Donald H. Light** is principal of D.H. Light Consulting Services, Menlo Park, California. His practice emphasizes distribution strategy.
- **David H. Maister** is president of Maister Associates in Boston. He is a specialist on managing professional service firms and has written extensively on this topic. Previously he served on the faculty of the Harvard Business School.
- **Richard Normann** is chairman of the Service Management Group, an international research and consulting firm headquartered in Paris. He is also author of *Service Management: Strategy and Leadership in Service Businesses* (Wiley, 1984).
- **A. Parasuraman** is professor of marketing at Texas A&M University. He has worked extensively in the area of service quality.
- **James Brian Quinn** is the William and Josephine Buchanan Professor of Management at the Amos Tuck School of Business Administration, Dartmouth College. He is an author and consultant in technological and strategic management.
- **Roger W. Schmenner** is associate professor of operations and systems management at the School of Business, Indiana University, Indianapolis. He has published widely in the field of production and operations management.
- **Benjamin Schneider** is professor of organizational behavior at the University of Maryland. He is also active as a consultant, particularly to financial service firms.
- **Gregory L. Schultz** writes for *Service Management* magazine and focuses on improving customer support services in high technology industries.
- **Ronald K. Shelp**, a business executive, writer, and lecturer, is vice president of Celanese Corporation in New York. He is author of *Beyond Industrialization: Ascendancy of the Global Service Economy* (Praeger, 1981).
- **G. Lynn Shostack** is managing director of The Coveport Group, Inc., a New York based consulting firm. Previously a senior vice president of Bankers Trust Company, she has published several articles on managing service delivery processes.
- **Michael R. Solomon** is associate professor and chairman, Department of Marketing, School of Business, Rutgers, The State University of New Jersey.
- The late **D. Daryl Wyckoff** was James J. Hill Professor of Transportation at Harvard Busi-

ness School at the time of his death in 1985. A specialist in the transportation and hospitality industries, he was a director of several companies.

- **Valarie A. Zeithaml** is visiting associate professor at Fuqua School of Business, Duke University. She has written extensively on consumer evaluation of services and on service quality issues and has consulted to major service companies.

Authors of the Cases
(if not previously listed above)

- **Clifford Baden**, Director of Programs in Professional Education, Harvard Graduate School of Education.
- **George B. Beam**, former casewriter, Colgate Darden Graduate School of Business Administration, University of Virginia.
- **Colin Carter**, former research assistant, IMEDE, Switzerland.
- **David A. Collier**, former associate professor,

Colgate Darden Graduate School of Business Administration, University of Virginia.
- **Shauna Doyle**, former research assistant, Harvard Business School.
- **Sula Fiszman**, former research assistant, Harvard Law School.
- **James R. Freeland**, professor of business administration, Colgate Darden Graduate School of Business Administration, University of Virginia.
- **John Klug**, former research assistant, Harvard Business School.
- **Robert J. Kopp**, assistant professor, Babson College.
- **Penny Pittman Merliss**, former research associate, Harvard Business School.
- **Rocco Pigneri**, former research assistant, Harvard Business School.
- **Kelley S. Platt**, M.B.A. Class of 1982, Fuqua School of Business, Duke University.
- **Marvin Ryder**, professor of marketing, McMaster University, Canada.
- **W. Earl Sasser**, professor of business administration, Harvard Business School.

INTRODUCTION

In October 1987, the world's stock markets endured what some wags described as "market meltdown," followed by a period of great volatility. This volatility was blamed, in part, on the impact of computerized trading technologies, innovative financial products, and a rapidly evolving global marketplace.

Managers of service businesses can be forgiven for feeling that the entire service sector has been going through an extended meltdown in recent years—not in the sense of a sudden decline, but more from the standpoint of the fast-changing shape and composition of service industries and radical changes in the ways in which they do business.

Consider some of the indicators:

• New airlines come and go with great rapidity, while some long-established firms adopt major changes in route structure and operational strategy or are merged out of existence.

• Financial service firms expand into banking, brokerage, and insurance activities that were previously denied them, as brokers and insurance companies muscle in on the bankers' turf.

• Realty firms and restaurants, once the epitome of local "mom-and-pop" operations, go nationwide.

• Large manufacturing firms derive a third or more of their revenues from the service businesses that they operate.

• The old healthcare system of hospitals and doctors' offices is augmented—and in part displaced—by a complex array of delivery systems that now embraces health maintenance organizations, out-patient surgicenters, chains of small walk-in medical centers, and expensive diagnostic equipment that travels by truck from one location to another.

- Service organizations once owned by the government are transformed into private enterprises, especially in Europe.
- Consumers everywhere decry an alleged decline in service quality across a broad cross-section of industries, lamenting the loss of the personal touch.
- Without intervention by service personnel, consumers conduct financial or other information-based transactions accurately and near instantaneously across thousands of miles.

FORCES FOR CHANGE

Why is the service sector in such a state of flux? What are the forces for change, the ingredients for success? Among the factors transforming the service sector of the economy are the following:

Reduced government regulation, especially in the United States, has already eliminated or minimized many constraints on competitive activity in such industries as airfreight; airlines, railroads, and trucking; banking, securities, and insurance; and telecommunications. Barriers to entry by new firms have been dropped in many instances, geographic restrictions on service delivery have been reduced, there is more freedom to compete on price, and existing firms often find themselves able to expand into new markets or new lines of business.

Relaxation of professional association standards, often under pressure from government agencies, has made it possible for professional service firms to engage in advertising and promotional activities that were previously prohibited. Among the types of professionals affected by such rulings are accountants, architects, doctors, lawyers, and optometrists, whose firms or practices now engage in much more vigorous competitive activity than previously.

Privatization of public corporations has been moving ahead at speed in a number of countries, with Great Britain being the most notable example. The transformation of such operations as national airlines, telecommunications services, and natural gas utilities into private enterprise services has led to restructuring, cost-cutting, and a more market-focused posture.

Computerization and technological innovation are radically altering the ways in which many services do business with their customers—as well as what goes on behind the scenes. Data-based services, such as information and financial service firms, are seeing the nature and scope of their businesses totally transformed by the advent of national (or even global) electronic delivery systems. But technological change affects many other types of services—from airfreight to hotels to retail stores. Implications include creation of new or improved services, ability to maintain more consistent standards through centralized customer service departments, replacement of personnel by machines for repetitive tasks, and greater involvement of customers in operations through self-service.

The growth of franchising is seeing large franchise chains replace or absorb a vast array of atomistic service businesses in fields as diverse as bookkeeping, car rentals, haircutting, muffler repair, plumbing, printing, quick service restaurants, and real estate brokerage. Among the implications are creation of mass media advertising campaigns to promote brand names nationwide (and even worldwide), standardization of service operations, formalized training programs, an ongoing search for new products, continued emphasis on improving efficiency, and dual marketing programs directed at customers and franchisees respectively.

The expansion of leasing and rental businesses represents a marriage between service and manufacturing businesses. To an increasing degree, both corporate and individual customers find that they can enjoy use of a physical product without actually owning it. Long-term leases may involve use of the product alone—such as a truck—or provision of a host of related services at the same time. In trucking, for instance, full-service leasing provides almost everything but the driver, including painting, washing, maintenance, tires, fuel, license fees, road service, substitute trucks, and driver safety programs. Personnel, too, can be rented rather than employed directly.

Service profit centers within manufacturing firms are transforming many well-known companies in fields such as computers, automobiles, and electrical and mechanical equipment. Ancillary services once designed to help sell equipment—including consultation, credit, transportation and delivery, installation, training, and maintenance—are now offered as profit-seeking services in their own right, even to customers who have chosen to purchase competing equipment.

Financial pressures facing public and non-profit organizations are forcing such organizations to cut costs, develop more efficient operations, and pay more attention to customer needs and competitive activities. Faced, in many instances, with declining sources of free or inexpensive labor (such as that provided by volunteers or members of religious orders), many nonprofit agencies are having to take a more businesslike approach to recruitment, training, and motivation of managers and staff members.

The internationalization of service companies is readily apparent to any tourist or business executive traveling abroad. Formerly domestic airlines and airfreight companies now have foreign route networks. Numerous financial service firms, advertising agencies, hotel chains, fast-food restaurants, car rental agencies, and even hospital groups now operate on several continents. This strategy may reflect a desire to serve existing customers better and/or a goal of penetrating new markets. Most Americans would be surprised—even shocked—to discover how many well-known service companies in the United States are owned by foreign investors (a direct consequence of massive trade deficits).

IMPLICATIONS FOR MANAGEMENT

Although no service organization is affected by all of these factors, few are untouched by any of them—and none will remain untouched. There's an old Chinese curse that wishes its recipient, "May you live in a time of change." Caught up in the turmoil of change, many managers must yearn for the good old days, when the behavior of competitors was more predictable—even implicitly agreed upon, when customers or clients were less demanding and more loyal, when

employees could be relied on to spend their entire careers within the same organization (or at least the same industry), when government regulations and professional standards discouraged both new market entrants and service innovations, and when established ways of creating and delivering services remained just that: established.

Many of the factors described above have served to stimulate competition, which, in turn, places a premium on encouraging innovation and improving cost efficiency. New technologies often provide solutions to both problems. But technology may require heavy capital investments, redefinition of jobs, and hiring or retraining of workers to ensure that the necessary human resources are available to operate and manage the new technical resources.

To recover these upfront investments, the service firm needs higher profits. Some profit improvement may come from cutting operating costs, but revenues also need to be increased. Effective marketing may enable the firm to grow by improving and expanding its product line, targeting new market segments, seeking new distribution and delivery systems, and employing both pricing and advertising strategies to expand its market share.

Increased size of operations—whether through internal growth, franchising, or mergers—allows service suppliers to achieve economies of scale. Capital expenditures can then be spread over a larger base of market transactions. At the same time, the firm can hire staff specialists to provide a long-term, strategic perspective and expert assistance to operating managers whose principal focus is on solving day-to-day problems.

Not every service organization is growing: some have cut back their operations in order to focus on the needs of specific types of customers, to specialize in certain types of services, and/or to reduce costs. Yet the survivors in most service industries will have to transform themselves in order to remain competitive and to incorporate modern technology. The service organization that emerges from this transformation will require a different and more sophisticated approach to management than its predecessor.

KEY DIFFERENCES BETWEEN MANUFACTURING AND SERVICE ORGANIZATIONS

Service industries have dominated most Western, industrialized economies for more than a quarter of a century. Yet policy makers, economists, and management educators have tended to focus on manufacturing, agriculture, and natural resources. It's only recently that the challenging task of how to manage service organizations more effectively has finally begun to attract the attention that it deserves.

Are the management skills developed in manufacturing organizations *directly* transferable to service organizations? I think not. Although there are some generalizable principles, it's my belief—and that of many other researchers and practitioners—that management tasks in the service sector differ from those in manufacturing industries in several important respects. As we shall see later in some of the readings, the differences are most marked in what might be termed the "front office," where customers interface with the service operation. "Back office" operations, by contrast, may be sealed off from the customer and managed in ways that are often not unlike a manufacturing plant. The major focus of this book will be on managing the front-office aspects of service businesses.

Among the characteristics distinguishing services management from manufacturing management are the nature of the product, the involvement of customers in the production process, greater importance of the time factor, difficulties in achieving and maintaining quality standards, the absence of inventories, and the structure of distribution channels. Let's look briefly at each, while recognizing that not all of these generalizations apply with equal force to all services.

Nature of the product. In contrast to manufactured goods, which are physical objects, services are performances which tend to be produced in real time—and often in the presence of the customer. Managing the creation and delivery of a performance is very different from managing the production and distribution of a manufactured product, which may be turned over to a wholesale or retail intermediary (a service business in its own right) for resale to the end user.

Customer involvement in production. Performing a service involves assembling and delivering the output of a mix of physical facilities, equipment, and mental or physical labor. In many service industries, customers are actively involved in helping to create the service product—either by serving themselves (as in laundromats, self-service cafeterias, or banks with automatic teller machines) or by cooperating with service personnel in settings such as full-service restaurants, hair salons, hotels, colleges, and hospitals.

Importance of the time factor. Many services are delivered in real time. Customers have to be present to receive service from airlines, hospitals, haircutters, restaurants, and many other types of organizations. There are limits as to how long customers are willing to be kept waiting for service to be provided; further, that service must be delivered expeditiously so that customers do not spend longer receiving service than appears reasonable to them. Even when the service operation takes place in the back office, customers have expectations about how long it should take to complete the task—whether it be repairing a machine, completing a research report, cleaning a suit, or preparing a legal document.

Quality control problems. Manufactured goods can be checked before they leave the factory, long before they reach the customer. But many services are consumed as they are produced, with final assembly taking place under real-time conditions. In these types of services, where the front office is the dominant portion of the service operation, the customer literally enters the service factory; both service personnel and other customers may become an integral part of the service experience. These factors make it hard for service organizations to control quality and offer a consistent product.

No inventories for services. Because a service is a deed or performance rather than a tangible item, it cannot be inventoried. The necessary equipment, facilities, and labor can be held in readiness to create the service, but these simply represent productive capacity, not the product itself. Unused capacity in a service business is a wasted asset. Demand that exceeds the firm's capacity to serve at any given time represents lost revenues that may never be recouped. An important task for service managers is to find ways of balancing supply and demand without the aid of inventories to act as a buffer.

Different distribution channels. Unlike manufacturers, which require physical distribution channels to move goods from factories to customers, service businesses either use electronic channels (as in broadcasting or electronic funds transfer) or else combine the service factory, retail outlet, and point of consumption into one. In the latter instance, service firms find themselves responsible for managing customer contact personnel (rather than contracting out this task to retail intermediaries). They may also have to manage the consumption behavior of their own customers to ensure that the operation runs smoothly and that one person's behavior doesn't irritate other customers who are present at the same time.

SCOPE OF THE BOOK

As the title of this book suggests, effective management of service businesses requires the integration of three key functions—marketing, operations, and human resources. Each function can be examined independently, of course, but effective implemen-

tation requires ongoing coordination between these three. In manufacturing firms, by contrast, marketing usually takes over only after the product leaves the factory gates, and it's the rare organization where production and operations personnel have direct contact with the customer on a regular basis.

The book is divided into eight parts:

• Part I—The Challenge of Services
• Part II—Understanding Services: Breaking Free from Industry Tunnel Vision
• Part III—Designing and Delivering Services
• Part IV—Managing Capacity and Managing Demand
• Part V—The Search for Service Quality
• Part VI—Customer Service
• Part VII—The Human Dimension in Services Management
• Part VIII—Organization and Integration

The sequencing of these parts reflects my experience in teaching courses and seminars in services management. The early parts provide an understanding of the service sector and a framework for analyzing service organizations. Later parts address specific management issues. Finally, Part VIII focuses on organizational issues and on how to integrate marketing, operations, and human resources.

With the exception of Part I, which is composed of readings only, the several readings in each part are followed by two or three cases. These cases are intended primarily for class discussion, but many of them are also useful and interesting for individual study. Brief synopses in front of each reading and case are designed to help the individual reader to identify materials of particular interest. There is an index at the end covering both readings and cases.

PART I
The Challenge of Services

The Service Economy Gets No Respect

RONALD K. SHELP

Many people still see service jobs as low paying and menial, service production as low in productivity and labor intensive, and service industries as parasitic. The author dispels these and other misconceptions, and emphasizes the importance of developing policies to nurture today's service-dominated economy.

As a businessman dedicated to developing international rules for services trade, I often get invited to the world's great spas where the movers and shakers hold their meetings. At places like Ditchley Park outside Oxford and Bellagio on Lake Como, I have raised with some very distinguished economists the basic question of whether the rule of comparative advantage in international trade applies to services. One can almost see the lights go on. Several participants seem to be reckoning that in the answer to that question may lie some future Nobel Prize.

You'll recall the rule of comparative advantage from basic economics says that countries should concentrate on producing whatever they can make most efficiently, based on their mix of land, labor, and capital, relative to other countries. But who remembers service examples ever being used to illustrate this principle? I always studied widgets. There seems to be an entire intellectual tradition of not thinking about services in our economic framework.

The second part of this intellectual tradition logically follows from the first: A bias has actually developed against services. Both Adam Smith and Karl Marx have at least one thing in common: They agree that services are parasitic. Marx and Smith describe services as living off those "productive" activities of the economy. This dogma has actually been put into practice in the Soviet Union and in certain other Socialist countries. Their economic measuring system is called the "Material Product System." Therein many services are not counted as contributing to production or wealth creation but instead are viewed as serving a welfare function. Services are seen only as a means to transfer wealth from the productive areas of the economy to the nonproductive.

This long neglect and bias against services was well summed up by the man whom many view as the father of service economics, Colin Clark, the Australian economist. Clark has said, "The economics of tertiary industries remain to be written. Many as yet feel uncomfortable about even admitting their existence."

Many American leaders seem to want the service economy to simply go away. The head of a large bank recently defined a service economy as one in which we take in each other's laundry. Former Secretary of State Henry Kissinger has been quoted as saying that a great nation cannot depend upon fast-food franchises for its survival. "The United States cannot turn itself into a service-industry country," Kissinger reportedly declared a few years ago.

"When you sell an insurance policy or a hamburger, you simply don't create the ripple of growth that happens when you manufacture an automobile, a steel pipe, or even a toothpick," argues Paul Tippett, chairman of American Motors. By the same token, New York investment banker Felix Rohatyn dismisses the service economy as a myth. "Is it rational, in the name of the mythical 'free market,'" Rohatyn asks, "to let our basic industries go down one after the other in favor of an equally mythical 'service society' in which everyone will serve someone else and no one will be making anything?"

The reality is that we already are a service economy and have been one for more than 40 years. However, we think about our economy, and develop policy to influence it, as if we were still strictly an industrial economy.

According to economists, a service economy is one in which more than one half the workers earn their livelihood in service industries. We became that kind of an economy in 1950, and today 73 percent of all working Americans are employed in service industries. So service employment has grown almost 50 percent since the United States first became a service economy.

We are a service economy by other measures as well—for example, the contribution of services to GNP. Today, 67 percent of U.S. production comes from service industries, an increase of about 33 percent since 1950.

The trend is equally apparent in our international commerce. In 1982 the United States had a $36-billion surplus in services trade. You probably did not hear much about that because most of the focus was on the deficit in goods trade.

These facts indicate just how much services have come to dominate our economy. Do the measures we use to gauge how the economy is doing reflect the trend?

Consider the leading economic indicators that come out every few weeks. One is the average manufacturing workweek. Others are new orders for plant and equipment, inventory levels, commodity prices. Are these measures really sufficient for an economy in which 73 percent of the people work in services and 67 percent of the GNP is produced by services?

This vision of our economy is held by others besides the government. On Wall Street the Dow Jones Industrial Average is the beacon that tells the rest of the world how capitalism is doing. Yet it was only recently that the first financial-services firm, American Express, was added to the Dow Jones list of 30 companies. There are one or two other service firms on it—Sears Roebuck, for example—but basically, the Dow Jones Average uses industrial firms to measure how the stock market is doing.

How many citizens are aware that between 1975 and 1982, while the news bemoaned the huge merchandise trade deficits, we actually had an overall balance of payments surplus in five out of eight of those years because of the mammoth services surplus? This same orientation toward goods trade permeates our perspective in dealing with our specific trading problems, for example competition from the Japanese. I wonder how many are aware that we actually have a services surplus with Japan.

This legacy explains why we are uncomfortable about being a service economy. The problem has led to a series of myths about our economy and about services.

Myth No. 1: A service economy produces services at the expense of other sectors.

This assertion makes about as much sense as arguing that an industrial economy produces only manufactured goods or an agricultural economy only agricultural goods. It is wrong to assume that because the proportion of jobs and output in the service sector has been growing, the American economy will ultimately produce nothing but services. In fact, the opposite is true. In the past 20 years, while service jobs have increased dramatically, so have manufacturing jobs. It is true that most of the new jobs in the statistics for manufacturing industries represent white-collar, front-office workers. Today, after a recession in which several million manufacturing jobs were lost, we have more workers employed in manufacturing than we did 20 years ago.

It is important to remember that with all of our problems we continue to be competitive in manufacturing industries. More than 20 percent of all U.S. industrial exports are from manufacturing industries, and one out of every six workers owes his job to manufacturing exports.

What is happening is exactly what occurred in agriculture between 1910 and 1981. Although the number of people in agriculture declined in that time from 10 million to 3 million, our production went up some 220 percent. Today, we are the greatest agricultural producer in the world, and yet we have relatively few farmers doing the producing. Similarly in manufacturing, although the percentage of American workers employed in this sector may continue to decline (but not necessarily the number of workers), our total industrial production

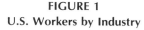

FIGURE 1
U.S. Workers by Industry

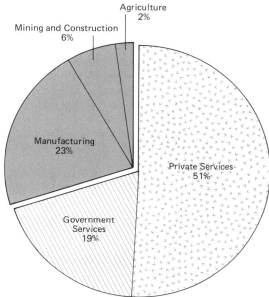

Note: The percentages of full-time employees in each sector includes part-time workers who have been lumped together in full-time units. Fractions have been rounded off and thus the sum comes to more than 100 percent. Other measures, which include other categories of workers, put the total majority of those in services at 73 percent.

SOURCE: U.S. Department of Commerce, Bureau of Economic Analysis.

should increase, especially if the appropriate technology is brought to bear.

Myth No. 2: Service jobs are low-paying and menial.

This view is reinforced by articles like th[e] one that appeared on the front page of *[The] New York Times* last year headlined, "Big [?] supplants Big Steel." The piece implied [that] unemployed steel workers had only o[ne al-] ternative in a service economy—sellin[g] burgers.

The intuitive support for this m[yth is the] belief that service workers are m[ostly wait-] bers, bootblacks, and sales clerk[s. A Labor] Department survey in 1982 seem[ed to show] that wage levels of service work[ers are lower] than those of manufacturing [workers, but] the data are not very accura[te] ment admits that only one third of firms covered in the wage survey are service firms. Further, the questionnaire is directed toward manufacturing, and service firms have trouble answering it. For example, it tries to distinguish between supervisory personnel and assembly-line workers. In a service firm, the person answering the questionnaire is supposed to decide if a computer programmer is a supervisory or nonsupervisory position. But service firms do not keep personnel records in the same way as manufacturing firms, so they either respond inaccurately or do not respond at all.

More than half of all service workers in this country are in highly skilled, white-collar occupations—lawyers, bank managers, and so forth. Yet the official data help support the conclusion that steel workers are paid better than these kinds of service workers.

Between 1977 and 1980, employment in fast-food franchises and eating and drinking establishments increased 18 percent. During the same period, business-service employment increased 32 percent, with computer and data processing up 64 percent. These kinds of jobs are thus more representative of work in a service economy.

Myth No. 3: Service production is primarily labor intensive and low in productivity.

That belief is disputed by a fascinating
nt study by the Department of Labor
ked 145 industries according to cap-
it of output and capital-labor rand that the majority of service
among the 20 percent that
intensive. There was not
in the least capital-in-

rable speculation
erican produc-
the shift to
er part of
hat ser-
ases
ger
clines
goods-
uld be at-
roducing in-

Myth No. 4: The growth of government in recent decades is the reason we are a service economy.

Long before President Reagan, the number of people employed in government was declining. Some three years ago we became a service economy without government. In other words, more than 50 percent of Americans work in private service industries.

If these myths can be dismissed, it will help focus economic analysis and policy-making. Fiscal policy is an excellent case in point.

Both Presidents Reagan and Carter had a business-tax policy predicated on more liberal depreciation provisions and credits for investment in plant and equipment to prime the economy. The proposal that was introduced by President Carter was signed into law by President Reagan, although in somewhat different form. But what do these tax advantages do for the economy if the majority of services, even the capital-intensive ones such as advertising and finance, invest little in plant and equipment? Was it the intention of the President to reallocate capital away from the service sector toward the industrial sector, or had it never been considered?

The tax cuts for individuals proposed by both Presidents also ignored the importance of services in the economy. Under President Reagan we have the three-phase supply-side tax cut. President Carter had his infamous $50 tax rebate. The idea in both cases was to stimulate demand. But for what?

The implicit thinking was to stimulate demand for durables. In service economies, however, people tend to spend more and more of their discretionary income on services instead of goods. Could the tax cut have thus inadvertently spurred the development of the service economy instead of doing what was intended? Is a $50 or $100 tax refund more likely to be spent on buying a Chinese dinner than applied to the purchase of a car or refrigerator? These are the questions that seem to never be asked in the policymaking process.

Our nearsighted, virtually exclusive focus on manufacturing and on high-tech tends to

make us forget about the problems of service industries. For example, how much attention has been given to protectionism abroad in services, compared with protectionism that hurts more traditional industries? The U.S. Trade Representative's office has compiled a list of some 200 pages of barriers that services face abroad. Have we tried to eradicate such barriers with the same indignant zeal with which we address steel subsidies or dumping of television sets?

An increasing number of foreign countries are placing restrictions on transborder data flows (TBDF) or, more simply stated, the movement of information across international boundaries. So, for example, if a firm wishes to transmit information from one country to another, it will encounter difficulties plugging into national systems. France has considered taxing computer tapes as they go across the border—not just on the value of the tape but on the value of the information thereon. These are but two examples of a series of restrictions that, if not brought under control, could affect the future competitiveness of many American service, manufacturing, and agricultural companies.

Similarly, has the current deregulation craze been carefully thought through to determine its impact on services? Recently, the U.S. trucking industry was deregulated. Immediately, Canadian and Mexican truckers could start competing with U.S. truckers, although Americans cannot do the same in Mexico and Canada because deregulation has not occurred there.

Other trends need to be closely examined. For example, everybody has always assumed that services are recession proof. While this has generally been accurate, it was not true in the last recession, for the first time. In the summer of 1982, just before we began to emerge from the recession, there were 400,000 service jobs lost between June and September.

The technological change occurring in service industries will have a dramatic impact on service jobs. Peter Drucker has estimated that word-processors, electronic banking, and other technological innovations will eliminate 15 million service jobs by 1996. That will have extraordinary implications for certain communities, especially cities like New York.

Yet another trend still only dimly perceived is that the linking of computers and telecommunications now permits much of service production to occur virtually anywhere. Citibank illustrated what can happen by moving its credit-card operations to South Dakota. But this technology also allows relocation of service production to Taiwan, Argentina, Korea, or the UK.

The relationship between high-tech and services has been largely overlooked. It is the computer industry that has spun off one of the fastest-growing service markets, computer software, which in just 15 years has become a $22-billion-a-year industry. Similar developments will occur in other countries.

These developments illustrate the changing mix in American industry. Consider Honeywell: Today, it is estimated that some 30 percent of its revenue comes from services, yet we think of it as mainly a high-tech manufacturing company. General Telephone and Telegraph has earned more than half of its revenues from services since 1974. In 1982, 10 industrial companies left the *Fortune* 500 to become service companies. That led *Fortune* to create its much vaunted list of 500 service companies.

So there is a quiet but dramatic evolution underway in American business. It makes distinguishing between service and nonservice firms more difficult, somewhat artificial, and less relevant. In short, it is time we faced up to the reality of the economy we have, instead of the economy we wish we would have but have not had for 40 years.

Will Services Follow Manufacturing into Decline?

JAMES BRIAN QUINN AND CHRISTOPHER E. GAGNON

Although new technologies have restructured most service industries, they have also made them more vulnerable to competitive attacks. Managers need to understand technical and competitive forces in order to boost service performance and finesse foreign competitors.

Although they probably know better, many executives still think of the service sector in terms of people making hamburgers or shining shoes. These images belie the complexity, power, technical sophistication, and economic value of activities that now account for more than 68 percent of the nation's GNP and 71 percent of its employment. Worse, they help perpetuate a set of myths about service industries that lead managers and policymakers to ignore their full potential. Worse still, such inattention and complacency threaten to undermine the competitive ability of these industries at a time when their importance to the national economy has never been greater.

Services are actually all those economic activities in which the primary output is neither a product nor a construction. Value is added to this output by means that cannot be inventoried—means like convenience, security, comfort, and flexibility—and the output is consumed when produced. Table 1 suggests the scale and power of services in the United States.

Now more than ever, we need a vital service sector. To suffer the beating there that we have already endured in manufacturing

TABLE 1

Components of U.S. Gross National Product

	BILLIONS OF 1985 DOLLARS
Total GNP	$3,998
Agriculture, forestry, and fishing	$ 92
Mining and construction	305
Manufacturing	796
Total products sector	$1,193
Transportation and utilities	$ 268
Communications	109
Wholesale trade	277
Retail trade	375
Finance, insurance, and real estate	627
Other services	639
Total private services sector	$2,295

SOURCE: U.S. Department of Commerce, Bureau of Economic Analysis. Revised figures, August 1986. The $510 billion difference between the sum of these two subtotals and GNP is predominantly government expenditures.

would be a national disaster. Even so, we dither and deny while warning signs appear. It is no small matter that net positive trade balances in services have fallen steadily since the beginning of the decade—from $41 billion in 1981 to $21.4 billion in 1985. Of the total, business services declined more than $9.3 billion between 1981 and 1985, when the net balance was a meager $0.2 billion. The most serious losses have occurred in travel and transportation-related industries. Although U.S. airlines have maintained a steady 38 percent to 40 percent of the world's revenue passenger miles during the past decade, its once powerful international carriers, Pan Am and TWA, have fared poorly at the hands of foreign competitors like Swissair and JAL, which have made heavy long-term investments in their fleets and paid close attention to the quality of care given passengers.

The threat to other services is real and immediate. These confrontations are not limited to markets abroad; we can lose over here too. Many U.S. markets for services are no safer from foreign competition than were domestic markets for manufactured goods. Indeed, foreign direct investment in the U.S. service sector has exploded since the mid-1970s, although the rate of increase has slowed a bit in recent years. It is sobering to realize that many of the great names in services—names like Twentieth Century-Fox, Stouffer's Hotels and Restaurants, Intercontinental Hotels, Saks Fifth Avenue, Gimbels, Marshall Field, Spiegel, A&P, Grand Union, and Giant Food—have foreign owners now. Even Goldman-Sachs has a new partial owner from abroad.

U.S.-based services offer even more opportunity for growth—and for mismanagement—than product-based industries did in the past. While there is still time, it is essential to take a hard look at how we think about services, how we manage them, and how much they contribute to the nation's economic health.

FACING THE FACTS

Many views of services do not jibe with the facts:

- Contrary to popular opinion, services are not responses to marginal demands that people satisfy only after they meet their product needs. People value services at least as highly as they do manufactured products and purchase them in much less cyclical patterns than manufacturers.
- Service companies produce value added at comparable or higher rates than do product companies.
- The service sector is at least as capital-intensive as the manufacturing sector, and many industries within it are highly technological.
- Service industries tend to be as concentrated as manufacturing and to have companies of sufficient scale to be sophisticated buyers and even producers of technology.
- Service industries lend themselves to productivity increases great enough to fuel continuing real growth in per capita income.

Services substitute directly for manufactured products across a wide spectrum. Few customers care whether a computer accomplishes a function by a hardware circuit or by its software. If anything, they may prefer the software approach—especially when, as

FIGURE 1
PIMS Value Added

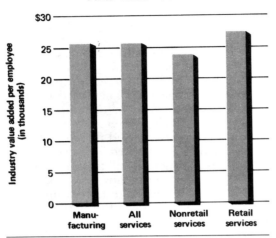

Note: This index is derived from an industry survey and calculations from the Profit Impact of Management Strategy (PIMS) data base. Strategic Planning Institute, Cambridge, Mass.

with CAD/CAM, it substitutes for production machinery at a fraction of the cost. In much the same way, self-service at retail levels can lower real costs for manufactured goods as much as can savings in the production process itself.

Such substitutions boost productivity and value added in real, concrete terms. In fact, our data indicate that measured value added in the service sector is at least as high as in manufacturing. (See Figure 1.) Moreover, services are less cyclical than manufacturing. In the last two decades, employment in services has advanced on average 2.1 percent during economic contractions and 4.8 percent during expansions. In contrast, in the goods-producing sector, employment has declined an average of 8.3 percent during recessions and increased only 3.8 percent during expansions. (See Figure 2.) These figures mean that people will stop buying many products before they will sacrifice service essentials like education, telephones,

FIGURE 2
Recession Resistance of Service Sector

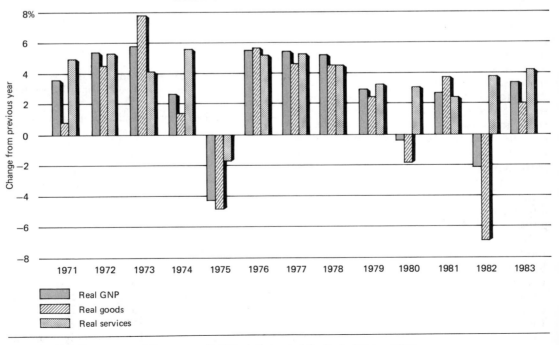

SOURCE: U.S. Department of Commerce, *Statistical Abstract of the United States,* 1984.

banking, health care, and police and fire protection.

Nor, as the evidence shows, is the service sector less labor-intensive or technologically based than manufacturing. Capital stock per service worker has been rising since the mid-1960s and has already surpassed that for manufacturing workers, and some service industries—notably rail and pipeline transportation, communications, public utilities, and air transport—are among the most capital-intensive of all industries.[1] In perhaps the most complete study of relative capital intensities in U.S. industry, nearly half the top 30 industries—out of 145 surveyed—were services.[2] Figure 3, based on the profit impact of management strategy [PIMS] data base, confirms these findings.)

The service sector is also a major market for high technology. The most recent studies available show that some 80 percent of the computing, communications, and related information technologies equipment sold in the United States during 1982 went to the service sector and that in Britain 70 percent of all computer systems sold in 1984 went to the service sector.[3] Contrary to the current stereotype that the service sector is much too small and diffuse to buy large technological

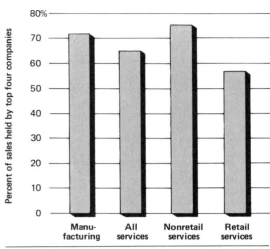

FIGURE 4
Concentration in Service Sector

SOURCE: PIMS data base, Strategic Planning Institute, Cambridge, Mass.

systems or to do research on its own, PIMS data suggest that concentration in the service sector is comparable to that in manufacturing and that, at the margin, services are about as attractive to capital as manufacturing is. (See Figure 4 and Figure 5.)

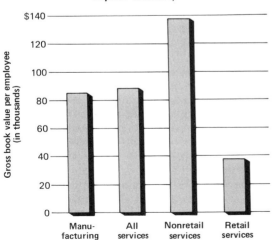

FIGURE 3
Capital Intensity

SOURCE: Calculated from PIMS data base, Strategic Planning Institute, Cambridge, Mass.

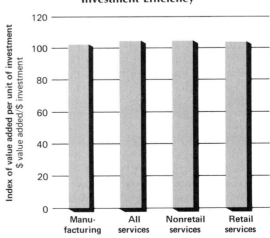

FIGURE 5
Investment Efficiency

SOURCE: Calculated from PIMS data base, Strategic Planning Institute, Cambridge, Mass.

TABLE 2

Productivity Increases in Service Sector

	PERCENTAGE OF AVERAGE ANNUAL IMPROVEMENT	
	1960-1983	*1970-1983*
Telephone and communications	6.1%	6.8%
Air transportation	5.8	4.5
Railroad (revenue traffic)	5.1	4.8
Gas and electric utilities	2.7	1.0*
Commercial banking		0.9†
Hotels and motels	1.6	0.8

*1981 data.

†1982 data.

SOURCE: Bureau of Labor Statistics, Office of Productivity and Technology.

Service industries have both the financial power and the structural rationale to buy technology as needed. Large banks, insurance companies, airlines, utilities, communications companies, hospitals, and retail chains all have the scale not only to purchase technology but also to help manage its conception, design, and development.

In turn, these combined infusions of capital and technology can raise levels of service productivity and per capita national income ever higher. According to the latest available studies, between 1975 and 1982 there was a 97 percent increase per service worker in new technology investment, which resulted in many service industries achieving significant productivity improvements.[4] In others, where improvements have not yet been impressive, the potential for productivity-enhancing automation remains quite high. (See Table 2.)

NEW TERMS OF COMPETITION

Although the effects of deregulation complicate the picture, most experts agree that new technologies have restructured the service industries extensively in recent years. Unfortunately, these technologies have also made the industries vulnerable to the same modes of attack that earlier so rapidly un-

dermined the nation's manufacturing capability. If executives understand the relevant technical and competitive forces, they can take advantage of some powerful opportunities to boost service performance and help develop switching and entry barriers that shut out foreign competitors. If executives do not comprehend these potentials or if they act with the complacency of manufacturing managers a decade ago, they will leave major portions of the U.S. economy wide open to foreign incursions.

What restructurings has technology brought? And what are their implications as opportunities or points of attack?

Economies of Scale

Every service industry we studied reported important new economies of scale driven by the application of new technologies. The first-order effect in most cases was a revised competitive structure characterized both by increased concentration and by increased fragmentation, niching, or segmentation. To realize the potential scale economies of new technologies, many intermediate and large companies in each service industry merged to form giant enterprises. But within each industry smaller companies also identified local niches—or specialized service needs—and concentrated successfully on these.

In the rental car industry, for example, the large companies, in conjunction with the airlines, could initially lock up virtually any long-distance traveler with their instantaneous guaranteed reservation systems. They even had international subsidiaries or affiliates connected electronically. Soon, niche operators proliferated under this pricing umbrella. Automated computer and telephone answering devices allowed both "superelegant" and "Rent-A-Wreck" extremes to serve local markets with office-in-the-home operations, and midsize operations like Alamo and Agency could segment target groups with particular needs like cut-rate and conference rentals.

Automation of the securities trading process, to cite another example, changed the entire structure of that industry in the mid-1960s and early 1970s. Under the old paper-based system, shares traded had to be physically delivered from the seller's agent to the buyer's. As daily volumes approached 12 million shares, only the big banks could hire and manage enough people to keep track of their securities trades each day. Smaller firms began to fail because they could neither control nor process their securities in a timely fashion.

Finally, Wall Street firms formed Central Certificate Services (later the Deposit Trust Company), which brought essentially all securities certificates under one roof. Rather than having to move shares physically, a single set of accounting entries could change their ownership. After five or six years, the system became totally electronic and smaller brokers could tie into the depository. Today, such automated clearinghouses handle virtually all private and government transactions.

New technology has also had scale effects on medical care. Because of the reimbursement system first in use, the original effect of capital-intensive technologies was to centralize treatment in the larger hospitals. Small practitioners and hospitals did not have enough patients to be able to afford constant updating of their diagnostic, surgical, and recovery equipment. This centralization led specialized medical practices to form around the biggest hospitals and spurred the creation of regional referral centers to handle particularly difficult cases. As a result, many smaller hospitals suffered, closed down, or joined cooperative networks with the larger centers.

The average cost of an inpatient stay soared from $729 in 1972 to $2,898 in 1984, when diagnosis-related group restrictions began to shift cost patterns. With patient care growing ever more impersonal in the large centers, new and less costly distribution systems have begun to emerge along both vertical (home care, primary care, specialty care) and horizontal (pediatrics, obstetrics, dermatology, internal medicine) axes. Such complex alternative systems as electronically linked HMO networks have grown almost ten times

in number since 1971, and the number of people they serve from 3.1 million to more than 13.6 million. Ambulatory surgical centers have exploded from 400 in 1982 to 1,200 today.

Management of these complex service systems has become so critical a factor in the health care industry that large private companies have found it profitable to apply their skills to both hospitals and other parts of the system. To obtain scale economies, insurance companies have integrated forward into health care management and some hospitals have begun to offer insurance.

Economies of Scope

Beyond its important effects on scale, technology often creates powerful second-order effects—economies of scope—that allow entirely new service products to move through established networks or systems with little added cost. Once debugged, communications and information-handling technologies permit the distribution of a much wider set of services to a more diffuse customer base, yet they often actually lower marginal costs on old products as equipment, development, and software investments are allocated over a broader base of applications. In addition, such new technologies frequently offer further strategic benefits in terms of more rapid new-product introduction or faster response to competitors' moves.

When Federal Express started its overnight small-package delivery business, it developed advanced computer communication systems to link its couriers' trucks with dispatchers. To prevent inflight delays, it installed the most up-to-date civilian flight-control system available. To track, control, and handle its packages and to manage its operations efficiently, Federal created its COSMOS electronic network. With these major subsystems in place, the company could, as opportunities arose, add overnight document delivery, large packages, international services, and finally, two-hour ZapMail document delivery, with costs lower than those of competitors.

Insurance companies first automated their backroom activities in the mid-1960s when their industry was stable and heavily regulated. Handling premium billings and collections brought them dramatic productivity gains. When wildly fluctuating interest rates hit the industry a decade later, the companies had to alter their products rapidly to attract new premiums and to offset the effects of customers borrowing against their policies at low interest rates. In such an environment, only companies with flexibly designed computer and control systems could design or deploy their products quickly enough to get a competitive edge. Previously, insurance companies had brought out new rate books only every three to five years. Successful industry executives said that without effective electronic and software systems, they could neither have conceived of the variety of new products needed in the 1970s nor have explained and introduced them to their widespread agent and customer bases.

Many smaller insurance companies, which could not afford the huge costs of sophisticated electronic networks, attest to this fact. They failed, sold out, merged, or concentrated on localized or specialized services falling outside the interests of larger companies.

Given both scale and scope economies as well as the relatively low expense of transporting services internationally, large technologically sophisticated U.S. companies like Citicorp and a deregulated AT&T should have powerful international advantages. But there is no reason to be complacent. The same is true for certain foreign competitors. Large Japanese and European banks have already expanded into U.S. markets. NEC has carved out a potent position at the crucial interface between computers and communications. And large European and Asian distribution companies have proved they have the talent and resources to acquire and manage underperforming U.S. retail networks.

Complexity

Technology in services permits the management of new levels of complexity. Law firms, for instance, can in a matter of hours complete more exhaustive background searches, prepare more intricate contracts, and document resulting settlements more thoroughly than they previously could in weeks. Computer models and data base networks allow specialists of all sorts to analyze much more complex problems. So powerful are some of these technologies that in some research fields, they can identify critical relationships and pose new hypotheses, not merely assist in analyzing and testing data. For instance, computerized models can now suggest feasible structures for complex but as yet unknown proteins, and gene machines can manufature them within hours for initial testing against potential antigens or biological insults.

On a broader scale, the velocity of transactions in monetary exchanges and commercial activity has increased so much that without well-developed electronic support systems, it is impossible to compete effectively in many markets. For example, annual world trade in products and services is perhaps $2.5 trillion to $3 trillion, but Eurodollar transactions alone aggregate some $75 trillion. A major stock exchange is open somewhere in the world all but six hours in the workweek, and these markets are instantly accessible from almost any point on the globe.

The shortened transaction times, heightened volatility, and sheer complexity inherent in these transactions simply overwhelm older modes of doing business. But the technologies that make such systems possible also have their own side effects, which further undermine established terms of competition, strategic management, and even economic policy-making. International capital markets are so closely tied together that it may be impossible for one country to create cost-of-capital advantages for its companies through its policy actions. Control of national economics may become equally problematic.

Within companies, the effects of complexity reinforce economies of both scope and scale. Companies can deliver better and more varied services with no significant cost penalties. They can simultaneously achieve a high degree of segmentation in their activities and lower their costs. Computerized reservation systems allow airlines to analyze their costs and their customers' buying behavior in such detail that they can optimize margins on each type of demand and meet each competitor's response. The resulting crazy quilt of prices leads customers to concentrate more on services provided, which offers the major carriers further opportunities to segment with services like specialized meals, wheelchairs, committed seat assignments, luggage verification, and even counseling for nervous passengers. Yet within a wide range of activities, marginal costs can actually drop as systems overheads are allocated over a wider base.

Similarly, bar-code scanners give retailers instant feedback on their sales and inventory movements—hence opportunities for much more control over inventory, margins, and even operating costs. Some retailers now go a step farther and sell this information to help suppliers and manufacturers fine-tune their own strategies. Their sophisticated information systems enable major chains to stock "superstores" with a variety of products that were previously uneconomical to keep under one roof and to branch out into retail drug, home center, mail order, or small specialty chains that may have higher value-added potentials.

Boundary Crossing

Still another effect of technology on competition in services is to break down many of the traditional boundaries among these industries. Some of the most obvious examples are in financial services. Many consumers now use their banks and brokers almost interchangeably because neither is seriously restricted in its scope of operations and consumers no longer care which intermediaries handle their investments. As a consequence, banks, insurance companies, and brokerage houses increasingly offer a similar range of financial products and services and compete head to head on the basis of location, knowledge, and cost.

At the same time, retailers and manufacturers like GM and Ford have also parlayed off their strengths in consumer credit to present similar financial service offerings. Their actions have eroded the distinction between financial services and product marketing to the point that the two are inseparable. In fact, General Motors Acceptance Corporation's $75 billion in assets and $1.02 billion in profits (more than one-fourth of the parent's earnings in 1985) have made it the nation's largest single holder of consumer debt.

The implications of information services technologies for competitive strategy in product-oriented companies like Exxon and Boeing are equally profound. These companies' profits can be made or devastated by how well they develop and deploy knowledge about supplier costs, new technologies, exchange rates, changing regulations, swap potentials, and political and market sensitivities. In the aggregate, more money is often made in the goods sector through information and services than through production activities. In fact, one study shows that about three-quarters of the total value added in the goods sector is created by *service* activities within the sector.[5]

Services and production are becoming so widely substitutable that distinctions between the sectors seem more arbitrary than helpful. Executives and policy analysts often view activities like product design, market research, accounting, and data analysis as product costs if they are carried out within manufacturing concerns but as services if they are provided externally. Internal salespeople are classified under manufacturing employment, but external sales representatives and wholesalers are called service providers. If a farmer harvests his own grain, the costs are production costs; if the farmer hires a professional combine operator, the activity is a service.

Measuring the service component of international trade is even more complicated. If a U.S. bank has a loan officer in its British subsidiary who relies heavily on analyses developed in New York for a deal consummated in London, is this an export? A return on investment abroad? Or just a local sale of services? In manufacturing, how much of a company's overseas income is due to its products rather than the embodied technology, training, systems, or service support the company extends from its U.S. base?

International Competitiveness

Perhaps the most crucial impact of service technologies will be on international trade. True, in 1980 worldwide service exports were only about 3.7 percent of GDP and those of the United States were only 1.4 percent. But worldwide service trade was growing at a 19 percent rate—much greater than world production's 14 percent growth rate.[6] In 1985, some 18 percent of the world's trade was in measurable services, whereas 49 percent was in manufactures and 33 percent in other goods.

First, service and support technologies related to products contribute much of their total value. Second, services have also vastly restructured the international manufacturing marketplace. Communication technologies, of course, permit manufacturers to coordinate their design, sourcing, distribution, and manufacturing strategies on a worldwide basis to minimize costs. But other services have affected manufacturers' costs and global trade patterns even more.

Cheaper and more flexible transportation systems have loosened geographic constraints on production and encouraged the transfer of skills, technology, and manufacturing knowledge among countries. Containerization and new onboard storage techniques (like that for liquefied natural gas) have made extensive world trade possible for such things as fragile high-technology goods, volatile chemicals and gases, and certain bulk items like coal. Computerized navigation and satellite communications systems have lowered transportation risks and insurance costs and allowed instant redeployment of in-transit inventories like oil to maximize margin gains.

Some consequences, though equally far-reaching, are less clear. In earlier years, the improvement of service-related technologies permitted manufacturing to migrate from industrialized countries to developing areas, where labor or materials costs were lower.

In the near future, however, these same technologies may place an even higher competitive premium on staying physically close to the marketplace to respond more rapidly to customers' service needs. This situation could lead to the "remanufacturing" of Western countries.

For example, at GM, Saturn's planned five- to eight-day cycle from order to delivery of an options-loaded vehicle may make it difficult for foreign plants to compete. The same may be true of just-in-time inventoried products throughout the U.S. production system. Japanese auto companies building cars in the United States are already bringing their suppliers here for just this reason. In the years ahead, manufacturing may actually return to the older industrialized economies because of the services needed to satisfy customers in a highly diffuse marketplace, where rapid and flexible responses create high-value premiums.

The inescapable fact is that services have become a critical cost dimension of a nation's manufacturing competitiveness. Services can dramatically raise or lower the real cost of producing goods domestically—through differences in transportation, communications, financing, insurance, and health care costs. Efficiency in these sectors also improves the real wealth of laborers for any given wage level and thus relieves upward cost pressures. While the Japanese have been superb in certain mass manufacturing fields, their productivity (in terms of GNP per person) has consistently lagged behind that of the United States, largely because we have a more productive service sector. (See Table 3.) Properly used, U.S. services offer our manufacturers unique international competitive advantages.

SOWING FOR THE HARVEST

The United States has painfully learned that its goods-producing industries are vulnerable to challenge from abroad. So too are the services on which much of the nation's economic health depends. Technology-driven changes in how these industries compete

TABLE 3
Productivity of Service Sector in United States and Japan

	VALUE OF OUTPUT PER LABOR HOUR*				UNITED STATES AS A PERCENTAGE OF JAPAN
	JAPAN		UNITED STATES		
	1970	*1980*	*1970*	*1980*	*1980*
Private domestic business	$ 3.59	$ 6.01	$ 9.40	$10.06	167%
Agriculture	1.37	2.38	16.53	18.36	771
Selected services:					
Transportation and communications	3.86	5.66	9.29	13.14	232
Electricity, gas, and water	14.01	19.74	21.98	25.38	129
Trade	2.88	4.53	6.88	7.92	175
Finance and insurance	6.69	12.03	8.21	8.20	68
Business services	3.39	3.60	7.69	7.59	211
Manufacturing	3.91	8.00	7.92	10.17	127

*In constant 1975 dollars.

SOURCE: *Measuring Productivity: Trends and Comparisons*, from the First International Productivity Symposium, Tokyo, Japan, 1983 (New York: UNIPUB, 1984).

provide great opportunities, to be sure, but they also open the door to new threats. It is difficult for well-run service establishments to maintain their competitive advantages when everyone can buy the same hardware and software and connect into the same networks and when suppliers of these new technologies have strong incentives to sell their products as widely and quickly as possible. Seemingly secure markets may be easy to invade.

The resulting losses could be tragic. On the one hand, our policies of deregulation in communications and financial markets may have given us a lead that, some say, other countries' more regulated sectors will find it difficult ever to close. But there is little room for complacency. Deregulation also opens domestic U.S. markets to foreign competition. And many countries and foreign companies have proved that their skills in managing service enterprises are formidable indeed—note only the Swiss PTT and Japan's NTT, Oberoi Hotels, Swissair and Singapore airlines, Barclays Banks and Lloyd's Insurance, and the spreading influence of the Japanese tourist and banking industries.

It will take hard and dedicated work not to dissipate our broad-based lead in services,

as we did in manufacturing. Many of the same causes of lost position are beginning to appear. Daily we encounter the same inattention to quality, emphasis on scale economies rather than customers' concerns, and short-term financial orientation that earlier injured manufacturing. Too many service companies have been slow to invest in the new market opportunities and flexible technologies available to them. They have stayed with their old concepts too long and have concentrated on cost-cutting efficiencies they can quantify rather than on adding to their product value by listening carefully and flexibly providing the services their customers genuinely want. Haven't we heard this once before?

The cost of losing this battle is unacceptably high. If service industries are properly nurtured, they will grow and generate much of America's future wealth. If they are misunderstood, disdained, or mismanaged, the same forces that led to the decline of U.S. manufacturing stand ready to cut them to pieces. With some 70 percent of the U.S. economy already in services—not including the three-fourths of all manufacturing costs that represent support services—the stakes are immense. It can happen here.

Notes

[1]Stephen Roach, "Information Economy Comes of Age," *Information Management Review*, January 1985, p. 9.

[2]Ronald Kutcher and Jerome Mark, "The Services Sector: Some Common Misperceptions Reviewed," *Monthly Labor Review*, April 1983, p. 21.

[3]Richard Kirkland, "Are Service Jobs Good Jobs?" *Fortune*, June 10, 1985, p. 38; and "Information Makes the Money Go Round," City of London survey, *The Economist*, July 6, 1985, p. 5.

[1]*U.S. National Study on Trade in Services* (Washington, D.C.: Office of the U.S. Trade Representative, December 1983), p. 24.

[5] Ibid., p. 21.

[6]Ibid., pp. 13, 16; "The World Is Their Oyster: A Survey of International Banking," *The Economist*, March 16, 1985, p. 5; *Euromoney Yearbook 1983* (London: EuroMoney Publications Ltd., 1983), sec. 1.3.

The Coming Service Crisis

WILLIAM H. DAVIDOW

Quality of service is about to become the decisive factor in corporate survival. Manufacturing firms will increasingly find that the services added to a physical good constitute the basis of competitive differentiation. Good service, tailored to customer needs, is particularly important for high technology products.

The storm clouds have begun to gather for the next great business clash between American firms and their overseas competitors. This time the battleground will be *service*.

We have been through this before, and most painfully with our Japanese counterparts. The first war was fought over manufacturing costs. Firms that could not keep their costs down and thus compete on retail price were obliterated. Look at pocket calculators. Video games. Computer memory.

The second battle—one the semiconductor industry will never forget—was about product quality. This threw the U.S. chip business into a tailspin from which it only recently recovered.

Now, before we have a chance to catch our breath, the fight is about to be joined again. Quality of service is about to become the decisive factor in corporate survival.

Service. It may seem like a rather prosaic, secondary field for such momentous events —but that is precisely the cavalier attitude we all share that has made service the Achilles heel of most businesses. Our neglect has set the stage for a life-threatening struggle.

So what? You might ask. Service is no big deal; I'll just add a few more people to maintenance, extend the warranties and put in a toll-free phone. Easy.

Not so easy. I submit that offering good service is one of the most difficult jobs in

"The Coming Service Crisis" by William H. Davidow, as published in the October 1986 *Field Service Manager*.

business. We only think it is easy because we *don't* know what service really is. *Believe me, great companies of the future do—and they are perfecting it.* That is why we are again heading towards the day, much like that devastating moment in the mid-1970s when H-P berated U.S. semiconductor makers for low quality, when we suddenly discover that competitors are once again beating the hell out of us in an area where we didn't even know we were competing.

What is service? Let me give a definition that will surprise you by its scope: 'Service is those things, which when added to a product, increase its utility or value to the customer.'

Amazed? Where's the mention of the 80-page manual and the extended service contract and the new delivery trucks and all the rest of the minor appointments we classify as service? They're in that definition . . . but there are a lot of other things like:

- Maintenance and repair.
- Customer information, such as application notes, delivery information, training and documentation.
- Improved administrative interface (i.e. ordering and billing).
- Performance to delivery commitments.
- Quick resolution of quality and application problems.
- Well trained and friendly customer support staff.

Wait a minute, you may be asking, outside of product development and manufacturing you've just about listed my whole business.

That's right. Now you see why you should start worrying.

If you cannot look at the above list without wincing, don't feel bad. You are in the majority. I have been there myself. You can call this section "A True Confession About Bad Service."

I joined Intel in 1973, and my first job was to take over the $100,000 per month 'design aids' business. It was not the most popular department at Intel—considered something of a backwater, as a matter of fact—but I believed in it. I thought I saw a

way to make design aids one of Intel's most important businesses.

My conversations with customers convinced me that what was really needed was in In-Circuit Emulator (ICE), sort of an X-ray machine for microprocessors. After quite a bit of convincing and lobbying, we finally got the go-ahead to build it.

The ICE was an instant hit. Sales skyrocketed, until orders were four times what we had forecast. We started moving 400 systems per month—a $100 million annual rate—and walking all over our competition.

We slapped each other on the back for the brilliance of our plan. We'd train our customers at our training center, sell them a development system to speed the design process, send in an application engineer to help with their application problems at the component or system level, and then sell them the microcomputer parts. We had a complete product and the best service in the industry.

And we were in for a very rude awakening.

As with any product, to remain competitive we had to upgrade, incorporate the newest technology. This was our Series II. We had fifty of these new models running like Swiss watches in our lab, so we were convinced the product was as solid as could be. We started shipping.

Within days the phone was ringing off the hook. Systems were failing everywhere.

The manuals were so inaccurate that if a customer were to follow it the machine wouldn't work. The drop in humidity with the approach of winter made matters even worse because the system was so sensitive to static that a well-charged engineer would wreck his or her newly-designed program.

It was at this moment that we realized just how lousy our service was. I learned five great lessons:

1. A service-oriented attitude will not assure good service. With all the problems in the design of our Series II, our service people could not have helped the hapless customers no matter how hard they tried.

2. If you eliminate the need for service, you are

giving good service. We had terrific—great—service on the original model because it worked so well it never needed service. Our customers assumed we had good service because they never had to call upon it.

It took a long time to pull ourselves out of this crisis. President Andy Grove even had to ask Chairman Gordon Moore to help me. We began with a program of quick fixes to level off the failure rate. Then, with some breathing room, Intel embarked on a program to design quality into its systems products. That was my next lesson:

3. Good service requires an excellent service infrastructure—that means training your employees, documentation, spare parts distribution, and most of all, enbuing everyone in the company with an attitude towards quality. In some companies this takes five to ten years. Some companies never get it.

It would take me several years, and a few more corporate battles to learn the final two lessons about service. After the above, the reader should find both self-evident:

4. Serviceability must be designed into a product.
5. Giving good service is a strategic problem.

As I said at the beginning of this article, the competitive battleground in high technology (as well as most businesses) has begun to shift. With the increasing standardization of products, technological innovation as the decisive competitive factor gave way to price. Price in turn, as profits were squeezed, gave way to quality. Now, with most of the world's competitors comparable in the quality of their products, the competition will shift to two new areas, service and marketing (the latter the subject of another discussion).

There is another explanation as well for the growing pre-eminence of service. It is that the world is becoming more complicated. Technology may be more powerful and more efficient than in the past, but it is also more difficult to service. For example, I used to be able to tune my 1961 Volvo myself; now even the dealer doesn't seem to be able to tune my new BMW.

The cost of technical service on high tech products now runs an estimated 1 percent per month. That's about one-half the price of the product in just four years and that

doesn't count the cost of down time in lost productivity—a manufacturing line for example might be shut down.

Try fixing your own VCR or compact disc player. Or try using a computer program without adequate supporting documentation or training. You will quickly appreciate why service has become so important.

Good service is intangible, yet it is of great value. It differentiates products that have grown more alike. It commands large price differentials. That should be enough to convince you right there.

Here's another nice characteristic: it lends itself nicely to economies of scale. A single applications note or manual can serve one or a million units.

But there is a down side as well. Good service can't be experienced until after the product is owned or purchased. Perception of service is all important. That's why people buy IBM, Mercedes and L. L. Bean. It takes a long time to gain that kind of reputation —and just a few blunders to lose it.

Do you give good service? Look around your company. How many indifferent or callous retail sales or service people does your company employ?

How many customer complaints are really ever answered?

How often does the company president actually deal with specific customer problems?

Would your company sacrifice short term revenues on a new product by holding back its introduction until the service program is in place.

Good service is not the result of a memo or a newly drafted corporate objective. It begins with the man or woman at the top setting an example, continues with the ongoing participation of management and ends with a corporate environment that demands good service be provided to the customers by all employees.

If you say that can't be done, look around you at examples from other industries. Why is it that the employees at Hyatt Hotel are so universally pleasant while their counterparts at other chains are as often as not indifferent? Why does Nordstrom's do so well at a time when other department stores are failing?

These firms have been successful because they recognize that an environment promoting service has a strategic value.

One of the most often heard raps against improving service is that it is expensive, that customers won't pay the incremental cost.

I submit the opposite is true. If they had to, customers would pay the difference . . . but in fact, good service, especially when combined with its antecedent of good quality, is actually *cheaper*.

Remember my experience at Intel. When you have high quality, as I did with the first product, the cost of giving good service is all but nil. High quality means complaint departments become smaller, fewer spare parts are needed, there are fewer inquiries about delivery problems. Good service *makes* money when quality is high.

But consider the flip side. It is impossible to provide good service on a low quality product. The service organization, no matter how large, soon becomes swamped. Customers become frustrated by the endless breakdowns. Worst of all, they quickly lose any loyalty they had to the product or its manufacturer. Just ask Xerox: 'good' service became 'bad' when higher quality copiers came along.

Quality and serviceability *must* be designed into a product. You cannot go back later. Sure, you say, but we do that at my company. Are you sure? Think about all the software programs introduced each year that are written in such a way as to be all but impossible to maintain and update. Remember the Chevy Monza in which you couldn't reach the spark plug? A dumb mistake, right? Well, Ford just did the same thing with the Aerostar. And I certainly can't throw stones. Remember that Series II of mine? You couldn't get to its power supply.

In conclusion, I appreciate that I have given few pragmatic solutions for how to deal with the impending service crisis. But unfortunately, the solution will vary with the company and its industry.

At least, I hope that I have convinced you of the pressing need to analyze your company's service program; to break out of the narrow-mindedness of perceiving service as merely repair and instead see it as a central part of the company's strategic competitive program.

All of us, no matter what our professions or industries, are in the business of satisfying our customers. Furthermore, most of us are committed to remaining in these roles and positions for the long-term. And that means we will have to fight.

The great warriors of the past, Alexander, Caesar, Napoleon, Patton, always tried to pick their ground to do battle. If those men were manufacturers, retailers, or restauranteurs today, they might well decide to fight on service. Some Japanese have already made such a decision. Your competitors down the street may be doing the same thing.

Side Bar 1

First, businesses start out competing with one another based on technology, if I can make steel and you can't, I get all the orders. But that situation never goes on for very long and pretty soon other people discover how to make steel and the technology becomes widely diffused. Say we have a situation where the battleground then shifts to cost, and cost is a weapon that we are all very familiar with in Silicon Valley. That's the weapon the Japanese have used in steel, ship building, television and radios. It is also the weapon the Koreans are using in steel, ship building, television and radio today. But after awhile a parity has been achieved in cost, because everybody learns how to manufacture about as well as everyone else or some kind of barriers get set up by governments that enable less efficient producers to exist. Once parity is achieved on the basis of both cost and technology, the battleground shifts to quality. That is the newest business craze that is sweeping companies in the world and it is as well, sweeping the world in consumer markets where customers and consumers have become more quality conscious and less cost sensitive.

Businesses now understand very well the cost of quality and I think most companies are rapidly achieving parity in the quality area today. I'm sure we'd expect to see the world competition shifting to a different area and the area it is going to end up in is the area of service and marketing. I think that service is going to become one of the most crucial areas of marketing in the future. And there is good reason for this because the importance of service to your customers is increasing. Think about our increasingly sophisticated products that can't be used effectively today without good service.

Side Bar 2

In the past, we have erred on the side of too narrow a definition for service. When I look at companies, they have Manufacturing Departments that build things, Engineering Departments that engineer things, Marketing Departments that sell things, and Quality Departments that insure the quality of your product going out the door. But I would submit to you that not one company that I know of has a comprehensive service department today. And as I look at most of these companies and most of these service issues, I would like to suggest to you that most of them fall clearly in the hands of marketing.

Side Bar 3

I have one example of a company that is giving bad service and I've chosen this example because it has disobeyed all five rules. It's not a manufacturing company, the company is People Express; they are giving bad service today. Department of Transportation complaints on People Express run 10.3 per 100,000 passengers, twice the rate of Pan Am, who I'm not too happy about. From November to January, they failed to board or denied boarding to 28,600 passengers; seven times the rate of Eastern Airlines which I feel is one of the worst. They are losing 14,000 bags a month and may make some of their customers unhappy. On the other hand, only 57 percent of their planes arrived on time during the month of March which made the ones who had their bags unhappy as well.

Side Bar 4

A good service attitude starts at the top and I would like to quote an interview that Mr. Burr, President of People Express had with Leslie Stahl on "Face the Nation" on March 23, 1986.

Burr: "We have a saying at People Express which is, that the sweetness of a low price is soon forgotten in the bitterness of a bad experience, and so you've got to have by far and away the best service."

Stahl: "You have the best service?"

Burr: "Absolutely!"

Stahl: "Come on, it's called "people distress". That's the joke about your airline; you are always overbooked. I can't start claiming you have the best service."

Burr: "We do, absolutely have the best service."[1]

Service can't start unless the guy at the top is willing to admit the problem and start working on it.

---

[1]*Editor's note:* Facing the prospect of bankruptcy, People Express sold out to Texas Air Corporation, and was absorbed into Continental Airlines in Feburary 1987.

Business Schools
Owe Students Better Service

CHRISTOPHER H. LOVELOCK

Management education is still strongly biased towards issues and problems in the manufacturing sector. Business schools need to reform their curricula in order to make a contribution to improving the quality of management in service industries.

In the continuing debate about the value and relevance of business education, an important question has been consistently overlooked: Do business school programs provide a balanced treatment of management issues across both the manufacturing and the service sectors? From the evidence available to me, I think the answer has to be no.

Business education in this country is geared toward meeting the training needs of manufacturing industries. A review of texts, cases and business curricula suggests that, across most management functions, only a small minority of illustrations deal with service enterprises. The problem is often most pronounced in introductory courses required of all students. In such courses, it's not uncommon to find examples drawn from manufacturing outnumbering those drawn from services by five to one. And yet the service sector, by many measures, now accounts for about two-thirds of economic activity in the U.S. Private-sector services alone account for roughly half the total GNP—more than double the value of manufacturing and construction industries.

Why is it that the service sector fails to receive coverage more closely proportionate to its size from business educators? Several possible hypotheses are suggested.

Could it be that business professors regard service and manufacturing companies

Reprinted with permission from *The Wall Street Journal*, February 10, 1984.

as broadly similar? Certainly, many academics believe that the principles of good management are not industry-specific and can be applied across industry and sectoral boundaries. By studying manufacturing companies, they argue, students should be able to learn principles that can be generalized and that also can be applied to services. (If this is the case, then of course the reverse also should hold true.)

A growing body of research suggests that managers in the service sector face many problems that are not commonly encountered by their colleagues in manufacturing. For instance, finished services normally cannot be stored; in the absence of inventories to buffer supply and demand, strategies must be developed to bring productive capacity and customer demand into balance at specific points in time. Service-management problems are particularly distinctive in "front-room" operations—those aspects of the service that are readily apparent to the customer. Operations personnel who are in contact with customers become part of the product and must be trained in marketing and customer-relations skills; customers entering the "service factory"—be it airline facilities, a hotel, a restaurant or a branch bank—must be managed in ways that preserve the efficiency of the operation without detracting from the quality of their experience. Managing quality control is particularly difficult for intangible services, especially when the service is delivered in real time by failure-prone human beings.

Alternatively, business educators may believe that the service sector is composed primarily of cottage industries and mom-and-pop operations that are neither large nor complex enough to merit academic study and research. A comparison of the *Fortune* Service 500 against the *Fortune* Industrial 500 quickly dispels that argument: More than 99 percent of the service companies would qualify for the industrials list in terms of size of assets, and 98 percent would qualify on number of employees. Comparing sales or operating revenues across sectors is problematic, as it is hard to make direct comparisons of the value added; but of the 400 non-

banking service organizations, 93 percent also would make the industrials list.

Some writers make the point that manufacturing organizations often include important service components and that the backroom operations of service companies closely parallel many manufacturing operations. Both points are valid. Yet how much coverage do we see in business curricula of the challenges of managing service divisions such as consulting, credit financing, education, and repair and maintenance—to name just a few—within manufacturing corporations? And how often do business courses probe management issues behind the scenes in service organizations?

Another plausible hypothesis for the limited coverage of services is that manufacturing-oriented curricula reflect student career goals. But this isn't the case either. Recent MBA placement statistics for seven major business schools show that 34 percent of graduates joined manufacturing companies, 28 percent joined financial-service firms, 11 percent went into consulting and 22 percent went to work for other service employers.

A final explanation for the relative lack of interest in service organizations among many business faculties could be that the instructors are the intellectual heirs of the 19th-century economists who believed that services that do not alter a physical product neither contribute to wealth nor create value.

Historically, service industries perceived themselves as unique. They preferred to train their own managers internally or to recruit from industry-specific programs in such fields as health administration and hotel management. Now they are turning to business schools for help in finding management solutions to such challenges as deregulation, the advent of new electronic technologies, the growth of franchising and the globalization of service competition. They recognize that effective management of such important functions as marketing, control, operations and human resources is crucial to meeting these challenges. But unless business educators reshape both their MBA and executive program curricula, service organizations are likely to be disappointed.

Business school faculties should review their curriculum materials—textbooks, cases and exercises—to determine if they overlook important service industries or ignore significant problems commonly faced by service managers. Employers in the service sector should be asking pointed questions of placement officers and faculties. Students and executive-program participants should evaluate their courses with reference to their relevance for a career in managing service enterprises. And alumni who have gone on to careers in service companies should take the initiative in offering suggestions for curriculum reform.

Until these imbalances in business education are corrected, business schools will fail to achieve their full potential for helping improve the quality of management in this country. And the initials MBA will stand simply for Manufacturing Business Administrator.

PART II
Understanding Services: Breaking Free from Industry Tunnel Vision

How Can Service Businesses Survive and Prosper?

ROGER W. SCHMENNER

Through the use of a service matrix, the author shows how service businesses can broaden their professional relationships with other services that have similar operations and managerial challenges, and in so doing, gain the economic foothold needed to survive and prosper.

Presently the service sector of our economy is characterized by both profusion and confusion. By profusion, I mean that it has done wonderfully well at generating jobs, for new kinds of services are sprouting continually. By confusion, I mean that service businesses seem to rise and fall from Wall Street grace with regularity. Moreover, as many are markedly entrepreneurial in spirit, they all claim to have idiosyncratic operations. For example, while manufacturing management enjoys the benefits of various professional societies (i.e., those for materials management, manufacturing engineering, industrial engineering, and quality control) whose roles are to find management principles that apply across many different kinds of manufacturing enterprises, service business management does not enjoy such cooperation. All too often, service companies view themselves as unique, and consequently they do not promote service operation management techniques with the same vigor as does the manufacturing sector.

Some manufacturers, of course, also claim that they are unique. However, over the years, manufacturers have been unified by their acceptance of certain terminology to describe generic production processes—job shop, batch flow, assembly line, continuous flow process. This not only helps to solidify manufacturers of sometimes widely divergent product lines, but it also helps to reveal the challenges manufacturers face.

THE CHARACTERISTICS OF A SERVICE BUSINESS

The confusion surrounding service operations can be lessened in part by looking at key aspects of service businesses that significantly affect the character of the service delivery process. Specifically, there are two elements that can be used to classify different kinds of service businesses. These elements will serve later as a springboard for investigating the strategic changes of service operations and the challenges that lie ahead for managers.

Labor Intensity

The first key element is the labor intensity of the service business process. Labor intensity is defined as the ratio of the labor cost incurred to the value of the plant and equipment. (Note that the value of inventories is excluded because the concept seems "cleaner" without taking inventories into account.) A high labor-intensive business involves relatively little plant and equipment and considerable worker time, effort, and cost. For example, professional services are typically a high labor-intensive business. A low labor-intensive business, on the other hand, is characterized by relatively low levels of labor cost compared to plant and equipment. Trucking firms with their breakbulks and other kinds of terminals, trailers, and tractors are an example. It is important to think of labor intensity as a ratio. Many, for example, think of hospitals as labor intensive —after all, hospitals are filled with nurses, technicians, orderlies, and doctors. Nevertheless, despite employing large numbers of people, a hospital has a comparatively low labor intensity because of the very expensive plant and equipment it must have. Table 1 documents the labor intensity of some broad service industries.

Consumer Interaction and Service Customization

The other key element of a service business is somewhat more confusing because it combines two similar but distinct concepts: (1) the degree to which the consumer interacts with the service process; and (2) the degree to which the service is customized for the consumer. This joint measure has a high value when a service evidences both a high level of interaction and a high level of customization for the customer. Similarly, when both individual measures are low, the joint measure has a low value. Where there is a mix of high interaction with low customization (or the other way around), the joint measure falls somewhere in between.

What exactly do these measures mean? A service with a high level of interaction is one where the consumer can actively intervene in the service process, at will, often to demand additional service of a particular kind or to request that some aspects of the service be deleted. However, high visibility or duration of contact with the process is not enough to indicate high interaction. College teaching, for example, is a highly visible service activity in that students are in class for long periods of time. However, seldom do student consumers actively intervene in the process. Thus college teaching has a comparatively low level of interaction.

A service with high service customization will work to satisfy an individual's particular, and perhaps full range, of preferences. A physician typically gives very individual, customized service. Furthermore, good physicians are always open to feedback from their patients and willing to rethink and modify the service they provide. College teachers, on the other hand, are reluctant to throw out the syllabus to accommodate student desires: they "teach what they know."

To clarify further this joint measure, consider the restaurant industry. At the low end of the spectrum are McDonald's and Kentucky Fried Chicken. Here, the consumer's

TABLE 1
Labor Intensity of Some Broad Service Groups

Low Labor-Intensive Services	Capital-Labor Ratio
Electric Utilities, Gas, Sanitation Services	14.21
Communications	5.31
Amusement & Recreation	2.49
Hospitals:	
—Teaching	1.59
—For-Profit	1.63
—All Other (e.g., community)	1.75
Auto & Other Repair	1.60
Transportation	1.27
Banking	1.20
Hotels, etc.	1.01

High Labor-Intensive Services	Capital-Labor Ratio
Security, Commodity Brokers	0.15
Insurance Agents & Service	0.18
Business Services (e.g., advertising, credit reporting, mailing & reproduction, building services, personnel supply, computer & data processing, management consulting & public relations)	0.42
Personal Services (e.g., laundry, photo, beauty/barber shops, funeral services)	0.53
Wholesale Trade	0.54
Retail Trade	0.62

Notes:

The labor intensities of specific types of service businesses are not routinely calculated. Most of the following estimates are based on 1980 data on depreciable assets (from the 1980 Statistics of Income, Corporation Income Tax Returns, Internal Revenue Service) and compensation to employees (from the Revised Estimates of the National Income and Product Accounts, Survey of Current Business, Bureau of Economic Analysis, U.S. Department of Commerce). The hospital estimates are based on data compiled by the American Hospital Association for 1981.

The calculations shown are capital-to-labor ratios (gross depreciable assets divided by compensation to employees) for very broad groups of service businesses. Services with capital-labor ratios greater than about 1 could be viewed as having "low labor intensity," while services with ratios less than 1 could be viewed as having "high labor intensity." By contrast, the average capital-labor ratio by this measure for manufacturing in 1980 was 1.90.

The service industry classifications are broad ones as a result of the Standard Industrial Classification codes.

interaction with the process is typically brief and controlled (i.e., order, payment, and pickup), and customization does not prevail. The service is prompt and courteous, but everybody is treated the same. At Burger King and Wendy's consumer interaction is similarly brief and controlled. However, these fast-food chains offer measurably more customization for the consumer—you can have a burger "your way." This process permits some customization.

Cafeterias provide even more customization for the consumer (i.e., the opportunity to choose from a wide range of foods) and a modest increase in interaction (e.g., as one proceeds down the line, one can often request the staff to replenish an item or to serve a rarer cut of roast beef). Next in line are restaurants with salad bars that have some waiter assistance. Such restaurants offer customization similar to that of a cafeteria but there is more customer interaction: the waiter can be called on, at will.

Finally, there are restaurants with extensive waiter services. Such restaurants typically permit a high degree of customization and interaction: the customer decides what he or she wants to eat and when he or she wants to be served (e.g., "We'd like to enjoy our cocktail now and order later"; "Coffee later, thank you"), and the waiter is on call, at will, to fill any particular desires. However, it should be noted that the haute-cuisine restaurant is not necessarily at the highest end of the customization/interaction spectrum, as some of them offer limited menus and many even decide the particular seating time. In this case, consumers are willing to trust the chef because of the food's known quality and the restaurant's ambience.

For many services, customization and interaction go hand in hand: if one is high, the other is high; if one is low, the other is low. There are services, however, where they differ. Insurance underwriting, especially at Lloyd's of London, offers considerable customization but a low degree of interaction with the client. On the other hand, an advertising agency typically is high on both customization and interaction. A travel agency provides a different example. The typical business traveler service is fairly standard and often involves merely presenting the schedule options to the traveler and issuing the ticket. Here, the degree of customization is not nearly as great as it is for planning a pleasure trip. On the other hand, business travel often demands rescheduling and a good deal of tinkering with timetables. Thus, business travel agency work often involves more interaction than customization.

OTHER SERVICE CLASSIFICATION SCHEMES

Other observers have sought to classify service operations, notably Richard Chase, David Maister, and Christopher Lovelock. Chase arrays various services along a continuum from high to low "contact."[1] For Chase, contact refers to the duration of a customer's presence in the service system. According to this scheme, hotels are high contact, "pure" services, while the postal service is low contact. Repair shops are medium contact services, lying in between the prior extremes.

Although Chase makes a useful distinction, his distinction is not as helpful as it could be. A number of services can be judged high contact even though they only "shelter the customer" and in the process have very

little interaction with the client. To use Chase's example, a hotel is a high-contact service, but, to me, hotels are vastly less demanding than are hospitals, primarily because hotels interact with customers in limited and very structured ways, whereas hospitals must interact with patients in irregular and frequently sustained ways. Hospital management is much more demanding, and is, therefore, worthy of classification apart from that of hotel management.

Chase's classification scheme becomes even more problematic when he turns to examining potential operating efficiency.[2] Here, Chase asserts that

$$\text{potential facility efficiency} = f \left(1 - \frac{\text{customer contact time}}{\text{service creation time}} \right).$$

By this mode of thinking, the greater the ratio of customer contact time to service creation time (a somewhat nebulous term that refers to the work process involved in providing the service itself), the lower is the potential efficiency of the service facility. If this is so, hotels have lower potential efficiencies than do either the postal service or repair shops. If I am not misinterpreting Chase, the implication of his assertion is curious. For many people, hotels are often viewed as considerably more efficient, and certainly more profitable, than the postal service or many repair shops. As far as I am concerned, contact time simply does not capture completely what is challenging about service sector management.

Maister and Lovelock come closer to the mark.[3] They use both the extent of client contact and the extent of customization to dimension a two-by-two matrix that distinguishes among the factory, the job shop, mass service, and professional service. Unfortunately, Maister and Lovelock do not spend much time either describing or pursuing this characterization. They do not identify particular services as belonging to one or the other of their matrix quadrants, and, therefore, it is difficult to take them to task. However, they do use client contact, and, as was discussed above, the notion of client contact may be fraught with more ambiguity than is necessary.

Here, I argue that services are better classified by using both the degree of labor intensity and the degree to which (1) the consumer interacts with the service and (2) the service is customized for the consumer. By expanding the two-by-two matrix, it is possible to analyze the challenges service managements face and the dynamics of operation changes in their businesses.

THE SERVICE PROCESS MATRIX

I have characterized services as being either "high" or "low" in terms of client interaction and customization. Naturally, not all service businesses fit cleanly into these extremes: there are many shades of gray. Nevertheless, these extremes are helpful in developing a two-by-two matrix that can categorize a whole host of diverse service businesses. Figure 1 displays a service matrix and indicates some of the classic service businesses that fit neatly in one of the four quadrants. As this figure shows, service businesses that have a relatively low labor intensity and a low degree of customer interaction and customization are labeled "service factories": airlines, trucking, hotels, and resorts are classic examples. As the degree of interaction or customization for the consumer increases, however, the service factory gives way to the "service shop," much as the line flow operation gives way to a job shop operation when customization is required in manufacturing. Service shops still have a high degree of plant and equipment relative to labor, but they offer more interaction and customization. Hospitals, auto repair garages, and most restaurants are examples of service shops.

"Mass service" businesses have a high degree of labor intensity but a rather low degree of interaction and customization. Many traditional kinds of services can be found in this category, such as retailing, wholesaling, schools of all types, and many services like laundry, cleaning, and many routine computer software and data-processing functions. If the degree of interaction with the consumer increases and/or customization of this service becomes the watchword, mass service gives way to "professional service": doctors, lawyers, accountants, architects, investment bankers, and the like are the archetypal examples.

CHALLENGES FOR SERVICE MANAGERS

Variations in the managerial challenges of different services stem from the high and low distinctions made of labor intensity and interaction/customization. For example, in the case of low labor intensity (e.g., hospitals, airlines, hotels), the choice of plant and equipment is heightened. Monitoring and implementing any technological advantages are also critical. In such low labor-intensive services, capacity cannot be augmented easily and so demand must be managed to smooth out any peaks and to promote off-peak times. The inflexibility of capacity also implies that scheduling service delivery is relatively more important for these low labor-intensive businesses than it is for others.

As for services with high labor intensity (e.g., stores, professional associations), managing and controlling the workforce becomes paramount. Hiring, training, de-

FIGURE 1
The Service Process Matrix

Degree of Interaction and Customization

		Low	High
Degree of Labor Intensity	Low	**Service Factory:** —Airlines —Trucking —Hotels —Resorts and recreation	**Service Shop:** —Hospitals —Auto repair —Other repair services
	High	**Mass Service:** —Retailing —Wholesaling —Schools —Retail aspects of commercial banking	**Professional Service:** —Doctors —Lawyers —Accountants —Architects

veloping methods and controls, employee welfare, scheduling the workforce, and controlling work for any far-flung geographic locations are critical elements. If new units of operation are contemplated, startup may become a problem and managing the growth of such units can often be difficult.

Different managerial challenges also surface when we consider the distinction made between high and low levels of consumer interaction and customization. When the degree of interaction and customization is low (i.e., airlines, retail stores, commercial banks), the service business faces a stiff marketing challenge. Such a business must try to make

the service it provides warm, even though it does not give all the personal attention that a customer might want. This means that attention to physical surroundings becomes important. In addition, with a low degree of interaction and with little customization, standard operating procedures can be instituted safely. In this type of service, the hierarchy of the operation itself tends to be the classic pyramid with a broad base of workers and many layers of management. Furthermore, the relationships between levels in the pyramid tend to be fairly rigid.

As the service takes on a higher degree of interaction and customization (i.e., professional associations, hospitals, repair

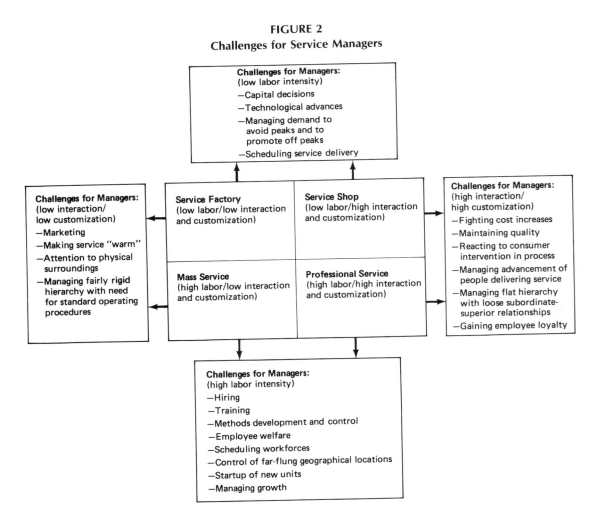

FIGURE 2
Challenges for Service Managers

Challenges for Managers:
(low labor intensity)
—Capital decisions
—Technological advances
—Managing demand to avoid peaks and to promote off peaks
—Scheduling service delivery

Challenges for Managers:
(low interaction/ low customization)
—Marketing
—Making service "warm"
—Attention to physical surroundings
—Managing fairly rigid hierarchy with need for standard operating procedures

Service Factory
(low labor/low interaction and customization)

Service Shop
(low labor/high interaction and customization)

Mass Service
(high labor/low interaction and customization)

Professional Service
(high labor/high interaction and customization)

Challenges for Managers:
(high interaction/ high customization)
—Fighting cost increases
—Maintaining quality
—Reacting to consumer intervention in process
—Managing advancement of people delivering service
—Managing flat hierarchy with loose subordinate-superior relationships
—Gaining employee loyalty

Challenges for Managers:
(high labor intensity)
—Hiring
—Training
—Methods development and control
—Employee welfare
—Scheduling workforces
—Control of far-flung geographical locations
—Startup of new units
—Managing growth

services), management must deal with higher costs and more talented labor. Managing costs effectively—either by keeping them down or by passing them on to consumers—becomes a significant challenge. Maintaining quality and responding to consumer intervention are also important. In addition, talented employees demand attention and expect advancement in the organization. In effect, what this all means for many service businesses with high interaction and customization is that the hierarchy of control tends to be flat and unlike the classic pyramid. As the relationship between superiors and subordinates tends to be much less rigid, management must continually strive to keep workers "attached" to the firm by offering innovative pay and benefits packages and by paying close attention to quality of worklife issues.

As Figure 2 demonstrates, the high versus low differentiation made for labor intensity and the degree of consumer interaction and customization yield distinct combinations of management challenges for the four service types identified. Typically, well-run service factories, service shops, mass-service firms, or professional firms pay close attention to all of the managerial challenges that apply to their quadrant of the matrix.

INNOVATIONS AND STRATEGIC CHANGES

Categorizing service businesses into quadrants can be used to investigate the strategic changes of service operations over time. At least some of the current confusion has occurred because service industries are changing rapidly. The most salient development in the service sector is vast segmentation and diversification. Services that were once clearly service shops or mass service firms are no longer clearly labeled as such. Service firms are spreading themselves out across the service matrix. Below are examples illustrating this trend.

Fast-Food Restaurants. A classic strategic change involved the development and evolution of fast-food restaurants. The traditional restaurant could be positioned as a service shop with relatively high customization and interaction for the consumer and a middling labor intensity. The elegant gourmet restaurant may even be classified as a professional service. On the other hand, with the advent of fast foods, interaction and customization for the consumer have been lowered dramatically, as has labor intensity. As a result, the restaurant industry today encompasses a wide diversity of operations.

Hospitals. Another interesting innovation within the service shop quadrant involved hospitals. The new kinds of hospitals developed by Humana, Hospital Corporation of America, and others are different from the traditional community hospital or university medical center. Whereas the traditional hospital (especially the university medical center) is set up to diagnose and treat any disease by investing in all of the latest equipment and technology, this new breed of hospital customarily deals with the more routine kinds of medical treatment: intensive care units and other high expense units for very sick or dying patients are often not a part of these hospitals. Very ill patients are referred to larger, and better-equipped hospitals. For its part, the new type of hospital offers a much lower cost service that is convenient for the consumer. In this respect, this new breed of hospital offers less customization but, at the same time, demands a higher degree of labor intensity. As Table 1 shows, there is a lower capital-to-labor ratio for "for-profit" hospitals than there is for traditional community hospitals. For-profit hospitals are not burdened with all the capital expenditures that are part of the traditional hospital. Table 1 also shows that teaching hospitals, perhaps for understandable reasons, are more labor intensive than are community hospitals.

Mass Services. Another series of changes occurred in some of the mass service operations. Retailing offers some interesting examples. The expansion of catalog stores (e.g., Best's), warehouse stores (e.g., Toys R Us), mail-order sales (e.g., L. L. Bean), and brand-name discounters (e.g., Loehmann's) has shifted the emphasis of traditional retailing operation toward a lower degree of labor intensity. This was made possible because such services provide less than department store-type "full service." On the other hand, the proliferation of boutiques and specialty operations within stores like Bloomingdale's is evidence of a different kind of change, one where interaction and customization are stressed. This often demands higher labor intensity (more than "full service"). By being more "professional"—frequently by putting salespeople on commission—such stores hope to convert more "browsers" into "buyers."

The deregulation of commercial banking and financial services also created some intriguing strategic operation changes within the mass service quadrant. Automation in commercial banking (i.e., automatic teller machines, electronic transfers, and other new technological advances) has made commercial banking less labor intensive. Indeed, credit-card operations and check clearing are now placed in their own facilities (often at quite a distance from the commercial banks themselves), and they do essentially the kind of work that one would expect in a service factory. A similar change is evident in some other financial service companies. One of the justifications given for the acquisition of Lehman Brothers Kuhn Loeb by Shearson/American Express was the fact that the trading operations of Lehman Brothers could be absorbed easily by slack capacity in the backroom operations at Shearson.

However, even though technological advances have made it possible for some aspects of commercial banking to become less labor intensive, there is still a move to customize other services even more. Customization in this business grew out of the removal of interest rate ceilings on certificates of deposit, the cessation of fixed brokerage commissions, the demise of Regulation Q, which affects interest rates on bank accounts, and the initial steps toward interstate banking. Moreover, many of the services that have been acquired by the "financial supermarket" companies are essentially services that will give those companies greater interaction and customization. Consequently, the increasing menu of services provided by the traditional brokerage houses may cause the old-time broker, who tried to be all things

to his client, to become an anachronism. Merrill Lynch, for example, is promoting both greater automation and increasing customization of its services.

CHOOSING APPROPRIATE OPERATIONS

Service-business innovations, which have resulted in increasing segmentation and diversification of this sector, point up the need to assess the industry's operational choices. The insights of Wickham Skinner are as relevant to service businesses as they are to manufacturing organizations.[4] Service operations, like factories, have to be tailored to do certain things well at the expense of doing other things well. Moreover, one cannot assume that the "formula" that has been so successful in one service business will necessarily carry over to another service business, even if that business is merely a segmentation of the old one. Thus, the more explicit a service business can be about the demands of the business in light of its operations choices, the more appropriate those choices are likely to be.

McDonald's, for example, has been adamant in maintaining its focus on the fast-food business and has resisted diversifying into other types of fast-food chains or service businesses. On the other hand, Toys R Us has moved away from the warehouse-type store operation and has ventured into children's clothing, Kids R Us. Recognizing that children's clothes cannot be sold like toys, the company has altered its operations to provide more interaction and customization. At Kids R Us, the store sizes and layouts are different, the workers (clerk-counselors and clothes "runners") that are hired and trained to provide a more personalized service are different, and the inventory control systems are different.

MOVING TOWARD THE DIAGONAL

Given the quickening pace of segmentation and diversification of service businesses, several observations concerning the dynamics of service processes bear mentioning. First, many of the segmentation steps that service businesses have taken have been *toward* the diagonal that runs from the service factory to the professional service firm. Figure 3 illustrates this move. Still, one may ask, What makes the diagonal so attractive to existing services? The answer seems to be better control. However, it should be noted that the kinds of controls needed for mass services are different from those needed for service shops.

On one side of the diagonal, mass service controls often relate to labor costs and efficiency, for these services are trying constantly to get a grip on labor scheduling and productivity. Here, plant and equipment are rarely constraints. For example, in retailing, labor is a critical variable cost, and, therefore, scheduling labor is an important ac-

FIGURE 3
Strategic Operation Changes within the Service Process Matrix

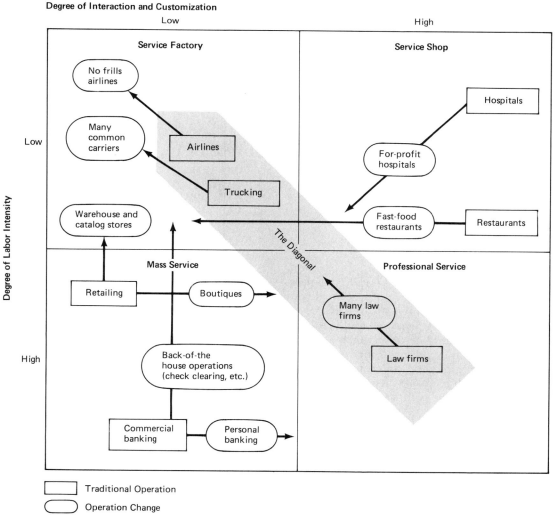

tivity. The increased use of point-of-sale terminals has permitted the tracking of sales of different items by 15-minute intervals throughout the day. Such information, in combination with sales per salesperson per hour (a productivity measure), is tremendously useful to inventory control, not to mention workforce scheduling. Moves toward more customization (e.g., the department store boutique and its commissioned salespeople) can also be understood as a move to increase control of the selling situation, with higher revenues, profits, and productivity as the end result.

On the other side of the diagonal, the service shop frets about control of the service itself. With this kind of service, plant and equipment are constant constraints. Therefore, there are concerns for how frequently unpredictable jobs (e.g., auto repairs, patients) can be scheduled through expensive capital equipment. Control is also affected by the uncertainty over when and how people can tell when a service is rendered satisfactorily. Hospitals, for example, have a high proportion of fixed costs and thus worry a great deal about capacity utilization. Current debates about who should dictate the utilization of hospital resources—administrative staffs or medical staffs—are, at the core, debates about resource control. In this context, one can understand pressures to provide less customized and/or interactive service (e.g., fewer tests, more ambulatory care).

The service factory and the professional service firm, on the other hand, suffer less from loss of control. Although control is still an issue for both kinds of services, for the professional service firm, control is more of an individual concern, relatively free of constraints of plant and equipment. The high degree of interaction and customization required of such firms is at least matched with a high degree of training and skill in the workforce.

The service factory can develop its "production process" to foster more control. The process that defines the service and the flow of information and materials is relatively smooth. In this regard, the service factory shares many of the benefits that manufac-

turing operations enjoy. The labor needed is well known for given levels of demand, and scheduling of labor, plant, and equipment is fairly straightforward.

Even though there are pressures for *existing* operations to move toward the diagonal, there is no reason to think that all service shops or mass service operations will become extinct. Many operations will be able to adhere to their traditional operations. Moreover, marketing pressures for increased customization and generation of completely new services are likely to replenish the supply of service shops or mass service operations. Witness, for example, the demand for luxury airplane travel or luxury hotel accommodation. These are new services that are rendered to particular market niches. Note too the recent change in how computers are sold—that is, through mass outlets as opposed to individual salespeople. The recent shift by J. C. Penney toward more "full service" is yet another example.

MOVING UP THE DIAGONAL

Another observation centers on some of the service businesses already located on the diagonal. The professional service firm and the service factory are not immune to strategic changes. Of those services that have changed their positions within the service process matrix, most have moved up the diagonal. Consider, for example, the changes that have occurred within many law firms over the last decades. The institution of paralegals and other lower cost labor and the increasing specialization of many law firms have driven many firms within that industry toward lower labor intensity and less customization (i.e., less full service). Similarly, other professional service firms have invested in equipment, much of it for word processing or data processing.

Commercial banking in California is an example of a service business in the throes of change. Given its faltering economic position, the state is currently applying pressure on bank loan portfolios. Deregulation has also pressed heavily on the industry. Banks have been forced to seek lower costs to compensate for the increased rates they have had to pay to attract funds. In addition, deregulation has permitted banks to explore new lines of business. Given these pressures, it is understandable that BankAmerica, for instance, closed 132 branches in 1984 and reduced its workforce by 4 percent. Such decisions reflect a move up the diagonal, away from the old "formula." Furthermore, the bank scouted out the insurance industry as a potential source of earnings.

In a similar vein, the deregulation of trucking and air travel has meant significant change for the service factories. Trucking deregulation has forced many of the old-line common carriers to invest dramatically in breakbulks and additional freight terminals for less-than-truckload shipments. While such capital investments have meant increased barriers to entry for trucking firms, these firms can no longer afford to offer as customized a service as they used to for their clients. Today, their services are more specialized. In addition, their pricing structures have been changed to encourage the clients to ship in particular ways. Consequently, common carriers are moving up the diagonal.

A similar story can be told of the airlines. Deregulation encouraged major airlines to shift to hub-and-spoke systems, which means that a number of "pushes" can be made from their major airport hubs during any day. Where once competition focused on time of day and elegant service, competition these days centers more on price and less on the number of flights and the optimum time of day. The result for most airlines has been both less customization and lower labor intensity, given the significant investments that have been made at the hubs.

But just as movement toward the diagonal does not necessarily mean that service shops and mass service firms will cease to exist, the move up the diagonal does not necessarily mean that professional service firms will become small service factories. There will always be some firms that will be able to maintain successfully a high labor intensity

and high interaction and customization. Furthermore, new professional services will spring up that will demand, at least initially, a combination of high labor intensity and high interaction and customization.

CONCLUSION

For many existing services, the pressures for control and lower costs will tend to drive them toward the diagonal and/or up it. For many service firms, such positions will be the most profitable ones. Understanding such pressures on a service operation is well advised because it can help existing service businesses anticipate the nature of competitors' changes as well as many of the management challenges they will face over time (see Figure 2). In fact, what will be demanded of many newly created service businesses will be very different from what was demanded of their predecessors. Therefore, companies that appreciate and anticipate these differences will be at a strategic advantage. Those businesses that are diversifying or segmenting will know that the old "formula" may have to be changed for the new business, and they will have more than an inkling about how such operations should change. Competing service businesses that understand these changes will have a better appreciation for competitor moves and will also better understand relative strengths and weaknesses of their own operations.

Service managers who continue to claim that their operations are unique may be left in the dust by those who see their operations as more generic. When service firms begin to appraise themselves as service factories, service shops, mass service, or professional services—much as manufacturers see themselves as job shops, assembly lines, continuous flow processes, and the like —the service version of the not-invented-here syndrome will fade away and management minds will be more receptive to general, and generalizable, service management concepts.

Notes

[1]R. B. Chase, "The Customer Contact Approach to Services: Theoretical Bases and Practical Extensions," *Operations Research* **29** (1981): 698–706; R. B. Chase, "Where Does the Customer Fit in a Service Operation?" *Harvard Business Review*, November–December 1978, pp. 137–142; R. B. Chase and D. A. Tansik, "The Customer Contact Model for Organizational Design," *Management Science* **29** (1983): 1037–1050; R. B. Chase and N. Aquilano, *Production and Operations Management* (Homewood, IL: Richard D. Irwin, 1985), ch. 3.

[2]Chase (1981).

[3]D. H. Maister and C. H. Lovelock, "Managing Facilitator Services," *Sloan Management Review*, Summer 1982, pp. 19–31.

[4]W. Skinner, "The Focused Factory," *Harvard Business Review*, May–June 1974, pp. 113–121.

The Customer Contact Approach to Services: Theoretical Bases and Practical Extensions

RICHARD B. CHASE

This paper reviews the underlying theory of the customer contact approach to services and suggests specific applications to a wide range of service systems. The approach holds that the potential efficiency of a service system is a function of the degree of customer contact entailed in the creation of the service product. A number of propositions about high contact systems are identified and some simple heuristics for service system design and operation are proposed.

There is probably no area of operations management (OM) of greater current interest than services. Some of the reasons for this are (1) the rapid growth of services relative to manufacturing in the last decade, (2) the pressures on service operations to become cost efficient in their production processes, and (3) the (debatable) point that most of the intriguing OM problems in manufacturing have been dealt with so extensively that few new major breakthroughs appear likely, thus services provide a fresh target for applications of OM concepts. However, despite these compelling reasons for studying services, there is still a real question as to how services should be approached as a distinctive OM subfield for both research and teaching purposes. What seems to be called for is the development and dissemination of one or more theories of OM in services. One such theory is the "customer contact" approach, which is the focus of this paper.

Before explaining the customer contact approach, however, it is useful to discuss briefly some of the other efforts which have been undertaken to categorize services according to some specific managerially useful dimensions.

The literature on services is diffuse, but it appears that service marketing specialists have given the most attention to developing service taxonomies and generating prescriptions relative to each service system category. A common theme running through these efforts is the classification of services into tangible and intangible components in order to help determine how to choose an effective marketing strategy. [See, for example, Rathmell (1966) and Shostack (1977b).] Eiglier and Langeard (1977) have proposed a classification scheme which, in addition to tangibility/intangibility, considers the effect of the organization and client interface and user participation on the customer's perception of the product. Thomas (1978) dichotomizes service into equipment-based and people-based service as a means of developing strategy.

With respect to OM, writers in the field tend to model service systems by drawing structural analogies with manufacturing systems: e.g., intermittent, continuous, and project flows, in Buffa (1975); and input, transformation, and output, in Wild (1977). Though helpful in understanding flow properties of given services, these types of analogies cannot account directly for the presence or absence of behavioral and marketing elements which are embodied in the service product. In this sense, they suffer from the same limitations as process charts and operations charts of work design—they describe only the physical aspects of what takes place, not the psychosocial dynamics of the environment where they occur.

Approaches which address these more subjective aspects of service production to a greater extent are given in Sasser et al. (1978) and in Levitt (1972). Sasser et al. provide a descriptive model which they label as "operating characteristics in a service environment." This model postulates causal relationships among three elements: the service concept, the service delivery system, and service levels. In their view, the service concept (i.e., facilitating good, explicit intangibles and implicit intangibles) dictates, and is defined by, the service delivery system (i.e., performance characteristics of materials, atmosphere and image of facilities, attitudes of

employees). Both of these elements in turn are used by management to create service levels (in terms of materials, facilities, and personnel), which are then communicated to the consumer (via advertising) to determine "consumer perceived service levels." Levitt, in contrast, offers a normative view of services, advocating that service managers take a manufacturing approach to services by substituting "technology and systems for people." The prime example of this design philosophy is McDonald's Hamburgers, where, as Levitt notes, "Through painstaking attention to total design and facilities planning, everything is built integrally into the machine itself, into the technology of the system." Levitt (1972, 1976) provides a variety of other examples to buttress his contentions.

Both of these views have advantages and disadvantages relative to further development of service theory for OM. Sasser et al. provide a descriptively valid model of what takes place in a service operation but do not articulate what, if any, design or operation criteria derive directly from their model. Levitt's philosophy does have implications for design and operations but it does not develop specific criteria for the organization of services or for measuring the effectiveness of service performance. In fairness, neither approach was presented as an all-embracing theory, but by virtue of their general coverage of services they must be considered as yardsticks by which to measure subsequent approaches.

In addition to these two preceding approaches to services (which seem to emphasize what will be termed "high contact" services in this paper), there have been some interesting papers focusing on "low contact" or back office operations in banking. [See Matteis (1979), Shostack (1977a), and Reed (1971).] Also, there is a very extensive literature on services which bears tangentially on OM issues in economics (Gartner and Riesman 1974), public administration (Quinn 1978), and organization theory (Schneider 1973). Finally, there are some direct applications of quantitative techniques to such service OM problems as staff scheduling (Buffa et al. 1976), vehicle deployment (Kolesar and Walker 1974), and check processing (Boyd and Mabert 1977). Space does not permit a review of these efforts.

CUSTOMER CONTACT APPROACH

The customer contact approach holds that a service system's potential operating efficiency is a function of the degree to which the customer is in direct contact with the service facility relative to total service creation time for that customer:

potential facility efficiency

$$= f \left(1 - \frac{\text{customer contact time}}{\text{service creation time}} \right).$$

Efficiency is seen as the ratio of outputs to inputs for a given service facility; it does not account for customer utility functions or for organization-wide production or marketing performance. Service facilities characterized by high customer contact are perceived as being inherently limited in their production efficiency because of the uncertainty that people introduce into the service creation process. This uncertainty derives from individual differences in customers' attitudes and behaviors. Systems characterized by low customer contact are seen as being essentially free of this type of uncertainty and therefore are capable of operating at high levels of production efficiency, analogous to that achieved in well-run manufacturing organizations. (See Chase 1978 and Chase and Aquilano 1977.)

THE TECHNICAL CORE AND DECOUPLING

The contact approach was formulated partly in response to insights by several writers on two general concepts of organization design—protection of the technical core, and selective decoupling of organizational units. As can be seen from the following brief review, these concepts themselves are highly interrelated. Thompson (1967) proposed that organizational rationality logically leads de-

signers to seal off the technical core (the production processes) of the organization from environmental influences. In Thompson's words, ". . . organizations seek to buffer environmental influences by surrounding their technical core with input and output components." The objective of this is to enable the core to produce ". . . at a continuous rate and with specified quality." Herbst (1974) defines the work domain of a team as consisting of a core region, a maintenance and service region, and an extra task region. He emphasizes that the mission of the last two regions is to facilitate performance of the core region. Miller (1959), in describing how systems can be differentiated, suggests that the management of operations is enhanced when homogeneous tasks are spatially and sequentially combined. Regarding decoupling, Simon (1969) has argued that complex systems can be disaggregated into stable subassemblies and that these are significant elements in any organization. Weick (1976) notes that "the coupling imagery gives researchers access to one of the more powerful ways of talking about complexity now available." Magee and Boodman (1967), in discussing the functions of inventory, emphasize its ability to decouple operations, making ". . . it unnecessary to gear production directly to consumption." (The implications of this observation relative to services are particularly intriguing.) Finally, there is Skinner's (1974) "plant-within-a-plant" concept (PWP) which makes operational both the technological core idea and decoupling, by advocating segmentation of a manufacturing facility "both organizationally and physically" into homogeneous units. "Each PWP has its own facilities in which it can concentrate on its particular manufacturing task using its own workforce management approaches, production control, organization structure, and so forth."

A CONTACT-BASED CLASSIFICATION SCHEME

In Chase and Chase and Aquilano it was proposed that common service systems could be grouped according to decreasing contact under three broad headings: pure services, mixed services, and quasi-manufacturing. Pure services include those organizations whose major production is carried on in the presence of the customers (medical care, restaurants, transportation, personal services); mixed services which commonly involve a mix of face-to-face contact and loosely coupled back office work (primarily branch offices); and quasi-manufacturing that entails virtually no face-to-face contact (home offices and distribution centers). Admittedly, pure services do have noncontact production, but their main business entails heavy customer involvement.

Following the basic premise of the approach, quasi-manufacturing service units are most amenable to a manufacturing rationale, mixed services are less so, and pure services hardly at all. Obviously, the classification scheme is highly simplified and at this time can be supported only on the basis of intuitive appeal and experience rather than directed research. However, for practical application specific cases can be incorporated readily within it and, perhaps most importantly, a working language and point of departure for service system study is available. (See Lovelock and Young 1979 for its use in a discussion of marketing strategy.)

DERIVATIVE PROPOSITIONS

One of the attributes of the contact view of services is that it leads fairly directly to some interesting propositions about the nature and limitations of high contact systems relative to low contact systems (and manufacturing systems). Table 1, containing a few representative propositions, is drawn from several sources (see Bessom and Jackson, Kolesar and Walker, Sasser 1976, and Chase and Aquilano) although only the latter identify them as propositions. (Some propositions taken from Chase and Aquilano have been modified in light of further examination.)

With reference to the propositions, it can be seen that each one has implications for one or more of the primary OM functions of planning, scheduling, and control. Also,

TABLE 1

OM Characteristics of High Contact Services— Some Propositions

1. The service product is multidimensional (time, place, atmosphere) and hence its quality is in the eye of the beholder.
2. The direct worker is part of the service product.
3. Demand for the service is often instantaneous and hence cannot be stored.
4. Because production is generally customer initiated, an optimal balance between service system demand and resources is difficult to achieve.
5. Changes in the capacity of the system affect the nature of the service product.
6. The production schedule has a direct, personal effect on the consumer.
7. Only part of the service can be kept in inventory.
8. Verbal skills and knowledge of policy are usually required of the service worker.
9. Wage payments must usually be related to labor hours spent rather than output.
10. It is assumed that service system capacity is at its long run level when the system first opens.
11. A service system malfunction will have an immediate, direct effect on the customer.
12. The location of the service system modifies its value to the customer.

they serve to illustrate some of the implicitly recognized but rarely articulated aspects of the marketing production interface.

APPLICATION OF THE CONCEPT

As mentioned earlier, typical service organizations have been placed under headings of pure service, mixed service, or quasi-manufacturing according to their dominant service product. However, since most service systems are really a mixture of high and low contact, the steps which follow are felt to be suitable for analyzing any service organization. The steps are:

1. Identify those points in the service system where decoupling is possible and desirable. (It will be necessary to trade off cost savings from operations improvement against marketing losses that result from changes in the nature of the services provided.)

TABLE 2
Contact Reduction and Improvement Strategies

Contact Reduction Strategies:

- Handle only exceptions on a face-to-face basis; all other transactions by phone, or better yet by mail.
- Use reservations or appointments-only systems.
- Decentralize using kiosks with one person for information handling (this takes pressure off the main facility).
- Use drop-off points such as automatic teller machines.
- Bring service to customer through postal rounds or mobile offices.
- Use a roving greeter or signs outside facility to act as buffers and information providers.

Contact Improvement Strategies:

- Take-a-number systems.
- Assign contact workers who are people-oriented and knowledgeable about service system processes and policies.
- Maintain consistent work hours.
- Partition back office from the public service counter; do not permit work breaks in front of the customer.
- Provide queueing patterns and signs to indicate standardized and customized service channels.

Low Contact Improvement Strategies (for back office or home office):

- Establish control points for items entering and leaving departments (log times and quantities to control work in process and provide a basis for capacity planning).
- Process standard items in an assembly line mode; customized items as whole tasks.
- Utilize manufacturing-based concepts such as standard times, cost centers, acceptance sampling techniques, and resource-oriented scheduling and dispatching criteria.

2. Employ contact reduction strategies where appropriate.
3. Employ contact enhancement strategies where appropriate.
4. Employ traditional efficiency improvement techniques (production control, industrial engineering, etc.) to improve low contact operations.

In carrying out Steps 2, 3, and 4, a number of widely used, common-sense heuristics come to mind (Table 2). The interesting thing about them is that a contact view of the world will lead the system designer or manager directly to them. On the other hand, without this perspective few organizations are likely to apply them all, or seek out others.

Of course, some companies have shown an understanding of the effects of customer contact and decoupling as illustrated by the following simple examples.

An international bank in Paris is in the process of physically relocating its back office (low contact) operations outside the city to take advantage of lower office space costs and to utilize a newly constructed building designed to handle paperwork in a factory-like way.

Benihana of Tokyo restaurants have flamboyant chefs cook all meals on a hibachi at the customer's table (thereby providing a "show"), while simultaneously eliminating the need for a large kitchen at their expensive downtown locations.

A local car wash, in response to declining business, shifted its high-seniority but less personable old-timers from customer contact points at the beginning and end of the process, to low contact points at intermediate stages. They were replaced by clean-cut college students who could relate well to the customers. (The sign on the car wash marquee subsequently read "Sudsiness with a Smile.")

FURTHER DEVELOPMENT OF THE CONTACT APPROACH

There are several aspects of the customer contact approach which need to be expanded and validated. One is the categorization itself. For instance, the distinction between pure service and mixed service is far from precise. How much back office work has to be done before a pure service becomes a mixed service, and vice versa? At what point along the contact continuum does the presence of the customer entail a shift in service policy? Likewise, what role does the extent of coordination required play in segmenting pure, mixed, and quasi-manufacturing services? That is, when does the need for tight coordination across the boundary between high and low contact operations change the nature of a given service (and hence its placement within the typology)? What is the effect on organization structure of decoupling by customer contact?

Regarding additional refinements, one possibility is the description of service systems using a taxonomical approach roughly similar to that used in job shop scheduling research. [See for example the four-parameter notation used in Conway et al. (1967).] Such a taxonomy might employ a set of descriptions such as: High (low) contact/Standardized (customized) service/Tangible (intangible) product dominant/Automated (nonautomated) technology. Obviously, a tight taxonomy would be of immense value in focusing OM research efforts and synthesizing results.

Finally, there is the need to test the propositions and heuristics proposed here. Do they hold across the entire range of services? Are there other variables or contingencies not yet identified which ultimately determine their applicability? Can both be used in some way to develop "true" principles of services?

CONCLUSION

In addition to explicitly advocating the customer contact approach, this paper has implicitly supported the feasibility of developing a general theory of services for OM. Thus, if the ideas presented here stimulate others to join in the development of alternative general approaches and theories, the objective of this paper will be more than met. The study of services is a fascinating activity; indeed, by virtue of being constantly involved with them in our everyday lives we become "experts" on them to some degree. Certainly the time is ripe for OM specialists to begin to study them in earnest.*

---

*ACKNOWLEDGMENTS: The author thanks Nicholas Aquilano, Dwight Smith, and the anonymous referees for their helpful and thought-provoking comments on the manuscript.

REFERENCES

BESSOM, R. M., AND D. W. JACKSON. 1975. Service Retailing: A Strategic Marketing Approach. *J. Retailing* **51**, 75–84.

BOYD, K., AND V. MABERT. 1977. A Two Stage Forecasting Approach at Chemical Bank of New York for Check Processing. *J. Bank Res.* **8**, 101–107.

BUFFA, E. 1975. *Operations Management: The Management of Productive Systems.* Wiley/Hamilton, New York.

BUFFA, E., M. COSGROVE, AND B. LUCE. 1976. An Integrated Work Shift Scheduling System. *Decision Sci.* **7**, 620–630.

CHASE, R. B. 1978. Where Does the Customer Fit in a Service Operation? *Harvard Bus. Rev.* **56**, 137–142.

CHASE, R. B., AND N. J. AQUILANO. 1977. *Production and Operations Management: A Life Cycle Approach*, rev. ed. Richard D. Irwin, Homewood, Ill.

CONWAY, R., W. MAXWELL, AND L. MILLER. 1967. *Theory of Scheduling.* Addison-Wesley, Reading, Mass.

EIGLIER, P., AND E. LANGEARD. 1977. A New Approach to Service Marketing. In *Marketing Consumer Services: New Insights, Report 77-115.* Marketing Science Institute, Boston.

GARTNER, A., AND F. RIESMAN. 1974. *The Service Society and the Consumer Vanguard.* Harper & Row, New York.

HERBST, P. G. 1974. *Socio-technical Design: Strategies in Multidisciplinary Research*, pp. 143–147. Tavistock Publications, London.

KOLESAR, P., AND W. WALKER. 1974. An Algorithm for the Dynamic Relocation of Fire Companies. *Opns. Res.* **22**, 249–274.

LEVITT, T. 1972. Production Line Approach to Service. *Harvard Bus. Rev.* **50**, 41–52.

LEVITT, T. 1976. The Industrialization of Services. *Harvard Bus. Rev.* **54**, 41–52.

LOVELOCK, C. H., AND R. F. YOUNG. 1979. Look to Customers to Increase Productivity. *Harvard Bus. Rev.* **57**, 168–178.

MAGEE, J. F., AND D. M. BOODMAN. 1967. *Production Planning and Inventory Control*, 2nd ed. pp. 20–21. McGraw-Hill, New York.

MATTEIS, R. J. 1979. The New Back Office Focuses on Customer Service. *Harvard Bus. Rev.* **57**, 146–159.

MILLER, E. J. 1959. Technology, Territory and Time: The Internal Differentiation of Complex Production Systems. *Human Rel.* **12,** 243–272.

QUINN, R. 1978. Productivity and the Process of Organizational Improvement: Why We Cannot Talk to Each Other. *Pub. Admin. Rev.* **38,** 41–45.

RATHMELL, J. M. 1966. What Is Meant by Services? *J. Marktg.* **30,** 32–36.

REED, J. 1971. Sure It's a Bank but I Think of It as a Factory. *Innovation* **23,** 19–27.

SASSER, W. E. 1976. Match Supply and Demand in Service Industries. *Harvard Bus. Rev.* **54,** 61–65.

SASSER, W. E., R. P. OLSEN, AND D. D. WYCKOFF. 1978. *Management of Service Operations*, pp. 20–21. Allyn & Bacon, Boston.

SCHNEIDER, B. 1973. The Perceptions of Organizational Climate: The Customer's View. *J. Appl. Psychol.* **57,** 248–256.

SHOSTACK, G. L. 1977a. Banks Sell Services—Not Things. *Bankers Magazine*, Winter, pp. 40–45.

SHOSTACK, G. L. 1977b. Breaking Free from Product Marketing. *J. Marktg.* **41,** 73–80.

SIMON, H. A. 1969. The Architecture of Complexity. *Proc. Am. Phil. Soc.* **106,** 457–482.

SKINNER, W. 1974. The Focused Factory. *Harvard Bus. Rev.* **52,** 113–121.

THOMAS, D. 1978. Strategy Is Different in Service Businesses. *Harvard Bus. Rev.* **56,** 158–165.

THOMPSON, J. D. 1967. *Organizations in Action*, pp. 14–37. McGraw-Hill, New York.

WEICK, K. E. 1976. Educational Organizations as Loosely Coupled Systems. *Admin. Sci. Quart.* **21,** 1–19.

WILD, R. 1977. *Concepts for Operations Management*. John Wiley & Sons, London.

Classifying Services to Gain Strategic Marketing Insights

CHRISTOPHER H. LOVELOCK

The diversity of the service sector makes it difficult to come up with managerially useful generalizations concerning marketing practice in service organizations. This article argues for a focus on specific categories of services and proposes five schemes for classifying services in ways that transcend narrow industry boundaries. In each instance insights are offered into how the nature of the service might affect the marketing task.

Developing professional skills in marketing management requires the ability to look across a broad cross section of marketing situations, to understand their differences and commonalities, and to identify appropriate marketing strategies in each instance. In the manufacturing sector many experienced marketers have worked for a variety of companies in several different industries, often including both consumer goods and industrial firms. As a result, they have a perspective that transcends narrow industry boundaries.

But exposure to marketing problems and strategies in different industries is still quite rare among managers in the service sector. Not only is the concept of a formalized marketing function still relatively new to most service firms, but service industries have historically been somewhat inbred. The majority of railroad managers, for instance, have spent their entire working lives within the railroad industry—even within a single company. Most hoteliers have grown up in the hotel industry. And most hospital or college administrators have remained within the confines of health care or higher education, respectively. The net result of such narrow exposure is that it restricts a manager's ability to identify and learn from the experience

Reprinted from *Journal of Marketing*, Vol. 47 (Summer 1983), 9–20, published by The American Marketing Association.

of organizations facing parallel situations in other service industries—and, of course, from marketing experience in the manufacturing sector. Conversely, marketers from the manufacturing sector who take positions in service businesses often find that their past experience has not prepared them well for working on some of the problems that regularly challenge service marketers (Knisely 1979, Lovelock 1981, Shostack 1977).

This article argues that development of greater sophistication in services marketing will be aided if we can find new ways to group services other than by current industry classifications. A more useful approach may be to segment services into clusters that share certain relevant marketing characteristics—such as the nature of the relationship between the service organization and its customers or patterns of demand relative to supply—and then to examine the implications for marketing action.

After briefly reviewing the value of classification schemes in marketing, the article summarizes past proposals for classifying services. This is followed by presentation and discussion of five classification schemes based on past proposals or on clinical research. In each instance examples are given of how various services fall into similar or different categories, and an evaluation is made of the resulting marketing insights and what they imply for marketing strategy development.

THE VALUE OF CLASSIFICATION IN MARKETING

Hunt (1976) has emphasized the usefulness of classification schemes in marketing. Various attempts have been made in the past by marketing theorists to classify goods into different categories. One of the most famous and enduring is Copeland's (1923) classification of convenience, shopping and specialty goods. Not only did this help managers obtain a better understanding of consumer needs and behavior, it also provided insights into the management of retail distribution systems. Bucklin (1963) and others have re-

vised and refined Copeland's original classification and thereby been able to provide important strategic guidelines for retailers. Another major classification has been between durable and nondurable goods. Durability is closely associated with purchase frequency, which has important implications for development of both distribution and communications strategy. Yet another classification is consumer goods versus industrial goods; this classification relates both to the type of goods purchased (although there is some overlap) and to product evaluation, purchasing procedures and usage behavior. Recognition of these distinctions by marketers has led to different types of marketing strategy being directed at each of these groups. Through such classifications the application of marketing management tools and strategies in manufacturing has become a professional skill that transcends industry divisions.

By contrast, service industries remain dominated by an operations orientation that insists that each industry is different. This mind set is often manifested in managerial attitudes that suggest, for example, that the marketing of airlines has nothing at all in common with that of banks, insurance, motels, hospitals or household movers. But if it can be shown that some of these services do share certain relevant marketing characteristics, then the stage may be set for some useful cross-fertilization of concepts and strategies.

How Might Services Be Classified?

Various attempts have been proposed in the past for classifying services and are outlined, with brief commentaries, in Table 1. But developing classification schemes is not enough. If they are to have managerial value, they must offer strategic insights. That is why it is important to develop ways of analyzing services that highlight the characteristics they have in common, and then to examine the implications for marketing management.

This article builds on past research by ex-

TABLE 1
Summary of Previously Proposed Schemes for Classifying Services

Author	Proposed Classification Schemes	Comment
Judd (1964)	1. Rented goods services (right to own and use a good for a defined time period) 2. Owned goods services (custom creation, repair or improvement of goods owned by the customer) 3. Nongoods services (personal experiences or "experiential possession")	First two are fairly specific, but third category is very broad and ignores services such as insurance, banking, legal advice and accounting.
Rathmell (1974)	1. Type of seller 2. Type of buyer 3. Buying motives 4. Buying practice 5. Degree of regulation	No specific application to services—could apply equally well to goods.
Shostack (1977)[a] Sasser et al.[a] (1978)	Proportion of physical goods and intangible services contained within each product "package"	Offers opportunities for multiattribute modeling. Emphasizes that there are few pure goods or pure services.
Hill (1977)	1. Services affecting persons vs. those affecting goods 2. Permanent vs. temporary effects of the service 3. Reversibility vs. nonreversibility of these effects 4. Physical effects vs. mental effects 5. Individual vs. collective services	Emphasizes nature of service benefits and (in 5) variations in the service delivery/ consumption environment.

Thomas (1978)	1. Primarily equipment-based
	  a. Automated (e.g., car wash)
	  b. Monitored by unskilled operators (e.g., movie theater)
	  c. Operated by skilled personnel (e.g., airline)
	2. Primarily people-based
	  a. Unskilled labor (e.g., lawn care)
	  b. Skilled labor (e.g., repair work)
	  c. Professional staff (e.g., lawyers, dentists)
		Although operational rather than marketing in orientation, provides a useful way of understanding product attributes.

Chase (1978)	Extent of customer contact required in service delivery
	  a. High contact (e.g., health care, hotels, restaurants)
	  b. Low contact (e.g., postal service, wholesaling)
		Recognizes that product variability is harder to control in high contact services because customers exert more influence on timing of demand and service features, due to their greater involvement in the service process.

Kotler (1980)	1. People-based vs. equipment-based 2. Extent to which client's presence is necessary 3. Meets personal needs vs. business needs 4. Public vs. private, for-profit vs. nonprofit	Synthesizes previous work, recognizes differences in purpose of service organization.
Lovelock (1980)	1. Basic demand characteristics —Object served (persons vs. property) —Extent of demand/supply imbalances —Discrete vs. continuous relationships between customers and providers 2. Service content and benefits —Extent of physical goods content —Extent of personal service content —Single service vs. bundle of services —Timing and duration of benefits 3. Service delivery procedures —Multisite vs. single site delivery —Allocation of capacity (reservations vs. first come, first served) —Independent vs. collective consumption —Time defined vs. task defined transactions —Extent to which customers must be present during service delivery	Synthesizes previous classifications and adds several new schemes. Proposes several categories within each classification. Concludes that defining object served is most fundamental classification scheme. Suggests that valuable marketing insights would come from combining two or more classification schemes in a matrix.

[a]These were two independent studies that drew broadly similar conclusions.

amining characteristics of services that transcend industry boundaries and are different in degree or kind from the categorization schemes traditionally applied to manufactured goods. Five classification schemes have been selected for presentation and discussion, reflecting their potential for affecting the way marketing management strategies are developed and implemented. Each represents an attempt to answer one of the following questions:

1. What is the nature of the service act?
2. What type of relationship does the service organization have with its customers?
3. How much room is there for customization and judgment on the part of the service provider?
4. What is the nature of demand and supply for the service?
5. How is the service delivered?

Each question will be examined on two dimensions, reflecting my conclusion in an earlier study (Lovelock 1980) that combining classification schemes in a matrix may yield better marketing insights than classifying service organizations on one variable at a time.

WHAT IS THE NATURE OF THE SERVICE ACT?

A service has been described as a "deed, act or performance" (Berry 1980). Two fundamental issues are at whom (or what) is the act directed, and is this act tangible or intangible in nature?

As shown in Figure 1, these two questions result in a four-way classification scheme involving (1) tangible actions to people's bodies, such as airline transportation, haircutting and surgery; (2) tangible actions to goods and other physical possessions, such as air freight, lawn mowing and janitorial services; (3) intangible actions directed at people's minds, such as broadcasting and education; and (4) intangible actions directed at people's intangible assets, such as insurance, investment banking and consulting.

Sometimes a service may seem to spill over into two or more categories. For instance, the delivery of educational, religious or entertainment services (directed primarily at the mind) often entails tangible actions such as being in a classroom, church or theater; the delivery of financial services may require a visit to a bank to transform intangible financial assets into hard cash; and the deliv-

FIGURE 1
Understanding the Nature of the Service Act

Who or What is the Direct Recipient of the Service?

What is the Nature of the Service Act?		People	Things
Tangible Actions		Services directed at people's bodies: ● Health care ● Passenger transportation ● Beauty salons ● Exercise clinics ● Restaurants ● Haircutting	Services directed at goods and other physical possessions: ● Freight transportation ● Industrial equipment repair and maintenance ● Janitorial services ● Laundry and dry cleaning ● Landscaping/lawn care ● Veterinary care
Intangible Actions		Services directed at people's minds: ● Education ● Broadcasting ● Information services ● Theaters ● Museums	Services directed at intangible assets: ● Banking ● Legal services ● Accounting ● Securities ● Insurance

ery of airline services may affect some travelers' states of mind as well as physically moving their bodies from one airport to another. But in most instances the core service act is confined to one of the four categories, although there may be secondary acts in another category.

Insights and Implications

Why is this categorization scheme useful to service marketers? Basically it helps answer the following questions:

1. Does the customer need to be *physically* present:
   a. Throughout service delivery?
   b. Only to initiate or terminate the service transaction (e.g., dropping off a car for repair and picking it up again afterwards)?
   c. Not at all (the relationship with the service supplier can be at arm's length through the mails, telephone or other electronic media)?
2. Does the customer need to be *mentally* present during service delivery? Can mental presence be maintained across physical distances through mail or electronic communications?
3. In what ways is the target of the service act "modified" by receipt of the service? And how does the customer benefit from these "modifications"?

It's not always obvious what the service is and what it does for the customer because services are ephemeral. By identifying the target of the service and then examining how it is "modified" or changed by receipt of the service act, we can develop a better understanding of the nature of the service product and the core benefits that it offers. For instance, a haircut leaves the recipient with shorter and presumably more appealingly styled hair, air freight gets the customer's goods speedily and safely between two points, a news radio broadcast updates the listener's knowledge about recent events, and life insurance protects the future value of the insured person's assets.

If customers need to be physically present during service delivery, then they must enter the service "factory" (whether it be a train, a hairdressing salon, or a hospital at a particular location) and spend time there while the service is performed. Their satisfaction with the service will be influenced by the interactions they have with service personnel, the nature of the service facilities, and also perhaps by the characteristics of other customers using the same service. Questions of location and schedule convenience assume great importance when a customer has to be physically present or must appear in person to initiate and terminate the transaction.

Dealing with a service organization at arm's length, by contrast, may mean that a customer never sees the service facilities at all and may not even meet the service personnel face-to-face. In this sort of situation, the outcome of the service act remains very important, but the process of service delivery may be of little interest, since the customer never goes near the "factory." For instance, credit cards and many types of insurance can be obtained by mail or telephone.

For operational reasons it may be very desirable to get the customer out of the factory and to transform a "high-contact" service into a "low-contact" one (Chase 1978). The chances of success in such an endeavor will be enhanced when the new procedures also offer customers greater convenience. Many services directed at *things* rather than at people formerly required the customer's presence but are now delivered at arm's length. Certain financial services have long used the mails to save customers the inconvenience of personal visits to a specific office location. Today, new electronic distribution channels have made it possible to offer instantaneous delivery of financial services to a wide array of alternative locations. Retail banking provides a good example, with its growing use of such electronic delivery systems as automatic teller machines in airports or shopping centers, pay-by-phone bill paying, or on-line banking facilities in retail stores.

By thinking creatively about the nature of their services, managers of service organizations may be able to identify opportunities for alternative, more convenient forms of service delivery or even for transformation of the service into a manufactured good. For instance, services to the mind such as education do not necessarily require attendance in person since they can be delivered through the mails or electronic media (Britain's Open University, which makes extensive use of television and radio broadcasts, is a prime example). Two-way communication hook-ups can make it possible for a physically distant teacher and students to interact directly where this is necessary to the educational process (one recent Bell System advertisement featured a chamber music class in a small town being taught by an instructor several hundred miles away). Alternatively, lectures can be packaged and sold as books, records or videotapes. And programmed learning exercises can be developed in computerized form, with the terminal serving as a Socratic surrogate.

WHAT TYPE OF RELATIONSHIP DOES THE SERVICE ORGANIZATION HAVE WITH ITS CUSTOMERS?

With very few exceptions, consumers buy manufactured goods at discrete intervals, paying for each purchase separately and rarely entering into a formal relationship with the manufacturer. (Industrial purchasers, by contrast, often enter into long-term relationships with suppliers and sometimes receive almost continuous delivery of certain supplies.)

In the service sector both household and institutional purchasers may enter into ongoing relationships with service suppliers and may receive service on a continuing basis. This offers a way of categorizing services. We can ask, does the service organization enter into a "membership" relationship with its customers—as in telephone subscriptions, banking and the family doctor—or is there no formal relationship? And is service delivered on a continuous basis—as in insurance, broadcasting and police protection —or is each transaction recorded and charged separately? Figure 2 shows the 2 × 2 matrix resulting from this categorization, with some additional examples in each category.

Insights and Implications

The advantage to the service organization of a membership relationship is that it knows who its current customers are and, usually, what use they make of the services offered. This can be valuable for segmentation purposes if good records are kept and the data are readily accessible in a format that lends itself to computerized analysis. Knowing the identities and addresses of current customers enables the organization to make effective use of direct mail, telephone selling and personal sales calls—all highly targeted marketing communication media.

The nature of service relationships also has important implications for pricing. In situations where service is offered on an ongoing basis, there is often just a single pe-

FIGURE 2
Relationships with Customers

Type of Relationship between the Service Organization and Its Customers

Nature of Service Delivery		"Membership" Relationship	No Formal Relationship
	Continuous Delivery of Service	Insurance Telephone subscription College enrollment Banking American Automobile Association	Radio station Police protection Lighthouse Public highway
	Discrete Transactions	Long-distance phone calls Theater series subscription Commuter ticket or transit pass	Car rental Mail service Toll highway Pay phone Movie theater Public transportation Restaurant

riodic charge covering all services contracted for. Most insurance policies fall in this category, as do tuition and board fees at a residential college. The big advantage of this package approach is its simplicity. Some memberships, however, entail a series of separate and identifiable transactions with the price paid being tied explicitly to the number and type of such transactions. While more complex to administer, such an approach is fairer to customers (whose usage patterns may vary widely) and may discourage wasteful use of what are perceived as "free" services. In such instances, members may be offered advantages over casual users, such as discounted rates (telephone subscribers pay less for long-distance calls made from their own phones than do pay-phone users) or advance notification and priority reservations (as in theater subscriptions). Some membership services offer certain services (such as rental of equipment or connection to a public utility system) for a base fee and then make incremental charges for each separate transaction above a defined minimum.

Profitability and customer convenience are central issues in deciding how to price membership services. Will the organization generate greater long-term profits by tying payment explicitly to consumption, by charging a flat rate regardless of consumption, or by unbundling the components of the service and charging a flat rate for some and an incremental rate for others? Telephone and electricity services, for instance, typically charge a base fee for connection to the system and rental of equipment, plus a variety of incremental charges for consumption above a defined minimum. On the other hand, Wide Area Telephone Service (WATS) offers the convenience of unlimited long-distance calling for a fixed fee. How important is it to customers to have the convenience of paying a single periodic fee that is known in advance? For instance, members of the American Automobile Association (AAA) can obtain information booklets, travel advice and certain types of emergency road services free of additional charges. Such a package offers elements of both insurance and convenience to customers who may not

be able to predict their exact needs in advance.

Where no formal relationship exists between supplier and customer, continuous delivery of the product is normally found only among that class of services that economists term "public goods"—such as broadcasting, police and lighthouse services, and public highways—where no charge is made for use of a service that is continuously available and financed from tax revenues. Discrete transactions, where each usage involves a payment to the service supplier by an essentially "anonymous" consumer, are exemplified by many transportation services, restaurants, movie theaters, shoe repairs and so forth. The problem of such services is that marketers tend to be much less well-informed about who their customers are and what use each customer makes of the service than their counterparts in membership organizations.

Membership relationships usually result in customer loyalty to a particular service supplier (sometimes there is no choice because the supplier has a monopoly). As a marketing strategy, many service businesses seek ways to develop formal, ongoing relations with customers in order to ensure repeat business and/or ongoing financial support. Public radio and television broadcasters, for instance, develop membership clubs for donors and offer monthly program guides in return; performing arts organizations sell subscription series; transit agencies offer monthly passes; airlines create clubs for high mileage fliers; and hotels develop "executive service plans" offering priority reservations and upgraded rooms for frequent guests. The marketing task here is to determine how it might be possible to build sales and revenues through such memberships but to avoid requiring membership when this would result in freezing out a large volume of desirable casual business.

HOW MUCH ROOM IS THERE FOR CUSTOMIZATION AND JUDGMENT?

Relatively few consumer goods nowadays are built to special order; most are purchased "off the shelf." The same is true for a majority of industrial goods, although by permutating options it's possible to give the impression of customization. Once they've purchased their goods, of course, customers are usually free to use them as they see fit.

The situation in the service sector, by contrast, is sharply different. Because services are created as they are consumed, and because the customer is often actually involved in the production process, there is far more scope for tailoring the service to meet the needs of individual customers. As shown in Figure 3, customization can proceed along at least two dimensions. The first concerns the extent to which the characteristics of the service and its delivery system lend themselves to customization; the second relates to how much judgment customer contact personnel are able to exercise in defining the nature of the service received by individual customers.

Some service concepts are quite standardized. Public transportation, for instance, runs over fixed routes on predetermined schedules. Routine appliance repairs typically involve a fixed charge, and the customer is responsible for dropping off the item at a given retail location and picking it up again afterwards. Fast food restaurants have a small, set menu; few offer the customer much choice in how the food will be cooked and served. Movies, entertainment and spectator sports place the audience in a relatively passive role, albeit a sometimes noisy one.

Other services offer customers a wide choice of options. Each telephone subscriber enjoys an individual number and can use the phone to obtain a broad array of different services—from receiving personal calls from a next-door neighbor to calling a business associate on the other side of the world, and from data transmission to dial-a-prayer. Retail bank accounts are also customized, with each check or bank card carrying the customer's name and personal code. Within the constraints set down by the bank, the customer enjoys considerable latitude in how and when the account is used and receives a personalized monthly statement. Good hotels and restaurants usually offer their customers an array of service options from which to choose, as well as considerable flexibility in how the service product is delivered to them.

But in each of these instances, the role of the customer contact personnel (if there are any) is somewhat constrained. Other than

FIGURE 3
Customization and Judgment in Service Delivery

Extent to Which Service Characteristics Are Customized

	High	Low
High	Legal services Health care/surgery Architectural design Executive search firm Real Estate agency Taxi service Beautician Plumber Education (tutorials)	Education (large classes) Preventive health programs
Low	Telephone service Hotel services Retail banking (excl. major loans) Good restaurant	Public transportation Routine appliance repair Fast food restaurant Movie theater Spectator sports

Extent to Which Customer Contact Personnel Exercise Judgment in Meeting Individual Customer Needs tailoring their personal manner to the customer and answering straightforward questions, contact personnel have relatively little discretion in altering the characteristics of the service they deliver: their role is basically that of operator or order taker. Judgment and discretion in customer dealings is usually reserved for managers or supervisors who will not normally become involved in service delivery unless a problem arises.

A third category of services gives the customer contact personnel wide latitude in how they deliver the service, yet these individuals do not significantly differentiate the characteristics of their service between one customer and another. For instance, educators who teach courses by lectures and give multiple choice, computer scored exams expose each of their students to a potentially similar experience, yet one professor may elect to teach a specific course in a very different way from a colleague at the same institution.

However, there is a class of services that not only involves a high degree of customization but also requires customer contact personnel to exercise judgment concerning the characteristics of the service and how it is delivered to each customer. Far from being reactive in their dealings with customers, these service personnel are often prescriptive: users (or clients) look to them for advice as well as for customized execution. In this category the locus of control shifts from the user to the supplier—a situation that some customers may find disconcerting. Consumers of surgical services literally place their lives in the surgeon's hands (the same, unfortunately, is also true of taxi services in many cities). Professional services such as law, medicine, accounting and architecture fall within this category. They are all white collar "knowledge industries," requiring extensive training to develop the requisite skills and judgment needed for satisfactory service delivery. Deliverers of such services as taxi drivers, beauticians and plumbers are also found in this category. Their work is customized to the situation at hand and in each instance, the customer purchases the expertise required to devise a tailor-made solution.

Insights and Implications

To a much greater degree than in the manufacturing sector, service products are "custom-made." Yet customization has its costs. Service management often represents an ongoing struggle between the desires of marketing managers to add value and the goals of operations managers to reduce costs through standardization. Resolving such disputes, a task that may require arbitration by the general manager, requires a good understanding of consumer choice criteria, particularly as these relate to price/value trade-offs and competitive positioning strategy. At the present time, most senior managers in service businesses have come up through the operations route; hence, participation in executive education programs may be needed to give them the necessary perspective on marketing to make balanced decisions.

Customization is not necessarily important to success. As Levitt (1972, 1976) has pointed out, industrializing a service to take advantage of the economies of mass production may actually increase consumer satisfaction. Speed, consistency and price savings may be more important to many customers than customized service. In some instances, such as spectator sports and the performing arts, part of the product experience is sharing the service with many other people. In other instances the customer expects to share the service facilities with other consumers, as in hotels or airlines, yet still hopes for some individual recognition and custom treatment. Allowing customers to reserve specific rooms or seats in advance, having contact personnel address them by name (it's on their ticket or reservation slip), and providing some latitude for individual choice (room service and morning calls, drinks and meals) are all ways to create an image of customization.

Generally, customers like to know in advance what they are buying—what the product features are, what the service will do for them. Surprises and uncertainty are not normally popular. Yet when the nature of the service requires a judgment-based, customized solution, as in a professional service, it is not always clear to either the customer or the professional what the outcome will be. Frequently, an important dimension of the professional's role is diagnosing the nature of the situation, then designing a solution.

In such situations those responsible for developing marketing strategy would do well to recognize that customers may be uneasy concerning the prior lack of certainty about the outcome. Customer contact personnel in these instances are not only part of the product but also determine what that product should be.

One solution to this problem is to divide the product into two separate components, diagnosis and implementation of a solution, that are executed and paid for separately. The process of diagnosis can and should be explained to the customer in advance, since the outcome of the diagnosis cannot always be predicted accurately. However, once that diagnosis has been made, the customer need not proceed immediately with the proposed solution; indeed, there is always the option of seeking a second opinion. The solution "product," by contrast, can often be spelled out in detail beforehand, so that the customer has a reasonable idea of what to expect. Although there may still be some uncertainty, as in legal actions or medical treatment, the range of possibilities should be narrower by this point, and it may be feasible to assign probabilities to specified alternative outcomes.

Marketing efforts may need to focus on the process of client-provider interactions. It will help prospective clients make choices between alternative suppliers, especially where professionals are concerned, if they know something of the organization's (or individual's) approach to diagnosis and problem-solving, as well as client-relationship style. These are considerations that transcend mere statements of qualification in an advertisement or brochure. For instance, some pediatricians allow new parents time for a free interview before any commitments are made. Such a trial encounter has the advantage of allowing both parties to decide whether or not a good match exists.

WHAT IS THE NATURE OF DEMAND AND SUPPLY FOR THE SERVICE?

Manufacturing firms can inventory supplies of their products as a hedge against fluctuations in demand. This enables them to enjoy the economies derived from operating plants at a steady level of production. Service businesses can't do this because it's not possible to inventory the finished service. For instance, the potential income from an empty seat on an airline flight is lost forever once that flight takes off, and each hotel daily room vacancy is equally perishable. Likewise, the productive capacity of an auto repair shop is wasted if no one brings a car for servicing on a day when the shop is open. Conversely, if the demand for a service exceeds supply on a particular day, the excess business may be lost. Thus, if someone can't get a seat on one airline, another carrier gets the business or the trip is cancelled or postponed. If an accounting firm is too busy to accept tax and audit work from a prospective client, another firm will get the assignment.

But demand and supply imbalances are not found in all service situations. A useful way of categorizing services for this purpose is shown in Figure 4. The horizontal axis classifies organizations according to whether demand for the service fluctuates widely or narrowly over time; the vertical axis classifies them according to whether or not capacity is sufficient to meet peak demand.

Organizations in Box 1 could use increases in demand outside peak periods, those in Box 2 must decide whether to seek continued growth in demand and capacity or to continue the status quo, while those in Box 3 represent growing organizations that may need temporary demarketing until capacity can be increased to meet or exceed current demand levels. But service organizations in Box 4 face an ongoing problem of trying to smooth demand to match capacity, involving both stimulation and discouragement of demand.

Insights and Implications

Managing demand is a task faced by nearly all marketers, whether offering goods or ser-

FIGURE 4
What Is the Nature of Demand for the Service Relative to Supply?

Extent of Demand Fluctuations over Time

	Wide	Narrow
Peak Demand Can Usually Be Met without a Major Delay	1 Electricity Natural gas Telephone Hospital maternity unit Police and fire emergencies	2 Insurance Legal services Banking Laundry and dry cleaning
Peak Demand Regularly Exceeds Capacity	4 Accounting and tax preparation Passenger transportation Hotels and motels Restaurants Theaters	3 Services similar to those in 2 but which have insufficient capacity for their base level of business

Extent to Which Supply Is Constrained

vices. Even where the fluctuations are sharp, and inventories cannot be used to act as a buffer between supply and demand, it may still be possible to manage capacity in a service business—for instance, by hiring part-time employees or renting extra facilities at peak periods. But for a substantial group of service organizations, successfully managing demand fluctuations through marketing actions is the key to profitability.

To determine the most appropriate strategy in each instance, it's necessary to seek answers to some additional questions:

1. What is the typical cycle period of these demand fluctuations?
   - Predictable (i.e., demand varies by hour of the day, day of the week or month, season of the year).
   - Random (i.e., no apparent pattern to demand fluctuations).
2. What are the underlying causes of these demand fluctuations?
   - Customer habits or preferences (could marketing efforts change these)?
   - Actions by third parties (for instance, employers set working hours, hence marketing efforts might usefully be directed at those employers).
   - Nonforecastable events, such as health symptoms, weather conditions, acts of God

and so forth—marketing can do only a few things about these, such as offering priority services to members and disseminating information about alternative services to other people.

One way to smooth out the ups and downs of demand is through strategies that encourage customers to change their plans voluntarily, such as offering special discount prices or added product value during periods of low demand. Another approach is to ration demand through a reservation or queuing system (which basically inventories demand rather than supply). Alternatively, to generate demand in periods of excess capacity, new business development efforts might be targeted at prospective customers with a countercyclical demand pattern. For instance, an accounting firm with a surfeit of work at the end of each calendar year might seek new customers whose financial year ended on June 30 or September 30.

Determining what strategy is appropriate requires an understanding of who or what is the target of the service (as discussed in an earlier section of this article). If the service is delivered to customers in person, there are limits to how long a customer will wait in line; hence strategies to inventory or ration demand should focus on adoption of reservation systems (Sasser 1976). But if the service is delivered to goods or to intangible assets, then a strategy of inventorying demand should be more feasible (unless the good is a vital necessity such as a car, in which case reservations may be the best approach).

HOW IS THE SERVICE DELIVERED?

Understanding distribution issues in service marketing requires that two basic issues be addressed. The first relates to the method of delivery. Is it necessary for the customer to be in direct physical contact with the service organization (customers may have to go to the service organization, or the latter may come to the former), or can transactions be completed at arm's length? And does the service organization maintain just a single outlet or does it serve customers through multiple outlets at different sites? The outcome of this analysis can be seen in Figure 5, which consists of six different cells.

Insights and Implications

The convenience of receiving service is presumably lowest when a customer has to come to the service organization and must use a specific outlet. Offering service through several outlets increases the convenience of access for customers but may start to raise problems of quality control as convenience

of access relates to the consistency of the service product delivered. For some types of services the organization will come to the customer. This is, of course, essential when the target of the service is some immovable physical item (such as a building that needs repairs or pest control treatment, or a garden that needs landscaping). But since it's usually more expensive to take service personnel and equipment to the customer than vice versa, the trend has been away from this approach to delivering consumer services (e.g., doctors no longer like to make house calls). In many instances, however, direct contact between customers and the service organization is not necessary; instead, transactions can be handled at arm's length by mail or electronic communications. Through the use of 800 numbers many service organizations have found that they can bring their services as close as the nearest telephone, yet obtain important economies from operating out of a single physical location.

Although not all services can be delivered through arm's length transactions, it may be possible to separate certain components of the service from the core product and to handle them separately. This suggests an additional classification scheme: categorizing services according to whether transactions such as obtaining information, making reservations and making payment can be broken out separately from delivery of the core service. If they can be separated, then the question is whether or not it is advantageous

FIGURE 5
Method of Service Delivery

	Availability of Service Outlets	
Nature of Interaction between Customer and Service Organization	Single Site	Multiple Sites
Customer Goes to Service Organization	Theater Barbershop	Bus service Fast food chain
Service Organization Comes to Customer	Lawn care service Pest control service Taxi	Mail delivery AAA emergency repairs
Customer and Service Organization Transact at Arm's Length (mail or electronic communications)	Credit card company Local TV station	Broadcast network Telephone co.

to the service firm to allow customers to make these peripheral transactions through an intermediary or broker.

For instance, information about airline flights, reservations for such flights and purchases of tickets can all be made through a travel agent as well as directly through the airline. For those who prefer to visit in person, rather than conduct business by telephoning, this greatly increases the geographic coverage of distribution, since there are usually several travel agencies located more conveniently than the nearest airline office. Added value from using a travel agent comes from the "one-stop shopping" aspect of travel agents; the customer can inquire about several airlines and make car rental and hotel reservations during the same call. Insurance brokers and theater ticket agencies are also examples of specialist intermediaries that represent a number of different service organizations. Consumers sometimes perceive such intermediaries as more objective and more knowledgeable about alternatives than the various service suppliers they represent. The risk to the service firm of working through specialist intermediaries is, of course, that they may recommend use of a competitor's product!

DISCUSSION

Widespread interest in the marketing of services among both academics and practitioners is a relatively recent phenomenon. Possibly this reflects the fact that marketing expertise in the service sector has significantly lagged behind that in the manufacturing sector. Up to now most academic research and discussion has centered on the issue, "How do services differ from goods?" A number of authors including Shostack (1977), Bateson (1979), and Berry (1980) have argued that there are significant distinctions between the two and have proposed several generalizations for management practice. But others such as Enis and Roering (1981) remain unconvinced that these differences have meaningful strategic implications.

Rather than continue to debate the existence of this broad dichotomy, it seems more useful to get on with the task of helping managers in service businesses do a better job of developing and marketing their products. We need to recognize that the service sector, particularly in the United States, is beoming increasingly competitive (Langeard et al., 1981), reflecting such developments as the partial or complete deregulation of several major service industries in recent years, the removal of professional association restrictions on using marketing techniques (particularly advertising), the replacement (or absorption) of independent service units by franchise chains, and the growth of new electronic delivery systems. As competition intensifies within the service sector, the development of more effective marketing efforts becomes essential to survival.

The classification schemes proposed in this article can contribute usefully to management practice in two ways. First, by addressing each of the five questions posed earlier, marketing managers can obtain a better understanding of the nature of their product, of the types of relationships their service organizations have with customers, of the factors underlying any sharp variations in demand, and of the characteristics of their service delivery systems. This understanding should help them identify how these factors shape marketing problems and opportunities and thereby affect the nature of the marketing task. Second, by recognizing which characteristics their own service shares with other services, often in seemingly unrelated industries, managers will learn to look beyond their immediate competitors for new ideas as to how to resolve marketing problems that they share in common with firms in other service industries.

Recognizing that the products of service organizations previously considered as "different" actually face similar problems or share certain characteristics in common can yield valuable managerial insights. Innovation in marketing, after all, often reflects a manager's ability to seek out and learn from analogous situations in other contexts. These classification schemes should also be of value to researchers to whom they offer an alternative to either broad-brush research into services or an industry-by-industry approach. Instead, they suggest a variety of new ways of looking at service businesses, each of which may offer opportunities for focused research efforts. Undoubtedly there is also room for further refinement of the schemes proposed.

REFERENCES

BATESON, JOHN E. G. (1979), "Why We Need Service Marketing," in *Conceptual and Theoretical Developments in Marketing*, O. C. Ferrell, S. W. Brown, and C. W. Lamb, eds. Chicago, American Marketing Association, 131–146.

BERRY, LEONARD L. (1980), "Services Marketing Is Different," *Business* (May–June), 24–29.

BUCKLIN, LOUIS (1963), "Retail Strategy and the Classification of Consumer Goods," *Journal of Marketing*, **27** (January), 50.

CHASE, RICHARD B. (1978), "Where Does the Customer Fit in a Service Operation?," *Harvard Business Review*, **56** (November–December), 137–142.

COPELAND, MELVIN T. (1923), "The Relation of Consumers' Buying Habits to Marketing Methods," *Harvard Business Review*, **1** (April), 282–289.

ENIS, BEN M., and KENNETH J. ROERING (1981), "Services Marketing: Different Products, Similar Strategies," in *Marketing of Services*, J. H. Donnelly and W. R. George, eds. Chicago: American Marketing Association.

HILL, T. P. (1977), "On Goods and Services," *Review of Income and Wealth*, **23** (December), 315–338.

HUNT, SHELBY D. (1976), *Marketing Theory*. Columbus, OH: Grid.

JUDD, ROBERT C. (1964), "The Case for Redefining Services," *Journal of Marketing*, **28** (January), 59.

KNISELY, GARY (1979), "Marketing and the Services Industry," *Advertising Age* (January 15), 47–50; (February 19), 54–60; (March 19), 58–62; (May 15), 57–58.

KOTLER, PHILIP (1980), *Principles of Marketing*. Englewood Cliffs, NJ: Prentice-Hall, Inc.

LANGEARD, ERIC, JOHN E. G. BATESON, CHRISTOPHER H. LOVELOCK, and PIERRE EIGLIER (1981), *Services Marketing: New Insights from Consumers and Managers*. Cambridge, MA: Marketing Science Institute.

LEVITT, THEODORE (1972), "Production Line Approach to Service," *Harvard Business Review*, **50** (September–October), 41.

——— (1976), "The Industrialization of Service," *Harvard Business Review*, **54** (September-October), 63–74.

LOVELOCK, CHRISTOPHER H. (1980), "Towards a Classification of Services," in *Theoretical Developments in Marketing*, C. W. Lamb and P. M. Dunne, eds. Chicago: American Marketing Association, 72–76.

——— (1981), "Why Marketing Management Needs to Be Different for Services," in *Marketing of Services*, J. H. Donnelly and W. R. George, eds. Chicago: American Marketing Association.

RATHMELL, JOHN M. (1974), *Marketing in the Service Sector*. Cambridge, MA: Winthrop.

SASSER, W. EARL, JR. (1976), "Match Supply and Demand in Service Industries," *Harvard Business Review*, **54** (November–December), 133.

———, R. PAUL OLSEN, and D. DARYL WYCKOFF (1978), *Management of Service Operations: Text and Cases*. Boston: Allyn & Bacon.

SHOSTACK, G. LYNN (1977), "Breaking Free from Product Marketing," *Journal of Marketing*, **41** (April), 73–80.

THOMAS, DAN R. E. (1978), "Strategy Is Different in Service Businesses," *Harvard Business Review*, **56** (July–August), 158–165.

Managing Facilitator Services

DAVID H. MAISTER
CHRISTOPHER H. LOVELOCK

This article examines a group of industries—including stock-brokerage operations, real estate, and travel agencies—that facilitate the buying and selling of goods and services. These facilitator industries exhibit many common features, such as the general types of services that they provide, their compensation structures, and the relationships found between the firms and their brokers and clients. By following developments in other facilitator services, managers of facilitator firms should be able to anticipate future trends in their own industries.

Part of the art of management is learning how to benefit from the experience of others: being able to recognize similarities in problems and situations that have been encountered before so that the lessons learned in those situations can be brought to bear on the problems at hand. Frequently, the search for common experiences reaches across industry boundaries. Consumer goods producers study each other's actions in the search for the common experiences of marketing such products. Manufacturers with assembly-line factories attempt to draw upon each other's experience with such operations. In each of these examples, the area of common ground that unifies the experiences is clear: consumer goods marketing in the former case, assembly-line operations in the latter.

The ability to classify industries in these ways is the result of many years of research. Over time we have learned that it is, indeed, a useful categorization to divide marketing into consumer marketing and industrial marketing; to divide operations into job shops, assembly lines, and continuous-flow types. However, much of what is known about such industry "types" has developed in the manufacturing sector. When we turn our attention to services, few such useful categorizations can be found.

Many authors have sought to develop useful generalizations about the entire service sector. Yet there is as much—or more—diversity among service businesses as there is among manufacturing firms, and few generalizations (whether about marketing, operations, or any other managerial topic) are likely to hold true for all services.

THE NATURE AND ROLE OF FACILITATOR FIRMS

This article examines a group of service industries that, we believe, have much in common with each other but are notably different from other types of services. They are what we term the facilitator service industries.

Who Are the Facilitators?

Facilitator services include those industries that are in the business of facilitating market transactions, the buying and selling of other goods or services. Prime examples of such industries are travel agencies, employment agencies, and real estate brokerage operations. The use of the word "broker" also suggests other types of facilitators, including stockbrokerage operations, insurance brokers, and even marriage brokerage and dating services.

Facilitators act as "experts for hire" in their respective markets, bringing buyers and sellers together and advising (perhaps at different times) both buyer and seller. Their fee, which is usually in the form of a commission, is earned when the buyer and the seller complete their transaction. This commission may be paid by the buyer, the seller, or both.

A distinction must be drawn between facilitator services and other intermediary functions, such as retail (or wholesale) merchandising. The latter involves taking possession of a physical product (on either a purchase or consignment basis) and then reselling it, thus serving as the distribution channel for some seller or group of sellers. Some brokerage operations may indeed engage in purchase and resale (travel agents

sometimes act in this way), but there is an important distinction between the two roles. The merchandiser is primarily a seller; the facilitator, primarily an *advisor*. In some industries these roles may sit happily together in one business; in others they are being forced apart.

The Facilitators' Role

Why do facilitators exist? Basically, the facilitators' services are required whenever there is some form of market "failure." In the economist's model, one of the preconditions for the successful functioning of a "free" market is perfect information. To make a wise purchase or sale decision, both buyer and seller need to be able to know who is in the market, what the range of offerings is, how the characteristics of different offerings compare, what their prices are, and so forth. When these conditions are absent, there is an opportunity for the facilitator, whose role is basically that of a market expert.

The facilitator's key stock in trade is *information*. A potential client who visits a real estate broker wants to know what houses or apartments are for sale, their condition, the current state of the market in terms of prices, and so forth. Similar types of informational services are provided by travel agents who assist customers in searching through alternative travel offerings, and by employment agencies which help job seekers uncover job opportunities. In providing these services, the facilitator adds value by assembling in one place a great deal of relevant information. Buyers (and sellers) *could* perform the "market search" for themselves, but the use of the agency or broker allows this search to be conducted much more efficiently.

However, this is only one component of facilitator services. In addition to simple information exchange, real estate agents, employment agents, and travel agents all offer *advice* (as, indeed, do stockbrokers and insurance brokers). Their clients seek assistance in evaluating alternative courses of action and the various factors that may influence the buying or selling decision. For instance, home sellers seek advice on current market values of homes in the area and the prices they should ask for their own homes. Meantime, home buyers seek advice on the quality of different neighborhoods and probable future trends in the values of different types of houses. The travel agent evaluates alternative vacation spots, the stockbroker advises on individual stocks and bonds, and the employment agency advises on the characteristics of individual companies.

The common thread running through these examples is that what is being sought in engaging the facilitator's services is not only efficient access to market information, but, more crucially, assistance in evaluating it. Whether the purchase (or sale) is a home, a vacation, a job, an insurance policy, or an investment, it involves a degree of risk for the client. In most cases, the client does not feel fully competent to appraise the available alternatives alone, and therefore seeks out expert assistance.

A third way in which facilitators add value to their clients is that they assist in *completion of the transaction*. Travel agents issue tickets and hotel vouchers; employment agencies forward resumes and employer information; stockbrokers handle the actual buying and selling of the securities. Increasingly, real estate agents are providing access to mortgage financing and assisting with (if not necessarily performing) the legal paperwork requirements necessary to complete the transaction.

PROBLEMS FOR FACILITATORS

It is important to stress the tripartite nature of the facilitator's services: information exchange, advice, and transaction processing. Many of the management problems (and opportunities) in facilitator industries derive from the interaction of these three elements and the attempt to balance them appropriately.

In most facilitator industries, commission or fee revenue is only obtained when the transaction is completed. The commission rate is usually standard across the industry, whether by legal fiat or entrenched industry

practice. All employment agencies tend to charge the same commission; for professional positions, this is normally 1 percent for every $1,000 of starting salary, up to a limit such as $30,000. Real estate agents charge 5 to 6 percent of the sales price of the home, and travel agents receive 7 to 11 percent of the sales price of the airfare, depending on the nature of the travel. Fixed commissions existed, of course, in the stockbrokerage industry until "Mayday"—May 1, 1975; later we shall review the impact of the abolition of fixed commissions. It should be noted here that events in the brokerage industry may serve as a foretaste of what other facilitators can expect when and if fee competition develops in their own industries.

The circumstances of providing *three* types (or levels) of service while being compensated for only one (the completion of the transaction) creates significant problems for the facilitator firm. A large amount of effort and cost may be invested in the provision of the first two levels of service (information and advice) without generating any corresponding revenues. Indeed, the need for this investment is often given as a reason for preserving the fixed commission system. In most facilitator industries, the return on the investment, when it comes, can be substantial. An employment agency's fee for successfully placing a candidate may be as high as $5,000; selling a house may result in commissions in excess of $10,000. But a great deal of speculative effort on behalf of a number of *potential* clients is necessary to reap the rewards from a single completed transaction.

Historically, this risk to the facilitator firm has been reduced by sharing it with the frontline work force. Real estate brokers, stockbrokers, employment agents, and insurance agents (although not travel agents) usually receive a substantial component (if not the majority) of their compensation in the form of shared commissions. In employment agencies and real estate, the norm has been as much as 50 percent of the commission earned by the firm, although proportions in other industries have varied.

Because of this traditional compensation system, relations between the individual broker and the facilitator firm are unlike employee-employer relations in many other industries. In fact, the firm is more dependent upon the individual broker than vice versa. It is the broker who undertakes most of the interaction with the client and who develops the loyalty of the client. The client may have little involvement with the firm as such: in many clients' eyes the broker handling their transactions *is* the firm. A classic syndrome in all of these industries is the talented broker with a loyal customer base who leaves the firm, taking along a customer following. Competition in these industries may often be as much to attract (and retain) quality employees as it is to attract clients.

Client-Broker-Firm Relations

What are the causes (and results) of the tripartite relationship formed by the firm, its brokers, and its clients in Figure 1? As we have seen, the "bond" between the broker and the client is often stronger than the bond between the client and the firm or the bond between the broker and the firm. This reflects the fact that in many facilitator services it is individual brokers rather than the firm

FIGURE 1
A Tripartite Relationship

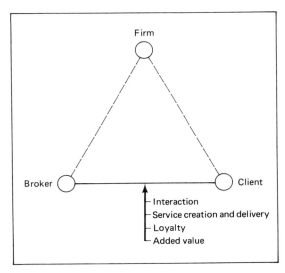

who add the most value in the delivery of the service. The broker is not only the salesperson, but also the producer of the service.

This is particularly true of those facilitator firms whose strategy is to place emphasis on the *advice* component of the facilitator's three services. A key characteristic of the advice function that distinguishes it from information exchange and transaction completion is that it is, by its very nature, a customizing process (if not necessarily a customized one). A crucial part of the interactive process necessary to delivery of the facilitator's services is a diagnostic stage in which the client's needs, wishes, and values (i.e., what constitutes a good home, vacation, job, investment goal, or insurance coverage?) are established. If this task is performed well, then succeeding tasks become much easier, if not routine. It is the ability and skill to diagnose and customize effectively that lie at the heart of the advice function; these activities have traditionally been assigned to frontline professionals in the typical facilitator service firm. Regardless of the firm's efficiency in assembling and disseminating relevant market information, or of its ability to establish routinized procedures to complete transactions, it is the interactive process termed "advice" that constitutes much of the added value of the firm. Providing this advice has traditionally been the function of the individual broker.

POSITIONING THE FACILITATOR FIRM

The relative emphasis given to information exchange, advice, and transaction processing is, of course, a strategic decision for the individual firm that serves to position itself in the marketplace. It is possible for the firm to specialize in one or more of these functions. The discount stockbrokerage operations that have spread since the ending of fixed commissions clearly are focused upon transaction processing, while "old-style" brokerage houses continue to emphasize their research and advice functions.

A policy of pursuing two strategies aimed

at different markets is exemplified by those travel agents that solicit both commercial (business travel) accounts and individual/family vacationers. In fact, these two types of accounts are distinctly different and should probably be managed separately. Commercial account business is transacted largely by telephone and made up of reasonably routine activities. The traveler, typically an executive, wishes to get from point A to point B. The agent takes the order by telephone, checks the flight schedule, and issues the ticket. Little or no advice is given. By contrast, a vacation traveler may visit the office and remain seated with the agent while a large number of options are reviewed and an extended debate takes place. In the former case, the service is primarily one of transaction processing, while in the latter the service emphasizes advice. As might be expected, those firms following high-advice strategies have a greater need for a "professional" work force, and have the most firmly entrenched commission system (and tripartite relations problem). Later we shall explore the techniques used by the management of such firms to overcome this problem.

EXPANSION AND DIVERSIFICATION STRATEGIES

In positioning itself in the marketplace, the facilitator firm first must choose which of the three tasks (information, advice, and transaction) to emphasize. However, since a firm only receives revenue when a transaction is completed, it also has a vested interest in ensuring that no "roadblocks" exist, for either buyer or seller, that prevent completion of the deal. Anything that may prevent this threatens the revenue stream. This is an incentive for the facilitator to expand its activities to remove these roadblocks, taking on additional components of the transaction task in a form of horizontal integration.

Consider, for example, the real estate industry, where difficulty in obtaining a mortgage loan has prevented many otherwise satisfactory sales transactions from being completed. Now there is a growing trend for realtors to provide access to mortgage funds

as part of their service offerings. In recent years Merrill Lynch has entered the real estate brokerage market, with the announced strategy of offering a full line of all services (from brokerage to mortgage financing to insurance) that might be required during a residential real estate transaction. Also led by Merrill Lynch, the securities brokerage industry is similarly diversifying its services with such offerings as "Cash Management Accounts" which allow the customer to move funds in and out of the securities market with the minimum of friction. In the employment agency field, some firms assist applicants in the preparation of resumes, or they check references for employers. In the travel agency business, firms long ago expanded their basic business of travel bookings to include reservations for hotels, car rentals, and other adjuncts to travel.

When additional services are added to facilitate successful completion of the primary transaction, the facilitator firm has to choose between offering the additional services as *separate* services or as a "bundle." In its early stages, a new service is frequently introduced as an ancillary service at no charge to the client (effectively "bundling" the existing and new services). For example, arranging mortgage loans was introduced by some real estate brokers solely to ensure that the home sale went through. Subsequently, as the firm expands its activities in this new way, a charge may be imposed for each separate service. Now the key advantage is that of "one-stop shopping" for an array of services.

A final stage is for the firm to get involved not only in assembling the product or service bundle, but also in modifying the package and taking a "position" in the actual creation of the services being transacted. A prime example is when travel agents create their own charter tours and offer them for sale in the marketplace. Investment banking firms, which facilitate large financial transactions such as mergers and acquisitions, also engage in this activity.

The Facilitator Life Cycle

In this review of facilitator firm activities, we have seen that the firm must choose the

TABLE 1
Stages in the Development of Facilitator Organizations

Passive brokerage	Basic information exchange (simple listings of would-be buyers and sellers)
Active brokerage	Attempts to match buyer and seller needs, involving advice and counseling
Multiservice brokerage	Wide range of services related to completed transactions offered to provide "one-stop shopping"
Packaging brokerage	Services and products from various sellers are commissioned or modified by broker

level of its involvement in the transaction it is attempting to facilitate. The various levels are summarized in Table 1. They are presented in the form of an industry "life cycle," since this is the way that many such facilitator industries have evolved. It is, however, not necessary for firms to go through all of the stages. In emerging facilitator industries, different firms may attempt to enter the market at different stages.

Apart from the levels of service shown in Table 1, the facilitator firm must make choices along another dimension in positioning itself in its industry. It must decide whether to target the buyers or sellers (or both) of the product it is attempting to facilitate. While realtors and employment agencies, of necessity, attempt to serve both buyers and sellers, travel agents target their services primarily at buyers of travel services, acting as a form of distributor for a large number of firms in the transportation, travel, and hospitality industries, rather than seeking exclusive franchises.

Serving Both Buyers and Sellers

A facilitator industry can only exist when it provides advantages to both buyer and seller. If there is some form of market failure (for example, sellers find it difficult to communicate with buyers), it is in the ultimate interests of both buyers and sellers that the market friction or barriers be overcome. One side or the other may have the power

and resources to accomplish this for itself: for example, the airline or insurance industries might decide to invest the resources to reach their market directly through their own consumer outlets. The travel agency and insurance brokerage businesses can exist only to the extent that they add value to both sides of the transaction they are facilitating. The interests, resources, and capabilities of both sides must be considered in defining the nature of the facilitator business.

The difficulty posed by this "middleman" function is best seen in the real estate or employment agency fields, where it is conventional for firms to acknowledge both sides of the transaction as their potential clients. The problem is that the services desired from the facilitator by the buyers are not necessarily compatible with those desired by the sellers. For example, in serving a job hunter well, a firm may offer assistance in resume preparation, advice on how to behave in an interview, and so forth. However, these services may not be in the best interests of the potential employer who wishes to be able to evaluate the "real" candidate, rather than a carefully packaged one. Similarly, in a residential real estate transaction, the broker's advice to sellers on how to smarten up their homes for profitable resale may not be in the best interests of buyers. Attempting to design services that will attract both buyers and sellers may even represent a conflict of interest on the part of the facilitator. This problem is recognized by investment bankers who have addressed it by forming separate departments for dealing with buyers and sellers and maintaining a "Chinese Wall" between these departments.

While the potential for conflict of interest is not as great in other facilitator industries as it is in investment banking, the lesson that the different interests of the two parties to a transaction might best be served by different departments is one that other facilitators might usefully consider. In real estate brokerage, for example, it is generally the practice that the same individual broker (at different times) will be required to act on behalf of a seller and a buyer. However, the way in which good service is rendered to those two groups, and the personal talents and skills necessary to their delivery may be quite distinct. Sellers wish for advice on how to present their home, what price to ask, and assurances that their privacy will not be interrupted too much as buyers are shown around. Buyers want detailed information not only about individual homes, but also about communities and availability of financing; they want to be able to make a detailed inspection of any property they are seriously interested in buying, and to be reassured as to the value of their prospective purchases. Even if the expertise (or knowledge) required to serve both groups well is sometimes the same, the process (interactive) skills necessary to deal with each group are not, and there may be great benefits to specialization.

The relative emphasis given by the firm toward buyer or seller groups may change over time. Consider, for example, an employment agency. In booming times when employees of a particular profession are scarce and job openings numerous, the firm needs to strengthen its ability to attract potential candidates. However, in recessionary periods when there is a glut of job seekers, the competitive position of the firm will be enhanced to the extent that it can provide superior service in meeting the needs of employers seeking to fill a position. Over time the firm must learn to balance its capabilities.

STEPS IN THE FACILITATING PROCESS

We have seen that the facilitator firm is defined by its ability to acquire market information and expertise (which are *not* the same), and to bring these to bear in matching the needs of buyers and sellers in order to complete a transaction. To review the management tasks this imposes on the firm, let us look at a conceptual model of the necessary steps in this process (see Figure 2).

FIGURE 2
The Facilitating Process

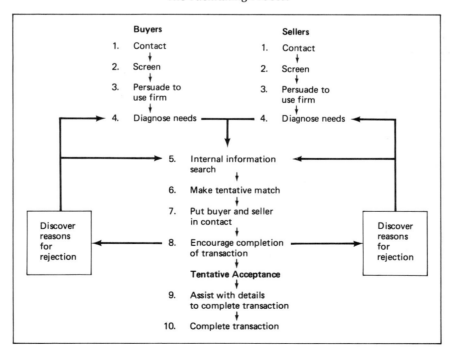

Encouraging Contact with the Firm

The first step, naturally, is to encourage both buyers and sellers to contact the firm: the primary marketing task. The approaches taken to accomplish this in various facilitator industries have varied widely, including reliance on personal contact and referral (widely encountered in old-style real estate and stockbrokerage firms), development of high-traffic retail office locations to attract walk-in clients (travel agencies), and use of mass-media advertising (which is increasingly common in all facilitator industries).

Screening Prospective Clients

The next step in the facilitating process should logically be one of screening. As noted earlier, facilitator firms can expend a great deal of time and effort on potential clients who do not ultimately complete a transaction. It is, therefore, crucial that the firm screen its potential clients so that this wasted effort is minimized. In some firms, a form of "coding" is employed that categorizes potential clients both by the probability of successfully helping them ("placeability" in employment agencies, available funds to spend or invest in real estate and stockbrokerage) and by the size of the resulting transaction. In old-style firms, this decision (on the amount of effort to expend, if any, on an individual potential client) is left up to the individual broker. At more "modern" (or "professional") firms, a formal system is employed. (If such a system is *not* used, then one of the crucial training tasks inside the firm is ensuring that new or junior brokers learn how to be selective in accepting or turning away prospective clients.)

Signing Up Clients

Just because a prospective client is attractive to the facilitator does not automatically mean that the reverse is true. The next task is to get the prospect to use the firm's services. Where personal referral is relied upon for developing contacts, the task of per-

suading the client to *use* the firm tends to be personal; however, there is an increasing trend to institutionalize this function through the means of giving away ancillary services and products. The task here is to get the client to "list" with the firm: to give the firm the opportunity to make a match. Many firms attempt to lock in clients with free services, such as securities research reports (stockbrokerage), home maintenance hints (real estate brokerage), free resume kits (employment agencies), and travel brochures (travel agencies).

In part, the function of these free products and services is to create an implicit sense of obligation in the potential client. They also serve to reinforce the facilitator firm's image of expertise, offering proof of the firm's knowledge of market dynamics. Some firms have taken this a step further by providing brief seminars: stockbrokers hold investment counseling evenings, real estate agents hold home improvement seminars, and one innovative employment firm (Scientific Placement) recently announced a seminar for corporations on how to improve their recruiting activities. By promoting the expertise of the firm, these activities strengthen the customer appeal of the firm as opposed to that of the broker.

Diagnosing Client Needs

The next step in the facilitating process is to diagnose the client's specific needs. It is at this stage that the crucial task of customization enters into the system. For most facilitator firms, this stage is the real test of the firm's effectiveness. Usually, good diagnosis directly affects the client's perception both of service quality ("That broker understood what we were looking for in a house"; "They didn't send me to any job interviews that weren't close to what I was looking for"), and of efficiency (no wasted effort in making matches that one or both of the parties would not realistically consider).

The diagnosis stage has a significant educational component. Clients often look to a facilitator firm for guidance in how to make a choice, advice on what to look for, and suggestions on how to appraise alternatives. Again this is not only an opportunity to provide service, but also an opportunity to improve the efficiency of the firm's performance. To the extent that clients' expectations as either buyers or sellers can be made more realistic, the probabilities of a successful match (and, hence, revenue to the firm) are enhanced.

Search for Potential Matches

The next step in the facilitating process is a search for potential matches. This is usually an *internal* process for the firm, as it "mines" its files for lists of buyers to offer sellers and lists of sellers to offer buyers. The computer revolution has the potential for greatly enhancing the efficiency of this process. Since the stock in trade of the facilitator firm is market information, the great advantage of the computer is that it allows firms to accumulate (and *access more efficiently*) larger quantities and types of information. Travel agencies are well along this road, thanks to the efforts of individual airlines in sharing access, through leased CRT units, to their schedule and seat availability information. (It is interesting to note, however, that as yet there is no *combined* data base for all airlines, so the full efficiencies in this regard have not yet been reaped.) The computer is also beginning to be used in real estate brokerage; there is much talk in that industry (and some progress) in computerizing the "multiple listing service" (homes available for sale) to which most agencies in a given locality usually subscribe. In the employment agency field, at least one agency has computerized its files on job openings and available candidates, leading to efficiencies in making "quality" matches.

Making a Tentative Match

The next stage in the facilitating process is making a "tentative" match and putting buyer and seller in touch with each other. In real estate and employment agencies, this is a physical phenomenon: the house buyer

must see the house and the job hunter must be interviewed by the potential employer. In a travel agency or stockbrokerage, this can be accomplished through paperwork: showing brochures of travel destinations and annual reports and research reports. It should be noted that, here too, the facilitator industries are learning from each other. Real estate agents and employment agencies are increasingly providing more information about specific homes and jobs in paper form. This enhances the service in the clients' eyes, saving travel time and providing more information to make a reasoned decision on whether to explore the match further. There is also speculation about—and some experimentation in—the use of video tapes or slide projection machines to show pictures of homes in the realtor's office. Once again, this represents an opportunity for the firm to provide service to its own brokers and add to value above that created by them. At the same time, it constitutes an additional fixed cost.

Encouraging Completion

The next step is to encourage the buyer and seller in a tentative match to complete the transaction (to buy *this* security, to accept *this* offer for the home, to go on *this* vacation, to hire *this* candidate). This stage of the process will never be completely institutionalized, since it involves skills in personal selling on the part of frontline personnel. Success comes in part from creating a feeling on the part of the buyer and seller that they cannot do better by continuing to search the market. The more the firm can subtly but effectively communicate its market expertise and the fact that it has done a complete market search on behalf of its clients, the easier it should be to convince the buyer and/or seller to close the deal.

Evaluating the Reasons for Failure

If the parties in a tentative match fail to "close," then it is important to learn why, so that the next attempted match (and future matches of a similar nature) can respond more closely to individual needs. This stage is difficult, but by no means impossible to institutionalize. If the firm is utilizing a computer data base, the relevant files can be updated so that the facts about what advantages and disadvantages are possessed by individual offerings (homes, jobs, stocks, travel destinations) can be disseminated through the firm. In the old-style firm, inefficiencies generally result as each of a number of brokers wastefully discovers independently how the market is reacting to a specific type of offering.

Assisting with Completion of a Match

The final stage in the facilitating process is to assist with the details of completion once a successful match has been accomplished. As noted already, firms are tending to become increasingly involved in this stage of the process through addition of ancillary services.

INSIGHTS AND TRENDS

What insights can be drawn from this analysis for managers of facilitator services? What trends can be anticipated in the future? A number of comments and caveats need to be made in the light of our review of the steps in the facilitating process. We recognize that not all steps will be of equal importance to all firms in all industries. In particular, as firms move through the life cycle referred to in Table 1, the relative importance of and the relative emphasis on different stages in the process will change. There is a trend towards significant changes in the way facilitator firms create and deliver their services, particularly as these relate to "de-professionalizing" the frontline tasks and embodying more of the added value in the systems and in the firms themselves. The extent of this trend varies across industries but it is present in all. Greater sophistication has come to the real estate business through the growth of large franchise systems (Century 21, formed in 1972, had obtained over 5,000 franchises by the late 1970s and was

sold for $90 million in 1979). Franchise systems are also beginning to develop in the employment agency field. Travel agencies, while becoming increasingly sophisticated from a technological standpoint, are still characterized by small operations displaying the relatively low level of managerial sophistication encountered in most small businesses. Stockbrokerage operations have become increasingly sophisticated and larger in scale. In part, this reflects a firm's ability to back up its frontline personnel with back-room activities.

Moves to Standardization

The differentiation between "front-room" (high customer contact) and "back-room" (low customer contact) activities is a crucial one. Much of the success in transforming the facilitator industries comes from two directions: standardizing the customer-contact process, and learning how to take more steps in the process into the back room. There they can be treated as production-type operations (Figure 3), and the lessons of modern production-line management methods can be brought to bear. As long as the process involves a high degree of customer con-

FIGURE 3
Alternative Directions for Facilitators

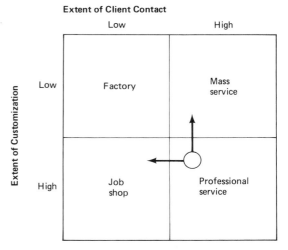

tact, there will be a premium on the process skills required by frontline personnel, and the firm's added value will be embedded mostly in its professionals.

Compensation Problems at the Management Level

One of the classic management problems inside facilitator firms derives from the high customer-contact nature of the businesses. There are a number of steps in the facilitating process where interactive skills between broker and client are critical. Such skills are not easily taught in schools; they are best learned from experience. A primary management task in facilitator firms is to coach new brokers, helping them to develop the key interactive skills necessary to the delivery of quality service. The reason that this has been a problem for many facilitator firms is that the compensation system has been based on commissions, even for managers. This raises a conflict for individual managers between allocating time on earning personal commissions, and allocating it to coaching, training, and managing.

Two steps are usually taken to address this problem. First, managers may be given an "override" commission based either on the sales commissions generated by the brokers working under their control, or on the profits (contribution to overhead) made by their office. This can be difficult to design and administer. Selecting the appropriate level to balance competing incentives may be problematic. Moreover, the appropriate override must reflect the training, coaching, and management needs of the specific office or group. The second approach to this problem is to "force" managers to give up their sales activities on being promoted, and to devote themselves exclusively to the managerial tasks. (This is, for example, how the problem is addressed at Merrill Lynch.) We predict that, as the shifts we have described take place and more of the firm's added value is embedded in its systems, the latter route will increasingly be the one that is taken.

Mass versus Professional Services

As Figure 3 suggests, the increasing application of hard and soft technologies in the facilitator industries will involve the firms in a shift in their target markets. Increasing standardization of procedure will involve less personalization, turning the firm into a mass service rather than a "professional" one. Consequently, there will still be a role for "old-style" firms at the upper end of the market. (This is the common view held about Century 21's success: that its methods of doing business appeal to the low- and mid-range home buyer, and that one way to compete against the firm is to preserve a people-intensive, nonstandardized approach in the premium market.)

Pricing Issues

The traditional pricing mechanism for facilitator firms has been the use of a commission structure that has tended to be standardized across all firms in each industry. This approach had the great advantage of simplicity but is now beginning to disintegrate. Deregulation of the airline industry is likely to result in a move away from the standard percentage commissions received by travel agents from the airlines (their biggest "selling" customers). In the stock-brokerage industry, discount brokers are now offering significant savings to customers who only want to buy and sell stocks and who have no interest in the ancillary services offered by most brokers.

As facilitators expand their range of services, there are likely to be moves to unbundle the services rendered and to start charging for each separately. Just as many stock-brokers now sell information and advice through the medium of "market letters" available only to subscribers, so other facilitators may start charging fees separately for the different components of their activities. However, for the information and advisory services to pay their own way, four criteria must be met. First, there must be no legal barriers to charging either prospective buyers or sellers for these services. Second, the facilitator firm that elects this strategy must be perceived as having a differential advantage over competing firms that choose not to charge for these services. Third, there should be a market demand for standardized information and advice of a more broadly defined nature than that required to complete a specific transaction. Finally, cost accounting procedures should be able to determine with a reasonable degree of accuracy what costs are associated with the provision of each service component.

Impact of the Computer

By accumulating market information and updating it rapidly and continually, the computer allows the firm to disseminate its market expertise rapidly throughout the firm; *all* frontline personnel can be made instant experts about the current state of the market. The expertise of the individual is converted into the expertise of the firm, improving its ability to deliver quality service consistently through *all* of its frontline personnel. With suitable software, the search activities themselves can be made more programmatic, by identifying key customizing variables that reflect the particular client's needs. For example, employment agencies try to identify for a job seeker openings offering the desired salary, location, type of work, level of responsibility, and so forth. Computer programs can be written to search the job-opening files and automatically generate a list of feasible matches. The same can be done in real estate brokerage.

If the most relevant "customizing variables" can be specified and programmed in advance, the firm becomes less dependent upon its frontline personnel to perform the customizing tasks. Not only is the market knowledge institutionalized, but so is much of the necessary expertise, namely, the individual *judgment* that previously had to be exercised by the frontline personnel. Customization can still be delivered, but it is no longer entirely dependent on the discretion and professional expertise of the brokers.

One final way in which the computer may be employed is in the *generation* of market knowledge. Through its capturing of market transaction information, the facilitator firm is well positioned with a large data base which it can routinely analyze to uncover market trends, demographic detail, and other matters. The firm can obtain market expertise not only passively (by accumulation), but also *actively* (by processing its available information).

The impact of such changes on the internal structure of facilitator firms will be drastic. We have already said that the firm will become less dependent upon its brokers; we expect this to be reflected not only in lower turnover in the broker ranks, but also in dramatic changes in the compensation system. With these new systems, a fundamental shift will take place in where (and how) the firm "adds value." In the old-style firm, as we noted, much of the added value was provided by the individual broker, and this justified the high commission structure. Now the added value is built-in to the firm and its systems, and a significantly lower commission structure will be necessitated.

The introduction of computer-based systems will add significantly to the fixed costs of the firms, transforming them from the high-variable-cost systems that were implied by the commission compensation systems. This will force the firms into more active marketing efforts to generate the revenues (and smooth the fluctuations in demand) necessary to cover these fixed costs. In turn, the necessity for these fixed expenditures will provide a driving force toward the large multi-site firm. In the past, most facilitator firms have been characterized by large numbers of small, single outlets. (In 1968 there were 6,000 authorized travel agencies in the U.S.; by 1977 there were 13,500. In the late 1970s there were more than 10,000 employment agencies and 150,000 real estate firms, of which some 80 percent were single-office outlets.) The drive to cover increased fixed costs may also lead to increased price competition. (In the past, firms responded to downturns by laying off brokers and weathering the storm by keeping fixed costs low.)

More Emphasis on the Advisory Function

One final trend should be noted. The ultimate impact of the combined computer and communications revolution may be to enable buyers and sellers to search for each other by direct access to a computer-based market file. While it may be possible to make a business of this by owning the data bank and charging an access fee, this development will threaten existing facilitator businesses. To the extent that existing facilitator firms have relied upon the information-exchange (market *knowledge*) service they provide, they may be threatened. Survival will require expansion of their advisory functions.

This trend toward *expertise* as the added value is notable. New specialist firms are springing up in many industries. For example, an article in the *New York Times* on June 5, 1981, described a new firm specializing in booking top-of-the-line hotel reservations. It is attempting to compete against travel agents, it appears, because of the latter's "generality" and their inability to bring specialist expertise to bear on advising the client well as to the quality of hotels in remote locations. Similarly, employment agencies are increasingly tending to specialize by type of job function, because such specialization gives them a greater ability to be expert advisors. In stockbrokerage, while specialization by firm is not necessarily taking place, there is a trend to specialization *within* the firm. Rather than the general broker handling all of the client's needs, market experts in each of the financial services are brought to bear on the client's specific problems, changing the relationship of client to broker and enhancing the bond linking client to firm and broker to firm. This will create new problems as the frontline broker is now required to cross-sell services and concentrate on process/interactive skills. As with the other changes outlined here, a fundamental realignment of relations (and compensation) between the firm and its personnel will be required.

CONCLUSION

In this article we have tried to demonstrate the commonality of tasks, problems, and opportunities faced by a group of industries engaged in facilitating market transactions. We have, of necessity, focused on what they have in common, rather than on what distinguishes them. Although the differences may be considerable, this article makes the case that managers in each of these facilitator industries should begin to watch each other more closely, and should reflect on how developments in the other industries might be relevant to their own.

Lex Service Group

CLIFFORD BADEN
COLIN CARTER

The senior management of a chain of motor vehicle distributors and service centers seeks to improve customer satisfaction. Attempts are being made to define and measure service.

The management of the Lex Service Group, a British-based company, was trying to define a policy for the implementation of the "service concept." Lex's growth had been very rapid over the past few years, with much of it due to acquisitions of service-oriented companies: car dealerships, travel bureaus, employment agencies, and hotels. Lex was committing itself increasingly to the service sector of the economy; the company had adopted the motto: "Lex is in the service business. Service means customer satisfaction." After several months of wrestling with the service concept, top management wanted to articulate a policy that would enable them both to measure and to manage the quality of service provided at the operating level of Lex.

MOTTO

COMPANY BACKGROUND

Lex was incorporated as Lex Garages in 1928, to build and operate parking garages and petrol stations in London. In 1945, Norman and Rosser Chinn bought control of the company and continued to expand Lex's activities in the parking, petrol (gasoline), car repair, and motor distribution businesses.

When Trevor Chinn, the son of Rosser, became managing director, he instituted a program to streamline and reorganize the company.

LEX DISTRIBUTORSHIPS

Most British motor car companies had a two-stage distribution system, with cars passing from the manufacturer through an area distributor to a local dealer.[1]

Each distributor had an exclusive franchise for a geographical area, with the right to supply all cars from a given manufacturer to dealers in his area. The distributor received a 4 percent commission on all dealers' sales in his area. The distributor could also retail cars to the public; Lex's distributorships tried to retail at least half the cars that they received from the manufacturers.

Lex owned distributorships for Morris (9), Austin (8), Rover (6), Triumph (5), Volvo (4), Jaguar (2), and Rolls-Royce (3), as well as 16 dealerships. As one London brokerage house noted, "By following a policy of selective acquisition and using advanced management techniques in a relatively unsophisticated industry, Lex has now become the leading motor distributor in this country."

All the Lex distributors and dealers had service garages attached to their new-car showrooms. A separate Parts Department provided parts to mechanics in the garages and also sold parts wholesale to other dealers; a small proportion of parts were also sold retail to the public. Each of Lex's car companies was thus in three different businesses: sales, service, and parts.

---

[1]Ford and Volkswagen had both changed to a one-stage system, with cars being sold through a few large dealerships.

THE SHIFT TO THE SERVICE CONCEPT

Mr. Chinn realized that rapid growth could not entirely be internally generated, but much would have to come from diversification. After considering various sectors of the economy, he settled on the service sector as the one that showed the greatest promise of growth into the future. The choice of the service sector also fulfilled one of Mr. Chinn's principal strategic goals, that of not tying up Lex's capital in fixed assets of an inherently obsolescent nature.

The commitment to a service strategy was sufficiently well-formed for Mr. Chinn to explain it to Lex's shareholders in the Annual Report.

> As the vehicle business is based on manufacturers' franchise arrangements, physical growth is not entirely at the sole discretion of a company such as Lex, and the strategic plans of the manufacturers concerned can impose limitations on our growth.
>
> While continuing to develop our existing motor vehicle distribution interests, we have, in order to meet our growth aspirations, started to diversify into other service businesses. We first moved into areas closely associated with existing activities such as vehicle leasing and retail distribution of tyres, oil and accessories, and then moved further afield as we sought a broad enough horizon of opportunity to ensure the continuing development of the Company in the years to come.
>
> It is our intention to become a diversified company operating in a number of major service industries. Each target industry will be selected on certain criteria:
>
> **a.** It must be large enough totally to allow Lex to establish a business entity complete in line and staff management of the highest calibre.
>
> **b.** It must have a growth potential in the coming decade which will enable us to maintain a rate of profit growth equal to that of our existing business.
>
> **c.** Lex must be able to establish itself among the market leaders of the industry.
>
> **d.** Lex must expect that within a reasonable time it will draw an important contribution

to Company profits from that service industry.

e. We will select industries that require a high level of service to customers that preferably are fragmented and operate on a decentralised basis and where accordingly profit improvement can be achieved through the exercise of modern management skills in the areas of planning, financial control, marketing, and personnel management.

Lex owned interests in several service-related industries: passenger car distribution and servicing, commercial vehicle distribution and servicing, freight and transportation, hotels and tourism, and employment agencies. However, 80 percent of Lex's profits were still derived from vehicle distribution and service. Mr. Chinn and his corporate staff believed that any steps taken to implement the service concept at Lex would first have to be proved effective in the motor side of the business.

ATTEMPTS TO DEFINE AND MEASURE SERVICE

At a corporate-level meeting in London, the top managers of Lex discussed the service concept and the company motto: "Lex is in the service business. Service means customer satisfaction." Those attending the meeting were unable to come up with a definition of service beyond "customer satisfaction," nor were they able to choose any measures that would allow Lex to quantify the service it was providing. Measurements such as the number of complaints received were felt to be negative indices; management hoped to be able to measure positive results.

At this meeting, the following directive was given to all the divisional managers.

Objective: To improve level of customer service satisfaction in every part of our company. Each General Manager is to report back to his Divisional Manager by 1st June outlining methods by which service to the customer is to be improved and causes of complaint eliminated. He is also to report specific steps which are being taken to improve communication between management and staff and management and customer to ensure that management is aware of customer complaints and can take speedy action to remove the cause.

Responses to this directive were received at company headquarters the second week in June. These responses varied in length from two to twelve pages; two of them are reproduced in *Exhibit 1*.

EXHIBIT 1

Sample Responses to Headquarters Request for Service Programs

To: Group Headquarters, London
Subject: Customer Satisfaction

The Group's standard of Service to its Customers must be of the caliber to ensure that Customers return to the Group each and every time they require Service, and knowing that the Service received is of the highest standard we will acquire, through the personal recommendations of our Customers, other Customers.

In order to achieve Customer Satisfaction, the following factors must be met:

1. Premises clean and businesslike and Reception points clearly marked so that the Customer can see exactly where he has to go to enquire for the Service required.
2. The Customer expects to be talking to a knowledgeable, helpful individual who shows complete interest in the Service requested and that at this particular moment the satisfaction of the enquiry is the most important task in the Employee's life.

3. Explain the operations or steps entailed in completing the service. After all, the Customer has called upon us to satisfy an immediate need and we should treat this with the importance it warrants.

4. Make sure that completion time is reasonably accurate. If things go wrong, let the Customer know. We have had to amend our plans because something has gone wrong; give the Customer a chance to amend his.

5. If an Estimate of charges is requested and a firm one can be given, then give it, and stick to it. If you cannot say so—make it quite clear that charges you are giving are an estimate because of this or that—Explain why.

6. Make sure that the Service is performed correctly.

7. If a Customer complains and you cannot give him satisfaction, make it easy for him to see your immediate supervisor. Never leave a complaint unresolved.

8. Telephone answering:

   a. Upon the receipt of each call, state the name of the Company, followed by—Good Morning/Afternoon—can I help you.

   b. Ensure that you know the names and extensions of all Employees.

   c. Ensure that you know what type of Service is carried out by each extension.

   d. If the line is engaged, say so, and offer to ring caller back.

   e. If caller decides to "hold on," keep advising that line is still busy until line is free, or offer to ring back.

9. Invoice presentation of highest order, avoid padding to justify price charged.

10. Correspondence to be concise and businesslike.

I feel that appropriate Notices should be displayed at points of Sale informing Customers that our aim is to give a First Class Service and if the Customer feels that he has reason to be dissatisfied with the Service, he should write to a "Customer Satisfaction" Department at Head Office. This would give Head Office an awareness and measurement of the standard of Service throughout the Group.

I believe that the quality of Service is remembered long after the amount charged is forgotten.

To: Group Headquarters, London
Subject: Service means Customer Satisfaction

To our customer service means friendly and professional attention, good availability of goods and services, completion of a supply or work contract within a specified period and a good appearance of the finished product. The service has to be courteous, prompt, honest, and reliable in all Departments of the business which preferably should be carried out in clean, cheerful and modern premises.

Any complaints should be given immediate attention with a fair and unbiased investigation at the highest company unit level.

WHY IS OUR SERVICE NOT ALWAYS AS GOOD AS IT SHOULD BE?

Service Department

1. Staff make promises which they are unable to keep or forget to take action.

2. They quote prices when they are not sure what the correct price is and without checking whether or not the repair is really necessary.

3. They do not check to see if the part is available.

4. They blame the Parts Department or the factory for problems rather than take a positive approach.

5. They do not always advise the customer in time regarding delays in completion of repairs.
6. They do not advise the customer at inception that we require payment on collection.
7. Telephone enquiries are not always answered as promptly as should be.
8. Cars sometimes handed over dirtier than they came in.
9. Failure to advise Accounts Department of action taken after dealing with a complaint.

Parts Department

1. Area of weakness in supplying special order parts and the customer not always advised when parts are in stock.
2. The telephone service not always as good as it should be with customers being kept waiting too long either (1) before phone answered or (2) whilst parts being located.

SUGGESTED REMEDIES

Service Department

1. Re-name Tester by calling him Quality Control Supervisor; otherwise only cars with running faults get tested.
   Have check sheet specifying certain known failures in service in addition to the actual repair:
   a. Cleanliness of car.
   b. Greasy steering wheel.
   c. Cleanliness of carpets.
   d. Use of paper car mats.
   e. Use of plastic seat covers (throw-away type).
   f. Use of wing covers.
   g. Oil and water levels.
   h. Tyre checks.
2. The Foreman to constantly supervise all work as it progresses and notify either Reception or Progress chaser of any delays and to notify customer.
3. Attach Customer Satisfaction card to all repaired cars and provide a handy receptacle for these, or send out regular mailing letters asking for comments on our servicing.
4. The retailing aspects of service and sales are complementary to each other and are better handled by one person in the Sales Department as they are stronger at this.
5. Service Managers to random check at least one car per day and report to General Manager on the quality of workmanship.
6. General Manager to check at least two cars per week to satisfy himself on the quality of work.
7. To ensure that all customers' complaints are dealt with promptly and sympathetically and if we are at fault to pass credit note immediately.
8. Notify customer of any work found and advise him or her whilst car in workshop and not when the car is called for; they may have returned a hire car.
9. Display all customer complaints on notice board highlighting to mechanic concerned. He would probably be more careful in future. Red label to be attached to work copy of repair order showing name of original mechanic.
10. Have all cars washed (with exception of very minor repair jobs).
11. Install Dynamometers and brake testing equipment to minimize road testing.
12. Train staff to be clean and tidy in themselves and habits by providing good facilities, i.e.,
    a. Rubbish bins.
    b. Clean toilets and washing facilities.
    c. Clothes lockers and changing rooms.
    d. Mess room.
13. Advertise and give guarantee of service (we do anyway, why not say so).

14. Have a good level of investment in special tools and any labor-saving devices, i.e., power wrenches, diagnostic equipment, etc.
15. Have customer participation suggestion box in reception area.
16. Ensure that mechanics attend specialized factory training courses.
17. Offer incentive to fitters who carry out complaint-free repairs on monthly basis.
18. Offer incentive to Quality Control for returning cars with genuine faults in repair. (This way he will look for faults instead of disguising them.)
19. Train Receptionist to remember customers' names and their car.
20. Return displaced parts to customer in plastic bag.

Parts Department

1. Ensure that the customer parts counter is always manned and to ensure that customers know that they have been noticed.
2. Questionnaire mailing to all parts customers.
3. Parts Marketing Manager and marketing representatives to report back all complaints.
4. Give help and advice to all do-it-yourself customers.
5. General Manager and Parts Manager to make random checks as to the promptness with which incoming telephone calls are dealt.
6. One telephone Salesman to be responsible for provision of all parts required for urgent use which are not at the time in stock.
7. Compilation of non-availability record.
8. Separate counter for orders telephoned in so that customers ordering by phone can have orders made up ready for collection to avoid waiting.
9. Investigate van routes, cut out non-paying, long-distance, time-consuming routes to give a better local service.
10. Ensure vehicles properly maintained to cut down "off the road" time. Consider incentives for well kept vehicles.
11. Employ women drivers, as it has been found that dealers prefer them to men.
12. Always try to reserve the last fast-moving item for workshop use.
13. Install interpretation section to Retail Parts Counter, so that customers who know their part numbers can be dealt with more quickly, and so that those who need specialist help can receive it.
14. Improve the level of skill in the Parts Department and to improve its image as the "cinderella" of the business.

MEASUREMENT OF OUR SERVICE

1. Service complaints as a percentage against retail sold hours or as a percentage of number of repair orders issued monthly.
2. Sales as a percentage against vehicles delivered retail.
3. Parts as a percentage against turnover in retail terms. (These percentage targets to be set after a trial period in the light of experience.)

As examples of the efforts being made toward customer satisfaction, some of the Divisional Managers sent copies of public relations material that had been developed at the divisional or local levels. These included a "Customer Satisfaction Card" (*Exhibit 2*) and an invitation to a free car inspection for vehicles over 12 months old (*Exhibit 3*).

At the same meeting in May, it was decided to try simultaneously another approach to gauging the effectiveness of Lex's customer service. Questionnaires were sent to over 1,200 customers of two Lex garages asking them to evaluate the quality of service they had received. Responses were collected at the divisional level and sent to company headquarters for evaluation (*Exhibit 4*).

With the responses to the questionnaires and the directives in hand, Mr. Chinn and his staff hoped to define some measures of service that would provide workable guidelines for people at the operating level of the company.

EXHIBIT 2

Customer Satisfaction Card

CUSTOMER SATISFACTION CARD

Help us to provide the kind of service you want for your vehicle. This is one of the most important aspects of our role as a Morris Distributor, and to assist us in appraising our standard of service and guide us in any improvements we make please put a tick in the appropriate box and return this card to us at your convenience.

Does our reception engineer usually attend to you promptly and courteously?   YES NO

Are we good at diagnosing what is wrong with your vehicle?   YES NO

Are you satisfied with the quality of our work?   YES NO

Do we usually complete the servicing on your vehicle when promised?   YES NO

Do we leave your vehicle in a clean condition after service?   YES NO

NAME _____

ADDRESS _____   **LEX**

EXHIBIT 3

Invitation to Free Car Inspection

BRITISH

LEYLAND

Distributors for Triumph Agents for Austin, Rover, Jaguar, Daimler

No Telephone #

Dear Customer,

   We are sure that you will be interested to know that we are running a Special Show and Service Week at our premises for one week only from 22nd to 27th November, inclusive.

   For many years now Standard-Triumph have been organizing Show and Service Weeks, and on the dates quoted, their Service Engineers will be available to carry out a free inspection on all Standard and Triumph cars over 12 months old and which are no longer enjoying the benefit of the Manufacturers Guarantee.

   If you would like a detailed report on the exact condition of your car, may we suggest that you telephone our Service Reception Department, so that a convenient time and date may be arranged.

   In addition to the Engineer's Services, we shall also have our own Special Show of Triumph cars, both on exhibition and for demonstration. If you would like to wait while your car is being inspected, or come and see us anyway during this special week, our sales staff will be pleased to answer any problems you may have.

   We look forward to the pleasure of your company during this special week.

                                        Yours faithfully,

                                        DIRECTOR

EXHIBIT 4

Report on Customer Service Questionnaire

This report covers the results of a survey carried out during early May amongst customers of Cheltenham Car Mart and Lex T.B.C. Kidderminster.

Background

A questionnaire was sent out, under cover of a personalized letter, to all customers who had used our service facilities during the three months' period February–April this year. The covering letter stressed that it was our continued aim to seek complete customer satisfaction and to this end would they please complete the attached questionnaire adding any suggestions which they thought might improve our customer service. A reply-paid envelope was enclosed.

At Cheltenham a total of 390 questionnaires was sent out, whilst at Kidderminster over 850 questionnaires were dispatched.

Findings

Question 1. Did you make a prior booking for your service?

	Cheltenham		Kidderminster	
Yes	152	95%	158	88%
No	7	5%	22	12%
Not completed	2		8	
Total	161		188	
Base for %	159		180	

Question 2. When did you last receive a service card or letter from us?

	Cheltenham		Kidderminster	
1 month	29	21%	113	66%
2 months	18	13%	24	14%
3 months	9	2%	10	6%
Never	85	60%	23	14%
Not completed	20		18	
Base for %	141		170	

Question 3. Has anyone from our Company ever contacted you by telephone about servicing your car?

	Cheltenham		Kidderminster	
Yes	20	13%	33	19%
No	131	87%	141	81%
Not completed	10		13	

Question 4. Were you satisfied with the reception you received from our staff when you arrived with your car?

	Cheltenham		Kidderminster	
Completely	140	89%	153	92%
Reasonably	16	10%	8	5%
Poor	1		4	2%
Bad	1		1	
Not completed	3		22	
Base for %	158		166	

Question 5. Was the work carried out to your satisfaction?

	Cheltenham		Kidderminster	
Completely	114	73%	112	63%
Partly	42	26%	55	31%
Not at all	1		10	6%
Not completed	4		11	
Base for %	157		177	

Question 6. Were there any grease marks on the steering wheel or seat when you collected the car?

	Cheltenham		Kidderminster	
Yes	4	3%	22	12%
No	156	98%	157	88%
Not completed	1		9	
Base for %	160		179	

Question 7. Was the car ready for collection when promised?

	Cheltenham		Kidderminster	
Yes	149	96%	146	84%
30 mins. late	6	4%	17	10%
1 hour late			1	
Over 1 hour late	1		11	6%
Not completed	5		13	
Base for %	156		175	

The Law Offices of Lewin & Associates

SULA FISZMAN
CHRISTOPHER H. LOVELOCK

A chain of legal clinics is losing money at several of its 18 offices. The managing partner is reviewing office procedures and seeking to increase the number of legal cases handled.

Elizabeth Lewin, managing partner of The Law Offices of Lewin & Associates, was concerned. It was January 1983 and business was in a precarious state for one of the largest law clinics in the United States. Four of the firm's 18 offices in the large midwestern city of Lakeshore were losing money, and two more were financially marginal. Altogether, the firm was losing somewhere around $15,000 per month. Over the next two months, Lewin and her associates needed to agree on a plan to increase the number of cases per office and to improve office efficiency.

THE FIRM

The Law Offices of Lewin & Associates (L&A) was founded in 1978, growing out of a long-held concern of Elizabeth Lewin with the limited accessibility of legal services. Lewin, then aged 33, was a graduate of the Stanford Law School who had worked in government agencies as well as for a major law firm in downtown Lakeshore. She believed strongly in the need for a full-service law firm devoted to handling the legal problems of middle-income people at affordable prices. Other investors, including several lawyers, ac-

This case was prepared by Research Assistant Sula Fiszman and Associate Professor Christopher Lovelock. Copyright © 1983 by the President and Fellows of Harvard College. Harvard Business School Case 9-583-122. Reprinted by permission.

cepted her invitation to invest capital in the new firm that she decided to found. It was agreed that only Lewin, who was named managing partner, would be involved in the day-to-day administration of the firm.

The partners sought to achieve economies of scale by modeling the new organization after successful retail chains. They intended to achieve these economies by:

- Opening a significant number of small neighborhood offices, to increase clients' accessibility to the firm.
- Creating a system of standardized forms and procedures for handling personal legal problems to achieve more efficient processing of clients' cases.
- Delegating routine administrative tasks to secretaries so that the more highly paid lawyers would be available for client consultation and for handling those tasks which only they were qualified to perform.
- Centralizing and computerizing the administrative functions, such as accounts payable, purchasing, and personnel hiring.
- Concentrating the work of attorneys on a limited number of recurring legal needs to take advantage of economies of scale and learning curve effects.
- Utilizing specialists who served more than one office to enable the firm to offer a broad product line.

The firm sought to target two very large market segments: (1) middle-income people who patronized traditional law firms, but could be served equally well through the new firm's less costly system; (2) people who did not use legal services as often as they needed them because the services were too expensive or inaccessible.

Lewin selected a product line that was general in that it covered every kind of personal legal service and specialized in that not all L&A lawyers handled all types of legal cases. For complex problems ranging from bankruptcy to consumer law, the firm had specialists located in various offices to whom its other lawyers referred these problems. This system enabled L&A to serve all clients and yet achieve the learning curve effects which occurred when a lawyer handled many similar cases. As one of the firm's attorneys said: "We are in law what family practitioners are in medicine."

Lewin spent her first six months preparing for the simultaneous opening of nine offices in October 1978. She noted that there were economies of scale involved for furniture and equipment purchases. "More important, though," she added, "it was the only way to make advertising economical." The firm's rapid development precluded any formal planning. "In general," Lewin said, "our offices were located with a view both to the population and a sense of the neighborhood we'd be serving." Offices were established in commercial buildings, shopping centers, and malls in downtown Lakeshore and its suburbs. Five offices were on the ground floor of the buildings they occupied, but this location did not seem to bring in more clients than offices situated on higher floors.

By late 1981, the firm had expanded to 11 offices. Lewin then arranged to open seven offices in the Valu-Rite chain of discount retail stores, which sold household items and clothing. The firm needed more suburban offices in Bulbeck County, south and west of Lakeshore, to spread advertising costs and to maximize advertising potential. Valu-Rite customers were the group at which L&A was aiming. "Putting offices in a chain store has great potential," said Lewin. "It offers us a convenient location and a captured client." Some L&A employees thought that the Valu-Rite image was negative; they were also concerned that the new offices were too near several existing offices and competed directly with them. *Exhibit 1* summarizes information on each of the 18 offices operated by Lewin & Associates in January 1983.

THE CHANGING FACE OF THE LEGAL PROFESSION

According to a 1971 article in the *American Bar Association Journal*, approximately 70 percent of the U.S. population lacked access to needed legal services, because they had too little money to afford the services yet not so little that they qualified for free legal aid.

It was estimated that one-third of all adults had never consulted an attorney and that less than one in five used attorneys to resolve consumer problems.

A number of legal clinics were established to remove some of the mystique from the law and to make legal services more accessible and affordable. However, a 1977 survey found that, of 33 legal clinics throughout the U.S., eleven were insolvent, five relied on subsidies to fund losses, fourteen were solvent, and only three could be described as prospering. Part of the problem was that state bar associations prohibited lawyers from using advertising to solicit professional employment. This barrier was eliminated in mid-1977, when the United States Supreme Court ruled in *Bates* v. *State Bar of Arizona*, 433 U.S.

EXHIBIT 1
Location and Characteristics of Lewin & Associates in Offices in Lakeshore Area, 1983

Location	Neighborhood	Employees		Type of Client	Average Consultations Per Month	Average Monthly Income
Market Street Lakeshore	Business	Atty.	2	Mixed ethnically	145	$19,600
		Sec.	2	Status: Professional		
1st Avenue Lakeshore	Business Residential	Atty.	2	Mixed ethnically	108	$17,800
		Sec.	2	Status: Middle management		
15th Avenue Lakeshore	Business Residential	Atty.	1	Mixed ethnically	49	$11,400
		Sec.	2	Status: Middle management		
Broadmoor	Residential	Atty.	2	Black	97	$18,000
		Sec.	2	Status: Blue collar		
Royal Highway	Residential	Atty.	2	White	87	$26,000
		Sec.	2	Status: Blue collar		
Town Park	Residential	Atty.	1	White	75	$20,900
		Secy.	2	Status: Blue collar		
Logan	Residential	Atty.	1	Mixed ethnically	66	$10,500
		Secy.	2	Status: Blue collar		
Green Lake	Residential	Atty.	1	Black/Hispanic	98	$ 8,400
		Secy.	1	Status: Middle management		
Black Plains	Residential Business	Atty.	2	Mixed ethnically	112	$10,500
		Secy.	1	Status: Professional		
Arlmont*	Residential	Atty.	1	Black	35	$ 7,900
		Secy.	2	Status: Blue collar		
Georgeville*	Residential	Atty.	1	Black	75	$11,200
		Secy.	1	Status: Blue collar		
Fittburg*	Residential	Atty.	1	White	129	$12,400
		Secy.	1	Status: Blue collar		
East Bulbeck	Residential	Atty.	1	White	29	$ 7,400
		Secy.	1	Status: Middle management		
Bulbeck Center*	Residential	Atty.	1	White	103	$13,100
		Secy.	1	Status: Blue collar		
Vienna*	Residential	Atty.	1	White	119	$16,800
		Secy.	2	Status: Blue collar		
Petit Lac*	Residential Business	Atty.	1	White	71	$ 9,000
		Secy.	2	Status: Middle management		
Plymouth	Business	Atty.	1	Mixed ethnically	32	$ 6,000
		Secy.	1	Status: Middle management		

*Denotes unprofitable or financially marginal office. (*Note:* Vienna and Fittburg were located in Valu-Rite stores.)

350 (1977), that lawyers had a constitutional right to advertise. Associate Justice Blackmun wrote:

> Since the belief that lawyers are somehow above trade has become an anachronism, the historic foundation for advertising restraint has crumbled . . . (I believe that advertising by lawyers would reduce the cost of legal services . . . without encouraging any more shoddy work than now exists.)

Two months later, the four-office legal clinic of Jacoby & Meyers in Los Angeles became the first law firm to advertise on television. Within 18 months, that firm had expanded to a total of 22 offices. An independent study reported that since the firm began its TV campaign, it had attracted approximately 2,500 new clients each month. By 1983, Jacoby & Meyers boasted a total of 63 offices in California and New York. Other multioffice legal clinics expanded rapidly. Hyatt Legal Services, based in Kansas City and affiliated with the H&R Block chain of income tax preparers, operated 114 offices in 14 states and Washington, D.C.

THE LAKESHORE AREA LEGAL MARKET

Although there were no other chains of legal clinics or law offices in the Lakeshore area, Elizabeth Lewin had noted increased television and newspaper advertising by law partnerships and solo practitioners. Most of these solo practitioners specialized in a particular area of law, such as personal injury, immigration, or bankruptcy. A few had formalized referral services from other attorneys on a statewide basis and offered a toll-free number for initial consultation. The *Lakeshore Area Yellow Pages* featured 30 pages of listings under the category of "Lawyers," including separate listings grouped by type of practice and by location of practice. There were a number of eye-catching display advertisements for lawyers in the *Yellow Pages*, including one for Lewin & Associates.

Consumer Use of Legal Services

A telephone survey of randomly selected Lakeshore area residents commissioned by Lewin found that fewer than half of the respondents had previously used legal services. These users were more likely to be middle-aged, male, white, with above-average incomes, and professionals or managers. Half of these individuals had used legal services at least twice before. The most frequent case types were business, real estate, personal injury, and divorces (*Exhibit 2*).

When previous users were asked how they chose their attorney, they listed, with equal frequency: quality, reputation, and fees. Among nonusers, the most cited criterion for future selection was fees. The survey revealed that 65 percent of respondents (mostly previous users) would refuse to consult a lawyer whose office was located in a depart-

EXHIBIT 2
Types of Legal Needs Encountered Among Residents of Greater Lakeshore

Type of Case	Percent of Total Cases Reported
Business	22.9
Real estate	20.0
Wills	15.9
Other	11.3
Personal injuries	8.7
Divorce	6.1
Criminal	3.8
Workers compensation	3.2
Estate	2.6
Motor vehicle	2.0
Landlord/tenant	1.2
Immigration	1.2
Malpractice	0.9
Social Security	0.6
Adoption	0.3
Employment	0.3
Name change	0.3
Guardianship	0
Bankruptcy	0
Unemployment	0

SOURCE: Telephone survey of 402 randomly selected residents of L&A's service area, 1982.

ment store. Eighty-nine percent of respondents said they did not believe that a price-quality tradeoff existed. The survey also asked what sources people would consider most helpful in finding an attorney: 76 percent of respondents cited referral from a friend or relative, 16 percent listed word-of-mouth, and 5 percent mentioned the *Yellow Pages*. However, combined mentions of all other media totaled only 3.5 percent. More than half the respondents said they would not feel comfortable consulting an attorney who advertised on television or in a newspaper. This feeling was unrelated to prior experience with lawyers. Aversion to advertising generally increased with income level and correlated with refusal to consult an attorney whose office was in a department store or shopping mall.

In contrast to the profile of the "typical" Lakeshore legal client, L&A records showed that the firm attracted a larger proportion of clients who had a below average income, were black, or aged between 25 and 35. Each of these groups was more receptive to legal advertising. Although half of the firm's clients had used an attorney before, only 3 percent had consulted L&A previously—a fact that Lewin attributed to the firm's relative youth. Some clients wanted a "second opinion" on a matter about which they had already consulted another attorney. The most frequent type of case brought to L&A was divorce (*Exhibit 3*).

When asked how they chose their attorney, L&A's clients most frequently cited fees (61 percent), personal attention (44 percent), and convenient location (36 percent). Those who listed fees were most likely to be young and white; there was no correlation between fee sensitivity and income level. Almost three quarters of the firm's clients had learned of L&A through TV advertisements, which emphasized fees and personal attention. Only 13 percent heard of the firm from a friend. Another 15 percent learned of L&A through the *Yellow Pages*. About 70 percent of clients came to the firm's offices directly from their homes; more than half of this group of clients lived 2 to 10 miles from the office in question.

EXHIBIT 3
Composition of the Firm's Caseload, Fall 1982

Type of Case	Proportion of Total Cases
Divorce	33.4%
Criminal	10.7
Money claims	7.3
Landlord/tenant	6.9
Wills	6.6
Bankruptcy	5.9
Real estate	5.5
Business	5.4
Personal injuries	3.4
Employment	2.0
Dept. of Motor Vehicles	1.9
Adoption	1.8
Name change	1.6
Immigration	1.2
Social Security	1.0
Workers compensation	0.8
Guardianship	0.7
Other	4.0

SOURCE: Company records.

Competition Among Providers of Legal Services

Providers of legal services in the Lakeshore area ranged from prestigious firms in downtown office towers to neighborhood solo practitioners. Lewin & Associates competed primarily with solo proprietorships, local partnerships, legal clinics, and do-it-yourself legal kits. Within this group it did not provide the lowest-priced services (*Exhibit 4*). Rather, it served those clients who could not or did not want to pay the high-priced prestige firms, yet did not seek out the lowest fees available.

The firm had had some difficulties with the organized bar. One attorney observed:

We're not well liked by the legal community because we take business away from the little guys. And judges have a bone to pick with Lewin & Associates from time to time. They see our ads on TV and become suspicious that the level of service is not what it should be.

Lewin acknowledged that her firm was encroaching on the turf of solo practitioners, but emphasized that L&A had tried to avoid antagonizing the bar through advertising:

We try to make our ads as informative as possible. We try to stay within all the guidelines that are required. And if something is potentially controversial, we'll analyze it and decide whether we think we're justified in trying it. There's no reason to make the legal community angry with us. We try to do things professionally.

ORGANIZATION AND MANAGEMENT

Lewin & Associates had developed a two-tiered system of management. Certain administrative functions were handled centrally. Individual offices were headed by a managing attorney who both practiced law and supervised office personnel and financial matters.

The head office employed six administrators. Two of these, Elizabeth Lewin and Gordon Kane, were attorneys. The major functions of the head office were pricing decisions, monitoring of office management, quality control, and attorney hiring, training, and compensation. It collected business statistics from the individual offices, handled client complaints, and coordinated advertising efforts with the firm's advertising agency. Excluding advertising costs, Lewin estimated that head office expenses consumed about 25 percent of the firm's total earnings. Lewin took responsibility for office locations and attorney incentive and compensation plans. She participated with her financial partners in decisions regarding financing and future growth strategies. Kane handled personnel hiring and supervision of individual offices.

Pricing

Each attorney had a fee manual which listed categories of cases, covering nearly every option a client might need, and identified the appropriate fees in each instance. Lewin determined the fee based on the dollar and cents costs of running the business and an evaluation of what the market would bear. The goal was to set a price in advance, rather than to charge on an hourly basis. L&A was not the cheapest legal service in the Lakeshore area. For example, the firm offered to undertake uncontested divorce for $328 plus court costs; individual practitioners charged from $100 to $700 (*Exhibit 4*). Kane trained new attorneys to use the fee manual. He went over fact patterns or situations that might be encountered, and

EXHIBIT 4
Comparative Fees for Different Types of Cases

Type of Case	Lewin & Assoc.	Solo Practitioners	Legal Clinic	D-I-Y Legal Kit
Uncontested divorce	$328	$100–700	$250–350	$99–150
Simple bankruptcy	459	500–750	350–550	N/A
Real estate closing	1% of value*	250 or 1% of value*	250 or 1% of value*	N/A
Legal name change	250	200–250	200–350	N/A
Wills:				
Single	60	0–200†	40–100	N/A
Reciprocal	110	0–300†	80–300	N/A

Note: Fees cited exclude court costs (where applicable).

*That is, 1% of the selling price of the property.

†Some practitioners made no charge for a will in expectation of subsequently handling the estate work.

SOURCE: Company records plus local research in Greater Lakeshore.

demonstrated how that case should be categorized.

On arriving at an L&A office, a new client was requested to complete a brief form and pay a $25 consultation fee. The client then met with an attorney for approximately 30 minutes to discuss the problem. After analyzing the case, the attorney selected the appropriate fee category, gave the client a written estimate, and sent a copy to the main office. Approximately one consultation in three resulted in a client's retaining L&A to handle the case.

For the estimated fee, the client would receive a certain number of the attorney's hours, at a rate averaging more than $100 per hour. If the required time exceeded that included in the fee, the client was charged for the balance at an hourly rate of $85, which approximated the actual cost to L&A of providing legal services. Lewin claimed that her firm's more efficient procedures enabled it to offer clients greater value for their dollar than conventional law firms.

If the nature of the case changed—for example, if an uncontested divorce became contested—the attorney had to file a case-type change form to adjust the fee as appropriate. Certain cases, such as legal name changes, were charged at a flat rate regardless of the amount of time spent. Wills were priced as loss leaders. Although fees on a few cases, such as contested divorces or felony charges, could be as high as $3,000 or more, the average case at L&A yielded fees to the firm of about $350.

There was still some variability in fee quotes. Kane explained that the difference could arise if one attorney was more optimistic about settling the case through negotiation while another foresaw lengthy litigation. In 1981, a disguised visit to two L&A offices by a reporter for the *Lakeshore Tribune* revealed a $600 variance in fee estimates to do a contested divorce. Kane believed that training had narrowed such differences. Fees were usually changed once a year. The situation would be reviewed if attorneys complained that a fee was too high and that they were not retaining clients, or if they claimed that a fee was too low for the time required. Proposed revisions were submitted to attorneys for comment.

Recruitment

Most attorneys at Lewin & Associates came to the firm from their own practice or from a small law firm. L&A's official qualifications were five years of general practice experience for a managing attorney and one to three years for an associate. Each attorney had a personnel handbook which outlined basic firm policies such as working hours and dress codes. Practicing law on the side was strictly forbidden. When Kane interviewed an applicant, he looked for attorneys with a broad base in general practice and experience in dealing with people:

> I look for someone with the ability to elicit facts from clients expeditiously and to tell clients what to expect in terms of representation and fees. I look for someone who is generally well-organized and has the ability to follow up, because what we are looking for is a solo practitioner in a sense.

Applicants who passed Kane's screen were then sent to visit managing attorneys of offices to which they might be assigned. The managing attorney determined whether the applicant would be able to retain clients and do a reasonable share of the work. About 30 percent of the firm's attorneys were women, none were black. There was a scarcity of black attorneys, Lewin explained, and most of them went to work for large firms.

Monitoring Office Management

Each office called the head office daily with figures on the number of appointments kept, the fees collected the previous day, and the number of appointments booked for the present day. Monthly rankings were assigned to each office based on number of clients, rate of retention, and profitability. Kane visited all offices periodically. Those with new attorneys or poor statistics were visited more frequently—for example, once a month—whereas a more established office might not be visited more than twice yearly.

By 1983, each office had enough of a track record to allow Kane to know if it should be doing better. He reviewed files to ensure that cases were being moved along expeditiously. Depending on the office, 50 to 150 files would be open at any one time. A file might remain open for anything from two weeks to as long as two and a half years. The average uncontested divorce case file remained open for 16 weeks.

L&A's policy required offices to call and confirm appointments, but not to call and inquire about an already missed appointment. "People feel that's a little too aggressive and pushy," said Lewin. To minimize the number of missed appointments, L&A policy required that offices schedule appointments at the earliest possible date, preferably the same day that a client called. Lewin commented:

> We have trouble with this. The attorneys in the offices don't really believe it, but the faster you get clients in after they phone, the less likely they are to be no-shows. Offices can be really lax about this sometimes. You can understand the tendency to say, "Oh no, another client—book them tomorrow, book them Wednesday." But that's not good for business.

When Kane had finished reviewing files at an office, he sat down with the managing attorney tò discuss his impressions and to make suggestions on how to manage the case load more efficiently. "One of the things I tell the attorney," he said, "is that we're a 'pay-as-you-go' law firm. The faster the work can be accomplished, the sooner the file can be closed and the better off that office is economically."

The firm had an of counsel[1] litigation specialist, whom Lewin urged the attorneys to use since she felt litigation was disruptive to an office. The more experienced attorneys, she said, would handle a case up to trial before turning it over to the specialist.

---

[1]An of counsel attorney is neither a partner nor an employee of the firm. He or she maintains a relationship not unlike that of a consultant, providing assistance to the firm on some matters, but working independently on others.

Both Lewin and Kane described the task of evaluating the quality of service as a matter of judgment. Kane observed that one of the most direct ways of evaluating an attorney's advice was being in the office frequently. "You have to have a feel for what goes on in an office: how does it look, how does the attorney handle his staff, how does he greet the client, how does he behave with the client?" The firm also relied on client complaints to alert it to problems, which Kane then investigated.

Every year, L&A reviewed the performance of each office and each attorney; this review was based on Kane's and Lewin's impression of the office, and the office statistics. The results helped the firm decide on salaries and on whether an attorney should stay with the firm.

Not all attorneys felt that the administrators were able to control quality effectively. Said one: "The administrators say they ensure consistency because of the forms, training, hiring process. But not really. They find out when there's a problem. They have carried some people for a long time when they've known the attorney had problems, when the problems were pretty consistent." Another attorney agreed that the firm's quality control was not that effective but felt, in general, that the attorneys had been good and hard working.

Attorney Compensation

After some experimentation, L&A had adopted a compensation formula whereby each office was assigned a certain gross earnings target per month, such as $12,000 for a one-attorney office. The attorney was paid a salary plus 10 percent of anything the office earned over that gross amount. The annual salary, including bonus, for a managing attorney, ranged from $27,000–$45,000; for an associate, it was between $17,000 and $22,000. The additional cost to L&A of benefits and payroll taxes amounted to about one fifth of the salary totals.

Lewin was still unsure whether the compensation scheme provided enough incentive for the attorneys "to go that extra mile which you really need to make these offices very effective." It appeared that the stronger offices were carrying the weaker, and Lewin felt that many managing attorneys had lost all sensitivity to the cost of their offices. She was not happy with the plan, stating that she wanted to see some change:

> This kind of firm really needs an entrepreneurial type of attorney. It's a retail business. You've got to be out there hustling. You've got to be on top of your office. It's a nickel and dime business in a way, with lots of small cases. So unless attorneys really feel they're going to be getting something out of the office, you're going to have a situation where you're not getting the maximum amount you can from each operation.

Monetary compensation was an especially important incentive, since L&A attorneys could not look forward to rising in the firm's ranks. Lewin had no plans for taking on new partners nor additional executive personnel. One managing attorney described his probable career path as: "Associate, manager, out . . . . I don't see my future with L&A. I can see myself opening a competitor and becoming an entrepreneur. I'm not crazy about the practice of law. I'd rather be the owner." The turnover rate was described variously by attorneys as "extremely high" and "not as high as you'd think."

INDIVIDUAL OFFICES

The typical L&A office was staffed by a managing attorney and a paralegal secretary. Where the volume of cases warranted it, an associate attorney and additional secretarial help were hired. Secretaries were paid, on average, $320 per week. Benefits and payroll taxes added another 21 percent to these wage costs. Most offices were small, ranging in size from 700 to 1000 square feet. Annual rental costs averaged $15 per square foot. Miscellaneous office expenses, such as supplies, copying, electricity, heating or cooling, telephone, etc., amounted to around $280 per week for the average office.

The managing attorney was responsible for office management and for compliance with firmwide policies with regard to the keeping of statistics, fee quotes, and appointment booking procedures. He or she also had full responsibility for handling the case load and supervising the associate attorney. The firm was considering extending office hours (currently Monday–Friday, 9:00 A.M.–5:30 P.M.) into two evenings each week and opening for a full day every fourth Saturday.

L&A offices were simple and unpretentious. The firm accepted credit cards. Wherever possible, all brochures and written materials, including legal documents, were prepared in straightforward language. Attorneys were encouraged to be direct and matter-of-fact in their dealings with clients.

The Market Street Office in Lakeshore

Four blocks from Union Station, across from a coffee shop and wedged between two banks, was the L&A office managed by Steven Farmann, who worked with an associate. Serving a substantial area of midtown Lakeshore, it had been one of the firm's highest-revenue offices, averaging a gross of about $19,600 per month with a record high month of $26,000 and a record low month of $14,000.

Farmann had held a responsible position in a family sportswear company before graduating from Illiana Law School. After passing the bar, he opened his own practice in a suburban town 20 miles from Lakeshore. For 10 months he worked as an attorney during the day and as a waiter at night for additional income. When he decided to marry, Farmann began applying for jobs in Lakeshore and joined Lewin & Associates.

The work itself could be repetitive, Farmann felt. What made it interesting was the variety of people: "At the bottom end, I see an alcoholic postal worker who wants a divorce. At the top end, I see a psychiatrist at a major hospital. I also see nurses, middle managers—mostly women—people who work for Blue Cross and in health-related fields." They came to Lewin & Associates, he thought, because they didn't know any lawyers, and had seen the firm's advertisements. Due to the nature of the cases—predominantly divorce—there was little repeat business from the same clients.

In summarizing his role, Farmann said:

> Once I became managing attorney, it became a challenge to bring the office from an average of $12,000 or $13,000 per month up to $20,000 or $21,000. So that's where I put all my energy. I got a paralegal who was like a diamond in the rough. She got so good at her job that I could give her verbal instructions and half an hour later something would be completed on my desk. This gave me time to sit with clients. L&A can succeed only if an attorney is in the office a maximum number of hours. An attorney can't afford to go to court to answer motions, go to trials, do real estate closures, because time is precious and should be spent in the office.

However, Farmann did not turn down cases involving court time: "I can't turn down clients because I have to make the money. It's all about making the money. I have a second attorney, so if I go to court, there's coverage here." He estimated that he spent only 5 percent of his time in court.

Despite Farmann's efforts, business during the third quarter of 1982 had not been good. The office scheduled as many appointments as possible, but there was an exceptionally high rate of missed appointments. Lewin estimated the firmwide average at 35 percent. Farmann attributed the increase in no-shows to the firm's austerity program under which radio spots replaced TV advertisements when the cost of television spots rose seasonally. He felt that radio advertising attracted a different kind of client, who was surprised, on calling for an appointment, to learn that the firm charged an initial consultation fee and who was less likely to keep an appointment.

Farmann had other concerns about the firm:

> The organization is so unusually informal that each office basically is fairly autonomous. The manual with fee schedules dictates the policies of the firm. But, whether we follow it closely varies office by office. There's no strict monitoring like Kentucky Fried. Lots of things go by the board here because we don't have the time.

Beth Lewin feels that if attorneys have direct control over costs, offices will be more profitable. But she needs to put more time into sitting down with the attorneys and figuring out what it is about their offices that isn't profitable in terms of time and consultation management. Most office expenses are fixed. The only thing to maximize is performance of individual attorneys and the head office administrators have us pigeonholed in such a way following their procedures that they lose a lot of people along the way. They've tried to standardize and make the operation so uniform that they don't take attorney preferences to heart. We're not pushing lingerie over the counter. I like to think of myself as a professional, not a retail store operator, and this as a law firm, not Valu-Rite or Sears.

In November 1982, about a month after making these observations, Farmann resigned to go back into private practice. Lewin remarked that she and Kane had not regarded Farmann as a good manager. The new managing attorney appointed to Market Street had taken the initiative in establishing a better work flow, thereby lowering costs, while also moving aggressively to increase revenues. The net result had been a significant improvement in profitability of this office, which had hitherto been operating at close to breakeven.

The Nuffield Street Office in Broadmoor

The Nuffield Street office was located on a side street just off a busy and colorful shopping street in Broadmoor, an old neighborhood just west of central Lakeshore. It was on the top floor of a three-story building populated by small retail businesses and fast-food chains. There was a family dental practice on the second floor. The waiting room had the same utilitarian carpeting found in nearly all L&A offices. Brochures were available on a small table. A receptionist sat behind a glass window. Hanging on the wall was a framed quotation from Abraham Lincoln. It read: "A lawyer's time and advice are his stock in trade."

Martha Ross was managing attorney at this office. She was also the firm's bankruptcy specialist. Ross, a graduate of Ohio State Law School, had worked for legal aid in Cleveland for two years, and then for a two-person firm in Lakeshore before joining Lewin & Associates in 1980. She had left the small firm because she felt she was being exploited, "doing 75 percent of the work for 25 percent of the income," as she put it. Discussing her work at L&A, Ross commented: "I kind of enjoy what I do. It really is my own office. I feel fairly entrepreneurial. I do basically what I want within certain guidelines which are rational, so there's no reason to argue." Six months had gone by since Lewin or Kane had been out to check on her office.

Ross supervised one general practice attorney, two bankruptcy attorneys (located in other offices), and three paralegal secretaries (two of whom worked in other offices). By early 1983, she was spending 75 percent of her own time on general legal work, the balance on bankruptcy work. The typical bankruptcy client had been out of work for six months and had just become employed again. Most had fallen in arrears on their mortgage payments and faced foreclosure, but given time, they would be able to pay off their debts. Chapter 13 of the Bankruptcy Code allowed them three years. Ross preferred to see as many first-time clients as possible, believing that she was best able to evaluate a case, establish a fee and make referrals where necessary. She remarked:

> I do virtually no routine work. The secretaries do all the routine work, all the pleadings, papers, simple matrimonials. I quickly skim it before it goes to court. Basically, it's all done by the secretaries. They've done it countless times, they're perfectly competent. When I have a question I ask them.

Three-quarters of the business that came into Ross's office consisted of matrimonial and family court cases. The rest included bankruptcy, real estate, and wills. Criminal cases were referred to the firm's criminal law expert in the First Avenue Office. Ross remarked:

> I don't turn anything down. The head office may encourage it indirectly. I think they're concerned about people getting caught in cases that are going to require a lot of time and take them out of the office. I wouldn't like what I'm doing if I was turning down everything that was a little complex and therefore interesting, leaving myself only uncontested divorces.

The area where Ross worked was largely populated by blacks. This was reflected in her client mix. Many clients worked for Lakeshore Transit, Henderson's Department Store, Union Electric, and the Illiana Telephone Company, all of which had offices nearby. Most clients' incomes ranged from $15,000 to $30,000. Many had pensions, some had credit union accounts, fewer than half owned homes.

Ross kept a record of the time she spent on each case on strips of paper attached to the side of her desk. Like the firm's other attorneys, she worked with L&A's standard fee schedule, but noted:

> I tend to give higher fee estimates than indicated by the schedule because experience tells me that it's really hard to explain to someone that what you said would be $1,000 will now be $4,000. If there's a real problem paying, I take less money up front. The general policy is to take at least half the fee in advance. I may take a quarter. Still, there are billing collection problems. Five percent, maybe, are bad debts.

COMMUNICATION EFFORTS

L&A's business was heavily dependent on advertising. Lewin estimated that the firm spent 12 percent of every dollar earned to cover advertising expenses. The firm's advertising agency selected advertising media by comparing efficiencies. The goal was to reach the largest number of potential clients for the least cost. Advertising was bought on a quarterly basis, with the same amount of money budgeted for each quarter. During the first and third quarters of the year, television advertising was relatively cheap, and so L&A ran about fourteen 30-second TV spots per week. During the second and fourth quarters, when TV advertising was seasonally more expensive, the firm switched to 60-second radio spots. Several attorneys noted a drop in business during the second and fourth quarters.

Lewin & Associates did not advertise on transit vehicles or on billboards. In 1978, the firm had run some full-page advertisements in the *Lakeshore Examiner*, a large circulation daily newspaper; these showed a man with a mask over his eyes saying, "The way lawyers charge, there ought to be a law." The advertising did not generate many calls to L&A offices. It did, however, offend many members of the legal community. Lewin remarked:

> We have not done print advertisement on a consistent basis. I think there might be some print opportunities we haven't taken advantage of. On the other hand, it's expensive and we face a lot of competition. Every other lawyer who advertises in print quotes specific fees. We don't want to do that. We're usually more expensive.

Community Contacts

Lewin said she would like to see her attorneys taking out local advertisements, joining more local neighborhood activities, and putting up billboards near their offices. However, she wanted to retain control over their efforts. One managing attorney observed that if the office were his own, he'd be out in the field more, making contacts and trying to get referrals. "I want to know why L&A has no community-based contacts and why they rely strictly on advertisements," he said.

Another attorney said he would not invest in local print advertising because it was expensive and not cost effective. He had thought about giving seminars on common legal problems for employees of major businesses in the area, but was not sure how to go about this. It had occurred to him to give discounts to members of large groups; this would re-

quire Lewin's approval and he had never pursued his idea so far as to ask for that.

A third L&A attorney said he had no time to organize meetings with local clubs and churches. "If the firm took one month's worth of advertising money," he remarked, "they could get a PR person for 12 months, but they think each individual attorney has enough time. An organization with these resources should do a lot more local PR."

THE PARTNERS DELIBERATE

After Lewin had summarized the firm's difficult economic situation, she and her financial partners considered possible solutions. One was to reduce the number of offices. However, the tension level among employees was rising as word spread that drastic changes were in the offing. Lewin worried about the impact of office closings on attorney morale. Reducing the number of offices would also increase the burden of advertising expense on the remaining offices.

The partners next considered changing the compensation plan to a 50–50 split of gross income between the managing attorney and the head office, with a guaranteed minimum salary of $2,000 per month. According to this plan, the managing attorney would be required to pay all office expenses out of the 50 percent share, including the salary of the associate attorney, if the office had one, and that of the office secretaries. The managing attorney would then take home whatever was left over as salary. Lewin felt that this arrangement would give the attorneys an incentive to keep office costs down. Any office which was not able to meet its expenses out of its 50 percent would be closed.

But the partners foresaw several problems. New offices would need to be carried until they could establish themselves. Moreover, the gross income of some offices was highly variable from month to month; employment contracts, hitherto unused at L&A, might be necessary to give attorneys the security they required. The location of new offices would become extremely important since these might dilute business at existing offices if established nearby. Further, the fee-sharing arrangements between the general practice attorney and the specialist might have to be changed.

The partners also considered providing additional services to increase volume. Tax service was one possibility. As Lewin per-

ceived it, the problem with this option was that L&A's image would then become blurred, and expensive changes in the advertising would have to be made. In addition, L&A personnel lacked the necessary expertise for complicated, specialized areas of the law, such as tax.

Costs

Managing Attorney	36,000
Associate	19,500
benefits	11,100
wages (Lawyers)	66,600
Secretaries (2)	19,360 x 2 (so aches)
	38720
Rent (ave sq. ft 850)	12,750.
Misc ($280 x 52)	14560
	$ 132,630.

Service Positioning Through Structural Change

G. LYNN SHOSTACK

The basis of any service positioning strategy is the service itself, but marketing offers little guidance on how to craft service processes for positioning purposes. A new approach suggests that within service systems, structural process design can be used to "engineer" services on a more scientific, rational basis.

When a firm or provider establishes and maintains a distinctive place for itself and its offerings in the market, it is said to be successfully positioned. In the increasingly competitive service sector, effective positioning is one of marketing's most critical tasks.

For some marketers (e.g., Ries and Trout 1981), positioning is strictly a communications issue. The product or service is a given and the objective is to manipulate consumer perceptions of reality. As Lovelock (1984) rightly points out, however, positioning is more than just advertising and promotion. Market position can be affected by pricing, distribution and, of course, the product itself, which is the core around which all positioning strategies revolve.

Apart from promotion, pricing, and distribution, the product is indeed a critical, manageable factor in positioning. Products often are engineered explicitly to reach certain markets, as the original Mustang was designed to reach the youth market and light beer was created to tap the calorie-conscious consumer. Sometimes products are invented first and positioned afterward. The Xerox copier and the Polaroid camera are examples of products that were first created, then positioned to various markets. Finally, an existing product may be changed in order to

Reprinted from *Journal of Marketing*, Vol. 51 (January 1987), 34–43, published by the American Marketing Association.

change its market position, as the Jeep was altered physically from a military vehicle to a vehicle for the family market.

Services are not things, however. Mc-Luhan (1964) perhaps put it best and most succinctly more than 20 years ago when he declared that the *process* is the product. We say "airline" when we mean "air transportation." We say "movie," but mean "entertainment services." We say "hotel" when we mean "lodging rental." The use of nouns obscures the fundamental nature of services, which are processes, not objects.

As processes, services have many intriguing characteristics. Judd (1964), Rathmell (1974), Shostack (1977), Bateson (1977), and Sasser, Olsen, and Wyckoff (1978) were among the first to ponder the implications of service intangibility, service perishability, production/consumption simultaneity, and consumer participation in service processes. They found that traditional marketing, with its goods-bound approaches, was not helpful in process design, process modification, or process control.

If processes are the service equivalent of a product's "raw materials," can processes be designed, managed, and changed for positioning purposes the way physical goods are? The purpose of this article is to take a closer look at processes as structural elements and suggest some ways in which they can be "engineered" for strategic service positioning purposes.

PROCESS CHARACTERISTICS

Processes have been studied for some time in disciplines other than marketing. Systematic, quantified methods for describing processes have been developed in industrial engineering (Deming 1982), computer programming (Fox 1982), decision theory (Holloway 1979), and operations management (Schroeder 1981), to name a few examples and well known authors in each field. Though their techniques and nomenclatures may differ, process-oriented disciplines share certain basic concepts. First, each of them provides a way of breaking any process down into logical steps and sequences to facilitate its control and analysis. Second, each includes ways to accommodate more variable processes in which outcomes may differ because of the effects of judgment, chance, or choice on a sequence. Finally, each system includes the concept of deviation or tolerance standards in recognition that processes are "real time" phenomena that do not conform perfectly to any model or description, but rather function within a band or "norm" of some sort.

Little process description can be found in marketing literature. However, several writers on services have drawn upon manufacturing sources in using the words "standardized" and "customized" to define the poles of a process continuum (see Levitt 1976; Lovelock 1984). "Standardized" usually implies a nonvarying sequential process, similar to the mass production of goods, in which each step is laid out in order and all outcomes are uniform. "Customized" usually refers to some level of adaptation or tailoring of the process to the individual consumer. The concept of deviation usually is treated as a quality issue, in reference to services that do not perform as they should.

COMPLEXITY AND DIVERGENCE

Extracting from various approaches, we can suggest two ways to describe processes. One way is according to the steps and sequences that constitute the process; the other is according to the executional latitude or variability of those steps and sequences. Let us call the first factor the complexity of the process and the second its divergence. Deviation, a real-time operating factor, can then be thought of as an inadvertent departure from whatever process model and standards have been established for the first two factors.

We can define a service's complexity by analyzing the number and intricacy of the steps required to perform it. Accounting, for example, is more complex than bookkeeping because accounting is a more elaborated process, involving more functions and more steps. Architecture is more complex than plumbing. Plumbing is more complex than lawn mowing.

Apart from complexity, however, some processes include a high level of executional latitude and others do not. The degree of freedom allowed or inherent in a process step or sequence can be thought of as its divergence. A highly divergent service thus would be one in which virtually every performance of the process is unique. A service of low divergence would be one that is largely standardized.

Every service can be analyzed according to its overall complexity and divergence. A physician's services, for example, are highly complex. They are also highly divergent. As the service is being performed, a doctor constantly alters and shapes it by assimilating new data, weighing probabilities, reaching conclusions, and then taking action. Every case may be handled differently, yet all performances may be satisfactory from the consumer point of view. Architecture, law, consulting, and most other "professional" services have similarly high divergence (as well as high complexity), because they involve a considerable amount of judgment, discretion, and situational adaptation.

However, a process can be high in complexity and low in divergence. Hotel services, for example, are a complex aggregation of processes, but hotels standardize these processes through documentation and establishment of executional rules for every sequence from room cleaning to checkout. Telephone services are also highly complex, yet telephone companies have standardized and automated them to ensure uniformity and achieve economies of scale.

Services also can be low in complexity but high in divergence. In process terms, a singer renders the service of entertainment in one step: singing. This service is infinitely divergent, however, because each execution is unique and unlike that of any other provider. A painter "merely" paints, a teacher simply "transmits knowledge," a minister "spreads the gospel." These services do not consist of orderly, mechanical procedures, but of unique performances. Services that involve interpretative skills, artistic crafting, or highly individualized execution often appear simple in process terms, yet are highly

FIGURE 1
Park Avenue Florist

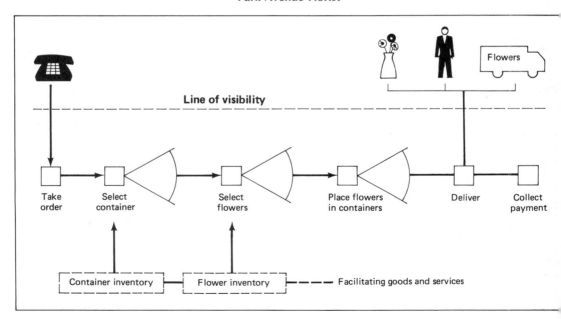

divergent in operation. In fact, for such services, defining "what" is done in process terms is often easier than describing "how" it is done.

BLUEPRINTING COMPLEXITY AND DIVERGENCE IN SERVICE SYSTEMS

Though processes can be reduced to steps and sequences, services must be viewed as interdependent, interactive systems, not as disconnected pieces and parts. One approach for visualizing service systems is a mapping technique called "blueprinting"

(Shostack 1984a,b). Blueprinting is a holistic method of seeing in snapshot form what is essentially a dynamic, living phenomenon.

For process design purposes, a blueprint should document all process steps and points of divergence in a specific service. This documentation must be carried to whatever level of detail is needed to distinguish between any two competing services. In other words, specific blueprints of real services are more productive than generic or generalized visualizations in working out position strategies based on process.

Figure 1 shows how one Park Avenue florist's service appears in blueprint form. The

FIGURE 2
Installment Lending: Bank X

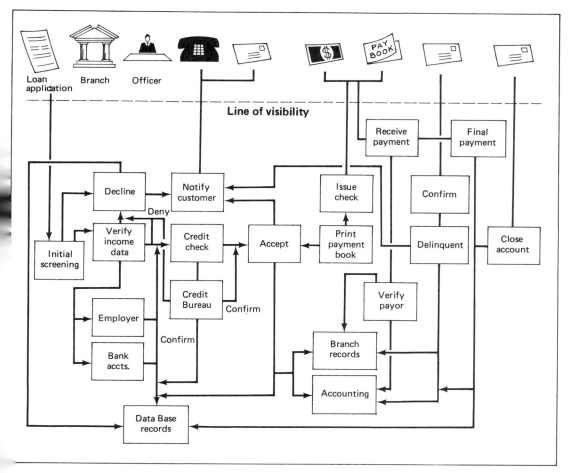

"fan" is borrowed from decision theory (see Holloway 1979) in which a fan attached to a circle is used to show a range of potential events that may occur, whereas a fan attached to a square denotes a range of potential actions that may be taken. This is a useful symbol for divergence and is used throughout the following illustrations. The florist provides a service of low complexity that is highly divergent. Though the process steps are few, the fans indicate broad executional latitude stemming from the judgment and decisions of the individual performing the service.

For comparison, Figure 2 illustrates a complex but standardized service—consumer installment lending at a large commercial bank. Here, the process has many more specific steps, but the steps are executed in a strict and unvarying manner. As Levitt would say, the service has been "industrialized" (1976). There is one and only one permissible manner and order in which the service is provided. Parts of the process have been automated for further conformity, and the bank's design for this service does not allow employees who are part of the service system to modify or change the service in any way. Such a service may not function perfectly at all times. However, as noted before, such quality failures represent deviation from a design standard, whereas true divergence is an integral part of the process.

Figure 3 shows yet another structure—the highly complex and highly divergent ser-

FIGURE 3
General Practitioner Services

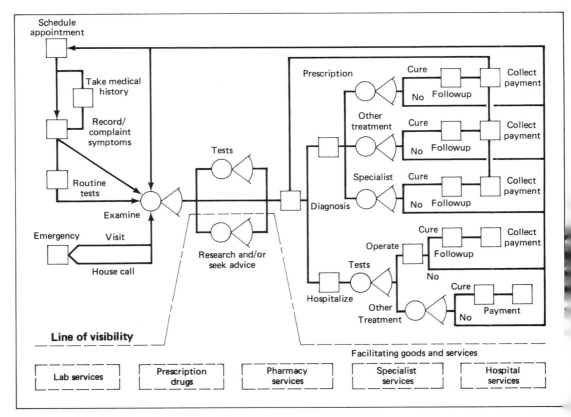

vice of a general medical practitioner. Here, not only is the process complex, but virtually every step involves variable execution.

Blueprints as a Tool in Consumer Research

It may be noted that this analytical approach is a useful and natural companion to market research. Lovelock (1984) noted the difficulty of researching service "attributes" for positioning purposes, which is caused at least partly by the inherent ambiguity and subjectivity of verbal descriptions. Blueprints provide visible portraits to which consumers can react, and which can facilitate exploration of more parts of the service system than just its processes. Blueprints can be used to educate consumers, focus their evaluative input on various aspects of the service system, elicit comparative or competitive assessments, and generate specific responses to contemplated changes or new service concepts. As Schneider and Bowen (1984) pointed out, regardless of whether consumers are privy to or even aware of all parts of the process, their awareness of its results and evidence makes them potentially valuable participants in the design of the entire system, not just those parts they see.

CHANGING THE PROCESS

Complexity and divergence are not fixed and immutable. They are factors that can be changed. Once a service has been documented accurately, it can be analyzed for opportunities either to increase or decrease one or both variables.

Alternative Directions for Structural Change

A change in overall complexity or divergence generally indicates one of four overall strategic directions. Each one has management consequences as well as certain market risks.

Reduced Divergence. Reducing divergence leads to uniformity which tends to re-duce costs, improve productivity, and make distribution easier. It usually indicates a shift to a volume-oriented positioning strategy based on economies of scale. The positive market effects of such a move can include perceived increases in reliability—more uniform service quality and greater service availability. However, reducing divergence also can have negative market effects. It dictates conformity as well as inflexibility in operating procedures. Customers may perceive the shift as one that lowers customization and limits their options, and may reject a highly standardized service even if it costs less.

Increased Divergence. Raising divergence is the service equivalent of creating a "job shop." Greater customization and flexibility tend to command higher prices. Increased divergence usually indicates a niche positioning strategy, dependent less on volume and more on margins. The market can respond positively to such a shift if the service taps a desire for prestige, customization, or personalization. Here, too, however, care is needed in making such a shift. A divergent service is more difficult to manage, control, and distribute. Moreover, customers may not be willing to pay the price that customization demands.

Reduced Complexity. Reduced complexity usually indicates a specialization strategy. As steps or functions are dropped from the system, resources can be focused on a narrower service offering (radiology, for example, versus general medical services). Narrowing the service offering usually makes distribution and control easier. Such a service can be perceived positively by the market if the provider stands out as an expert. However, reduced complexity also can cause a service to be perceived as "stripped down" or so limited that its specialized quality is not enough to overcome the inconvenience or price of obtaining it. Reducing complexity can be competitively risky if other providers continue to offer a broader, more extensive full-service alternative.

Increased Complexity. Higher complexity usually indicates a strategy to gain greater penetration in a market by adding more services or enhancing current ones. Supermarkets, banks, and retailers have expanded their service lines with this strategic goal in mind. Increasing complexity can increase efficiency by maximizing the revenue generated from each customer. In contrast, too much complexity can be confusing to customers and can cause overall service quality to fall. Thus, a highly complex service system may be vulnerable to inroads by competitors who specialize.

MARKETING STRATEGY AND STRUCTURAL CHANGE

Service industries offer numerous examples of changes in complexity and divergence and how they affect market position. Barbering, for example, is a relatively simple service, but beginning in the 1970s some providers began to reposition it. They added processes borrowed from women's beauty salons, such as tinting, body perms, and backcombing, redefined their mission, and transformed "hair cutting" into "hair styling"—a more complex, divergent service structure. Hair styling tapped or created a new market segment of men willing to pay substantially higher prices for a more elaborated process and carved a niche in the market through structural differentiation.

In retailing, there are many examples of adding to the complexity of service systems. Supermarkets began as specialty food stores and have added banking services, pharmacist services, flowers, books and magazines, and even food preparation to their basic food retailing structure. In the fast-food industry, what were once simple hamburger outlets have become providers of breakfast, dining room services, and even entertainment. Retailing also affords many examples of reducing complexity, as evidenced by the emergence of businesses specializing only in pasta, only in cookies, and only in ice cream.

For examples of lowered divergence, we need only to look at professional services. Legal services, for instance, have historically had both high complexity and high divergence. A consumer needing legal assistance first had to seek out and select an attorney, and was then dependent upon the variable performance of that individual. Over the past few years, however, this service has been repositioned through the actions of business-minded entrepreneurs who perceived a market need for less complex, less divergent alternatives. The result has been the creation of legal "clinics" and chains that offer a limited menu of services executed uniformly at published rates. This repositioning not only has opened a new market for legal services, but also has had and will continue to have a profound effect on the positioning strategies of traditional law firms.

A similar downshifting and repositioning of traditional personal accountant services was effected by the innovations of H & R Block, which tapped a vast market of consumers who did not require the variable and costly services of a personal accountant, but who were willing to pay someone else to prepare their tax returns.

Most of these examples are based on entrepreneurial response to the perception of an unmet market need. What is perhaps less clearly recognized is that such changes need not be intuitive or accidental. They can be made deliberately to support explicit positioning or competitive strategies.

IMPLICATIONS OF SERVICE SYSTEM CHANGES

Let us assume that Figure 1 is an accurate representation of a specific florist's service. Assume further that in an analysis of competitors, very similar structures were found. One strategic option to reposition and differentiate the service would be to re-engineer it as a less divergent system. Figure 4 illustrates a redesigned blueprint that accomplishes this objective. The number of container choices has been limited to two; there are only two groups of flowers and only two choices of arrangement for each group. Thus, only eight combinations are possible.

Obviously, the new design has implica-

FIGURE 4
Florist Services: Alternative Design

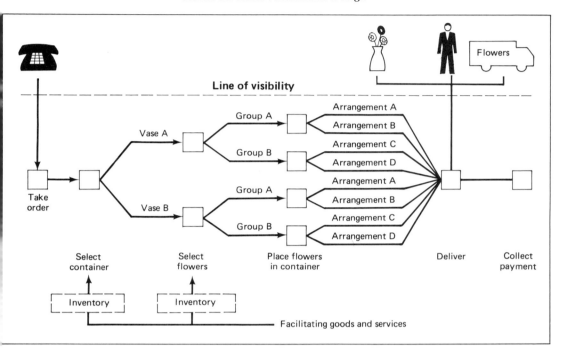

tions for inventory management as well as productivity. Inventory can be ordered in larger, more economic quantities. More arrangements can be produced by the florist because the process is more standardized. These two effects will lower prices and potentially allow the service to be repositioned to a broader market. The new structure also will allow wider service distribution, because simpler blueprints are easier to replicate. FTD (Florists' Transworld Delivery) arrived at a similar conclusion and expanded florist services from a local craft into a national service industry.

However, if all the florists in a particular market had structures similar to Figure 4, a logical positioning strategy might be to move toward the design shown in Figure 1—a highly artistic, high-priced structure. Alternatively, a marketer might choose to increase complexity alone, through retailing a selection of plants and supplies, or to increase both complexity and divergence by offering flower arranging classes.

Identifying and Evaluating Strategic Choices

Services can be structurally evaluated on a stand-alone basis and also as members of service families. Within a service family, a marketer can consider positioning strategies based on structural complementarity, structural diversity, and overall developmental direction.

In Figure 2, a bank's consumer installment lending service is diagrammed. This service, of course, is only one of a constellation of services that constitute consumer banking. Though consumer banking, in its totality, is an extraordinarily complex service system, most blueprints of its component services would show low divergence

FIGURE 5

Relative Positions Based on Structural Analysis

High Complexity

● Hospital services
○ General practitioner: diagnosis and treatment
● Specialist: treatment only
● Diagnostic services only

● Forensic-Testing Lab

Low Divergence ———————————————— High Divergence

● Outpatient clinic: Limited treatment; e.g., Broken bones / Minor burns only

● Retailer of orthopedic supplies

● X-ray lab

● Medical Counseling

Low Complexity

stemming from 20 years of effort to standardize and automate the service system.

One strategy for a bank with this structure is to continue increasing complexity by adding more subservices while continuing to minimize divergence through standardization and automation. For a competitor, an equally valid strategy would be to adopt the counterposition, which would call for increasing the customization of services. The latter strategy is evident in banks offering "private" banking, an integrated package of services for the upscale market that includes such divergent services as customized lending, portfolio management, and financial planning.

The general practitioner previously described also has numerous strategic choices. Figure 5 illustrates the relative structural positions held by a number of medical service providers, including the general practitioner analyzed in Figure 3. From the present position, he/she can move in any direction on the scale by adding or deleting service functions to create a new family. Depending on the complexity and divergence of these functions, the overall service system's complexity divergence will change, thus altering its relative position.

For example (Figure 6), retailing or-

thopedic supplies would add complexity to the doctor's overall service system, but little divergence. Adding counseling, in contrast would add considerable divergence, but little operational complexity. Conversely, if minor surgical procedures that have been performed in the office were eliminated, the service system would be reduced in both complexity and divergence and move closer to the position held by diagnosticians, who perform no treatment themselves. At the ex-

FIGURE 6

Positional Shifts Through Structural Change

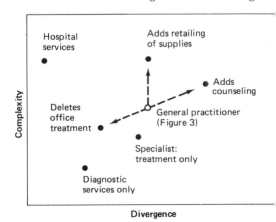

FIGURE 7
Structural Alternatives

Lower Complexity/Divergence	Current Process	Higher Complexity/Divergence
No reservations	Take Reservation	Specific table selection
Self-seating. Menu on blackboard	Seat Guests, Give Menus	Recite menu: Describe entrees and specials
Eliminate	Serve Water and Bread	Assortment of hot breads and hors d'oeuvres
Customer fills out form	Take Orders	At table. Taken personally by maitre d'
	Prepare Orders	
Pre-prepared: No choice	• Salad (4 Choices)	Individually prepared at table
Limit to four choices	• Entree (15 Choices)	Expand to 20 choices: Add flaming dishes; Bone fish at table; Prepare sauces at table
Sundae bar: Self-service	• Dessert (6 Choices)	Expand to 12 choices
Coffee, tea, milk only	• Beverage (6 Choices)	Add exotic coffees; Wine list; Liqueurs
Serve salad and entree together: Bill and beverage together	Serve Orders	Separate course service: Sherbet between courses; Hand grind pepper
Cash only: Pay when leaving	Collect Payment	Choice of payment. Including house accounts: Serve mints

treme position, complexity and divergence could be lowered to the point where only the simple service, such as X-rays, is provided in a completely standardized way. Consumer research can be instrumental in facilitating this strategic process, and blueprints are a useful tool for focusing consumer input and response to new structural concepts.

In simplified terms, Figure 7 shows some changes that a midpriced family restaurant might consider to alter complexity and divergence for competitive purposes. Any prospective change or mix of changes can be compared with competitors' offerings to determine which mix is most likely to provide the maximum competitive differentiation.

Positioning charts are a useful tool for market analysts wishing to compare the perceived performance of competing services on two or three attributes simultaneously. Examples of such charts (also known as perceptual maps) are given by Tybout and Hauser (1981) and Lovelock (1984). Blueprinting works well in tandem with this technique by serving as a focal point for determining which parts of the service system or process components are important to the market, and in evaluating change across many elements of the system.

IMPLEMENTING CHANGE

Though processes are intangible, the means by which services are rendered are very real. There are only two, people (both providers and consumers) and facilitating goods. Any shift in overall complexity or divergence, or the introduction of any new process design, must be implemented with a clear understanding of the potential impact on these "producers" of the process.

Role of Service Employees and Customers

Considerable attention has been paid to people in the service system. Whether they are providers or consumers, the management and control of human behavior is a critical factor in process design, change, and operating quality. Mills (1985) suggests that management controls over service employees should depend on the structure of the service system. For low-contact, standardized services, behavior can be controlled through mechanistic means, such as rules and regulations. However, for high-contact, divergent services, Mills suggests that employee self-management and peer-reference techniques are more effective. Smith and Houston (1983), in contrast, propose that a script-based approach to managing customer and employee behavior can help to control expectations as well as process compliance. Bowen and Schneider (1985) speak of "boundary spanners," that is, employees with high customer interaction, as a valuable source of design information and as change agents whose acceptance and commitment are critical to success in altering any process. Schneider and Bowen (1984) as well as others (Berry 1983; Heskett 1986) stress that employee involvement and "internal" marketing to employees are important factors in ensuring successful service operations. Deming (1982), however, argues that both behavior and motivation are controlled by the design of the process itself and that if the process is properly designed, high motivation and effectiveness will be the natural results.

In terms of consumer participation, Lovelock and Young (1979), Chase (1978), Bateson (1985), and others have discussed whether and how to involve consumers in the service process, and the management of their involvement. Chase argues that consumer participation should be kept to a minimum in the interests of greater process efficiency. However, as we have seen, process design offers many routes to market success. A service (self-service gasoline stations, for example) can be designed for maximum consumer participation and still be profitable. In fact, Bateson's (1985) work suggests that consumers can be segmented on the basis of control needs, resulting in services that are designed to capitalize profitably on the consumer's own desire for participation.

These brief descriptions illustrate the richness and diversity of current thought about the human side of service systems. Our purpose here is not to choose one approach over another, but to underscore the fact that people are just as important as structural design. If people issues are not addressed effectively, even the best design will fail.

Role of Facilitating Goods

Facilitating goods are also important in structural planning. Educational services, for example, can be rendered by a human being who lectures in a traditional classroom setting. Education also can be rendered via videotape, television, computer, and book, to name just a few alternative facilitating goods. For the designer of a new or different educational service, any of these choices will yield a different service structure. These structures will differ in complexity and divergence, as well as in cost dynamics, distribution constraints, and market position.

Sometimes facilitating goods are used as a replacement for human performance to reduce divergence. Computers are the prime example of a good that has been used in this way to standardize service systems. However, simplification is not the only use for technology. Technology also can be used to increase complexity and divergence. When bank automated teller machines first were introduced, for example, they could deliver only simple cash dispensing and deposit services. Now, technology has allowed the addition of funds transfer and investment services to the system, increasing its overall complexity. Tomorrow, what are called "smart" cards will make possible the delivery of a wide range of credit, payment, and information services. Ultimately, technology may even make possible a degree of customization (i.e., divergence) that only human providers can now deliver.

For all these reasons, the consideration of changes to any service structure demands an appreciation of the interrelatedness and intricacy of service systems. Unlike a product, a service cannot be engineered and then made in a factory. "Producing" a service is a dynamic, continuous event.

CONCLUSION

Though our discussion focuses on process design, other elements of the service system can and do affect market position. Advertising and promotion are, of course, powerful forces in the positioning process. American Express, for example, has repositioned its credit services to women solely through advertising.

Distribution channels also affect market position. Marketing stock brokerage through Sears stores is one example of positioning a service to a new, broader consumer base through a change in distribution channels. Moreover, as Shostack (1985), Blackman (1985), and others have noted, various forms of physical service evidence, from the environment in which a service is rendered to the correspondence, brochures, signage, and even people to which a customer is exposed, can affect position. Facilitating goods also can affect position, even without process change. A provider who substitutes limousines for taxicabs, for example, may succeed in charging higher prices and tapping a different market for exactly the same transportation service.

In short, the issues involved in service positioning are numerous, and this discussion by no means encompasses all of the subjects relevant to the positioning process. In a structural sense, however, processes themselves appear to have characteristics that not only affect market position, but also can be deliberately and strategically managed for positioning purposes. By manipulating complexity and divergence, a service marketer can approximate some of the product analysis and design functions that are traditional in product marketing. Moreover, the use of blueprints provides a mechanism through which services can be "engineered" at the drawing board, as well as a tool for identifying gaps, analyzing competitors, aiding in market research, and controlling implementation.

The marketplace affords evidence that both complexity and divergence are concepts that are understood and employed in service industries. Though the practice is not formalized, it works. How much more powerful the result might be if marketers brought a professional discipline, capable of crafting service systems on a rational basis, to bear on the service positioning task!

For managers in service industries, taking a structural approach can help increase their control over some of the most critical elements of service system management. For marketers, process design may be a tool that can substantially increase their impact and role in the service sector and help service marketing come of age.

REFERENCES

BATESON, JOHN E. G. (1977), "Do We Need Service Marketing?" *Marketing Consumer Services: New Insights*, Report #77-115. Cambridge, MA: Marketing Science Institute.

———— (1985), "Perceived Control and the Service Encounter," in *The Service Encounter*, John A. Czepiel et al., eds. Lexington, MA: Lexington Books.

BERRY, LEONARD L. (1983), "Relationship Marketing," in *Emerging Perspectives on Services Marketing*, Leonard L. Berry et al., eds. Chicago: American Marketing Association, 25–28.

BLACKMAN, BARRY (1985), "Making a Service More Tangible Can Make It More Manageable," in *The Service Encounter*, John A. Czepiel et al., eds. Lexington, MA: Lexington Books.

BOWEN, DAVID E. and BENJAMIN SCHNEIDER (1985), "Boundary-Spanning-Role Employees and the Service Encounter," in *The Service Encounter*, John A. Czepiel et al., eds. Lexington, MA: Lexington Books, 124–47.

CHASE, RICHARD B. (1978), "Where Does the Consumer Fit In a Service Operation?", *Harvard Business Review*, 56 (November–December), 137–42.

DEMING, W. EDWARDS (1982), *Quality, Productivity and Competitive Position*. Cambridge, MA: Massachusetts Institute of Technology, Center for Advanced Engineering Study.

FOX, JOSEPH M. (1982), *Software and Its Development*. Englewood Cliffs, NJ: Prentice-Hall, Inc.

HESKETT, JAMES L. (1986), *Managing in the Service Economy*. Boston: Harvard Business School Press, 45–74, 117–34.

HOLLOWAY, CHARLES A. (1979), *Decision Making Under Uncertainty: Models and Choices*. Englewood Cliffs, NJ: Prentice-Hall, Inc.

JUDD, ROBERT C. (1964), "The Case for Redefining Services," *Journal of Marketing*, 28 (January), 58–59.

LEVITT, THEODORE (1976), "The Industrialization of Service," *Harvard Business Review*, 54 (September/October), 63–74.

LOVELOCK, CHRISTOPHER H. (1984), *Services Marketing, Text, Cases, & Readings*. Englewood Cliffs, NJ: Prentice-Hall, Inc., 55–56, 133–39.

———— and ROBERT F. YOUNG (1979), "Look to Consumers to Increase Productivity," *Harvard Business Review*, 57 (May–June), 168–78.

McLUHAN, MARSHALL (1964), *Understanding Media*. New York: McGraw-Hill Book Company.

MILLS, PETER K. (1985), "The Control Mechanisms of Employees at the Encounter of Service Organizations," in *The Service Encounter*, John A. Czepiel et al., eds. Lexington, MA: Lexington Books.

RATHMELL, JOHN M. (1974), *Marketing in the Service Sector*. Cambridge, MA: Winthrop Publishers, Inc.

RIES, AL, and JACK TROUT (1981), *Positioning*. New York: McGraw-Hill Book Company.

SASSER, W. EARL, JR., R. PAUL OLSEN, and D. DARYL WYCKOFF (1978), *Management of Service Operations: Text, Cases, and Readings*. Boston: Allyn & Bacon.

SCHNEIDER, BENJAMIN, and DAVID E. BOWEN (1984), "New Service Design, Development and Implementation," in *Developing New Services*, William R. George and Claudia Marshall, eds. Chicago: American Marketing Association, Proceedings Series, 82–102.

SCHROEDER, ROGER G. (1981), *Operations Management*. New York: McGraw-Hill Book Company.

SHOSTACK, G. LYNN (1977), "Breaking Free From Product Marketing," *Journal of Marketing*, 41 (April), 73–80.

———— (1984a), "A Framework for Service Marketing," in *Marketing Theory, Distinguished Contributions*, Stephen W. Brown and Raymond P. Fisk, eds. New York: John Wiley & Sons, Inc., 250.

———— (1984b), "Designing Services That Deliver," *Harvard Business Review*, 62 (January–February), 133–39.

———— (1985), "Planning the Service Encounter," in *The Service Encounter*, John A. Czepiel et al., eds. Lexington, MA: Lexington Books, 243–53.

SMITH, RUTH A. and MICHAEL J. HOUSTON (1983), "Script-Based Evaluation of Satisfaction with Services," in *Emerging Perspectives on Services Marketing*, Leonard Berry et al., eds. Chicago: American Marketing Association.

TYBOUT, ALICE M. and JOHN R. HAUSER (1981), "A Marketing Audit Using a Conceptual Model of Consumer Behavior: Application and Evaluation," *Journal of Marketing*, 45 (Summer), 82–101.

Franchise Prototypes

KEVIN FARRELL

When entrepreneurs develop a prototype service operation, they may spend months or years hammering out the details that make the service work well and efficiently. A smoothly running prototype business can often be cloned through franchising, although some adaptation may be needed from one location to another.

Entrepreneurs are discovering the key to building successful big franchises quickly: perfecting the prototype. Investing years, and sometimes millions of dollars, in a pilot unit is profitable for franchisors in virtually every retail business. From ice cream to computers to such brand-new concepts as gift-wrap and packaging franchises, entrepreneurs are learning that if they develop a well-oiled model unit that can be replicated with ease, where the pieces are in place and the bugs eliminated before a single franchise is sold, the world will buy.

The rewards of getting it right the first time can be great. It took three years and $1.6 million for Steven B. Heller, 43, and James J. Edgette, 42, to fashion a model of their retail computer store, Entré Computers. But the work, which involved endless research, paid off handsomely. Barely one year after they began franchising, Entré has sold well over 200 franchises, and is selling them at a rate of 10 a month. "A prototype will enable you to do a tremendously refined job of opening a center," says Edgette. Ron Berger, 35, devoted a year and a half and spent $700,000 to develop a solid prototype for National Video Corp., a Portland, Oregon-based renter of video equipment. Within three years National Video sold 500 franchises. "I would counsel anyone who wants to go into franchising to devote a great deal of time and effort to making absolutely sure the prototype is as efficient as possible before launching into franchise sales," he says. And Ron Strunk, 28, projects he will sell his 200th Phone Source phone store franchise by 1985, scarcely two years after he opened his prototype store in Omaha. Such success stories are not uncommon today, as franchising continues to pull in nearly one-third of all retail sales. Consumers spent an estimated $436 billion in franchise units in 1983, nearly 13 percent more than 1982.

In its development stage, a prototype becomes a hands-on experiment for the entrepreneur. It is a time to make mistakes, to work out the kinks, and to determine how to sell the franchises. It is not an easy process. It takes months in some industries, years in others, and still a prototype is seldom cast in stone; it is constantly modified as business develops. But the rewards of having a workable prototype are invaluable. In addition to smoothing out an operating system, having a solid model makes it that much easier to sell franchises and impress bankers and backers.

And entrepreneurs are devising their winning formulas in a variety of ways. Not surprisingly, the formulas often seem to have little in common. For some, a prototype unit is basically an opportunity to test design ideas. For others, it is an occasion to draw up training procedures for management and employees, or to create financial goals and a system for realizing them, or to fine-tune distribution and marketing techniques. Clearly, prototypes have different functions for different franchisors, but are in some way or other a proving ground for the entrepreneur's concepts.

Franchisors have always struggled to get the kinks out of their operations. But what today's high-speed franchisors do differently is get a headstart on problems that may surface when, for example, the company has dozens of franchises and suddenly discovers its method of inventory control is ineffective, or that poorly trained employees are alienating customers. "We want to make the mistakes, not our franchisees," says Michael J. Coles, 39, chairman of Atlanta-based The Original Great American Chocolate Chip Cookie Inc., a 1977 startup that now has 200 units either open or under construction.

In addition, the prototype affords the entrepreneur an opportunity to discover if, in fact, a business can be cloned through franchising. Says Martin Boehm, a research analyst for the International Franchise Assn., a Washington trade group representing 381 franchisors: "It has to be simple enough to teach someone how to run it, someone else has to be able to run it, and it has to be profitable enough so the profits can be split."

In some cases, franchisors have been accused of using the prototype as a misleading sales tool to attract franchisees. For instance, in 1978, the original management of Command Performance Hair Salons built a prototype store in a busy San Diego shopping center, and spent relatively large sums of money to advertise and promote the unit, according to Timothy H. Fine, a San Francisco attorney. Fine represents 19 Command Performance Hair Salon franchisees in a suit against the franchisor's former management charging fraud and misrepresentation in the sale of franchises. The present defendants deny the charges. Fine says franchisees bought Command Performance franchises based on impressive sales records of the prototype. His clients claim that the franchisees could not match the prototype's sales figures on their own because of competition from other nearby Command Performance units which were eventually built, and because the 4 percent-of-sales ad budget required by the franchisor was much less than was spent to promote the prototype.

According to the franchisees' lawsuit, Command Performance heavily promoted its San Diego prototype between November, 1978, and August, 1979. During that period, they claim, the store sometimes pulled in weekly gross receipts of more than $12,000. The franchisees contend that sales at the prototype declined steadily as the promotion budget dropped, and as competing Command Performance franchises were built. By 1982, they claim, the prototype's weekly receipts dropped to as low as $2,000.

In 1981, the original management of

Command Performance left the company and the parent corporation, First National Services Corp., filed for bankruptcy under Chapter XI. The company has since been taken over by some of the owners of Andover, Mass.-based Docktor Pet Centers Inc. and existing Command Performance franchisees. William J. Wright, one of the original Command Performance managers named as defendants, declines to comment on the pending suit.

A former vice-president of Command Performance, Adrian Deacon, says: "It was not a premeditated plan to run the volume of that store up to sell franchises," adding, "we were not pumping any more money into that store than into any others." He says franchisees were only required to spend 2 percent of sales on company advertising campaigns, which he agrees was too small. He adds that it is difficult to judge how many stores will saturate a market. "When you're doing a threshold business, how do you know what's too close?" he says.

A MISLEADING TOOL

"A prototype generally can be a misleading thing," says Fine. "It may have no bearing in real life. It also can be very dangerous. It can be misused by the franchisor to promote sales that are inflated." Adds Edgette of Entré Computers: "A prototype should be something that proves the system works. It should absolutely not be used as a sales tool. That's a dangerous road to follow."

Different entrepreneurs seem to learn different lessons while proving their systems work. Tom Sizer, 42, bought Pac N-Send, an existing 16-unit packaging, gift-wrapping, and shipping business in Florida, from founder Bruce Young in April, 1983, believing he could sell franchises nationally. He changed the name to P.k.g.'s, hired Young as chairman, and then built a model unit in Orlando. There, he discovered subsequent outlets would need to be strictly uniform in appearance "to avoid looking like a mom-and-pop operation," he says. Also, he learned from his prototype that franchisees should

be freed of most operating responsibilities so they could concentrate on selling the service. "The thing we learned was that the store should be a complete turnkey operation, meaning everything down to postage stamps all the way up to cabinetry should be supplied by us. That frees the franchisee to just sell the service," he says. Sizer collects an average 3½ percent royalty from 25 franchises opened in less than a year, and plans to open 150 franchised units by January, 1985.

But others have learned that it won't always work to have a standard operation and standard appearance. Once the Entré Computers prototype in Tysons Corners, Va., was working, "We learned that you can't cookie-cutter the sales process in our industry, it must be tailored for the individual center," says Edgette. "Selling a [computer] system to a farmer in Iowa is different from selling one to a government consulting firm in suburban Washington," he says. National Pet Care Centers Inc., Newport Beach, Calif., which sells franchises of its pet hospital to existing veterinarians (in much the same way Century 21 sells franchises to realtors), also learned that a prototype can't always be reproduced. "We don't and won't have a prototype unit in terms of design and decor," says co-founder Douglas S. Keane, 37. "But we will have a prototype in terms of the systems we use."

Sometimes the point is that the hard-and-fast rules franchisors are searching for are *not* the answer. For instance, Martin Byrne, 46, who created a concept for John Phillip Tuba ice cream restaurants, realized he should offer a flexible program for franchisees. Depending on how much they plan to spend, franchisees can open either a simple ice cream shop, or a store with ice cream and a take-out menu for food, or a full-service restaurant with an ice cream stand, robotic entertainment, and video games. The startup costs range from $95,000 to $430,000. Byrne has sold 14 franchises since January, and says the flexible plan enables him to penetrate markets relatively quickly.

When entrepreneurs develop a prototype, they may spend months, or even years, hammering out the details that will eventually make it relatively simple to adapt from location to location. In part, it is the gift of time—time to solve a sticky problem. For Strunk, it was a chance to test out design schemes for the Phone Source until he hit upon one that appealed to both men and women. After six months, he settled on a decor based on cedar shelves and cubed glass. For Daniel Rhode, president of King of Prussia, Pa.-based Sparks Tune-Up, it was a chance to establish a one-price auto tune-up. The goal was to offer tune-ups for any car at a price of $44.90. However, after six months of molding a system at the Reading, Pa., prototype—learning how much they could afford to pay mechanics and how many tune-ups a mechanic could do in a day— Rhode realized he could lower the price to $39.90. In two and a half years, he opened 40 franchised units.

A startup franchisor with little or no experience is taken more seriously by financiers if he or she can point to a successful prototype. Byrne had a working prototype of his middle-level John Phillip Tuba franchise—the restaurant with an ice cream stand—when he sought a $200,000 loan from a St. Petersburg, Fla., bank to equip a prototype for his larger franchise, the restaurant with entertainment. "The bank flew five of its officers down to Fort Lauderdale to see our prototype before they would approve the loan," he says. When Strunk wanted an equity partner for franchising the Phone Source, he showed his prototype unit to Gerald Bogard, an Omaha financial adviser who, after seeing the prototype in operation, invested $30,000 for 50 percent equity interest. Then, Strunk discussed his business plan with a local banker and trotted him through the prototype unit. The banker offered Strunk a $75,000 line of credit.

GAINING FINANCIAL CREDIBILITY

A working model also makes it easier for franchisees to finance their franchise. Explains Berger, founder of National Video: "A young franchisor doesn't have a good record, and when someone wants to buy a franchise, the bank says to a potential franchisee, 'Are you sure this guy's going to be around [very long]?' But a prototype can convince the bank that the franchise is a good investment."

Having a prototype provides the credibility that may be needed to move into a prime location. That's why David Glassman, 32, and Steven Shoeman, 34, co-founders of All American Hero, a hoagie shop franchise, used their prototype to gain acceptance in regional shopping malls, which are virtually impossible to enter without a track record. The prototype was set up in the "food court" of Fort Lauderdale's Hollywood Mall at a cost of $60,000. The unit was treated as an experiment. Food and labor costs were scrutinized and operations continually altered until the founders developed a formula that resulted in operating margins of 24 percent, relatively high for the restaurant industry. At that point, Glassman and Shoeman invited mall developers and managers to view the prototype. "You have to have them on your side to get into their prime locations," says Glassman. All American Hero has expanded to 30 franchise units—most in large shopping malls—each averaging $350,000 in revenues. Glassman has 15 more units under construction, and anticipates the chain will double in units each year the next three years.

Entrepreneurs come upon their winning formulas in a variety of ways. Ray Jacobs, 47, founder and president of America's Number One Software Dealer Inc., never intended to franchise. He spent $7,500 to open a 1,000-sq.-ft. software store in Teaneck, N.J. When he saw "people coming in here from over 50 miles away," he knew the store was "franchiseable." He hired a franchise consultant who helped him through the legal maze required to register and sell franchises. And he learned that the stores could locate in "secondary" space, relatively inexpensive strip shopping centers. Since January, he has sold 50 franchises.

Franchisors who create a prototype can use it as a "university" where franchisees can learn the system. As business develops in the

---

EVALUATE THE PROTOTYPE CAREFULLY

An individual looking to buy a franchise still in the prototype stage generally has the advantage of getting in on a good deal, since the prices for franchises typically shoot up after the franchisor achieves success. But early franchisees should be doubly cautious in scrutinizing a prototype. So how can you tell if it can be replicated?

First, find out if the advertising and promotion money being spent on the prototype exceeds the percentage that is called for in the franchise agreement. A franchisor may require a franchisee to spend 4 percent of sales on advertising, for instance, when he or she is spending 10 times that amount to promote a company-owned prototype. The result of the high advertising budget may be much more business in the prototype than you would draw with your relatively low budget, according to Timothy H. Fine, a San Francisco-based attorney who represents franchisees and franchisee trade groups.

Next, try to determine how the franchisor intends to authorize the location of franchises. A prototype may rack up impressive sales, if it is the only unit of its kind within a five-mile radius. Will the franchisor promise not to permit another unit to be built within five miles of your store?

The Federal Trade Commission requires that a franchisor provide you with a Franchise Offering Circular before you buy a franchise. The circular spells out a franchise's investment costs and estimated operating costs. But check the circulars of other franchisors in the industry (they are public documents) and compare their operating costs with the costs of the prototype you are shown. For instance, a franchisor may spend a greater portion of his or her prototype's budget on labor or goods than a competitor spends. In such cases, chances are the franchisor is providing extraordinary services to his prototype that you wouldn't receive as a franchisee, according to Fine.

Also try visiting the prototype when the franchisor is absent from the premises. "If it runs the same way when he isn't there [as it does when he is]," says Craig Slavin, president of Franchise Architects, a Chicago franchise consulting firm, "then it indicates the franchisor has perfected the prototype." Finally, keep in mind that if the prototype is geographically distant from your proposed store, there may be difficulties. "You may have to get the franchisor to your unit immediately if a problem crops up," says Paul J. Stewart, president of Franchise Associates Inc., a Dallas consulting firm, "and he better not be in San Diego if you're in Bangor, Me."

K.F.

---

model store, training procedures are changed and updated.

But for all the work and worry, the rewards of building a successful prototype can be great. Entré Computers collected $30,000 franchise fees from each of the 55 stores it sold in fiscal year 1983, its second year of operation. Also, it collected royalties of 8 percent on the estimated $39 million total sales of the 59 operating stores. The fees and royalties added up to $3.8 million. In addition, Entré's company-owned prototype earned profits of $750,000 on sales of $4.5 million. In all, the company's profits were $1.7 million. And the profits should continue rolling in, as Entré anticipates opening its 200th unit by the end of fiscal 1984 in August. Together, co-founders Heller and Edgette personally own slightly more than half the company's stock. They filed for an initial public offering last October, and hope to raise at least $20 million for working capital for expansion into foreign markets, and to construct an automated warehouse. If the offering is successful, it would leave Heller and Edgette each with 21.4 percent ownership of a company valued at $140 million.

Even for smaller franchisors, the rewards multiply as units expand. Strunk collected franchise fees of $10,000 from each of the 10 units opened in 1983, and he is raising that fee to $15,000 for the six additional stores he intends to add in 1984. He collected royalties of 3 percent on total franchise sales of $750,000 in 1983, and estimates those sales will increase to $4 million in 1984. He figures his modest profits in 1983 of $10,000 will jump to $120,000 in 1984 as units and sales are added. He owns 50 percent of the company.

Berger, who owns approximately one-third of National Video, expects to see profits of

$250,000 on total sales of $4 million from his 190 franchise units for fiscal 1984. But with a $15,900 franchise fee and 3.9 percent royalties from software sales, he estimates his company will earn $12.7 million on sales of $54 million by yearend 1987, when he anticipates having 6,000 stores in operation. And for 1984, the first full year of franchising P.k.g.'s, Sizer expects profits of $350,000 on total franchise sales of $3.5 million. He collected royalties averaging 3½ percent from each of the 25 units for a total of $100,000 in royalties. Also, he collected $7,500 franchise fees from each of the 10 units that were not Pac N-Send franchises he converted. Those rewards should build as the franchise gains momentum. Sizer hopes to have as many as 100 units in place by yearend 1984, and as many as 350 in three to five years. "Having a prototype," says Sizer, "makes all the difference."

A Guide for New Distribution Channel Strategies for Service Firms

DONALD H. LIGHT

Service firms that successfully develop new methods for distributing their products will have a clear competitive advantage. This article presents a schematic for understanding service distribution channels and explores issues in designing and selecting channels.

The pursuit of distribution channel strategies by firms in various service industries has led companies in new and unfamiliar directions.

Doing what they do best, American Airlines and United Airlines have spent millions of dollars developing their on-line reservation systems to better serve (and, some might say, control) independent travel agents. The system gave priority listings to flights of these airlines when agents requested travel information via computers. The airlines were told by the Civil Aeronautics Board that those systems created some very unfriendly skies for competing carriers and had to be modified.

More than 70 percent of bank executives queried in a poll a few years ago said that they planned to enter the insurance industry. They indicated a desire to put another product line through their high-cost brick-and-mortar branch networks, even though at the time of the survey, basically everyone who needed insurance could easily buy it.

Most national stock brokerage firms have vastly expanded their product offerings, making each broker a miniature financial supermarket. This led a Paine Webber branch manager to say, in effect, no thank you to selling a new product—"We get a new product every day—it's really mind-boggling. My brokers all complain there's so much to choose from, it confuses them."

There is little to guide executives of airlines, banks, stockbrokerages, and other service firms as they struggle with the strategic problem of service distribution. Even the idea of "distributing" an intangible service is a little hard to get a handle on. There is a well-developed field within marketing that deals with distribution channels. But with few exceptions, that literature concentrates on the tactical problems of distributing physical products.[1] This article attempts to meet the needs of executives who develop strategies for delivering services.

SERVICES VS. PRODUCTS

It is easy to intuitively understand how products are made, distributed, and used. Somewhere, a factory manufactures a tangible, physical product. The product is handled by various shippers, wholesalers, and warehouses. Eventually, it finds its way to a retail location, where a customer buys it, takes it home, and uses it.

An attempt to describe services in a similar way runs into immediate difficulties. A service is not a tangible object that is physically manufactured. No one ships services by common carrier or stores them in service warehouses. When a customer buys a service, there is nothing to take home and put in the upstairs closet.

If a service is not a product, what is it? The creation, distribution, and consumption of a service together constitute an integrated process.[2] The purchaser of a service enters into a *relationship* with the service firm and its intermediaries. The value of an insurance policy to the policyholder comes from the agent's advice about what coverages to buy, and the psychological comfort provided by the insurance company's ability to pay for losses if and when they occur.

A service is intangible, even though physical objects play a role in the creation/distribution/consumption process. The fact that insurance companies and agents need buildings, computers, and desks to give their advice and fulfill their promises is a secondary concern to the policyholder.

Notwithstanding these differences between services and products, it would be wrong to assume that there is an unbridgeable strategic chasm between services and products. In fact, many of the concepts and approaches this article develops for services are easily transferable to the world of products.

A SCHEMATIC FOR A SERVICE DISTRIBUTION CHANNEL

The service/product differences do imply that service distribution channels have some unique characteristics. Figure 1 shows these features. It has three major sectors, which are shown across the bottom of the exhibit:

- The channel participants and their relationships
- The various functions that the participants perform using material and technological supports
- The service that they create

The distribution channel has three kinds of participants: service firms, intermediaries, and customers. Each participant is in a buying and selling relationship with up-channel and down-channel participants. Each participant has its own capacities and objectives, which results in a characteristic channel mix of power, conflict, and cooperation.

The participants also perform certain functions that add value to the service. (One way of thinking about a service is to consider it as the summation of all the value that channel participants have added to it.) In performing these functions, the participants use many kinds of material and technological supports: paper and pencil, sophisticated computer networks, buildings, automobiles, etc.

The service itself has various elements: price, availability, and so forth. Customers distinguish between the services offered by various firms in terms of these elements: how much each costs, its particular features, and where and how it can be purchased.

FIGURE 1

General Schematic for a Service Distribution Channel

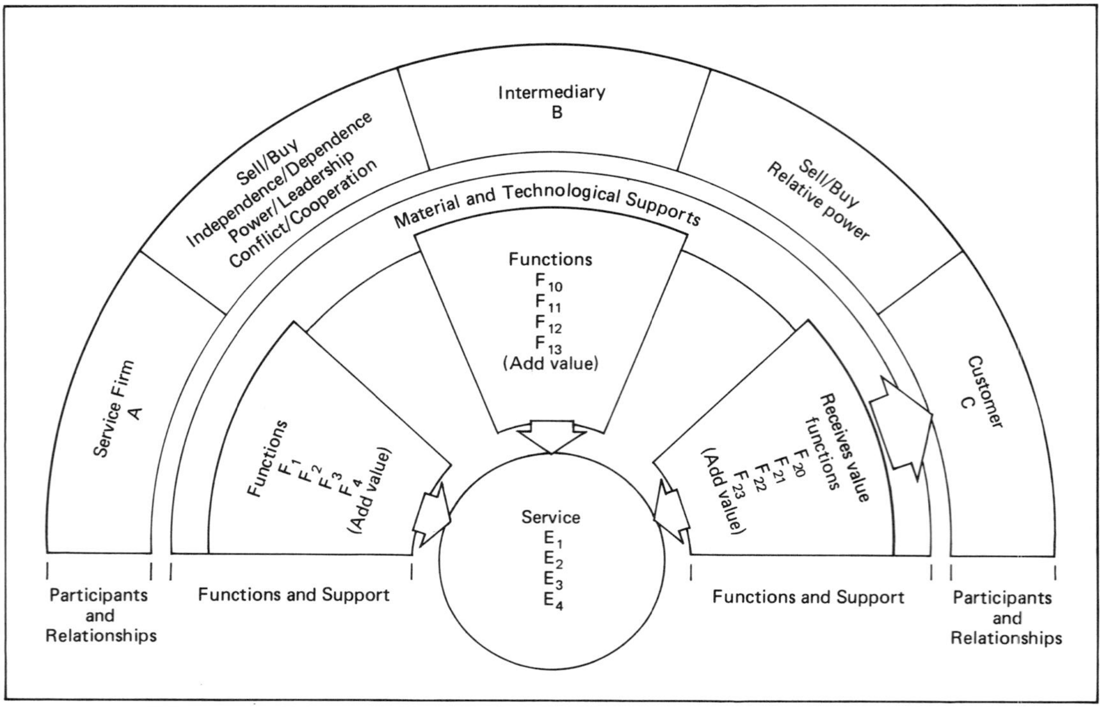

SOURCE: SRI International.

A Distribution for Homeowners Insurance

Figure 2 shows the *participants* in a distribution channel for homeowners insurance: the insurance company (the service firm), the agent (the intermediary), and the policyholder (the customer). In this particular channel, the intermediary is an independent agent (i.e., an independent contractor who represents more than one insurance company).

The *relationship* between the company and the agent is frequently characterized by conflict. Counterbalancing the power of the independent agent to place business with any of several companies is the power of the company to determine the service's elements (the policy's price, coverages, etc.) and to set the level of the agent's compensation.

The relationship between the agent and

the policyholder has much less conflict—even though both have their own sources of power (the agent's ability to influence the rate the insurer will charge a particular customer, and the policyholder's ability to purchase his policy from this or another agent).

Numerous *functions* are allocated among the insurance company, the agent, and the policyholder (e.g., accepting or declining risks, adjusting claims, providing advice on alternate coverages, giving notice of losses). In order to perform these functions, the company and agent use various *material and technological supports*: home offices, pricing manuals, telephones, etc.

Using the Schematic

A service firm manager can use the schematic to illustrate how his distribution channel differs from his competitors'. A planner

FIGURE 2

Insurance: An American Agency System Company and Its Independent Agents

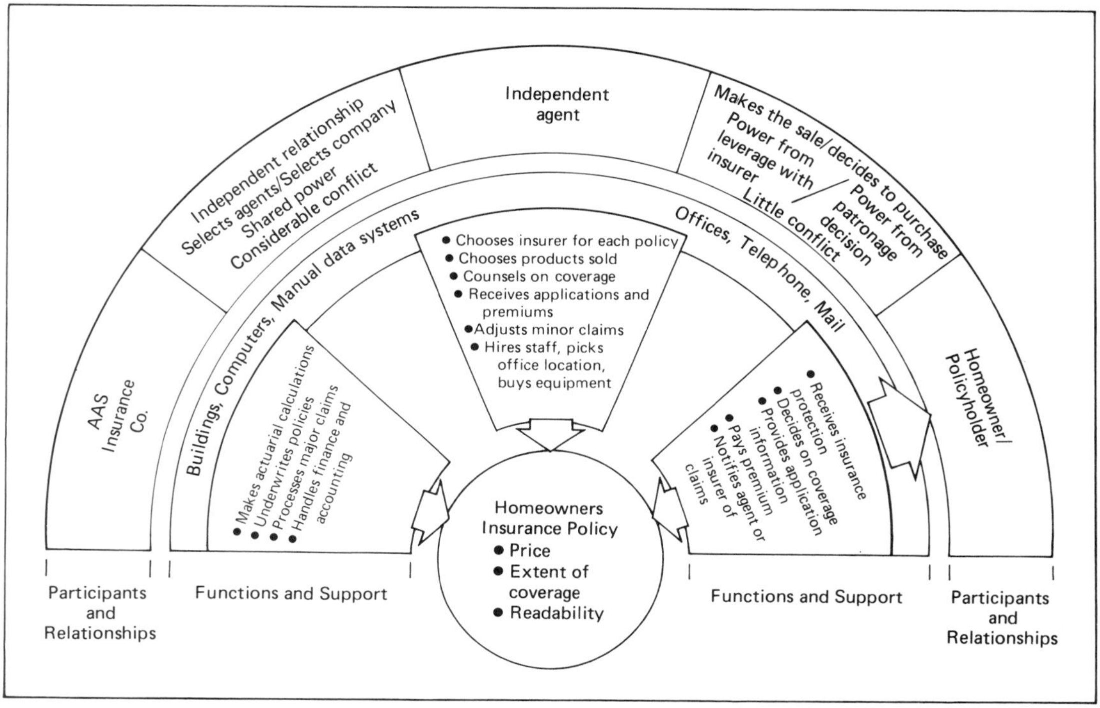

Independent
agent

Independent relationship
Selects agents/Selects company
Shared power
Considerable conflict

Makes the sale/decides to purchase
Power from
leverage with
insurer
Little conflict
Power from
patronage
decision

Offices, Telephone, Mail

Buildings, Computers, Manual data systems

Homeowner/
Policyholder

AAS
Insurance
Co.

- Chooses insurer for each policy
- Chooses products sold
- Counsels on coverage
- Receives applications and premiums
- Adjusts minor claims
- Hires staff, picks office location, buys equipment

Makes actuarial calculations
Underwrites policies
Processes major claims
Handles finance and accounting

- Receives insurance protection
- Decides on coverage
- Provides application information
- Pays premium
- Notifies agent or insurer of claims

Homeowners
Insurance Policy
- Price
- Extent of coverage
- Readability

Participants
and
Relationships

Functions and Support

Functions and Support

Participants
and
Relationships

SOURCE: SRI International.

can use the schematic to create alternative channel strategies (e.g., by varying the types of intermediaries or the allocation of functions among the participants).

The schematic also makes it easier to understand how structural shifts can occur throughout an entire industry. For example, using an independent agent to distribute homeowners insurance was the dominant channel during the first half of this century. But shortly after World War II, companies like Allstate, State Farm, and Farmers used a different channel, exclusive agents, to win well over half of the personal lines market. Their channel had several advantages: better control of the underwriting functions, a lower cost of sales, and, in some cases, better prices for certain risks.

In more recent years, another personal insurance channel is gaining share: direct response marketing used by companies like GEICO and USAA. This channel does not use any kind of agent as an intermediary. Instead, it sells by using the mail and sophisticated telemarketing centers. In the future, Bank of America and Chemical Bank may sell insurance to their home banking customers through a telephone link to their personal computers.

MULTIMARKETING

What Is Multimarketing?

Up to this point, service distribution strategies have been discussed from the viewpoint of a single service firm distributing one service through one type of intermediary to one type of customer. A simple example is

TABLE 1
Multiple Manifestations of Multimarketing

Approach	Service/ Product	Types of Intermediaries	Customers
All roads lead to Rome	Same	Different	Same
Different strokes for different folks	Same	Different	Different
Customer is king	Different	Different	Same
Fill up the pipeline	Different	Same	Different
All things to all people	Different	Different	Different

an airline selling tickets through travel agents to business travelers. But what if a firm has a more complex strategy?

An airline might provide special charters as well as its regularly scheduled flights. It might sell tickets using its own ticketing offices and inbound phone lines as well as independent travel agents. It may eagerly seek vacationers and students in addition to its bread-and-butter business travelers.

Multimarketing occurs when a service firm varies its service, intermediary, and/or customer segments.[3] Table 1 shows the five combinations of these elements, which constitute the major forms of multimarketing. Each combination provides its own competitive advantages and has its own vulnerabilities.

All Roads Lead to Rome

With the "all roads lead to Rome" approach, the service firm sells the same service through various kinds of intermediaries to the same set of customers. A firm using "all roads lead to Rome" wants to reach a target set of customers through every (reasonable) available means. For example, the film *Testament* (about a small town in California after a nuclear war) was made for television and later became available on video cassettes for purchase or rental.

"All roads lead to Rome" has two related vulnerabilities: some of the intermediaries may prove to be inefficient, and the systems may be complex and difficult to manage. No

intermediary provides guaranteed profits. For example, the producers of *Testament* might be losing their shirts on cassette sales and rentals. Additionally, each distribution channel demands its own set of skills from successful participants. The more types of intermediaries a firm has, the more types of management skills and systems it needs to successfully control and manage all of its channels.

Different Strokes for Different Folks

In "different strokes for different folks," the firm sells the same service through several types of channels to different sorts of customers. The producers of *Testament* might feel that there is another customer segment that they are not reaching through television broadcasts and cassettes, namely the people who like to go out to see a movie. The solution is simple (and was actually done): release *Testament* to selected neighborhood theaters.

A firm pursuing a "different strokes for different folks" strategy believes that different types of intermediaries have particular advantages in reaching different, target customer segments. Such an advantage might be based on knowledge of a geographic market (using one film distribution company for the U.S. market and another for Europe). Or it might be based on certain skills or a favorable customer image.

"Different strokes for different folks" shares the same potential vulnerabilities as "all roads lead to Rome," namely, inefficiency and management complexity. It adds a third vulnerability, the need to understand several distinct market segments. If the firm is lucky, its target segments will be similar enough (in-home movie viewers and in-theater movie viewers) for this not to pose major problems. But a U.S. film producer who wants to crack the African market will probably have to do a fair amount of homework first.

The Customer Is King

In this approach, a firm sends different services through different types of channels to reach the same customer. Consider a youth-oriented record company that makes rock videos for MTV, sells records and tapes through retail outlets, and sends its groups on national concert tours. Some firms using "the customer is king" may be pursuing a classic diversification strategy: trying to leverage its current customer base by selling new kinds of services to them.

If the firm knows its customers quite well, "the customer is king" approach frequently works. All the same, there are the pitfalls of intermediary inefficiency and management complexity. There is also the possibility that the service firm will not understand the new channels or services well enough. Such a firm may find its old customers less than eager to buy services that are poorly designed or delivered.

Fill Up the Pipeline

In the fourth approach, the firm sells different services through the same intermediary to different customer segments. Television network programming clearly illustrates "fill up the pipeline." It uses the same intermediary (national network broadcasts) to send programs (*Good Morning America*, *Star Trek* reruns, and *General Hospital*) designed to meet the tastes of distinctly different viewing populations.

Firms that are "filling up the pipeline" may be trying to use available capacity profitably. They may also be seeking that most elusive goal, synergy. The capabilities of the intermediary are the key to making this strategy work. Successful intermediaries will gain in power vis-à-vis the service firm, but if sales are rolling in, the service firm may not care.

All Things to All People

Last, there is "all things to all people." This involves sending different products through different intermediaries to different customer segments. This is a fairly pure diversification strategy. CBS sells television programs, records, films, and even computer software through multiple intermediaries to a variety of customers. It is betting that it knows a broad industry (like enter-

tainment) well enough to compete in many phases of it.

The major vulnerability of "all things to all people" is organizational. A holding company or conglomerate is the most likely user of this strategy. The key question is whether corporate-level managers can make correct resources and staffing decisions across a broad range of businesses or industries.

POWER, CONFLICT, AND COOPERATION

Power

Distribution channel studies frequently discuss power, conflict, and cooperation.[4] The same concepts, though not always with these labels, play an important role in the day-to-day operating realities of service firm managers and planners.

Power is usually defined as the ability of one participant to influence another's actions. Power in a distribution channel could mean many things: the ability of a hospital to decide which physicians are members of its staff, or the ability of an airline to determine what promotional materials its travel agents will use.

Someone has to decide how each distribution channel component works: which participants perform what functions using various technological and material supports to produce a service with certain elements. Is finding the source of power simply a matter of identifying the participant who is making all of these decisions?

In practice, power is usually shared. Some channel participants do have more power than others, but their freedom of action is limited by a pervasive reciprocity found throughout the channel. An insurance company may think that it has the sole authority to hire and fire agents, but any agent worth his salt can find other companies to represent. A movie studio may believe that it alone chooses its scripts, directors, and stars, but a studio that has produced a series of dogs soon finds that the owners of the best first-run theaters are booking other studios' films for next Christmas.

Conflict and Cooperation

Conflict and cooperation coexist in most channels. For a channel to work at all, its participants must cooperate. Stockbrokerage firms and their account executives agree on the allocation of functions: the former makes the actual trades while the latter solicits orders from their clients. At the same time, it is a rare channel that does not have some disagreements among its participants —the stockbrokerage firms want to set production quotas for its account executives, who in turn would like a more generous commission structure.

Conflict and cooperation are two ends of a spectrum. On any given issue, two participants may find themselves at one end or the other. The total relationship is much more complex, because there will usually be dozens of issues that are important to the service firm and its intermediaries. Furthermore, service firms may have hundreds or thousands of intermediaries. Out of 5,000 account executives, 4,000 might be quite satisfied with the commission structure, but 1,000 might be bitterly unhappy.

Why Conflict Occurs

One major cause of conflict comes from within a channel; another comes from outside. Internally, power is unevenly distributed among channel participants, each of whom has its own perspective and agenda. Externally, the viability of the channel may be in doubt because of competitive or environmental developments.

Within a channel each participant is likely to have its own ideas on how to maximize revenue or profit for the channel as a whole, and will almost certainly have its own notion on an appropriate division of profits and losses. It is also human nature for participants to think largely about their own interests while assuming that the channel as a whole will muddle through.

Similarly, any aspect of channel design can be a ground for controversy. The travel agent could sell a lot more tickets to Hawaii if the airline would just extend its low-cost package into the winter season. The independent insurance agent is sure he could be much more efficient if only had the right kind of computer link to the insurance company. On most issues, one participant is going to be more powerful than others. The airline, not the travel agents, will decide on the length of the promotion. The insurance agent, if he is important enough to the company, may be able to insist that the insurance company tie its computer to his.

Pressure from *outside the channel* can also cause conflict. Efficient HMOs (health maintenance organizations) might operate at full capacity, leaving fee-for-service hospitals and physicians with empty beds and waiting rooms. The fee-for-service hospitals might respond by opening their own freestanding primary care clinics (which could compete directly with their own affiliated physicians). The affiliated physicians might in turn perform laboratory and diagnostic procedures in their own offices rather than admitting those patients to the hospital.

Changes in the regulatory environment can also disrupt channel relations. A few years ago the Civil Aeronautics Board revised its rules, which had effectively prohibited airlines from selling tickets through anyone other than travel agents. Suddenly, banks, Ticketron, corner supermarkets, and, most important, corporate travel departments all became possible intermediaries.

Under the watchful eyes of travel agents, no major airline has used these alternative intermediaries to any significant degree. Interestingly, the travel agents themselves have forestalled possible direct deals between airlines and large corporate customers by rebating a portion of their commission to those large customers.

MANAGING CONFLICT

Distribution channel conflict is inherently neither good nor bad. Given the diversity of people and organizations, it is not realistic to have a goal of totally eliminating conflict. Probably, a channel participant's best course of action is to seek to manage it actively.

The first step in managing conflict is to

know when it is occurring. Sometimes the signal may be loud and clear (e.g., when a large group of physicians start admitting their patients to other hospitals). Other times, the signal might be more subtle (e.g., physicians may still admit their routine, short-stay patients to their old hospital, but send their more complex cases to a new one).

A second step is to understand the conflict's causes. As outlined above, a wide variety of internal and external factors could be responsible. Some causes could be unintended or uncontrollable. Others might result from a participant's deliberate action.

A third step is to estimate the consequences. No hospital can afford the wholesale desertion of its physicians. On the other hand, some hospitals might feel they are better off with shorter, less complex cases. (Current Medicare reimbursement procedures tend to penalize hospitals for treating patients with complex conditions.)

The last step is to decide whether to accept the conflict or to lessen it by moving the relationship toward the cooperation end of the spectrum. Figure 3 shows how a participant's relative power could influence this choice.

If a participant is powerful, it may decide to accept (or even increase) the level of conflict for Darwinian reasons. The less fit channel participants will eventually weaken and leave; thus, a more fit (compatible) group would remain. For example, a strong insurer could require its agents to meet certain sales quotas, knowing that the smaller and weaker agents will eventually terminate their contracts. On the other hand, a powerful participant may choose to increase the level of channel cooperation. A painless way of doing this is to restructure incentives to promote the types of behavior the powerful participant would like to see. An insurer whose agents are unhappy about their level of compensation could increase commissions on those lines of insurance it is especially good at underwriting while lowering commissions for less profitable lines.

Participants with less power have less attractive choices. They may have to accept conflict because, at least in the short run, they have no viable alternative. If they want to increase the level of cooperation, the only available path may be capitulating to the agendas of the more powerful participants —which could mean lower revenue or profits.

FIGURE 3

Conflict/Cooperation Strategy Choices

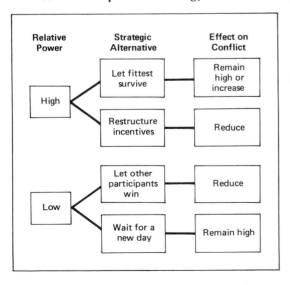

DESIGNING DISTRIBUTION CHANNELS

What Is Channel Design?

Every service firm has a stake in making its distribution channel strategy a potent competitive weapon. There are many ways that distribution channels can contribute to a service firm's overall success or failure. Braniff Airlines claimed that it went into bankruptcy because (among other things) the automated travel agent reservation system of its arch-rival, American Airlines, unfairly discriminated against Braniff's flights. (Such discrimination is the basis of the CAB's charge mentioned at the beginning of this article.)

Practically anything in a distribution channel is fair game for the strategist and designer. There are potential design variables within each major sector of the service distribution channel schematic (Figure 1). Those variables include:

- The number of intermediaries
- The types of intermediaries
- The allocation of value-adding functions among the channel participants
- The kinds of material and technological supports that the participants use
- The service itself—its elements and the dimensions of those elements

The five multimarketing approaches in Figure 3 also provide design possibilities. For example, a service firm using "all roads lead to Rome" employs various intermediaries to send the same service to a given set of customers. Since the firm has already invested in business systems for each type of intermediary, a logical channel redesign possibility would be "different strokes for different folks." In that strategy, the firm could seek diversification by using its several types of intermediaries to send its service to new customer segments.

Sometimes it is useful to distinguish between tactical and strategic decisions. A tactical design decision for an insurance company using independent agents is the selection of the specific agencies with which it will contract. A strategic decision (actually made by Continental Insurance[5]) is to cancel the contracts of one-fourth of its agents who produced unprofitable business.

Who Designs Distribution Channels?

When asked this question, the typical channel participant would probably say, "No one." Tradition, custom, and inertia provide the seemingly obvious answers for who does what with whom in a channel. However, more and more companies are finding it to their advantage to influence deliberately what goes on in their channels.

By definition, the most powerful participant in a channel has the greatest opportunity to make design decisions. This is probably, but not always, the service firm. Home Box Office (an intermediary) provides an exception to the rule. It takes a very active role in telling its service firms (the movie studios) what to produce for its viewers.

Individual intermediaries, who are very small compared with their service firm, will frequently band together to promote their joint interests. A major insurance agent trade group, the Independent Insurance Agents of America, recently hired a consultant to make recommendations for better ways of allocating marketing functions among agents and companies.

Even the most powerful participant does not have unlimited design flexibility. When American Airlines tried in August 1983 to cut the commissions it paid to travel agents, it quickly backed down when no other major carrier followed suit.[6] A powerful participant, if it is wise, will realize that it can achieve its own ends only through cooperation with the other participants.

Three Ways of Designing Channels

An organization can design channels driven by (1) goals, (2) strategies, or (3) marketing compatibility.

A *goal-driven* process starts with the firm's overall goals and designs the channels, which increase the likelihood of obtaining the goals. For example, a service firm could have a challenging growth goal that might be extremely difficult to reach if it were restricted to a single channel and a single customer group. Such a firm might start by considering the five multimarketing approaches. Another firm, like the USAA Insurance Company, might place great emphasis on serving its policyholders. It would therefore design its channel to include high-quality telecommunications equipment and well-trained service representatives.

A *strategy-driven* process searches for sustainable competitive advantages. Merrill Lynch's Cash Management Account (CMA) provides a brilliant example of such a channel strategy. Merrill (and every other national retail stockbroker) finds its power over its account executives limited by the executives' ability to jump to another firm, taking many of Merrill's best customers with them. With the CMA, Merrill introduced a product that appealed precisely to those key customers, a product they could not get if they followed their account executives elsewhere. It took other firms several years to develop comparable products. During that time, Merrill enjoyed relatively greater customer loyalty and more power vis-à-vis its account executives.

Channel designs driven by *marketing compatibility* are concerned with the fit among the service, the intermediary, and the customer. Twenty years ago, Louis Bucklin described three kinds of retail outlets and products: convenience, shopping, and specialty.[7] As the name implies, consumers buy convenience products and services (e.g., newspapers, dry cleaning) in neighborhood outlets that keep suitable hours. Consumers will compare prices and other product features when shopping for goods and services like home appliances and automobile insurance. They will seek out specialty goods or services, like heart transplants, in the specific locality they are offered.

Certain combinations of these kinds of products and outlets imply certain kinds of approaches to channel design.[8] Firms selling convenience products through convenience outlets will normally use intensive distribution (i.e., they will try to get as many intermediaries as possible). Selective distribution (choosing a limited number of intermediaries in a given area) is compatible with shopping services. Exclusive distribution (giving a single intermediary rights to a particular geographic market, or customer segment) often fits specialty products.

Choosing Designs

How does a service firm manager choose among all the possible distribution strategies? The short answer is: It all depends. It depends on the internal resources of his firm and the external constraints imposed on it.

Some channel strategies may require substantial capital investments (e.g., telecommunications equipment). Others, like many of the multimarketing strategies, will require specific management skills. Such requirements will not be a problem if the firm can meet them with currently available or easily obtained resources. If not, the firm should proceed with great caution.

Other channel strategies may capitalize on changing consumer needs. As consumers grow more familiar with a product, the intermediary's functions may become simplified. Innovative firms may introduce less costly types of intermediaries—as was seen in the earlier discussion of homeowners insurance.

Finally, no channel can succeed unless the service firm and its intermediaries add the right kinds of value to create an appropriately priced service that meets the needs of a viable number of customers.

Design or Be Designed Against

One of the truisms in insurance is "select or be selected against." In other words, a company must either carefully select the good risks it wants to insure or else a great many poor risks will find their way onto its books. The same principle applies to service firms wondering whether it is worth bothering about channel schematics, power, conflict, cooperation, and multimarketing.

There are always reasons not to rock the boat, to put out today's fires, and let precedent and inertia determine channel design. The danger is that regulatory or technological change may be destroying the underpinnings of a comfortable, known system. What is even more likely is that aggressive competitors are finding ways of increasing the effectiveness of *their* channels at the expense of the status quo firms.

Notes

[1]See, e.g., D. J. Bowersox et al., *Management in Marketing Channels* (1980); L. W. Stern and A. I. El-Ansary, *Marketing Channels* (2d ed. 1982). One strategically oriented exception is W. A. DeBord, "Dealer Network Strategic Planning," *Journal of Business Strategy*, Fall 1984, pp. 32–40.

[2]The discussion in this and the next two sections is adapted from D. H. Light and G. Warfel, *Distribution Strategies for Services*, Business Intelligence Program, SRI International, pp. 3–6. Exhibits 1 and 2 are used with permission from SRI.

[3]The term "multimarketing" occurs in an excellent article by R. E. Weigand, "Fit Products and Channels to Your Markets," *Harvard Business Review*, Jan.–Feb. 1977, pp. 95–105.

[4]A good recent survey is in J. F. Gaski, "The Theory of Power and Conflict in Channels of Distribution," *Journal of Marketing*, Summer 1984, pp. 9–29.

[5]L. Gubernick, "Shoot the Stragglers," *Forbes*, Dec. 31, 1984, p. 62.

[6]D. Rothbart, "Competition in Bonus Commissions to Agents Disrupts Airline Industry," *Wall Street Journal*, Aug. 31, 1983, p. 23.

[7]L. P. Bucklin, "Retail Strategy and the Classification of Consumer Goods," *Journal of Marketing*, Jan. 1963, pp. 50–55.

[8]Bowersox, note 1 supra, at 202–203.

Benihana of Tokyo

W. EARL SASSER
JOHN KLUG

An innovative, limited menu restaurant, started by a young Japanese entrepreneur, has grown into a chain of 15 restaurants, five of which are franchised. The service concept represents a production-line approach to service and the owner believes there are significant opportunities for future expansion.

"Some restaurateurs like myself have more fun than others," says Hiroaki (Rocky) Aoki, youthful president of Benihana of Tokyo. Since 1964 he had gone from deficit net worth to becoming president of a chain of 15 restaurants that gross over $12 million per year. He sported a $4,000 sapphire ring, maintained a $250,000 home, and kept five cars including three Rolls-Royces. One wall of his office was completely covered with photographs of Rocky with famous personalities who had eaten at a Benihana. Rocky firmly believed: "In America money is always available if you work hard."

BACKGROUND

By 1972 Benihana was basically a steakhouse with a difference—the food was cooked in front of the customer by native chefs and the decor was that of an authentically detailed Japanese country inn. From a humble 40-seat unit opened in midtown Manhattan in 1964, Benihana had grown to a chain of 15 units across the country. Nine were company-owned locations: New York (3); San Francisco; Chicago; Encino and Marina del Rey, California; Portland, Oregon; and Honolulu. Five were franchised: Boston, Fort

This case was made possible by the cooperation of the Benihana Corporation and Russ Carpenter, Executive Editor of the magazine *Institutions/Volume Feeding*. It was prepared by John Klug, Research Assistant, under the direction of Assistant Professor W. Earl Sasser. Copyright © 1972 by the President and Fellows of Harvard College. Harvard Business School case 9-673-057. Reprinted by permission.

Lauderdale, Beverly Hills, Seattle, and Harrisburg, Pennsylvania. The last unit, Las Vegas, was operated as a joint venture with Hilton Hotels Corporation. Rocky, who was a former Olympic wrestler, described his success as follows:

> In 1959, I came to the United States on a tour with my university wrestling team. I was 20 at the time. When I reached New York, it was love at first sight! I was convinced that there were more opportunities for me in America than Japan. In fact, the minute I was able to forget that I was Japanese, my success began. I decided to enroll in the School of Restaurant Management at City College basically because I knew that in the restaurant business I'd never go hungry. I earned money those early years by washing dishes, driving an ice cream truck, and acting as a tour guide. Most importantly, I spent three years making a systematic analysis of the U.S. restaurant market. What I discovered is that Americans enjoy eating in exotic surroundings but are deeply mistrustful of exotic foods. Also I learned that people very much enjoy watching their food being prepared. So I took $10,000 I had saved by 1963 and borrowed $20,000 more to open my first unit on the West Side and tried to apply all that I had learned.

The origins of the Benihana of Tokyo actually date back to 1935. That was when Yunosuke Aoki (Rocky's father) opened the first of his chain of restaurants in Japan. He called it Benihana, after the small red flower that grew wild near the front door of the restaurant.

The elder Aoki ("Papasan"), like his son who was to follow in the family tradition, was a practical and resourceful restaurateur. In 1958, concerned about rising costs and increased competition, he first incorporated the hibachi table concept into his operations. Rocky borrowed this method of cooking from his father and commented as follows:

> One of the things I learned in my analysis, for example, was that the number one problem of the restaurant industry in the United States is the shortage of skilled labor. By eliminating the need for a conventional kitchen with the hibachi table arrangement, the only "skilled"

person I need is a chef. I can give an unusual amount of attentive service and still keep labor costs to 10–12 percent of gross sales (food and beverage) depending on whether a unit is at full volume. In addition, I was able to turn practically the entire restaurant into productive dining space. Only about 22 percent of the total space of a unit is back of the house, including preparation areas, dry and refrigerated storage, employee dressing rooms, and office space. Normally a restaurant requires 30 percent of its total space as back of the house. [Operating statistics for a typical service restaurant are included in *Exhibit 1.*]

> The other thing I discovered is that food storage and wastage contribute greatly to the overhead of the typical restaurant. By reducing my menu to only three simple "Middle American" entrees—steak, chicken, and shrimp—I have virtually no waste and can cut food costs to between 30 percent and 35 percent of food sales depending on the price of meat.

> Finally, I insist on historical authenticity. The walls, ceilings, beams, artifacts, and decorative lights of a Benihana are all from Japan. The building materials are gathered from old houses there, carefully disassembled, and shipped in pieces to the United States where they are reassembled by one of my father's two crews of Japanese carpenters.

Rocky's first unit on the West Side was such a success that it paid for itself in six months. He then built in 1966 a second unit three blocks away on the East Side simply to cater to the overflow of the Benihana West. The Benihana East quickly developed a separate clientele and prospered. In 1967, Barron Hilton, who had eaten at a Benihana, approached Rocky concerning the possibility of locating a unit in the Marina Towers in Chicago. Rocky flew to Chicago, rented a car, and while driving to meet Mr. Hilton saw a vacant site. He immediately stopped, called the owner, and signed a lease the next day. Needless to say, a Benihana didn't go into the Marina Towers.

The number three unit in Chicago had proved to be the company's largest moneymaker. It was an instant success and grossed approximately $1.3 million per year. The food and beverage split was 70/30 and management was able to keep expense percent-

EXHIBIT 1
Operating Statistics for a Typical Service Restaurant

	Ranges (Percent)
SALES	
Food	70.0–80.0
Beverage	20.0–30.0
Total sales	100.0
COST OF SALES	
Food cost (percent of food sales)	38.0–48.0
Beverage cost (percent of beverage sales)	25.0–30.0
Cost of total sales	35.0–45.0
Gross profit	55.0–65.0
OPERATING EXPENSES	
Controllable expense	
Payroll	30.0–35.0
Employee benefits	3.0–5.0
Employee meals	1.0–2.0
Laundry, linen, uniforms	1.5–2.0
Replacements	0.5–1.0
Supplies (guest)	1.0–1.5
Menus and printing	0.25–0.5
Miscellaneous contract expense (cleaning, garbage, extermination, equipment rental)	1.0–2.0
Music and entertainment (where applicable)	0.5–1.0
Advertising and promotion	0.75–2.0
Utilities	1.0–2.0
Management salary	2.0–6.0
Administration expense (including legal and accounting)	0.75–2.0
Repairs and maintenance	1.0–2.0
Occupation expense	
Rent	4.5–9.0
Taxes (real estate and personal property)	0.5–1.5
Insurance	0.75–1.0
Interest	0.3–1.0
Depreciation	2.0–4.0
Franchise royalties (where applicable)	3.0–6.0
Total operating expenses	55.0–65.0
Net profit before income tax	0.5–9.0

SOURCE: Bank of America, *Small Business Reporter*, Vol. 8, No. 2, 1968.

ages at relatively low levels: food (30 percent), labor (10 percent), advertising (10 percent), and rent (5 percent).

The fourth unit was San Francisco and the fifth was a joint venture in Las Vegas in 1969. By this time literally hundreds of people were clamoring for franchises. Rocky sold a total of six until he decided in 1970 that it would be much more to his advantage to own his units rather than franchise them. Following are the franchises that were granted: Puerto Rico (not successful due to economic turndown), Harrisburg, Fort Lauderdale, Portland (company bought unit back), Seattle, Beverly Hills, Boston.

The decision to stop franchising was made because of a number of problems. First, all the franchises were bought by investors, none of whom had any restaurant experience. Second, it was difficult for the American investor to relate to a predominantly native Japanese staff. Finally, control was considerably more difficult to maintain with a franchisee than a company employee manager. During the period to 1970 several groups attempted to imitate the Benihana success. One even included a group with intimate knowledge of the Benihana operation who set up in very close proximity to one Benihana unit. They, however, folded within the year. Bolstered by the confidence that the Benihana success could not be easily replicated, management felt that one of the classic pressures to franchise was eliminated— i.e., to expand extremely rapidly to preempt competitors.

The amount of space devoted to the bar/lounge/holding area accurately indicates when the unit was built. When Rocky opened his first unit, he saw the business as primarily food-service sales. The Benihana West had a tiny bar that seated about eight and had no lounge area. Rocky quickly learned that this amount of bar space was insufficient, and at the second unit, Benihana East, he doubled the size of the bar/lounge area. But since the whole unit was larger, the ratio of space was not too different. A typical floor plan is included as *Exhibit 2*.

His third Manhattan operation, called Benihana Palace, opened in 1970. Here, the

EXHIBIT 2

A typical Benihana floor plan

Benihana West on West 56th Street in Manhattan, which replaced the original restaurant Rocky opened, is typical of the standardized 112- to 120-seat restaurant with a 55- to 60-seat cocktail lounge. The typical Benihana operation has 5,000 to 6,000 square feet.

2 Towel Washer by Hamilton
3 Work Table, custom
4 Work Table, custom
5 Three Compartment Sink, custom
6 Double Overshelf, custom
7 Double Slant Overshelf, custom
8 Rice Stocker, custom
9 Rice Cooker
10 Range With Oven by Vulcan Hart
11 Stock Pot Stove by Vulcan Hart
12 Swing Faucet
13 Exhaust Hood, custom
15 Reach-in Refrigerator by Traulsen
16 Scale by Howe Richardson
17 Combination Walk-in Cooler-Freezer by Bally
18 Adjustable Modular Shelving by Market Forge
19 Adjustable Modular Shelving by Market Forge
20 Shelf, custom
21 Dishwasher with electric booster by Champion
22 Soiled Dishtable with Pre-Rinse Sink, custom
23 Slant Overshelf, custom
24 Clean Dishtable, custom
25 Exhaust Hood, custom
26 Double Wallshelf, custom
27 Twin Soup Urn by Cecilware
28 Single Tea Urn by Cecilware
29 Towel Warmer
30 Water Station with Sink, custom
31 Rice Warmer
32 Utility Table, custom
33 Double Wallshelf, custom
34 Two Compartment Sink, custom

35 Overshelf custom
46 Work Table, custom
37 Open-Front Cold Cast with Adj. Shelves by Tyler
38 Double Overshelf, custom
39 Pre-Check Register by NCR
40 Utility Table with Dipperwell, custom
41 Double Overshelf, custom
42 Ice Cream Dipping Cabinet by Schaefer
43 Ice Cream Storage Cabinet by Schaefer
44 Double Wallshelf, custom
45 Reach-In Freezer by Traulsen
46 Ice Cube Maker by Kold Draft
47 Ice Crusher by Scotsman
48 Adjustable Modular Shelving by Market Forge
49 Pass-Through Refrigerator by Traulsen
50 Sake Warmer
51 Cash Register by NCR
52 Underbar Workboard by Perlick
54 Back Bar Refrigerator by Perlick
56 Underbar Bottle Cooler by Perlick
57 Remote Soda System Dispensing Station by Perlick
58 Remote Soda System Power Pak with Stand by Perlick
59 Pre-Check Register by NCR
60 Cash Register by NCR
61 Shelving, custom
62 Glasswasher by Dorex
63 Time Clock
64 Telephone Shelf Booth
65 Platform Truck by Roll A. Liss
66 Utility Table, custom

EXHIBIT 2 (continued)

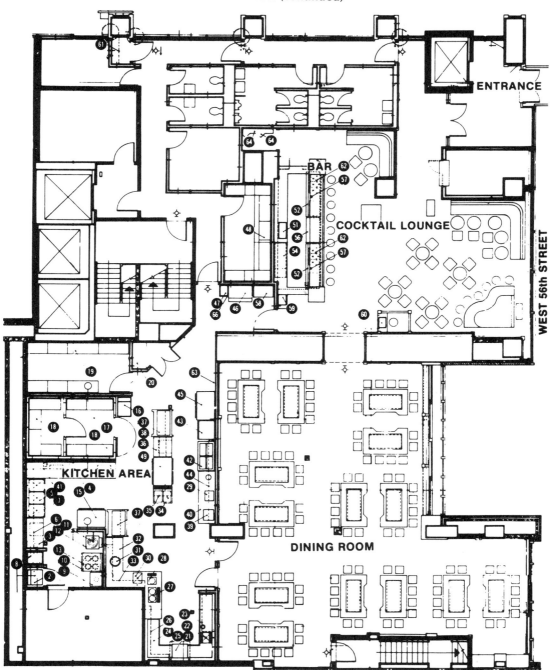

bar/lounge area was enormous, even in ratio to size. Figures from 1972 bear out the wisdom of the growth. At West, beverage sales represented about 18 percent of total sales. At East, they ran 20–22 percent. And at the Palace, they ran a handsome 30–33 percent of total sales. The beverage cost averaged 20 percent of beverage sales.

The heart of the "show biz" was in the dining area. The "teppanyaki" table was comprised of a steel griddle plate, with a 9½-inch wooden ledge bordering it to hold the ware. It was gas-fired. Above every table was an exhaust hood to remove cooking steam and odors and much of the heat from the griddle. Service was provided by a chef and waitress; each such team handled two regular tables.

The four food items—steak, filet mignon, chicken, and shrimp—could either be had as single entree items or in combinations. A full dinner had three, with the shrimp as appetizer. The accompaniments were unvaried: bean sprouts, zucchini, fresh mushrooms, onions, and rice.

Normally, a customer could come in, be seated, have dinner, and be on his or her way out in 45 minutes, if need be. The average turnover was an hour, and up to an hour and a half in slow periods.

The average check, including food and beverage, ran about $6 at lunch, about $10 at dinner. These figures included one drink (average price $1.50) at lunch, an average of one-plus at dinner.

The big purchase was meat. Only U.S.D.A. Prime Grade, tightly specified tenderloin and boneless strip loins were used. The steaks were further trimmed in house. Only a bit of fat at the tail was left, which was for effect only. When the chef began cooking the meat, he dramatically trimmed this part off and pushed it aside before cubing the remaining meat.

The hours of operation for the 15 units varied according to local requirements. All were open for lunch and dinner, though not necessarily every day for each. Lunch business was important; overall it accounted for about 30–40 percent of the total dollar volume despite a significantly lower check average. Essentially the same menu items were served for both meals; the lower menu price average at lunch reflected smaller portions and fewer combinations.

SITE SELECTION

Because of the importance of lunchtime business, Benihana had one basic criterion for site selection—high traffic. Management wanted to be sure that a lot of people were nearby or going by both at lunch and at dinner. Rent normally ran 5–7 percent of sales for 5,000–6,000 square feet of floor space. Most units were located in a predominantly business district, though some had easy access to residential areas. Shopping center locations were considered, but had not been accepted by 1972.

TRAINING

Because the chef was considered by Benihana to be a key to its success, all of them were very highly trained. All were young, single, native Japanese and all were "certified," which meant that they had completed a three-year formal apprenticeship. They were then given a three- to six-month course in Japan in the English language and American manner as well as the Benihana form of cooking, which was mostly showmanship. The chefs were brought to the United States under a "trade treaty" agreement.

Training the chefs within the United States was also a continuous process. In addition to the competition among the chefs to perfect their art in hopes of becoming the chief chef, there was also a traveling chef who inspected each unit periodically and was involved in the grand opening of new units.

While Benihana found it relatively difficult to attract chefs and other personnel from Japan due to the general level of prosperity there as well as competition from other restaurants bidding for their talents, once in the United States they were generally not anxious to leave. This was due to several factors. One was the rapidity with which they could rise in the American Benihana operation versus the rather rigid hierarchy based on class, age, and education they would face in Japan. A second and major factor was the paternal attitude that Benihana took toward all its employees. While personnel were well paid in a tangible sense, a large part of the compensation was intangible, based on job security and a total commitment of Benihana to the well-being of its employees. As a result, turnover of personnel within the United States was very low, although most did eventually return to Japan. To fully appreciate the Benihana success, the unique combination of Japanese paternalism in an American setting must be appreciated. Or, as Rocky puts it: "At Benihana we combine Japanese workers with American management techniques."

ORGANIZATION AND CONTROL

Each restaurant carried a simple management structure. It had a manager ($15,000/year), an assistant manager ($12,000/year),

EXHIBIT 3

Benihana Organization Chart

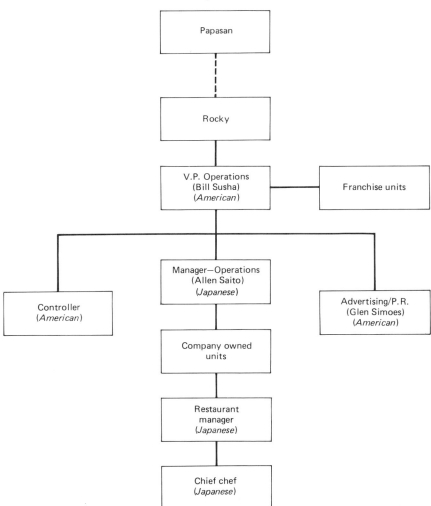

and two or three "front men" ($9,000/year), who might be likened to maitre d's. These front men were really potential managers in training. All managers reported to the manager of operations Allen Saito who, in turn, reported to Bill Susha, vice president in charge of operations and business development (see *Exhibit 3*).

Susha came to Benihana in 1971, following food and beverage experience with Hilton, Loew's, and the Flagship Hotel Division of American Airlines. He described his job as follows:

> I see management growth as a priority objective. My first step was to establish some sort of control system by introducing sales goals and budgets. At the most recent manager workshop meeting in New York—with managers from all over the country—I asked each to project his sales goal on an annual basis, then break it out by month, then by week, then by day. After I reached agreement with a manager on the individual quota figures, I instituted a bonus plan. Any unit that exceeds its quota on any basis—daily, weekly, monthly, yearly—will get a proportionate bonus, which will be prorated across the entire staff of the unit. I've also built up an accounting staff and controller to monitor our costs. It's been a slow but steady process. We have to be very careful to balance our need for control with the amount of overhead we can stand. We can justify extra "front men" standing around in the units. At the corporate level, however, we have to be very careful. In fact, at present the company is essentially being run by three people—Rocky, myself, and Allen Saito.

ADVERTISING POLICY

Rocky considered that a vitally important factor in Benihana's success was a substantial investment in creative advertising and public relations. The company invested 8–10 percent of its gross sales on reaching the public. Glen Simoes, the director of advertising and public relations, summed it up:

> We deliberately try to be different and original in our advertising approach. We never place advertisements on the entertainment pages of newspapers on the theory that they would be lost among the countless other restaurant advertisements.
>
> We have a visual product to sell. Therefore, Benihana utilizes outstanding visuals in its ads. The accompanying copy is contemporary, sometimes offbeat. A recent full-page advertisement which appeared in the *New York Times*, *Women's Wear Daily*, and *New York Magazine* did not contain the word "restaurant." We also conduct a considerable amount of market research to be sure we know who our customers really are.

Exhibit 4 shows the results of one market research survey. *Exhibit 5* is a further discussion of Benihana advertising policy. *Exhibits 6, 7, 8,* and *9* are examples of Benihana advertising copy.

EXHIBIT 4

What the Customers Think

Every foodservice operator thinks he knows why customers come to his operation. Benihana, which has served two-and-a-quarter million customers in eight years, a high percentage of which were repeat business, thought it knew.

But when he joined as v-p of operations a year-and-a-half ago, Bill Susha wanted to be sure the hallowed presumptions were true.

He devised a questionnaire, and arranged that it be handed to departing customers. A remarkable number took the time to fill out and return the form.

The percentage figures shown here are averages of six stores. While there were many variations from unit to unit, the general thrust was constant, so the six-store figures have been averaged to save space.

EXHIBIT 4 (continued)

The six units included the three in New York City, plus Chicago, Encino, Cal., and Portland, Ore. The questions and averages are as follows:

Are you from out-of-town?

Yes	38.6%
No	61.4

Here on:

Business	38.7%
Pleasure	61.3

Do you live in the area?

Live	16.0%
Work	35.9
Both	45.1

Have you been to a Benihana in another city?

Yes	22.9%
No	77.3

How did you learn of us?

Newspaper	4.0%
Magazine	6.9
Radio	4.6
Recommended	67.0
TV show	1.0
Walk by	5.0
Other	11.5

Is this your first visit?

Yes	34.3%
No	65.7

What persuaded you to come?

Good food	46.7%
Service	8.2
Preparation	13.1
Atmosphere	13.3
Recommendation	5.7
Other	13.1

Food was:

Satisfactory	2.0%
Good	20.1
Excellent	77.9

Portions were:

Satisfactory	21.8%
Good	33.0
Excellent	45.4

Service was:

Satisfactory	9.8%
Good	21.6
Excellent	71.3

Atmosphere is:

Satisfactory	6.3%
Good	29.9
Excellent	63.2

Would you consider yourself a lunch or dinner customer?

Lunch	17.3%
Dinner	59.0
Both	23.7

Which aspect of our restaurant would you highlight?

Food	38.2%
Atmosphere	13.0
Preparation	24.6
Service	16.3
Different	2.2
Friendly	2.4
Other	3.3

How frequently do you come to Benihana?

Once a week or more	12.1%
Once a month or more	32.5
Once a year or more	55.6

Age:

10-20	4.2%
21-30	28.3
31-40	32.0
41-50	21.4
51-60	10.1
60 and over	4.0

Sex:

Male	71.4%
Female	28.6

Income:

$ 7,500-$10,000	16.8%
$10,000-$15,000	14.2
$15,000-$20,000	17.3
$20,000-$25,000	15.0
$25,000-$40,000	17.9
$40,000 and over	18.7

Occupation:

Managerial	23.0%
Professional	26.6
White Collar	36.9
Student	6.9
Housewife	5.0
Unskilled	1.1

EXHIBIT 5
Summary of Benihana Marketing Philosophy

No icky, sticky, slimy stuff

"Part of what makes Benihana successful," Rocky Aoki believes, *"is our advertising and promotion. It's different, and it makes us seem different to people."*

Indeed it is, and does. Much of the credit belongs to Glen Simoes, the hip director of advertising and public relations for Benihana of Tokyo. With a background mostly in financial public relations, Simoes joined the chain a little over two years ago to help open the flagship Benihana Palace. Since then, he's created a somewhat novel, all-embracing public relations program that succeeds on many levels.

"My basic job," he explains, *"is guardian or the image. The image is that of a dynamic chain of Japanese restaurants with phenomenal growth."* Keeping the image bright means exposure. Part of the exposure is a brilliant advertising campaign; part is publicity.

Each has its own function. Advertising is handled by Kracauer and Marvin, an outside agency, under Simoes' supervision and guidance. Its function is to bring in new customers.

"Our ads," Simoes points out, *"are characterized by a bold headline statement and an illustration that make you want to read on. The copy itself is fairly clever and cute. If it works properly, it will keep you reading until you get the message—which is to persuade a stranger to come into Benihana.*

"The ads are designed to still fears about icky, sticky, slimy stuff," he adds. *"We reassure folks that they will get wholesome, familiar food, with unusual, unique and delicious preparation, served in a fun atmosphere. We want to intrigue the people celebrating an anniversary or taking Aunt Sally out to dinner. A Japanese restaurant would normally never cross their minds. We're saying we're a fun place to try, and there's no slithery, fishy stuff.*

"We have an impact philosophy. We go for full pages in national publications on a now-and-then basis, rather than a regular schedule of small ads. We want that impact to bring the stranger into Benihana for the first time. After that, the restaurant will bring him back again and again, and he will bring his friends.

"We do a good media mix," Simoes concludes. *"We advertise in each of the cities in which we operate. Within each market we aim for two people: the resident, of course, but even more, the tourist-visitor. With them you know you're always talking to new people. We appear in city entertainment guides and work with convention and visitor bureaus to go after groups and conventions."*

The second factor is publicity. Here, the intent is not the quantity of mentions or exposure, but the type. As Simoes sees it, *"We are building. Each mention is a building block. Some are designed to bring customers into the store. Some are designed to bring us prospective financing, or suppliers, or friends, or whatever. We work many ways against the middle. And the middle is the company, the people, Rocky, the growth and all of it put together that makes the image."*

Introducing Benihana of Tokyo.

Publicity takes many forms, it's media stories, and TV demonstrations. Simoes cites clipping and viewing services to prove that every day of the year, something about Benihana appears either in print or on radio or TV, a record he believes is unique. Publicity is department store demonstrations, catering to celebrities, hosting youth groups, sending matchboxos to conventions and chopsticks to ladies' clubs, scheduling Rocky for interviews and paying publicists to provide oneliners to columnists.

But no engine runs without fuel. And Rocky believes that advertising and promotion are a good investment. Believes so strongly, in fact, that he puts an almost unprecedented $1 million a year into advertising, and probably half that again into promotion, for a total expenditure of nearly 8% of gross sales in this area.

A few months back, Simoes, wholeheartedly pitching his company to a skeptical magazine writer, said heatedly there are *"at least 25 reasons people come to Benihana."* Challenged on the spot, he came back a few days later with a list of 31. They are:

1) the quality of the food; 2) the presentation of the food; 3) the preparation of the food; 4) the showmanship of the chef; 5) the taste of the food; 6) authenticity of construction; 7) authenticity of decor; 8) continuity of Japanese flavor throughout; 9) communal dining; 10) service—constant attention.

11) Youthfulness of staff; 12) frequent presence of celebrities; 13) excitement created by frequent promotions; 14) type of cuisine; 15) moderate price; 16) the uniqueness of appeal to the five senses; 17) the recent growth in popularity of things Japanese; 18) quick service; 19) unusual advertising concept; 20) publicity.

21) No stringent dress requirements; 22) recommendations from friends; 23) the basic meal is low-calorie; 24) banquet and party facilities; 25) the presence of Rocky Aoki, himself; 26) chance to meet people of the opposite sex; 27) the presence of many Japanese customers (about 20%); 28) locations in major cities giving a radiation effect; 29) acceptance of all major credit cards; 30) the informality of the dining experience; and 31) the use of the restaurant as a business tool.

Benihana, New York's first Japanese restaurant devoted to hibachi cooking, proudly announces a grand total of 13 imitators.

Come see what the imitators are trying to imitate.

The Mission of Rocky Aoki

I was so dazzled by the knifework. I almost forgot to eat the results.

EXHIBIT 6

Benihana Advertising

Go forth now and cook amongst the Americans.

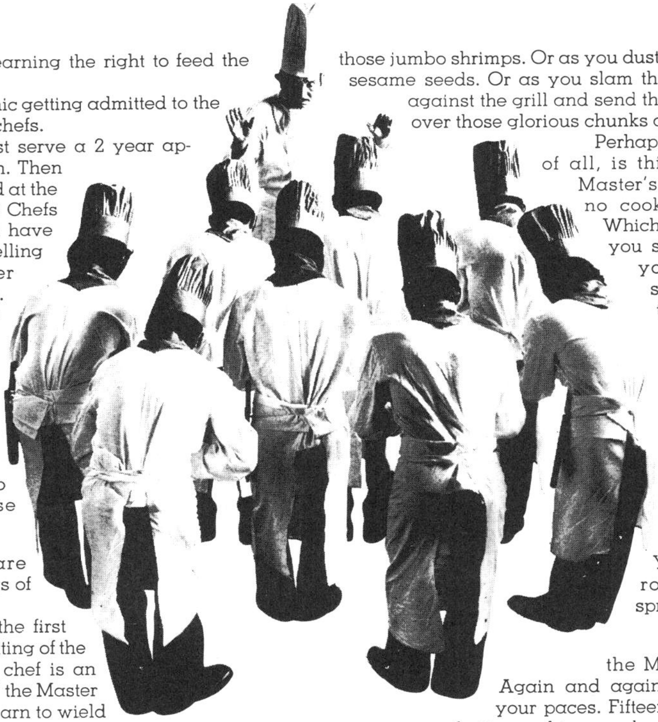

It's not easy earning the right to feed the people of America.

No, it's no picnic getting admitted to the league of Benihana chefs.

First, you must serve a 2 year apprenticeship in Japan. Then you must be accepted at the Benihana College of Chefs in Tokyo. There you have to spend fifteen gruelling weeks under Master Chef Shinji Fujisaku. You don't graduate unless the Master certifies that you've become an absolute whiz at Benihana's special style of Hibachi cooking (Japanese grill cuisine as opposed to classical Japanese cuisine.)

And what are some of the teachings of the Master?

Well, one of the first has to do with the cutting of the meat. "A Benihana chef is an artist, not a butcher," the Master says. So you must learn to wield a knife with dazzling grace, speed and precision. Your hands should move like Fred Astaire's feet.

You also learn that to a Benihana chef, Hibachi cooking is never solemn. As the Master says "It's an act of pure joy." So joy, really, is what you must bring to the Hibachi table. A joy that the people around you can see and feel. A joy they can catch as you sauté those jumbo shrimps. Or as you dust that chicken with sesame seeds. Or as you slam that pepper shaker against the grill and send the pepper swirling over those glorious chunks of steak.

Perhaps most important of all, is this saying of the Master's: "Benihana has no cooks. Only chefs." Which means that while you should be joyous, you must always strive for perfection. So you learn everything there is to learn about sauces and seasonings. You labor to make your shrimp the most succulent shrimp anyone's ever tasted. Your sirloin the most delicious and juicy. Your every mushroom and beansprout a song.

Over and over the Master drills you. Again and again you go through your paces. Fifteen exhausting, perfection-seeking weeks.

But the day comes when you're ready. Ready to bring what you've learned to the people of such faraway places as New York, Chicago and Los Angeles.

It's a great moment.

"Sayonara, Honorable Teacher," you say.

"Knock 'em dead, Honorable Graduate," he replies.

BENIHANA of TOKYO

New York—Benihana Palace 15 W. 44 St., 682-7120 • Benihana East 120 E. 56 St., 593-1627 • Benihana West 61 W. 56 St., 581-0930
Boston, Harrisburg, Fort Lauderdale, Chicago, Seattle, Portland Ore., San Francisco, Las Vegas, Encino, Marina Del Rey, Beverly Hills, Honolulu, Tokyo.

EXHIBIT 7

Benihana Advertising

THEATER OF THE STOMACH

It's a little scary at first.

There you are sitting around this enormous table (which turns out to also be a grill) when suddenly he appears. A man dressed like a chef but with the unmistakable air of a samurai warrior.

He bows. Just to be on the safe side, you bow back.

Smiling inscrutably, he takes out a knife. You make a grab for your chopsticks.

He reaches into the cart he's wheeled in. From it he brings out rows of these really beautiful fresh whole shrimps.

Suddenly, the man turns into a kind of whirling dervish. Zip.

Zip. zip...his knife flashes through the rows like lightning. The shrimps (now cut into bite-size morsels) seem to dance to the center of the grill. He presses on. With magnificent, sweeping gestures he adds freshly ground pepper to the shrimps. Then butter. Then soy sauce. The action never stops. He even spins around and throws sesame seeds out from over his shoulder.

At last comes the moment of truth. He flips a sizzling shrimp directly on your plate. You taste it. You have a small fit of ecstasy.

Naturally, that's just the first scene. The show goes on this

way...course after course after course. He performs. You eat. He performs again. You eat again. Steak. Chicken. Mouth-watering vegetables of every variety. You've never had such a feast, you've never seen such choreography.

Finally, it's over. He bows. You sigh. He thanks you. You thank <u>him</u>. He walks off.

If you weren't so full you'd get up and give him a standing ovation.

BENIHANA of TOKYO

EXHIBIT 8

Benihana Advertising

Two philosophies of the steak.

The basic philosophy of the American restaurant.

The chef throws a slab of raw steak into the kitchen broiler.

It sits there until it's rare, medium or well-done.

The waiter brings it to your table.

You eat it.

The Benihana philosophy.

The chef comes right up to your hibachi table. (Why shouldn't you see the man who's actually creating your meal?)

He bows. (There's no reason why a chef can't be a gentleman.)

He sets the raw steak in front of you. (Isn't it nice to see for yourself that you're getting the very freshest, prime cuts?)

He asks you how you want it. (There's no luxury like the luxury of dealing directly with your chef.)

He cuts your steak into bite-size morsels. (Why should you have to perform any labor?)

His knife begins a snappy, rhythmic attack on the onions. (We believe there's as much drama in a dancing onion as in a dancing chorus girl.)

He slams the pepper shaker against the grill. (It's not good for a chef to suppress his excitement.)

As he cooks he adds all kinds of Japanese sauces and seasonings. (No, Worcester sauce is not part of our theory.)

At last he puts the sizzling steak directly on your plate. (The world's fastest waiter couldn't serve you better.)

You eat it. (Tell us. Has there ever been a more palatable philosophy?)

BENIHANA of TOKYO

New York—Benihana Palace 15 W. 44 St., 682-7120 • Benihana East 120 E. 56 St., 593-1627 • Benihana West 61 W. 56 St., 581-0930
Boston, Harrisburg, Fort Lauderdale, Chicago, Seattle, Portland Ore., San Francisco, Las Vegas, Encino, Marina Del Rey, Beverly Hills, Honolulu, Tokyo.

EXHIBIT 9

Benihana Advertising

The Mission of Rocky Aoki

When Rocky Aoki, owner of Benihana, came to America about ten years ago, this was how a great many Americans felt about Japanese food:

(1) It wasn't as good as Chinese food.

(2) It was mostly sukiyaki and soup that tasted like hot brown water.

(3) If you ordered anything besides sukiyaki, you'd wind up with raw, slithery fishy things.

(4) OK, the food was very prettily arranged. But you walked out twice as hungry as when you walked in.

"My task is clear," said Rocky. "I'm going to change the way Americans think about Japanese food. I'm going to introduce hibachi cooking to America."

(Hibachi cooking or cooking on a grill, is nothing at all like the highly stylized classical Japanese cuisine.)

And so, in 1964, Rocky opened the first Benihana. It broke all the rules. You couldn't get sukiyaki there. Or raw fish. There wasn't even a conventional kitchen. You just sat around this big hibachi table—a combination grill and dining table—and waited for your chef to appear.

When he did, he came bearing a feast. Basket upon basket of beautiful fresh meat, poultry and vegetables. Then, right in front of you, he sprang into action. Slicing, seasoning and cooking, he prepared your meal with a speed and skill bordering on wizardry.

It was hard to believe. No exquisitely carved carrot slices. No wispy vegetables arranged in perfect flower patterns. Instead, solid food in abundance. Jumbo shrimps sauteed with lemon. Succulent chunks of steak. Young chicken dusted with sesame seeds. Mushrooms, scallions, beansprouts—served not together in some kind of mish-mash, but individually. It was enough to bring joy to the most jaded gourmet, bliss to the most ravenous appetite.

Well, the first New York Benihana was an enormous success. Within a year, Rocky had to open another one. That too became a smash. Soon Rocky was opening a Benihana in Chicago. And then one in San Francisco. And then another in Las Vegas. Today Rocky has Benihanas all over the United States.

When he opened his third New York Benihana—the Benihana Palace—Rocky Aoki declared: "I'll consider my mission accomplished when everyone in America has tried hibachi cooking at least once."

Come in and give a nice Japanese boy a break.

BENIHANA of TOKYO

No slithery, fishy things.

New York — Benihana Palace 15 W. 44 St., 682-7120 • Benihana East 120 E. 56th St., 593-1627 • Benihana West 47 W. 56th St., 581-0930

Atlanta, Boston, Fort Lauderdale, Harrisburg, Chicago, Denver, Bethesda Md., Bala Cynwyd Pa., Seattle, Portland, Ore., San Francisco, Las Vegas, Encino, Beverly Hills, Marina Del Rey, Miami, Houston, Honolulu, Tokyo, Toronto.

FUTURE EXPANSION

Bill Susha summed up the problems of the future as he saw them:

I think the biggest problems facing us now are how to expand. We tried franchising and decided to discontinue the program for several reasons. Most of our franchisees were businessmen looking for investment opportunities who did not really know and understand the restaurant business—this was a problem. The Japanese staff we provided were our people and we have obligations to them that the franchisee could not or would not honor which at the time made us unhappy. The uniqueness of our operation in the hands of novices made control more difficult. Finally, we found it more profitable to own and operate the restaurants ourselves.

Presently, we are limited to opening only five units a year, because that is as fast as the two crews of Japanese carpenters we have can work. We are facing a decision and weighing the advantages and disadvantages of going into hotels with our type of restaurant. We are presently in two Hilton Hotels (Las Vegas and Honolulu) and have recently signed an agreement with Canadian Pacific Hotels. What we have done in these deals is to put "teeth" in the agreements, so that we are not at the mercy of the hotel company's management.

Further, one of our biggest constraints is staff. Each unit requires approximately 30 people who are all Oriental. Six to eight of them are highly trained chefs.

Finally, there is the cost factor. Each new unit costs us a minimum of $300,000. My feeling is that we should confine ourselves to the major cities like Atlanta, Dallas, St. Louis, etc., in the near future. Then we can use all these units to expand into the suburbs.

We've been highly tempted to try to grow too fast without really considering the full implications of the move. One example was the franchise thing, but we found it unsatisfactory. Another example is that a large international banking organization offered to make a major investment in us which would have allowed us to grow at a terrific rate. But when we looked at the amount of control and autonomy we'd have to give up, it just wasn't worth it, at least in my mind.

Another thing I'm considering is whether it's worth it to import every item used in construction from Japan to make a Benihana 100 percent "authentic." Does an American really appreciate it and is it worth the cost? We could use material available here and achieve substantially the same effect. Also, is it worth it to use Japanese carpenters and pay union carpenters to sit and watch? All these things could reduce our costs tremendously and allow us to expand much faster.

Rocky described his perception of where the firm should go:

I see three principal areas for growth: the United States, overseas, and Japan.

In the United States we need to expand into the primary marketing areas Bill talked about that do not have a Benihana. But I think through our franchises we also learned that secondary markets such as Harrisburg, Pennsylvania, and Portland, Oregon, also have potential. While their volume potential obviously will not match that of a primary market, these smaller units offer fewer headaches and generate nice profits. Secondary markets being considered include Cincinnati and Indianapolis.

The third principal area I see for growth is in suburbia. No sites have yet been set, but I think it holds a great potential. A fourth growth area, not given the importance of the others, is further penetration into existing markets. Saturation is not a problem as illustrated by the fact that New York and greater Los Angeles have three units each, all doing well.

We are also considering someday going public. In the meantime, we are moving into joint ventures in Mexico and overseas. Each joint venture is unique in itself. We negotiate each unit on the basis that will be most advantageous to the parties concerned, taking into account the contributions of each party in the form of services and cash. Once this is established, we agree on a formula for profits and away we go.

Four deals have not been consummated. Three are joint ventures out of the country. An agreement has already been reached to open a Benihana in the Royal York Hotel, Toronto, Canada. This will provide the vanguard for a march across Canada with units in or outside Canadian Pacific Hotels.

Second is a signed agreement for a new unit in Mexico City. From here, negotiations are under way on a new hotel to be built in Acapulco. Benihana stands ready to build and operate a unit in the hotel or, if possible, to take over management of the entire hotel. These units would form a base for expansion throughout Mexico.

The third extraterritorial arrangement was recently signed with David Paradine, Ltd., a British firm of investors headed by TV personality David Frost. Again, this is a joint venture with the Paradine group to supply technical assistance, public relations, advertising, and financing, and Benihana the management and know-how. This venture hopes ultimately to have Benihana restaurants, not only throughout Great Britain, but across the Continent.

Rocky also had a number of diversification plans:

We have entered into an agreement with a firm that is researching and contracting large food processors in an effort to interest them in producing a line of Japanese food products under the Benihana label for retail sale. There has been a great deal of interest and we are close to concluding a deal.

I worry a lot. Right now we cater to a middle-income audience, not the younger generation. That makes a difference. We charge more, serve better quality, have a better atmosphere, and more service. But we are in the planning stages for operations with appeal to the younger generation.

For instance, there is no Japanese quick service operation in this country. I think we should go into a combination Chinese-Japanese operation like this. The unit would also feature a dynamic cooking show exposed to the customers. Our initial projections show margins comparable to our present margins with Benihana of Tokyo. I see a check of about 99¢. We are negotiating with an oil company to put small units in gas stations. They could be located anywhere—on turnpikes or in the Bronx. I think we should do this very soon. We might call it the "Orient Express." I think I will get a small store in Manhattan and try it out. This is the best kind of market research in the United States. Market research works in other coun-

tries, but I don't believe in it here. We are also negotiating for a site on Guam and to take over a chain of beer halls in Japan.

The restaurant business is not my only business. I went into producing; I had two unsuccessful Broadway shows. The experience was very expensive, but I learned a great deal and learned it very fast. It's all up to the critics there. In the restaurant business, the critics don't write much about you if you're bad; but even if they do they can't kill you. On Broadway they can. They did.

I promoted a heavyweight boxing match in Japan. It was successful. I am going into promoting in the entertainment field in Japan. I am doing a Renoir exhibition in Japan with an auction over television. I am thinking about buying a Japanese movie series and bringing it here. I am also thinking of opening a model agency, probably specializing in Oriental models.

My philosophy of the restaurant business is simply to make people happy. We do it many ways in Benihana. As we start different types of operations, we will try to do it in other ways. I have no real worries about the future. The United States is the greatest country in the world to make money. Anybody can do it who wants to work hard and make people happy.

Russ Carpenter, a consultant and editor for *Institutions/Volume Feeding* magazine, summed up his perceptions as follows:

I basically see two main problems. What is Benihana really selling? Is it food, atmosphere, hospitality, a "watering hole" or what? Is having entertainment in the lounge consistent with the overall image? All the advertising emphasizes the chef and the food, but is that really what the public comes for? I don't know. I'm only raising the questions. The other thing is how do you hedge your bets? Is Benihana really on the forefront of a trend of the future with their limited menu, cooking in front of you, and Oriental atmosphere, or is it just a fad? This relates to whether the firm should emphasize restaurant operations only.

Chandler Trust Company

ROGER W. SCHMENNER
KELLEY S. PLATT

The operations division of a bank must come up with a new and faster method of processing interbank transactions.

Alexander Chase was winding down his 1981 summer internship in the Banking Operations Division of Chandler Trust Company and would soon return to his second year at the well-known southern business school he attended. His boss, Judith Stoddard, asked to see him as soon as possible. Alex knew from his brief experience at Chandler that when the boss came looking for him it had to be important. Ms. Stoddard was a First Vice President of the Bank and was in charge of a staff group that supported the Operations Division. This group, of which Alex was a part, was responsible for all automation projects undertaken in the Division. To date this had included word processing, micrographics, and some computer system automation.

"Alex," said Ms. Stoddard, "since you are almost finished with your other projects and you will be with us for another two weeks, I'd like you to undertake a special project. This is very different from anything you've done before, and as you will see when I outline the problem further, it is essential that we have your report within one week. As you probably know, CHIPS (Clearing House Interbank Payments System) is changing on October 1, 1981 to a same-day settlement system instead of its current next-day settlement. This means that our transactions will all have to be processed by 4:00 P.M. on the

This case was prepared by Kelley S. Platt, under the supervision of Associate Professor Roger W Schmenner.

EXHIBIT 1

New CHIPS Deadlines

The following times will be strictly adhered to after October 1, 1981.

Eastern Time

7:00 A.M.	CHIPS opens for storage and sending of payment messages.
9:00 A.M.	Fedwire opens nationwide for funds transfer
11:00 A.M. 1:00 P.M. 3:00 P.M.	Exchange of fedwire payments and CHIPS messages.
4:30 P.M.	CHIPS cut-off for payment messages. Fedwire cut-off (nationwide) for interdistrict transfers between federal districts. Fedwire cut-off (2nd district) for intradistrict 3rd-party transfers. (Each district's option.) (Use of Fedwire for bank settlements continues.)
4:45 P.M.	CHIPS completes providing net settlement information to participants.
5:00 P.M.	CHIPS settlement process begins.
5:45 P.M.	CHIPS cut-off time for any settling participant to notify New York clearing house that it is unwilling to settle net position of any participant for which it settles.
6:00 P.M.	CHIPS settlement. Fedwire cut-off (all districts) for intradistrict third-party fedwire payments.
6:30 P.M.	Fedwire closes for all transactions (including two-party bank settlements).

SOURCE: Internal memorandum 10, Chandler Trust Company.

day that they are received, if we are to settle with our clearing banks by the time the Federal Reserve closes at 6:30 (see *Exhibit 1*). You've been in that department before and have seen how things are done now, so you know that the present system is unlikely to work. I want you to come up with a plan for meeting these new CHIPS deadlines.

"I'm sure that David Winter or Brett Johnson will be able to give you some background information on the department. They have come up with some ideas on what might be done but I'll count on you to develop a comprehensive proposal."

SAME-DAY SETTLEMENT[1]

CHIPS (Clearing House Interbank Payment System) was a group of 100 financial institutions in New York. It served as an elec-

tronic payment mechanism for its participants to make payments to each other. All transactions were currently processed one day and the funds became available about 10:00 A.M. the next day. Banks' positions with each other were determined by their net credit or debit position vis-à-vis every other bank at the end of the banking day. These positions were "settled" by transferring funds on deposit with the Federal Reserve System to balance out the accounts. Federal Reserve funds were transferred by means of an electronic payment system called the Fedwire. See *Exhibit 2* for additional definitions. A bank's net position with other banks was balanced out by transferring funds over the Fedwire before 10:00 A.M. on the second day. Fedwire transfers were for immediately available funds because the transfer involved only a movement of funds from one bank's account at the Fed to another.

CHIPS was important because of its size —55,000 transactions totalling $150 billion

[1]*Source:* Chase Manhattan, N. A. publication.

EXHIBIT 2

Definition of Terms

Same day funds are funds available for transfer today in like funds or withdrawal in cash, subject to the settlement of the transaction through the payment system used.

Next day funds are funds available for transfer today in like funds and available the next business day for transfer in same day funds or withdrawal in cash, subject to the settlement of the transaction through the payment system used.

Federal funds are funds on deposit at a Federal Reserve Bank in the United States. They are a subset of same day funds and only those funds transferred via the Fedwire are immediately collected. All other federal funds payments are subject to final settlement/collection.

Immediately Available Funds—see Federal funds (settlement is simultaneous with the execution of the transaction).

Settlement refers to the balance amounts (resulting from payments drawn on and made to banks through a payment system) that are presented to the Federal Reserve System for debiting or crediting the lawful reserve accounts of the banks on the payment system that settle in this manner. Settlement is completed when all of the appropriate debit or credit entries have been made across the Lawful Reserve Accounts.

The worldwide definition of *value date* is the date when the receiving bank has use of the funds. In the U.S. we also make the funds available to the beneficiary at the same time. This is due to our accounting procedures which have not been geared to posting future values as is customary in other countries.

SOURCE: Internal memorandum 9, Chandler Trust Company.

to $160 billion dollars per day. Over 90 percent of the world's foreign exchange business was done through CHIPS. It was the major vehicle for the world's Eurodollar market, including Eurodollar loans, speculative investments, and time deposits. CHIPS was also an important settlement system for international trade transactions.

The growth of the Eurodollar market had led to instability in foreign exchange and Eurodollar interest rates because of the present next-day settlement system.[2] Funds invested on Friday earned an extra two days interest because the trade would not be completed (settled) until Monday. There existed many opportunities for arbitrage because of the time zones and the one-day lag between

processing a transaction and actually having the funds available for use. To eliminate the arbitrage opportunities, the CHIPS system was to begin same-day settlement of all transactions on October 1, 1981.

Same-day settlement would require that all transactions be processed by 4:30 each day. At that time the participants would have two hours (4:30–6:30 P.M. EST) to settle with each other over the Fedwire. At the same time the banks would have to settle their reserve deposit requirement with the Federal Reserve Bank. The primary result would be the standardization of Eurodollar and foreign exchange rates.

The implications of same-day settlement for the processing of funds transfers centered on the reliability and timeliness of the transfer and advising system.[3] Input pro-

---

[2] Eurodollars, euroyen, or euromarks for example, are any currency which is deposited in a bank outside of its home country, e.g., U.S. dollars on deposit in U.S. banks' foreign branches or in foreign banks.

[3] The advising systems generate written records that verify a payment has been made or received. The output is an "advice."

cessing deadlines would be earlier. It would be more difficult to make corrections in transactions while they were being processed. Error corrections the next day, after the transaction was settled, would be about six times more expensive than currently because compensation would have to be paid for the interest that the injured party would have earned overnight had the transfer been properly made.

COMPANY BACKGROUND

The Chandler Trust Company was a small wholesale bank. Headquartered in New York, Chandler had an Edge Act subsidiary in

---

EXHIBIT 3
Funds Transfer Department Staffing

Job Description (current staffing levels)   Total 24

CHIPS Terminal Operator (4) Enters all CHIPS payments into terminals, releases payments after verification, gives incoming tickets to incoming clerk. Requires training in terminal operations.

CHIPS Checker (2) Checks the written copy of stored CHIPS payments against the cable or written instructions for accuracy. Errors are corrected by deleting the whole transaction from the system and reentering it.

CHIPS Final Checker (1) Second check on all payments before they are released.

CHIPS Incoming Clerk (2) Receives incoming CHIPS tickets from CHIPS terminal operator. Matches against advice if the bank has been told the money is coming. Prepares cables to advise of receipt if none exists. Prepares credit forms for account to receive money.

Setup Clerk (1) Receives all payment and receipt instructions. Highlights key information, i.e., names, addresses, account numbers, type of transaction.

Blocking Clerk (1) Ensures sufficient funds available for transfer by monitoring the accounts of the Bank's clients (manual process).

Clearing Bank Clerk (2) Maintains ledgers to monitor balance of all banks that use Chandler as their access to the CHIPS network.

Balance Reporting Clerk (1) Monitors balance and records transactions of a large foreign bank. Advises bank by cable of all transactions.

Fed Funds Clerk (1) Separates all fed funds payment tickets. Types necessary advices.

Fed Funds Checker (2) Checks all machine Federal funds entries against payment instructions before release from Federal funds terminal.

Fed Funds Position Sheet (2) One incoming, one outgoing, records and tallies banks' own position at the Federal Reserve by adding all payments in and subtracting all transfers out. Advises senior management of position throughout the day.

Proof Sheet Clerk (1) Posts all internal payments and transfers for data entry into demand deposit accounting system.

Fedwire Operators (2) Enter all Federal Funds Transfers into system. After verification, release payments into system.

Typists (2) Prepare cables. Type payments tickets. Break apart multipart forms and distribute to parties involved in transaction. File copies of all transactions.

Supervisors (2) One is a Fed Funds position sheet clerk and one is a Clearing Bank clerk. Responsibilities split into Fed Funds staff and CHIPS staff.

Miami which could only carry out international banking activities. Its overseas operations included branch offices, affiliated banks (that were part of the Chandler Group, the parent organization of Chandler Trust Company, but were separately incorporated and capitalized), and subsidiaries of the Chandler Group.

Chandler's customers included small to medium-sized multi-nationals, foreign companies, local and regional banks in the U.S. and many foreign banks and government agencies. Because of its emphasis on international business, Chandler's operations were geared to processing large volumes of foreign exchange transactions, loans, and securities investments denominated in Eurodollars or foreign currencies. Much of the Eurodollar activity was channeled, for tax purposes, and to avoid interest rate restrictions imposed by the Federal Reserve Board, through Nassau or the Cayman Islands.

The Chandler Trust Company had built its reputation on customizing its services to meet its clients' needs. Prompt and efficient response to customer inquiries was of utmost importance. Many of Chandler's customers relied on the bank to invest all of their available funds every night. These amounts changed from day to day and, as a consequence, the investments had to be made over again every day. To do this, the bankers had to have accurate and timely information on their clients' balances.

The headquarters office of Chandler employed approximately 500 people. One-third of these were actually involved in the company's operating divisions. The operating departments of Chandler were divided according to the function that they performed. For example, the Foreign Exchange Department processed the paper work to support all the foreign currency deals that the bank or its clients made. The actual transferring of funds from one account to another or to other banks was done by the Funds Transfer Department (see *Exhibit 3* for staffing). It acted as a service center for the other operating departments (see *Exhibit 4* for floor plan).

EXHIBIT 4
Floor Plan—Funds Transfer Department

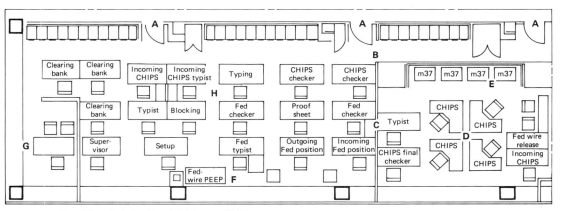

Current floor plan is from blueprint of the area. All fixtures are to scale. The following are key items:

A. Exterior doorways onto open corridor. Free access through these doorways.

B. Interior doorway to machine room.

C. Wall 36″ in height with glass panel to ceiling to block off machine room. Machine room has raised floor.

D. CHIPS machines for entering and deleting payments from the CHIPS system. Must remain on a raised floor.

E. Back-up CHIPS machines.

F. Fedwire machines for fed payments. Do not have to be on raised floor.

G. Department head's office.

H. All desks are of a standard size and freely moveable. Titles identify function performed at that desk and do not necessarily correspond to individual employees.

SOURCE: Blueprints of the area.

DEPARTMENTAL BACKGROUND

David Winter, Assistant Treasurer, was part of the Operations Division staff group at Chandler. When Alex asked about the functions of the Funds Transfer Department, David explained that, "the prime function of the department is to transfer and receive funds on behalf of the bank's customers and operating departments. The department interfaces with two automated systems to perform its function: the Clearing House Interbank Payment System (CHIPS) and the Federal Reserve Funds Transfer System (Fedwire). Treasurers' checks are also used to make payments. The choice of payment method is dictated by the payment instructions and the nature of the transaction.

"In addition, the department performs a wide range of other services including:

- teller facilities such as check cashing, check certification, accepting deposits, and receiving documents.
- monitoring the balance of our accounts at other banks and keeping those balances at levels specified by senior management.
- monitoring continually our balance at the Federal Reserve Bank and keeping senior management and the money traders apprised of the bank's position as necessary.

"Since the department's activities involve direct communication with the bank's customers and correspondents, careful attention to detail and a high degree of accuracy are mandatory."

"How many of these transfers or payments does the department make, David?"

"I believe those figures run about 17,000 Fed payments and 20,000 CHIPS payments per month. Our Financial Control Department produces a monthly production activity report for the Fed section (see *Exhibit 5*) and the CHIPS section of the department (see *Exhibit 6*). We've experienced an historical growth of 10–15 percent annually over the last four years. I expect that this rate will double when we move to same-day settlement. Our operation is pretty hectic on a busy day.

"The biggest problem I see with this same-day settlement thing is maintaining a high level of accuracy. If we make a mistake and don't transfer the right amount of funds, or don't make the cut-off time, we can be liable for paying compensation claims because somebody else should have been earning interest on that money. It doesn't sound like much, but with interest rates at 18 percent, the overnight interest on a $10 million transfer is $4,931.51, and we transfer hundreds of millions every day.

"Accuracy is also important to our internal auditors. They are always after us to improve our internal processing controls. Sometimes I think the only way we could ever satisfy them is to track each transaction

EXHIBIT 5
Production Activity Report (Banking Operations Division)

Department: Funds Transfer
Section: Federal Funds   Month ending: _____

Tasks	ACTUAL ACTIVITY			STANDARD ACTIVITY		TASK UNIT COST	
	Current Month	Prior Month	Year to Date	Current Month	Year to Date	Actual	Standard
Incoming payments	4,644	3,991	13,033	4,337	12,986	$ 1.69	$ 1.62
Outgoing payments	3,753	3,297	10,410	3,505	10,378	3.84	3.69
Control fed funds	8,397	7,288	23,443	7,843	23,367	.63	.62
Proof sheet	22	18	61	21	61	239.03	228.40
Collection	174	187	367	162	554	10.90	10.49
Return items	1	1	3	1	3	467.74	571.58
Certification	1	1	3	1	3	262.21	320.73

FEDWIRE NOT BMD.

EXHIBIT 6
Production Activity Report (Banking Operations Division)

Department: Funds Transfer
Section: CHIPS   Month ending: _____

Tasks	ACTUAL ACTIVITY			STANDARD ACTIVITY		TASK UNIT COST	
	Current Month	Prior Month	Year to Date	Current Month	Year to Date	Actual	Standard
Payment and transfer	7,818	7,179	14,997	9,229	28,350	$5.02	$3.67
Payment check	666	647	1,313	787	2,494	6.48	4.76
Clearpay draft	59	67	126	70	285	9.39	6.86
Clearpay memo	111	74	185	131	344	5.14	3.73
Federal funds (setup)	3,083	2,468	5,551	3,637	10,699	1.02	.74
Incoming payment	8,094	7,272	15,366	9,552	28,664	1.13	.83
Certification	104	55	159	122	326	3.97	2.92
Clearing accounts	2,603	2,164	4,767	3,072	8,779	7.74	5.68
Special accounts	678	546	1,224	800	2,285	7.63	5.61

SOME PROBS I CHIPS PROD.

every step of the way through the department with checks and counterchecks along the way. Lately, they've been complaining about the department's security. All of the doors are open to the hallway and there is no door to the machine room."

Brett Johnson was an Assistant Treasurer. Part of his responsibilities included coordinating the plans for same-day settlement, the upcoming change in the CHIPS payment system. Alex approached Brett for advice on the current status of the Funds Transfer Department. "The work flow in the department is fairly standardized, Alex. David and I did a situation analysis of the area last spring. We drew flow charts that trace the processing of the four major types of transactions they handle: CHIPS payments and CHIPS receipts (see *Exhibit 7*), and Fed payments and Fed receipts (see *Exhibit 8*). The current processing is broken down by task within the payment process.

"In a typical payment one clerk receives the payment instructions in the form of a cable, a telephone message, or written instructions from another department in the bank. The setup clerk "sets up" the payment by highlighting or underlining the pertinent information which includes the type of payment (Fed or CHIPS), the amount, the debit party, the paying bank, the beneficiary, and any references. Next the blocking clerk verifies that there are sufficient funds in the account to cover the transaction (blocking). If the funds are not there the clerk will check to see if there is an advice of funds to be transferred into the account on that day. If not, and the transfer exceeds the client's overdraft facility, then the clerk must call the account officer to have the transfer approved.

"If the transaction involves a Fed payment or receipt then the Fed position clerk will record it on their position sheet. This is a large ledger on which they keep a tally of the bank's deposits and withdrawals in its account at the Federal Reserve.

"CHIPS and Fed payments must be entered into their respective automated payment systems. This is done by the CHIPS terminal operators and the Fedwire operator respectively. In both systems the information is entered into the machine and a paper copy or CRT screen image is created. This copy will be verified twice before the payment message is actually sent electronically.

"There are separate clerks to check the accuracy of CHIPS and Fed payments against the cable or other instructions which created the payment. Final checkers also check only CHIPS or Fed payments although there is very little training needed to learn to check either type of payment.

2 pymt systems

EXHIBIT 7

Funds Transfer Department—CHIPS Payment Flow

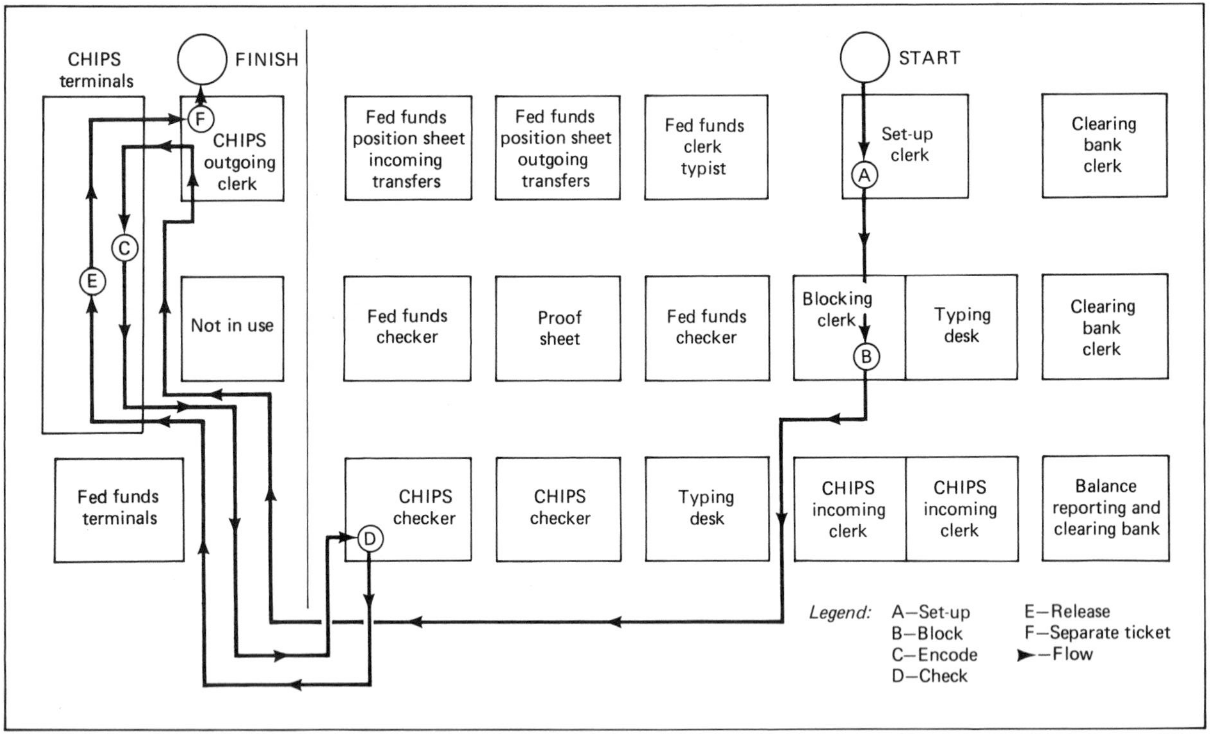

EXHIBIT 7 (continued)

Funds Transfer Department—CHIPS Receipt Flow

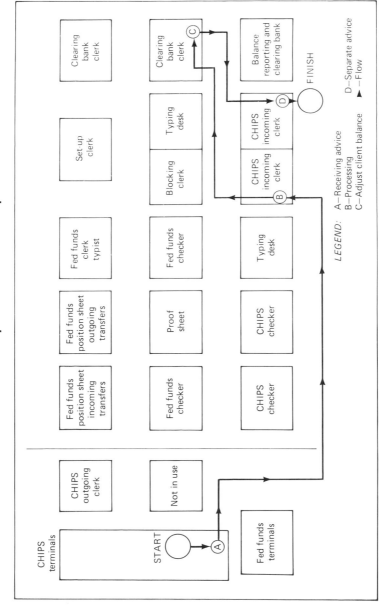

LEGEND: A—Receiving advice
B—Processing
C—Adjust client balance
D—Separate advice
—Flow

SOURCE: Internal memorandum.

EXHIBIT 8

Funds Transfer Department—Federal Funds Receipt Flow

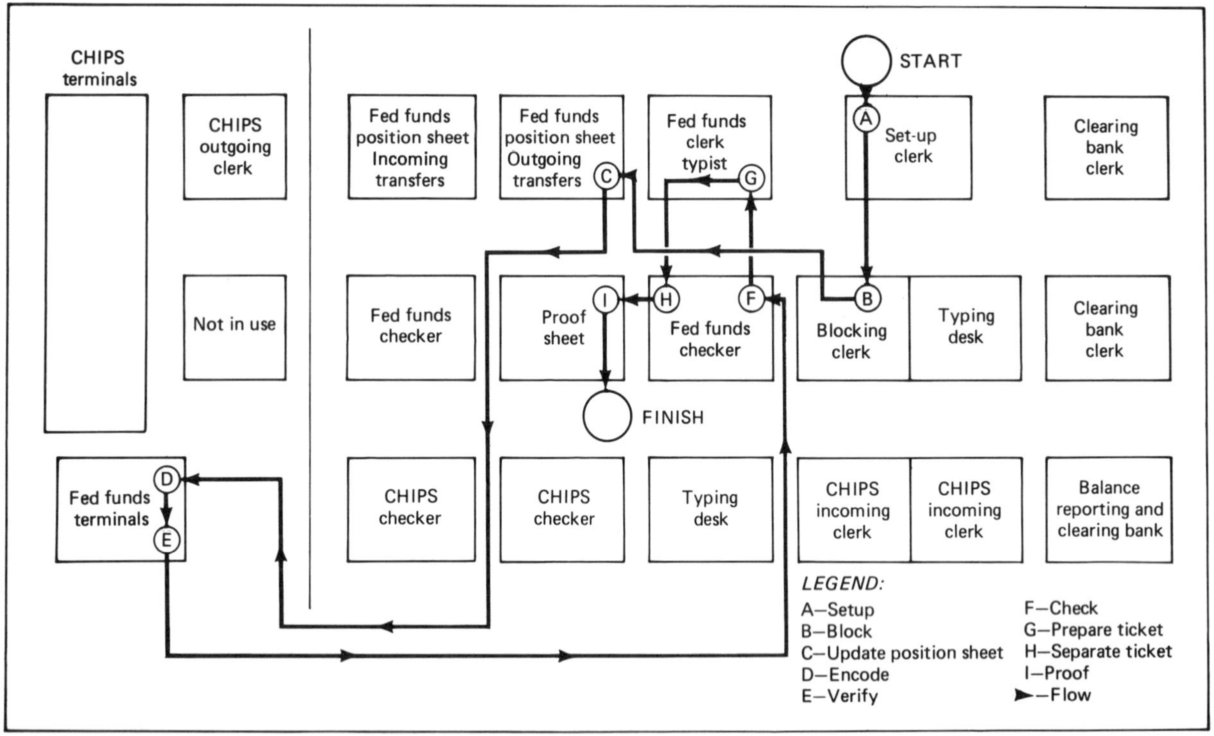

LEGEND:

A—Setup
B—Block
C—Update position sheet
D—Encode
E—Verify
F—Check
G—Prepare ticket
H—Separate ticket
I—Proof
►—Flow

SOURCE: Internal memorandum.

EXHIBIT 8 (continued)

Funds Transfer Department—Federal Funds Payment Flow

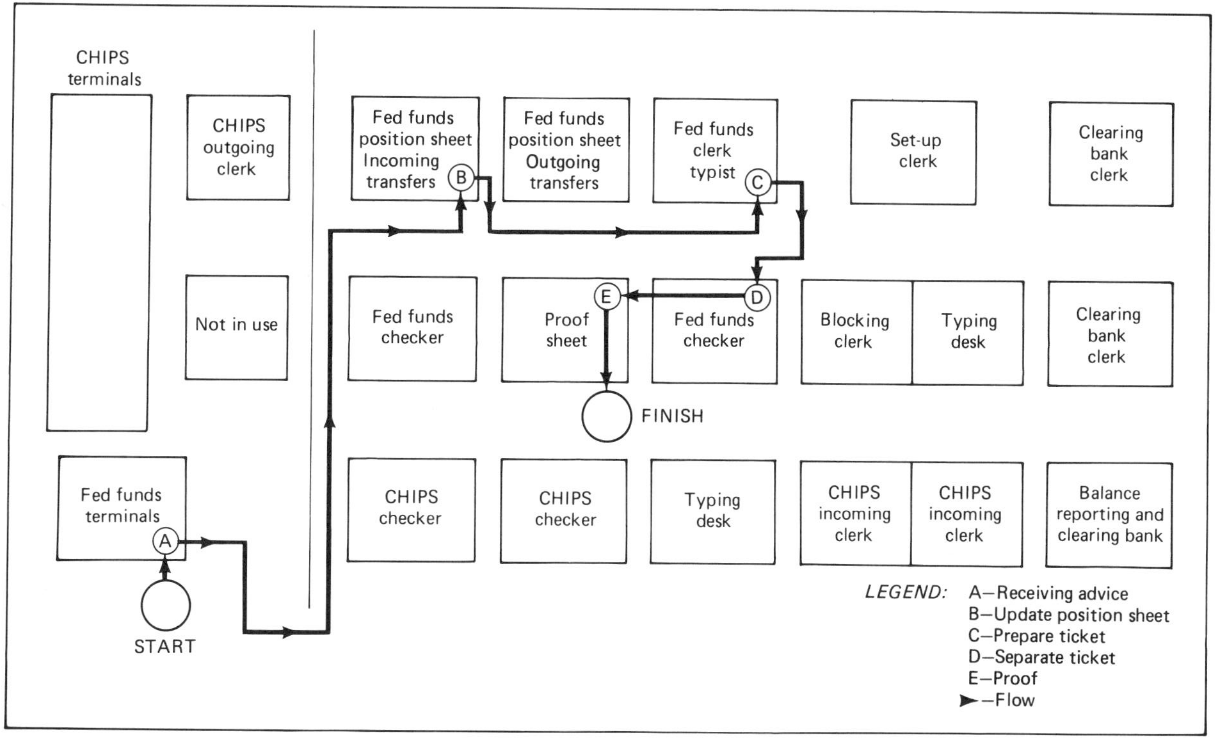

LEGEND: A—Receiving advice
B—Update position sheet
C—Prepare ticket
D—Separate ticket
E—Proof
▸—Flow

"The next step involves entering the proper information into the automated system to release the payment so that it can be sent. This is done by one of the terminal operators, but not the one that entered the message originally.

"Finally, the paper ticket that is the bank's record of the payment is separated ("broken down") into nine pieces that are then sent to various parts of the bank for safekeeping. Some customers have standing orders that they are to be cabled whenever any funds are moved into or out of their accounts. When this is the case, the CHIPS or Fed checker who has broken down the ticket will indicate that on the ticket and give it to a typist to type up the cable.

"You can see that several people must handle each transaction that the department processes. The processing starts and stops many times as the message is moved from the top of one pile to the bottom of the next pile at every step along the way. The floor plan indicates the physical flow of each transaction. You can see how many times it "walks" across the room before it is finished. (See *Exhibits 4, 7,* and *8.*) It didn't use to be that way when we were smaller and one person could do several of the steps as long as someone else checked the accuracy of her work. I think our clerks are going to need track shoes come October first if we don't do something about the work flow in here."

"Several ideas have been suggested for what to do in that department, Alex. Maybe they'll help you with your recommendations.

- First, we could move some desks around so the clerks don't have to do so much walking. Keep in mind though that the CHIPS machines have to stay in their own room and that security in the department is key.

- Second, we can add extra people to help with the processing, but it would be hard to justify without an increase in volume. The question then is where to add them. The Financial Control department did a time and motion study in there last year which gives some figures on how long it should take to do each job. (See *Exhibit 9.*)

- Third, we could add word processors to replace some of the manual record keeping. I really think they would help for maintaining our position at the Fed and for maintaining our clearing and foreign bank accounts. Having those balances anytime during the day is going to make a difference to the customers. Of course this option raises the question of what to do with the clerks' time if it's quicker to maintain balances on a word processor than a ledger sheet. In any case we can't afford to lose any business because of same-day settlement.

"I'm sure you must be full of ideas of what we can do in there, Alex. I hope this information will be of some help to you in making your recommendations."

EXHIBIT 9
Capacity Planning Data

Activity	Average Time Required per Transaction
Setup	1 minute
Block	60–75 seconds
Check	45 seconds
Process payment	2–5 minutes*
Verify payment	1 minute
Final check	2 minutes

*Approximately one-third of all payments are of a simple nature which require substantially less processing time. Average 90 seconds each.

SOURCE: Case writers' estimates based on internal work measurement study.

Delta Video Store

MARVIN RYDER

A Canadian entrepreneur has been running a store specializing in videocassette and VCR rentals for over three years. During the past 18 months, she has faced increasing competition from a nearby variety store that has expanded into the same line of business. She wonders whether to purchase an automatic videotape vending machine in order to be able to offer 24-hour service.

Susan Howard, owner of Delta Video Store of Hamilton, Ontario, was considering the purchase of a "Video Vendor" machine. Operating in the manner of a soft drink vending machine, the "Video Vendor" would allow Susan's customers to rent videotapes twenty-four hours a day. It was April 1986, and though she was not being pressed to make a decision by the selling company, Susan had heard rumors that a competing store two blocks away was considering a similar purchase.

THE VIDEO INDUSTRY IN CANADA

In 1981, video cassettes were only available for purchase to the 230,000 people who owned a video cassette recorder (VCR). Yet in five years, the rental of video cassettes had grown to become a $200 million dollar per year industry in Canada alone. That dollar rental figure was equivalent to the total revenues of movie theatres in Canada. Five million people in Canada owned a VCR by 1986. The rapid growth in rentals could be attrib-

This case was prepared by Professor Marvin Ryder of McMaster University in Hamilton, Ontario. Copyright © 1986 by Marvin Ryder.

uted in part to the decline in VCR price from over $2000 in 1976 to $400 ten years later.

One in five Canadian homes owned a VCR in 1986. There was a cultural bias with 22 percent of English-speaking homes owning a VCR as compared to 14 percent in French Canada. The percentage of ownership was highest for people 35 to 49 and lowest for people over 65. The Prairie provinces experienced a greater percentage penetration while the Atlantic provinces recorded the lowest penetration. As well, homes with children and/or with a family income over $25,000 were most likely to own a VCR.

In the United States, 1985 cassette rentals totalled $2.8 billion dollars and this was expected to grow to $20 billion dollars by 1995. The 1995 rental figure would be: (1) equal to total television advertising revenue; (2) three times movie theater box office revenue; and (3) ten times Cable TV revenue. It was expected that, by 1995, 85 percent of Americans would own a VCR and those people would spend 25 percent of their television viewing time watching rented videos. Currently the average American VCR owner spent 6.9 hours per week recording and playing shows. (See *Exhibit 1* for a list of the most bought and rented video cassettes of 1985.)

When video cassettes first became available in 1964, they were manufactured in many different sizes and formats. There were dozens of VCR machines on the market and no standard had been agreed upon. By 1986, three standards had emerged in the marketplace: Beta with 9 percent of sales, VHS with 90 percent of sales, and 8 mm with 1 percent of sales. "Beta" format had been developed by Sony, the largest seller of VCR machines and many experts felt that it had the best performance.

As Sony had tried to keep the Beta secret to itself, many competitive VCR manufacturers had championed the non-secret VHS format. Slightly larger than Beta format tape, VHS had grown considerably by being the first to introduce stereo sound to video cassettes.

A third format emerged in 1985. A considerably smaller 8 mm tape was introduced. By switching to this type of video cassette, VCR's and video cassette cameras could be drastically reduced in size. Industry experts agreed that by 1995, only one format would survive but they were unsure as to which it would be.

Because of the growth in the video rental market, the number of retail outlets offering video cassettes for rent grew at a tremendous rate. Specialty video rental stores became quite common with over 1500 in Canada by 1986. Carrying 400–800 titles and several dozen VCR's, these stores served the needs of many different customers from film buff to bargain hunter.

Many other retail stores used video rentals to supplement their regular income. It

EXHIBIT 1
The Most Purchased and Rented Video Cassettes of 1985

Rentals	*Purchases*
1. *The Karate Kid*	1. Jane Fonda's Workout
2. *The Falcon and The Snowman*	2. Prince and The Revolution
3. *A Soldier's Story*	3. We Are The World, The Video Event
4. *Starman*	4. *Pinocchio*
5. *Desperately Seeking Susan*	5. Wrestlemania
6. *The Flamingo Kid*	6. Prime Time
7. *A Nightmare on Elm Street*	7. WHAM! The Video
8. *The Terminator*	8. *Singin' In The Rain*
9. *Pinocchio*	9. *Star Trek 3: The Search for Spock*
10. *The Mean Season*	10. The Jane Fonda Workout Challenge

SOURCE: Billboard Magazine, Sept. 21, 1985.

was not uncommon to find television stores, appliance dealers, computer stores, and variety stores all carrying video cassettes and VCR's for rent. These outlets carried fewer titles (mostly the older movies) and had fewer VCR's for rent, but they had succeeded at the expense of the specialty store by offering more convenient hours. In renting a video cassette, one would have to get to the store before closing time and then return the cassette the next day. Even with 9:30 AM. to 9 P.M. hours, specialty stores could not compete with the long hours (and sometimes 24-hour service) offered by most convenience stores.

DELTA VIDEO STORE

Delta Video Store operated in the east end of Hamilton. Opened in 1983, Susan Howard's store specialized in video cassette and VCR rentals. She had over 1,800 movie titles, some in Beta format and the others in VHS format. Some titles were available in both formats. She had not yet received any 8 mm titles and had not had any demand for them. Besides popular and classic American movies, Susan stocked music videos and a selection of Italian language films. The latter had been very popular with the ethnic population in the neighborhood. Susan also had 25 Beta and 20 VHS VCR's for rent. She found that she replaced 8 VCR's each year.

In the fall of 1984, a variety store, two blocks away, also began to offer video cassette and VCR rentals. In the past year and a half, Susan had noticed a steady decline in her rental business. (See *Exhibit 2* for income statements.) She attributed this partly to the variety store's longer hours (8:00 A.M. to 12:00 A.M. as compared to her hours of 9:30 A.M. to 6:00 P.M.) and partly to the multiple copies

EXHIBIT 2

Delta Video Store: Income Statements for 1983, 1984, and 1985

(Year end is January 31 of subsequent year)

	1983	1984	1985
REVENUES			
Video Cassette Rentals*	$88,200	$121,274	$112,713
Video Cassette Sales*	4,713	8,586	8,625
Interest Income		1,076	1,820
VCR Rentals*	31,206	35,632	32,171
TOTAL REVENUES	$124,485	$166,568	$155,329
EXPENSES			
Labor	$6,976	$22,972	$24,028
New Movie Purchases	37,478	45,886	48,823
Rent	12,000	12,000	12,000
Loan Repayment†	13,200	13,200	13,200
Depreciation—VCR's	5,500	4,625	4,127
Depreciation—Fixtures	7,000	5,600	4,400
Advertising	4,376	3,783	4,016
VCR Repair & Replacement	2,712	3,334	3,121
Miscellaneous	2,273	2,469	2,708
TOTAL EXPENSES	$92,515	$113,850	$117,504
Profit Before Taxes	$31,970	$52,718	$37,825

*Average Cassette Rental Charge: 1983—$2.15; 1984—$1.94; 1985—$1.86
  Average Cassette Selling Price: 1983—$84.23; 1984—$75.68; 1985—$71.88
  Average VCR Rental Charge per day: 1983—$11.17; 1984—$9.34; 1985—$8.69

†To help start up the store, Susan Howard borrowed $50,000 from a bank with a 15% interest charge.

of popular titles that they kept on hand. For a popular recent movie like *The Breakfast Club*, she carried four copies of the film (two in Beta and two in VHS). As the variety store kept movies in their rental pool for a shorter time, they had eight copies of the film available. If people didn't want to go hunting for a video cassette of a popular recent film, they looked first at the variety store. If people were looking for a film that was somewhat out of the mainstream, they would come to Susan's store first.

THE "VIDEO VENDOR"

The "Video Vendor" was available for purchase from Video Vista Inc., a firm located in Burlington, Ontario. Susan had received a package of information in the mail outlining the product and what it had to offer. According to the introductory offer:

A "Video Vendor" provides customers with convenient 24-hour access to the latest movie releases, using Automated Teller Machine technology. . . . With "Video Vendor" you can operate a video store capable of renting or selling movies as well as replacing them for the next customer. Every function that up until now has been done manually is now fully automatic including your inventory and accounting information.

The "Video Vendor" advantages are: 1. no labour costs; 2. minimal rental expense (only 16 square feet are required) and your overhead is less than $2.00 per hour . . . . The opportunity to enter the video business has never been more affordable. With "Video Vendor" you can compete with any video store at less than 10 percent of store cost.

A list of the "Video Vendor" service functions is included in *Exhibit 3*, while a picture of the "Video Vendor" machine appears in *Exhibit 4* and one store location appears in *Exhibit 5*. The machine had been developed in the United States by a company located in Skokie, Illinois. Video Vista president David Cranston had discovered the "Video Vendor" when he attended a video convention in Chicago during June of 1985. Acting on his business judgment, Cranston acquired the exclusive Canadian rights to distribute the machine.

The machine was eight feet long. Behind two locked bulletproof plastic doors, there were slots for 320 movies (40 per shelf for 8 shelves). Although Beta and VHS tapes were different sizes, both could be accommodated in the "Video Vendor". At the right hand side, one could find the nerve center of the machine. Special computer hardware operated the machine.

Infrared sensors detected when someone approached the machine and a message appeared on a computer screen. The "Video Vendor" operated in the same manner as an automated banking machine. A credit card (Mastercard, Visa or one issued by the store) was passed through a reader. From the magnetic strip on the back of the card, the customer's name and account number was recorded. A maximum of 5,000 accounts could be handled by one "Video Vendor" machine. The account number was checked for unreturned tapes or unpaid charges. If any existed, a client could not check out any new tapes. Otherwise, the customer was free to make up to two movie selections.

Before processing the selections, the customer needed to deposit cash. The machine would accept $1, $2, and $5 bills. Any overpayments would be credited to the person's account. A robotic arm would then pick the cassette from the shelf and take it to a receptacle that the customer had access to. The next day, when the tape was returned, the robotic hand could "read" the label and return the tape to the shelf. The microcomputer would then credit the return to the person's account. The "Video Vendor" was not capable of VCR rental yet.

Although the machine had "adult" video cassettes, only people over nineteen were allowed to rent them. (People had to be over nineteen to have a credit card or to join the company's adult video club.) Cranston indicated that over 60 percent of video cassettes were rented by children who were encouraged to get a video club card. Children as young as 9 years had membership cards and operated the machine.

EXHIBIT 3

"Video Vendor" Service Functions

WHEN THE CASH DOOR IS OPENED THIS MENU APPEARS:

SERVICE MODE

1. Bookkeeping	7. Tape prices	13. Early Timer	19. Store Code
2. Show Totals	8. Extra Day Charge	14. Customer/Tape	20. Set Clock
3. Add Credits	9. Lock Out Tape	15. Horiz. Count	21. Title Editor
4. Add Debits	10. Price List	16. Vert. Count	22. Switch Test
5. Add Customer	11. Lock Out List	17. Access Count	23. Disk I/O
6. Delete Customer	12. Customer List	18. Area Code	24. Return Tape

Amplification of Above Menu

1. BOOKKEEPING

A tape is printed with all the movies listed and how many times they were rented and the last date they were rented. The customer who has, or had, the tape last is also printed, and, the status of that tape—in, out or lock (see 9 lock out tape). Total rentals for the period are printed at the bottom of this list.

The second part of bookkeeping prints out all customers who do not have a zero balance, and the last date a movie was rented by that customer. Credit and the debit columns are both totaled.

The third part of bookkeeping would only be printed if you have studio releases in your machine. This list identifies all these special movies and how many times each has been rented.

The fourth part is the bookkeeping totals.

Total customers. Total sales is printed (this cannot be reset). Total service credits given this period. Last service date.

Note: "This period" refers to the last date this program was run. When completed, memory is cleared of totals except for the total sales.

2. SHOW TOTALS

This lists the following totals to the screen. Total customer. Total sales. Total movies rented this period. Total service credits given this period. Total sales this period.

3. ADD CREDITS

This allows you to add credits to a customer's account. ($2.00 would be entered as 200)

4. ADD DEBITS

This allows you to debit a customer's account. ($2.00 would be entered as 200)

5. ADD CUSTOMERS

This allows you to add customers. There are 3 ways to add account numbers.

a. Add all 5000 random accounts by entering 5000.

b. Add any specific number of random accounts by entering any number between 1 and 4999 (the number of accounts you actually want).

c. Add any specific account number by entering the 8 digit number.

6. DELETE CUSTOMERS

This allows you to delete customers. Simply enter the customer's assigned account number.

7. TAPE PRICES

You can set an individual price for every tape in the machine. This price can only be in increments of a quarter. If no specific prices are set, prices default to $2.00.

8. EXTRA DAY CHARGE

The price you charge for extra days can be changed. If no specific price is set, the default price is $2.00.

EXHIBIT 3 (continued)

9. **LOCK OUT TAPE**
   This allows you to lock out a specific tape location from being rentable.

10. **PRICE LIST**
    Will print out all movies and their prices.

11. **LOCK OUT LIST**
    This prints out a list of all locked out locations.

12. **CUSTOMER LIST**
    This prints out a list of all active account numbers being used.

13. **EARLY TIMER**
    The amount of time you have to return a movie for full credit can be adjusted. If no specific time is set the default time is 15 minutes.

14. **CUSTOMER TAPE**
    You can look up the records of a particular customer or tape.

15. **HORIZONTAL COUNT**
    This is where you adjust the dimension from home position to the first shelf from the bottom.

16. **VERTICAL COUNT**
    This is where you adjust the dimension from home to the first division on the right.

17. **ACCESS COUNT**
    This is where you adjust the dimension from home to access door.
    Note: The dimension is displayed as pulses and a pulse is equal to approximately .0014 inches.

18. **AREA CODE**
    This is where you set up the first 3 digits of the 14-digit account number. (For the machine code.)

19. **STORE CODE**
    This is the next 3 digits of the account number.

20. **SET CLOCK**
    This allows you to set the time and the date.

21. **TITLE EDITOR**
    This allows you to change the title lines on the receipt.

22. **SWITCH TEST**
    This is a service function in which the switches can be manually tested with the results displayed on the monitor.

23. **DISK I/O**
    This allows you to initialize, format, and copy disks to and from the bubble memory unit.

24. **RETURN TAPE**
    This allows you to change the records in memory to read that a tape has returned, without going thru the actual return procedure. (This is used when a customer who has a tape out has been deleted.)

    During power up, diagnostic tests are performed on the electronics and if any problems are encountered they are displayed on the monitor.

25. **CREDIT CARD READER**
    Can be programmed to accept your own magnetically encoded membership card as well as any major credit card to identify user and obtain a security deposit. All movie rental fees are paid by cash.

EXHIBIT 4
The ''Video Vendor''

EXHIBIT 5
A Typical Store Location

Along with the promotional material, Susan received some financial data which is presented below.

Initial cash investment per machine	$10,000
Government backed Small Business Loan arranged through a bank using the Video Vendor as security	$23,000
Total Investment	$33,000

This money would be invested as follows:

Purchase of one "Video Vendor" automatic vending machine	$22,828*
Purchase of 160 movies:	
40 new releases @ $80 each	$3,200
30 adult releases @ $40 each	1,200
60 used releases @ $30 each	1,800
30 kids releases @ $20 each	600
	6,800

*If someone wished to purchase 5 or more machines, the price declined to $20,000 per machine.

Opening Expenses	1,850
Cash on hand	1,522
Total Expenditures	$33,000

Operating expenses were also given:

	Opening Month	Subsequent Months
Loan Repayment (over 36 months)	$750	$750
Location Rent	200	200
Labels for new releases	0	180
Machine Service Contract	0	106
Machine Insurance	106	106
Advertising	400	100
Printing	300	0
New Movies	0	3200
Miscellaneous	94	58
Total monthly expenses	$1850	$4700

To give some idea about potential revenues the following chart was provided:

Rentals per Day	At $2.00 Each	At $3.00 Each	At $4.00 Each
10	$600	$900	$1200
20	$1200	$1800	$2400
30	$1800	$2700	$3600
40	$2400	$3600	$4800
50	$3000	$4500	$6000
60	$3600	$5400	$7200
75	$4500	$6750	$9000
100	$6000	$9000	$12000

Revenues are for a 30 day month. To calculate any number in chart use the following formula: 30 × Rentals per day × Rental charge per movie.

Susan talked with some of the customers of the "Video Vendor" to find out their reaction to the machine. Susan felt that the most popular movie titles were overpriced at $4.00, yet no customer complained about the price. Instead, the most frequently heard complaint was that there were not enough "good" movies available for rent. The other major area of complaint concerned the machine itself. If the machine jammed, no one could rent or return a movie. This was very inconvenient as it meant people had to go away and return at a later time. As well, the machine sometimes "ate" the customer's money and either gave them no credit for putting money into the machine or gave them credit for the wrong amount.

The most popular feature was the twenty-four hour availability of the machine. For people who worked, most stores were closed by the time they had decided to rent a tape. As well, many people used the machine as it was one of the few sources of Beta format movies. Only people with a VCR could use the machine as it did not rent cassette players.

THE COMPETITION

Susan faced increased competition from a Mac's Milk Convenience Store just down the street. This store carried video cassettes but she had heard that Mac's was test marketing a different type of video vending machine in Oakville and, based on that test, Mac's might be introducing the machines throughout Ontario.

The vending machine they were considering was manufactured by Videovend Box Office Limited in Toronto. Resembling a soft drink vending machine in size, the Videovend product was quite different. The machine operated only with a credit card. All rentals were charged to a customer's account —no cash had to be put into the machine.

The machine held 105 titles and carried a VHS and Beta copy of each. When renting a movie for $2.99, one had a $125 purchase option. If someone did not return a title within a week, they were simply billed for the purchase price plus seven days' rental. Across the top of the machine, three rows of videocassette box fronts were on display. This gave more information about the movie than the title along could convey.

The 105 titles (3 rows of 35 titles each) rotated automatically to show the machine's contents. Once one was ready to make a choice, one could manually cause the display to move and indicate a choice. If the choice was available for rent, the cassette would be chosen and deposited into a drop box and a receipt issued. Otherwise the machine would indicate that the selection was unavailable. Because of the metal casing, one could not see how the machine operated inside.

In talking with the Mac's clerk, Susan was told that the store and the head office had been impressed with the performance of the vending machine. Because a clerk was on duty 24 hours a day, any jam in the machine could be taken care of immediately. There were only two drawbacks. Only 35 percent of the population carried a valid Visa or MasterCard. Mac's was eliminating a lot of customers this way. Second, each credit card transaction required a computer call to the credit card company's head office for validation. Each call cost $0.22.

CONCLUSION

Susan realized that the purchase of a "Video Vendor" could have both positive and negative consequences on her business. By installing a credit card access door, placing the "Video Vendor" in the front of her store and installing some sliding doors to secure the other part of her store, Susan would be able to serve her customers 24 hours a day and that should help recoup some of the lost business. As well, not all the expenses listed in the "Video Vendor" prospectus would apply to her. She also felt that she could recoup 30 percent of the tape purchase cost by re-selling videotapes 60 to 90 days after purchase.

On the other hand, she would cannibalize much of her present video cassette rental business. She would also have to remodel the front of her store to accommodate the "Video Vendor." She also realized that this machine was a step-up in technology and she might have some problems with it. Yet those problems might not be that much different from training new employees. She even wondered if she should eliminate the other aspects of her business and concentrate solely on the "Video Vendor".

A recent article she had read in the Financial Post contained an interview with Dalton McArthur, president of Canada's largest video cassette distributor. McArthur declared that the new automatic vending machines had good potential but cautioned: "It is one thing for them to work in a factory but another for them to work in the field. I think they have some use on the ground floor of a major department store. But I don't think they will replace specialty stores. There will always be a place for the video specialty store with personal service."

As a final complicating factor, Susan feared that the Mac's convenience store down the street was contemplating the introduction of a video vending machine. If they introduced one while she did not they would further erode her business. Yet, if both Susan and the variety store had a video vending machine, Susan would gain no competitive edge.

PART IV
Managing Capacity
and Managing Demand

Strategies for Managing Capacity-Constrained Service Organizations

CHRISTOPHER H. LOVELOCK

A major problem facing managers of capacity-constrained service organizations is how to balance demand against available capacity. Unlike manufacturing firms, service organizations cannot rely on inventories of finished products to act as a buffer between a constrained level of supply and a fluctuating level of demand. Opportunities may exist to manage both capacity and demand.

One important characteristic that distinguishes service organizations from manufacturing firms is the former's inability to inventory finished products. In the manufacturing sector, imbalances between supply and demand are usually irregular and temporary phenomena, since inventories can generally be employed as a buffer between the two. It is only during periods of resource shortages that marketers of physical goods need to develop strategies for dealing with scarcity (Kotler and Balachandran, 1975; Monroe and Zoltners, 1979).

The lack of inventories of finished services is not a problem for all service businesses. However, it raises significant issues for management in capacity-constrained service organizations that regularly face significant variations in demand levels. This happens in such important industries as transportation, lodging, food service, repair and maintenance, entertainment, and health care, and in many professional and commercial services. Financial success in these industries is, in large measure, a function of management's ability to use productive capacity—staff, labor, equipment, and facilities—as efficiently and as profitably as possible. When demand is low, productive capacity is wasted, since a service business

Adapted from an article by the author in *Service Industries Journal*, November 1984, by permission of Frank Cass & Co. Ltd., publishers.

cannot normally store its product as inventory; and when demand is so high that it exceeds the organization's ability to meet it, potential business is likely to be lost.

One solution to the demand problem, which falls within the province of operations, is to tailor *capacity* to meet variations in demand (Sasser, 1976). Another solution which should logically be entrusted to marketing is modifying *demand* to match available capacity. (Many service organizations, of course, seek to manage both demand and capacity.)

STRATEGIES FOR MANAGING CAPACITY

Two basic alternatives present themselves in capacity management. The first is a strategy of *level capacity* in which the same amount of capacity continues to be offered, regardless of variations in demand. The second is a *chase demand* strategy under which the amount of capacity is varied in response to changes in the level of demand.

As noted earlier, productive capacity is composed of several elements, typically including labor (management, professionals, and other employees), physical facilities (buildings and land), and equipment used in creating and delivering the service. The type of physical elements used varies widely according to the nature of the service, but is often divided into discrete elements such as rooms (as in a hotel, college, or hospital), seats (in a restaurant, theater, aircraft, or train), and equipment (such as automatic teller machines or repair tools).

By flowcharting the process of service creation and delivery, managers can determine what productive elements are involved at each stage in the process—in both the front and back offices. Such analysis often identifies potential bottlenecks, representing steps that have a lower capacity than those which precede or follow them. Increasing capacity to serve higher levels of demand may require simply adding personnel or equipment (or both) at a specific bottleneck, as opposed to increasing capacity at every stage in the process.

Sasser (1976) and Fitzsimmons and Sullivan (1982) suggest several actions that managers can take to adjust capacity to match fluctuating levels of demand:

1. *Schedule downtime during periods of low demand.* To ensure that 100 percent of capacity is available during peak periods, scheduled repair and maintenance activities should be conducted when demand is expected to be low. Employee vacations should also be taken during such periods.

2. *Using part-time employees.* Many service businesses hire extra workers during their busiest periods. Examples include postal workers and store clerks at Christmas time, extra lifeguards during summer weekends, and additional hotel employees during vacation periods.

3. *Renting or sharing extra facilities and equipment.* To avoid over-investment in fixed assets, a service organization may be able to rent extra space or machines at peak times. Sometimes service firms with complementary demand patterns enter into formal sharing agreements.

4. *Cross-training of employees.* Even when the service delivery system appears to be operating at full capacity, certain elements—and their attendant employees—may be underutilized. If employees can be cross-trained to perform a variety of tasks, they can be shifted to bottleneck points as needed, thereby increasing total system capacity. In supermarkets, for instance, the manager may call upon stockers to operate cash registers when checkout lines start to get too long. Likewise, during slow periods, the cashiers may be asked to help stock shelves.

Whether a service organization pursues a strategy of level capacity or elects to chase demand, its managers need to understand and forecast the forces determining demand. It also helps to be able to identify opportunities for smoothing out the peaks and valleys of demand through active management of demand.

UNDERSTANDING THE PATTERNS AND DETERMINANTS OF DEMAND

The search for demand management strategies should start with an understanding of what factors govern demand for a specific service at a given point in time. Managers should address the following questions:

I. Does the level of demand for the service follow a regular *predictable* cycle?
   A. If so, is the duration of that cycle:
      1. One day (varies by hour).
      2. One week (varies by day).
      3. One month (varies by day or by week).
      4. One year (varies by month or by season; or reflects annually occurring public holidays).
      5. Some other period.
   B. What are the underlying causes of these demand variations?
      1. Employment schedules.
      2. Billing and tax payment/refund cycles.
      3. Wage and salary payment dates.
      4. School hours and vacations.
      5. Seasonal changes in climate.
      6. Occurrence of public holidays and so forth.

II. Are changes in the level of demand largely random in nature? If so, what are the underlying causes?
   A. Day-to-day changes in the weather affecting relative use of indoor and outdoor recreational or entertainment services.
   B. Health events whose occurrence cannot be pinpointed exactly (for example, heart attacks and births affecting the demand for hospital services).
   C. Calls for assistance resulting from accidents, acts of nature, and certain criminal activities requiring fast response by emergency services.

III. Can demand for a particular service over time be disaggregated by market segment to reflect such components as:
   A. Use patterns by a particular type of customer or for a particular purpose;
   B. Variations in the net profitability of each completed transaction?

Disaggregating Demand by Market Segment

Generally, marketing efforts can do little to smooth out *random* fluctuations in demand over time, since these are usually caused by factors beyond the service organization's control. However, detailed market analysis may sometimes reveal that a predictable demand cycle for one segment is concealed within a broader, seemingly random pattern, and can thus be addressed by marketing strategies. For instance, a repair and maintenance shop may know that a certain proportion of its work consists of regularly scheduled contractual business, representing routine preventive maintenance. The balance may come from "walk-in" business and emergency repairs, and it may be hard to predict or control the timing and volume of such work.

The ease with which total demand can be disaggregated depends on the nature of the records kept by the service organization. If each customer transaction is recorded separately, and backed up by detailed notes (as in a hospital visit or accountant's audit), then the task of understanding demand is greatly simplified. For subscription services, where each customer receives itemized monthly bills, managers can gain some immediate insights into usage patterns. If the identity of the subscriber is known, consumption of the service can be related to type of user (household versus commercial or industrial), geographic location, and total usage volume. Some services—such as telephone—even have the ability to track subscriber consumption patterns by time of day. Although these data may not always yield specific information on the purpose for which the service is being used, it is often possible to make informed judgments about the volume of sales generated by different user groups. Similarly, if there are variations in the prices charged to different customers (and/or the costs incurred in serving them), then managers can assess the relative profitability of serving various customer segments.

Analysis may also show that part of the demand for a particular service is undesirable—for instance, calls to emergency services to rescue cats from trees. Demand that represents a poor fit with institutional goals may constitute a special problem for public and nonprofit organizations which define their missions in nonfinancial terms. Although discouraging undesirable demand through marketing campaigns or screening procedures will not eliminate random fluctuations in the remaining demand, it may bring the peaks of that demand within the service capacity of the organization.

When demand for a service fluctuates widely but follows a predictable pattern over a known cycle, it may be economically worthwhile to develop marketing strategies designed to smooth out major fluctuations over time. However, no strategy is likely to succeed unless it is based on an understanding of *why* customers from a specific market segment choose to use the service when they do. For example, most hotels find it difficult to convince business travelers to remain on Saturday nights, since few executives do business over the weekend. Instead, hotel managers should consider promoting use of their facilities for other purposes at weekends, such as conferences or pleasure travel. Similarly, attempts to get commuters on public transport to shift their travel to off-peak periods will probably fail, since the timing of most commuter travel is determined by people's employment hours. Instead, marketing efforts should be directed at employers to persuade them to adopt flexitime or staggered working hours (Lovelock and Young, 1979).

STRATEGIES FOR MANAGING DEMAND

At any given point in time, a fixed-capacity service organization may be faced with one of four conditions:

1. Demand exceeds maximum available capacity with the result that potential business may be lost.
2. Demand exceeds the optimum capacity level; no one is turned away, but all customers are likely to perceive a deterioration in the quality of service delivered.
3. Demand and supply are well balanced at the level of optimum capacity.
4. Demand is below optimum capacity and productive resources are under-utilized; this poses the risk (in some instances) that customers may find the experience disappointing or have doubts about the viability of the service.

Note the distinction between *maximum available* capacity and *optimum* capacity. When demand exceeds maximum capacity, some potential customers may be disappointed because they are turned away—and their business may be lost forever. However, when demand is operating between optimum and maximum capacity, there is a risk that all customers being served at that time may receive inferior service and thus become dissatisfied.

The optimum level of capacity is likely to vary from one service business to another and even from one market segment to another. Sometimes optimum and maximum capacities are the same. For instance, at a live performance in a theater or sports arena, a full house is generally regarded as very desirable, since it stimulates the players and creates a sense of excitement and audience participation, thereby enhancing the service experience. In other cases, however, customers may feel that they get better service if the facility is not operating at full capacity. The quality of restaurant service, for instance, often deteriorates when every table is occupied. Passengers traveling alone in aircraft with high-density seating usually feel more comfortable if the seat adjacent to them is empty. When repair and maintenance shops are fully scheduled, delays may result if there is no slack in the system to allow for coping with unexpected difficulties in completing particular jobs. Hence, smoothing demand to the optimal level may be a desirable goal even for service organizations that rarely encounter demand in excess of maximum available capacity.

Optimizing the use of capacity requires looking at the *mix* of business obtained as well as the total volume. Some market segments may be more desirable than others because the customers fit particularly well with the organization's mission, reinforce the ambience that the service organization is trying to create, have needs that match the professional skills and interests of staff members, or pay higher rates and are more profitable. Marketing managers should examine the components of overall demand and seek to stimulate or discourage demand from particular segments on a selective basis.

Five common approaches to managing demand can be identified. The first, which

TABLE 1
Alternative Demand Management Strategies for Different Capacity Situations

Approach Used to Manage Demand	Capacity Situation Relative to Demand		
	Insufficient Capacity (Excess Demand)	Sufficient Capacity* (Satisfactory Demand)	Excess Capacity (Insufficient Demand)
Take no action	Unorganized queuing results. (May irritate customers and discourage future use.)	Capacity is fully utilized. (But is this the most profitable mix of business?)	Capacity is wasted. (Customers may have a disappointing experience for services like theater.)
Reduce demand	Pricing higher will increase profits. Communication can be employed to encourage usage in other time slots. (Can this effort be focused on less profitable/desirable segments?)	Take no action (but see above).	Take no action (but see above).
Increase demand	Take no action (unless opportunities exist to stimulate (and give priority to) more profitable segments.	Take no action (unless opportunities exist to stimulate (and give priority to) more profitable segments.	Price lower selectively (try to avoid cannibalizing existing business; ensure all relevant costs are covered). Use communications and variation in products/distribution (but recognize extra costs, if any, and make sure appropriate trade-offs are made between profitability and usage levels).
Inventory demand by reservation system	Consider priority system for most desirable segments. Make other customers shift (a) outside peak period or (b) to future peak.	Try to ensure most profitable mix of business.	Clarify that space is available and that no reservations are needed.
Inventory demand by formalized queuing	Consider override for most desirable segments. Seek to keep waiting customers occupied and comfortable. Try to predict wait period accurately.	Try to avoid bottleneck delays.	Not applicable.

*"Sufficient capacity" may be defined as *maximum available capacity* or *optimum capacity*, depending on the situation.

usually reflects the absence of any strategy, involves taking no action and *leaving demand to find its own levels*. This approach does have the virtue of simplicity; eventually customers may learn from experience or word-of-mouth when they can expect to stand in line to use the service and when it will be available without delay. The second and third strategies involve *managing demand*: taking active steps to reduce demand in peak periods and to increase it when demand is low, respectively. The fourth and fifth approaches involve *inventorying demand*. This objective can be accomplished either by introducing a *reservations system* or by adopting a *formalized queuing system* (or by a combination of the two).

Table 1 links these five approaches to three alternative demand/capacity situations and offers a strategic commentary on each of the 15 resulting cells. To achieve the best results over the duration of the demand cycle, service organizations should consider using a combination of two or more of the options described.

Managing Demand

The *product demand cycle* is the periodic cycle influencing demand for a particular service; it may vary in length from one day to 12 months. In many instances, multiple cycles may operate simultaneously. For example, demand levels for public transport may vary by time of day, day of week, and season of year. The demand for service during the peak period on a Monday in summer may be different from the level during the peak period on a Saturday in winter, reflecting day-of-week and seasonal variations jointly.

Many permutations may exist. For instance, two time-of-day periods (peak and off-peak), two day-of-week periods (weekday and weekend), and three seasonal periods (peak, shoulder, and off-peak) can be combined to create 12 different demand periods. In theory, each of these periods might have its own distinct demand level (at a particular price) and customer profiles. By careful analysis of both the demand level and the mix of business in each demand period, a manager can determine whether there are close similarities between any of the demand periods. This would make it possible to collapse the framework into clusters of cells, with each cluster receiving a distinct marketing treatment in order to optimize use of available capacity and achieve the most desirable customer mix. During the 1960s, the Canadian National Railway developed such an approach for pricing its passenger services. The entire year was divided into 162 "red" (or bargain) days, 143 "white" (or economy) days, and 60 "blue" (or standard) days—essentially representing dates on which rail travel was in low, average, or high demand—with prices being set accordingly and communication efforts publicizing the dates through the use of an eye-catching red, white, and blue calendar (Harvard Business School, 1966).

Inventorying Demand for a Service

Service businesses, for the most part, can rarely inventory supply, but they can often inventory demand.[1] This can be done by asking customers to wait in line on a first-come, first-served basis (queuing), or by offering them the opportunity of reserving space in advance.

A marketing approach to queuing involves determining the maximum amount of time that people will wait for service and then finding ways to make this time pass quickly and pleasantly. Strategies for accomplishing this include agreeable surroundings (for example, a comfortable temperature, a seat, and restful music), taking preliminary information from the customer, disseminating advance information on the service, promoting other products offered by the organization, or offering supplementary services (for example, entertainment, reading materials, or food and drink).

Market segmentation may sometimes be used in designing queuing strategies so that certain users of the service obtain a higher priority than others. This may be based on the importance of the customer (or the job), how long it will take to provide service (with "express lanes" for shorter jobs), or faster service in return for a premium price.

Usually goods that require servicing can be kept in a waiting line longer than people can. But sometimes their owners do not wish to be parted from them for long. Households with only one car, for example, or factories with a vital piece of equipment often cannot afford to be without such items for more than a day or two. So a reservations system may be necessary for service businesses in fields such as repair and maintenance. By requiring reservations for routine maintenance, management can keep time free for handling emergency jobs at premium

---

[1]Inventorying the supply of a service is usually only possible for repair and maintenance services involving homogeneous, interchangeable goods. For instance, an industrial service shop may handle large numbers of identical electric motors. Regular customers who bring in such a motor for repair can be given a substitute motor, already serviced and sitting on the shelf, then billed subsequently for the work on their own motor, which will be offered later to another customer bringing in a similar piece of equipment at some future point in time.

prices which yield a much higher contribution margin.

Taking reservations serves to pre-sell the service. In theory, it benefits customers by avoiding the need for queuing and, to help the service firm balance capacity, guaranteeing service availability at a specific time. Demand can be deflected from a first-choice time to earlier or later times, and even from first-choice locations to alternative locations. However, problems arise when customers fail to show up or when service firms over-book. Marketing strategies for dealing with these operational problems include requiring an advance fee for all reservations (not always feasible), cancelling nonpaid reservations after a certain time, and providing compensation to victims of overbooking.

ASSET REVENUE GENERATING EFFICIENCY

Ideally, capacity-constrained service firms would like to be operating at a high level of capacity (which, as discussed earlier, may or may not be 100 percent of available capacity) at all times outside scheduled downtime periods. Many capacity-constrained service organizations use percentage of capacity sold as a measure of operational efficiency. For instance, transport services talk of the "load factor" achieved, hotels of their "occupancy rate," and hospitals of their "census." Similarly, professional firms can calculate the proportion of a partner's or an employee's time classified as billable hours, and repair shops can look at utilization of both equipment and labor. However, by themselves, these percentage figures tell us little of the relative profitability of the business attracted, since high utilization rates may be obtained at the expense of heavy discounting.

What is needed, then, is a measure of the extent to which the organization's assets are achieving their full revenue-generating potential. This must take into account the relationship between the average price actually obtained per unit of service and the maximum price that might potentially have been charged—what might be termed the unit price efficiency rate. By multiplying the capacity utilization rate by the unit price efficiency rate, we can derive an index of *asset revenue-generating efficiency* (ARGE). Consider, for example, a 200-room hotel where all rooms carry a maximum posted price of $100. If only 60 percent of rooms is occupied one night, with 60 rooms being sold at $100 and another 60 at $60, then the average unit price efficiency rate is 80 percent and the ARGE is $(0.6 \times 0.8) = 48$ percent. Another way to arrive at the ARGE is to divide total revenues received ($9,600) by the theoretical maximum revenues that could have been obtained by selling all rooms at the highest unit price ($20,000).

Improving Advance Sales Decisions

The value of the ARGE approach to performance measurement is that it forces explicit recognition of the opportunity cost of accepting business from one segment when another might subsequently yield a higher rate. Consider the following problems facing sales managers for different types of capacity-constrained service organizations:

1. Should a hotel accept an advance booking from a tour group of 200 room-nights at $60 each when these same room-nights might possibly be sold later at short notice to business travellers at the full rate of $100?
2. Should a railway with 30 empty freight cars at its disposal accept an immediate request for a shipment worth $300 per car or hold the cars idle for a few more days in the hope of getting a priority shipment that would be twice as valuable?
3. How many seats on a particular flight should an airline sell in advance to tour groups and passengers traveling at special excursion rates?
4. Should an industrial repair and maintenance shop reserve a certain proportion of productive capacity each day for emergency repair jobs that offer a high contribution margin and the potential to build long-term customer loyalty, or should it simply follow a strategy of making sure that there are sufficient jobs, mostly involving routine maintenance, to keep its employees fully occupied?

5. Should a computer service bureau process all jobs on a first-come first-served basis, with a guaranteed delivery time for each job, or should it charge a premium rate for "rush" work, and tell customers with "standard" jobs to expect some variability in completion dates?

Good market information supported by good marketing sense is the key to making appropriate decisions in such instances. The decision to accept or reject business should represent a realistic estimate of the probabilities of obtaining the higher rated business, together with a recognition of any incremental costs involved.

Based upon past experience and an understanding of current market conditions, prices can be set that reflect the demand curves of different market segments. At the same time, "selective sell" targets can be assigned to advertising and sales personnel, reflecting how management expects to allocate available capacity among different market segments *at a specific point in time*. These allocation decisions by segment also constitute vital information for reservations personnel, indicating when to stop accepting reservations from certain segments. To simplify the task, customers from different segments can be assigned different telephone numbers or mailing addresses for making reservations.

Allocating Capacity Over Time by Service Class

Service organizations often offer different classes of a particular service, with the premium version containing added value elements such as more comfort, more speed, and extra amenities. Marketers of multiclass services often develop a framework for establishing pricing policy and capacity allocation decisions by both service class and time period. Figure 1 shows a hypothetical example in which three service classes—top-of-the-line, standard, and budget—have been combined with four time periods—peak, first shoulder, off-peak, and second shoulder—to form 12 cells, each of which may require a distinctive marketing approach. The size

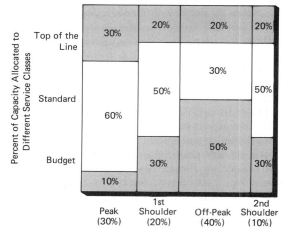

FIGURE 1
An Example of Capacity Allocation

Percent of Capacity Allocated to Different Time Periods Within the Product Demand Cycle

of each cell reflects the percentage of total capacity allocated to it over the duration of the product demand cycle (in this case, one year). For instance, top-of-the-line/peak has been assigned 9 percent (30 percent × 30 percent) of total annual capacity. Clearly, accurate demand forecasting and understanding of customer behavior are important to this assignment process. Fine tuning can be achieved by monitoring results and changing capacity allocations, prices, and other marketing actions for future demand cycles.

This type of exercise may need to be performed separately for each operating unit (for example, each service facility in a chain of repair shops or each corridor in a transportation system). Relevant criteria include strength of market demand, competitive price levels, quality of product relative to the competition, and variations in cost structure. Alternatively, individual units can be clustered into similar groups (for example, hotel units located at airports versus hotels located in central business districts) for the purpose of establishing appropriate marketing programs. The challenge is to be responsive to individual market situations but to avoid creating a pricing scheme so complex that it confuses customers, intermediaries, and service personnel alike (as many airline pricing schemes are alleged to do).

In order to ensure that profitability goals are met, the marketer must not only set an appropriate price but also understand the variable cost per sales unit, such as a seat, a room, or a specific repair task. This cost is likely to vary by service class when extra value is added by providing extra service, such as more floor space, more personal attention, or use of superior equipment. In some instances, however, as in theaters with identical seat sizes, the extra value to customers is created by better locations, and no extra costs are incurred by the marketer. Additionally, a decision must be made on how to allocate fixed costs among the different cells. When the marketer would like to price close to variable cost in order to stimulate off-peak demand for budget-class service, it may be appropriate to allocate no fixed costs to that cell at all. (However, all fixed costs must be allocated and recovered *somewhere* within the matrix!) The final issue is to recognize that 100 percent utilization of the assigned capacity within each cell may not be achieved. Hence, cost allocations per sales unit must reflect the anticipated utilization rate in each cell. Again, this places a premium on accurate forecasting.

MODIFYING MARKETING MIX ELEMENTS TO MANAGE DEMAND

All the elements of the marketing mix have a role to play in stimulating demands during periods of excess capacity and in decreasing it (demarketing) during periods of insufficient capacity.

Price is often the first variable to be proposed for bringing demand and supply into balance, but product and distribution modifications and communication efforts can also play an important role. The relative effectiveness of each depends both on the underlying causes of demand variations and on the nature of the demand cycle. Although each element is discussed separately below, effective demand management efforts often require changes in two or more elements jointly.

Product Variations

Although pricing is the most commonly advocated method of balancing supply and demand, it is not quite as universally feasible for services as for goods. A rather obvious example is provided by the respective problems of a ski manufacturer and a ski slope operator during the summer. The former can either produce for inventory or try to sell skis in the summer at a discount. If the skis are sufficiently discounted, some customers will buy before the ski season in order to save money. However, no skiers would buy ski lift tickets for use on a midsummer day at *any* price. To encourage summer use of the lifts, the operator has to change the product by installing an alpine slide or by promoting the view at the summit. Solutions of a similar nature have been adopted by tax preparation firms that now offer bookkeeping and consulting services to small businesses in slack months, and by landscaping firms in many parts of the U.S. and Canada that seek snow removal contracts in the winter. These firms recognize that no amount of price discounting is likely to develop business out of season.

Although many service offerings remain unchanged throughout the year, others undergo significant modifications according to the season. Hospitals, for example, tend to offer the same array of services throughout the year. By contrast, resort hotels sharply alter the mix and focus of their peripheral services such as dining, entertainment, and sports to reflect customer preference in different seasons.

There can be variations in the product offering even during the course of a 24-hour period. Restaurants provide a good example, marking the passage of the hours with changing menus and levels of service, variations in lighting and decor, opening and closing of the bar, and presence or absence of entertainment. The objective may be to appeal to different needs within the same group of customers, to reach out to different customer segments, or to do both, according to the time of day.

Different versions of the same service can also be offered simultaneously in response to variations in customer preferences and ability to pay. For example, airlines offer first-class, business-class, and tourist-class service; hotels have different room and service categories; and theaters and concert halls offer different seating categories. To reflect variations in demand among different customer groups over the course of the product demand cycle, some service marketers vary the mix of capacity allocated to the different product categories (for example, by adding or removing first-class seats from an airliner). But when the capacity mix is fixed—as it is in hotels and concert halls—changes in category allocations are tantamount to price increases or decreases (for example, when hotels charge only the price of a regular room for a suite).

Another form of product variation reflects the customer's need for speedy service. Examples include different priority classes for surgery, airfreight service, printing, and computer processing. Higher-priority classes have first claim to the limited productive capacity available.

Variations in Distribution

Rather than seeking to modify demand for a service that continues to be offered at the same time in the same place, it may be worthwhile to respond to market needs by modifying the time and place of delivery.

Four basic options are available. The first option represents a strategy of no change: regardless of the level of demand, the service continues to be offered in the same location at the same times. By contrast, the second strategy involves varying the times when the service is available to reflect changes in customer preference by day of week, by season, and so forth. For instance, theaters often offer matinees over the weekend when people are free during the day as well as in the evening; during the summer in hot climates, banks may close for two hours at midday while people take a siesta, but remain open later in the evening when other commercial establishments are still active.

The third strategy involves offering the service to customers at a new location. One approach is to establish mobile units that will take the service to customers, rather than requiring them to visit fixed-site service locations, as an inducement to use. Mobile libraries and vans equipped with primary care medical facilities are two examples that might be emulated by other service businesses. A cleaning and repair firm that wishes to generate business during low-demand periods could offer free pickup and delivery of movable items that require servicing.

Alternatively, a viable strategy for a service whose productive assets are mobile may be to follow the market when that, too, is mobile. For instance, some car rental services establish seasonal branch offices in resort communities. In these new locations, it may be necessary to change the schedule of service hours (as well as certain product features) to conform with local needs and preferences. This results in a fourth strategy that involves simultaneous variations in both scheduling availability and location. One New England airline, for instance, operates between Boston and Cape Cod in the summer; in the winter, the aircraft and crews move to Florida and operate a different route network and schedule down there.

Pricing

For price to be effective as a demand management tool, the marketing manager must have some sense of the shape and slope of a product's demand curve (that is, how the quantity of service demanded responds to increases or decreases in the price per unit) *at a particular point in time*. It is important to determine whether the aggregate demand curve for a specific service varies sharply from one time period to another. If so, significantly different pricing schemes may be needed to fill capacity in each time period.

To complicate matters further, there may be separate demand curves for different segments *within* each time period, reflecting variations in the need for the service or ability to pay between various customer groupings.

One of the most difficult tasks facing service marketers is to determine the nature of all these different demand curves. Research, trial and error, and analysis of parallel situations in other locations or in comparable services are all ways of obtaining an understanding of the situation. This information is needed not only for demand management purposes, but also to maximize profits in service businesses (or to optimize the social value of a public or nonprofit service).

Many service businesses explicitly recognize the existence of different demand curves for different segments during the same period by establishing distinct classes of service, each priced at levels appropriate to the demand curve of a particular segment. In essence, each segment receives a variation of the basic product, with value being added to the core service in order to appeal to the higher-paying segments. For instance, top-of-the-line service in airlines offers travelers larger seats, free drinks, and better food; in computer service bureaus, product enhancement takes the form of faster turnaround and more specialized analytical procedures and reports.

In each case, the objective is to maximize the revenues received from each segment. However, when capacity is constrained, the goal in a profit-seeking business should be to ensure that as much capacity as possible is utilized by the most profitable segments. For this reason, various usage conditions may have to be set to discourage customers willing to pay top-of-the-line prices for trading down to less expensive versions of the product. Airlines, for instance, may insist that excursion tickets be purchased 21 days in advance and that the passenger remain at the destination for at least one week before returning—conditions that are too constraining for most business travelers.

Communication Efforts

Even if the other variables of the marketing mix remain unchanged, communication efforts alone may be able to help smooth demand. Signing, advertising, and sales messages can remind prospective customers of the peak periods and encourage them to avoid these in favor of the uncrowded, off-peak times when service is, perhaps, faster or more comfortable. Examples include postal service requests to "Mail Early for Christmas," public transport messages urging noncommuters—such as shoppers or tourists—to avoid the crush conditions of the commuter hours, and communications from sales reps for industrial maintenance firms advising customers of periods when preventive work can be done quickly. In addition, management can ask service personnel—or intermediaries such as travel agents—to encourage customers with discretionary schedules to favor off-peak periods.

If there are changes in pricing, product characteristics, and distribution, it is vital to communicate these clearly to the target markets. Obtaining the desired response to variations in marketing mix elements depends, of course, on fully informing customers about their options.

INFORMATION NEEDS

It is clear that managers in service organizations require substantial information if they are to develop effective demand and capacity management strategies and to monitor subsequent marketplace performance.

The information required includes:

1. Historical data on the level and composition of demand over time, including responses to changes in price or other marketing variables.
2. Forecasts of the level of demand by segments under specified conditions.
3. Ability to distinguish between periodic cycles and random fluctuations in demand on a segment-by-segment basis.
4. Good cost data to enable the organization to distinguish between fixed and variable costs and to determine the relative profitability of incremental unit sales to different segments and at different prices.
5. In multisite organizations, identification of

meaningful variations in the levels and composition of demand on a site-by-site basis.

6. Customer attitudes toward queuing under varying conditions.

7. Customer opinions on whether the quality of service delivered varies with different levels of capacity utilization.

Where might all this information come from? Although some new studies may be required, much of the needed data is probably already being collected within the organization—although not necessarily by marketers. As Little (1979) has noted:

> A stream of information comes into the organization from the world at large in many ways . . . especially from distilling the multitude of individual transactions of the business. . . . The amount of data handled by a large company is staggering. Business runs on numbers. Sales alone have vast detail.

Most service businesses collect detailed information for operational and accounting purposes. Although some do not record details of individual transactions (examples include urban public transportation, cinemas, and sports arenas), a majority can identify specific customers with specific transactions. Unfortunately, the marketing value of these data tends to be overlooked and they are not always stored in ways that permit retrieval and analysis for marketing purposes. Nevertheless, the potential exists to re-format collection and storage of customer transaction data in ways that would provide marketers with some of the information they require, including how existing segments have responded to past changes in marketing variables.

Other information may have to be collected through special studies, such as customer surveys, or reviews of analogous situations. On the other hand, information on competitive performance must be gathered on an ongoing basis, since changes in the capacity or strategy of competitors may require corrective action.

The ultimate goal is to develop a marketing decision support system that organizes the different databases within a service organization and then combines them with models and analytical techniques that can be directed at forecasting demand by segment under alternative assumptions. These projections can then serve as the basis for developing the most appropriate demand and capacity management strategy at specific points in time. Ongoing data collection should quickly reveal whether actual performance met the projections. By monitoring performance in this way, and by evaluating the reasons for significant deviations, management should be able to improve its strategies in the future.

CONCLUSION

Managers of capacity-constrained service organizations often face the problem of balancing demand against available capacity, especially when the level of demand varies sharply over a reasonably predictable time cycle. However, it is not enough just to maintain high levels of utilization. If the organization is to meet its goals, action must be taken to attract the most appropriate type of business at specific times. Such efforts require breaking down existing and potential demand over time and by segment. This analysis will make it possible for management to establish time-based priorities, stating how much demand is sought from various segments at particular points in time. Establishing such objectives allows management to create a precisely scheduled marketing program to attract the most desirable segments at the busiest time, to encourage lower-priority segments to use the service when capacity is more freely available, and to actively discourage use (or misuse) of the service by unwanted segments.

Marketing strategies for managing demand to match capacity include taking steps to increase or decrease demand, as appropriate, or introducing such procedures as reservations and customer-oriented queuing. Each element of the marketing mix has a role to play in helping the service organization make optimum use of its capacity, and often the best results are achieved when several elements are used in conjunction with each other.

The availability of good data for planning and evaluation purposes is central to creation of effective capacity planning and demand management strategies. Many service organizations already collect much of the needed data, but store it in formats that meet the needs of the operations and billing departments, rather than of marketing. An integral part of the shift to a greater marketing orientation in service businesses is reevaluation of current data collection and storage procedures.

Because capacity-constrained service organizations tend to have heavy investments in fixed facilities and equipment, and incur substantial fixed labor costs, even modest improvements in capacity utilization can have a significant effect on the bottom line. Similarly, changes in the mix of business to emphasize the most profitable segments during periods of excess demand can also have an important impact on profits. The service organization that can combine a strong marketing management orientation with the marketing decision support systems needed to develop effective demand management strategies will thus be well placed to achieve—or improve upon—success.

REFERENCES

FITZSIMMONS, JAMES A., and ROBERT S. SULLIVAN, 1982, *Service Operations Management.* New York, McGraw-Hill.

Harvard Business School, 1966, "Canadian National Railways," 9–513–038, Boston: Harvard University, HBS Case Services.

KOTLER, PHILIP, and V. BALACHANDRAN, 1975, "Strategic Remarketing: The Preferred Response to Shortages and Inflation," *Sloan Management Review*, Fall.

LITTLE, JOHN D. C., 1979, "Decision Support Systems for Marketing Managers," *Journal of Marketing*, Summer.

LOVELOCK, CHRISTOPHER H., and ROBERT F. YOUNG, 1979, "Look to Consumers to Increase Productivity," *Harvard Business Review*, May–June.

MONROE, KENT B., and ANDRIS A. ZOLTNERS, 1979, "Pricing the Product Line During Periods of Scarcity," *Journal of Marketing*, **43** Summer.

SASSER, W. EARL JR., 1976, "Match Supply and Demand in Service Industries," *Harvard Business Review*, November–December.

The Psychology of Waiting Lines

DAVID H. MAISTER

Waiting for service is an almost universal phenomenon. This article presents eight propositions about the psychology of queues, each of which offers insights to service organizations seeking to reduce customer dissatisfaction with waiting times.

In one of a series of memorable advertisements for which it has become famous, Federal Express (the overnight package-delivery service) noted that: "Waiting is frustrating, demoralizing, agonizing, aggravating, annoying, time consuming, and incredibly expensive."[1] The truth of this assertion cannot be denied; there can be few consumers of services in a modern society who have not felt, at one time or another, each of the emotions identified by Federal Express's copywriters. What is more, each of us who can

recall such incidents can also attest to the fact that the waiting-line experience in a service facility significantly affected our overall perceptions of the quality of service provided. Once we are being served, our transaction with the service organization might be efficient, courteous, and complete; but the bitter taste of how long it took to get attention pollutes the overall judgment that we make about the quality of service.

The mathematical theory of waiting lines (or queues) has received a great deal of attention from academic researchers, and their results and insights have been successfully

---

[1]*Fortune*, 28 (July 1980), p. 10.

---

applied in a variety of settings (Buffa, 1983). However, most of this work is concerned with the *objective reality* of various queue-management techniques: for example, the effects upon waiting lines of adding servers, altering "queue discipline" (the order in which customers are served), speeding up serving times, and so on. What has been relatively neglected is much substantive discussion (at least in management literature) of the *experience* of waiting.[2] Depending on the context, a wait of ten minutes can feel like nothing at all, or it can feel like "forever." Accordingly, if managers are to concern themselves with how long their customers or clients wait in line for service, then they must pay attention not only to the actual wait times but also to how these are perceived. They must learn to influence how the customer feels while waiting.

In this chapter I shall discuss the psychology of waiting lines, examining how waits are experienced, and shall attempt to offer specific managerial advice to service organizations about how to improve this aspect of their service encounters.

THE FIRST AND SECOND LAWS OF SERVICE

Before discussing the laws of waiting, it is necessary to consider two general propositions about service encounters and how these are experienced. The first of these is what I call "The First Law of Service," expressed by the formula: Satisfaction equals perception minus expectation. If you *expect* a certain level of service and *perceive* the service received to be higher, you will be a satisfied customer. If you perceive the same level as before but expected a higher level, you will be disappointed and therefore a dissatisfied customer. The point is that both what is perceived and what is expected are psychological phenomena—they are not reality. Hence,

there are two main directions in which customer satisfaction with waits (and all other aspects of service) can be influenced: by working on (1) what the customer expects and (2) what the customer perceives.

Sasser, Olsen, and Wyckoff (1979) provide good examples of managing both the perception and the expectation of waiting times. For the former, they offer the example of:

> the well-known hotel group that received complaints from guests about excessive waiting times for elevators. After an analysis of how elevator service might be improved, it was suggested that mirrors be installed near where guests waited for elevators. The natural tendency of people to check their personal appearance substantially reduced complaints, although the actual wait for the elevators was unchanged. (1979, 88)

As an illustration of how expectations can be explicitly managed, they note that:

> some restaurants follow the practice of promising guests a waiting time in excess of the "expected time." If people are willing to agree to wait this length of time, they are quite pleased to be seated earlier, thus starting the meal with a more positive feeling. (1979, 89)

This last example deserves further exploration. When I have discussed this anecdote with a variety of serving personnel, they always reaffirm its wisdom. As one waiter pointed out to me: "If they sit down in a good mood, it's easy to keep them happy. If they sit down disgruntled, it's almost impossible to turn them around. They're looking to find fault, to criticize." As a result of these conversations, I offer my "Second Law of Service": It is hard to play "catch-up ball." There is a halo effect created by the early stages of any service encounter. Consequently, if money, time, and attention are to be spent on improving the experience of service, then the largest payoff may well occur in the early stages of the service encounter. In most cases, this will include a waiting experience.

---

[2]A notable exception is the brief discussion given in Sasser, Olsen, and Wyckoff (1979). A good summary of the work of psychologists in this area is provided by Doob (1960).

THE PRINCIPLES OF WAITING

Having established the importance of perceptions and expectations in the experience of waiting, we now turn to a series of propositions about the psychology of queues, each of which can be used by service organizations to influence their customers' satisfaction with waiting times.

Proposition 1: Unoccupied Time Feels Longer than Occupied Time

As William James, the noted philosopher, observed: "Boredom results from being attentive to the passage of time itself." The truth of this proposition has been discovered by many service organizations. In various restaurants it is common practice to hand out menus for customers to peruse while waiting in line. Apart from shortening the perception of time, this practice has the added benefit of shortening the service time, since customers will be ready to order once they are seated. A similar tactic is to turn the waiting area into a bar, which adds to revenues as well as occupies time. Use can be made of posters or reading material, and even shifting lights, rolling balls, and other "adult toys" to distract the customer's attention away from the passage of time. Theme restaurants (such as Victoria Station) which provide interesting memorabilia to examine are also applying the lesson of occupying waits as a means of enhancing the service.

In some situations, such as telephone waits, it is difficult to fill up time in a constructive way. The familiar "muzak" played by some organizations when their telephone-answering agents are busy is, to many people, an added annoyance rather than a benefit. In large part, this is because the activity of listening to music is totally unrelated to the service activity to come, whereas the use of menus and bars cited above successfully integrates the waiting experience into the total service experience. This suggests that the activity provided to fill time should (1) offer benefit in and of itself, and (2) be related, in some way, to the ensuing service encounter. The best example of this I ever encoun-

tered in relation to telephone waits is the story of the sports team that, when lines were occupied, played highlights of the previous week's game. In one memorable incident, a caller was transferred from the queue to the receptionist, whereupon he screamed, "Put me back, (so-and-so) is just about to score!"

It should also be noted, however, that there can be circumstances where a service may choose to fill time with an unrelated activity. In certain medical or dental waiting rooms, there appears to be a conscious attempt to distract the patient's attention from the forthcoming activity, perhaps on the grounds that to remind the patient of what is about to occur might heighten fears and hence make the wait more uncomfortable. Even in this context, it is possible to provide service-related distractions. Many medical clinics provide instructional videotapes, weighing machines, eye charts, and other self-testing equipment in the waiting room. Time can be occupied not only with distractions, but also with movement. In this regard, it is interesting to note the difference between the multiple-line system at McDonald's restaurants (where each server has a separate line of people waiting) and the multistage system at Wendy's restaurants (where the first server takes the order, the second prepares the burger, the third the drink, and so forth). In the former system, where one server handles the total request of each customer, the physical line is shorter but it moves only sporadically. In the latter system, where each customer is passed through a number of stages, the physical line is longer but it moves (in smaller steps) more continuously. The customer in the latter situation can see signs of "progress."

A similar attention to the sense of movement can be seen at Disneyland, where the length of the line for a given ride is often disguised by bending it around corners so that the customer cannot judge the total length of the line. Because of the rate at which Disneyland can load people onto the rides, the actual wait is not that long. However, the sight of a large number of people waiting might make it seem long. By focusing the customer's attention on the rate of progress rather than the length of the line, the waiting experience is made tolerable.

Proposition 2: Preprocess Waits Feel Longer Than In-Process Waits

One of the other virtues of handing out menus, providing a bar, and other methods of service-related time fillers is that they convey the sense that the service has started. People waiting to make their first human contact with the service organization are much more impatient than those who have begun the service process; preprocess waits are perceived as longer than in-process waits. One's anxiety level is much higher while waiting to be served than it is while being served, even though the latter wait may be longer. There is a fear of being forgotten. (How many times has the reader gone back to a maître d' to check that his or her name is still on the list?) Many restaurant owners instruct their service staff to pass by a table as soon as the customers are seated to say: "I'll be with you as soon as I can, after I've looked after that table over there." In essence, the customer's presence is being acknowledged. This lesson is applied by those mail-order houses that send a quick acknowledgment of an order with the message that: "Your order is being processed. Expect delivery in four to six weeks." Even if the "four to six weeks" message was in the initial advertisement or catalog (another example of managing expectations), the customer who has sent in a check may well be concerned that the order did not arrive. The acknowledgment of receipt assures the customer that service has begun. One walk-in medical clinic that I studied decided to introduce a triage system whereby all patients were first met by a nurse who recorded the patient's name and symptoms and decided whether or not the patient could be treated by a registered nurse practitioner or should be seen by a doctor. Even though the addition of this step in the process had no impact on the time it ultimately took to see a medical service provider, it filled up otherwise unoccupied waiting time and surveys showed that patients were pleased with

"reduced waiting times." The patients felt they had been entered into the system.

Proposition 3: Anxiety Makes Waits Seem Longer

A large part of the concern that we feel to "get started" is attributable to anxiety. In the cases cited, the anxiety was about whether or not one had been forgotten. Anxiety can, however, come from other sources. Nearly everyone has had the experience of choosing a line at the supermarket or airport, and stood there worrying that he had, indeed, chosen the wrong line. As one stands there trying to decide whether to move, the anxiety level increases and the wait becomes intolerable. This situation is covered by what is known as "Erma Bombeck's Law": The other line always moves faster. On a recent (open-seating) Eastern Airlines shuttle flight, my fellow passengers formed an agitated queue at the boarding gate long before the flight was due to depart, leading the attendant to announce: "Don't worry, folks, the plane's a big one; you'll all get on." The change in atmosphere in the waiting lounge was remarkable. Similar efforts to deal with customer anxiety can be seen when airlines make on-board announcements that connecting flights are being held for a delayed flight, when movie theater managers walk down the line reassuring patrons they will get in, or when customer service agents in airport lobbies reassure waiting patrons that they are indeed waiting in the correct line and have sufficient time to catch their flight.

One of the poorest examples I know of managing anxiety is when I am on standby for a flight, and the agent takes my ticket. Now I am anxious not only about whether I will get on the flight, but also about whether I will get my ticket back. I have been asked to give up control of the situation. At least if I had my ticket I could change my mind and go to another airline. The prescription for managers resulting from this discussion is: ask yourself what customers might be worrying about (rationally or irrationally), and find ways to remove the worry.

Proposition 4: Uncertain Waits Are Longer Than Known, Finite Waits

The most profound source of anxiety in waiting is how long the wait will be. For example, if a patient in a waiting room is told that the doctor will be delayed thirty minutes, he experiences an initial annoyance but then relaxes into an acceptance of the inevitability of the wait. However, if the patient is told the doctor will be free soon, he spends the whole time in a state of nervous anticipation, unable to settle down, afraid to depart and come back. The patient's expectations are being managed poorly. Likewise, the pilot who repeatedly announces "only a few more minutes," adds insult to injury when the wait goes on and on. Not only are the customers being forced to wait, but they are not being dealt with honestly.

A good example of the role of uncertainty in the waiting experience is provided by the "appointment syndrome." Clients who arrive early for an appointment will sit contentedly until the scheduled time, even if this is a significant amount of time in an absolute sense (say, thirty minutes). However, once the appointment time is passed, even a short wait of, say, ten minutes, grows increasingly annoying. The wait until the appointed time is finite; waiting beyond that point has no knowable limit.

Appointment systems are, in practice, troublesome queue-management tools. They suffer from the problem that some customers may make appointments without showing up (a problem endemic to airlines, hotels, dentists, and hair cutters) and also from the fact that it is often difficult to decide how far apart to schedule appointments. If they are too far apart, the server is left idle waiting for the next appointment. If they are too close together, appointments begin to run behind and, since they cumulate, tend to make the server further and further behind. This is a particularly acute problem because a customer with an appointment has been given a specific expectation about waiting times, and a failure to deliver on this premise makes the wait seem longer than if no appointment had been made. This does not mean that appointment systems should never be used. They are, after all, a way of giving the customer a finite expectation. It should be recognized, however, that an appointment defines an expectation that must be met.

Proposition 5: Unexplained Waits Are Longer Than Explained Waits

On a cold and snowy morning, when I telephone for a taxi, I begin with the expectation that my wait will be longer than on a clear, summer day. Accordingly, I wait with a great deal more patience because I understand the causes for the delay. Similarly, if a doctor's receptionist informs me that an emergency has taken place, I can wait with greater equanimity than if I do not know what is going on. Airline pilots understand this principle well; on-board announcements are filled with references to tardy baggage handlers, fog over landing strips, safety checks, and air-traffic controllers' clearance instructions. The explanation given may or may not exculpate the service provider, but it is better than no explanation at all.

Most serving personnel are repeatedly asked about the circumstances in waiting situations. The lack of an explanation is one of the prime factors adding to a customer's uncertainty about the length of the wait. However, knowing the length of the wait is not the only reason a customer wants an explanation. As the Federal Express advertisement points out, waiting is also demoralizing. Waiting in ignorance creates a feeling of powerlessness, which frequently results in visible irritation and rudeness on the part of customers as they harass serving personnel in an attempt to reclaim their status as paying clients. In turn, this behavior makes it difficult for the serving personnel to maintain their equanimity. For example, on a significantly delayed flight, one cabin attendant was forced to announce to the passengers: "Please pay us the courtesy of being polite to us so that we can reciprocate in kind."

Naturally, justifiable explanations will tend to soothe the waiting customer more than unjustifiable explanations. A subtle illustration of this is provided by the practice of many fast-food chains which instruct serving personnel to take their rest breaks out of sight of waiting customers. The sight of what seems to be available serving personnel sitting idle while customers wait, is a source of irritation. Even if such personnel are, in fact, occupied (for example, a bank teller who is not serving customers but catching up on paperwork), the sight of serving personnel not actually serving customers is "unexplained." In the customer's eyes, he or she is waiting longer than necessary. The explanation that the "idle" personnel are taking a break or performing other tasks is frequently less than acceptable.

Proposition 6: Unfair Waits Are Longer Than Equitable Waits

As Sasser, Olsen, and Wyckoff (1979) note, one of the most frequent irritants mentioned by customers at restaurants is the prior seating of those who have arrived later. They observe: "The feeling that somebody has successfully 'cut in front' of you causes even the most patient customer to become furious. Great care to be equitable is vital" (1979, 89).

In many waiting situations, there is no visible order to the waiting line. In situations such as waiting for a subway train, the level of anxiety demonstrated is high, and the group waiting is less a queue than a mob. Instead of being able to relax, each individual remains in a state of nervousness about whether their priority in the line is being preserved. As already noted, agitated waits seem longer than relaxed waits. It is for this reason that many service facilities have a system of taking a number, whereby each customer is issued a number and served in strict numerical order. In some facilities, the number currently being served is prominently displayed so that customers can estimate the expected waiting times.

Such systems can work well in queuing situations where "first in, first out" (FIFO) is the appropriate rule for queue discipline. However, in many situations customers may be ranked in order of importance, and priorities allocated that way. A good example is a walk-in medical facility which will frequently break the FIFO rule to handle emergency cases. Also familiar is the example of the restaurant that has a finite supply of two-person, four-person, and large tables, and seats customers by matching the size of the party to the size of the table. A final example is the use of express-checkout lanes in supermarkets, whereby customers with only a few items are dealt with by a special server.

All of these cases represent departures from the FIFO system. In some, the priority rules are accepted by the customers as equitable and observed—for example, the supermarket express checkout. In other illustrations, such as the restaurant with varying sizes of tables, the priority rule that seats customers by size of party is less accepted by the customers, and frequently resented. The rule may serve the restaurant, but the customer has a harder time seeing the equity benefit. Similarly, special service facilities for important customers may or may not be accepted as equitable. For this reason, many service facilities physically separate premium servers (for example, first-class airline check-in counters) from the sight of regular customers so that the latter will not resent the special service rendered.

A slightly different example of the equity problem in queue management is provided by the serving person who is responsible not only for dealing with customers present in the serving facility, but also for answering the telephone. How many of us have not had the experience of waiting while a receptionist answered the telephones, and consequently felt a resentment that some distant customer was receiving a higher priority than we who have made the effort to come to the service facility? The example can be extended to those people who answer their telephone while you are in their office. By answering the phone, they are giving you a lesser priority than the random caller.

The main point to be stressed here is that the customer's sense of equity is not always obvious, and needs to be explicitly managed. Whatever priority rules apply, the service provider must make vigorous efforts to ensure that these rules match with the customer's sense of equity, either by adjusting the rules or by actively convincing the client that the rules are indeed appropriate.

Proposition 7: The More Valuable the Service, the Longer the Customer Will Wait

The example of the supermarket express-checkout counter reminds us that our tolerance for waiting depends upon the perceived value of that for which we wait. Special checkout counters were originally provided because customers with only a few items felt resentful at having to wait a long time for what was seen as a simple transaction. Customers with a full cart of groceries were much more inclined to tolerate lines. Airlines, too, have discovered this principle and provided separate lines for those with simple transactions (such as seat selection), medium-difficulty transactions (baggage check-in), and complex transactions (ticket purchase or modification). Specialization by task does not necessarily reduce the aggregate amount of waiting in the system; however, it serves well to allocate the waiting among the customer base. That perceived value affects tolerance for waits can be demonstrated by our common experience in restaurants—we will accept a much longer waiting time at a haute cuisine facility than at a "greasy spoon." In universities, there is an old rule of thumb that if the teacher is delayed, "You wait ten minutes for an assistant professor, fifteen minutes for an associate professor, and twenty minutes for a full professor." This illustrates well the principle that tolerance for waits depends upon perceived value of service—perhaps with the emphasis on the perception.

It follows from this principle that waiting for something of little value can be intolerable. This is amply illustrated by the eagerness with which airline passengers leap from their seats when the airplane reaches the gate, even though they know that it will take time to unload all the passengers ahead of them, and that they may well have to wait for their baggage to arrive at the claim area. The same passenger who sat patiently for some hours during the flight suddenly exhibits an intolerance for an extra minute or two to disembark, and a fury at an extra few minutes for delayed baggage. The point is that the service (the flight) is over, and waiting to get out when there is no more value to be received is aggravating. A similar syndrome is exhibited at hotel checkout counters. Just as preprocess waits are felt to be longer than in-process waits of the same time duration, so are postprocess waits; these, in fact, feel longest of all.

Proposition 8: Solo Waits Feel Longer Than Group Waits

One of the remarkable syndromes to observe in waiting lines is to see individuals sitting or standing next to each other without talking or otherwise interacting until an announcement of a delay is made. Then the individuals suddenly turn to each other to express their exasperation, wonder collectively what is happening, and console each other. What this illustrates is that there is some form of comfort in group waiting rather than waiting alone.

This syndrome is evidently in effect in amusement parks such as Disneyland, or in some waiting lines to buy concert tickets when a sense of group community develops and the line turns into almost a service encounter in its own right; the waiting is part of the fun and part of the service. Whatever service organizations can do to promote the sense of group waiting rather than isolating each individual, will tend to increase the tolerance for waiting time.

CONCLUSION

The propositions presented here are by no means meant to be an exhaustive list of all the psychological considerations involved in managing customers' acceptance of waiting time. Not discussed, for example, is the importance of explicit apologies and apologetic tones in preserving the customer's sense of valued-client status. Similarly unmentioned are cultural and class differences in tolerance for waiting. It is said of the English, for example, that if they see a line they will join it. I hope, however, that the managerial reader will have gained a greater appreciation both for the psychological complexity of queues, and for the fact that the psychological experience of waiting can be managed. The propositions given here can be researched not only by academics for their general applicability, but also by managers for application in specific service situations. The main point of this chapter is that the waiting experience is context specific. By learning to research and understand the psychological context of their own waiting lines, managers can have a significant impact upon their customers' satisfaction with the service encounter.

REFERENCES

BUFFA, E. S. (1983), *Modern Production/Operations Management*. New York: John Wiley and Sons.

DOOB, L. W. (1960), *Patterning of Time*. New Haven, Conn.: Yale University Press.

SASSER, W. E., R. P. OLSEN, AND D. D. WYCKOFF (1978), *Management of Service Operations: Text, Cases and Readings*. New York: Allyn and Bacon.

The Parker House:
Sales and Reservations Planning

PENNY PITTMAN MERLISS
CHRISTOPHER H. LOVELOCK

The management of a successful hotel finds itself on the horns of a dilemma. A large tour group seeks to make a major booking, with the possibility of additional bookings at two other hotels in the same chain. Yet management is reluctant to allocate too much of the hotel's capacity to this type of client, preferring to attract business travelers who pay top rates and are more consistent with the image desired for the Parker House.

"Could I speak to you for a minute, Mac?"

Robert McIntosh, general manager of the Parker House, Boston's oldest hotel, looked up from his desk. William Murphy, the hotel's director of sales, was standing in the doorway. McIntosh smiled. "Any time, Bill," he replied, hoping no more surprises had surfaced since last week, when a group of athletes sponsored by one of the hotel's leading corporate clients had smoked enough marijuana to render their rooms uninhabitable for 24 hours. Or perhaps another VIP was complaining about the need to book early at the Parker House; the hotel was often filled to capacity during the fall season, and early October 1979 was proving to be no exception.

"We have got a problem on our hands with TransAm Tours," Murphy began. "My sales force has been doing its best to cut down on tour groups, especially since the hotel's done such a good job of attracting clients who will pay the full rate. Some of our other properties—I am thinking of the Berkshire Place in Manhattan—can't afford to turn down a lot of tour business."

McIntosh nodded. He was well aware of the Parker House's 85 percent occupancy

This case was prepared by Research Assistant Penny Pittman Merliss and Associate Professor Christopher H. Lovelock. Copyright © 1980 by the President and Fellows of Harvard College, Harvard Business School case 9-580-152.

rate, significantly above the national average and the second highest in the Dunfey Hotels system.

"Well, I just got a call from Harvey Kimball" [Dunfey's national tour sales director], Murphy continued. "He's worked out a deal with TransAm Tours for next summer and fall. They've agreed to block out approximately 2,000 guest nights at the Berkshire Place, weekends as well as midweek, from June through October 1980. The problem is that TransAm is trying to leverage the Berkshire deal into roughly 4,000 guest nights with us during the same period. Now, not only are we trying to avoid tour groups—we're also trying to maximize our room revenues. On the other hand, Mac, the Berkshire is a Dunfey hotel, and it needs our help. What do you think we should do?"

DUNFEY CLASSIC HOTELS

The Parker House, wholly owned by the Dunfey corporation, was the most profitable of the company's 23 hotels. Generally considered to be the flagship of the corporation, it was the premier member of Dunfey's Classic Hotels division, directed by Yervant Chekijian. Management felt that the Classic hotels—each of which was a unique unit—offered discriminating travelers a welcome opportunity to escape the monotony of the chains. The Classics also provided a retreat from the noise and crowds of conventions. As Chekijian explained:

> A Dunfey Classic is not a convention hotel. While we will accommodate small executive and professional groups, our marketing approach is not to pack the house with large groups. We are seeking a quiet, peaceful atmosphere. . . . Our feeling is that corporate travelers who are regular customers of the hotel will appreciate knowing that they can get rooms with us even if the rest of the town is sold out to a convention.

Each Classic hotel was a formerly elegant property located in the city center which had fallen into decay prior to Dunfey's purchase.

The renovation process involved more than refurbishment of facilities. In the words of William Dunfey:

> A Dunfey Classic hotel is not just an old hotel that we've slapped a new coat of paint onto. Even though some of the properties may have been neglected or run down when we took over, they all had a tradition of excellence and quality. Turning them into Classic hotels involves restoring that level of service as well as restoring the physical plant.

In keeping with Dunfey management's belief in the individuality of the Classic hotels, each had a very different decorating scheme. The Berkshire Place, in Manhattan, where major renovations were completed in May 1979 at a cost of over $9 million, had a contemporary tone, with large green plants, hand-woven Oriental rugs, and imported Italian marble columns and floors in the lobby. The Ambassador East, in Chicago, restored a year earlier for over $7 million, was decorated in a mixture of eighteenth-century English antiques and Oriental and contemporary accessories.

Renovations at the Parker House had been designed to establish the air of understated luxury considered most congenial to cultivated New England tastes. Old oak paneling and rich Oriental carpets decorated the lobby; burnished, ornately patterned brass doors glowed on the elevators; a two-tiered brass chandelier was suspended from the elaborately carved central wooden ceiling. Encouraged by the success of the first round of room renovations, completed in 1975, the Dunfey management began even more luxurious redecorating in 1979. The cuisine served in Parker's Restaurant, reopened in 1975, had become widely recognized for its excellence among Boston diners; according to *Boston* magazine, Parker's was one of the ten best restaurants in the city and offered the best Sunday brunch in town.

Situated on the Freedom Trail, a self-guided walking tour through the heart of historic Boston, the Parker House was closer to Boston's financial, governmental, and trade centers than any other major hotel in the city. Much of the waterfront area, once decayed, now contained new apartments, offices, shopping areas, and parks; the recently restored Faneuil Hall-Quincy Market retail and restaurant complex, which had become enormously popular, was less than a ten-minute walk from the hotel. However, between mid-1981 and late 1982, three new luxury hotels were scheduled to open in the same general area of the city as the Parker House. Offering a combined total of over 1,200 rooms, these new hotels would be operated by Inter-Continental (a subsidiary of Pan Am), Meridien (a subsidiary of Air France), and Marriott Hotels, respectively.

THE PARKER HOUSE: FROM BANKRUPTCY TO REVIVAL

The Parker House was the oldest continuously operating hotel in the United States. The original building, constructed in 1855, quickly attracted a large and cosmopolitan clientele. The hotel had been almost totally rebuilt in 1927, but during the fifties and sixties it fell into decline. By 1969, occupancy at the Parker House was down to 35 percent, and the hotel that had hosted Presidents was forced to declare bankruptcy.

The Parker House was rescued by Dunfey Hotels, a privately owned chain. In 1975, the Dunfey family hired the former head of Sheraton's international marketing, Jon Canas, as vice president of sales and marketing. Canas brought a strong marketing orientation to the organization and recruited a number of experienced hotel executives.

Well aware of the heavy fixed costs of operating a hotel, Canas and his team knew that their major source of profits lay in room sales rather than food and beverage revenue. Accordingly, they went after all the business they could find: tour groups, conventions, training sessions, anything to "keep the lights on." As occupancy rose, they began to upgrade the appearance of the Parker House, renovating, restoring, and finally repositioning rooms, restaurants, and public areas. Room prices rose accordingly, and

many of the customers who had initially enabled the hotel to survive were replaced by less price-sensitive corporate clients. Successful renovation of the Parker House, combined with Canas's marketing efforts and the improving national economy, led the Dunfey hotels' revenues to double in three years; chain-wide occupancy rates went from 56 percent in 1975 (when the industry average was 62.5 percent) to a projected 76 percent in 1979. At the Parker House, the net earnings of the hotel in 1979 (after deducting all operating costs, depreciation, and amortization), were projected to reach $1.19 million—up from $1.05 million in 1978.

Target Marketing

The key to successful marketing, in the opinion of Dunfey management, was segmentation. Ron Gustafson, Dunfey's manager of sales administration, stated:

> What we want to say is, "We are this type of a hotel: now what do we need to do to reach these segments?" First we canvass an area door to door. We talk to customers and find out their needs. Then we tell them our story, we bring them down and show them the hotel. Then, when business begins to pick up, we try to monitor whether we're taking share from the correct hotels. We want to build our business with the correct market segments—not just fill rooms—because we're building for the future and the profile of customers we take in has a tremendous impact on creating a position for the hotel in the minds of the customers. For example, if our hotel is in the luxury class appealing to the upscale business executive and professional traveler, we don't want the badge-and-bottle conventioneers running around the lobby because, frankly, it destroys the atmosphere.

Extensive segmentation was very unusual in the hotel business. Most hotels segmented their guests into two or three categories: tourists, corporate travelers, and groups. However, the Parker House segmented its clients as follows:

1. *Pure Transient*—the customer, either tourist or corporate traveler, who simply picked up

the phone and made a reservation at the rack rate,[1] attracted through general advertising or word of mouth. No direct sales effort reached this person.

2. *Outside Reservation*—the customer whose room (also at rack rate) was arranged through Dunfey's toll-free reservations number, often used by travel agents for their clients. This number, operated for Dunfey Hotels by an independent reservation service, cost the Parker House $100 per month, plus $5.43 for each individual reservation thus made. Management was interested to see how well this service performed.

3. *Executive Service Plan (ESP)*—consisted of executives traveling singly or in groups smaller than ten who reserved their rooms through an unlisted number and paid rack rate. Because this group was, to a large extent, drawn to the Parker House as a direct result of personal sales calls by ESP representatives, it was important to measure the success of the sales effort.

4. *Special Transient*—a limited category composed of friends of management, favored travel agents, etc. This segment was traced so that the lower rates charged to it would not skew other rate data. The hotel tried to limit these bookings to slow periods, such as weekends or the first quarter of the year.

5. *Patriot*—the government segment. The Parker House had 36 extremely small rooms, each containing a single bed, which were offered to government employees for a price considerably below the rack rate. In 1979 7,000 room nights in this category were billed. This segment was also traced primarily to avoid skewing more significant data.

6. *Mini-Vacation*—a standard weekend package comprising two nights (Friday-Saturday or Saturday-Sunday) and two breakfasts. In spring 1980 its cost would be $88.

7. *Classic Package*—the luxury weekend package, including a wine and cheese platter in the room, Godiva chocolates in the evening, sheets turned down before bedtime, dinner at Parker's Restaurant. In spring 1980 this package would cost $186.

8. *Corporate Groups*—corporate clients reserving rooms at the same time in blocks of ten or more. It was very unusual for the Parker House to book sleeping space for groups of over 150 people, though meetings of up to 500 were accepted.

9. *Associations*—professional associations reserving rooms at the same time in blocks of ten or more. Like those of corporate groups, their rates varied, depending on the time of the year and the desirability of the groups. Medical associations, for example, were highly prized, because they spent heavily on food and beverage and often planned their meetings during the weekends, when the hotel's occupancy dropped.

10. *Bus Tours*—the hotel attempted to limit these groups to weekends and the months of July and August, traditionally slower periods. The Parker House also tried to upgrade its bus tours from American groups to European, Japanese, and other foreign tourists, who were willing to pay higher rates.

11. *Airline*—these 117 small rooms, overlooking airshafts, were secured through annual contracts with airlines using Boston's Logan International Airport and were occupied seven nights a week. The rate was somewhat cheaper, but European and other foreign airlines were courted because they were willing to pay more for the rooms than American carriers.

The other categories were: *permanent residents* (at present, the Parker House had none); *complimentary rooms,* provided free of charge, sometimes to compensate for a previous error made by the hotel; and *house use rooms,* given to employees who were forced to stay overnight or who wished to appraise the hotel's service. A quarterly breakdown of room revenue by segment is presented in *Exhibit 1.*

In some cases the market was segmented further by seasons of use, geography, and industry. The hotel also segmented its referrals. When all rooms were full, or when a guest was turned away because of overbooking, management made sure that well-heeled transients and top-rated corporate clients were referred to Boston's best hotels, such as the Ritz, the Copley Plaza, and the Hyatt Regency, the latter across the river in Cambridge. More price-sensitive guests were directed to middle-rank hotels or motor lodges.

---

[1] The published rate charge for each accommodation, as established by hotel management.

EXHIBIT 1
The Parker House Room Revenue by Segment, 1978 (quarterly)

Segment	(1) Jan.–Mar.	(2) April–June	(3) July–Sept.	(4) Oct.–Dec.	Total
1. Pure transient	$ 448,087	$ 335,103	$ 387,227	$ 338,141	$1,508,558
2. ESP	382,287	605,889	594,414	594,224	2,176,814
3. Mini-vacation*	45,894	48,855	40,098	67,388	202,235
4. Patriot and airline	243,438	247,121	251,300	252,002	993,861
5. Associations and corporate groups	156,500	314,541	208,669	276,268	955,978
6. Bus tours	12,819	64,914	172,910	83,388	334,031
7. Other†	38,095	21,353	23,276	32,555	115,279
Total	$1,327,120	$1,637,776	$1,677,894	$1,643,966	$6,286,756

*The only weekend package plan available in 1978.
†Includes Special Transients and Outside Reservation System guests.
SOURCE: Company records.

Pricing varied for each segment and depended to a great extent on competition. Boston hotel rates in general were much lower than rates at similar hotels in New York City. Competitive information was gathered at regular intervals. Projected rack rates at the Parker House for fall 1980 are reproduced in *Exhibit 2*.

One of the most important benefits of the detailed segmentation employed by the Parker House management was the guidance it offered to the sales division. Jon Canas commented:

> With the rooms merchandising plan you know what to ask sales and reservation people to do. In general, in the industry, salespeople do not know who to see, they do not know how many rooms are available, and they definitely do not know what rate to charge. At Dunfey we want to provide these guidelines as closely as possible in order to maximize our profitability and productivity.

The Sales Division

The Parker House sales division was led by Bill Murphy, who had previously directed sales at the Ambassador East in Chicago. He directed a group of five salespeople and eight inhouse telephone and clerical staff. Direct sales efforts were targeted toward the most desirable market segments, according to the hotel's mission statement. The sales manager handled professional associations; the corporate sales executive covered corporate groups; and the two ESP account executives, Lyssa O'Neill and Pamela Roberge, were responsible for sales to individual business travelers. Since most ESP reservations were made by secretaries or corporate travel managers, O'Neill and Roberge directed the majority of their calls to people in these positions. All three of these sales efforts—corporate, professional, and ESP—were directed only toward room sales; banquets were handled by another representative who also reported to Murphy.

One of the hotel's goals for 1980 was to shift its market base toward customer segments more likely to pay full rates. Very seldom were all 546 rooms in the Parker House sold at the rack rate; most often about 30 percent were discounted. In an attempt to raise room sales efficiency[2] and reduce discounting, management had decided to aim for a lower occupancy rate—83.5 percent—in the hope of bringing in more guests at rack rate and raising revenues and profits.

---

[2]Defined as the ratio of total room sales revenue over a period divided by the potential revenues that might be obtained if all available rooms were sold at full rates during the same period.

EXHIBIT 2
Projected Parker House Room Rates, Fall 1980

Room Category	Number	RATE Single	Double	Furnishings
1. Standard	130	$70	$80	Double bed, clock radio, color TV, Drexel furniture, Thermopane windows, individually controlled heat and air conditioning. The least expensive room available to ESP clients.
2. Deluxe	181	80	90	Similar to standard; larger room.
3. Top of the line	20	90	100	King-size beds; other furnishings similar to standard; larger room.
4. Mini-suite	48	105	115	Very large room (often constructed from two smaller rooms, with a wall removed) with walk-in closets and dividers between living and sleeping areas.
5. Parlor suite	16	$125		Living room, bedroom (1 or more), and some kitchen facilities such as a sink or wet bar.
6. Deluxe suite	2	250		Larger rooms, complete kitchen facilities, luxurious furnishings.

The latest renovations and rate increases were an essential part of this strategy. As Yervant Chekijian put it: "We are going to have no compromises on our product offering, and at the same time, we are not going to apologize for our rates."

Executive Service Plan

Because rates for tours, groups, and associations were often discounted, but ESP clients were always charged the rack rate, the ESP plan was considered the key to the hotel's new room sales efficiency target. Designed to make it convenient for individual corporate travelers to use the hotel, the plan included a direct unlisted telephone number reserved for ESP clients (out-of-town customers could call collect); "preferred" (i.e., larger) rooms; preregistration to ensure easy check-in; an express check-out service; bill-back privileges; a welcome packet, including a complimentary newspaper each morning (to be picked up in the lobby); and a special ESP privilege on Friday and Saturday nights entitling the spouse of an ESP guest to stay at the hotel free of charge.

Direct sales calls were an essential element of ESP marketing strategy. The Parker House sales division kept files on 710 ESP companies, categorized as red, blue, green, or yellow depending on how frequently their employees used the hotel. Red clients, who booked over 150 room nights annually, were called on monthly; blue clients (75-150 rooms annually), every two months; green clients (25-75 rooms annually), every three months; and yellow clients (less than 25 rooms annually), once or twice a year. In order to cover these accounts, ESP reps Roberge and O'Neill made approximately 40 calls (including 16 key accounts) weekly.

The ESP job was the hotel's entry-level sales position. Selling to groups and associations, according to Dunfey management, required dealing with experienced travel and convention planners and was handled by more senior members of the sales staff. In fact, since many of the ESP accounts were steady clients of the Parker House, and the demand for hotel space in Boston was high for a large part of the year, the ESP reps tended to view their job as customer service or client education rather than sales. "As salespeople we're not strictly solicitors at all," said O'Neill. "We're more personal contact. We are the company's liaison to the hotel, and they can call us if they have a problem. They know our faces, our names."

During and immediately after the original renovation of the hotel, ESP reps had been given a quota of 25 new accounts per week to solicit. By late 1979, demand for the Parker House had increased to the point that management instituted an account evaluation program. Roberge explained:

> It's reached the point where we've had to look at an account and say, OK, these people have only used the hotel three times in the past year—to accommodate them on these three nights we may be shutting out somebody who uses us 1,500 room nights a year. We're going to try to be a little more selective about sales calls.

Neither ESP representative considered it very difficult to distinguish the hotel's most valuable clients. Commented O'Neill:

> The least desirable people are those who are very price-sensitive and concerned about the rates. For instance, one guy who ran a shoe outlet wanted to have a function here and bring his own liquor and his own dry snacks. People like that—or people who have reservations made on short notice in spring and fall only—I really want to discourage because the hotel is full during that time and their volume is nothing we can put our finger on. I'll bring up rates during the call, which is something a salesperson usually doesn't do. Alternatively, I would encourage such a client to go through the front desk or the 800 number, which offers the smaller, less expensive rooms that we don't sell to ESP guests.

Allocation of Capacity

The sales staff saw one of its major challenges as determining how many rooms should be set aside for clients desiring long lead time, how many rooms should go to shorter lead-time groups, and how much capacity should be saved for walk-in business. Faced with average occupancy rates ranging from 90–97 percent, Monday–Thursday, during many periods in 1978–79, many clients tried to book well in advance.[3] The Parker House, however, refused to quote rates more than six months in advance and had set a 45-day maximum on advance banquet bookings at lunch; such banquets could

potentially interfere with the needs of groups booking rooms as well as meal service. Jon Canas summed up the situation:

> Consider New England during the middle of October. For us success at this time is to have 100 percent walk-in transient business at the rack rate—and to have raised the rate the day before! It wouldn't be to our best interest to have booked a group at a very low rate way in advance when we know we're going to get this excellent, high-rated transient business at this time of year. On the other hand, there are cases which crop up when it's necessary to give people a discount in the middle of October—when you could have had the highest rate—in order to get that business back on January 2 when you will otherwise have nothing. So, it's a constant game of balancing.

Customer complaints to the sales division usually centered on one of two problems: room availability or the difficulty of getting through to the ESP office on the phone. Both Roberge and O'Neill made a point of frequently reminding their accounts about the hotel shortage in Boston. There were a total of 6,925 rooms in the city; all major hotels were fully booked for close to 90 days of the year. The sales division published a special quarterly newsletter for ESP clients which publicized problem dates, and also kept a waiting list, again for ESP accounts, after space closed. An extra telephone line had been added to the ESP office in fall of 1979; in February 1980 a recorded announcement would be introduced which would take and hold calls when all reservationists were busy.

The hotel continued to solicit some new business, primarily in New York City, where Roberge and O'Neill had recently traveled on a sales trip. It was hoped that the highly desirable, less price-sensitive accounts solicited there would crowd out smaller, rate-conscious clients and increase the number of ESP guests in the hotel.

ESP Sales Calls

Lyssa O'Neill was the senior Parker House ESP account executive. Her talent for sales had surfaced in grade school; at age eleven,

---

[3]Occupancy rates Friday–Sunday during the same periods averaged 80–83 percent.

she had sold 165 boxes of Girl Scout cookies in five days. Reviewing her background, she commented:

> In high school and college I waitressed a lot and was an assistant manager at one restaurant, which really brought a lot to this job as far as knowledge of food and beverage is concerned. Being a waitress, I think, is one of the best possible kinds of experience for dealing with people—dealing with their objections, pampering them, understanding their needs. Minimization is a big part of this job—how we softsoap people, deal with complaints, get them to realize how the hotel's "batting average" outweighs isolated incidents.

O'Neill had begun her career with Dunfey as an in-house ESP reservations manager, answering the phones. After nine months she was promoted to account executive, and she expected to receive another promotion in early 1980, after a year's experience on the job. Her present salary consisted of a base rate plus a quarterly incentive, tied to the occupancy rate of the hotel as well as the number of ESP bookings she brought in through her own calls.

A week of sales calls for O'Neill typically began on the preceding Friday afternoon. After reviewing company files pulled by a secretary, she compiled a detailed itinerary listing the 16 key accounts she planned to cover and her objective in visiting each one. Next to a major accounting firm's name, she noted: "Meet new contact in Personnel; check on volume potential for first quarter." For a medium-sized bank she wrote: "Major contact back from maternity leave; reaffirm and probe future needs." She assessed a small brokerage firm as: "An inactive yellow account; determine potential through contact before killing." A copy of this itinerary was sent to Murphy before the calls began. At the end of the week, when O'Neill had covered all 16 key accounts as well as about 24 others, she sent another copy of the itinerary to Murphy, along with copies of 16 key call reports. The call report was a detailed description of the sales call, followed by a plan for future action. As O'Neill described it:

We write up a call report on every complaint or problem that comes into the office; we also write up a call report after every sales visit. These enable every person who's picking up an account to know what this customer does, what their travel trends are, which person in the office is making reservations. They also help when you are going out on a call and you are aware that this company has had problems. They feel very good when you go in and say, I understand you have had difficulties—how is everything going now?

After completing the call reports, O'Neill selected a date for the next sales call, based on the account's volume, and wrote the date in the file and on a separate index card. Through these index cards, filed chronologically, the ESP reps kept the coming weeks' schedules at their fingertips and could tell the secretaries exactly which files to pull.

Except for Friday afternoons, when she planned the upcoming week, and Monday mornings, which she spent in departmental sales meetings, O'Neill was out every day from 10–12 and 2–4, calling on accounts. Her midday lunch period was frequently spent meeting clients and giving them lunch and tours of the hotel. Very often the people she brought in were secretaries. O'Neill felt that by targeting the people who actually made reservations, rather than restricting her contact to those who stayed in the hotel, she pulled in a significantly greater number of ESP rooms.

O'Neill felt she could number her difficult clients almost on the fingers of one hand:

> I feel there are three basic ingredients in dealing with this job: a sense of respect, a sense of discretion, and a sense of humor. I have had only a few really unpleasant experiences since I have been here in which customers were downright rude. Some people, for instance, don't realize that a hotel is a business with a limited capacity. They think of it as a personal service—"Don't tell me you're sold out. Don't tell me there isn't a room in the place."

Managers believed that no other hotel in Boston offered significant competition to the Parker House's ESP account coverage program. The Sonesta, across the river in Cambridge, sent representatives out to corporate accounts about once every two months; other hotels invited clients to occasional public relations functions. As O'Neill saw it, the Parker House corporate plan was by far the most attractive in Boston.

Tour Groups

Although Harvey Kimball, Dunfey's director of tour sales, maintained his office at the Parker House, the greater part of his marketing efforts were directed toward other Dunfey hotels which considered tours an important part of their business mix. His task was to uncover leads; it was the responsibility of the individual hotel's Executive Operating Committee (EOC), aided by the regional director of sales, to decide whether the business was good for the hotel. Kimball received a yearly salary, plus a bonus based on the number of room nights he brought in.

Janet Morin, the Parker House tour coordinator, was a secretary in the general manager's office who received no incentive and made no direct sales calls of any kind. "It really isn't necessary," she stated. "The tour wholesalers call us—in fact, I usually get about 18 calls a day and end up referring most of them to the Park Plaza,[4] which is more eager to get tours than we are." Rates for groups of 15 or more varied according to the time of year, ranging from $44 to $58 (single), with a $10 additional charge per person for double, triple, and quadruple occupancy. The hotel did not encourage tours during the middle of the week, because ESP and transient guests brought in much more revenue. During the weekend, however, ESP guests almost vanished, and as Morin noted, "We need anything we can get." During 1979, tour rooms as a percentage of total rooms sold monthly ranged from 0.3 percent to 11 percent; tour room revenues as a percentage of total monthly revenues ranged from 0.3 percent to 8 percent.

---

[4]A large hotel, not part of the Dunfey organization, located on the fringe of the downtown area.

Tours usually reached the hotel in groups of 46, a standard bus load. Most tour group guests were older people who preferred not to drive themselves, and they spent relatively little money in the hotel. "Our restaurants are in the moderate to expensive range," Morin explained, "and tour operators want the least expensive rate they can get on everything. They'll put inexpensive restaurants on the itinerary and herd the group in and out." The one meal which tour groups usually ate in the hotel was breakfast, and this had caused problems in the past, according to Morin:

> We charge the tours a prepaid flat rate of $5 for breakfast. We used to omit a service charge, until the waitresses started complaining that the groups would never tip—apparently they assumed that the $5 covered service. Now we add a 15 percent service charge to their bill.
>
> The breakfast scene is at its worst in the fall. We may have several tours in the hotel and they'll all come down for breakfast at 8:15 or 8:30, because their buses leave at 9. You have hundreds of people waiting to eat breakfast, lines in the lobby, buses leaving at 9, people getting edgy, and then if they have to miss breakfast to catch the bus they all want vouchers for another meal. It gets very confusing.

Tour wholesalers also tended to submit their passenger lists to the hotel at the last minute, a habit which both the sales division and the front desk found intensely annoying. "We like to get a rooming list three weeks beforehand for forecasting," Morin explained, "but tour groups will sell space in a tour till the day they leave. They'll send us a list with four names on it to meet the deadline, and then they'll give us any excuse to keep putting more names on. That's okay on weekends, but terrible on weeknights." Tours also often failed to meet their pre-established check-in times of 1 p.m. Groups coming in late were asked to wait in their buses until the lobby was clear of other tours, "but they always get out anyway and end up crowding around the desk," according to Morin.

Despite these frustrations, Morin felt that tour wholesalers offered one advantage to the hotel in addition to raising weekend occupancy: they did occasionally bring in corporate bonus trips. Fifty top sales representatives from a large corporation, for example, might be rewarded with a weekend in Boston and brought to the hotel in a group. Since corporations were less price-sensitive than tourists, the hotel could charge rack rate for each room.

TransAm Tours [disguised name] operated out of the West Coast and put together packaged tours for travel agents and individuals. This firm was considered a relatively "exclusive" tour wholesaler by the Parker House. "They're price-sensitive," Morin commented, "but their customers aren't." TransAm tourists were flown to Boston and then put aboard a bus which would transport them through New England. A typical group would come in late Thursday night, spend Friday exploring Boston and return after dinner, spend Saturday in New Hampshire, return to the hotel Saturday night, and leave early Sunday for Vermont. "They don't spend any money in the hotel, outside breakfast," Morin noted, "because they're never here."

Advertising, Promotion, and Customer Relations

The Parker House advertising strategy, as devised by Bill Murphy and Dunfey's senior marketing executives, was twofold. The hotel was promoted locally, as an individual property, and nationally, as a Dunfey Classic hotel. Although the need for strong promotion had been questioned, Paul Sacco, Dunfey's corporate director of sales, felt the Parker House's high average occupancy rate was very deceptive:

> The hotel is favored with a very heavy demand on Monday, Tuesday, and Wednesday nights. But we fight like hell to get people to stay on Sunday night, and we beg them to stay over Thursday and check out Friday—maybe stay for the weekend, bring their spouse. When we have an occupancy in the high 90s Sunday through Saturday, we will be satisfied. That's not presently the case.

Bill Murphy added:

> It's important not to look at it as though we do not need to sell any more. Actually, we have to work even harder—it's easier to get soft at the top. Our sales reps don't have a quota of 25 new accounts per week any more, but they do have a firm quota of 40 calls. That's necessary just to keep up with movement within firms and within the city.

All promotion at the Parker House was based on an Advertising Action Plan, again developed jointly by the hotel's EOC and corporate headquarters. This plan, which was revised every four months, set specific advertising and direct sales targets and established the budget and media through which these goals would be reached. Classic hotel advertising, budgeted at close to $800,000 in 1979, promoted the Parker House, the Berkshire Place, and the Ambassador East as a group, and was supervised by Dunfey's director of advertising and public relations.

The Classic hotels advertisement was designed to upgrade and promote the Dunfey corporate image while it simultaneously linked the three hotels as a group. A four-color, one-page ad, it first appeared in mid-1979 in the Boston, New York, Chicago, and Los Angeles editions of leading national news and business magazines. Local promotion of the Parker House as a Classic hotel was particularly important, according to Dunfey's advertising director:

> The Boston market is a very important source of guests for New York and Chicago. The Dunfey corporate image still needs to be supported. And also, though from a rooms point of view and an occupancy point of view they may not seem to need it, the combination of the Parker House with the Ambassador and the Berkshire is helping to further position the Parker House, further upgrade its image . . . as well as positioning Dunfey.

Local promotion for the Parker House was supervised by Bill Murphy, whose combined advertising and sales budget totalled approximately $260,000 in 1979. Except during December, January, and February, when occupancy averaged 75 percent, promotions (such as parties for clients or inexpensive desk items for travel agents) were not a major concern at the hotel.

Management placed a good deal of emphasis on customer reaction to the hotel. Questionnaires were distributed to clients after banquets; they were also placed prominently in every room. The cards were signed by Roy Dunfey, vice president of employee and guest relations, and designed to be mailed directly to him. Although comments were not tabulated by segment, it was McIntosh's opinion that bus tours complained the most. As he put it: "They are on limited budgets, they have high expectations because their vacation is a big thing for them, they have time on their hands for complaining, and they give lots of reinforcement to each other's objections."

THE CONTINUED DEBATE

The Parker House's dislike for tour groups was not totally shared in Dunfey headquarters, and by mid-October 1979, as the deadline for responding to TransAm's offer approached, discussions grew increasingly heated. From the beginning, there had been no doubt that the Berkshire Place business would be accepted. TransAm had originally offered to pay a flat $25 (double), mid-week and weekend, for 2,000 Berkshire guest nights. After bargaining the rate up to $55, Dunfey sales executives felt that the revised contract was almost indispensable, considering the Berkshire's occupancy rate: 60 percent in July 1979, 70 percent in August (breakeven was about 62 percent). Then came a strong intimation from TransAm that the Berkshire business might ultimately depend on a guarantee of all 4,000 guest-nights requested at the Parker House.

In the discussion that followed, Terry Flahive, Dunfey's regional director of sales for New England, argued in TransAm's favor, telling Paul Sacco, the corporate director of sales:

We're desperate for business in New York. From a corporate point of view, we want those room nights to make the Berkshire Place successful. I think we're going to have to bite the bullet at the Parker House, even though it might be bad rooms merchandising.

Sacco tended to agree. As he pointed out to Bill Murphy:

It isn't actually a big bite, because we definitely want the business at the Berkshire Place, and at the Parker House we want the weekends. What we're arguing about is weeknights, midweek, and the question is whether we should cut some of that revenue in order to capture the rest.

Murphy, on the other hand, was strongly opposed. He knew that the Parker House had already accepted a number of other advance tour bookings:

We're already booked very heavily to other tour brokers, and if we accept TransAm for every date they've requested, we're going to be rolling the dice a little bit, hoping we get some cancellations. What is even more important, in my opinion, is that if we add another tour group of this volume, we're going against the entire mission of the hotel.

TransAm's specific Parker House room requests are reproduced in *Exhibit 3*. Approximately half of these requests were accepted immediately, at a rate of $32/39, single/double (weekend) and $53/61 (weekday). TransAm then requested that the hotel accept the company's remaining tour bookings at a rate of $32/39 (weekend) and $63/73 (weekday); it was implied that all TransAm business would hinge on the hotel's acceptance of this latest offer.

Murphy and Flahive immediately began an intensive review of the specifics of the TransAm proposals, attempting to calculate exactly how much tour space was available and how much revenue the tours might generate, compared with expected transient and corporate business. The key to establishing room availability was the Group Rooms Con-

EXHIBIT 3
Transam's Requested Bookings at the Parker House, June–October 1980

	S	M	T	W	T	F	S
June					□26 a	□27 a	
July			1	2	3	4	5
	6	7	8	9	○10 a	○11 a	12
	13	14	15	16	17	18	19
	20	21	22	23	□24 a	□25 a	26
	27	28	29	30	○31 a		
August						○1 a	2
	3	4	5	6	○7 a	○8 a	9
	10	11	12	13	14	15	16
	17	18	19	20	□21 b	□22 b	23
	24	25	26	27	28	29	30
	31						
September		1	2	3	□4 a	□5 a	6
	7	8	9	10	□11 a	□12 a	13
	14	15	16	○17 *	△18 b	◇19 d	△20 a
	○21 a	22	○23 *	□24 *	△25 *	◇26 c	□27 a
	○28 *	○29 *	○30 *				
October				□1 *	△2 *	◇3 *	□4 *
	○5 *	○6 *	○7 *	△8 *	△9 *	◇10 b	□11 b
	○12 *	○13 *	○14 *	□15 *	△16 b	◇17 d	□18 a

Bookings Requested by TransAm Tours for Specific Dates:

○ One group (2 singles, 20 doubles, 1 complimentary for tour escort).

□ Two groups (4 singles, 40 doubles, 2 complimentary).

△ Three groups (6 singles, 60 doubles, 3 complimentary).

◇ Four groups (8 singles, 80 doubles, 4 complimentary).

Parker House's Initial Response to TransAm Requests:

[a] All reservations requested for that date were immediately accepted by the hotel.

[b] Only one group of requested bookings was accepted.

[c] Only two groups of requested bookings were accepted.

[d] Only three groups of requested bookings were accepted.

[*] None of requested bookings were accepted.

SOURCE: Company records.

EXHIBIT 4
Extract from Group Rooms Control Log

Type of Group	Gross	Net	S	M	T	W	T	F	S	Rates
*Number of rooms requested** — Day Aug.			17	18	19	20	21	22	23	
SST†			193	135	135	135	140	253	258	
Assoc./Corp.‡										
Definite	800	500	125	125	125	125				53/61
Tentative	600	600	100	100	100	100	100	100		NRQ#
Tours										
Definite	52	40					40			28/31/36
Tentative	169	164					47	72	45	NRQ

Type of Group	Gross	Net	S	M	T	W	T	F	S	Rates
Number of rooms requested — Day Aug.			24	25	26	27	28	29	30	
SST†			103	110	75	75	90	233	258	
Assoc./Corp.‡										
Definite	200	160	40	40	40	40				NRQ
Tentative	0	0								
Tours										
Definite	25	20					20			28/31/36
Tentative	632	593	25				67	238	263	28/43

Type of Group	Gross	Net	S	M	T	W	T	F	S	Rates
Number of rooms requested — Day Sep.			21	22	23	24	25	26	27	
SST			128	100	75	75	90	233	258	
Assoc./Corp.‡										
Definite	267	220				70	70	70	10	58/68
Tentative	100	80			80					NRQ
Tours										
Definite	50	40						20	20	28/31/36
Tentative	827	769		114			35	311	309	28/43

Type of Group	Gross	Net	S	M	T	W	T	F	S	Rates
Number of rooms requested — Day Sep./Oct.			28	29	30	Oct. 1	2	3	4	
SST†			138	90	75	75	75	218	238	
Assoc./Corp.										
Definite	298	293	50	60	50		61	61	11	NRQ
Tentative	0	0								
Tours										
Definite	225	198					20	45	133	NRQ
Tentative	576	500		85	20			185	210	30/43

Type of Group	Gross	Net	S	M	T	W	T	F	S	Rates
Number of rooms requested — Day Oct.			5	6	7	8	9	10	11	
SST			108	75	75	75	75	218	238	
Assoc./Corp.										
Definite	69	54					18	18	18	50/58
Tentative	0	0								
Tours										
Definite	200	170		40			20	45	65	28/43
Tentative	689	650		90	40		25	220	275	28/43

EXHIBIT 4 (continued)

Type of Group	Number of rooms requested Gross	Net	Day Oct. SST	S 12 148	M 13 50	T 14 50	W 15 60	T 16 60	F 17 208	S 18 188	Rates
Assoc./Corp.											
Definite	120	90							45	45	NRQ
Tentative	0	0									
Tours											
Definite	75	70		20					25	25	28/49
Tentative	717	659		162	20			22	226	229	33/46

*Gross = the number of rooms reserved by a group; net = salesperson's estimate of the number of rooms a group would actually occupy.

†SST = "selective sell target," the optimum number of rooms to be sold to associations, corporate groups, and tours.

‡Assoc./Corp. = professional or special-interest associations and corporate groups.

#NRQ = no rate quoted.

SOURCE: Company records.

trol Log (GRC), which listed "selective sell targets" for groups broken down by room night. By starting with the total number of rooms in the hotel (546) and subtracting projected transient, ESP, "patriot," and airline business, the sales department could apportion a certain number of rooms each night to be sold to groups of all kinds, including corporate groups, associations, and tours. GRCs for the remaining dates requested by TransAm are reproduced in *Exhibit 4*.

Potential TransAm revenues were then compared to the revenues to be derived from the sale of comparable rooms at projected summer and fall 1980 rack rates (*Exhibit 2*). Since it was not possible to know how guests would make their choices between room categories (e.g., standard vs. deluxe vs. top of the line), an average of standard and deluxe rates was used for calculations.

Murphy felt he was faced with three questions. Did the Parker House have space for TransAm on the dates not yet accepted (*Exhibit 3*)? Would the TransAm business be as profitable as reservations which might be booked simultaneously by other segments? And how many tours could the Parker House accept without altering the desired positioning of the hotel?

As he wrestled with these issues, the phone rang. Harvey Kimball was on the line. "Bill, I just talked to TransAm Tours," he announced. "They told me they're in the process of putting things together for Chicago —and under certain circumstances, might consider booking at the Ambassador East. Can we give them the go-ahead for the Parker House?"

University Health Service: Walk-In Clinic

SHAUNA DOYLE
ROCCO PIGNERI
DAVID H. MAISTER

The administrator of a walk-in health clinic is evaluating the performance of a triage system designed to reduce delays experienced by patients seeking different types of treatment. She wonders whether further changes are needed.

Kathryn Angell stared out her office picture window, oblivious to the bustle on Mount Auburn Street. In July 1979, shortly after receiving her Master's degree in Health Policy and Management from the Harvard School of Public Health, Angell was hired into a new University Health Service position as Assistant Director for Ambulatory Care. A major objective of the new position was the reorganization of the Walk-In Clinic—the exact topic of Angell's thesis.

As the chief administrator of the clinic, responsible for its daily functioning, the organization of medical and support services and its overall planning, the emphasis of Angell's position was clearly placed on the improvement of the delivery of medical care through better services coordination and the implementation of new programs. Soon after assuming her duties in July 1979, Angell implemented a triage system in the Walk-In Clinic, whereby arriving patients were screened by a triage coordinator to determine whether they should be treated by a nurse practitioner or a physician. After almost a year's operation under the new system, Angell's concern shifted from implementation to evaluation of the clinic's performance.

This case was prepared by Shauna Doyle, Research Assistant, and Rocco Pigneri, Research Assistant, under the direction of Assistant Professor David H. Maister. Copyright © 1981 by the President and Fellows of Harvard College, Harvard Business School case 9-681-061. Reproduced by permission.

THE UNIVERSITY HEALTH SERVICE

The University Health Service offered medical care to Harvard University students, staff, faculty and their dependents who elected certain health care plans in which the services of UHS were included. Since the system was prepaid for over 90 percent of the potential users, UHS operated primarily as a health maintenance organization.

The medical services provided to patients by UHS included surgical and 24-hour emergency facilities, an inpatient infirmary, four outpatient clinics (including the Walk-In and three primary care clinics associated with specific Harvard professional schools), mental health services, laboratory and x-ray facilities, and a variety of other specialized services. Patients were free to choose a personal physician, who could be seen by appointment and who would, if necessary, refer the patient to an appropriate specialist. Ailments of an acute or emergency nature were treated by the outpatient clinics.

For the 1979–1980 fiscal year, UHS was budgeted approximately $10 million to meet its total health care expenses (*Exhibit 1*). Of the $10 million, the Walk-In Clinic, including its emergency facilities, expended approximately 20 percent, including salaries to its medical professionals and clerical staff as well as its portion of overhead and supplies.

Physicians worked 46 forty-hour weeks in the year. Of the 40 hours, approximately 12 were spent in the Walk-In Clinic, 16 hours in meeting patients by appointment in the physician's office, 5 hours on duty at the UHS infirmary, and 7 hours on administrative and other matters. Included in the time for appointments (which were normally scheduled by the physician's secretary in half-hour intervals) were two half-hour periods per week known as "reserve time." These were periods when the doctor might ask patients to come to see her or him in the office, perhaps to check on the progress of treatment. Reserve time differed from regular appointments in that patients could not, by themselves, book appointments at these times: only the physician could schedule them. The physician could sometimes see up to 4 patients in one half-hour of reserve time. By well-established precedent, all UHS doctors were required to undertake duty in the Walk-

EXHIBIT 1
Income and Expense Statistics

INCOME	1979–80	%1978–79	%1979–80
Student health fee	$3,390,023	38.2	34.4
Student insurance	1,636,925	17.3	16.6
Harvard University			
Group Health Program	900,212	7.0	9.1
Payroll assessment	1,589,497	16.9	16.1
Care for Medicare	252,074	1.6	2.5
Radiation protection	435,603	3.8	4.4
Other services	1,628,448	15.2	16.9
Total	$9,832,782	100.0%	100.0%
EXPENSE			
Salaries, wages & benefits	$5,223,685	53.5	53.7
Student insurance	1,636,925	17.2	16.8
Building operations & maintenance	388,870	4.3	4.0
Medical/dental supplies	278,987	2.3	2.8
Outside laboratories	176,309	2.2	1.8
Malpractice insurance	49,048	1.1	.5
All other	1,967,436	19.4	20.4
Total	$9,721,260	100.0%	100.0%

In Clinic. Doctors who were associated with UHS on a part-time basis were normally allocated a proportionate share of their time in the clinic. While exceptions existed, most doctors preferred seeing patients in their office to Walk-In Clinic duty—partly because of the hectic pace of the Walk-In Clinic, but also because in their appointments they could deal with patients they knew and with whose medical records they were familiar. Salaries for physicians ranged from $35,000 to $55,000 for primary care physicians. Nurses were paid a range of $16,000 to $26,000, depending upon their level of practical experience. For both physicians and nurses, UHS incurred additional costs of 18.5 percent of salary in the form of benefits.

THE WALK-IN CLINIC

The Walk-In Clinic at the Holyoke Center provided the most comprehensive ambulatory care of the four walk-in clinics by offering the patient a portion of the total available UHS services. Patients with acute medical and surgical problems, who had not chosen a UHS personal physician, or who were unable to wait for appointments with their personal physicians, were served on a first-come, first-served basis Monday through Friday, 8 A.M. to 5:30 P.M. The clinic was also open on Saturday mornings, 8 A.M. to 12:45 P.M. Emergencies, of which there were relatively few, were of course treated immediately.

In 1979, over 37,400 patients visited the Walk-In Clinic for treatment of problems ranging from common ailments such as colds, nausea, and respiratory illnesses to those with more serious problems such as acute appendicitis and chest pains. Of the patients who visited the clinic, 67 percent were students, 23 percent staff, and 10 percent dependents and Medex and Medicare subscribers. One UHS study, conducted in 1980 over a three-week period, demonstrated that an average of 143 patients were seen per day (*Exhibits 2 and 3*).

Staffing levels for the Walk-In Clinic were scheduled on the basis of past experience

EXHIBIT 2
Daily Average of Patient Visits
by Day of the Week

Monday	163
Tuesday	151
Wednesday	136
Thursday	137
Friday	128
Average	143

Average Number of Patient Arrivals per Hour

8–9 A.M.	18.2
9–10 A.M.	17.6
10–11 A.M.	16.8
11–12 noon	15.2
12–1 P.M.	11.8
1–2 P.M.	16.9
2–3 P.M.	16.2
3–4 P.M.	15.9
4–5 P.M.	11.6
5–6 P.M.	2.8

EXHIBIT 3
Patient Distribution by Reason for Visit*

Reason	Percent of Total
Emergency	1.4
Medical: initial visit** *for spec complaint*	41.3
Medical: return visit	11.3
Medical: specific provider	24.0
Surgical: initial visit**	0.1
Surgical: return visit	0.8
Lab result	2.0
Premarital test	0.4
Blood pressure	2.2
Prescription: confirmed diagnosis	0.8
Prescription refill	2.0
Administrative	1.0
Other	1.7
Unspecified (missing)	11.0
	100%

*As indicated by the patient.

**Initial visit for the specific complaint: this is not to be interpreted as the patient's first visit *ever* to the Walk-In Clinic.

EXHIBIT 4
University Health Service—Walk-In Clinic:
Medical Professional Scheduling 1979 Walk-In Clinic

	Monday		Tuesday		Wednesday		Thursday		Friday	
	# MDs	# NPs	# MDs	# NPs	# MDs	# NPs	# MDs	# NPs	# MDs	# NPs
8–9 A.M.	2	2	2	2	2	2	2	2	2	2
9–10 A.M.	2.5	4	3	4	2.5	4	2	4	2.5	4
10–11 A.M.	5	4	4	4	5	4	5	4	5	4
11–12 noon	3	4	3	4	3	4	3	4	4	4
12–1 P.M.	3	2.5	2	2.5	2.5	2.5	3	2.5	2.5	2.5
1–2 P.M.	3	2.5	3	2.5	3	2.5	2	2.5	3	2.5
2–3 P.M.	3	4	4	4	3	4	3	4	4	4
3–4 P.M.	4	4	4	4	4	4	4	4	4	4
4–5 P.M.	3	2.5	2	2.5	2	2.5	3.5	2.5	3	2.5
5–6* P.M.	1	2	1	2	1	2	1	2	1	2

MD = Medical Doctor.
NP = Nurse Practitioner.
*The clinic admitted its last patient at 5:30 P.M. Staff were required to stay until 6 P.M.

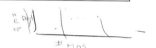

with peak periods of patient visits, which typically occurred between 10 A.M. and 4 P.M., according to the generally accepted impression of the UHS staff (*Exhibit 4*). No set criteria existed for establishing staffing levels; only minor adjustments were made year-to-year, at times that were felt to be too busy. Twenty-two physicians treated all patients in the clinic as part of their overall UHS responsibilities, and were scheduled by Ms. Angell for specific hours throughout the week, usually in blocks of 3 to 4 hours at a time. The Walk-In Clinic was also staffed by two registered nurses and eleven nurse practitioners, the latter being registered nurses with additional medical training capable of treating minor ailments without direct consultation with a physician. In a small number of cases, nurse practitioners also treated patients by appointment. Nurses and nurse practitioners worked 8-hour shifts, including one hour for lunch.

Nurse practitioners staffed the UHS emergency room at nights and weekends, and performed a variety of semiadministrative duties, such as receiving test results over the phone. Approximately 45 percent of nurse practitioner hours were available to treat patients in the Walk-In Clinic.

The Walk-In Clinic had 12 rooms available for seeing patients, 4 for nurses and 8 for doctors. However, 3 of the doctors' rooms were permanently assigned to individuals as their UHS offices, and were only available for Walk-In Clinic use at the times when those three individual physicians were scheduled for Walk-In Clinic duty.

PRE-TRIAGE ORGANIZATION

Before the triage system was instituted, a typical patient's visit to the Walk-In Clinic proceeded in the following way. On arrival, the patient signed in at the front desk, by providing basic identification information on a small, sequentially numbered sheet, and was then asked by a receptionist to take a seat in the waiting area. The receptionist next requested the patient's record from the Medical Records Department, who retrieved and sent down the record to the Walk-In Clinic in approximately 8–9 minutes. The receptionist then brought the record to the "medical desk" where a clerk checked to ensure that the patient's address and phone number were current and that all recent lab reports were present. When checking was completed, which took approximately 5 minutes, the clerk placed the record and the numbered sheet in a pile ordered according to the arrival of patients. Each patient was subsequently seen by the first available nurse when his or her medical record reached the top of the pile. If the problem was minor (such as a cold), the nurse would treat the patient definitively. However, if, after the nurse had done all she or he could, it was still necessary for the patient to see a physician, the patient would return to the waiting area and the nurse would put the record in a pile for the physicians, again according to the order of initial arrival. The patient would be seen, in turn, by the first available physician.

Widespread dissatisfaction had developed concerning the Walk-In Clinic. Waiting time between sign-in and treatment constituted the major complaint, specifically the waiting time to the first contact with a professional staff member capable of assessing the patient's problem. This time period averaged 23 minutes; however, as many as 22 percent of all patients who saw a nurse had to wait over 35 minutes for this first contact. A study of the Walk-In Clinic done in November 1978 found that patients who requested specific nurses or physicians at sign-in waited an average of 40 minutes before seeing the desired staff member; this group comprised approximately 19 percent of the total patient load. If a nurse had to refer a patient on to a doctor, an average of 10 minutes elapsed between the end of the nurse visit and the meeting with the doctor. Some patients complained that the length of their wait often had no relation to the nature of the visit such as a 55-minute wait for a prescription renewal. Other patients reportedly decided to avoid potential visits to the Walk-In Clinic because of the anticipated wait. Consequently, patients viewed the Walk-In Clinic as cold, inefficient, and impersonal since there was such a time gap between sign-in and treatment.

Members of the UHS administrative and medical staff also expressed feelings that the Walk-In Clinic could function better than it had. Sholem Postel, M.D., the Deputy Director and Chief of Professional Services (physicians and nurses) at UHS, and the person to whom Angell reported with respect to the Walk-In Clinic, commented on the pre-triage system's problems:

> All the nurses were involved in seeing all the patients initially. This created a bottleneck as each nurse independently decided the extent of care for a patient and then provided as much of that care as possible before, if necessary, having the patient wait to be seen by a physician for the rest of the care. This led to inconsistency and too much variation in treatment, given the different skills and experience levels of individual nurses. Furthermore, though nurses saw 100 percent of the patients, they treated only 40 percent definitively. The result: duplicated efforts (time, questions and examinations) for 60 percent of our patients.

THE TRIAGE SYSTEM

To overcome these problems, a "triage system" was introduced in September 1979 by the UHS administration. The system was defined as "the preliminary evaluation and referral of patients to the necessary health resource, based on decisions about the nature of the patients' problems and knowledge of the priorities and capabilities of the available health care resources."

Under the triage system, the patient upon arrival filled out an Ambulatory Visit Form (AVF) which requested the patient's reason for visit as well as identification information (*Exhibit 5*). If the patient checked off "emergency care," the front desk personnel immediately notified a physician, nurse practitioner or triage coordinator who then more thoroughly assessed the patient's condition. In most cases, however, the front desk simply reviewed the AVF for completeness and requested the patient's record from Medical Records. Upon arrival of the record in 8–9 minutes, the appropriate clerical personnel matched the record with the AVF, ensured that all personal information and prior tests were properly filed and updated in the record, and then placed them chronologically in a "triage pile."

In turn, one of two "triage coordinators" called for the patient and provided the initial contact. The two triage coordinators were both highly experienced registered nurses. It was felt that experience was necessary so that they could make accurate assessments and preliminary diagnoses. The triage coordinator visited with the patient in a private room and, on the basis of the immediately available information and a brief discussion with the patient, summarized the nature of the patient's problem. If the triage nurse, in determining the severity of the patient's problem, decided the ailment warranted more immediate care, she would then put the patient ahead of others waiting to see a physician.

As one triage coordinator explained:

> My duties are to determine the chief complaint of the patient and to triage him or her to an MD or nurse practitioner. I'll spend 3–4 minutes per patient in an average encounter and I rarely have to deviate from this—only when people are unable to clearly describe their symptoms or when they overestimate the severity of their illness. However, there is no time constraint in determining the status of a patient.

The triage coordinator did not treat the patient but determined, according to guidelines and her discretion, whether the patient needed to see a nurse practitioner or a physician in the Walk-In Clinic and whether the problem could be better handled by an appointment or referral to another service within UHS. Patients were triaged to a nurse practitioner if their ailments fell under one of thirteen categories (*Exhibit 6*). All other ailments outside the guidelines required the attention of a physician, unless the triage nurse, by using her discretion, felt a nurse practitioner could treat the problem. If, however, the nurse practitioner attended a problem which was not included under the thirteen categories, a physician was required to countersign the treatment. This required the nurse to find a doctor who would sign the medical record, thereby authorizing the treatment recommended by the nurse. In some cases, the doctor might choose to meet with or examine the patient before signing. Other doctors would sign without examining further. Expansion of the guidelines beyond the thirteen specific ailments would, by state law, require the drafting of detailed treatment guides so that a nurse practitioner could be allowed to treat the patient without consulting a physician. The UHS planned on such expansion in the near future. However, it was not known how many patients this might affect.

After the visit with the triage coordinator, the patient returned to the waiting area while his/her record was placed by the triage nurse chronologically in either the nurse practitioner or the physician "pile," unless more immediate care was deemed necessary by the triage coordinator. As physicians and nurse practitioners then finished with their previous patient, they summoned the next patient in their respective piles for treatment. Although significant variation existed, MDs saw an average of 3.10 patients per hour while approximately 1.83 patients per hour were seen by nurse practitioners.

When the triage system was instituted, it was expected that the waiting time to see a triage coordinator would be about 15 minutes, and waiting time to be seen by a nurse practitioner or a physician would be less than 10 minutes. A 1980 UHS study reported, however, that patients waited a mean length of 19.7 minutes to the point of being triaged and a mean time of 18.6 minutes from the start of the patient's visit with the triage coordinator to the point of being seen by either a nurse practitioner or a physician. The average total waiting time was 37.5 minutes, including the actual time to be triaged (*Exhibit 7*). Approximately 67 percent of the patients were triaged to a physician whereas 33 percent were triaged to a nurse practitioner. Ms. Angell commented,

> When we introduced the triage system, we thought the nurse practitioners would accept more of the patient load and leave the physicians more time on a per patient basis. Unfortunately, it has not worked out that way. Among the reasons for this might be the fact that, as we discovered, the triage coordinators

→ add sign delays.

EXHIBIT 5

Ambulatory Visit Form

Nº 82336

UNIVERSITY HEALTH SERVICES : WALK-IN CLINIC

AMBULATORY VISIT FORM

FOR PATIENT USE: PLEASE FILL OUT THIS SECTION COMPLETELY

TIME & DATE

UHS/ HARVARD I.D. NO.

NAME: PLEASE PRINT

First　Middle　Last

BIRTHDATE　Mo.　Day　Yr.

MALE ☐
FEMALE ☐

LOCAL ADDRESS

PHONE DURING THE DAY

LOCATION OF VISIT:
☐ Holyoke Center　☐ Law School
☐ Business School　☐ Medical Area

IS THIS YOUR FIRST VISIT TO
A UHS FACILITY? YES ☐

IF YOUR MEDICAL RECORD IS KEPT AT A UHS FACILITY OTHER THAN
HOLYOKE CENTER, PLEASE CHECK HERE: BUSINESS ☐　LAW ☐　MEDICAL AREA ☐

STATUS
☐ H/R UNDERGRAD., CLASS
☐ GRAD. SCHOOL (Name)
☐ LESLEY COLLEGE
☐ EPISCOPAL DIVINITY SCHOOL
☐ STAFF WITH HARVARD BC/BS
☐ STAFF WITH HARVARD UNIVERSITY
　GROUP HEALTH PROGRAM (HUGHP)
☐ STAFF WITH NO HARVARD INSURANCE
☐ HARVARD MEDEX
☐ MEDICARE (ONLY)

☐ STUDENT DEPENDENT WITH UHS COVERAGE
☐ STUDENT DEPENDENT WITH UHS COVERAGE
　– UNDER 14 YEARS OLD
☐ HUGHP DEPENDENT
☐ HUGHP DEPENDENT–UNDER 14 YEARS OLD
☐ MEDEX DEPENDENT
☐ SUMMER SCHOOL: STUDENT
　　　　FACULTY　　FAC. DEPENDENT
☐ NON-MEMBER OF HARVARD UNIVERSITY
☐ OTHER

FOR WALK-IN PATIENTS ONLY

The following information is designed to help us treat you promptly and efficiently.
All information will be kept confidential. If you do not wish to complete the rest of
the form, please check "personal" and you will be seen in turn.

WHAT IS THE REASON FOR YOUR VISIT?　PLEASE CHECK:

☐ I NEED **EMERGENCY** CARE.

☐ BLOOD PRESSURE CHECK **ONLY**

PRESCRIPTION(S) ONLY
☐ DIAGNOSIS CONFIRMED; INSTRUCTED
　TO OBTAIN PRESCRIPTION
☐ PRESCRIPTION REFILL:
　UHS　　　OTHER

GENERAL MEDICAL PROBLEM
☐ FIRST VISIT FOR THIS PROBLEM
☐ RETURN (REPEAT) VISIT FOR THIS
　PROBLEM
☐ TOLD TO SEE:
　　　　NURSE OR DOCTOR

GENERAL SURGICAL PROBLEM
☐ FIRST VISIT FOR THIS PROBLEM
☐ RETURN (REPEAT) VISIT FOR THIS
　PROBLEM
☐ TOLD TO SEE:
　　　　NURSE OR DOCTOR

ADMINISTRATIVE PROBLEM
☐ SPORTS CLEARANCE
☐ MEDICAL EXCUSE FOR EXAM
☐ MEDICAL FORMS TO BE COMPLETED

☐ PERSONAL

☐ OTHER

LABORATORY PROCEDURES ONLY
☐ LAB RESULTS DESIRED
☐ PREMARITAL TESTS DESIRED
☐ PREGNANCY TEST REQUISITION

FOR UHS USE ONLY

TRIAGE TIME　　TIME PT. SEEN

PROVIDER 1　NUMBER
NAME

PROVIDER 2　NUMBER
NAME

TYPE OF CONTACT
☐ WALK-IN
☐ APPOINTMENT
☐ BROKEN APPOINTMENT
☐ CANCELLED BY UHS
☐ CANCELLED BY PATIENT
☐ LEFT BEFORE BEING SEEN
☐ RESERVE
☐ OTHER

SERVICE
☐ MEDICAL
☐ SURGICAL
☐ EMERGENCY
☐ ALLERGY
☐ DENTAL
☐ DERMATOLOGY
☐ EYE
☐ EAR, NOSE, & THROAT
☐ GASTROENTEROLOGY
☐ GYNECOLOGY

☐ IMMUNIZATION
☐ MENTAL HEALTH
☐ NEUROLOGY
☐ NUTRITION
☐ OBSTETRICS
☐ ORTHOPEDICS
☐ PEDIATRICS
☐ PHYSICAL THERAPY
☐ UROLOGY
☐ OTHER

☐ INITIAL VISIT FOR THIS PROBLEM

☐ RETURN VISIT

Please circle as many lab test boxes as apply.

HEMATOLOGY
PROVIDER NO.:
1　2
☐ ☐　COULTER CBC
☐ ☐　DIFFERENTIAL
☐ ☐　OCCULT BLOOD (GUAIAC)
☐ ☐　PLATELET COUNT
☐ ☐　PROTHROMBIN TIME
☐ ☐　RETICULOCYTE COUNT
☐ ☐　SEDIMENTATION RATE
☐ ☐　OTHER

CHEMISTRY
PROVIDER NO.:
1　2
☐ ☐　BILIRUBIN
☐ ☐　BLOOD GLUCOSE
☐ ☐　BLOOD UREA NITROGEN (BUN)
☐ ☐　CHOLESTEROL
☐ ☐　CREATININE
☐ ☐　ELECTROLYTES
☐ ☐　SGOT
☐ ☐　SMA 12/60
☐ ☐　T₃ UPTAKE
☐ ☐　T4
☐ ☐　TRIGLYCERIDES
☐ ☐　URIC ACID
☐ ☐　OTHER:

SEROLOGY
PROVIDER NO.:
1　2
☐ ☐　HETEROPHILE
☐ ☐　RPR
☐ ☐　RUBELLA
☐ ☐　OTHER:

BACTERIOLOGY
PROVIDER NO.:
1　2
☐ ☐　CERVICAL/URETHRAL CULTURE
　　　　& GRAM STAIN
☐ ☐　STOOL FOR CULTURE
☐ ☐　STOOL FOR OVA & PARASITES
☐ ☐　THROAT CULTURE
☐ ☐　URINE CULTURE
☐ ☐　OTHER:

MISCELLANEOUS
PROVIDER NO.:
1　2
☐ ☐　BLOOD TYPE & RH
☐ ☐　ELECTROCARDIOGRAM
☐ ☐　MONILIA
☐ ☐　PAP SMEAR
☐ ☐　PATHOLOGY
☐ ☐　PREGNANCY TEST
☐ ☐　PULMONARY FUNCTION
☐ ☐　TRICHOMONAS (WET PREP)
☐ ☐　URINALYSIS
☐ ☐　OTHER:

are sometimes classifying patients as "MD/NP" (physician/nurse practitioner) to maintain the flow when they feel the practitioners are backed up. The MD's share of patients thus gets increased in overload situations. We did not want to have "MD/NP" as a classification, and have asked the triage coordinators to stop using it. When in doubt, they are to triage the patient to a nurse practitioner.

Among the patients who were initially seen by a nurse practitioner, about 5 percent were then referred to a second provider, usually a physician. Either the patient would remain in the NP's room while the NP fetched an MD, or, if longer MD treatment time was anticipated, the patient would join the MD waiting line, their file being placed in the MID pile according to the AVF number. Thus, if any other patient still in the MD queue had arrived before the referred patient, that other patient would be seen first. Though the mean times to be triaged to an MD or NP were relatively equal (approximately 19 minutes), as would be expected, the mean waiting time to see a physician was much longer (25.2 minutes) than the mean waiting time to see a nurse practitioner (6.7 minutes).

It was suspected that one of the factors creating differences in the waiting time to be seen by a physician versus a nurse practitioner was the percentage of patients who asked to see a specific provider of medical care. This percentage increased, for physicians in particular, after the institution of the triage system to a total of 24 percent of all patients. These patients still had first to see a triage nurse, who might attempt to dissuade them from waiting for a specific provider. If, however, the patient chose to wait, he or she did not obtain any priority over patients who were ahead in the system. For almost one-third of the physicians, more than 40 percent of the patients they saw in the Walk-In Clinic specifically asked for them (*Exhibit 8*).

Though the waiting time for triage was the same for the patients who asked for a specific physician or nurse practitioner and for patients who did not, the waiting time to be seen by the specific provider requested was 8.6 minutes longer on average for the

EXHIBIT 6

Categories Treatable Under Guidelines by Nurse Practitioners

1. Acute viral respiratory illness (primarily colds)
2. Amenorrhea (missed menstruation)
3. Cerumen (wax in ears)
4. Enterobiasis (pinworms)
5. Lower urinary tract infection (females)
6. Mononucleosis
7. Nausea, vomiting, diarrhea
8. Pediculosis capitus (lice)
9. Pediculosis pubis (lice)
10. Pharyngitis (sore throat)
11. Rubella (German measles)
12. Seasonal rhinitis (hayfever)
13. Vaginitis (vaginal infection)

EXHIBIT 7

Percentage of Patients Waiting, by Time Waited

Interval (minutes)	Waiting Time to be triaged	Waiting Time to be seen (after triage)	Total Waiting Time
0–4	1%	24%	0%
5–9	8	14	3
10–14	24	12	7
15–19	25	11	10
20–24	19	9	10
25–29	11	8	14
30–34	6	8	11
35–39	2	5	10
40–44	1	4	8
45–49	1	3	6
50–54	1	2	7
55+	1	0	14
	100%	100%	100%
Average	19.7	18.6	37.5

patients who asked. But as Mary Dineen, Supervisor of Outpatient Nursing, commented:

It seems doctors are allowed "walk-in appointments" with their own regular patients. Patients whose doctors have heavily booked appointment schedules become aware of the doctor's walk-in schedule and come into the

Physician*	Total No. of Patients Seen	No. of Patients Who Asked to See Specific MD (%)	Total No. of Hours	No. of Patients Seen per Hour	Calendar Days to First Available Appointment
Zuromskis	113	33 (29.2)	36	3.14	9
Bogota	50	23 (46.0)	17	2.94	24
Wellington	89	— —	18	4.94	5
Byrd	76	26 (34.2)	33	2.30	15
Recife	78	48 (61.5)	24	3.25	25
Brunei	113	45 (39.8)	36	3.14	17
Lobito	28	10 (35.7)	6	4.67	21
Santiago	91	43 (47.3)	29	3.14	3
Hobart	59	27 (45.8)	24	2.46	28
Seoul	90	34 (37.8)	28	3.21	5
Kingston	113	26 (23.0)	25	4.52	7
Java	78	16 (20.5)	27	2.89	13
Rome	74	32 (43.2)	19	3.89	7
Ottawa	82	31 (37.8)	26	3.15	5
Caracus	53	17 (32.1)	18	2.94	7
Manila	25	18 (72.0)	9	2.78	23
Durban	48	41 (85.4)	18	2.67	29
Luanda	61	5 (8.2)	21	2.90	8
Papua	34	— —	9	3.78	—
Glasgow	35	2 —	9	3.89	12
Cristobal	33	3 (9.1)	19.5	1.69	2
Aukland	16	1 (6.3)	12.5	1.28	—
	1439	481 (33.4)	464	3.11	17

*Some names in this exhibit have been changed.

Walk-In Clinic at prearranged times to meet. This may be a necessary evil to some degree, but today, for example, two of the five doctors on duty are 100 percent occupied with "walk-in appointments." This decreases our available MD resources by 40 percent for true walk-in patients today and fills up our waiting room.

Peter Zuromskis, M.D., a physician in the Walk-In Clinic, also suggested reasons for the misuse of the walk-in operation:

My evaluation of the dissatisfaction our patients have sometimes expressed with this system is that it represents an approach to acute ambulatory care which is quite different from that which they have previously experienced. Patients understandably find appealing the nostalgic image of the general practitioner who knows his patients well and is able to provide advice and treatment of minor illnesses in his office with an apparent minimum of clerical encumbrances. This is clearly impossible in a clinic which provides the volume and variety of medical care services that UHS offers to a large and heterogeneous population with a wide variety of diseases, from relatively minor complaints to major medical emergencies. Our aim is not and should not be to provide an atmosphere reminiscent of the country doctor's office, but rather to provide the best possible care to all our patients, particularly to those whose medical needs are most urgent.

Although people, for the first time ever, had been giving unsolicited praise to the new system, Angell knew that it still had problems and didn't always work as it had been designed. Some patient complaints still noted "excessive" waiting times and misunderstanding of the triage systems illustrated by the following specific, though not average, opinion submitted to the UHS Patient Advocate:

> In order to see a doctor about a very simple problem (a mild sore throat), I have seen a "triage nurse" (who stamped my form and passed me on) and a "nurse practitioner" (who looked, felt, and probed, but dared not offer an opinion). I am now 30 minutes into my visit, much handled, but not within sight of a doctor.

The medical, clerical, and administrative staff within the Walk-In Clinic, however, felt that although the efficiency of the clinic was still at less than a desirable level, the triage system was an improvement. As Warren Wacker, M.D., the Director of UHS, commented:

> Right now, I'm satisfied with the results of the triage system and I expect the system to be operating very well in another year. Of course, we'll have to resolve some sticky issues in the meantime. For instance, we need to expand the 13 nurse practitioner guidelines and further define the roles of nurse practitioner and physician within the Walk-In Clinic. Another item is how do we educate students in the Walk-In Clinic concept? Expectations of traditional medicine don't fit with the walk-in concept.

ANGELL'S DILEMMA

Angell now had the difficulty of sorting through a year's performance data, the concerns raised by several distinct groups associated with the clinic, and her own subjective observations. What changes needed to be made, if any? Were waiting times now acceptable? What was, after all, acceptable? Ms. Angell knew that work was in progress to expand the 13 nurse practitioner guidelines, but would this be enough to solve any remaining problems?

Among her biggest concerns was the issue of "walk-in appointments." She commented:

> We have tried in the past to ask the doctors to refrain from encouraging their patients to meet

them in the Walk-In Clinic. However, we have not had very much success, since the practice continues. Some of the doctors feel that they want *their* patients to see only them. Part of this is for medical reasons (the doctors wish to check on their patient's progress) and part of it is a general philosophy that medical care involves more than just treatment, and that personal relationships add to both the quality of health care and the patient's perception of good service. Many patients, perhaps appropriately, have the attitude of wanting to see "*my* doctor." Apart from the fact that you can never dictate to doctors, the UHS has always had a philosophy of not trying to tell physicians how to practice medicine.

Part of the problem is the general availability of appointment time. All our patients have the freedom to select their own "personal physician" from among any of our doctors. However, this often means that some are overloaded. Our overall staffing level at UHS is set approximately to provide one physician per 2,000 people covered by our various health plans. At the moment, the only way we try to limit the number of patients "assigned" to any given doctor, is by pointing out to the potential patient the difficulty of getting an appointment with an overloaded physician, and this is generally only done if the patient asks about it. We do not know how many patients each doctor is seeing as the patient's "personal physician," since this is an arrangement made by the doctor and the patient and not a formal "assignment."

There are a number of potential alternatives for dealing with this problem. We could try to educate our patient public on the separate purposes and missions of doctor appointments and the Walk-In Clinic—try to get them to use each appropriately. We could ask the triage coordinators to be a little more aggressive in asking patients who request a specific physician whether they really need to see that person and suggest alternatives. Ultimately, we could establish a firm policy of not accepting specific physician requests in the Walk-In Clinic.

Angell had these questions and more to consider over the next two weeks. At that time, she would share her findings and proposals with Ms. Dineen and Dr. Postel, since they would all have to agree on necessary changes and be involved in their implementation, if any changes were to succeed.

PART V
The Search for Service Quality

Why Is Service So Bad?
Pul-eeze! Will
Somebody Help Me?

STEPHEN KOEPP

Frustrated American consumers wonder where the service went. The economic upheavals of the 1970s and new technology seem to be at the root of the deteriorating quality of service in the U.S. Many service workers are poorly trained and overworked, but the increasing emphasis on price competition also means cutbacks in service personnel.

For Harry Hapless, it was a rough day in the service economy. His car, a Fiasco 400, started sputtering on the highway, so Harry pulled into a gas station for help. "Sorry, no mechanics, only gas!" shouted the attendant. "How can you call this a service station?" yelled Harry. He went to the bank to get some emergency cash for a tow truck, only to find the automatic teller machine out of order, again. "Real nice service!" he muttered. Then Harry decided to use a credit card to buy a tool kit at the Cheapo discount store, but he couldn't find anyone to wait on him. "Service! Anyone, please! Help me!" was his cry.

It had been a trying day indeed, Harry thought as he rode a bus home, but at least he could look forward to a trip to Florida the following week

with his wife Harriet. That is, until Flyway Air called: "Sorry, Mr. Hapless. Due to our merger with Byway Air, your Florida flight has been canceled." Harry got so angry he was going to call the Federal Aviation Administration immediately. But just then his phone went dead—no doubt because the Bell System had been split up, he imagined. Well, that was the last straw. A few minutes later a wild-eyed Harry burst into the newsroom of his local newspaper. "I've got a story for you!" he cried. "There is no more service in America!"

More and more consumers are beginning to feel almost as frustrated as Harry Hapless. Personal service has become a maddeningly rare commodity in the American market-

208

place. Flight attendants, salesclerks and bank tellers all seem to have become too scarce and too busy to give consumers much attention. Many other service workers are underpaid, untrained and unmotivated for their jobs, to the chagrin of customers who look to them for help. The concept of personal service is a difficult quantity to measure precisely, to be sure; the U.S. Government keeps no Courtesy Index or Helpfulness Indicator among its economic statistics. But customers know service when they miss it, and now they want it back. Says Thomas Peters, a management consultant and co-author of *In Search of Excellence:* "In general, service in America stinks."

Economic upheaval is to blame. First came the great inflation of the 1970s, which forced businesses to slash service to keep prices from skyrocketing. Then came deregulation, which fostered more price wars and further cutbacks. Meanwhile, service workers became increasingly difficult to hire because of labor shortages in many areas. At the same time, managers found that they could cut costs by replacing human workers with computers and self-service schemes. It all makes perfect bookkeeping sense for businesses, but the trend has left consumers without enough human faces to turn to for guidance in spending their billions of dollars on services. Americans tolerated, and even welcomed, self-service during an era of rising prices, but now a backlash is beginning. Result: some companies are scrambling to make amends, and "quality of service" is on its way to becoming the next business buzz phrase.

Ominously, the rising clamor suggests that something fundamental may be wrong in the vaunted U.S. service economy, in which the country has put so much hope for future prosperity. If service industries are beginning to dominate the economy, one might ask, why is there so little good service to be found? Is America in danger of becoming the no-can-do society? The question is becoming increasingly urgent. As manufacturing has declined in relative importance, the service sector has become the engine of U.S. economic growth. Of 12.6 million new jobs created since the end of the last recession, in 1982, almost 85 percent have been in service industries as opposed to goods-producing fields.

Sloppy service could become more than just a domestic annoyance. Economists have begun to warn that slipping standards could cost the U.S. its international competitive standing in services and thus worsen the country's trade problems. Japanese banks, for example, have already made inroads into the U.S. market. In the November-December [1986] issue of the *Harvard Business Review*, Professor James Quinn and Researcher Christopher Gagnon of Dartmouth's Amos Tuck School of Business contend that many U.S. service businesses have developed the same shortsighted habits and inattention to quality that American manufacturers have been guilty of—with disastrous results. "While there is still time," they write, "it is essential to take a hard look at how we think about services, how we manage them, and how much they contribute to the nation's economic health."

The potential of service businesses losing touch is chilling because it was the U.S. that practically invented the concept of good service on a mass-market scale. The country's huge appetite for reliable service gave rise to such pioneers as AT&T, IBM, American Express, McDonald's and Federal Express. But many U.S. companies today are failing to achieve the right balance of high-tech expedience vs. personal attention. "The state of service is pretty bad," admits Kenneth Hamlet, president of the Holiday Inn Hotel Group.

Among consumers, swapping horror stories about their confrontations with poor service has become a cathartic exercise. Many have never obtained satisfaction for their gripes, despite exhausting efforts. Kevin Kinnear, a Chicago software engineer, became increasingly angry with each of four trips to his car dealer to get the cruise control repaired on his 1985 Buick Century. Finally, he gave up when the mechanics made it clear that they no longer wanted to deal with his problem. Jane Ullman, a Santa Monica, Calif., sculptor, thought her refrigerator problems were over when deliverymen installed a new deluxe model in her kitchen. But her woes were just beginning; the workmen broke the refrigerator's copper pipes, which took several visits from repairmen to fix. "People have learned to take shoddy service in stride," she says wearily. Even when they speak up and get their money back, consumers often come away with a feeling of being abused. Earlier this month, when a Los Angeles homemaker took back a foul-smelling piece of fish to a supermarket on the city's west side, she got a refund only after answering brusque questions and signing papers. At no time did anybody apologize or give the slightest sign that they regretted spoiling her dinner.

Some of the longest, most tortured consumer stories involve home delivery. When Tony and Sandra Cantafio of Redondo Beach, Calif., bought a bed last October, they had to wait four weeks for it to arrive because of lost paperwork and other snafus. The result for Cantafio was an aching back from sleeping on the sofa. But there was another pain: to get the bed finally, Cantafio had to take an entire day off from his job as an aerospace executive because the deliverymen refused to predict what time they would arrive at his home.

In other cases, workers spoil an otherwise fine job with an almost creatively bad gesture. A Manhattan woman who bought carpet from a tony department store was pleased that the two installers were so friendly and efficient, but puzzled about why they left "like two robbers in a getaway car." Later she discovered the reason: they had used her bathroom as a dumpster for a three-foot pile of carpet clippings and packing material.

Sometimes consumers encounter sales clerks who cannot find the "on" button on electronic equipment they are selling. A clerk handling vacuum cleaners in a department store confesses to a customer, "I don't know a damn thing about these." Over in the shoe department, clerks nowadays may simply dump boxes at customers' feet rather than helping them with the merchandise.

Consumer grief is even becoming part of the pop culture. Comedian Jay Leno says that when he chided a supermarket clerk for failing to say thank you, she snapped, "It's printed on your receipt!" The film *Back to the Future* cracked up its audiences with a scene in which Michael J. Fox's character, who has traveled back in time, walks past a 1950s-era filling station and is flabbergasted to see four cheery attendants in neatly pressed coveralls. Like a pit crew at the Indianapolis 500, they dash up to a car and proceed to fill the gas tank, check the oil, clean the windows and polish the chrome.

Current U.S. levels of service sometimes appear lax to Americans when they return home from trips to Japan and Western Europe. While no country boasts the highest standards in every field, other cultures are more demanding of some services than America is. Most European countries insist on timely and efficient service on their railroads and airlines, which receive state subsidies to assure that performance. Americans who visit London typically come away with fond memories of the city's excellent taxicabs and subway system. The shortage of personal attention comes just when U.S. consumers are enjoying a cornucopia of novel products and services. Thus the deterioration of basic, personal service is taking the fun out of the new offerings. Shoppers can now find ten kinds of mustard and a dozen varieties of vinegar in a supermarket, but where is a clerk who can give a guiding word about these products? Airlines offer a bonanza of cheap fares, but many travel agents no longer want to be bothered handling such unprofitable business. That leaves consumers on their own, so they have to grab brochures and do their homework if they hope to make a correct decision. To take advantage of consumer advances today requires a tougher and smarter buyer.

Yet a growing number of shoppers have no time to get smart. Two-income householders have become hooked on convenience. Their expectations of quick, personal service have risen at a time when they are less likely to find it. Result: growing friction between harried workers and hurried customers. Says Irma Reyes, a New York City bank teller: "We try to service customers within three minutes after they walk into the bank, but they expect you to work miracles for them. Some customers get annoyed simply because you ask for identification."

The widespread perception of poor service has reached most corners of the U.S. because some of the worst offenders are national chains. Yet big-city consumers more frequently encounter poor service because some businesses feel they have an abundant supply of customers and thus are not dependent on long-term relationships with the shopper. Says Paul Schervish, a sociology professor at Boston College: "The situation is adversarial in a peculiar way. The seller acts as though the customer's gain is his or her loss and not mutually beneficial." In small towns with a more limited pool of shoppers, by comparison, buyer and seller have a long-term expectation of encountering each other again.

The simple reason that service workers have so little attention to give is that businesses often overwork them to save labor costs and keep prices low. Flight attendants, for example, once had time to chat with their passengers, but now their work is so speeded up that they can barely make sure all seat backs and tray tables are in their upright positions. If today's jumbo jets were staffed at the levels of a decade ago, an airline-union official says, the planes would carry 20 flight attendants instead of 12 to 14.

Service workers who handle customers over the telephone have been speeded up most of all. Any consumer who regularly talks to rental-car reservations clerks or mail-order takers probably feels the rush. Reason: computers monitor the workers' calls to measure performance. If a phone operator spends too much time with one customer, it spoils his or her average and standing on the job. Operators have been known to fake a disconnection when customers ask questions that are too complicated. Observes Harley Shaiken, professor of work and technology at the University of California at San Diego: "These assembly-line methods increase profits by boosting productivity, but there is a long-term hidden cost—the decline in service."

Many businesses would hire more service workers if they could, but a post-baby-boom shortage of young workers has created a critical scarcity of labor to handle minimum-wage ($3.35-an-hour) positions in restaurants and stores. Moreover, many salesclerks, delivery-truck drivers and other service workers are unmotivated because of the low pay and lack of career path in their jobs. Says journalist David Halberstam, whose recent best seller *The Reckoning* chronicled the decline of America's auto industry: "The main questions are: Does this job lead to anything? Does it have any dignity? No. We are dividing ourselves along class lines by education."

Too many service workers lack any pride or satisfaction in their jobs, especially in a society that, like America's, puts so much emphasis on speedy upward mobility. Says Thomas Kelly, an assistant professor at Cornell University's School of Hotel Administration: "In our culture, these jobs are not considered a worthwhile occupation. When workers view giving service as beneath them, it shows." The problem is notable among restaurant waiters, whose jobs were once regarded as legitimate careers. Now most waiters spend too little time in their jobs to become seasoned. "Sometimes I miss the graying at the temples among my staff," says Joseph Baum, co-owner of Manhattan's service-minded Aurora restaurant.

Businesses in general spend too little time training and motivating their front-line employees, whom they treat as the lowest workers on the ladder. The tendency has been to economize on the training process by designing service jobs to have the fewest possible skills. That keeps employee mistakes at a minimum, but it may hurt morale and make it difficult for workers to use their heads to solve unusual consumer problems when they arise. "Service people can become so robotized in their actions that they greet any customer request with a standardized response," write Karl Albrecht, a management consultant, and Ron Zemke in their 1985 book, *Service America! Doing Business in the New Economy.*

Too much of the training tends to dwell on handling the machinery of a job rather than the feelings of the customers. Cashiers must typically type a multidigit inventory code into a computer just to sell a 50¢ birthday card. That process reduces the number of accountants needed back at corporate headquarters but does nothing to help either the customer or the salesperson's sense of worth. Confesses an Avis car-rental clerk at a desk in a posh Los Angeles hotel: "The computer training was real good. I know how to do all this technical stuff, but nobody prepared me for dealing with all these different types of people."

Consumers want smiles more than ever because they have become strongly resentful of machines, even though computers have made services more efficient in many respects. Behind-the-scenes mainframes enable auto-rental firms, for example, to keep a customer's account information on file so that making a reservation takes only 30 seconds on the telephone. No one would want to give up such conveniences, yet the more that computers come into play in handling consumers, the more customers crave reassurance that humans will intervene when help is needed. Gripes Howard Mileaf, a New York City lawyer and Chemical Bank customer: "I used to have the illusion that a real person was looking after my account, but now I know better!"

Some computer-buff managers tend to impose technology almost compulsively, whether it is appreciated or not. When Virginia Boggs of Bellflower, Calif., went to a department store to buy a wedding gift, the clerk told her to go to a nearby computer and punch in the bride's name to learn her silver pattern. Boggs, who is computer-illiterate and proud of it, refused. "I don't even use the computer in my own business," she said. "Why should I run theirs?"

Disgruntlement with services runs almost counter to the prevailing attitude about products. Consumers show a reasonable level of satisfaction with the merchandise they buy, thanks largely to technological advances. But the harsh world of the service economy intrudes once again on their contentment when a modern product suffers a breakdown. In a sense, consumers are victims of high-tech bounty. "The complexity of technology has increased much more rapidly than the ability of the consumer or the service personnel to keep track of it," says Stephen Brobeck, executive director of the Consumer Federation of America. Products have become so diverse and complex that friendly neighborhood repair shops can no longer provide service. In most cases, everything from videocassette recorders to food processors must be sent to regional repair centers. Autos have become such sophisticated machines by and large that only dealers with space-age diagnostic devices can fix them.

The heyday of personal service probably came early in the postwar era, when labor was relatively cheap and prices were fairly stable. Businesses could afford to lavish attention on customers, who in turn shopped for the most personable service. Music stores, for example, provided record players so that customers could give disks a spin before buying them, and drugstores offered free delivery. But during the decade of rampant inflation in the 1970s, when prices rose 87 percent, consumers became willing to give up service in return for the lowest possible price tag. They began buying in bulk, bagging their own groceries and shopping in warehouse-like mega-stores.

As discount chains like K mart and Wal-Mart flourished in the retail industry, rivals were forced to cut their payrolls to stay competitive. In that environment, in which shoppers began to think of brand-name products as commodities, businesses that still offered knowledgeable sales help were taken for a ride by consumers and competitors. Shoppers quickly learned to visit a service-minded store for a free lesson about a particular product, then go down the street to a discount house to buy the item for 25 percent less. The headaches often come later, because discounters tend to offer very little follow-up service. Says Butch Weaver, a second-generation appliance repairman and president of a Maytag store in Gaithersburg, Md.: "A lot of this the public has done to themselves. If they're going to go for these cut-rate prices, something's got to give, so it's usually service."

Businessmen point out, of course, that self-service has spawned great conveniences, ranging from simpler telephone-connecting jacks to coin-operated car washes and even videocassette vending machines. Many storekeepers say that self-service often enables customers to meet their needs faster than would be possible if they relied on clerks. At Child World, a chain with 134 stores, the company last fall arranged toys in "learning centers," where customers can examine and play with the products. Says President Gilbert Wachsman: "The shoppers are out more quickly. It reduces our expenses, and we pass the saving on to the customers." Fayva, a discount shoe chain where consumers select their choices from the rack, has grown to 650 stores in 15 years.

A Kroger grocery store in Morrow, Ga., has taken the self-service concept to an extreme. Customers check out their own merchandise by scanning the price codes with electronic readers. Human clerks collect the payment, and computerized sensors monitor the flow of merchandise to check for any fraudulent item switching.

But while consumers will embrace self-service if they think they are getting a bargain, they usually demand attention if they believe it is included in the price tag. Shoppers generally put up with the scarcity of sales help in low-end stores but quickly grow impatient when the trouble arises at mid-price and prestige retailers. Says John D. C. Little, a professor at M.I.T.'s Sloan School of Management: "Stores will have problems if they pretend to be up-market but aren't." He chides pricey department stores like Bloomingdale's for sometimes providing less service than their upscale image leads customers to expect.

While inflation taught consumers to be more price conscious, it was deregulation that forced banks, airlines and other industries to streamline their services so they could survive the new competition. Many banks, locked in an expensive battle to offer the highest interest rates for savers, found they could no longer afford to provide cheap or free services to small-account holders. By raising service charges dramatically, some banks actively discourage small accounts, because the profits in serving them are slim or nonexistent. Most depositors must wait in line to see a banker, while big-account holders are whisked into private offices.

Yet just like retail stores, banks are offering a trade-off that they believe most customers will accept: more products in exchange for less personal service. Today's depositors with as little as $500 to invest will find that banks give them more possibilities than ever before. Banks now offer an array of money-management accounts and even discount stock-brokerage service. Banks have vastly improved upon old-time bankers' hours of 9 a.m. to 3 p.m. New York's Citibank boasts that 80 percent of its depositors use its 24-hour automatic-teller machines and that more than half of all customers say they no longer need to venture inside the bank.

Deregulation has prompted airlines to make daring experiments with service, sometimes to harrowing ends. People Express provided an example of just how far consumers can be pushed in a trade-off for low fares. Its aggressively no-frills service, featuring such hassles as on-board ticketing and extra fees for checked baggage, gave the airline a negative image among business flyers and probably hastened its demise. Its rival, Texas Air, which officially bought People Express [in January 1987], prevailed partly by making a point of offering low fares without reducing service below generally accepted levels. The airline-merger boom, too, has disrupted service in the airline industry, as huge airlines combine their schedules and crews. The Department of Transportation announced earlier this month that complaints about poor airline service, especially delays, increased 30 percent during 1986.

A prime indignity for airline customers is to be bumped, or denied a reserved seat, because the carrier has booked too many passengers on a flight. Overbooking is a product of fare wars; because airlines are collecting less per seat, they want to ensure a full load to make a profit. The practice of overbooking crops up in other businesses when managers want to make the most of a prime-time rush of customers. At peak times popular hotels and restaurants sometimes bump customers who show up even modestly late for their reservations.

For many consumers the breakup of the Bell System in 1983 contributed to the decline of Western civilization. The split of old reliable Ma Bell into seven regional operating companies left many customers convinced that they were worse off, even though long-distance competition has brought better rates. Indeed, according to a scorecard published in November [1986] by *Communications Week*, local service and repair are now fairly inconsistent across the U.S. The trade publication gave the top grade of A-minus to Ameritech, which serves Illinois, Indiana, Ohio, Wisconsin and Michigan. The lowest grade of C-plus went to Southwestern Bell (Arkansas, Kansas, Missouri, Oklahoma and Texas) and NYNEX (New York and New England).

Consumers miss the personal touch in health care especially. Technology has brought great improvements in curative powers, but patients wish they could get more attention from their doctors rather than being seen mostly by nurses and technicians. Says Victoria Leonard, executive director of the National Women's Health Network: "We see doctors not answering questions, giving curt answers, not spending enough time with patients. Years ago a doctor was more of a family adviser. Now medicine tends to attract the person who enjoys the high-tech procedures. Almost by definition, that's not a people person."

Sensitive to the mounting criticism, the business world is starting to make amends. Says Alan Raedels, professor of business administration at Oregon's Portland State University: "If stores are competing with the same products at basically the same price, then the next major battlefield is going to be service." Claims Steve Shelton, who represents an association of Southern California gas-station operators: "The market is begging for attention today. Motorists seem tickled when someone is actually giving old-fashioned service and cares about the condition of their car." Quality-service gurus like John Tschohl of Bloomington, Minn., are now in heavy demand to give speeches to top managers.

Says he: "We teach them the financial impact of good customer service. They're interested only in hard dollars and cents."

One company that seems to have come to this conclusion the hard way is Sears, the largest U.S. retailer. Sears managed to smudge its image in recent years by grouping its salesclerks around cash registers for fast check-out, which reduced the number of employees who were in the aisles to answer questions. Sears still helped customers in its custom-drapery departments, for example, but left buyers of prepackaged drapes to struggle for themselves. Now the company apparently believes it went too far. "We've been looking at service in the past 18 months with heightened intensity," says Everett Buckardt, a Sears vice president. "We have put more people on the sales floor."

Other examples are multiplying. In Miami all 5,000 of the city's cab drivers are required to take a three-hour course in courtesy called Miami Nice, which has reduced the rate of customer complaints by 80 percent. To do better in the highly competitive health-care industry, California's Santa Monica Hospital Medical Center put its 1,500 employees through a two-day seminar on customer service. One result: the hospital changed its emergency-room admission procedure to one in which staffers "greet and comfort" patients before bothering them with the paperwork.

Nearly all the experts agree that the way to improve America's service industry is to understand the lot of the front-line worker. At this point, too few businesses recognize that many service workers are doing a relatively new, difficult kind of work that could be called emotional labor, a term coined by Arlie Russell Hochschild, a Berkeley sociology professor, in her 1983 book, *The Managed Heart: Commercialization of Human Feeling.* Just as factory workers can become estranged from the products they manufacture, says Hochschild, service workers can feel distanced from their put-on emotions. Flight attendants, for example, often feel that their smile belongs to the company. One solution Hochschild recommends is for businesses to give employees a chance to rest and recharge their smiles by temporarily rotating to less stressful jobs.

Cosmetic approaches will not do. K mart, for one, tried to cue its employees to be more personable by putting TYFSOK on their cash registers, which was supposed to remind them to thank customers for shopping K mart. But some harried clerks reportedly mocked the procedure by blurting "Tyfsok!" at puzzled customers. Other companies have tried to get across an impression of personal service with tired slogans to the effect that "people are our most important asset."

But American business had better deliver the real thing, because shoppers like Arlene Cantlon of Riverdale, Ill., are starting to make a scene. Cantlon lost her temper recently in a Venture Stores discount outlet because the chain was making a habit, in her opinion, of failing to have advertised goods in stock. "I asked to speak to the salesgirl in the shoe department, but nobody knew where she was. I waited 35 minutes while they looked for her. Nobody could find her, so I asked to see the store manager. At this point, I had a crowd of customers cheering me on. One woman told me, 'It won't do any good, but good for you!' " Cantlon finally got her audience with the manager, and got some of the merchandise she wanted as well. It was a notable victory, but it need not be all that rare. American consumers would be well advised to follow Arlene Cantlon's example and make noise if they really want their satisfaction guaranteed.

Quality Counts in Services, Too

LEONARD L. BERRY
VALARIE A. ZEITHAML
A. PARASURAMAN

Quality is essential when service is what is being sold. The authors identify ten determinants of service quality and offer important advice to managers on how to improve quality and customer satisfaction.

The issue of product quality has come to the forefront in American industry. One reason for this is the rise of the "get my money's worth" consumer, a value-seeking shopper who thinks in terms of total use cost ("What will this product cost me over the total period I will be using it?") rather than just initial acquisition cost. According to a Whirlpool Corporation study, nearly four out of five American consumers claim to be more demanding about quality now than in prior years.[1]

Most published work on product quality focuses on manufactured goods. The subject of service quality has received less attention.

This distinction is important because some of the quality-improving strategies available to manufacturers (for example, better vendor management) may be inappropriate for service firms. Services are performances, not objects. They are often produced in the presence of the customer, as in the case of air travel or a medical exam. Because of the labor intensity of many services, quality can vary considerably from one firm to another and from one situation to the next within the same firm.

To learn more about the subject of service quality, we recently conducted a series of consumer focus group interviews and ex-

Business Horizons, May–June 1985. Copyright 1985 by the Foundation for the School of Business at Indiana University. Reprinted by permission.

ecutive interviews in four service sectors: retail banking, credit cards, securities brokerage, and product repair and maintenance. Our objectives were to better understand the nature and determinants of service quality from both consumer and executive perspectives, to find out more about what causes service quality problems, and to propose strategies for dealing with these causes. Our research was exploratory and, in this phase, restricted to consumer services.

The four service sectors we studied vary along key dimensions used to categorize services.[2] For example, retail banking and credit card services provide immediate customer benefits, while securities brokerage and product repair services provide more enduring benefits. A nationally recognized company in each of the four sectors participated in the study. In-depth interviews were held with operations, marketing, customer relations, and senior executives in the firms. A total of 14 executive interviews were conducted, each lasting one to two hours. The interviews were based on a common set of open-ended questions.

We also conducted 12 consumer focus group interviews, three for each of the four services being studied. Eight of the focus groups were held in a metropolitan area in the southwest; the other four were spread across the country. All focus group participants were current or recent users of the service being discussed. In the interviews, they discussed their experiences and perceptions concerning the service in general, rather than the specific service of the participating firm, the identity of which was not revealed.

WHAT IS SERVICE QUALITY?

Just what is service quality? Philip Crosby defines quality as conformance to specifications.[3] Christian Gronroos distinguishes between "technical quality" (*what* is delivered) and "functional quality" (*how* it is delivered). He believes the "how" of service delivery— for example, the appearance and behavior of a restaurant waiter—is critical to percep-

tions of service quality.[4] Jarmo Lehtinen views service quality in terms of "process quality" and "output quality." Process quality is judged by the customer *during* the service. Output quality is judged by the customer *after* the service is performed. The barber's conversation and apparent skill during the haircut involve process quality; the appearance of the hair after the haircut involves output quality.[5]

We asked each executive we interviewed to define service quality. A banker said that it "is setting standards regarding customer needs and meeting them." A securities brokerage executive answered, "Service quality is true representation of the client's interest first and foremost." A product repair executive responded, "Service in a reasonable amount of time at a reasonable cost by a competent technician who does it right the first time."

From the focus group interviews, we identified ten determinants of service quality. Virtually all comments consumers made in these interviews about service expectations, priorities, and experiences fall into one of these ten categories. Although the relative importance of the categories would vary from one service industry to the next, we believe the determinants of service quality in most (if not all) consumer service industries are included in the list.

- *Reliability* involves consistency of performance and dependability. It means that the firm performs the service right the first time. It also means that the firm honors its promises. Specifically, it involves:
  - accuracy in billing;
  - keeping records correctly;
  - performing the service at the designated time.
- *Responsiveness* concerns the willingness or readiness of employees to provide service. It involves timeliness of service:
  - mailing a transaction slip immediately;
  - calling the customer back quickly;
  - giving prompt service.
- *Competence* means possession of the required skills and knowledge to perform the service. It involves:
  - knowledge and skill of the contact personnel;

- knowledge and skill of operational support personnel;
- research capability of the organization.
- *Access* involves approachability and ease of contact. It means:
  - the service is easily accessible by telephone (lines are not busy and they don't put you on hold);
  - waiting time to receive service is not extensive;
  - hours of operation are convenient;
  - location of service facility is convenient.
- *Courtesy* involves politeness, respect, consideration, and friendliness of contact personnel (including receptionists, telephone operators, and so forth). It includes:
  - consideration for the consumer's property;
  - clean and neat appearance of public contact personnel.
- *Communication* means keeping customers informed in language they can understand. It also means listening to customers. It may mean that the company has to adjust its language for different consumers—increasing the level of sophistication with a well-educated customer and speaking simply and plainly with a novice. It involves:
  - explaining the service itself;
  - explaining how much the service will cost;
  - assuring the consumer that a problem will be handled.
- *Credibility* involves trustworthiness, believability, honesty. It involves having the customer's best interests at heart. Contributing to credibility are:
  - company name;
  - company reputation;
  - personal characteristics of the contact personnel;
  - the degree of hard sell involved in interactions with the customer.
- *Security* is the freedom from danger, risk, or doubt. It involves:
  - physical safety (will I get mugged at the automatic teller machine?);
  - financial security (does the company know where my stock certificate is?);
  - confidentiality (are my dealings with the company private?).
- *Understanding the customer* involves making the effort to understand the customer's needs. It involves:
  - learning the customer's specific requirements;

- providing individualized attention;
- recognizing the regular customer.
- *Tangibles* include the physical evidence of the service:
  - physical facilities;
  - appearance of personnel;
  - tools or equipment used to provide the service;
  - physical representations of the service, such as a plastic credit card or a bank statement;
  - other customers in the service facility.

FOUR CONCLUSIONS

Analysis of our data leads us to conclude the following about the concept of service quality.

1. Consumer perceptions of service quality result from comparing *expectations* prior to receiving the service and actual *experiences* with the service. If expectations are met, service quality is perceived to be satisfactory; if unmet, less than satisfactory; if exceeded, more than satisfactory. The expectations/experiences connection is consistent with Gronroos's conclusions based on research he performed in Europe.[6]

2. Quality evaluations derive from the service process as well as the service outcome. The validity of Lehtinen's process quality/output quality scheme is underscored in our research by the large number of focus group comments relating to the *interpersonal behaviors* of the service provider, such as politeness, willingness to help, trustworthiness. The manner in which the service is performed can be a crucial component of the service from the consumer's point of view.

3. Service quality is of two types. First, there is the quality level at which the regular service is delivered (such as the bank teller's typical handling of a transaction). Second, there is the quality level at which "exceptions" or "problems" are handled (when, for example, the monthly credit card statement is incorrect, or the broker bought the securities but the instructions were to sell them). Delivering good service quality requires strength at both levels.

4. When a problem occurs, the low contact service firm becomes a high contact firm.

Credit card service is a good illustration. Usually, the credit card user has no personal contact with the credit card company. There is contact with the merchant at checkout but none with the credit card company unless there is a problem. The problem may be noticed by the company (the user exceeds the credit limit) or by the user (an error in the statement), but in either case personal contact between company and customer may result. We have learned that interactions between customer and company representatives can—and do—figure prominently in the quality image of so-called low-contact firms. Time and time again, credit card and product repair focus group participants emphasized interpersonal factors when discussing how service providers responded to an exception.

Figure 1 shows how service quality evaluations are a function of the expectations consumers bring to the service situation and the process and output quality they perceive they receive. These relationships hold whether the service performed is the regular service or in response to an exception.

WHAT CAUSES SERVICE QUALITY PROBLEMS?

Our research reinforces the conclusion from a study of manufacturing companies, "that the seeds of quality problems are widely distributed."[7] However, studies of manufacturing firms and service firms produce some different "seeds." The most frequently mentioned sources of quality problems in the manufacturer study were workmanship/work force, materials/purchase of parts, control systems, product design, and maintenance of process equipment.[8] The primary causes of service quality problems surfacing in our research are, in key respects, quite different.

INSEPARABILITY OF PRODUCTION AND CONSUMPTION AND LABOR INTENSITY

Goods are manufactured in a factory, then sold, then consumed. For many services the sequence is reversed. First the service is sold, then it is produced, often in the presence of

FIGURE 1

Continuum of Perceived Service Quality

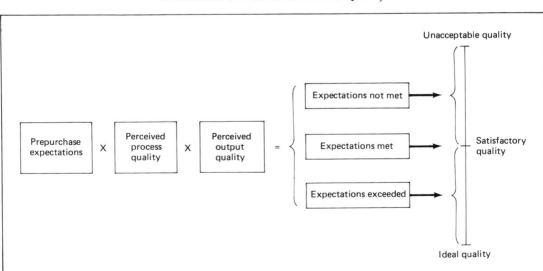

the customer. Frequently, production and consumption are inseparable. Customers cannot be transported by an airline without being on the airplane. They cannot have their teeth cleaned without going to the dentist's office. In effect, for many services the customer is *in the factory*. The customer experiences firsthand the production of the services. How service personnel conduct themselves, how they speak, even how they dress, all potentially shape the customer's perceptions of service quality.

The inseparability characteristic would not figure so prominently in matters of service quality, however, if most services were not so labor intensive. The extensive involvement of people in the production of a service introduces a degree of nonstandardization that doesn't exist when machines dominate the production process. As a securities brokerage executive put it: "Trying to maintain service quality when you have five thousand entrepreneurs (brokers) out there is difficult. Their levels of knowledge vary greatly. Getting five thousand to do it right all the time is hard."

Many factors can interfere with a satisfactory experience when service producer and service consumer are in direct contact. It is particularly troublesome—and yet quite common—when the backgrounds of those delivering the service and those buying it are quite different. The service personnel with whom consumers interact (bank tellers and credit card operations clerks, for example) are frequently among the least educated and lowest paid employees in their companies. Both the bank and the credit card issuer participating in our study voiced concerns about personnel who respond to customer inquiries but have a poor command of the English language.

The problem of service worker backgrounds involves low wages, insufficient talent pools for certain "non-glamorous" service jobs, not enough (or the wrong kind of) training, high turnover rates, and other factors. A bank operations executive enumerated several of these points: "Turnover is high and a lack of experience results. A person who normally would keep a position for 18 months has to move upward before he is ready. And this has an impact all the way down the line. You have limited staff because of unfilled openings and inadequately prepared staff because people have to get up the learning curve when they are new."

If a worker in a manufacturing plant has difficulties with the language, is poorly dressed, or has body odor, the customer won't know about it. With most services, however, the worker's language skills, dress, and odors are *part of the customer's experience*. The presence of the customer during production of the service—which is frequently labor-intense and hence subject to variability—causes quality problems unique to services.

INADEQUATE SERVICE TO INTERMEDIATE CUSTOMERS

In each of the companies we studied, the quality of service the consumer received depended in part on the quality of operational support the service personnel received. In effect, these customer contact personnel—the branch office banker, the stockbroker, the repair technician, the merchant accepting the credit card—are *intermediate customers* of various support services that pertain to the services they themselves perform. If the quality of intermediate service is poor, the quality of service rendered the ultimate consumer is likely to suffer.

Customer-contact personnel provide the link between company and customer. They sell and/or perform the service. To the consumer, they *are* the company. When something goes wrong—a lost stock certificate, an ordered appliance part that doesn't arrive—it is the contact person, who may be totally blameless, to whom the customer will likely turn.

For service quality to be satisfactory, customer contact personnel must be willing and able to perform the service. The repair technician needs to have the right diagnostic tools. The branch banker needs a prompt response from operations to the customer's inquiry. The merchant needs fast access to credit card purchase authorizations. We found evidence that intermediate service quality problems result in problems at the consumer level. The comment made by a securities brokerage executive illustrates the concept of intermediate customer service:

I wish I could take our 2,000 + operations people and let them see the reality of the broker in the office and the problems he faces. For instance, the broker comes to the office on Monday morning when the market is going up, and he thinks it's going to be a great week. The first call he gets is Mrs. Smith, who hasn't received her dividend check. He spends 30 minutes with her and then he can't get the problem fixed at headquarters.

For many service companies, two sets of service quality customers must be satisfied. In addition to the ultimate consumer, the intermediate customer—the contact person who depends upon support services provided elsewhere in the organization—must be served. The consumer's perceptions of service quality depend on it.

COMMUNICATION GAPS

Communication gaps were a major factor in service quality problems surfacing in our research. These gaps were of several types. One type is when the firm overpromises. Another is when the firm fails to stay in touch. The comment by a repair customer illustrates both problems: "I was told I would be the first call tomorrow. At 12:30 the next afternoon I called to ask them when their day started."

Another gap occurs when company communications are not understood. A brokerage customer said, "When the broker talks to you, you feel like he's talking to another broker." A credit card customer complained of "this mysterious thing called average daily balance."

Still another gap is when the company does not listen. One of several recurring themes in complaints to the bank in our study is, "My instructions to the bank were not followed." A second recurring theme: "I get no response."

A disproportionate number of service quality problems seem to arise from failure to stay in touch with customers until a problem is fully resolved, to communicate in nontechnical rather than technical language, to develop employee listening skills in training, and to moderate customer expectations.

SERVICE PROLIFERATION AND COMPLEXITY

Another source of service quality problems is too much *newness* in the service line—too many new services, too much added complexity with existing services. Change, in effect, outstrips organizational capacity to handle it. All of the companies we studied were characterized by extensive "net additions" to their service lines during the period in which we conducted our research. In the case of the financial firms, a clear impetus was deregulation. In the case of the repair firm, the impetus was electronics technology and its new product offspring: videocassette recorders, home computers, touch-sensitive, electronically timed washing machines.

In discussing the sources of service quality problems, a product repair executive stated: "We may not have all the specifications needed to train technicians before a new product is marketed. Some technicians may never be capable of being trained to service these new 'hi-tech' products. These products are coming too fast." On the same subject, a securities brokerage executive said:

All the new services bring with them new quality problems. When you are no longer a broker and not quite a bank, you're "in-between" and there are no "in-between" people to hire—so you have to make them. We've taken our best brokerage clients and hooked on a credit card, and we don't know enough about minimizing mistakes. Learning the process has taken a couple of hairs off my head.

Clearly, new products are vital to a firm's long-term success. However, our research underscores the importance of service firms being prepared to provide the service before marketing it. New services—or enhanced existing services—offer both additional marketing opportunity and additional opportunity for things to go wrong. Too much newness can do more harm than good.

VIEWING CUSTOMERS AS STATISTICS

Services are performed for individuals. It can be difficult to keep this perspective in mind when every working day a bank processes over one million checks, a credit card issuer receives thousands of telephone calls from customers, a brokerage firm executes 300,000 + transactions, and a repair firm has rooms full of appliances awaiting repair.

When a service firm has many customers, there is a tendency to view them as statistics, foregoing the opportunities that are sometimes present to individualize the service. However, many consumers desire a personalized and tailored approach to the service. A bank customer says: "Somebody in the bank should know you." A credit card customer: "They should know you're good for the bucks. They should know that, if I want to exceed my credit limit, I'm good for it." A securities customer: "The broker has to understand your situation, your objectives. Is the money for play, for risk, or is it for the kids' education?"

Repetitive tasks, more problems to solve than staff to solve them, sheer size and magnitude of operations, improper selection, training, compensation, and supervision of service workers—all contribute to a *service insensitivity* we found in our research. A product repair executive discussed the problem this way: "We tend to forget to put ourselves in the customer's shoes. All we see are broken appliances. We forget sometimes about how the customer feels, about his concerns, and we don't take the time to allay these concerns." A bank operations executive said:

> Operations personnel can be insensitive. They see so many problems that they lose sensitivity. For example, one hundred dollars doesn't seem

as important as one thousand dollars, but it's critical to the customer out one hundred dollars. Nevertheless, a situation where the bank has shortchanged a customer one hundred dollars may be put on the back burner because of other problems involving more money.

While the customer interacts with a small set of firms for a given service, the service firm interacts with a large set of customers. Treating individual customers as individuals is not automatic. When the lines in the bank lobby are backed up to the door, when the credit card customer telephones to indicate the charges on his statement belong to someone else and it's the forty-third such call received that day, the potential for treating the customer as a statistic—and for the customer to be disappointed—is high.

SHORT-RUN VIEW OF THE BUSINESS

Too much emphasis on short-term profitability in a service firm may be reflected in lower service quality assessments from the customer. A short-run view can affect service quality in several ways. First, it can lead to too many cost-reducing moves and their consequences, such as reducing the number of bank tellers (and lengthening the lines at the teller windows) or drawing down the spare parts inventory (and delaying the completion of certain repair jobs). Second, it can encourage transactions that are not in the best interests of the customer; for example, account churning by the stockbroker.

In the focus group interviews, *credibility* of the service firm proved to be a major determinant of service quality perceptions, especially in the securities brokerage and product repair groups. Two themes prevailed: Are they honest? Do they care about my welfare? These remarks from customers are typical:

- "If a broker is going to make a recommendation to a client, it should be an honest recommendation based on facts, not based on commissions to be received. Honesty is the basis of the whole thing."

- "If I find a good, honest repairman, I won't even experiment with anyone else."
- "When you have a problem, they treat you like you have a disease."
- "Everyone has the best products and service departments before you buy. Once you buy and sign your check, you go down the drain."

Taking a short-run view to conducting business is a well-known problem about which much has been written. The problem can be particularly acute in service businesses, however, because service is what is being sold. If you jeopardize the service in a service business, you jeopardize the business.

IMPROVING SERVICE QUALITY

Materially improving service quality is a long-term, multifaceted task. To approach this task on a short-term, unidimensional basis is to invite failure. What ideas might be incorporated into a service company's quality improvement planning?

Identifying Primary Quality Determinants. Earlier we presented the determinants of service quality found in our research. Improving service quality begins with a company using research to identify the quality determinants most important to market segments of interest. It is necessary to find out if the mix of primary quality determinants changes when it is an "exception" rather than a routine service. The next step involves assessing how the company and its competitors are rated by target markets on the key quality determinants. Isolating quality determinants important to the customer and in need of improvement by the company provides a focus for a quality improvement program. Because market priorities may change, they need to be tracked over time.

Managing Customer Expectations. The expectations consumers bring to the service situation play a pivotal role in the quality perceptions they ultimately develop. Avoiding the promotional temptations to overpromise can help a company achieve a good quality image. Raising expectations to un-

realistic levels may lead to more initial business, but it invariably fosters customer disappointment and discourages repeat business. The "on-time" airline, the "no surprises" hotel chain, and the "it will be ready by five" auto repair shop risk their reputations for quality every time they fall short of these promises. It is better, we believe, to excel in the primary quality determinant areas, to exercise prudence and caution in promoting these attributes of performance, and to let repeat patronage and word-of-mouth build the business. It is better to exceed customer expectations than to let the customer down.

Managing Evidence. Closely associated with the notion of managing expectations is the notion of managing evidence. While the former is concerned with assuring realistic expectations prior to the service situation, the latter is concerned with shaping perceptions during and after the service. Because a service is a performance and cannot be sensed as goods can, consumers tend to be especially attentive to tangibles associated with it for clues about its nature and quality.[9] Managing evidence means making sure that these tangible objects convey the proper clues. The tangibles to be managed could include the physical service facility, the appearance of service providers, devices or equipment used in performing the service, account statements, and the firm's logo.

Consider the case of the product repair service. The appearance of the technician is a clue. Is he neat and clean? Does he look "professional"? Another clue is his attitude. Is he courteous? Is he interested? Does he appear to know what to do? Still another clue is the technician's equipment. Is it impressive? Is it modern? All of these tangibles can make an impression about the quality of service rendered. If managed properly, they can support the intended quality image; if neglected, they can suggest a lower quality than desired. Planning the tangible and intangible elements of the service so they are *reinforcing* can help a service company improve its quality image.

Educating Customers about the Service. A service firm can enhance its credibility for "being on the customer's side" by helping consumers through education. More knowledgeable customers are likely to make better decisions, leading to greater satisfaction.

Customer education can take several forms. The firm can educate consumers to perform certain services themselves. Whirlpool, for example, has developed a do-it-yourself kit and a series of pamphlets for buyers of its appliances.[10] The firm can also help customers to know when to use the service. For instance, in our product repair focus groups, a number of participants expressed the desire for information that would help them decide whether to fix an appliance or replace it. Finally, the firm can educate consumers on how to use the service. Crocker Bank, for example, sponsored a "wait reduction" educational program, suggesting various strategies customers could use to minimize delays in banking transactions.

Although not directly related to customer decision making, some service companies could improve quality perceptions by explaining to customers the underlying rationale for policies that could frustrate them. A banker in our study said: "Lots of problems arise because people don't understand bank policies—for example, our policies on funds availability. We don't teach our customers how to use us well or why we do the things we do."

Developing a Quality Culture. Superior service quality on a sustained basis requires that quality become imbedded in a company's culture, that quality become *valued*.

Building a culture for quality involves establishing specific quality standards, hiring personnel with the capacity to meet those standards, training them to meet the standards, checking to see that they meet the standards, and rewarding them when they are successful. There is a quality loop, and the loop must be closed.

At American Airlines, which has had a formal quality program for more than 30 years, the vice president of passenger services makes a weekly presentation to top management on the company's quality performance. Data is collected by a quality consultant who rides the planes to check on service performance and take photographs. Data also comes from customer opinion surveys and from various electronic measurements (for example, the elapsed time before reservation phones are answered). American has scores of service standards for every facet of the operation. Reservation phones should be answered within 20 seconds at least 80 percent of the time; doors should be opened for deplaning within 70 seconds after the aircraft parks at the gate. Employee compensation, including incentives and merit raises, is tied to achievement of the standards.[11]

Commitment to quality needs to pervade an organization. It starts at the top but cannot end at the top. Quality happens in the trenches. In reviewing published case histories of companies known for service of high quality, we noted one constant: the *pervasiveness* of quality consciousness in these companies. At Wachovia Bank, which thoroughly pretests new serivces and technologies even if it means entering the market later than competitors, quality is part of the culture.[12] So is it at Disney, which puts all of its theme park employees through "Traditions I," a day-long course on the company's history and central values; in general, the enterprise places a premium on fielding well-trained, neatly groomed, unfailingly cheerful "cast members" (as they are called at Disney).[13]

Automating Quality. Replacing or supplementing human efforts with automated systems can minimize the chances of error in producing a service. For instance, the repair firm in our study has developed a computerized system that produces daily printouts of the repair jobs promised for the next working day in each service location. The securities brokerage industry is developing technology offering on-line editing of transactions entered into remote data input devices. In other words, if a broker in Des Moines enters a transaction containing an error, the order is not accepted until the error is corrected.

A key to making the right decisions about technology is understanding the customer's priorities well enough to know which aspects of the service require the human touch and which lend themselves to automation. Finding the optimum mix of "high-touch" and "high-tech" can pay off in better service quality.

Following Up the Service. Following up on services performed can help isolate aspects of the service that require improvement. Several possibilities exist. The company can take the initiative and contact all customers, or a sample of them, to determine their level of satisfaction with the service. An automobile repair firm that solicits feedback from every fourth customer is using this approach. A second option is to make it easier for customers to communicate with the firm when the need arises. Companies that sponsor toll-free telephone lines are using this approach.

Contacting customers and making it easier for customers to contact the firm are complementary strategies. Service companies should consider using both. The strength of the first strategy is that it represents a systematic approach for monitoring service quality. The second option affords the opportunity to get back in the good graces of unhappy customers who otherwise may be lost to the firm forever.

Soliciting feedback from contact personnel concerning the quality of intermediate customer service is also recommended. Surveys and small group discussions involving contact personnel can uncover conditions preventing them from offering higher quality service.

The service quality challenge is to meet —or better yet, exceed—customer expectations. For most firms, this is a complex undertaking. Most service businesses are labor intensive and the service is subject to variability. Customers are frequently present when the service is performed, in effect witnessing its production. Even if customer contact personnel have the talent, training, and motivation to deliver high-quality service, they may nonetheless be dependent on "good service" from the operations part of the firm to be fully effective.

There are no formulaic answers to this challenge. Part of the solution is recognition by management that high quality can contribute significantly to bottom-line performance. Part is recognition that delivering high-quality service touches everyone in the organization and is not limited to a quality assurance department. Part is recognition that many steps can be taken to improve quality and that they need to be melded into a cohesive whole. Improving service quality requires formalization, planning, and coordination. Most of all, it requires total commitment. Anything less is not enough.

Notes

[1] "America's Search for Quality," Whirlpool Corporation, 1983:3.

[2] Christopher H. Lovelock, "Classifying Services To Gain Strategic Marketing Insights," *Journal of Marketing*, Summer 1983:9–20.

[3] Philip B. Crosby, *Quality Is Free* (New York: McGraw-Hill, 1979): 17.

[4] See Christian Gronroos, *Strategic Management and Marketing in the Service Sector* (Boston: Marketing Science Institute, May 1983), Chapter 4.

[5] Jarmo R. Lehtinen, "Customer Oriented Service System," Service Management Institute Working Paper, Helsinki, Finland, 1983.

[6] Gronroos, Chapter 14.

[7] Frank S. Leonard and W. Earl Sasser, "The Incline of Quality," *Harvard Business Review*, September–October 1982: 164.

[8] Leonard and Sasser: 164.

[9] Leonard L. Berry, "Services Marketing Is Different," *Business*, May–June 1980: 26.

[10] "Whirlpool: A Marketing-Minded CEO Tries To Set Sales Spinning," *Business Week*, May 16, 1983: 50–51.

[11] Based on remarks by William E. Crosby, vice president of passenger services for American Airlines, in Robert C. Lewis and Bernard H. Booms, "The Marketing Aspects of Service Quality," in Leonard L. Berry, G. Lynn Shostack, and Gregory D. Upah, eds., *Emerging Perspectives on Services Marketing* (Chicago: American Marketing Association, 1983): 100–102.

[12] See "Interview: John G. Medlin, Jr., President, The Wachovia Corporation," *United States Banker*, October 1983: 22–28, 74.

[13] See Norwood W. Pope, "Mickey Mouse Marketing," *American Banker*, July 25, 1979: 4, 14; and Pope, "More Mickey Mouse Marketing," *American Banker*, September 12, 1979: 4, 14.

New Tools for Achieving Service Quality

D. DARYL WYCKOFF

Service operations can be managed for both quality and cost control without treating staff members like "cogs." Implementing some new quality-management techniques can turn service staff into thinking workers who find ways to exceed the quality standards set for them, while they delight customers with attentive service—as occurred at Rusty Pelican Restaurants and Midway Airlines.

Where manufacturing techniques have been applied to the service industries for improved consistency and productivity, services have too often become standardized, and personal interaction lost.[1] Particularly in the hospitality industry, some managers and customers feel that the loss of the personal touch is too severe a penalty to pay for productivity gains through "production-line" approaches. In the effort to improve some aspects of service, other important service qualities were sacrificed. Customers now ask where the *service* has gone from the service industries.[2] As Stanley Marcus remarked about the large hotel and fast-food chains, "They have perfected training methods to provide the guest with adequate but imper-

[1]Theodore Levitt, "Production-Line Approach to Service," *Harvard Business Review,* September–October 1982, pp. 41–52.

[2]See: Barbara Tuchman, "The Decline of Quality," *New York Times Sunday Magazine,* November 2, 1980, p. 38; Jeremy Main, "Toward Service without a Snarl," *Fortune,* March 23, 1981, p. 58; and Frank S. Leonard and W. Earl Sasser, "The Incline of Quality," *Harvard Business Review,* September–October 1982, pp. 163–17

sonalized attention and unvarying hamburgers."[3]

The distortion of services to allow the application of production methods is only one problem attendant on the use of manufacturing concepts. Another problem is that the types of production concepts applied have often been steeped in "Taylorism," an attitude that workers are unintelligent and unthinking cogs who must be told what to do to make the machine run.[4]

Fortunately, more recent manufacturing techniques stress the thinking, quality-oriented worker. These new methods give caring workers the tools for self-improvement in delivering service quality—and substantially reduce the need to denigrate service quality by sacrificing customization, choice, flexibility, and personalized services.

This article discusses these new techniques, using the experience of two firms, Rusty Pelican Restaurants and Midway Airlines, as examples of how service firms can apply these concepts.

IMPROVING ON EXCELLENCE

Rusty Pelican is a group of full-service restaurants that serve well-prepared, fresh seafoods in a setting of "sophisticated casualness." Originated in California, the company was one of the first to sense consumers' demand for lighter, more healthful foods, and their turning away from the limited menus of theme restaurants and from heavy meals of red meat. A typical Rusty Pelican restaurant might serve as many as 25 different varieties of fresh fish, which can be prepared in any of several ways, accompanied by fresh vegetables. The restaurants are pleasing to the eye and are often located in unusual and striking settings, such as on a waterfront.

A major component of Rusty Pelican's service strategy is hiring knowledgeable servers to provide attentive and personal-

ized cocktail and food service. Maintaining the firm's service standards is a significant challenge, because of the wide variety of seafood offered (and the fact that the availability and prices of seafood items change daily), because of the alternatives in preparation, and because the service style of sophisticated casualness requires a delicate balance to provide the appropriate pacing.

By most measures, Rusty Pelican was a success. The company was doing well financially, it received positive customer comments, and the number of repeat customers was large. Management recognized, however, that the service was too inconsistent in some of the restaurants and seemed too mechanical in others. The company was providing coaching and training, of course, but many of the employees were not really convinced that one way of providing the service was necessarily better than another. Performance, while generally good, was more a matter of the enthusiasm of a given staff or particular individuals than the result of design.

Management was concerned about how to recruit and train enough capable servers, especially since it didn't seem appropriate in this market segment to resort to a paramilitary-style application of detailed handbooks and industrial engineering, as has happened in many restaurant chains. The company also realized that increasing server productivity would reduce the number of servers needed and increase the individual servers' earnings through tips. Management set a goal of increasing productivity by ten to 20 percent. It chose a self-improvement strategy to achieve this goal.

Skills. Rusty Pelican hired a consultant to meet with small groups of employees and discuss how they believed they could increase productivity without reducing service quality. At this stage, most of the attention was devoted to how servers could improve their selling and merchandising skills to increase sales per employee hour. The groups decided to pay particular attention to their communication skills.

The results of this effort were measured

---

[3]Stanley Marcus, *Quest for the Best* (New York: Viking Press, 1979), p. 42.

[4]Also called scientific management, this approach breaks every job into small elements.

by the employees against the targets they had set for themselves. Productivity improvements were seen almost at once, partly because the employees wanted to see how much improvement they could bring about. Management's original targets for productivity improvements were easily met and sustained. In informal interviews, customers also rated the service quality as being higher.

Rusty Pelican then anonymously conducted a customer-satisfaction study, and found that the firm's service was rated significantly higher than that of competing restaurants. The company could easily have been satisfied with this result, but there was better news. Research had shown that customers were willing to pay considerably more for innovative service.

With the servers' assistance, the company began to examine every step in its service process to find opportunities for improvement and to pinpoint instances of failures. The servers identified several bottlenecks that were causing service problems. More space was needed in the kitchen to assemble orders, for example, and rearrangement of the bar and service bars would allow the cocktail servers to achieve their goals for prompt service.

Employees began to coach each other, and the experiences of team problem-solving promoted greater teamwork on the job. As the servers became more productive and quality-minded, they began to find that they could deal with more detail. Rather than simply going through the motions of service, they were *thinking* about service as they delivered it.

FROM WHOLESALE SKIES TO EXECUTIVE SKIES

Midway Airlines began life as a no-frills airline spawned by deregulation. Midway had dubbed its service the "wholesale skies"—a play on the "friendly skies" slogan used by United Airlines. Midway provided a simple service at cut-rate fares, a strategy that succeeded only as long as the major air carriers ignored Midway (i.e., while their own ca-

pacity was heavily utilized). At that point, Midway was easy to ignore, for it was small in comparison with the large trunk carriers that were focusing on long-haul competition.

The "wholesale passengers" were mostly price-sensitive, of course, and demonstrated little loyalty when another airline brought prices down to meet or beat Midway's fares. During periods of heavy traffic, therefore, Midway picked up the low-fare traffic that spilled over from regular-fare carriers. When traffic fell and other airlines offered low fares, Midway's traffic would disappear. The company was in what is known as a "stalled-market" position.[5] If Midway continued to hold this position, the best the company could hope for was meager earnings (with good luck) or great losses (with bad luck).

Breakout. To get *un*stalled, management initiated a "breakout strategy" by repositioning its service to attract the frequent traveler. Research had shown that this market was so badly served by most carriers that many travelers' feelings toward the airlines had gone beyond frustration to outright hostility.

In addition to examining its own customer feedback, Midway undertook formal market research. One step was to run full-page ads (without company identification) in *The Wall Street Journal* and the business sections of other newspapers, inviting experienced travelers to help design an airline that could deliver quality service.

The response was conclusive. Frequent travelers did not want lavish foods or liquor, but they *did* want reliability, timeliness, and comfort. Two-abreast seating was important to the respondents, for example, because they were crowded when they sat in rows of three and couldn't get any work done. Sufficient facilities for carry-on baggage were important, but so was reliable and fast baggage service. Simple, well-prepared food was preferred to more elaborate, reheated "mystery meals." Reliable, on-time departures and ar-

---

[5]This position is also called "stuck in the middle." Michael E. Porter, *Competitive Strategy* (New York: Free Press, 1980), pp. 41–44.

rivals were deemed vital, and knowledgeable and efficient cabin crews and ground staff were considered important to assure smooth services and to help when problems arose.

Businesslike. As a result of these findings, Midway removed some seats and added substantial carry-on luggage facilities. Aircraft interiors and exteriors and crew uniforms were redesigned to convey a new businesslike image. The gate areas were redesigned to provide work stations for passengers. Simple, excellent food offerings of salads, cold meats, and homemade-style breads were substituted for reheated meals, thereby avoiding the systematic destruction of food texture, flavor, and color that is inevitable with rewarming. The meals were presented in specially designed plastic boxes that resembled the sophisticated Japanese *bento* lunchboxes. Since there was no heating and the packaging was done in advance, the cabin crews could serve an entire meal in minutes.

These quality improvements (mostly in product design) answered only part of the challenge of repositioning. Midway felt these steps would help, but the most difficult part of the breakout strategy would be to change the company's culture from that of the "wholesale skies" to one of "executive skies." The mechanical product redesign provided some signals of change to the staff, but the real alterations in service had to come from the employees themselves.

The employees had been involved in the process right from the beginning, working through councils and committees on the redesign of the facilities, aircraft, and uniforms. They had struggled over the marketing research and had worked with designers who translated customer requirements into designs.

Next they turned to service delivery, by establishing priorities for action. It would be wishful thinking to expect to bring everything up to a high quality standard at once, but the most important service-quality issue identified in the marketing research was timely departure. This issue was to receive primary attention.

The first step toward achieving high levels of on-time service was to examine all the causes of late flights. Analyzing different aspects of the operation through flow charts revealed that there were about 30 causes of late departures. The employees identified failure patterns and suggested and implemented corrective actions. Soon the employees felt that their original performance targets for departures had been too modest. They questioned the traditional airline practice of considering any flight operating within 15 minutes of schedule as on time, and changed that standard to five minutes for Midway.

Baggage handling, announcements, onboard services, and the like soon received treatment similar to that of scheduling. A new sense of pride became the company's hallmark, and new quality measures were rapidly added by the employees, who suggested that the performance standards could be tightened further.

There were some interesting side effects of the quality program. Employees' absentee rates dropped by nearly half. Turnover of flight attendants and agents was reduced by 25 percent. Midway was experiencing a phenomenon that has been witnessed in other companies: quality-improvement programs frequently produce positive side effects.

TOOLS FOR QUALITY SERVICE

In both of the cases described here, customers recognized that there had been substantial improvements in service quality. In both cases, customers were willing to pay a premium, because the quality change enhanced their perception of the value of the service. This concept, service quality, may be defined as follows:

> Quality is the degree of excellence intended, and the control of variability in achieving that excellence, in meeting the customer's requirements.

This definition of quality is useful, because it incorporates the following three components: *design quality,* or the intended degree of excellence; *conformance quality*, or the minimizing of variance from the intended design; and *fitness of design*, or the extent to which the product meets the customer's needs.

In fact, it is important to focus first on the last point—namely, on the customer's needs, which usually take two forms. The first are the basic *substantive* needs. To satisfy substantive needs, for instance, hotels provide shelter, restaurants provide food, and airlines provide transportation. In most cases, customers can readily determine through simple observation whether they have received a substantive service.

The second category, *peripheral* needs, goes beyond the needs met at the substantive level. The service attributes that meet these needs surround and complete the substantive service. These needs must not be ignored.[6] Peripheral service attributes (e.g., security, promptness, interpersonal relations) fulfill such needs as the need for a sense of control, for a feeling of trust and confidence, or for a sense of belonging, self-fulfillment, and self-esteem.[7]

STANDARD AND CUSTOM

Two distinctions in services have important implications for service-quality management. The first is whether a particular service is standard (routine) or custom (nonroutine), and the second is the degree

to which the "back-room" parts of the service can be isolated from the customer, so that front-room operations can be minimized and controlled.[8]

Production approaches are often more easily applied to standard or routine services. Indeed, some service companies have *made* their services standard just so production methods could be applied. McDonald's did this with food service, Midas with automobile repair, and H&R Block with accounting services. The problem with these firms' rigid approach is apparent: gone is the chance for custom or nonroutine service. But service variety and service quality need no longer be mutually exclusive; using some new techniques of quality management, one can now deliver variety in service at a given quality standard.

The new methods used in manufacturing easily improve the production-oriented standardized services, but the Rusty Pelican example shows that the thinking employee can also manage a greater range of nonroutine services when given the opportunity.

Front and Back. Whereas past efforts at service management rested on the conceptual division of service into back-room and front-room operations and an emphasis on the back of the house (which was presumed easier to manage with standard production methods, being out of the customer's sight), the new quality-management techniques often stress front-room operations—helping employees manage and improve human-interaction processes.

NEW APPROACHES TO QUALITY MANAGEMENT

Managers have learned a great deal in the past two decades about quality management in manufacturing. In some cases, old truths have been rediscovered or restated in ways that make more sense in modern settings; in other cases, old beliefs have been turned up-

---

[6]For a more detailed discussion of this view of service, see: W. Earl Sasser, R. Paul Olsen, and D. Daryl Wyckoff, *Management of Service Operations* (Boston: Allyn and Bacon, 1978), pp. 177–179. For other views of the concept of a constellation of attributes for each quality, see: Corwin D. Edwards, "The Meaning of Quality," *Quality Progress*, October 1968, pp. 36–39.

[7]For a complete discussion of the needs fulfilled by peripheral services, see: Robert C. Lewis, "The Positioning Statement for Hotels," *The Cornell Hotel and Restaurant Administration Quarterly*, 22, No. 1 (May 1981), pp. 51–61; Leo M. Renaghan, "A New Marketing Mix for the Hospitality Industry," *The Cornell Hotel and Restaurant Administration Quarterly*, 22, No. 2 (August 1981), pp. 30–35; and Theodore Levitt, "Marketing Intangible Products and Product Intangibles," *Harvard Business Review*, May–June 1981.

[8]Christopher H. Lovelock, *Services Marketing* (Englewood Cliffs, NJ: Prentice-Hall, 1984), p. 5.

side down. The following statements summarize current thinking on the topic of quality management.

- *Quality exists only to the extent that a product or service meets the customer's requirements.* Therefore, design quality must begin with a thorough understanding of those requirements.
- *A product or service of high quality is the result of a total system of quality throughout every aspect of the firm.* A quality orientation and commitment in every part of the firm—by every employee and every supplier—is central to delivering a quality product or service.
- *The costs of poor-quality products and services outweigh the costs of good-quality products.* Doing things right the first time yields substantial reductions in total costs by cutting the costs of inspection, internal failure, and external failure.
- *Management must go beyond thinking of inspection merely as sorting out the good products and services from the bad or as preventing bad products from reaching customers.* Management must instead view inspection primarily as a tool to measure whether the production process is able to deliver the intended products or services—if the process is not capable of producing the desired quality consistently, why not?—and whether the process is under control. Examination of product problems has been simplified by improved means of process analysis and statistical process-control methods.

The following is a closer look at each of these four propositions.

SQUARE ONE

It is a marketing fundamental that one must start with customer requirements. There have been many departures from this principle in the service industries, however, partly because customers' requirements for services may be difficult to identify and articulate, and also because customers' wants are complex and multidimensional.[9] Perhaps for these reasons, service firms have often been dominated by creative individuals who have an intuitive concept of the services desired by customers. We remember those whose intuition was right—James Nassikas of the Stanford Court, Fred Smith of Federal Express—and we forget (or never know) the multitude who guessed wrong.

Even when intuitive concepts work, their creators may not know why. A mysticism often develops around details that are actually of little consequence to the customer. Because the interior of his first successful pizza store was decorated in a shade of green paint purchased from an Army surplus store, for example, "Shakey" Johnson insisted that the same color paint be used for all subsequent Shakey's Pizza Parlors.

It takes courage to reexamine the offerings and make changes, particularly when a firm has been successful. United Parcel Service, a company founded to deliver packages under contract from downtown department stores to uptown customers, made this reexamination when it observed the movement of retailers to the suburbs after World War II, and accordingly modified its entire service strategy to provide common-carrier service for all types of shippers to all destinations.

Unstated Needs. One must be imaginative in how one goes about learning of customers' requirements, because customers do not always *know* what they need or want. For example, the introduction of the "800" telephone number was important to Holiday Inns' ability to satisfy the customer's need for a familiar service in an unfamiliar location. Yet in consumer research of the time, customers did not explicitly ask for this innovation that proved so vital. Likewise, years ago, few customers even conceived of a reliable, nationwide, overnight parcel-delivery service. But they did have requirements for communication and document delivery that Federal Express was imaginative enough to detect.

In other cases, consumers *do* know what they want and articulate it—but are still left dissatisfied. As an example, such professionals as architects and doctors are now sometimes the targets of lawsuits by unhappy clients and patients. The professionals' fre-

---

[9]This concept is known as a "bundle of desires." Lawrence Abbott, *Quality and Competition* (New York: Columbia University Press, 1955), pp. 30–31.

quent reaction has been to have their clients sign releases rather than to find ways to win loyalty and confidence (i.e., to start with customer requirements).

Many recent management texts have stated that, in "excellent" firms, the customer is prominent in the minds of everybody at all levels. Despite the occasional difficulties, reviewed here, of emphasizing customer needs, service industries can also benefit from this attitude.

TQC

Many Japanese firms have enthusiastically embraced the concept of *total quality control* (TQC).[10] TQC rests on the belief that quality-control techniques or methodology must be used to raise the level of quality for every corporate activity, with a result of better yields, greater efficiency, higher productivity, and lower costs. TQC broadens the definition of quality management to cover all aspects of corporate existence, and quality control becomes the responsibility of everyone in the firm—not just an isolated step in the production line. For the company that practices TQC, accuracy in typing letters, politeness in answering the phone, and fussiness in cleaning the offices are just as important as meeting design and conformance quality standards in its products and services. Each activity represents a commitment to quality. Professional telephone manners do not substitute for poor product or service quality, of course, but care in all operations communicates a message of quality to employees and customers.

Because TQC emphasizes the exchange of information through the entire firm from the bottom up as well as from the top down, it depends heavily on informed, thinking, and involved workers. This does not mean that TQC leads to undisciplined operations—in fact, it promotes strict adherence to standards—but it encourages

continual reexamination of processes and standards and embodies a formal method for changing operations as needed to improve quality and productivity. TQC rejects the notion of doing just enough to get by.

The Japanese "quality circle" builds broad participation in quality thinking. The quality circle is based on a long Japanese tradition of looking down into an organization to find answers to problems, and the quality circle stimulates the initiative for improvement at every level of the company. Although it reflects unique aspects of Japanese culture that are not readily exported, the quality-circle concept may be adapted to any setting, as long as "one respects the brain power of human beings."[11] Regardless of what it is called, the success of this structure stems from employee involvement on a regular and ongoing basis, and simply giving trendy new names to tired old organizational structures will not guarantee quality.[12] As seen in the Rusty Pelican and Midway cases, employees participated in a quality-circle process without ever using that term.

COST OF QUALITY

The concept of the *total cost of quality* provides a framework for analyzing the expenses associated with providing a product or service that meets given standards. The total cost of quality is made up of four components. *Assurance costs* are those expenses associated with inspection, testing, and collecting and processing quality-control data. *Prevention costs* are the expenses incurred in avoiding poor quality (e.g., the cost of training programs, quality-improvement pro-

---

[10]This is sometimes called company-wide quality control.

[11]Kaorn Ishikowa, quoted in: Sud Ingle and Nima Ingle, *Quality Circles in Service Industries* (Englewood Cliffs, NJ: Prentice-Hall, 1983), p. 8.

[12]For example, see: Elizabeth Faulkner, "Will Quality Circles Work in American Food-Service Operations?," *Restaurants & Institutions*, September 15, 1983, p. 149; Keniche Ohmoe, "Why Quality-Control Circles Succeed," *Asian Wall Street Weekly*, April 5, 1982, p. 12; and Wayne S. Rieker, "QC Circles and Company-Wide Quality Control," *Quality Progress*, October 1983, pp. 14–17.

TABLE 1

Hypothetical Comparison of Two Cost-Control Strategies

The following calculations of the total cost of quality show that the low-price strategy described in the accompanying text is actually more costly than a policy of purchasing a more expensive product and investing in preventive measures.

"LOW-COST" STRATEGY

Lettuce purchased for salad:	$30,000/year (a savings of $9,000 over premium grade produce)
Salads made:	120,000/year
Yield of usable lettuce:	75%
Cost of salad:	$0.25
Salads rejected by food servers:	6,000/year
Salads rejected by customers:	3,000/year
Average cost of placating customers:	$.75/upset customer

COST ANALYSIS (ANNUAL FIGURES)

Cost Category	Item	"Low-Cost" Strategy	Alternative Strategy
Prevention costs:	Lettuce price premium	$ 0	$ 9,000
	Purveyor meetings	0	100
	Employee training	0	100
Assurance costs:	Receiving inspection	0	100
	Chef's inspection	1,800	900
Internal-failure costs:	Lost lettuce	7,500	500
	Server rejections	1,500	100
External-failure costs:	Customer rejections	750	100
	Placating customer	2,250	100
Total cost of quality		$13,800	$11,000

grams, process modifications, and vendor-qualification programs). *Internal-failure costs* arise from scrapping or reworking faulty products that are intercepted before they reach the consumer. *External-failure costs* stem from defective products that reach the consumer.

Management's objective is to minimize the sum of these costs. The simple example in Table 1 shows how this concept is applied. Imagine that a restaurant buys standard-grade lettuce to avoid the 30-percent premium for perfect lettuce. The company also reduces training costs by not telling kitchen helpers how to inspect the lettuce when it is received. (As standard grade, it can hardly be rejected anyway.) Predictably, some heads regularly fail to meet the freshness-quality requirements for salads, and although the chef spends some time inspecting the produce, he is so rushed that some salads are invariably made with wilted lettuce. Needless to say, either servers or customers reject these salads.

The alternative scheme illustrated in Table 1—spending *more* on the product and on assuring its quality—shows substantially reduced *total* costs. In this case, as is so often true, doing it right the first time saves money by obviating the need for greater spending in other quality-cost categories.[13] Reworking products, recalling defective materials, and placating unhappy customers are expensive. Perhaps the highest cost of all occurs when an unhappy guest never returns but takes every chance to tell friends about a terrible hotel or restaurant.

STATISTICAL PROCESS CONTROL

Among the most important advances in quality management has been the adoption of concepts of *statistical process control*. Statistical process control has changed the role of inspection from one of sorting out good and bad products to that of managing the production process by assessing whether the process is under control and by determining the process's capability when under control. This change in inspection's role has great significance for the service manager. Instead of depending on final inspection, often believed to be impractical in service delivery, operators can manage the service-delivery process, whether custom or standard in nature.

The first step in statistical process control is to chart the process in the form of a table or flow chart. A flow chart helps depict the complete process that must be managed. Rusty Pelican started with the flow chart shown in Figure 1, and expanded it to several pages of detailed design-quality specifications and standards.[14]

The initial standards the Rusty Pelican servers established are listed in Table 2. The next step—applying these standards—was critical to Rusty Pelican's success. Restaurant employees were shown how to measure themselves, rather than being evaluated by

FIGURE 1

Restaurant Flow Chart

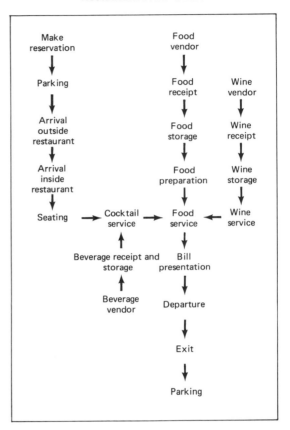

an inspector. In some cases, a control chart (a simple record of activity) is useful for monitoring performance.[15] The key to successful use of control charts is that they are based on data collected and recorded by involved employees who view the results as an opportunity for learning and self-improvement rather than reprimand. Again, such self-inspection reduces the need for inspec-

[13]See: Jack Campanella and Frank J. Corcoran, "Principles of Quality Costs," *Quality Progress*, April 1983, pp. 16–22; and Charles A. Aubrey II and Debra Zimbler, "The Banking Industry: Quality Costs and Improvement," *Quality Progress*, December 1983, pp. 16–20.

[14]See: G. Lynn Shostack, "Designing Services That Deliver," *Harvard Business Review*, January–February 1984, pp. 133–139.

[15]For additional background on the use of control charts, see: Armand V. Feigenbaum, *Total Quality Control* (New York: McGraw-Hill, 1983), pp. 345–369. For a detailed discussion of quality measurement in the service industries, see: Everett E. Adam, Jr., James C. Hershauer, and William A. Ruch, *Productivity and Quality: Measurement as the Basis for Improvement* (Englewood Cliffs, NJ: Prentice-Hall, 1981).

TABLE 2

Rusty Pelican Service Standards

FOOD-SERVICE STANDARDS

1. **First contact**—cocktail server speaks to customer within two minutes of customer seating.
2. **Cocktails delivered**—beverage service at table within four minutes of order. If no beverage order, request for food order within four minutes of first greeting.
3. **Request for order**—within four minutes after beverage service, customer should be asked whether he or she cares to order.
4. **Appetizers delivered**—salad, chowder, or wine delivered within five minutes.
5. **Entree delivered**—entree served within 16 minutes of order.
6. **Dessert delivered**—dessert and coffee or after-dinner drinks served within five minutes after plates are cleared.
7. **Check delivered**—check presented within four minutes after dessert course or after plates are cleared if no dessert.
8. **Money picked up**—cash or credit cards picked up within two minutes of being placed by customer on table.

COCKTAIL-SERVICE STANDARDS

1. **First contact**—greeting given and cocktail order taken; seafood bar, happy-hour specials, and wine-by-glass menus presented within two minutes.
2. **Cocktails delivered**—cocktails delivered within five minutes after first contact.
3. **Seafood bar delivered**—seafood bar and happy-hour specials delivered within seven minutes of first contact; ten minutes for cooked items.
4. **Next contact**—check for reorder of cocktail, seafood bar, customer satisfaction, and table maintenance within five minutes from delivery of first cocktail.

---

tors (or spies in the skies, as airline staffers call them).

Figure 2 shows the type of control chart used by Midway's employees to monitor their scheduling performance. The chart tells an interesting story, because simply measuring and tracking this critical feature of service quality caused some improvement. An enthusiastic management team was able to gain considerable additional improvement with "locker-room pep talks." Even with this enthusiasm, however, it was difficult to maintain consistent performance. More study was needed to reveal the causes of service failures.

Fishbones. Midway applied another tool of statistical process control, cause-and-effect analysis (also called "fishbone analy-sis").[16] This technique may appear at first glance to be mechanistic, but its results are usually worthwhile, for the analysis stimulates creative responses from employees and managers.

The initial fishbone analysis of Midway's delayed flights is shown in Figure 3. The cause-effect diagram starts with the effect—namely, delayed flight departures. Then major categories of causes are listed on the "spine." To get the analysis started, it is often useful to start with the five broad causal categories illustrated in Figure 3: material, personnel, procedure, equipment, and "other."

---

[16]First developed by Kaorn Ishikowa of Tokyo University, fishbone analysis was first applied at Fulsai Ironworks in 1953.

FIGURE 2

Control Chart of Midway Airlines Departure Delays

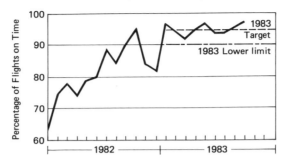

FIGURE 3

Portion of Midway Airlines Fishbone Analysis—Causes of Flight Departure Delays

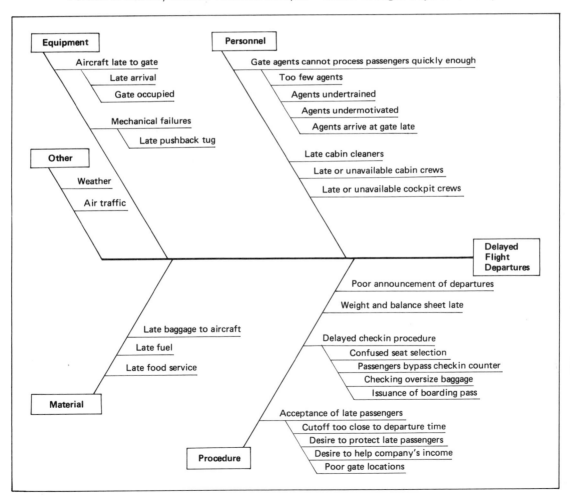

TABLE 3
Pareto Analysis of Flight Departure Delays

ALL STATIONS, EXCEPT HUB			NEWARK			WASHINGTON (NATIONAL)		
	Percentage of Incidences	Cumulative Percentage		Percentage of Incidences	Cumulative Percentage		Percentage of Incidences	Cumulative Percentage
Late passengers	53.3	53.3	Late passengers	23.1	23.1	Late passengers	33.3	33.3
Waiting for pushback	15.0	68.3	Waiting for fueling	23.1	46.2	Waiting for pushback	33.3	66.6
Waiting for fueling	11.3	79.6	Waiting for pushback	23.1	69.3	Late weight and balance sheet	19.0	85.6
Late weight and balance sheet	8.7	88.3	Cabin cleaning and supplies	15.4	84.7	Waiting for fueling	9.5	95.1

There may be several factors contributing to each cause.

Because of their personal experience, Midway's employees had little difficulty suggesting the causes of late departures. One problem, late arrival of passengers, quickly received considerable attention when it was discovered the company's policy on how to handle late passengers was vague. It was essential to determine how significant late arrivals were as a cause of late flights. To answer this, Midway applied "Pareto analysis," a technique that arranges data so that problems are ranged in order of importance.[17]

Discipline. The Pareto analysis revealed that nearly *90 percent* of the departure delays for all airports other than the hub were accounted for by only *four* of the many causes listed in Figure 3. The actual causes of late departures for one month of operation are listed in Table 3 in order of their frequency. Obviously, accommodating late passengers *was* a major cause of flight delays. These were not passengers who were late from connecting flights; they were simply passengers who were casual about getting to the airport. Individual gate agents had been making their own decisions about what was best for Midway in these circumstances. Most agents were anxious that Midway not lose the fares of the latecomers, and most agents were also sympathetic to the late passenger (although they forgot the inconvenience to the many passengers who had made the effort to arrive on time). Midway established a policy that it would operate on time and give top service to passengers who were ready to fly on schedule. This discipline was appreciated by the passengers, and the number of late passengers soon declined.

The delays in "pushback" (moving the aircraft away from the gate with motorized tugs) were reduced by better scheduling of tugs in some locations and by working more closely with subcontractors in other locations. Similar programs were initiated with cabin-cleaning contractors and fuel suppliers, and the Midway staff placed greater priority on promptly supplying the plane's weight and balance calculations to the pilot.

More specific information was generated by "stratification," dividing the data into useful subcategories or segments. Different patterns showed up in the Pareto analysis when the data were separated into different services, times, or locations. In Table 3, for instance, note the difference in problems of Newark departures and Washington depar-

[17]Named for Vilfredo Pareto, the 19th-century economist and social scientist. The Pareto rule, also referred to as the "80-20 rule," assumes that in a normal population roughly 80 percent of sales come from 20 percent of customers, or in this case, that 80 percent of the failures come from 20 percent of the causes.

tures. These differences could not have been discerned in the "total station" data.[18]

In January 1983, once the flight-departure process was under control, the company set control limits. At first, the *minimum* performance standard was set arbitrarily at 90-percent on-time flights, as shown in Table 4. Soon there were data showing that this lower limit was too generous (but it was probably a good place to start). The company shortly decided that any month that the on-time record was more than three standard errors from the *target* of 95 percent, the process was out of control.

UNCONTROLLED AND UNSTRUCTURED

Measuring the service customer's satisfaction levels is still one of the most subjective and difficult parts of quality management in services. Some service organizations mistakenly rely on unsolicited comments. This is unfortunate, because such a sample is uncontrolled and unstructured.[19] Comments are most likely to come from customers who are writing about exceedingly bad or exceedingly good experiences. Sometimes the comments come from crank letter writers. Worse, many customers who have bad experiences never tell the management; they just complain to their friends and switch their patronage.

The only satisfactory alternative to unreliable surveys is a controlled sample that is carefully examined for bias. Studies like this are usually tedious and expensive, and often the testing itself can damage the quality of the service experience. But these studies may be an important "reality check" of whether the service is satisfying customers' needs.

Rusty Pelican decided a short in-house restaurant survey was important. While management acknowledged the risk of disrupting a diner's experience, the need for reliable customer feedback was critical. Likewise, Midway found that passengers are quite willing to complete in-flight surveys, partly as a distraction during the flight, and the response rates have been high.

Incomplete. There were two shortcomings with the in-house surveys administered by Midway and Rusty Pelican. First, the companies did not get information about the perceptions of nonusers. Second, the surveys did not capture customers' reactions to the whole service experience, since the questionnaires were given out during the meal or flight (not afterward). Both Midway and Rusty Pelican gained additional information from focus-group research (i.e., interviews with groups of customers).

Although critical, measuring only one's own service quality is not sufficient. Some rude surprises can come to light in surveys of competitors' service offerings. Singapore Airlines, for example, thought it saw steady improvement on every measure of its in-flight services. Several competing airlines, however, were rapidly closing the lead Singapore had established, and it appeared that Singapore might shortly lose its competitive advantage in cabin services. Fortunately for Singapore Airlines, it observed this developing pattern and moved into a quality-improvement program at once.

One final observation: In those companies where the top officers personally made the investment to learn and understand the application of process control to quality management, process control has nearly always been successful. Whether the officers'

---

[18]The other tool frequently used to capture variations that may be lost in averages is the "histogram" or scatter diagram. The histogram shows variability in conformance quality by plotting information on a graph. The time it takes to deliver baggage after landing, for example, could be plotted for every flight. The result should be a mass of dots near the time established in the performance standard. If the diagram shows many dots falling below the standard—a trend that might be obscured in averages if many dots also fell *above* it— management would be alerted and could take corrective action.

[19]For a specific discussion of this problem, see "Improving Guest Surveys" in the *Notes* section of the November 1984 issue of the *Cornell Hotel and Restaurant Administration Quarterly*.

personal understanding was the critical factor or was just interpreted by employees as a sign of the company's commitment to quality management, the effort paid off.

BEYOND TAYLORISM

When the service businesses have adopted a production-line approach in recent years, the result has frequently been standardized services and diminished personal interaction. The new lessons for quality management learned in manufacturing industries have changed this mechanistic approach to one of cultivating thinking employees, backed up with management methods that enable them to understand, control, and improve the service-management process.

These techniques are not constrained or dictated by the size of the firm. While many of the quality-management methods described in this article may seem to be statistical tools oriented toward industrial engineering, their real strength lies in their ability to augment the human role in the service-delivery system. These tools can give small firms the same efficiency advantages enjoyed by large companies, while large firms can regain some of the flexibility and service quality seen in small firms.[20]

Designing quality around customers' requirements may seem axiomatic, but it has been forgotten or ignored by too many managers and servers; quality is more than slogans and press releases. It requires a company-wide investment in defining and articulating what quality service means, and providing the resources to produce that quality. All parts of the enterprise must be committed to *measuring* quality, because improvement is possible only when quality is measured.

Improving the quality of service is often a slow process. Some of the *fastest* process-control implementations have taken over two years; many will take longer. And recognition by *customers* of an improvement in quality takes still longer. The market is often slow to acknowledge quality changes. As a result, management may think it has gotten away with reduced quality if there is no short-term evidence of a loss in market share. Unfortunately, when the market is lost it may not be regained for years after the quality is restored.

---

[20]G. Michael Hostage, "Quality Control in a Service Business," *Harvard Business Review*, July–August 1975, pp. 98–106.

"It's Not My Job, Man"

MORTIMER R. FEINBERG
AARON LEVENSTEIN

The weak links in a service organization are usually at the points where departments are supposed to meet. Management must train and motivate employees to work for the company, not just their departments, if they are to serve customers well.

It's a familiar story: The restaurant patron asks a passing waiter, "Can you tell me the time?," and the answer comes back, "Sorry, sir, this isn't my table."

Or the airline passenger asks a flight attendant, "Where's seat 12A?," and is told, "I'm not on duty." The executive who recounted this episode insisted: "So long as she's wearing the airline uniform she's on duty! She's still a company representative."

In another example, Agfa-Gevaert's chief executive officer, Robert A. M. Coppenrath, cites the unanswered ringing of the telephone, which he labels "a corporate offense." He tells his people: "There's no such thing as 'it's not my phone.' Every telephone in the company is our phone. Don't let phones ring."

Situations like the ones described above arise from the notion that "it's not my responsibility." The weak links in an organization are usually at the point where departments are supposed to meet. It's at these joints that institutional arthritis attacks. When departments are separated like national frontiers, fully equipped with barbed-wire fences, bristling watchtowers, and buried mine fields, serious losses occur.

To be sure, refusal to assume any responsibility beyond that explicitly listed in

Reprinted by permission of Dr. Mortimer R. Feinberg, Chairman of the Board, BFS Psychological Associates, New York, and the *Wall Street Journal*. This article first appeared in the *Wall Street Journal*, November 11, 1985.

the job description or organization manual may be due to laziness or unconcern. But often the reasons are quite substantial: respect for the jurisdiction of colleagues or peers; fear of being labeled an empire-builder, turf-snatcher, or imperialist; lack of familiarity with the organizational structure; and failure of top management to clarify policy, particularly in such matters as centralization vs. decentralization.

People are reluctant to accept responsibility if it is not accompanied by an express delegation of authority. The successful executives, however, are usually those who believe that their responsibility exceeds their authority. They consider themselves responsible not only for the unit over which they preside, but for the company's success as a whole.

All too often, people who lack authority withhold action because they feel they don't have the information or other resources needed to act. They may assume that others are better qualified to handle the problem. Management has no right to expect employees to step into situations for which the company has given them no training.

Still another factor may be concern over who will get the credit if the outcome is successful—or the blame if it is not. James Robbins, president of Cox Cable Communications, places the onus on higher management to recognize when cooperative action is necessary and to assign primary responsibility. In such cases a superior must specify who is in charge and who is expected to work with him or her. Robbins argues that responsibility can be shared but that authority should always remain undivided.

Theoretically, efficiency is served by departmentalization, specialization, and division of labor. The goal, however, can be achieved only if management strives for coherence by constantly reminding people that they are not isolates working in their own cubbyholes, but parts of a larger whole. Here is what executives, conscious of the problem, recommend:

- From the very beginning of a relationship with employees, even in the hiring interview, it is important to stress that the individual will be *working for the company*—not for just a division, department, unit, or particular supervisor.

- By presenting *prospects for advancement,* the company can demonstrate that looking beyond the narrow confines of the immediate assignment will open windows of personal opportunity.

- In the course of periodic employee appraisals, cooperation with others and the display of initiative in discovering and filling gaps should be treated as *major performance criteria.* Managers should seek every opportunity to reward subordinates for contributions that benefit the whole organization.

Lyman Wood, president of Brennan College Books, in evaluating his managers, asks: How frequently do they communicate with other managers about filling organizational voids? He calls this type of person a "breaker-up of hardpan"—the layer of earth that's so tough the rain can't get through to nurture the roots. Such managers are tagged for ultimate promotion; in the meantime, they are rewarded with extra bonuses, and the president seeks out special occasions to maintain contact with them.

- The *image of the customer* must be kept vivid in the attention of all members of the organization. Joseph McEvoy, chief financial officer of Saks Fifth Avenue, says that the enlargement of personal responsibility is furthered by stressing that "it's the customer who pays your salary."

McEvoy cites the following example from department-store experience: Customers frequently make inquiries about their charge accounts but by understandable error may reach somebody in accounts payable. The natural tendency is to respond: "Sorry, you have the wrong department. Call this-and-this number." Instead, the preferable procedure is to ask for the customer's telephone number and then have the right person call him or her back, rather than compelling the customer to make two calls.

- People must be kept informed about the *needs of other departments* if they are to be able to spot significant gaps and communicate appropriately across departmental frontiers.

Many procedures are available for this purpose. Job rotation, especially for junior executives, helps to broaden perspective. Lending personnel to other departments in periods of shorthandedness, rush orders, or vacation time contributes to overcoming the provincialism that blocks initiative and cooperation.

- *Compensation systems* can be used to get people to think beyond their own bailiwick in terms of total company needs; group incentive plans and companywide profit-sharing programs provide an economic motivation for reaching out to others with supportive action and suggestions.

- Finally, management must *instruct its people* on how it wants them to behave when a no man's land appears on the landscape.

Centel of Virginia

JAMES R. FREELAND
GEORGE B. BEAM

The management of a telephone company is studying the possibility of introducing quality circles in an effort to increase productivity and improve worker participation and morale.

Dan Martin sat in his office considering the alternatives before him. He had just made a presentation to the division vice-president and his department heads of the Central Telephone Company of Virginia on quality circles, a form of participative problem solving being used by an increasing number of American companies. In his presentation Dan had also recommended the specific implementation plan Centel should use. Daryl Ferguson, the Division Vice-President, and Don Roberton, the Customer Services Manager, believed Centel would make better use of quality circles by changing the concept to fit the structure and work flow at Centel. They were basing their beliefs primarily on the Fall Rush Program at the University of Virginia. Dan Martin had studied the concept of quality circles and was not sure how successful the program would be if changed. Mr. Ferguson asked him to reanalyze the situation taking into account the differences in a service company like Centel and a manufacturing company (where quality circles first originated). Dan knew he had to either come up with a new plan or better defend his old plan and soon. Mr. Ferguson wanted his new recommendations within one week.

Case prepared by George B. Beam under the supervision of Professor James R. Freeland, The Colgate Darden Graduate School of Business Administration, University of Virginia. Copyright 1980 by the Colgate Darden Graduate Business School Sponsors, Charlottesville, Virginia. Reproduced by permission.

COMPANY BACKGROUND

The Central Telephone Company of Virginia was one of seventeen divisions of the Central Telephone & Utilities Corporation (Centel). With corporate headquarters in Chicago, Centel had eleven divisions offering phone service throughout the country. Together, these divisions constituted the fifth largest telephone system in the U.S. Centel also owned and operated electric utilities in Colorado and Kansas. Through its subsidiary Centel Communications Company, the company was involved in other communications-related businesses including cable television, the sale of business communication systems, and the design and marketing of acoustic enclosures for public telephones. Telephone revenues comprised over 70 percent of total sales for the corporation.

Centel of Virginia was the third largest subsidiary of the Central Telephone & Utilities Corporation. Covering a service area of 6,070 square miles, Centel served 142,600 customers in 29 counties throughout the State. For organizational purposes the service areas were broken down into geographic territories. Charlottesville was the location of the division offices and the customer services offices for the surrounding area. Other customer services offices served the Martinsville/Lexington area and the remaining Centel service area in Virginia. Centel employed 1,460 employees in Virginia of which 77 percent were hourly. Most of the hourly workers were represented by the International Brotherhood of Electrical Workers (IBEW). In 1980 Centel's management had a good working relationship with the Union. Centel had rarely had to lay off workers in the past, except for the '73–'74 recession, but with the rapid gains in tele-

EXHIBIT 1
Division Organization Chart

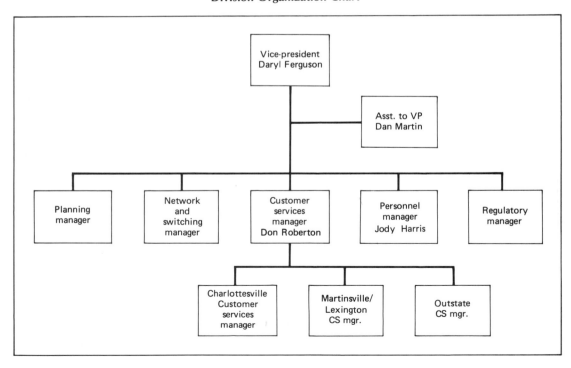

communications technology over the past few years, the practice could change. Turnover was very low and the average worker had been with Centel approximately seven years.

An organization chart of the division management is shown in *Exhibit 1*. Mr. Ferguson had been the head of the Virginia division for almost two years. Mr. Ferguson brought a number of new managers when he came to Virginia. In particular the department heads of Customer Services and Network & Switching who between them had 96 percent of the hourly workforce were replaced by Mr. Ferguson.

The Virginia division had experienced problems in the past which had affected service to customers and management-employee relations. The division management had changed a number of times over the past 10 years. It seemed that as soon as the employees had become accustomed to one management, they were replaced by another team. Service suffered and the gap between management and workers had widened.

Mr. Ferguson and his new managers had made progress in improving the relationship between management and workers. In the winter of 1979, Mr. Ferguson and other managers started meeting with first line supervisors and hourly workers. These meetings became known as Skip Level Meetings and they had a positive effect on the workers. The workers aired their gripe or question, and the attending managers tried to give them an answer. The new attitude of the workers was that "this management cares but let's wait awhile longer before we trust them completely." Because of the success of the program, Mr. Ferguson decided to continue Skip Level Meetings provided they would only be held when scheduling of the managers and workers permitted.

Though progress had been made, there still remained some areas where improvements could be made. One particular area was in the communications and coordination at the lower levels between different groups. The Fall Rush Program demonstrated there were problems in this area that could be corrected.

FALL RUSH PROGRAM

In September of 1979 Mr. Ferguson received a phone call from a professor in the Sociology Department at the University of Virginia. He was calling to complain about Centel's service. Centel's work load typically increased 50 percent during the period August through September when students at the University of Virginia returned to school, so these types of complaints were not uncommon. It was during this conversation that the professor suggested a way that might help Centel improve service in the future to its customers in the Charlottesville area during the Fall Rush. He suggested to Mr. Ferguson that Centel organize two groups of employees from all areas of the company to meet during the spring of 1980 to discuss how Centel could better prepare for the Fall Rush. The groups would be composed of hourly workers and managers chosen by upper management. The professor would provide two sociology graduate students who would serve as facilitators for the two groups. Mr. Ferguson was impressed with the approach and gave the go-ahead for the program.

From January to March the two seven-member teams met weekly to review the results of the 1979 Fall Rush and analyze specific problem areas identified by division management. The first couple of meetings were unproductive as the team members argued over which group in the company was responsible for a particular problem. A number of times the facilitator in each group had to interject to get his team back on the right track.

After the first couple of meetings, the group began to be more productive. In March each group made a presentation of their analysis and recommendations to Mr. Ferguson and Mr. Roberton. The recommendations of both teams were well received. The two teams were then combined into one team that was to come up with a detailed plan for improving service during the Fall Rush. Work continued for another month at the end of which another presentation was made. A number of the recommendations

EXHIBIT 2

Centel's New Fall Rush Procedure for Incoming Students

August 1, 1980

Dear Student:

Welcome back to Charlottesville. Centel looks forward to serving your telephone needs, and to help start the semester out right, we've made some changes this year to make applying for service easier and faster.

Centel's temporary business office will be in a new location this year. We have leased space in the former Sears building (1105 West Main Street) and we'll be open at this site from August 11 through September 15, just to handle student applications. Our hours are 8:30 a.m. to 5 p.m., Monday through Friday. There is plenty of free parking at our new location, which is also on the University bus route.

There are several reasons why we need more space this year. We're taking a larger staff consisting of experienced service representatives, clerks, and storeroom personnel. They will be able to process your orders more quickly, give you a telephone, and in most cases, provide service at your residence in one to three days.

Our temporary office is air conditioned and more spacious than our permanent business office on Arlington Blvd., so you'll be served in comfort.

In order to accomplish our goal of providing you quicker and better service, we'll need your help. First of all, we expect all students to make applications for service at the temporary business office (TBO) location. (Only permanent-resident customers will be served at our Arlington Blvd. location.) Beginning August 11, phone or in-person applicants will be asked to go to the TBO. Secondly, while you're waiting (hopefully the wait will be short) we will ask you to complete your own Service Application Card which will save time when you get to the Service Representative.

There are some additional facts we'd like you to know about our operations this year. In approximately 2500 addresses where students are normally housed, we have left the number and equipment in place. This means that if you move into one of these locations, you will have the telephone number of the student who lived there previously. The advantage of this is that we'll have a good chance of providing same-day service. At locations not "dedicated," we still hope to be able to provide three-day service.

Also, our lease instruments are now limited to standard desk and wall models in black or white (rotary or Touch Call). We will, however, offer phones in a variety of colors for sale to students at a reduced rate. These phones will be refurbished (cleaned and repaired lease instruments that have been returned to the telephone company), but will carry a full one-year guarantee. You can save on your monthly bill by owning your own telephone.

Enclosed is a handbook that Centel has produced especially for students in our serving areas. We hope you'll take the time to read it—it will provide the answer to a lot of your questions. If you need additional information or have questions, please call the business office.

We hope to see you at our temporary business office.

Sincerely,

Larry L. Gorby

Larry L. Gorby
Customer Services Manager

were accepted and implemented in the summer of 1980. One of these was a letter (shown in *Exhibit 2*) sent to every returning U.Va. student detailing Centel's new Fall Rush operations.

At the conclusion of the fall rush, the Fall Rush Program was declared a tremendous success. The program saved Centel an estimated $88,000, but more importantly, Centel's image was greatly enhanced by the better coordination and service offered students. The members of the Fall Rush Program groups were also enthusiastic. One member commented that it was the first time division management had listened to the supervisors' and workers' suggestions.

QUALITY CIRCLES

The Fall Rush Program convinced Mr. Ferguson that an ongoing group participation program could definitely benefit Centel. He had heard about a program used by the Japanese called "quality circles" but was not sure if that was a program Centel could use. He asked his assistant, Dan Martin, a new MBA out of the Darden School at the University of Virginia, to research major elements of the Japanese productivity system including quality circles and study some companies in the U.S. that had implemented a quality circle program. Finally, he wanted Dan to develop an implementation plan that could be initiated within the next six months if Centel chose to use quality circles.

Dan began his research by finding as many articles as he could on quality circles. As it turned out there were many due to the success of the Japanese and the new emphasis on productivity in American industry. After learning as much as he could from the articles, Dan called the American Productivity Center in Houston. From them he learned about three consulting firms on the West Coast which specialized in coming into companies and implementing quality circles. All three firms were established by the original Lockheed team that went to Japan to learn about quality circles and then returned to

Lockheed and started their own program. Dan also contacted two companies on the East Coast which had implemented a QC Program. After visiting these companies he felt he understood what made quality circles work. He now needed to determine if circles would work at Centel.

Dan felt the best way to find out if circles would work at Centel was to talk to the managers and hourly people at all levels in Centel. He specifically concentrated only on the Charlottesville area because he felt it would be the best place to start a program with the division offices there and the success of the Fall Rush Program. If it turned out the program was successful in Charlottesville, it then could be expanded to other areas. Dan also talked to the IBEW Union manager. All the managers and the union manager were receptive to such a program. Dan was really surprised the union manager was for it because his research indicated that most unions take a negative approach to such a program.

The two hourly workers Dan talked to had mixed feelings about quality circles. One felt such a program was needed because there were a number of times he had made suggestions to his supervisor and no one took any action. The other worker felt quality circles would just be another management program that would fail like all the others. Because the circles would be strictly voluntary, Dan was not worried by the last worker's comments. He knew only workers who wanted to participate would.

Dan Martin was convinced quality circles would benefit Centel, but what bothered him was the differences in a manufacturing environment where circles were being used exclusively, compared to a service environment like Centel. Dan knew quality circles should be made up of people with common work-related problems. This was so everyone in the group would be able to contribute in analyzing the problem. In a manufacturing company quality circles were formed from one supervisor's work group because most of the group's problems were within their common work area. This could be an assembly line, a machine, or a procedure. In a service company like Centel this was not the case. *Exhibit 3* shows the work flow in Centel's customer services department for getting one phone hooked up. For the phone to be installed properly, it was important that each of the four groups coordinate their work with the other groups and communicate any problems. If one group had a problem then all the groups had a problem. Thus, in Centel the majority of work-related problems that had the greatest effect on service were *intergroup* rather than *intragroup* problems as in a manufacturing company.

MEETING

Dan knew Centel would eventually have quality circles made up of workers from different groups, but he was hesitant to recommend that approach at the outset. From his research he had determined that two of the most important characteristics of quality circles were that the groups chose their own problems to analyze and that all problems analyzed would be common to the group. With intergroup circles Dan was worried members might choose problems that were not common to all members. He knew this problem could be alleviated by allowing management to choose the problems to be analyzed, but that would undermine the whole concept of quality circles being the workers' program rather than a management-imposed program. One indication of this was that one worker who participated in the Fall Rush Program said he resented management telling him what problems to analyze. Dan felt once some workers had gotten experience in a quality circle made up of members from the same work group,

EXHIBIT 3
Service Order Flow

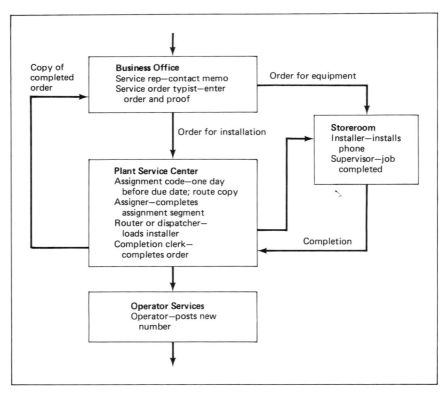

they would better understand how to function in an intergroup circle. He knew from talking with a number of supervisors there were a number of problems that could be work-group analyzed.

Dan prepared the implementation plan (see Appendix) and sent it to Mr. Ferguson and his department heads. Mr. Ferguson called for a meeting with his department heads and Dan to go over the implementation plan. Mr. Ferguson and Mr. Roberton said they felt Centel should go right to intergroup circles. They felt the greatest problems to be addressed were in this area and that the Fall Rush Program had shown such a concept could work at Centel. They both felt they did not have the six months Dan had recommended before going to intergroup circles.

Dan and Jody Harris, the Personnel Manager who would be responsible for the program, did not agree. They felt Centel should get some experience with the QC program as used by other companies before making any changes. Dan tried to point out the differences between the Fall Rush Program and quality circles and explain why he did not recommend intergroup circles to begin with. Mr. Ferguson, still unconvinced, asked Dan to reanalyze the situation and, if necessary, come up with a new plan.

DECISION

Dan returned to his office and thought over what had transpired. He knew why Mr. Ferguson and Mr. Roberton wanted to use intergroup circles, but it bothered him that they did not have six months before forming such circles. Dan wondered if increasing productivity was their only reason for wanting to implement a quality circle program? Dan felt a circle program should be started to increase worker participation and morale. Productivity increases were a benefit of the program and were a primary reason for management implementing such a program. If increasing productivity was the *only* reason Centel wanted to implement circles, Dan was worried what would happen if the program did not generate the magnitude of cost savings ideas the Fall Rush Program had. Whatever their reasons, Dan knew he would have to come up with a new plan or be better prepared to defend his old plan to Mr. Ferguson next week.

APPENDIX

Quality Circle Implementation Plan

September 30, 1980

TO: Daryl Ferguson
FROM: Dan Martin
SUBJECT: QC Implementation at Centel

I recommend that Centel implement a pilot Quality Circle program in the Charlottesville offices of Customer Services and Network & Switching. I first would like to list my reasons for making such a recommendation, followed by some of the problems identified to me by some Centel managers. Finally, I will list the implementation program I recommend Centel use if they choose to have a Quality Circle program.

During the past month, I spent time talking to a number of Centel managers and the IBEW Union Manager in the Charlottesville area. In our meetings, I presented the QC concept and got their reactions to such a program. Also, I talked to these managers about their work environment and how compatible it was to a QC program. A number of strengths and weaknesses of the program as it pertains to Centel were identified.

APPENDIX (continued)

I believe Centel should implement a pilot QC program in the Charlottesville area because:

1. Every manager and supervisor I talked to was favorable toward such a program. There were some problems identified, but all managers and supervisors said they would be willing to support such a program in their area under the right conditions. Also, the managers I talked to felt there were definitely a number of areas where employees could identify problems and make recommendations that would benefit Centel.

2. The IBEW Business Manager is in favor of the program and would like to see it implemented. Even though it is strictly voluntary, he was not sure if the hourly people would accept it, but he said the Union would take no action against the program.

3. The Fall Rush Program has made a favorable impression on the people involved in the program and on a number of employees who did not get to participate in the program now that management has used some of the recommendations of this program. According to first line supervisors, a number of employees feel the current management team will listen to employees' suggestions. Also, I believe the Fall Rush Program has established the idea of participative problem solving at Centel.

4. The Charlottesville area has closer contact with the division offices than any other Centel service area. The QC program will require a number of management meetings in the pre-implementation phase. These meetings will require less management time if the program is implemented in the Charlottesville area due to less traveling.

5. The skip level meetings have given employees a medium for airing grievances. Skip level meetings should be continued. This will help prevent Quality Circles being used by employees as a gripe session.

Some of the problems that will have to be addressed before Centel implements a Quality Circle program are:

1. What would be Centel's policy toward a Circle recommendation that eliminated someone's job?

2. What will Centel's policy be toward scheduling QC meetings? Will they be held during normal working hours or overtime? All the managers believed the program would benefit their area, but they could not see how they could schedule 8-10 people from one work group to meet for one hour each week and still meet their workload.

3. Since the normal workload goes up 25-50 percent during August and September, what would be Centel's policy toward circles meeting during the Fall Rush?

These were the problems identified by the managers I talked to. After the Steering Committee is formed, these should be the first issues they should consider after choosing a facilitator.

QC IMPLEMENTATION PLAN

Below are the steps I recommend to implement a pilot Quality Circle Program at Centel. See the estimated timetable in Table 1 and the estimated costs in Table 2.

1. Hire a consulting firm to make an in-house presentation on Quality Circles to all managers in Customer Services and Network & Switching in the Charlottesville area. If scheduling is a problem the seminar can be presented at night or twice during the work day. I recommend the consulting firm Quality Circle Institute of Red Bluff, California, as a first choice and J. F. Beardsley and Associates of San Jose, California, as a second choice. They both have good programs, but the former is much cheaper.

2. Hire same firm to implement Quality Circles in Charlottesville offices of Customer Services and Network & Switching. The consulting firm will send preliminary information concerning the formation of the Steering Committee, criteria for selecting a facilitator, and information on the formation and training of Quality Circles.

3. Form the Steering Committee, composed of the department heads of Customer Service, Net-

APPENDIX (continued)

work & Switching, and Personnel, the Charlottesville Customer Services Manager, Union Representative, Facilitator (after he is chosen), and the Division Vice-President.

4. Have the Steering Committee select one full-time facilitator and either a second full-time or part-time facilitator. The second facilitator can be used as a substitute at the beginning and then as a full-time facilitator when the program grows.

5. Facilitators begin training with consultant. The Union representative can be included in the training, but he indicated to me at our meeting he was not interested in participating. The Steering Committee begins to meet regularly to prepare guidelines and objectives of Centel program. Consultant will help Steering Committee identify areas to consider.

6. Steering Committee, Facilitator, and Consultant Design Implementation Program for Centel. The program should identify departments that will have pilot circles, schedule for circle meetings, and schedule for group leader training.

   Based on my study of the Charlottesville area, I recommend that a pilot program of six circles be initiated. I would put two circles in both the Charlottesville Customer Services Business Office and Plant Service Center. Because Centel desires to have them in Network & Switching also, I would organize two circles in Northern and Southern.

7. The facilitator should collect some pre-implementation data so as to later demonstrate a before and after comparison. I could not identify any data that Centel presently has to do this. Thus, I would recommend the Personnel Department administer a simple questionnaire to determine employees' attitudes in the Business Office, Plant Service Center, and Network & Switching.

8. The facilitator will next distribute Quality Circle literature to managers of the Business Office, Plant Service Center, and Network & Switching. Though I have already talked to most of these managers, it gives them an opportunity to review materials on circles and ask questions. It will then be up to the managers to select the pilot program circle leaders from the interested supervisory volunteers.

9. The Steering Committee will meet with the pilot program managers and circle leaders to discuss the program and answer any questions. This meeting is necessary to show middle managers and group leaders that the program has top management support.

10. The facilitator and consultant begin Circle Leader training. The Steering Committee and consultant make final review of circle policy, guidelines, and implementation plan.

11. Second level managers of pilot program departments conduct Quality Circle familiarization meetings with employees. The facilitator and possibly a representative of the Steering Committee should be there. Workers should be allowed to openly discuss the program and ask questions.

12. Circle leaders talk to each employee individually in their work groups to find out if employee is interested in voluntarily participating in the group.

13. The facilitator and circle leaders begin group training with training materials supplied by the consulting firm.

This concludes the pilot circle implementation plan. Circles will continue training for one hour each week during the first two months of the program. After two months, the circles will begin to identify problems in their work area and choose the ones they want to work on. The facilitator should schedule circle presentations to management on either recommendations or status once every three months. Members of the Steering Committee or pilot group managers should try and attend all or part of a circle's meeting at least once in the first three months of the program.

After the pilot program gets started, the Steering Committee needs to address the issue of circle expansion. How fast will circles be allowed to grow and in what areas are two primary considerations. Expansion should not be allowed until after approximately three months to give Centel management and employees a chance to experience the program.

The facilitator will meet with all the pilot circles during the first months to help the circle

APPENDIX (continued)

leader. After approximately three months, the facilitator should prepare a report for the Steering Committee on circle activities and any cost savings realized to date. Any problems in implementing the pilot circles should be identified in this report so the Steering Committee can make modifications to the program before future circles are added. Also, after three months of circle activities, the Steering Committee should meet with the managers and leaders of the pilot circles to discuss the attitudes of circle members, non-circle members, and middle management.

During the first six months, the facilitator will be able to contact the consulting group about any implementation problems and, if needed, have them send someone to Charlottesville. At the end of six months, the consultant will return to Centel to make an evaluation of the program and, along with the facilitator, establish goals for the program for the next year.

Once Centel has experienced some success with the pilot program, I would recommend the Steering Committee form two or three interdepartment groups between the Business Office, Plant Service Center, Storeroom, and possibly Operator Services. A number of people who took part in the Fall Rush Program said there are communication problems between groups that would be alleviated by intergroup interaction on problem solving. I do not recommend interdepartment groups initially because I feel the program must be accepted in its original form before making variations to it. Once employees become experienced in identifying and solving problems in their work groups, I feel they will be ready to tackle the more difficult task of interdepartmental problems.

I have tried to make my implementation steps as specific as possible. Once a consulting firm is retained and a facilitator hired more detail can be incorporated into the plan as Centel begins to get into the preliminary implementation phase. It will be up to the Steering Committee to add more detail and make modifications to the program as information becomes available.

TABLE 1
Implementation Timetable Guideline

Action	By Whom	Approximate Working Days
Decision to start.	Division Vice-President	0
Contact consultant to arrange for in-house seminar and implementation. Hopefully, seminar can be scheduled within next 20 days.	Assigned Individual	1
Receive and review preliminary information from consultant concerning organization of steering committee and choosing facilitator.	Assigned Individual	5
Form steering committee and initiate first meeting.	Assigned Individual	8
Steering committee selects facilitator and works on circle objectives and guidelines.	Steering Committee	18
Facilitator begins training with the instructor/consultant. Also, the two work on setting up implementation program to be presented to steering committee.	Facilitator	18
Facilitator collects preimplementation data for before and after comparison.	Facilitator	23
Distribute Quality Circle literature to pilot group managers.	Facilitator	28
Pilot group managers and supervisors meet with steering committee to discuss program and answer any questions.	Steering Committee and Pilot Group Managers	30
Select pilot program circle leaders from interested supervisory volunteers. Begin leader training.	Pilot Group Managers Facilitator	31
Managers conduct Quality Circle familiarization meetings with employees. Facilitator, Circle leaders, and a member of the steering committee participate as speakers.	Managers Facilitator	35

APPENDIX (continued)

Leader contacts each employee to determine circle membership.	Leader	37
Leader and facilitator begin weekly Circle meetings and initiate member training.	Facilitator, Leader	38
Circles learn problem solving techniques from training sessions.	Facilitator, Leader Group Members	78
Facilitator makes progress report to steering committee and arranges Circle presentation.	Facilitator	100
Steering committee decides on program expansion and makes revisions to policy/procedures.	Steering Committee	3 Months

TABLE 2
Cost Analysis—Quality Circles

A. One time costs:

Consultant seminar presentation	$ 500
Consultant implementation cost	3,950
Consultant expenses (estimate only)	4,000
	$8,450

B. On-going costs:
Full-time facilitator
Loss of production due to Circle meetings
Management expenses for participation on steering committee

— as program expands price will go ↑

Broadway Pizza

DAVID A. COLLIER

The president of a chain of pizza parlors that combines food service with family-oriented entertainment is wondering why sales are declining. He asks the vice-presidents of each department to identify and evaluate possible reasons and then jointly prepare a set of recommendations.

"Why are sales declining?" asked Mr. Dick Baldwin, the President of Broadway Pizza, at the beginning of the monthly executive meeting. After pondering the question for a moment, Mr. Larry Corea, the Vice-President of Marketing said:

I used to feel very confident about the soundness and uniqueness of the Broadway Pizza concept. (See *Exhibit 1*.) Now I'm beginning to wonder if this service delivery system isn't more complicated than we thought. Combining robotic entertainment and food service under one roof may be too tough to pull off. From the customer's viewpoint are we a pizza parlor, a community gathering place, an entertainment center and amusement park, a fantasy place for kids aged 3 to 12 years old, an arcade, or a place for parties? I think we are all of these things to our customers. Thus, our marketing and advertising programs are complex. Or maybe we're just a fad that has begun to lose its appeal.

Mr. Baldwin turned to Mr. Eugene Bell, the Vice-President of Operations, and asked,

Case prepared by Associate Professor David A. Collier, The Colgate Darden Graduate School of Business Administration, University of Virginia. Names, places, and some numbers have been disguised. Copyright 1984 by The Colgate Darden Graduate Business School Sponsors, Charlottesville, Virginia. Reproduced by permission.

254

EXHIBIT 1

The Concept

I. UNIQUENESS OF THE BROADWAY PIZZA CONCEPT

Broadway Pizza stores are *not fast-food restaurants;* they are a *totally unique concept combining food service* with *technological entertainment* oriented toward *families.* The ways in which Broadway Pizza stores are unique are as follows:

1. Our stores are oriented toward families. Demographic and income trends for families are favorable, and parents are once again looking for activities to participate in as a family unit. Children under the age of 18 are not allowed in without a parent, to ensure that a store does not become a "hangout."

2. Our stores are local *entertainment centers* that are relatively inexpensive. A family of four can have a very enjoyable unplanned outing lasting two hours for about $18.00. The children are able to enjoy the restaurant and run free rather than have to "sit still" as in most restaurants.

3. The concept makes use of recent breakthroughs in semi-conductor and electronics technology. Children of today are as accustomed to home computers and electronic video games as kids of 15 years ago were to TV, and they seem to be prepared to participate in the increasing levels of sophistication that will surely come. *Electronic entertainment* in robots, games, and video systems is in its infancy, and we should benefit from growth in all three areas.

4. The robotics also provide us with characters that can be actively promoted much like McDonald's "Ronald McDonald." Each Broadway Pizza store has character costumes, and every hour one of the employees makes an appearance, much like Mickey Mouse at Disneyland. The characters are extremely successful attractions at the store and in the community, because they can be touched and talked to, whereas Ronald McDonald is limited to television commercials and very infrequent appearances.

5. Broadway Pizza is a company of extremely creative people. It is likely to stay at the forefront of new developments in technological entertainment, character development, and labor-saving food service procedures.

II. BROADWAY PIZZA vs. ARCADES: THE DIFFERENCES

1. The only business of most arcades is to sell game plays. At Broadway Pizza, however, sales of food and beverages typically account for 75 percent or more of sales. Games are *less* than 25 percent of sales. Our *primary* function is as a *restaurant.*

2. Arcades primarily attract young males from 15 to 24 years old. Broadway Pizza attracts families with children ages 2 to 14. It caters nearly exclusively to families and groups. Children under the age of 18 are not allowed in the restaurant unless accompanied by a parent or guardian.

3. Arcades often become "hangouts" and promote an atmosphere that is conducive to this image by permitting smoking and eating. At Broadway Pizza no drinking, eating, or smoking is allowed in the games or rides areas. The atmosphere is oriented toward *young* children by using walkaround characters, computer-controlled animated characters, and play areas.

4. Secondary entertainment features at arcades may include pinball machines, pool tables, and hard liquor. Broadway Pizza has none of these. They are primarily fun-filled restaurants with a variety of entertainment attractions.

5. Parents who have taken their children to Broadway Pizza say it most reminds them of Disneyland and they rarely, if ever, mention arcades.

SOURCE: Company 10-K Report.

"What about food quality and customer service levels? Are they problems?" Mr. Bell responded:

> Dick, our survey of adults during peak-demand periods indicated some initial problems with pizza quality, but our new pizzas have corrected this problem. Our ratings on friendly employees, nice family atmosphere, and birthday/special occasions are all very high, so I don't think customer service levels are the problem. Although the parents indicate they want separate rooms with lower noise levels, I

sometimes think the layout of the store is too complicated.

(A summary of the Peak-Hour Adult Customer Survey is shown in *Exhibit 2*, and a typical store layout in *Exhibit 3*.)

"Well, I think the real problem is repeat business, not complexity, not store layout, not food quality, and not service levels," commented Brenda Layman, the Vice-President of Finance.

EXHIBIT 2

Peak-Hour Adult Customer Survey Summary*

This survey is based on 750 completed telephone interviews with adult customers of Broadway Pizza. Customer information cards completed in the stores were the basis for this phone survey. The stores surveyed were moderate to large size (190 to 400 seating capacity), geographically dispersed throughout the United States, and in operation for one year or more. Some totals exceed 100 percent due to multiple responses.

A. *Distance Traveled*
Over half (53.5%) of Broadway Pizza's adult peak-hour customers traveled six miles or less to get to the store. Over one-fourth (27.7%) traveled ten or more miles. First-time patrons were twice as likely as repeat customers to travel more than 10 miles to visit a store.

B. *Sex, Age, and Income of Adult Customers*
There were more female customers (59.7%) than male customers (40.3%) during peak hours. Peak-hour adult customers consisted of 12.6% for the 18–24 year old age range, 45.9% for the 25–34 age range, 29.6% for the 35–44 age range, and 11.9% for 44 years of age. The mean household income for peak-hour customers was $27,507, compared with a national mean of $21,063.

C. *Children as Customers*
Eight out of ten (82.5%) of Broadway Pizza's peak-hour adult customers had children living at home. The age of the children living at home who visited Broadway Pizza were: under 3 (33.0%), 3–5 (41.3%), 6–10 (50.5%), 11–14 (28.2%), and over 15 years of age (15.9%). The parents' child suggested they visit Broadway Pizza 42.6% of the time, the parents 42.6% of the time, relatives 8.1% of the time, and other 6.7% of the time. There were 4 people in a party (i.e., per visit) 65.2% of the time.

D. *Why Go To Broadway Pizza?*
The most important factors were: to entertain children (86.5%), animated character shows (65.3%), walk-around characters (53.8%), pizza (51.3%), arcade games (39.8%), and food other than pizza (18.5%). The frequency of visits to Broadway Pizza within the last month were as follows: once (57.9%), twice (24.3%), three times (8.1%), four times (5.8%), five or more times (3.0%), and no answer (0.9%). Over three-fourths (77.4%) of all peak-hour customers said they definitely would return to Broadway Pizza. Most peak-hour customers (83.6%) had recently been to a restaurant other than Broadway Pizza that served pizza. The other restaurants that served pizza that they most often named were as follows: Pizza Hut (26.5%), Showbiz (11.0%), Pizza Time Theatres (10.7%), Pizza Inn (10.3%), Shakey's (8.1%), Godfather's (6.5%), Round Table (6.2%), Straw Hat (6.1%), Circus Playhouse (0.3%), Other/Local (68.0%).

EXHIBIT 2 (continued)

E. *Amount Spent on Last Visit to Broadway Pizza*

Amount Spent	Food & Drink	Rides & Games	General Store/Misc.
$ 0	0.5%	12.4%	73.5%
$ Under $5	2.5	37.6	21.0
$ 5 to 10	15.9	35.8	3.8
$ 11 to 15	34.9	6.5	0.4
$ 16 to 20	19.6	4.9	0.4
$ 21 to 25	9.9	1.1	—
$ 26 to 30	5.7	0.4	—
$ Over 30	8.9	0.5	—
Don't Know	2.1	0.8	0.9
Mean Amount Spent Per Check	$16.98	$5.97	$0.95

F. *Pizza Preference (Prior to New Pizza Introduction)*
Of those customers who had recently been to other restaurants that served pizza, 38% stated a preference for the Pizza served at Broadway Pizza. The elements of competitive pizza that made it better than Broadway Pizza in the minds of the customer were: thicker crust (36.0%), more cheese (36.0%), and more toppings (30.9%). Customers appeared to be more impressed by quantity than quality of toppings.

G. *Evaluation of Overall Service Delivery System*
Peak-hour adult customers rated 13 aspects of Broadway Pizza on a scale from poor (1) to excellent (4). The results were as follows:

Variable	Mean Rating
Variety of Entertainment for Children	3.8
Staff Courtesy/Friendliness	3.6
Variety of Arcade Games	3.5
Appearance/Decor of Restaurant	3.5
Cleanliness	3.4
Number of Arcade Games	3.4
Speed of Food Service	3.2
Pizza Quality	3.2
Location of Restaurant	3.2
Maintenance of Arcade Games	3.1
General Food Quality	3.1
Price of Games	2.9
Price of Food	2.6

*The peak-hour survey included customers after 5:00 P.M. on weekdays and Saturday and Sunday. A nonpeak survey primarily for lunch customers was also performed, but the results are not presented.

We need to increase the frequency of visits customers make to Broadway Pizza. We don't get enough repeat business, and that gets back to Larry's idea about our stores being a fad.

After Brenda's comment, Dick evaluated what he had heard and concluded, "O.K., I want each of you to evaluate potential reasons for our sales decline in your area of responsibility during the next two weeks. Then get together and develop a final set of recommendations. Be ready to present them at our next monthly executive meeting. Now let's talk about next month's advertising plans."

EXHIBIT 3
Typical Broadway Pizza Store Layout

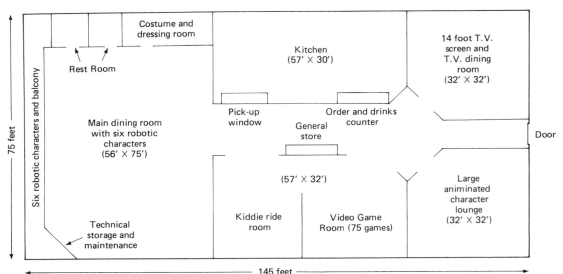

STORE DESIGN CONCEPTS AND LAYOUT

To the founders of Broadway Pizza, the concept of a family-oriented entertainment and food service business, as documented in *Exhibit 1*, seemed to take advantage of modern eating habits and technological innovations. Mr. Baldwin and a group of investors had founded the company in 1980 as a franchise of the national corporation, Broadway Pizza and Restaurants.

The layout of the store was based on a concept called "center-of-the-action." That is, a customer standing in the main hallway was given a visual taste of each attraction from a single vantage point (see *Exhibit 3*). In fact, most stores were designed so that when customers were placing an order at the counter they could see into each room of Broadway Pizza. In general, stores ranged from 8,000 to 12,000 square feet depending on building and lot constraints. Building a new store required an investment of $800,000 to $1 million. Twenty of the 40 stores were built from the ground up, and the rest were located in leased space. Annual rental costs ranged from $8 to $20 per square foot of

space. Broadway Pizza stores could accommodate 300 to 400 customers.

The typical Broadway Pizza store contained computer-controlled animated characters with voice and music synchronized to animated movements in the main dining room and the large character lounge. Generally, six colorful animated robots were located in the main dining room. They performed skits from a balcony stage. The audience enjoyed songs like "Hello Dolly," "Summertime," and "Yankee Doodle Dandy" while the robots moved their satin lips, heaved oversized bosoms, winked at the audience, told jokes, and talked to the audience. The robots could be programmed for up to 20 different routines. The kids, especially the younger ones, seemed fascinated, and the parents seemed to enjoy watching their kids have fun. The maximum seating capacity of a typical main dining room was 200. The lounge contained one huge animated character and about 60 seats. In the lounge, a six-to-nine foot tall character performed a skit when you put a coin or token in the coinbox.

Birthday and school-sponsored parties were an important part of Broadway Pizza's business. Stores averaged from 40 to 100 parties per month. Often two or three parties would be going on simultaneously. Broadway Pizza received a substantial amount of free and positive publicity in newspapers, on local television and radio, and in local magazines because of these parties and activities.

The game and ride rooms generally had about 75 video games and rides. Skeeball, Pac-Man, Centipede, and Asteroids were just a few of the video games available. The video games accepted quarters or free tokens given with food purchases and parties. The rides included a Ferris wheel, miniature helicopters, rocket ships, and a ball crawl (i.e., thousands of large, plastic, multi-colored balls in a huge container through which children crawled).

The TV dining room featured a 14-foot-wide television screen. This room had a maximum seating capacity of 48 seats. It was popular with parents as a place to escape the noise, eat pizza, and watch television while their kids enjoyed the other activities of Broadway Pizza.

The kitchen area included a counter to order meals, a salad bar, and a customer pick-up window. The counter area had five cash registers but most of the time only one or two were used. Customers placed their orders, received their drinks, trays, napkins, forks, etc., at the counter, and moved to the salad bar or pick-up window to receive the rest of their order. The modern pizza ovens cooked the pizzas in 6 minutes.

MARKET ANALYSIS

Vice-President of Marketing, Larry Corea, had identified five factors that he thought influenced demand for Broadway Pizza's entertainment and food services:

1. Metropolitan population within a 3-mile radius of the store. The number of families was considered a better indicator of store revenue than area population if available (i.e., single vs. family population).

2. Number of customer visits per year (i.e., frequency rate).

3. Average transaction dollars per visit per family.

4. The concept of Broadway Pizza as defined in *Exhibit 1*. Is it correct and sellable in the market place?

5. Aging of Broadway Pizza stores. Do customers get bored in our stores?

Larry wanted to evaluate each of these factors but had not had time to figure out a sound evaluation methodology. Most of his time was spent on local advertising programs to boost store revenues. With 40 stores open or opening, he was working 60 hours a week.

In general, store revenue was highest in the second quarter, moderate in the first and third quarters, and lowest during the fourth quarter. Approximately 80 percent of store revenue was collected after 5:00 P.M. Friday, Saturday, and Sunday sales accounted for almost two-thirds of total store revenue. During the last 18 months, sales revenue per store on a system-wide basis had declined from $33,000 per week ($1,683,000 per year) to $27,000 per week ($1,377,000 per year).

OPERATIONS

Eugene Bell, the Vice-President of Operations, and Brenda Layman, the Vice-President of Finance, had reviewed the operating budgets of many stores. They found the staffing levels for peak and nonpeak periods to be efficient, and customer service levels seemed to be high at all operating hours. Direct labor hours were based on the store manager's estimate of daily sales. Forecasts of daily store sales and the associated direct labor hours had been within ± 5 percent of actual experience. The two vice-presidents also compiled the investment and cost information for a typical Broadway Pizza store, shown in *Exhibit 4*, and found the national restaurant data, as documented in *Exhibits 5 and 6*.

Eugene did a stopwatch study on a sample of customers and found they averaged two hours in the store on their initial visit and

EXHIBIT 4

Investment and Cost Structure of a Typical Broadway Pizza Store

Investment	Percentage
Robotic characters	35
Kitchen equipment	16
Other attractions	14
Building costs	32
Research, development, architect, etc.	3
Total	100

Revenue	Percentage
Total revenue*	100
Food & beverage revenue	75
Game revenue	25
Cost as Percentage of Sales	
Cost of goods	21
Labor including benefits	25
Franchise fee to parent company	6
Marketing and advertising	5
Depreciation	5
Rent	8
Utilities	4
Interest	5
General & administrative	8
Maintenance and repairs	4
Subtotal	91
Income before taxes	9

*Cost/Revenue structure at the $33,000 per week or $1,683,000 per year sales level.

EXHIBIT 5

United States National Food Service Trends: Weekday versus Weekend Eating Out Patterns

Category	Weekday	3-Day Weekend
Fast Food	50%	50%
Family	44	56
Coffee Shop	59	41
Dinner House	45	55
All Restaurants	47	53

SOURCE: H. E. Lane and M. van Hartesvelt, *Essentials of Hospitality Administration* (Reston, Va.: Reston Publishing, 1983), p. 268.

1.5 hours for repeat visits. Also, customers did not seem to wait at the counter once their order was placed but wandered around the

EXHIBIT 6

Statement of Income and Expenses for a Typical 150-Seat Restaurant

Sales	Percentage
Food	70%
Beverage	30
Total Sales	100
Cost of sales	
Food	27%
Beverage	7
Total cost of sales	34
Gross profit	66
Controllable expenses	
Payroll including benefits	26%
Direct operating expenses	6
Advertising and promotion	2
Music and entertainment	2
Utilities	4
Administrative and general	6
Repairs and maintenance	2
Total controllable expenses	48%
Income before rent or occupation costs	18%
Rent or occupation costs	2
Depreciation	3
Total occupation costs	5
Income before taxes	13%

SOURCE: H. E. Lane and M. van Hartesvelt, *Essentials of Hospitality Administration* (Reston, Va.: Reston Publishing, 1983), p. 270.

store—sometimes playing games or watching the robotic characters perform. Sometimes a pizza got cold because they were involved in store activities and did not pick it up promptly.

Concerning the evaluation of store managers, Eugene noted, "At first, most store managers focus their attention on food services and ignore the automation. They leave it up to the store maintenance technician to test the robotics and software at 8:00 A.M. each morning, to do preventive maintenance, order parts, and groom the robotic characters. They quickly realize they must manage the automation side of the business too."

Each Broadway Pizza store had its own robotic maintenance technician who worked 40 hours per week. The average salary of a robotic technician was $25,000 per year. Sometimes a technician would handle two stores if they were in close proximity to each other and/or a store was temporarily without a technician. A considerable amount of time was required by the technician to set up, test, and debug a new skit (i.e., software program) or change robotic characters between stores. Management felt that to vary the skits and characters in each store once every few months was a necessary part of their business.

THE END OF THE DAY

Dick glanced at his office clock. It was 9:00 P.M. He hadn't even had dinner! He had spent most of the day working on the advertising plans on a store-by-store basis with Larry. He didn't begin reading the proposed new wage and salary review system for store and sales managers until 6:00 P.M. Being the president of a young service firm placed great demands on his time.

As he packed his briefcase and left the office, he pondered the day's meeting. Everyone was working hard. The most troublesome issue of all was the question, "Why are sales declining?" Then he thought, "Once we know the answer to this question, what can I do about it?" He would await the recommendations of his two vice-presidents at the next monthly executive meeting and then he must act quickly.

PART VI
Customer Service

Developing and Managing the Customer-Service Function in the Service Sector

CHRISTOPHER H. LOVELOCK

The customer service function is changing dramatically in many service businesses. This article reviews the steps necessary to transform customer service into a responsive activity that enhances the firm's competitive posture.

Customer service has suddenly become a rather universal term. In service organizations, it was once largely restricted to booths in big retail stores, where customers could get information, obtain refunds, and file complaints. Today, the term seems to be ubiquitous. The tellers at my bank are now known as customer service representatives. If I call Federal Express Corporation to ask them to pick up a package, I will be speaking to a customer service agent in one of three computerized telephone centers across the United States. And when I flew People Express [now merged into Continental Airlines], I was likely to find both the agent at the gate and one or more of the flight attendants on board the aircraft sporting badges that identified them as customer service managers.

Is this just one more case of euphemistic new names for old jobs, or is the nature of the jobs themselves changing? In my opinion, it's about 20 percent of the former and 80 percent of the latter.

Defining Customer Service in Service Organizations

One of the most fundamental concepts in analyzing service operations is the distinc-

---

tion between the "front office" and the "back office" (Chase 1978). Front-office procedures are those experienced by the consumer. In some instances, they represent a very small proportion of the service firm's total activities. For instance, the extent of personal contact between customers and their credit-card company is limited to receiving and paying a monthly statement, and perhaps an occasional letter or telephone call when problems arise. All the processing of credit-card applications, the credit checks, and the processing of credit card slips takes place behind the scenes. In a hotel, by contrast, the customer is exposed to the physical facilities and to numerous hotel personnel, ranging from telephone-reservation agent to front desk, from bell hop to room service, and from waitress to concierge.

Recognizing the importance of these front-office interactions to customer satisfaction, I define customer service as follows:

> Customer service is a task, other than proactive selling, that involves interactions with customers in person, by telecommunications, or by mail. It is designed, performed, and communicated with two goals in mind: operational efficiency and customer satisfaction.

This definition is much broader than the traditional view of customer service as a strictly reactive function that simply responds, on an exception basis, to customer problems or complaints. Essentially, it embraces all personnel whose jobs bring them into contact with customers on a routine as well as an exception basis. Such personnel become part of the overall service product, even though their jobs may have been defined in strictly operational terms. Hence the need to balance operational efficiency against customer satisfaction.

BETTER CUSTOMER SERVICE AS A RESPONSE TO COMPETITIVE PRESSURES

As the service sector becomes more competitive, the need for meaningful competitive differentiation is sharpened. To an increasing degree, this differentiation includes a search for superior performance on supplementary product elements, especially those included under my expanded definition of customer service.

Insights from Federal Express

A good example of focusing on customer service as a point of differentiation is provided by Federal Express. Finding that its once-unique overnight-package-delivery system had been emulated by numerous competitors, who used alternative operational procedures to create the same core product, Federal Express executives rethought their competitive stance. They redefined *service* as "all actions and reactions that customers perceive they have purchased" and proceeded to develop a sophisticated, centralized customer-service function to handle information provision, order taking, tracing, and problem solving.

Previously, most of these tasks had either been handled by operations personnel working out of local Federal Express stations, or by sales representatives. A toll-free number in Memphis, Tennessee also handled calls from customers who wished to speak directly with a customer-service agent (CSA) in the Memphis head office. Modern computer technology enabled the company to develop a professional customer-service function located at four interlinked call centers across the country. Electronic "order blanks" on cathode-ray tube (CRT) screens replaced paper records, and a sophisticated information and retrieval system allows CSAs to call up data on a regular customer simply by keying in that customer's account number. Since all packages are now computer coded and pass through optical scanners at each stage in the transportation and sorting process, information on package movements can be entered in the central computer and is easily accessible to CSAs for tracing purposes. Problems that are beyond the capabilities of a CSA to solve are transferred promptly to specialist personnel.

The customer-service department at Federal Express has grown into a management function that is independent of operations and sales but works closely with each; customer service has taken over certain routine tasks and simple problem-solving efforts from both sales and operations, leaving each of these departments to focus on the tasks that they are uniquely qualified to perform. Routine customer contacts from operations personnel are now limited to the pick-up and delivery of packages by the couriers.

Federal Express executives believe that their customer-service department provides a higher level of service than competitors can provide. They also note that it would be extremely expensive for competitors to install the equipment and systems needed to duplicate the Federal Express approach.

Customer Satisfaction and Customer Service

As Czepiel (1980) has emphasized, the managerial process necessary for integrating operations and marketing in a service business consists of four tasks:

1. Research and monitoring to determine customer needs, wants, and satisfaction levels.
2. Identifying from among these the sources of customer satisfaction (or dissatisfaction).
3. Setting service-level standards.
4. Designing technology and jobs to meet these standards.

Historically, many service organizations have been operations driven rather than marketing driven. As such, only limited efforts were made in the past to measure customer satisfaction through formal research. At the credit-card division of American Express (AMEX), for instance, customer service was measured by the manifestation of customer complaints through letters and telephone calls (Anonymous 1982). AMEX made what was, for them, the radical departure of viewing and measuring customer service as perceived by the customer. This led to the recognition that the customer-service department was only the "catcher's mitt" for problems that arose in other departments such as data processing, mail room, new accounts, and accounts receivable. New programs were then put into place to set

standards, improve work procedures, foster teamwork between departments, and monitor performance. The output of the back office was categorized into what American Express termed "service elements," such as processing applications, issuing new cards, responding to billing inquiries, authorizing charges on accounts, and issuing replacement cards. More than one hundred and eighty measures were developed to track the level of each service element against previously established quality-assurance standards.

The company claims that substantially improved efficiency, productivity, and service levels have resulted from its quality-assurance program. Interestingly, the refocusing of company attention on customer needs has also improved employee morale in both the front and back offices.

Like the credit-card division of American Express, many other service firms have a large back office and a small front office. In such firms, customer service is most appropriately viewed as the output of the operations department (Loud 1980), and will usually be channeled through a limited number of individuals.

In organizations that provide services to customers in person, the front office is relatively much larger. Customers are likely to come into contact with a greater number of service personnel, whose services may be delivered sequentially and independently of each other. Airline service provides a good example, with customers first making inquiries and reservations, then checking their baggage, getting seat assignments, being checked at the gate, receiving on-board service in flight, and retrieving their baggage at the destination airport (a task that may or may not entail further contact with service personnel). Each of these activities is an operations task that is secondary to the core product of physically transporting passengers and their bags between two airports. But these secondary tasks have great potential to generate customer dissatisfaction if performed poorly. Poor performance may include bad manners as well as substandard operational execution. In this instance, the responsibility of an expanded customer-service function might be to develop a stronger customer perspective on the part of all these service personnel, including recruitment guidelines, training, performance monitoring, obtaining customer feedback, and then redefining tasks and retraining the personnel as appropriate.

A distinctive characteristic of the organizational structure at People Express was its continuing rotation of customer-service managers (CSMs) through a series of jobs—reservations agent, gate agent, flight attendant—in order to develop a more cohesive perspective of how these jobs fit together from a passenger perspective. CSMs were also required to work in staff departments such as marketing and accounting several days a month.

DEVELOPING THE CUSTOMER SERVICE FUNCTION

The nature of the customer-contact function inevitably varies by service industry and by type of organization. Among the factors that serve to shape the tasks performed and the place of customer service within the organization are the following.

1. Presence or Absence of Intermediaries. Some customer-contact tasks are often more efficiently performed by intermediaries. Usually these relate to initial contacts by customers prior to delivery of the core service. Examples include travel agents and theater-ticket agencies that provide information and advice, make reservations, and collect payment. Some smaller hotel chains offer a toll-free telephone reservations service but contract out this task to a specialist firm. Although this strategy weakens the control of the firm over performance of key customer-contact tasks, it may result in better service at a lower cost.

2. High Contact Versus Low Contact. The more involvement the customer has with the service firm, the greater the number of customer-contact points and the more likely these are to take place in locations that are geographically far removed from the head office. This situation offers more opportunities

for mistakes or poor service to occur and is thus more complex to manage. By contrast, low-contact services entail few interactions with customers, with contacts often being limited to mail and telephone interactions with personnel located in a central office, where management controls can be much tighter.

3. Institutional Versus Individual Purchases. Greater variability is likely to be introduced into customer-service activities when dealing with members of the general public (who are often infrequent users of a particular service) as opposed to working with managers or employees of institutional customers. The latter are likely to purchase in greater volume and with greater frequency, but there may be multiple contact persons within the client organization. This requires particularly good record keeping on the part of the service deliverer.

4. Duration of Service Delivery Process. The longer it takes for service delivery to be completed, the more likely it is that customers will require information on work in progress—such as estimated completion dates, projected costs, and so forth. Good internal monitoring systems are required to generate and communicate the needed information.

5. Capacity-Constrained Services. In most instances, this group of services will need to offer either a reservation system or a queuing-control mechanism. The former requires on-line access to a reservations data base, and is usually handled by telecommunications; the latter requires friendly but firm interactions with customers standing in line, with realistic projections of the estimated wait for service.

6. Frequency of Use and Repurchase. When the bulk of consumption is accounted for by repeat use, it is important to separate proactive selling (which is expensive and requires more training) from simple order taking. As in the Federal Express example cited earlier, a computerized data base allows immediate access to customer records. To stimulate repurchase, some service businesses encourage their customer-contact personnel to remember regular customers and to offer them special recognition and favors. A good information system, which identifies repeat users, can be employed to brief staff members who might not otherwise be aware that a specific customer merited special treatment.

7. Level of Complexity. Some services are simple to use and easy for the operations department to deliver. Other services are more complex, with the result that inexperienced users require assistance. A related problem in complex services is the prevalence of Murphy's Law: There are lots of things that can go wrong, and sooner or later something will (usually at a most inconvenient moment). Complex services, therefore, require customer-contact personnel who can provide information and help to educate the customer. They also require contingency plans for problem resolution, necessitating careful training of personnel on what actions to take when a particular problem arises. Superior performance by service personnel in restoring operations (or providing an acceptable alternative) can create a very favorable impression in customers' minds, distinguishing the excellent organization from the mediocre ones.

8. Degree of Risk. Service managers must understand the consequences for customers of a service failure. Contingency planning is often required by government regulation where personal safety is a factor. Other consequences for customers may range from personal inconvenience to monetary loss. The higher the probability of a service failure and the more serious the consequences to customers, the more important it is to employ mature, well-trained contact personnel who are able to behave calmly and tactfully when faced by upset customers, as well as being able to resolve the problem as quickly as possible.

Assignment of Tasks to Customer Service

The array of tasks that may fall under the rubric of customer service is quite broad. An important question for any service organization that is developing or expanding its customer-service function is: Which specific tasks should be performed by and assigned to customer service?

The potential array of customer-service tasks can be divided into selling-related activities and nonselling activities, and also into customer-initiated interactions and firm-initiated interactions. The potential exists for customer-service personnel to get into selling-related activities, but this should be seen as an adjunct to their work, not its principal focus. For instance, a customer-contact employee might mention new services in the course of delivering service; or information on new service features might be included with a bill or documentation of account activity. As the number of retail-banking products expands, tellers are being encouraged (or required) to inform customers of these new services. Similarly, airline and hotel reservations personnel will sometimes attempt to encourage callers to make additional purchases. There is, however, a risk of annoying customers who may resent such a continual sales push.

Note that service delivery may be initiated by the organization or by the customer. An example of the former is provided by delivery of airline meals; the assumption is that the passenger will take a meal tray unless he or she declines the opportunity. Although customer service has historically focused on reactive problem solving and responding to complaints, progressive service firms sometimes seek to identify the potential for a problem before it occurs. For instance, if a flight is rescheduled, the airline should call passengers with reservations so that they have the opportunity to revise their plans. Rather than waiting for complaints, some firms regularly contact (by telephone or mail) all customers (or a sample of customers) who have recently purchased a service to determine if they are satisfied. This is, of course, a form of market research but it may serve to uncover simmering problems before they reach a boil, as well as identifying service features that customers appreciate.

Conducting a Customer-Service Audit

To determine the appropriate nature and scope of its customer-service function, each service organization should conduct a customer-service audit to determine the current situation. The following is an outline of a basic format for such an audit, although greater detail will be required to cover the situation in any specific organization.

- Identify customer-contact tasks (other than sales), for example:
    Information, reservations
    Service delivery tasks
    Billing and customer-record transmittal
    Problem solving, complaint handling
- Review standard procedures for each task
    Written standards (procedures manual) for each task
    Oral/written instructions (ad hoc)
    Availability (hours/days, locations)
    Interactions with other personnel
- Identify performance goals by task
    Specific quantitative goals
    Qualitative goals
    Contribution to related activities
    Contribution to long-term success of system
- Identify measures of performance by task
    Dollar based
    Time based
    Management/supervisor evaluations
    Customer evaluations
- Review and evaluate personnel elements
    Recruiting/selection criteria and practices
    Nature, content of training
    Job definition, career path (if any)
    Interactions with other employees
    Nature of supervision, quality control
    Evaluation procedures
    Corrective actions available
    Employee attitudes, motivation
    Hours, extent of paid/unpaid overtime
- Identify and evaluate support systems
    Instruction manuals, brochures, form letters
    Office facilities, furnishings, layout
    Office equipment (phones, computers, word processors)
    Vehicles and equipment for repair/maintenance

Radio communications
Record-keeping materials (for example, log books)

The audit begins by identifying all customer-contact tasks and the standard procedures prescribed for each. It then considers performance goals for each task and current measures of performance. Next comes a detailed review and evaluation of all personnel elements, and finally identification and evaluation of support systems available to customer-contact personnel. To determine the current utilization of customer-service personnel, it is useful to maintain a log of all calls to customer service (in person, by telephone, or by mail). The format for a simple customer-service log should include space for information on the date and time of the call, information on the caller, the reason for the call, and the disposition of that call.

The findings of the audit will establish the current situation and provide a basis for planning the future scope and quality of the customer-service function. Since customer service is potentially an important tool in competitive differentiation, an appraisal should also be made of competitors' customer-service efforts.

Guidelines for Effective Program Implementation

Once the customer-service program has been designed, it must be implemented effectively. Careful consideration should be given to each of the following tasks. (Several of these guidelines are derived from Takeuchi and Quelch [1983] but have been adapted to allow for effective implementation of customer-service programs in service-industry settings.)

1. Recruit the Right Employees. Individuals whose jobs require them to interact with customers must possess both the right technical skills and aptitudes and also appropriate personal characteristics. Depending on the job, the latter may include appearance, mannerisms, voice, personality, and so forth.

2. Train Employees Properly. First, the training must develop the necessary level of technical proficiency to perform specific tasks properly. Second, employees must be instructed in personal appearance and/or telephone manner, behavior toward customers, and use of correct language. Finally, skills in handling anticipated situations must be developed, particularly as these relate to personal interactions under difficult or stressful situations. The use of role-playing exercises is often very helpful.

3. Educate the Customers. They should know how to use and how not to use the service. It is helpful to offer customers information in printed form; good signing is very important at service delivery sites and on self-service equipment. In large service facilities, customer-service desks or booths should be available to help customers with queries or problems. When customers and the service organization transact remotely, consideration should be given to establishment of toll-free telephone numbers that customers can call.

4. Educate All Employees. They should view customers with problems as a source of useful information for the firm rather than as a source of annoyance. Internal marketing programs may be needed to change negative employee attitudes and to communicate procedures for effective interactions with customers who have experienced difficulties.

5. Be Efficient First, Nice Second. The ultimate objective of a customer-service program is to resolve the problem, not to provide cheerful sympathy. While basic courtesy is important to convey a caring attitude and to mitigate consumer confusion or anger, too much friendliness can be inefficient. At busy times, especially, when other clients may be waiting in line or on hold, the primary responsibility of a customer-service representative is to resolve the problem quickly.

6. Standardize Service Response Systems. Use of a standard form for handling inquiries and complaints provides a checklist for the customer service agent (CSA) and facilitates entry of the data into a computer system. This not only expedites follow-

through, but also facilitates monitoring of changes in the mix and level of customer-initiated contacts. Effective response also requires rapid forwarding to specialist personnel of sophisticated problems that the CSA cannot handle.

7. Develop a Pricing Policy. Quality customer service does not necessarily mean free service; consideration should be given to charging for certain categories of service that have traditionally been offered free of charge. This is especially necessary if delivering the service in question costs the company money or if customers abuse the service relationship (for example, calls to directory assistance for telephone numbers that are already in the phone book, frequent requests for copies of mislaid bank statements, deinstallation of cable-television connections for the summer followed by reinstallation in the fall).

8. Involve Subcontractors if Necessary. Fast, quality response is sometimes more easily and cheaply obtained by subcontracting certain customer-service functions to outside firms. Examples include use of travel agents for airline information and reservations, and use of an independent reservations service for toll-free hotel telephone reservations. The negative side of such an approach is that the primary service supplier loses control over the quality of customer service, may fail to capture the valuable marketing information inherent in customer-service calls, and may even find the subcontractor actively promoting the competition.

9. Evaluate Customer Service. Quantitative performance standards must be set for each element of the customer-service package. Actual performance should be measured against those standards and reasons for any variances determined. In addition, efforts should be made to solicit customers' opinions on customer-service elements at regular intervals. This may be done by distributing comment forms to all customers and relying on those who experience above-average or below-average service to respond with compliments or complaints; this is the strategy adopted by most hotels, which leave guest comment cards in each room. It can also be used quite inexpensively by firms that have an ongoing relationship with their customers and send out monthly statements; a short survey could be enclosed, say, once a year. Alternatively, a service firm may choose periodically to survey a representative cross section of customers to solicit their appraisals and suggestions.

10. Affirm Good Work. Superior performance by customer-contact employees should be recognized. Initiative should be rewarded. Employee feedback and suggestions should be encouraged. Many service managers are quite removed from their customers and fail to recognize the insights that employees may develop from their day-to-day contact with customers.

11. Take Corrective Actions to Improve Defective Customer Service. Such actions may include retraining employees, reassigning employees who are unsuited to perform customer-contact tasks but are otherwise motivated and proficient, and terminating incorrigibles. It may also be necessary to revamp support systems, restructure the work environment, and reassign responsibilities within the customer-service group to improve efficiency. Finally, in order to catch problems before they become too serious, it may help to develop improved performance monitors.

CONCLUSION

The customer-service function is changing dramatically in many service businesses. It is evolving from a purely reactive function, often grudgingly performed, to a responsive and even proactive function designed to enhance the firm's competitive posture. Previously haphazard procedures are being standardized and professionalized. Modern computer technology is an important factor in improving the efficiency and effectiveness of customer-service activities.

As service firms grow larger and as the number of each firm's service delivery sites increases, the customer-service function is becoming an important element in knitting the service organization together. It also serves to ensure that operations managers recognize the need to strive for both customer satisfaction and operational efficiency.

The more customers are exposed to high-quality execution of customer-service tasks, the more they will come to expect it of all service suppliers. Many service firms survived in the past with inadequate or mediocre performance of customer-service activities. However, they are liable to find themselves severely disadvantaged in the future unless they take steps to develop and implement an improved customer-service function.

REFERENCES

ANONYMOUS (1982), "How American Express Measures Quality of Its Customer Service," *AMA Forum* **71** (March): 29–31.

CHASE, RICHARD B. (1978), "Where Does the Customer Fit in a Service Operation?" *Harvard Business Review* **56** (November–December): 137–142.

CZEPIEL, JOHN A. (1980), *Managing Customer Satisfaction in Consumer Service Businesses.* Cambridge, Mass.: Marketing Science Institute.

LOUD, JAMES F. (1980), "Organizing for Customer Service," *Bankers Magazine* (November–December): 41–45.

TAKEUCHI, HIROTAKA, and JOHN A. QUELCH (1983), "Quality Is More than Making a Good Product," *Harvard Business Review* **61** (July–August): 139–145.

Making Service
A Potent Marketing Tool

*Spending heavily on customer care is becoming good business.
Both service companies and manufacturing firms are coming
to recognize that improving the quality of customer service not
only builds customer loyalty but also generates valuable market
information. This article describes the strategies adopted by
several well-known corporations.*

Stranded in a hotel in war-torn Beirut last
September, the Lebanese-born sister of a
Midwest orthodontist was frantic. Her local
bank had closed down, leaving her with no
funds and no way out of the country. Her
brother, an American Express Co. cardholder, contacted the company's Southern
Region Operations Center in Fort Lauderdale, Fla., for help. Twenty-eight telexes
later—via increasingly disrupted communications lines among Florida, Beirut, the
woman's hotel, and Bahrain, where a branch
of American Express International Banking
Corp. (AEIBC) was located—an agreement
came through for the bank to cash a $3,000
check—enough to pay the hotel bill and book
sea passage to Cyprus, since airlines were
shut down, too.

Over several different shifts, AmEx's service personnel followed through to provide
the funds in one day. They checked the
cardholder's credit, and AEIBC insisted on and
obtained special authorizations not only from
the card division but from bank headquarters to cash a check that would surely bounce.
The company increased the already high cost
of its rescue operation by awarding "Great
Performer" checks to the two employees most
instrumental in getting approvals and arranging for the cash to be brought to the
stranded woman.

The communication lines, computers, data

banks, personnel, and specialized training that back up that kind of service are expensive. They cost AmEx $150 million per year. But at least some companies, including AmEx, GE, Sony, IBM, Procter & Gamble, and Whirlpool, recognize the need for providing such service today, not only because it ties customers more closely to them, but also because the close interaction with customers provides them with enormous amounts of market information that helps them increase profits. Among the things they learn through their service operations:

- Demographic information.
- The impact of their advertising.
- Identification of problem merchandise by model, type of defect, and area of distribution for rapid feedback to manufacturing operations.
- Clues to customer concerns.
- The life-expectancy of their products.
- Assessments of the do-it-yourself competence of customers to determine what can be repaired at home.
- Ideas for potential new products and services.

Clearly, capturing that market data can best be done on computers, and companies see their service operation as the point of contact. "Service is our most strategic marketing weapon," says Louis V. Gerstner Jr., chairman and chief executive officer of AmEx's Travel Related Services Co., the company's most profitable division. "It's the only way we can differentiate our product in the marketplace."

STILL RARE

General Electric Co. sees it that way, too. Within the last three years, GE has built, almost from scratch, one of the most sophisticated service centers in the country. Others, as diverse as Westinghouse, Wachovia Bank, Noxell, Southland, and some auto companies, have been beefing up their service capabilities, too.

Using service as an active marketing tool is still a rare phenomenon, however. For years, customer service and the complaint department were synonymous at most companies—relegated to a back room and staffed with low-paid, indifferent clerks. Top management took an interest in the customer service department only if its costs got out of hand.

That may be changing. Sparked by some landmark studies commissioned by the White House Office of Consumer Affairs in 1979 and fueled by the widespread use of the minicomputer and the burgeoning of toll-free telephone numbers, a new attitude has been born: Companies are now actively soliciting complaints from customers. And growing numbers of businesses are beginning to perceive buyers' views as integral to the design, manufacture, and sale of products and services.

AmEx's Gerstner sees the service function elevated to full marketing status, where it will be used as the central contact with customers. At GE's three-year-old Answer Center in Louisville, N. Powell Taylor, its manager, has found that 25 percent of callers ask pre-purchase questions about products. Considering that GE's center will field some 2.4 million calls this year, up from 45,000 in 1981, there is potential for 500,000 purchases. Another 25 percent ask trained technicians how to repair appliances. About 20 percent of Whirlpool's calls are from do-it-yourselfers, too. The feedback helps identify what parts fail in older models. Fewer than 10 percent calling GE want to air complaints. On a typical day a few weeks ago, GE was deluged by calls responding to a television ad. The center maintains a flow chart on when advertising will appear and staffs accordingly. Vivitar Corp. modified a flash unit for its cameras on the basis of service department reports. Sony Corp. had redesigned TV sets on the market within three months of learning from its service center that customers wanted an easier hookup to computers when they used their screens as monitors.

Much of the impetus for establishing such centers was generated by Technical Assistance Research Programs Inc. (TARP), a Washington consulting firm hired by the

---

A GM Plant with a Hot Line Between Workers and Buyers

Labor and management at General Motors Corp.'s Fiero plant in Pontiac, Mich., are running an unusual customer service. Volunteer workers are calling a random group of customers to get feedback—problems, likes, and dislikes—on the new Fiero, GM's moderately priced, plastic-bodied, two-seater sports car. The car was introduced by Pontiac last fall, and by January the program was in full swing.

Under the program, 50 workers each follow five Fiero buyers for a year, surveying them with phone calls every three months. Workers on the assembly line, such as John Hughes, who installs trim, make the calls on their own time, usually from home, and Pontiac pays the phone bill. The information they glean is fed back to the plant—to line operators and to departments where the problems may have originated. It is also sent to service experts who educate dealers about repairs. But the primary goal of the program is to get information to the assembly plant where problems can be isolated and corrected immediately.

No Waiting

"With the car as new as it was, we thought we needed immediate feedback on problems identified by the customer," says Frank L. Slaughter, who was the director of quality control when the program was designed and is now the assistant director of salaried personnel. "We didn't want to wait 6 to 12 months for information from dealers to filter through. And if we want to have credibility, we ought to involve the people who have ultimate responsibility for building the cars. So why not involve them in calling the customers?"

Although UAW Local 653 supports the program, the international union is decidedly more aloof. Its position has long been that quality is a responsibility of supervisors and plant managers.

The program stems from a 1983 survey by professional service representatives of the new owners of Pontiac's midsize 6000 STE. The volunteer program's cost is minimal—perhaps $15 to $20 in phone bills per worker. But the benefits are high. For example, the calls turned up the fact that windshields were cracking in the upper corner. Line workers discovered that some tabs holding the windshield to the frame were creating excess pressure. They corrected the trouble and alerted service people in the field to the problem. "We were able to feed this to the service guys instead of vice versa," notes Slaughter.

Could the Fiero program be duplicated elsewhere? Slaughter thinks that it can, noting that hard times have created a spirit of teamwork at the plant. "Adversity is the mother of invention," says Slaughter. "There's a good working relation between the salaried and hourly people. All of them feel that if they want to remain employed, they have to come up with a way to put out a high-quality product. They want their reputation to be: 'We are concerned, we have ownership of what we do, and we are proud of it.'"

White House to assess service in the U.S. TARP's findings were eye-opening, suggesting that corporations were inadvertently losing many of their customers. For example, among buyers who faced a major problem—defined as costing $142 or more —with a consumer product, fewer than one in six complained to the manufacturer; they believed their complaints would not be satisfied. And 90 percent of disgruntled buyers did not repurchase from the offending company. That contrasts sharply with the 54 percent who remained loyal when their complaints were satisfactorily handled.

TARP went on to quantify the value in revenues from each loyal customer: Adjusted for inflation since 1979, auto makers could count on $142,000 over a satisfied buyer's lifetime; appliance makers would get $2,840 over 20 years; banks could expect $568; and supermarkets looked forward to $22,000 over a five-year period.

Careful customer service yielded other benefits, too. When companies were accessible, buyers asked broad questions, such as how to use, repair, or buy products—thus saving the company money on warranty calls, increasing sales of parts, and often boosting other sales.

PROHIBITIVE PRICE

Significantly, companies as diverse as GE, AmEx, GM's Buick, and Coors mentioned the TARP studies when discussing their service operations. To make their companies more accessible, they began to advertise toll-free phone lines. But more than phone lines are needed, as several companies are discovering. The 800 numbers can be an added source of customer frustration unless they provide fast and efficient response. A number of companies that have installed the lines do not cover them continuously—or at the times when customers would be most likely to use them. Sony's lines are manned only from 9 A.M. to 8 P.M. on weekdays, making it difficult for a customer to get direct help in hooking up a videocassette recorder, for example, on a weekend, when he is most likely to buy it and bring it home. Sony Vice-President John F. Spruce admits that Tsukasa Kimura, the consumer service company's president, has been pushing him for broader service hours but that he has been resisting because of the cost.

Even International Business Machines Corp., whose crack service operations have long been the benchmark against which other high-tech companies measured themselves, has limited access to its 800 number for users of its mass-marketed PCjr. Service hours are 10 A.M. to 7 P.M. on weekdays only. An IBM spokesman maintains that the PCjr is marketed for business and education as well as home use and that the company constantly monitors its phone lines. "We'll know immediately if a change of hours is appropriate, and we'll act accordingly," he says. However, since the literature that accompanies the PCjr lists the hot-line hours, it is unlikely that home users—who are most likely to sit down at their computers before or after those hours—would call.

Part of the reason for the limited calling hours is price. The phone lines themselves can cost millions of dollars per year. Sony's Spruce, for example, scotched a plan to switch phone calls to its Western center when its Eastern center closed for the night because of the price tag: $88,000 per month.

Adding shifts of service personnel, and training and monitoring them, is expensive, too—another concern that makes many companies draw back. And the training is essential. At GE, AmEx, and Sony, it is intensive, formal, and psychologically—as well as technically—oriented. Its main emphasis is on accuracy. AmEx draws most of its customer service staff from other areas of the company. Even so, it provides six to eight weeks of special training for each service specialist. Supervisors, drawn from the group, spend one full day a week for nine months learning how to teach and motivate their small staffs. GE provides a four-to-six-week program, with two to three hours per week of training for managers and technical specialists. "The idea," says Taylor, "is to make our service representatives 'perfect people' —empathetic, knowledgeable, fast, and efficient." Sony hires only recent college graduates. "That way they're not tainted by other company experiences. We want to develop them in our own way," says Spruce.

All are trained to use the computer to call up comprehensive information on which their answers are based. Their responses are carefully monitored by supervisors to ensure accuracy, courtesy, and speed. The computer can capture pertinent details, providing the company with data on the caller as well as the problem or request.

To create such interactive services, no expenditure can be spared. Says GE's Taylor: "Take out any element and the whole system can fall." It is not surprising that many companies are reluctant to make the investment. Says AmEx's Gerstner: "Because of the structure of most companies, the guy who puts in the service operation and bears the expense doesn't get the benefit. It'll show up in fewer complaints; it'll show up in marketing, even in new product development. But the benefit never shows up in his own P&L statement. Adds Karen E. Gillam, supervisor of Whirlpool's 24-hour "Cool-Line": "It's definitely a burden operation, but we recognize there is a return on it."

Not every company agrees, a fact noted in a recent Harris Poll that showed most consumers believe service is worse than it was 10 years ago. Says Gerstner: "Most companies are unwilling to make such a huge in-

Customers: P&G's Pipeline to Product Problems

One of the first mass marketers to establish a broad service operation, Procter & Gamble Co. is celebrating the 10th anniversary of its 800-number service this year [1984]. While it has been a leader in consumer services—it hired its first expert in 1941—its current operation is not as fully computerized as some of the hard-goods makers. P&G first experimented with the phone-line idea in 1971, and by 1979 it began implementing a plan to have an 800 number on every P&G consumer product sold in the U.S.

Last year, P&G received 670,000 mail and phone contacts about its products—the overall figure this year is running 17% ahead of that. And according to G. Gibson Carey, P&G division manager for general advertising, the calls fall into three broad categories: requests for information, complaints, and testimonials.

Early Warning Signal

P&G employs 75 people in its service department, 30 of whom handle calls; the rest answer letters and help collate information for other departments. Phones are manned weekdays from 9:30 A.M. to 7:30 P.M. Employees receive three to five weeks of training. Besides instruction on how to deal with people over the phone, the training includes the history of each product, the company's marketing and advertising strategy for it, and what happens if it is misused. Telephone representatives have reference manuals and access to technical staff but no computers to help answer questions. Information from P&G customers is tallied by hand and computerized later.

Most callers dial the company with the product package in hand. And every product has a code printed on it identifying the plant, the manufacturing date, and sometimes even the shift and the line on which it was made. Thus, if P&G has supplied defective packages, as happened not long ago with one product, it can trace the problem's source quickly and correct it.

Because of the calls it received on various products, P&G has:

- Included instructions for baking at high altitudes on the Duncan Hines brownies package.
- Added a recipe for making a wedding cake to the information on its white cake mix package.
- Told users what to do if Downy liquid fabric softener accidentally freezes (numerous customers had that problem during a cold spell).

"As a general rule, we don't look at [consumer service] as a source for new product ideas," Carey concedes. Information from the calls first goes to product-development personnel who track quality control. Each division and top management get a separate report. P&G also surveys customers to determine whether callers were satisfied with the treatment they received.

Carey says the 800-number service is "a distant, early-warning signal" of product problems. Without it, "we wouldn't find out about them for weeks or months." And, he points out: "There's a whole lot of enlightened self-interest in this."

vestment even though it makes marketing less expensive in the long run." Even after the investment is made, "you've got to keep the pressure on," says James D. Robinson III, AmEx's chairman. "People do what management inspects—not what it expects."

So when AmEx provides the kind of costly, computerized service that rescued the stranded woman in Lebanon, it is not only taking very seriously American Management Assns. studies showing that a satisfied customer tells three people about a good experience while a dissatisfied one gripes to 11. AmEx offers the service also because of its direct and indirect effects on the bottom line.

Replacing lost or stolen cards within 24 hours anywhere in the world costs AmEx more than $5 million annually. Nevertheless, AmEx likes its investment. A card in a business executive's or vacationer's hands brings in revenue. AmEx's same-day response on billing problems means faster turnover of receivables. Decreasing from 32 days to 15 the time it takes to process new applications has given the company 17 more days of revenues. Signing on new restaurants, hotels, and shops in 9 days instead of 25 has meant 16 extra days of commissions. But even more important, customers like prompt service, and it is far less expensive to hold on to established customers than to lure new ones.

NEW TARGETS

Added value comes when AmEx service operations poll customers to ask what new services they want and where. By continually collating such information, AmEx can cut its advertising expense, keep research costs in check, and target new markets—such as recent college graduates, women, and the highly affluent—with exquisite precision.

Although AmEx has made no direct correlation between such service and its market share, its record clearly provides a clue to why its Travel Related Services (TRS)—cards, traveler's checks, and travel arrangements—beset by competition and considered a mature business just five years ago, has been growing consistently at a 20 percent annual rate. That jumped to 40 percent in 1984's first quarter. Indeed, even with all of American Express's glamorous acquisitions over that period, TRS still provided more than half of the company's $515 million income last year.

Ironically, some companies have been pushed into adding service not to find new customers or to hold on to loyal ones but to win back dissatisfied ones. U.S. auto companies, for example, began taking service and quality more seriously in about 1980—when Detroit's four-year sales depression began.

Product quality and service are closely intertwined in the car business, according to J. David Power, president of J. D. Power & Associates in Westlake Village, Calif. Power has conducted market research for Japanese and domestic auto makers since 1968, and he currently produces an annual Customer Satisfaction Index that tracks, among other things, service-related issues. Mercedes-Benz gets the highest rating. Toyota Motor Corp. is second-best, and Ford Motor Co. is the only U.S. auto company to garner an above-average rating. American Motors Corp. comes in last.

Power notes that sloppy quality on the assembly line can lead to chronic problems that are difficult for car dealers to fix—badly designed latches that break easily, water leaks that are due to poorly fitting doors, and so on. "When manufacturers get those nuisance problems under control," says Power, "it's easier for dealers to do better servicing."

Toyota, now the biggest importer of cars to the U.S., with sales of nearly 556,000 units a year, illustrates his point. In 1968, Toyota was selling only about 70,000 cars a year in the U.S. Then, the cars were not especially well made, very durable, or spectacularly serviced. Toyota hired J. D. Power to conduct more than 100 market studies; a pivotal one concluded that Volkswagen was then outselling other European cars in the U.S. because of its superior service system.

Toyota decided to follow suit in 1969. It hired Norman D. Lean, formerly the national service training manager for Ford, specifically to improve service operations. (Lean subsequently headed Toyota's U.S. operations until taking early retirement last November.) Comments Power: "Toyota decided to put more emphasis on parts and service. They doubled or tripled their budget. It's bearing fruit for Toyota now."

GM's Buick Motor Div. claims it is the only auto maker with a toll-free phone system to handle customer complaints and inquiries. Its system, known as Customer Assistance Center (CAC), went national late last year. CAC, like a similar phone-in service designed to answer questions from Buick service mechanics, operates weekdays, 8 A.M. to 8 P.M.

CAC began to evolve in 1980 when Buick reviewed its standing in the customer satisfaction ratings compiled by GM for its five auto divisions. At that time, Buick was receiving about 80 phone complaints daily—and taking 25 to 30 days to resolve them. Now everything is electronic, and the period from initial call to final repair is less than 10 days. Local dealers get feedback and can contact the customer within 24 hours of the first call.

Buick launched pilot tests of CAC in Boston in 1981 and began expanding the system nationwide six months later. "We wanted to get closer to our customers," says Darwin E. Clark, assistant general sales manager for service, who set up the system. He says that one-third of customers with a problem call the manufacturer first. Under the old system, they were likely to lose patience because it took Buick so long to handle a complaint. "Now we're able to respond in one or two days," he says. "Customers can see we're interested in them."

KEEPING FAITH

Clark claims that most of the calls are for information. But Buick's GM customer sat-isfaction index has improved 10 points since CAC was started, although Clark notes that other factors are involved. Buick is only now trying to measure the precise effect of the center. Clark acknowledges that other auto makers have tried hot lines before and dropped them after a year or less. "We have no intention of backing off," he declares.

At the heart of all of these systems is enlightened self-interest—the knowledge that by serving customers well, companies serve themselves. GE's Taylor suggests that the new emphasis on quality service can serve to restore faith in institutions. AmEx's Gerstner sums it up: "In the old days," he says, "the mom-and-pop stores knew their customers intimately, and instinctively matched their service to each customer. Part of it was to generate goodwill, and part was genuine friendship. That's what we're trying to do—run AmEx's service like a huge mom-and-pop drugstore."

Customer Service: Who Delivers?

JACK FALVEY

The common belief is that by declaring customer service to be a goal, and then rooting on the employees, the mission will be accomplished. It's not that simple . . . Encourage and reward good customer contact. Instead of asking customers what went wrong, why not ask them what went right?

Almost everyone will admit that the most critical ingredient in business is a customer. Entry into the *Fortune* 500 is not determined by the number of MBAs on the payroll, the return on investment, or the latest in high technology. It is determined by one element only: the dollar amount of sales to customers.

You can do almost everything *wrong* in business and still succeed if you serve the customer. You can do just about everything *right* in business and fail if you do not take care of their needs, wants, desires, and emotions.

This truism is known to every business executive. It is stated in annual reports, found in philosophies of operation, has a chapter in every pop-management book, and is denied by no one.

But, customer service, even in marginal form, seems to have a very difficult time finding its way to actual customers. Why is that? What must one do to serve the customer?

The common belief is that by declaring customer service to be a goal, and then rooting on the employees, the goal will be accomplished.

Although that strategy has done great things for the customer service, meeting

This article has been reprinted through the courtesy of Halsey Publishing Co., publishers of Delta Air Lines' *SKY* magazine.

speakers, and motivational film industries, it has done little for customers. It doesn't require a genius to figure out why, or what to do about it. It does require considerable time, effort, and cost to make real progress in better treatment of customers.

First, consider who actually delivers customer service. In the fast-food industry, it's usually a 15-year-old adolescent (and they do a pretty good job at it). In the banking industry, it is the teller or loan officer. In every business, the switchboard operator or receptionist (anyone who answers a phone) is in charge of the delivery of customer service—and this collective effort has not been strong. Delivery and repair personnel have more customer contact than an entire management team; still many are ill-prepared for the day-to-day challenges of this unwanted task.

Pronouncements come down from the top of organizations, and customers are handled at the bottom of organizations. Is it any wonder that the customer suffers? The distance (sometimes measured in light-years) between both will often determine results.

The much-maligned American automobile industry is a classic case study. The Japanese did not out-produce, out-engineer, out-sell, or out-automate our people in Detroit. What they did do was provide what the consumer wanted at a level of quality demanded after years of having to buy cars from Detroit that didn't work very well. Lack of international organizational management, not lack of communication, causes poor customer service.

Here are some things that can be done to treat customers with the care and respect they deserve:

- Don't let anyone near a customer until they know what they are doing. Trainees must be closely supervised, and then certified as able to deal with customers. If management will not make that investment, they deserve the lost business that results.
- Determine just who deals with customers. Switchboard, delivery, maintenance, security guards, et al, must be managed in ways that will increase customer responsiveness.

- Although eight hours is considered a full day's work in office and factory, two or three hours of customer contact may be all that should be expected of people during that eight-hour day. Staffing and duties should be set up accordingly. Dealing with a tired, overloaded person is not in the best interest of either a customer or the company.
- Encourage and reward good customer contact. Instead of asking customers what went wrong (the hotel room comment cards), why not ask them what went right—or better still, who did something right for you?
- If and when a good customer action is identified, the hero or heroine of the day, week, or month should then be held up for all to see as an example of what the business is all about.

I found a customer service team in a most unlikely place.

Cable TV is not known for its responsiveness to the consumer, so when a local cable company began hooking up homes in our area, I was prepared to protect my rights. First of all, they did a neat, quick job of installation, but as with most new systems, a bug developed after a couple of days. A call to the company not only brought a courteous telephone answer, but a serviceman in 15 minutes.

All this must have been an accident. Wrong. The bug was fixed in about a half hour, but then a power loss brought the system down. The serviceman said that when the power returned, it should all work properly. About an hour later, I received a call from the customer service person asking if the repairman had been there and if everything was fixed. I couldn't believe the call. I said yes, the system went down, but that it should be all right when the power came back. She said that the power was now on, and would I go take a look? I did; and the bug had come back with the power. She said no problem, she would call the truck and the serviceman would be back in 15 minutes. He was. He fixed everything again. This time it held. Another half hour later, the telephone rang asking if everything was now in order. It was. All except my mind, which was suffering from consumer shock.

If customers are as important as management says they are, why not manage to that principle?

Would you let a trainee mess with a costly production machine? Would you let a foreman deal with your banker? Would you like your doctor to have worked a full seven hours in surgery before he operated on you?

Instead of running a meeting on customer service, try letting your management team work a full shift in contact with customers.

Overstaff your switchboard and overbuild your telephone system to take care of incoming traffic. Cut shift time, increase breaks, and set a standard of completing actions for everyone who picks up a phone. More than 70 percent of business calls are not completed. That means that, most of the time, whoever answers a phone must deal with some kind of follow-up. How about a callback system where the person taking the message calls back at the end of the day to check completion?

Of course, this takes time and costs money. But customer service is not a free lunch. The stakes are very, very high.

Prevention through supervision, training, staffing, reorganizing, and the demanding of superior performance are the preventative drill, but what do you do when the customer gets a raw deal?

The answer is: everything. Throw out the procedures manual and make it right. Cost is relative. Think of what is spent in advertising just to attract an unidentified potential consumer and make that person a customer. When you get people face-to-face with a problem, aren't they worth their weight in gold to keep?

Remember the rule of 250. Everyone has an average of 250 personal friends or contacts and anything of either a positive or negative nature is likely to be eventually shared with that same number of people—plus the ripple effect of whatever those contacts pass on to their network of 250.

A customer, if maltreated and disgruntled, is a walking time bomb. Whether you get a positive or negative detonation is up to what you do.

Customer service is not a cost; it is an investment. It produces returns that can be measured. Go talk to your customers and find out who in your organization is doing something right. Search that person out and make him or her the star of the day.

The base of all business is the customer. Those who continually invest in finding and maintaining that base will almost always be successful.

Federal Express:
Customer Service Department, I

PENNY PITTMAN MERLISS
CHRISTOPHER H. LOVELOCK

A rapidly expanding airfreight business seeks to improve the quality of customer service. Various technological solutions have been proposed, including a centralized, computerized order-entry system. But operations and sales personnel are both concerned and raise numerous objections.

By the end of 1978, the five-year-old Federal Express Corporation, which had lost approximately $29 million in its first 26 months of operations, was being hailed by the business press as one of the great success stories of American entrepreneurship. The Memphis-based air freight company had become the nation's premier carrier of small packages requiring overnight delivery, controlling approximately 30 percent of the market. Volume had grown from the 15 packages carried when operations began on April 17, 1973, to over 43,000 nightly. On the average, revenues had been increasing at a rate of over 50 percent per year since 1974.

Pleased as they were by Federal's phenomenal expansion, several of the company's marketing executives expressed concern about its effect on customer service. Market research commissioned privately revealed that more than one customer felt that Federal was paying a high price for its growth. The shipping manager for one industrial parts distributor complained:

I don't think they're as congenial as they were when they first broke open the door, rushed in, and promised you the world. They did try for the first year and a half. But since they established themselves, it's been downhill. Be-

This case was prepared by Penny Pittman Merliss, Research Assistant, under the direction of Associate Professor Christopher H. Lovelock. Copyright © 1980 by the President and Fellows of Harvard College. Harvard Business School Case 9-581-017. Reprinted by permission.

fore, they were willing to come in and talk to you once in a while. Now I've had to wait over six weeks for someone to come out and they said they were shorthanded.

I have no real complaint against them, because percentage wise, it's just unreal, the service they've given me. But as far as getting anyone to answer a question, it's part of every big company and I call it growing pains.

COMPANY BACKGROUND

Federal Express was incorporated in 1971 by Frederick W. Smith, Jr., the 27-year-old heir of the founder of Dixie Greyhound Bus Lines. Borrowing a concept developed by United Parcel Service, he designed a nationwide air service network to resemble the spokes of a wheel, with Memphis, Tennessee, as hub. Each night, after packages had been collected from customers by the company's pickup vans (deadlines ranged from 7:00 P.M. in New York City to 4:30 P.M. on the West Coast), Federal Express aircraft stationed throughout the U.S. were loaded with cargo and then flown to Memphis, where the packages were unloaded onto an 800-foot-long conveyor system. As huge clocks overhead counted down the minutes till deadline, the loading crews sorted packages according to destination and reloaded them. The planes then flew to their destination cities, where the packages were delivered by Federal Express couriers by noon of the following day.

Federal Express began operations with six aircraft and 150 employees, serving 18 cities. By November 1978 the company served 148 markets (including Canada) and employed 4600 people. Although initial losses were staggering, Federal Express passed the breakeven point in mid 1975 and cleared $3.6 million in fiscal 1976, its first profitable year. By the end of fiscal 1978, profits exceeded $20 million (*Exhibit 1*).

EXHIBIT 1
Federal Express Corporate Financial Summary, 1974–78 (in thousands)

	FISCAL YEAR ENDING MAY 31				
	1974	*1975*	*1976*	*1977*	*1978*
OPERATING RESULTS					
Operating revenues	$17,292	$43,489	$75,055	$109,210	$160,301
Operating expenses	26,137	47,613	65,210	95,608	134,024
Operating income (loss)	(8,845)	(4,124)	9,845	13,602	26,277
Other charges, net	(4,521)	(7,393)	(6,210)	(5,390)	(5,693)
Income (loss) before income taxes	(13,366)	(11,517)	3,635	8,212	20,584
Income taxes	—	—	(2,032)	(4,243)	(6,980)
Income (loss) before tax benefit of loss carryforward	(13,366)	(11,517)	1,603	3,969	13,604
Tax benefit of loss carryforward	—	—	1,982	4,185	6,425
Net income (loss)	($13,366)	($11,517)	$3,585	$8,154	$20,029
FINANCIAL POSITION					
Current assets	$ 7,891	$ 9,481	$14,725	$20,349	$ 30,370
Property and equipment, net	59,701	59,276	55,297	53,616	71,813
Total assets	70,697	70,193	71,229	75,321	106,291
Current liabilities	9,136	11,818	12,954	18,658	22,741
Long-term debt	51,605	59,892	56,186	46,229	30,825
Stockholders' investment	9,956	(1,517)	2,089	10,434	52,725

SOURCE: Company records.

EXHIBIT 2
Federal Express Primary Services, Fiscal Years 1974–78

	Arrival Time	Weight Limitation	RATES†		AVERAGE DAILY VOLUME					AVERAGE VARIABLE COSTS/ PACKAGE	
			1976	1978	1974	1975	1976	1977	1978	1976	1978
Priority One	Noon of day after pickup	70 lb	$23.56	$28.12	2,467	6,159	10,301	13,947	17,684	$10.60	$12.27
Courier Pak*	Noon of day after pickup	2 lb	$12.50	$14.00	187	549	1,077	2,632	6,759	$4.25	$ 4.75
Standard Air Service	Second business day after pickup	300 lb per shipment; 70 lb per item	$12.62	$14.75	1,456	4,356	3,214	5,352‡	5,073	$9.21	$10.13

*Shipped in a waterproof, tear-resistant envelope, provided by Federal Express.

†Rates for Priority One and Standard Air Service varied according to package weight and distance carried; figures shown here are systemwide averages. Priority One rates were discounted, based on the total number of Priority One packages tendered to Federal Express from one shipper on any single business day.

‡Inflated by United Parcel Service strike.

SOURCE: Company records.

Station/Customer Interface

Through field stations located near 120 airports, Federal Express served over 10,000 communities—reaching, according to company estimates, about 80 percent of the nationwide demand for air express services. By fall of 1978, it was estimated that about 18 percent of Federal's customers used the company's services each day. To accommodate this demand, Federal's fleet of pickup and delivery vans had been increased to over 900. Station clerks were receiving over 15,000 "on-call" pickup requests per day, in addition to the 2,200 customers who had arranged for permanent daily pickups. Approximately half of the company's employees worked in stations outside the Memphis headquarters.

Stations were classified according to package volume. An "A" station like Boston might handle 1,500 packages nightly and employ 15 people; Peoria, Illinois, a "D" station, employed 5 people and handled 50 packages or fewer. Because orders for service were made by telephone, customers almost never visited a station; "on-call" customers were linked to the company through their courier, and larger customers with standing pickup orders were visited by sales representatives as well. By the same token, dispatchers and station agents rarely met their customers. Station managers, on the other hand, often accompanied couriers or salespeople on their rounds.

Services

Federal Express offered three primary services to its customers: Priority One, Courier Pak, and Standard Air Service (*Exhibit 2*). Incremental services available at extra cost included Restricted Articles Service, providing special handling for hazardous cargo; Signature Security Service, a special-handling procedure that included signed receipts from everyone having custody of a package; and Saturday Delivery Service. The decision to use Federal Express as a carrier could be made by any of a variety of people, varying somewhat according to the service chosen. A traffic manager, mailroom supervisor, or shipping clerk usually placed Priority One and Standard Air Service orders; executives or their secretaries were more likely to call for Courier Pak pickups. Similarly, standing orders were customarily handled through company traffic or mailrooms, and on-call, intermittent requests for pickup usually came from managers, clerks, or secretaries.

All Federal Express shipments were originally transported in small Dassault Falcons (converted executive jets), which had a cargo capacity of 6,200 pounds. Smith had chosen the Falcon in order to escape federal regulation by the Civil Aeronautics Board (CAB); the CAB controlled the rates, routes, and services of all aircraft carrying over 7,500 pounds of freight. But by mid-1976, the same regulatory loophole which had made Federal Express possible was limiting its growth and inflating its costs. Unable to use large aircraft, the company was sending as many as six fully loaded Falcons nightly to a single city, wasting $25,000 a night as well as thousands of gallons of fuel. Smith and his associates took their case to Congress, lobbying heavily for a bill that would permit Federal Express to buy bigger jets. What they won, in November 1977, was a much greater victory: the total deregulation of the air freight industry.

AIR FREIGHT SHIPPING IN THE U.S.

The U.S. air cargo industry was estimated at $1.2 billion in 1978. Although air freight was the most expensive way of shipping small packages, users considered it a good value. One study revealed that fast delivery, reduced probability of loss, and protection of fragile items were the three major incentives that moved shippers to choose air freight. Most air shipments were small; 90 percent were composed of individual pieces weighing less than 70 pounds.

Originally dominated by the scheduled passenger airlines ("trunk carriers"), the air freight industry opened up in 1974–1975 as rising fuel costs led the trunks to substitute more profitable passenger traffic for freight. Although freight continued to be carried in the bellies of passenger aircraft, by fall 1978, only five major U.S. airlines continued to fly all-cargo freighters; 81 percent of their capacity was concentrated among four cities: New York, Chicago, Los Angeles, and San Francisco.

Competition

Federal Express was not the only company to move into this breach. In September 1976, Connecticut-based Emery Air Freight, the nation's leading air freight forwarder,[1] opened a network covering 21 cities. Service was provided by 16 chartered aircraft, ranging from four-engine jets to small single-engine aircraft. Within two years Emery's revenues had risen from $305 million to $413 million. In September 1978 the company began to offer, in addition to its heavy-cargo shipping, a one-day small-package service called Emery Express. This service was available to 35 cities initially, and the company planned to reach 100 within a year. Emery promised later pickup (7:30 P.M.) and earlier delivery (11 A.M.) than Federal, as well as 5–10 percent lower rates. "Our unique selling proposition is that Emery is the only company a shipper can turn to for all weights, all markets, and same-day service," an Emery marketing executive explained.

Other significant competitors included Seattle-based Airborne Freight, also cheaper than Federal, which handled about 2.2 million pieces in its express service during 1978, and the U.S. Postal Service's Express Mail, which handled 7.7 million pieces in 1978 and projected 12 million for 1979. Express Mail, limited to material under 70 pounds, was considerably cheaper than either Federal Express or Emery, but delivery beyond the destination post office was promised only by 3 P.M. the following day. The Postal Service also charged extra for pickup. According to some users, avoiding the pickup charge often meant waiting in long lines to drop off shipments at the post office; however, consignees willing to pick up their packages at the post office could receive them by 10 A.M. of the day after shipment. USPS offered a full refund on any delayed packages.

Smith felt that the impact of competition on Federal Express remained minimal and that his rivals' promotion of their express services benefited the entire industry. Annual unit growth rates for the air express package market were averaging 15–20 percent. Since users of air express services were predominantly fast-growing, service-oriented businesses, it was anticipated that rapid growth would continue. Indeed, some industry analysts felt that Federal's quality service was creating its own demand, leading some companies to develop business strategies based on Federal's performance capabilities. The firm's package volume increased 34 percent in the fiscal year ending in May 1978; the number of Federal Express customers increased 66 percent in the same period.[2] New users accounted for 83 percent of the company's increase in revenues in fiscal 1978, and no single customer represented more than 2 percent of Federal's business.

Developments after Deregulation

Contrary to predictions, deregulation of the air freight industry led only a handful of new competitors to enter the field, most of them regional charter and air taxi services. As one industry observer pointed out:

Unlike the trucking industry, where capital requirements are low and new operators can easily obtain financing, the airline industry is very capital-intensive. A new Boeing 747 jet freighter now costs more than $50 million, and there are few markets, if any, that could support the 250,000-lb. capacity of a jumbo jet freighter

---

[1]Freight forwarders, the wholesalers of the industry, arrange pickups and delivery for customers as well as retailing cargo space on commercial aircraft.

[2]Each one of an organization's branches and offices using FEC's services was considered a separate account by Federal Express.

that are not already being served by existing airlines.[3]

Immediately following deregulation, Federal arranged to augment its fleet of Falcons with 10 secondhand Boeing 727s, a move designed to increase its service to cover 300 U.S. cities. The 727s, costing a total of about $40 million, had a freight capacity of 40,000 pounds each. In April 1978 the company went public, increasing equity from $25 million to $49 million, and began planning to enlarge the Memphis hub to a capacity of 120,000 packages per night. (Projections of future volume are presented in *Exhibit 3*.) In addition, Federal Express had begun to expand its network of downtown convenience centers in major market areas. These locations allowed customers to drop off packages in the late afternoon and early evening, after regular pickup deadlines had passed.

EXHIBIT 3
Average Daily Package Volume*

Fiscal Year	Volume
1974	4,110
1975	11,064
1976	14,592
1977	21,931
1978	29,516
1979†	45,000
1981†	65,000
1983†	104,000

*Based on five-day weeks.
†Projections.
SOURCE: Company records.

CUSTOMER SERVICE AT FEDERAL EXPRESS

As the company's growth continued and field operations became more and more efficient, Smith and his associates began to turn their attention to marketing and, particularly, customer service, a relatively neglected function within the corporation. J. Vincent Fagan was given responsibility for marketing and quickly developed advertising campaigns that came to be acknowledged as the most successful in the industry. In order to coordinate promotion and sales, Smith assigned the sales department to Fagan in 1975, and in 1977 Fagan also assumed responsibility for customer service, with the title of senior vice president-marketing, sales, and customer service. Summarizing this integration, Fagan explained:

> The thinking was that marketing and sales were responsible for price, promotion, and product. Customer service was the one remaining function that looked as though it had overall control over product and a need for consistency. When customer service consisted of a local station with a battery of busy phones, no one knew what kind of service the customer was getting—there was no control. We knew how good our package delivery was, we knew whether planes were arriving on time, but we had no overall way to measure or control customer service.

Early Customer Service Structure

From the beginning, Federal Express had made the assumption that the group of people moving the shipments—the field personnel—should also provide information and assistance to customers. According to one senior company executive, this assumption was rooted in Federal's anonymous paperwork and control system, derived from United Parcel Service. As he explained package tracking by the "exception" system:

> The logic is that since we are a wholly controlled entity—since we own the trucks as well as the planes and the package never leaves our hands—then once we have the package, it can't get lost on another carrier's airplane (as Emery's can) or go to another trucking company. In essence, it's got to be somewhere in the system. Thus we can make the assumption that if we know all the packages which didn't get to where they were supposed to go, then everything else will arrive on time. So if a package that was supposed to go to Des Moines ends

[3]"Why Nobody is Rushing into Air Freight," *Business Week*, November 6, 1978, p. 190.

up in Detroit, it's the responsibility of the people in Detroit to call up Des Moines and let them know about it, so they'll be ready when the customer calls in.

Since there was no way anyone could be certain of where a package was in the system on any given day, requests for information had been transferred to field personnel "because they probably have as good an idea of what's going on as anyone else." Once the source of operational information was transferred to the field, it appeared to be a logical and cost-effective step to make the station also responsible for informational tasks, answering questions on rates and features of service.

Initially, customer service was provided both locally and through Memphis headquarters. In the field, telephone clerks (known as station agents) took orders for service, traced missing packages, and answered questions about rates, delivery, and insurance. The great majority of traces were handled by contacting the other station involved in the shipping; only rarely did a package have to be traced through Memphis. Complaints were dealt with by station managers in the smaller stations, or by station agent supervisors.

The Memphis service group, known as Customer Service Agents (CSAs), performed the same functions handled by station agents: taking orders, answering questions, tracing packages. Memphis CSAs were reached through a toll-free number, which according to one station manager was used "mostly by people who don't know or don't want to look up their local station. They seem to feel that if they call the corporate office they'll get faster service." Orders taken in Memphis were relayed electronically to the local stations via Datacom, a system similar to Telex.

Need for Turnaround

Although Federal's customer service structure appeared acceptable on paper, by 1977 it was considered a problem by almost everyone in the company. Fagan recalled:

At the station level, there was no consistency whatsoever. Customer service was an ad hoc, local option system; training consisted of a single sentence—"answer the phones as best you can." Station managers were using customer service people for all kinds of jobs—unloading trucks, sluicing down floors, grabbing the phones.

Recognizing the depth of the problem, Fagan assigned responsibility for the customer service department to Heinz Adam, who had joined the company in 1976 as director of marketing administration and supervised the strategy which led Courier Pak's average daily volume to increase by over 500 percent in two years. Adam took the job of vice president-customer service under protest in March 1978, well aware of the challenges he faced:

Corporate customer service has traditionally been a very defensive function—a bunch of far from dynamic older people usually drawn from the secretarial ranks, sitting in a back room trying to make nice-nice for everyone else's screw-ups. Their usual job is to try to compensate for salesmen who make big promises that the company can't keep; customers complain that orders aren't arriving, and customer service people try to speed up production. When I took over this job, that's exactly what I found: 45 Florence Nightingales who spent most of their time tracing lost orders, listening to complaints, and giving out information. A very defensive bunch of people.

Adam felt that the group handling written communications needed at least as much improvement as the other agents:

When I took over, the answering of written complaints was essentially being handled by women who worked in the sales department. A customer would write in to Fred Smith, say, complaining about a bill or a lost package or a goofy courier, and he would be answered by the sales manager and his secretary. It was one girl typing on the typewriter, one guy dictating letters, and the financial department saying, whatever you do, apologize but don't give any money back. The typography was bad—even Xeroxed letters were used—the language was bad, and there was no system at all. I inherited eight boxes of correspondence that was nine months old and hadn't been answered because they couldn't get to it.

Problems in customer service were also affecting Federal's sales force. Jack McHale, a corporate sales executive, recalled:

Back in fall of 1977, we had just reorganized sales and set up a system where we had about 110 sales representatives, working in local stations, who reported to regional sales managers, who reported to the regional vice president of operations. Each sales rep, as is true now, had a goal of 25 calls weekly, and at that time any account was fair game—even shippers who only used us three times a year would get a sales call if they wanted one. Now, of course, personal calls are restricted to high-volume and potentially high-volume accounts.

The problem was that every time there was any sudden change in volume, resulting from a strike at United Parcel Service for instance, customer service just couldn't handle it, and we'd be pulled inside. The reps would have to answer the phones and before you know it, they'd be trying to sell over the phone, not just addressing the customer's information request, and the call backup would only get worse. Sometimes we were not only answering the phones but helping the couriers make pickups and deliveries.

Within the station, pickup orders for dispatchers as well as telephone messages for sales reps were recorded by station agents on preprinted cards. Adam explained:

They simply had phones with push buttons, and when a call came in, a light would go on, and the agent would take the call. If it was an established customer, she'd then go over to a big tub file and pull the customer's card for company data—otherwise, she'd take the information over the phone. When she was done, assuming it was a pickup order, she gave it to the dispatcher. It was like the airlines 25 years ago. They too had a tub file and they'd just check off seats till the plane was booked up.

The flow of paperwork thus generated was growing steadily, especially in major markets. The New York station, for example, handled 1,600 dispatch orders and messages daily by mid-1978.

CENTRALIZING CUSTOMER ORDERS AND REQUESTS

As early as May 1975, before Adam even joined the company, Federal Express management began to realize that their present customer service system was not equipped to handle an order volume growing by 50 percent a year. Recalling his initial approach to the problem, Sydney Tucker Taylor, vice president of operations for ten Southern states, illustrated the company's predicament by sketching an hourglass:

On one side you have demand—20 million packages a year, 50 million, one day 100 million; on the other is our ability, through the expansion of our transportation network, to meet that demand. The bottleneck is the finite number of phone lines that link the two.

We had enough trucks, we had enough people, but we didn't have enough phone lines. We had all these planes and couriers, but we still couldn't meet demand, and the reason was, people couldn't get through to us.

Heinz Adam saw the problem as a reflection of company priorities:

Initially there were three major objectives at Federal Express. First, the establishment of an airline: hiring the pilots and mechanics, buying the planes, and so forth. Second, the establishment of a reliable pickup and delivery service, which meant building up a trucking company. Third, in 1976, the decision to tell the world we're in business—build up our marketing and communications program.

We got a lot of customers that way, but the problem was that they couldn't communicate with us. There were 120 separate order entry points, one for each city, with no communication between them. Customers got different answers to their questions—assuming they didn't get a hold or a busy signal.

It was a system built on moving packages; the people in the field were hired because they had the ability to run trucking operations.

Taylor summarized:

> We had placed primary communication and customer service responsibility on the field, and the net effects were no improvement whatsoever in operational communications (same day tracing); skyrocketing field communications costs (for which we tended to blame field discipline); and total confusion in communications—we had inside sales reps, outside sales reps, CSAs, station agents, supervisors, service clerks, and trainers, all giving the customers inconsistent messages.

Assigned by Fred Smith to break up the service bottleneck at Federal Express, Taylor examined the ordering and reservations systems of a variety of service organizations: commercial airlines, car rental agencies, hotel chains. "There were two elements to the problem," he recalled. "One, to get the customer to call you, to open up access to the system, and two, once you've got the information, getting it to the courier so he can make a pickup." Thus the airline model was only partially useful, since airlines simply stored reservations in a computer and waited for passengers to appear at the airport. Avis and Hertz had a task more similar to that faced by Federal Express—taking a reservation, and then, through instant communication with the right branch office, making sure that a car was ready.

In December 1976 Taylor presented his findings to Smith and the company's senior executives, making the following recommendations:

- That service at Federal Express be redefined as all actions and reactions which customers perceived they had purchased;
- That these actions include providing documentation and information on shipments as well as delivering them;
- That customers' needs for information be served through a centralized telephone system to handle all orders and requests.

Potential Benefits

A central order-entry system, Taylor believed, offered significant benefits to Federal Express as well as to customers. It would not only be a more efficient source of information for dispatchers than the tub-file method, but would also give station managers and supervisors more time for planning, executing, and supervising station operations. According to Taylor's estimates, the average manager spent two to two-and-a-half hours per day on the phone with customers discussing tracing, billing, and service problems which eventually had to be solved in Memphis.

Moreover, centralizing the order-taking process would facilitate more rational and realistic personnel planning in the stations. As Taylor put it:

> One of the critical problems of field productivity rests with the company's inability to plan field staffing requirements. If those requirements were solely a function of volume, the task would be straightforward. The fact is that the "telephone answering" aspect of Federal Express is a function of service level, not volume. Anyone who has ever been in a city station when the morning's aircraft is three hours late, or the previous evening's departing flight missed the sort, needs no convincing of this.

The aggregate service level at Federal Express, Taylor noted, was predictable, even though specific service problems in a given station were impossible to anticipate. Centralized order entry and customer service, he felt, would allow the local station to staff for volume, and the customer service department to staff for predictable aggregate service level.

Taylor also predicted that the centralized system would give the local sales reps time to make the phone calls (on a private line) required to keep in touch with their 250–300 assigned accounts. He pointed out:

> Since its inception, the local field sales program has floundered. The major reason rests with the physical impossibility of coming anywhere close to achieving the desired number of sales calls when the sales reps are in the local office answering the phone.

Furthermore, a computer-based order-entry system would provide specific data, to be used for management planning, regarding the nature and number of phone calls received by the stations. By learning exactly how many calls an agent should be able to handle and by forecasting staffing needs more precisely, Taylor felt the company would realize substantial productivity gains—possibly as much as $7 million annually.

To centralize the order-entry process, Taylor envisioned a network of four or five regional call centers distributed around the country. When the system was fully developed, he argued, it could operate as follows:

A prospective customer calls a local number, wanting information on Federal Express. The call is answered at any one of five service centers and routed to a CSA by an automatic call distributor. The CSA, seated at a video terminal, can call up rate and service information and relay it to the customer. If the customer asks for a pickup, the CSA will press a key and an "order blank" will flash onto the screen. After the CSA types in the order, it is immediately transmitted by the computer to a printer in the local station, and the dispatcher receives the request for pickup. If an established customer calls, the CSA can display and confirm all information required to make the pickup, and provide the local dispatcher with the same information.

Testing the New Service Concept

Taylor's new service concept, christened "Project Sydney," was first tested in April 1977. Data processing personnel designed a software package which utilized Federal's existing Burroughs computer to link the telephone lines of the Newark, New Jersey, station to a central answering facility in Memphis. Taylor and his associates prepared for the test with painstaking care. Afraid lest Newark customers be taken aback by the Southern accents of the Memphis CSAs (a problem described in internal memos as the "ken ah hep ya syndrome"), they circulated exhaustive lists of New Jersey town and street names and drilled the CSAs in proper pronunciation. Letters were sent to customers explaining the change; heavy-volume shippers received personal calls from salespeople.

Focus group interviews conducted before the test revealed consistent opposition among customers, all of whom felt it was important for customer service to be available locally. One woman commented:

When I come to work in the morning, I do two things: I make a cup of coffee, and I call my Federal Express station to check on my packages.

Yet, probing further, the interviews also revealed that what was really important to customers was a responsive answer to their questions, not geographic proximity.

The strongest objections came from Federal's own station personnel. Taylor recalled:

The people out in the field thought it was the dumbest thing they ever heard of. For a very valid reason: one of the things you lose when you centralize this operation is the personal touch. The problem is that with Federal Express growing the way it is, you can't keep that anyway. Eventually the New York City market, for example, gets so big that you can't talk to Debbie every time even if the phone's being answered locally. In many places those good old days were dead already, but people out in the field were reluctant to recognize that. They didn't want some strange woman with a Southern accent in Memphis talking to their friends in Newark.

To many people's surprise, customer reaction to the test of the new system was favorable. Federal Express had spared no expense training the 27 CSAs in Memphis who took over the Newark phones; customers sensed a new aura of professionalism and responded to it. Surveys conducted shortly after the test revealed that even the "ken ah hep ya syndrome" had turned out to be a nonissue; almost two-thirds of those surveyed had been unaware that they were talking with CSAs outside Newark, not even noticing the Southern accents. Forty-four percent of respondents had observed a difference in service and praised Federal's speed and courtesy, as well as the drop in busy signals. Within 12 weeks, volume in the Newark station had risen 4 percent—and station personnel had changed their minds about the new system. One sales rep remarked: "I love it. The phones don't ring."

Encouraged by these developments, Taylor and the Project Sydney team added Chicago to the system. This time difficulties arose, particularly in the dispatching of orders; the fault lay not in the CSAs nor in the program but in the Burroughs computer, which had reached the limits of its capacity. (In addition to the order-entry tests, the computer was also handling flight scheduling and the company's accounting functions.) Management then decided to abandon Taylor's original concept of four or five large call centers in favor of 20–30 smaller ones, which could also be spread across the country but would use mini-computers. Accordingly, Federal Express arranged to lease the new equipment—only to be informed by the manufacturer a few days before the scheduled delivery date that part of the necessary hardware had not yet been developed.

RECOMMENDATIONS AND DEBATE

By this time, Federal's data processing executives had become convinced that the Burroughs computer would not be able to handle the company's continued growth, even without the burden of Project Sydney. They urged that the company set up a data processing "think tank," charged with developing a totally new software package to satisfy all Federal's data processing and customer service needs.

The data systems division also recommended that Federal Express purchase the recently introduced IBM 30XX System. Designed for scientific computation and business data-communication networks, the 30XX System offered up to 16.8 million characters (megabytes) of main memory and included two IBM 3033s and two 3031s. The package, which cost $7.5 million, also included communications units, operator consoles, and power and cooling units.

Several Federal Express executives were concerned by the long waiting period required for delivery of the 30XX. First deliveries were scheduled for the third quarter of 1979, and there was already a waiting list.

Even IBM salespeople had initially expressed doubt as to whether the company needed such extensive processing capacity; as one remarked, "a lot of agencies in the U.S. government don't use two 3033s." When IBM learned of the proposed new application of the 30XX System, however, they encouraged Federal Express to obtain the equipment and proposed several ways to obtain delivery early enough to start developing the new software package as planned.

At the same time that Data Systems presented its recommendations, Fagan, Taylor, and Adam urged that Taylor's original plan for four to five regional call centers controlling all Federal Express customer service functions be implemented as soon as possible. In a memo to the company's senior information systems executive, Fagan and Taylor declared:

> The fact is that we are rapidly reaching a point in our major cities where we cannot handle any more on-call pickups. At a point somewhere between 900 and 1,200 on-call pickups per day, the combination of our need to answer the telephone intelligently and politely, our need to access relevant customer information, and our need to communicate with the driver puts an absolute limit on our volume growth.

Internal Resistance

The most immediate opposition to both the data processing expansion and the call centers came from the company's financial officers. Reviewing the initial plans for Project Sydney, which forecast a total net cash requirement of almost $10 million between 1979 and 1984, Federal's manager of financial analysis had commented:

> Regardless of the merit of the proposal, the financial implications are nothing less than astounding: since the origination of Federal Express, no capital expenditure program, with the exception of aircraft fleet additions, has required more funding.

The financial analyst had insisted that a joint research project be undertaken by Operations Research and Finance to define the exact correlation between increased profitability and increased service level. He also wanted to see concrete evidence of predicted productivity improvements, warning that "gut feel and intuition no longer should suffice in a corporation of our sophistication." These studies were not carried out. However, in October 1977, in response to the financial division's continued requests, the operations research and planning division, working with Taylor and Fagan, produced a detailed projection of the costs for a centralized order-entry system using four call centers.

Unfortunately, Taylor's initial vision of a

$7 million annual productivity savings had proved impossible to substantiate. He had simply guessed that station personnel could answer only about 65 calls per person per day, as compared to 110 for a CSA at a call center. But in reality, it appeared that a station clerk could handle at least the same amount of calls as a call center agent, although the former's accuracy was considerably less reliable. The new projections indicated an increase in net operating cost, after taxes, of $1,301,961 in FY 1981, declining slightly to $1,252,441 for FY 1983 (*Exhibit 4*). These figures did nothing to allay

EXHIBIT 4
Project Sydney Projected Profit and Loss Statement
(all dollars expressed in annual terms)

	FY1981	FY1983
OPERATING DOLLARS SAVED		
CSA salaries and fringe benefits	$ 8,235,000	$12,060,000
Overhead	480,718	627,635
Total (1)	$ 8,715,718	$12,687,635
Operating dollars saved/package	$.53	$.48
OPERATING COSTS		
Depreciation and amortization:		
Equipment	$ 22,488	$ 30,172
Software development	260,000	260,000
Computer installation	10,000	10,000
Personnel costs:		
Fixed	660,000	660,000
Variable	6,318,100	8,723,100
Computer personnel	350,000	350,000
Support costs:		
Data conversion	47,803	62,461
CRT installation	22,860	19,209
Computer hardware	594,615	594,615
Automatic call distributor	292,318	371,648
Rent and utilities	334,862	415,540
CRTs	391,166	544,839
Supplies	80,153	110,888
Line cost	2,281,147	3,373,048
Total operating cost (2)	$11,292,653	$15,156,310
Total operating cost/package	$.68	$.57
Imputed interest (3)	26,986	36,206
Net cost before taxes: (2) + (3) − (1)	$ 2,603,921	$ 2,504,882
Income tax savings	1,301,961	1,252,441
Net cost after tax savings	$ 1,301,961	$ 1,252,441
Net after-tax cost/package	$.08	$.05

SOURCE: Company records.

the misgivings of Federal's financial executives.

Company executives opposed to the project also pointed out that simply adding personnel and a Collins Automatic Call Distributor to each of Federal's six major markets (New York, Chicago, Los Angeles, San Francisco, Boston, and Washington, D.C.) would remove much of the order-taking burden from present employees—at a fraction of the cost required in the same period for a network of four call centers.

The productivity problem was complicated by the fact that both Fagan and Adam felt it would be a major mistake in labor relations to lay off any personnel. Federal Express employees were not unionized, and the company made it a point to keep relations smooth through profit sharing, opportunities for stock purchase, tuition refunds, aircraft jumpseat privileges, and heavy internal promotion. Heinz Adam described the dilemma:

> Management is saying to me—okay, are the call centers going to save people? And I have to say no, people are currently answering all these phones, but we're not going to just get rid of them with the new system, we're going to find other work for them. Firing these people is absolutely not an option—misgivings about the new system are causing attitudinal problems anyway.

Any reduction in the labor force, Adam felt, should come through attrition and the hiring of temporary workers to replace those who left a station within six months before it went online. He added:

> Besides, when a company is growing as fast as Federal Express is, finding adequately trained people to support that growth is one of management's biggest problems. We have these people, and if Project Sydney were implemented we could divert them to other jobs.

Doubts from the Field

Federal Express salespeople expressed the greatest opposition to Project Sydney; as they saw it, their carefully cultivated contacts would be turned over to a faceless person in another state. One sales rep in Boston worried:

> What about the big customer who usually calls in past our formal cut-off time and always gets service because of his account status? What about anyone who calls in past the deadline? Are those customers just going to be referred to a downtown convenience center, even if they're out in the sticks? How can somebody in Memphis who doesn't know the area, doesn't know where the trucks are, make judgments like that?

The anonymity of the new system provoked other fears. Customers who were known to the local stations were never asked to repeat details about themselves or their companies when placing orders; Memphis CSAs would be required to review at least some of this information with each call. Moreover, despite favorable customer reaction to the Newark test, many station personnel wondered how shippers would respond to an impersonal, faraway voice on the phone. Pointing to the success in Newark, Fagan insisted that this was an invalid concern:

> People will give up the luxury of personal contact and the security of the local operation, the mom and pop thing, if instead they get a very professionally run organization. They may be on guard because of the previous bad service record of computers, but we'll just have to prove ourselves.

In an attempt to allay the fears of sales and station personnel, Taylor drew up another list of the new system's operational advantages. As he saw it, Project Sydney could generate a tentative invoice that could be altered when the packages were picked up if they were different than described. The invoices would provide advice to flight scheduling, indicating unusual peaks and valleys in the system (outbound and inbound) prior to departure. By calling up records on their video screens, CSAs could keep "call for pickup" time under 60 seconds for established customers and could also check credit risks on the first call for billable se vice. Finally, the computer could generate constantly updated customer mailing lists for marketing purposes.

Additional Concerns

Other executives argued that the new system might make Federal Express dangerously dependent upon the telephone company. As even Taylor admitted, the phone company did string cables across bridges—and a bridge washout could paralyze a call center for six hours or more. The short-term answer to this problem, he felt, was an elaborate overflow and diversion system that would direct other call centers to pick up the slack. Long term, Taylor visualized an independent satellite communications system for Federal Express.

Heinz Adam refused to see the company's reliance on AT&T as a significant problem:

> We will depend on them to some extent, but we're not unique in this respect—so do the car rental agencies, the airlines, the credit card companies. Suppose some lines do go down—through coordinated effort and a good backup system we can handle it. For a good commercial company like Federal Express, the phone company will break their backs to get the repairs done. There's a certain paranoid quality to too much of this "what if that happens" thinking. The key to the whole problem is good, sane, nonoverreactive management.

GOING TO THE BOARD

As the time to present Project Sydney to the board drew nearer, Federal Express's financial executives remained unconvinced of the system's ultimate value and skeptical of its forecast costs (which had assumed 6 percent annual inflation). To many minds, the opportunity costs of the new system were almost as unsettling as the debatable financial data. A decision to go ahead with Project Sydney would seriously retard the development of a larger data processing and operational software package for the company—perhaps by as much as two years.

Since the vast majority of customer complaints concerned tracing, Federal Express was particularly interested in the development of an optical scanning system for packages to ensure a reliable documentation and tracking process and to simplify package loading and manifesting operations. The company also hoped to improve dispatcher-to-courier communications, possibly by installing computer-linked printers or video terminals within delivery vans. These projects would have to wait if Project Sydney were implemented.

Time to Act

No other company within the air freight industry had developed anything similar to Project Sydney. Emery had attempted to computerize its tracing process, with mixed results. Yet Heinz Adam felt that adoption of Taylor's concept was essential, not only for meeting customer needs but for maintaining Federal's positioning as the leader in the industry. Facing a pile of memos asking for more data on the new system, Adam was ready to blow up:

> So many people want a black and white solution to this problem, but how many times in the real world do you have that situation? Once you know you have the money to do something, it comes down to politics, proper interpretation of attitudes, and crystal ball gazing. These guys keep saying to me—Heinz, put together some numbers and show us that this will make fiscal sense. I can't—there isn't any way. I can show that the online city stations are growing faster than the others, but this incremental growth is only marginal—one to two percent.

In Fagan's view, one of the greatest benefits of the new system would be consistency:

> Centralized order-entry creates quality control assurance—you know your product's the same everywhere in the country. It's like McDonald's—you get the same hamburger everywhere you go. What if it is cheaper to have customer service in the field? Can you measure that trade-off in dollars?

Adam was even more vehement. Gazing up from his desk at the large map of the U.S. tacked on his wall, where a constantly multiplying stream of red pins gave visual proof of the extent of Federal's growth, he argued:

> Most decisions are based on return on investment—if we spend this money, it's a good investment because we're going to make money. Well, in this case, if we *don't* spend the money, we aren't going to grow. Look at it this way— it's only going to cost us a nickel a package to ensure that we go from 35,000 packages to infinity. That's different than saying if we buy a DC-10 instead of flying three 727s wingtip to wingtip, we can save money because it's less expensive to operate the DC-10.

We've got another problem here. Within the corporation, there's a very negative attitude about customer service, and there has been for as long as I've been here. The reasons for that are very complex, but they boil down to the tremendous difference between what our own people expect of us and what we are in fact able to do. At one time, I'll admit, the customer service department wasn't very reliable—but it's improved tremendously in the past year. My people can handle the order processing job—the tests have proved it.

There's never been an emphasis on customer service here, just a policy that if all else fails, give it to customer service. The fact is, if the service problems were simple we would never get involved. The station managers and sales force and billing office would take care of things themselves.

Federal Express:
Customer Service Department, II

PENNY PITTMAN MERLISS
CHRISTOPHER H. LOVELOCK

Management has adopted a computerized system known as COSMOS to improve the company's handling of customer orders and requests for information. Sales representatives are worried that the firm's newly enlarged customer service department is coming between them and their customers. They seek special treatment for large customers but the vice president-customer service is opposed.

"Let me be blunt about it," declared Jack McHale, manager of strategic sales planning for the Federal Express Corporation (FEC). "Customer service is the scourge of sales."

THE IMPACT OF COSMOS

By the late spring of 1980, it was clear that relations between FEC's sales and customer service departments, frequently somewhat strained, were being further taxed by the introduction of a centralized, computer-based order-entry system named COSMOS.

Customers who had previously placed pickup orders with local station clerks now conducted their business through toll-free calls to customer service agents (CSAs) in regional call centers located in Somerset, New Jersey and Memphis, Tennessee; a third center was scheduled to open in Sacramento, California in August. The CSAs also provided general information on Federal Express service and received tracing requests.

COSMOS, installed in 1979 at an initial cost of $5.6 million, offered distinct benefits to the company (greater operational efficiency, greatly expanded capacity for growth)

This case was prepared by Penny Pittman Merliss, Research Assistant, under the supervision of Associate Professor Christopher H. Lovelock. Copyright © 1981 by the President and Fellows of Harvard College. Harvard Business School case 9-581-102. Reprinted by permission.

and also to its customers (standardized, faster, more consistent response to calls). The main working room of each call center was specially designed to reduce noise; it held approximately 180 CSAs and 14 supervisors. CSAs worked in brightly colored hexagonal "pods," each equipped with six individual working bays. In addition, the Memphis call center contained 84 agents who specialized in tracing and 14 "executive desk" assistants who handled calls requiring more follow-up, such as complaints.

CSAs were trained to use their own judgment in deciding whether to hand a difficult caller over to a supervisor or executive assistant. But only a tracing agent, working with FEC's invoice adjustment department, could authorize a refund. Requests by customers for late pickups were passed to station dispatchers, who decided whether or not couriers' schedules could accommodate last-minute calls.

J. Vincent Fagan, senior vice president—marketing, sales, and customer service, felt that COSMOS had increased FEC's consistency in training and service, as well as creating checks and balances for the operating departments. "For example," he noted, "if we find through customer input to CSAs that a certain station can't handle its volume, the company can correct that." Although company market research had not revealed that customers perceived substantial differences between COSMOS and the earlier, fragmented system, Fagan was convinced that the adoption of COSMOS had been operationally imperative.

Yet many Federal Express salespeople still had misgivings about the new system, which was being progressively introduced in FEC's 141 stations. In areas already on-line, customer-station telephone contact had been eliminated almost entirely by COSMOS. Station phone numbers were now unlisted, and employees were instructed not to give the numbers to customers.

"At first," commented Fagan, "the sales reps were worried that having agents answering the phones from a central location might confuse customers in another part of the country. That fear turned out to be groundless, but there's still a problem, be-

cause now customer service has become a middleman between the sales force and the customers. Since customers can't call stations directly anymore, they have to leave a message at one of the call centers if they want to reach a sales rep."

Differing Perspectives on Customer Service

It was generally agreed at Federal Express that customer service had been a relatively inefficient, unprofessional function prior to March 1978, when Heinz Adam assumed control of the department and its 45 employees. But corporate surveys of Federal's sales representatives in late 1979, when CSAs numbered almost 400, indicated that the sales force's opinion of customer service was still very low. McHale noted:

> Any salesman will look at customer service and tell you—dammit, they just don't react like I would react to my customer. We're really a little worried about all these calls going through the call centers. When a customer calls just to give a message, or to discuss what looks like an easy problem, he may still want to see a sales rep personally. What's happening now is that a lot of these problems are being handled in the call centers, without our even knowing about them. The customers can get a little irritated because the sales rep never returns their calls—and the sales rep is really irritated because he never knew the customer had a problem.
>
> It's very tough selling service. You're only as good as your performance on the last shipment. Some people in the company say, "Gee, we've got advertising and customer service; we don't need sales reps. What are they doing?" Well, we're doing this: we're maintaining the business. A lot of sales reps make service calls on customers who've demanded to see them, who don't want to talk to the customer service center. They'll tell you: "I give you ten packages a day, I want to see a sales rep."

Heinz Adam, vice president of customer service, saw the situation from a different perspective:

> We're helping the sales reps by taking their calls, not hurting them, because we've trained our agents to screen customers and try to de-

termine an account's potential volume before passing the call on. A lot of people call up and say, "I'd like to see a salesman." Well, see a salesman for what reason? Have you got 20 packages a day to give us, or do you want a free lunch?

Quite frankly, what happened before was that the field people would take messages and the salesmen would run out and make calls and find out that a lot of messages were really questions like, "Hey, could you tell me, do you serve Albuquerque?" Our agents have cut the sales reps' message volume by 75 percent, and now the calls they're getting are, in fact, real problems. The recession is also something that's cutting into their calls, which they don't seem to recognize; their assumption, their paranoia, is that we're not allowing customers to contact the sales force.

The other thing that's really interesting here is that now the salesmen have to work. They can't spend eight hours returning calls and giving out rate information—they've got to get out and hustle. We're not held in the highest esteem because we're taking away their cotton candy.

Federal Express sales managers tended to respond to Adam's comments by pointing out that CSAs, many of whom had come up through the secretarial ranks, received only three weeks of training before assuming their new jobs (reservations agents for the airlines, in contrast, received approximately eight weeks of training). Summing up the situation, McHale declared:

> Customer service does a heck of a job taking orders. Even the tracing function, which still needs work, is improving. Heinz is really turning the department around, and it's only natural for him to want to expand the CSAs' responsibilities. But with a recession in sight, our salesmen are under a lot of pressure to perform, and the last thing we should have to worry about is some kind of middleman standing between us and our customers.

Adam, on the other hand, was convinced that the CSA's expanded role would benefit Federal Express. He wondered how to bring the sales department around to his point of view.

RESPONDING TO THE RECESSION

In addition to dealing with sales department concerns over the role of customer service agents, Heinz Adam also found himself at odds with the other department over a plan to use COSMOS to give preferential treatment to high-volume customers.

As summer drew closer, it was becoming clear that the deepening U.S. economic recession, which had already resulted in the layoff of over 200,000 auto workers and caused a sharp decrease in consumer spending, would cast its shadow over Federal Express as well.

Only a few months earlier, company management had felt that Federal's business was largely recession-proof, and announced plans to add 8 used DC-10s and 23 used 727s to its existing fleet of 15 second-hand 727s, 5 new 737s, and 32 Falcons. By June, two DC-10s and two additional 727s had already joined the fleet. Average daily package volume now exceeded 68,000, a 48 percent increase over the past fiscal year; annual revenues for the fiscal year ending May 31, 1980 reached $415 million, a 61 percent increase over fiscal 1979 (see *Exhibit 1*). But, as Adam admitted:

> We've had an average 50 percent annual growth in revenues since 1974, and suddenly we're facing a slowdown in certain segments of our business. The customers that we call "on-call" customers, who use us irregularly and place their orders through our central computerized system—COSMOS—are increasing at a good rate. These are professional service and high-technology firms. But the big industrial shipper—who arranges a standing pickup order through our sales department—is giving us less business.

During 1979–80, the company's advertising in the business media had emphasized the simplicity of using Federal Express (*Exhibits 2 and 3*) and the value of this service for emergency shipments (*Exhibit 4*). A new print advertising campaign, scheduled to begin in business publications at the end of June, focused instead on the importance of not keeping people waiting for vital documents and supplies; it suggested that Fed-

EXHIBIT 1
Operating Results and Financial Position, 1976–80
(in thousands)

	FISCAL YEARS ENDING MAY 31				
	1976	*1977*	*1978*	*1979*	*1980*
OPERATING RESULTS					
Air freight revenues	$75,055	$109,210	$160,301	$258,482	$415,379
Operating expense	65,210	95,608	134,024	216,330	346,416
Operating income	9,845	13,602	26,277	42,152	68,963
Other expenses (net)	6,210	5,390	5,693	6,329	7,628
Income before income taxes	3,635	8,212	20,584	35,823	61,335
Income taxes	2,032	4,243	6,980	14,400	22,605
Income before tax benefit of loss carryforward	1,603	3,969	13,604	21,423	38,730
Tax benefit of loss carryforward	1,982	4,185	6,425	—	—
Net income	$ 3,585	$ 8,154	$ 20,029	$ 21,423	$ 38,730
FINANCIAL POSITION					
Current assets	$14,725	$ 20,349	$ 30,370	$ 48,975	$ 85,454
Property and equipment (net)	55,297	53,616	71,813	123,844	277,702
Total assets	71,229	75,321	106,291	179,823	398,127
Current liabilities	12,954	18,658	22,741	40,067	58,775
Long-term debt	56,186	46,229	30,825	45,729	145,562
Common stockholders' investment	(16,561)	(8,216)	38,294	76,789	171,589

SOURCE: Company records.

eral Express was a new business tool that companies could use to improve their productivity (*Exhibit 5*).

Preferential Treatment Plan

As Federal's sales department received more and more pressure to meet goals, Jack McHale had devised a way to use the capabilities of COSMOS to boost sales revenues. Examining the "order blank" (*Exhibit 6*) that appeared on the video terminals used by customer service agents, McHale felt that COSMOS could be programmed to identify high-volume customers. In his words:

Right now, when the customer data come up on the screen, there's no way for the CSA to know whether this person has been shipping two packages a year, or 500. At present, we have about 4,000 key accounts which repre-sent less than 2 percent of the total account numbers, and they account for almost 45 percent of the business. It's very important that the customer service people realize that these accounts deserve special treatment.

I don't know what the phraseology would be, but I'd like to hear a CSA say something to a big customer like, "We recognize that you're a very good customer of ours, one of the better customers in the Hartford area. And I'm going to let your sales representative"—we may be able to put his name in the COSMOS file—"I'm going to let Joe Smith know about your problem (or your order) and I'll continue working on it too."

Adam was totally opposed to the plan, though he admitted that the programming required to implement it should be minimal. Shaking his head, he stated firmly:

If we're doing our job right, that kind of sys-

EXHIBIT 2
Advertising in *Wall Street Journal*, August 1979

FEDERAL EXPRESS CAN TAKE THE STUFF OFF YOUR DESK

AND SEND IT CLEAR ACROSS THE COUNTRY TO SOMEBODY ELSE'S DESK, OVERNIGHT.

Announcing a novel solution to the paper explosion. It's called Federal Express COURIER PAK? and it comes in three sizes: envelope, box and tube.

Here's what you do. When you have some documents, artwork, contracts, reports, blueprints, print-outs or any papers that absolutely, positively have to be somewhere else overnight, just pick up the phone and call us. We come to your office and give you a supply of boxes, tubes, and envelopes to put them all in, and we take them off your back.

That night we fly them in our own planes and we deliver them in our trucks right to the other person the morning of the next business day.

That's all there is to it. It's simple, safe, convenient, and it's absolutely, positively overnight.

Our Courier Pak service is exactly the same as our regular overnight package service: same trucks, same planes, same reputation for delivering on time.

And we don't charge a fortune for it either. For example, one Courier Pak envelope with up to 2 lbs. of paper, picked up, flown, and delivered to any of more than 10,000 cities and towns coast to coast is only $16.00. And if we pick up more than one, you're entitled to discounts of up to $6.00 per Courier Pak.

We're in the white pages under Federal Express, or call our toll-free number (800) 238-5355.

Give us a call the next time the paper explosion starts to blow you away.

WE'LL EVEN GIVE YOU THE CONTAINER TO SHIP IT IN, FREE OF CHARGE.

FEDERAL EXPRESS
WHEN IT ABSOLUTELY, POSITIVELY HAS TO BE THERE OVERNIGHT.

EXHIBIT 3
Advertising in *Wall Street Journal,* April 1980

Even if you're way above the day-to-day details of business, you can still use Federal Express.

Because even a big shot uses the telephone, and that's all it takes to use Federal Express.

All you do is pick up the phone and we come to your office or mailroom and pick up the envelope or package.

Then we fly it overnight in our own planes and deliver it door to door the next morning to any of more than 10,000 cities and towns in the U.S. and Canada.

It's as simple and easy as that. No complicated forms, red tape or shipping lingo involved. What we've done is taken the mystery and complication out of air express and made it available to anyone in the company with an urgent problem.

The cost is reasonable too. Our prices start at only $16.00, including pickup and delivery.

So the next time you have something that absolutely, positively has to get somewhere overnight, just pick up the phone and call your mailroom supervisor or call us direct.

We're listed in the white pages under Federal Express. Or call our toll-free number at (800) 238-5355.

If that's easy enough for the chairman of the board, you can handle it too.

FEDERAL EXPRESS
WHEN IT ABSOLUTELY, POSITIVELY HAS TO BE THERE OVERNIGHT.

©1979 Federal Express Corp. Federal Express overnight air service is a door-to-door service with packages scheduled to be delivered to the consignee's address by 12:00 noon the following business day after pickup by or tender to Federal Express.

For a copy of our latest annual report please write to: Mr. Daniel N. Copp, P.O. Box 727, Dept. 371, Memphis, TN 38194

EXHIBIT 4
Advertising in *Wall Street Journal*, April 1980

WHEN IT ABSOLUTELY, POSITIVELY HAS TO BE THERE OVERNIGHT.

For a copy of our latest annual report please write to: Mr. Daniel N. Copp, P.O. Box 727, Dept. 371, Memphis, TN 38194

© 1980 Federal Express Corporation. COURIER-PAK® is a registered trademark of Federal Express Corporation. All services are subject to the current Federal Express Corporation. Service Guide. Monday through Friday. Saturday delivery by special request only, and at an additional service charge.

EXHIBIT 5

Advertising Planned for Business Publications, June 1980

WAITING IS FRUSTRATING, DEMORALIZING, AGONIZING, AGGRAVATING, ANNOYING, TIME CONSUMING, AND INCREDIBLY EXPENSIVE. IT'S ALSO UNNECESSARY.

Waiting.

It's another cost of doing business today. Because business is spread out all over the country.

And it takes time to get things from one part of the country to the other, sometimes days and days.

And that gets expensive. For instance, every time an executive sends a letter, a document, or a report to another city, someone has to wait for it.

This slows down the whole project which affects productivity, which affects profit, which affects the entire performance of the company.

And when you're talking about skilled labor waiting for a part for a machine or computer, you're talking big money for each day of waiting.

Fortunately, there is an alternative.

Next time, instead of waiting for something from somewhere else, tell them to send it Federal Express and you'll have it overnight.*

For as little as $19.00, the report you called Phoenix for on Monday can be in your hands on Tuesday.

The part sitting on a shelf in Pittsburgh on Thursday can be in your assembly foreman's hands in Los Angeles on Friday.

With Federal Express you don't have to wait for anything anymore.

Imagine what that could do to this country's productivity figures if everyone used Federal Express to eliminate waiting.

Imagine what that could do to your profit statement if you used Federal Express more and more.

Look at Federal Express as not just a service to use in an emergency, but also as a way to eliminate the frustration, the annoyance, and the expense of waiting, and you'll start to see Federal Express the way we envisioned it in the first place.

Federal Express is really a new tool that can and is revolutionizing the way America does business, as did the phone, the copy machine, the computer, and jet travel.

In a very real sense, it's the next tool that's needed now that we can pick up the phone and talk to anyone and now that we can get on an airplane and go meet with anyone.

Thanks to Federal, you can now have things sent to you from practically any place in the country overnight.

So pick up the phone and call us at 800-238-5355 and we'll pick up, fly and deliver your package or envelope overnight.

With no waiting, and all the mental and physical problems that go with it.

After all, why wait when you don't have to?

FEDERAL EXPRESS
WHY WAIT WHEN YOU DON'T HAVE TO?

For a copy of our latest annual report please write to: Mr. Daniel N. Copp, P.O. Box 727, Dept. 371, Memphis, TN 38194

*Monday through Friday. Saturday delivery by special request at an additional service charge. © 1980 Federal Express Corporation. All services are subject to the current Federal Express Corporation Service Guide.

EXHIBIT 6

Federal Express Information and Dispatch Request Form

PICKUP INFORMATION AND DISPATCH REQUEST[1]
STATION IDENTIFICATION

Customer Detail Information

Shipper # _____ Shipper _____ Zip Code _____

Pickup Address _____ City _____ State _____ Company Closing Time _____

Contact [Name] _____ Area Code ____ Phone _____ Extension ___ Status ____

List Ret[2] _____ Collect Cash _____ Type of Commodity[3] _____ Type Req (A/C/D/S)[4] _____

Customer Request Information

Rate _____ Dispatch _____ Cust/Svc[5] _____ FEC Account # _____ Cust Sply[6] _____

Missed Pickup

Package Information

Time Package to be Ready _____ Package Rate _____ Type of Service _____

Destination Zip Code _____ Total Number of Packages _____ Total Weight _____

Next Day Pickup? _____ Cust Supplies[7] _____ CSA Remarks _____

Dispatch # _____ Area _____ Courier Route #[8] _____ Pick-up Date _____

---

[1]The caller was first asked for an FEC account number. When this was typed in, the bulk of the other information (excepting details of the specific shipment to be picked up) was automatically retrieved from the computer's memory, displayed on the screen, and double-checked by the CSA with the customer.

[2]Agent file search tool.

[3]Papers, machinery, art work, etc. Foodstuffs and poisons could not be carried on the same day of the week.

[4](a) Add to record; (c) change record; (d) delete record; (s) show (display) record.

[5]Customer request to see sales representative.

[6]Bulk supplies (e.g., 100 airbills, 50 service guides) to be sent to customer.

[7]Unit supplies to be brought by courier.

[8]Automatically displayed.

SOURCE: Federal Express Corporation.

---

tem should be totally unnecessary. I believe we should have service levels so high that we don't need to differentiate between the large and the small, between Leibowitz & Katz and General Motors or IBM.

The sales department is getting beaten on by everybody because the big accounts are suffering, and I would love to help them. But let me point out a few other problems with this idea, aside from my personal objections.

First, when you're dealing with 400 agents, it's difficult to teach them double standards in three weeks of training. It's a logistics problem, and

it's also a very dangerous step. I certainly don't want them to start thinking they only have to try hard when one of these "special" guys comes on the screen. Besides, how do you set up this treatment in the first place? How do you tell an agent, "Hey, make your voice sound nicer if it's IBM versus Leibowitz & Katz?"

McHale was aware of Adam's objections, but he still felt his plan held potential. "Federal Express has invested millions of dollars in the COSMOS system," he observed, "and right now the onus is still on sales to identify preferred customers, because the COSMOS file contains no package volume or revenue data.[1] Our present daily call volume is about 50,000, and CSAs are handling almost half

those calls.[2] Many customers even have to go through a CSA to reach a sales rep. I see no reason why those agents shouldn't have a much clearer idea of what kind of potential business they're dealing with."

---

[1]Volume and revenue data were generated by the financial department's data processing system, separate from COSMOS; there were no plans to make financial files available to Adam's CSAs.

[2]100 of the 141 Federal Express stations were not yet on-line to COSMOS; it was expected that all stations would be on-line by 1983. Adam estimated that by the end of May 1981, 85 percent of Federal Express orders would be processed through call centers.

PART VII
The Human Dimension in Services Management

Getting People to Grow

RICHARD NORMANN

Proper training of service personnel is vital to the success of all service organizations. In the best service companies, internal training programs fulfill a precise and well-understood purpose related to the firm's overall strategy.

Even fairly "conservative" types of service company are beginning to understand the meaning of the "moment of truth" [when the service provider and the customer come into direct contact with each other in the service "arena"]. One large bank has invented the slogan "The difference in money is people."

Since much of the quality of a service company depends on what happens at the moment of truth, several ways of assuring the required quality have evolved. The following are examples of such approaches:

- Trying to remove as much of the production as possible from the moment of truth; locating more of the production in the back office, perhaps in machines.

- Reducing the discretion allowed to the contact personnel; standardizing their situation and their behavior.

- Making it possible for the contact staff to use their discretion as creatively as possible, i.e., improving their ability to solve problems and to treat each situation in a customer-oriented way.

In the present chapter we shall be preoccupied mainly with the third of these approaches.

EDUCATION

The importance of developing and educating the people who will be supplying services is so great that many service companies organize their own schools. Hotel chains, as well as relying on well-known schools such as Cornell University, organize schools of their own. Examples are the Holiday Inn University and Marriott's "Learning Center." McDonald's has its own impressive "Hamburger University." Control Data has about a hundred learning centers which are used for clients and for their own personnel. And there are many other examples.

One of the tasks of these institutions is to teach the *technical skills* needed in the particular business. In "universities" or "learning centers" of this kind, employees are taught such things as accounting systems in hotels, underwriting procedures for facultative reinsurance risks, or cash management techniques. Operational rules which have proved efficient in the running of a local establishment, in whatever service business it may be, are stored and transmitted to new employees.

But there is more to education than mere technicalities. It is especially important in service operations, where the moment of truth necessarily implies a great deal of uncertainty and where situations are difficult to program completely, that employees are also taught various *interactive skills*. Many airlines provide their cabin staff with training in transactional analysis, to help them to cope with difficult demanding clients in unexpected situations. Many companies also use role play, creativity techniques, and conflict simulation as educational tools. Not a few even advertise the fact that they have such educational programs, trying to communicate to the customer that their service delivery system is designed to cope with almost any situation that could possibly arise.

Depending on the type of service business, the emphasis may be on either of these aspects, the technical or the interactive. McDonald's, the prototype of the "industrialization" and standardization of services to achieve a cost-effective level of quality, is

an interesting example. The contact staff at McDonald's learn to have eye contact with every customer—and the training is so efficient that I have never known it to fail. You could almost certainly go to any of the thousands of McDonald's anywhere in the world and turn to any of the employees in them and you would always make eye contact. When I recently visited a New York suburb, however, and asked for a Big Mac in a McDonald's at 9 o'clock in the morning, the employee was thoroughly startled and appeared to be completely flummoxed. Obviously the programming had never envisaged a customer so uneducated as not to know that McDonald's doesn't serve hamburgers for breakfast. (It is also part of the story that I was then served an American breakfast far better than I ate in any of the well-known hotels which I visited during a 10-day trip.)

It seems that, at least at present, the ideas upon which most advanced service companies are basing their internal training have a distinctly behavioral bias. In many areas it has been popular (and generally useful) to teach concrete technical skills on the one hand and on the other various ideas and techniques to improve self-insight and to change attitudes, especially in interpersonal relations. The popularity of transactional analysis is an example of this last. No doubt the theory was that a change in attitudes would induce a change in behavior. Now, however, the prevailing doctrine tends to emphasize concrete behavioral skills, with a view to molding behavioral patterns into "role models" for different types of jobs (Rosenbaum, 1982). Our own experience suggests that long-term effectiveness is best served by a combination of "personal growth technique" and "behavior modelling" inputs, complementing each other but perhaps with the stress on one or the other depending on the particular business and personnel category involved.

For companies which understand the effectiveness, in business terms, of their employees' personal growth, training is by no means the only instrument available. Personal development issues may be discussed regularly as part of individual performance reviews (formal reviews may be made as often as four times a year in some companies). Another approach is reflected in the following observation that stems from a large international service company:

> It is essential to perpetuate the enthusiasm of the employees, and we have a number of programs for that. We have one service, for example, which allows any employee or family member of an employee to call and talk about any problem—alcohol, family, insurance, . . . Anything that would influence the image or productivity of the company or the employee—for 24 hours a day, seven days a week, from anywhere in the world.

A third function of training is to infuse the employees with values, and to focus their attention on such things as being crucial to the success of the business.

Even though there is an impressive list of "universities" and "learning centers" in service organizations, most of the training probably takes place on the job. Services cannot easily be demonstrated to customers; the provision of services cannot easily be taught. In both cases there is no substitute for real-life experience. Mentor and master–apprentice systems, whether formalized or not, are therefore often to be found in service organizations.

THE TARGETS OF EDUCATION

There is no doubt, as we have seen in our work, that well-designed educational programs for *contact personnel* can often have a profound and immediately positive effect on the performance of a whole company. And yet we often find that we have to warn clients against adopting such measures. Contact-personnel training is a superb instrument in the service organization provided it is very well designed and adapted to the unique situation and business of the company and provided it is regarded as an integral part of a system of change rather than some kind of universal weapon. The three following comments, issuing from top executives in

three very large and successful international service companies, illustrate these points:

> We have found that when training tends to break down is when it is event-oriented rather than part of a larger program.

> We have given this course to all of our contact personnel, and it has worked out very well. But I can tell you from experience: if this course is the *only* thing you plan to do about better service—by all means don't give it!

> Courses only have value if the superiors of the participants can be brought to share the same values. When one of our international units wants education for its front-line people we say yes, we will be happy to give it, but not unless we have had sessions with the superiors and top executives also.

Various studies have shown that it is almost impossible to develop—and even more to maintain—a particular kind of climate and relationship between front-line personnel and customers unless the same climate and basic values prevail in the relationship between front-line personnel and their supervisors (Schneider, 1980). If one behavioral code and one set of values prevails inside the organization and another in external contacts with clients, the contact personnel will find themselves in a more or less impossible "double bind" position. The ambiguity of the situation will tend to reduce the quality of the service, as well as work motivation and client satisfaction, with easily discernible effects on the bottom line. Climate is crucial, and climate must be pervasive. (Anyone who has ever entered a French bank and studied the perfectly visible, deadly formal, and almost deliberately destructive relationship between the front-line personnel, their superiors, and the superiors of the superiors—all sitting one behind the other—will immediately give up any idea of obtaining good service there.)

In fact, supervisory roles are among the most difficult to fill in most service industries. Supervisors so obviously affect the behavior of the front-line personnel, but their own situation often lacks many of the excitements and rewards associated with customer contact.

TAILORED EDUCATION PROGRAMS

In the best service companies internal training programs fulfill a precise and well-understood purpose related to the total business situation and strategy of the company. *Operational* needs at the various levels will have been analyzed and programs designed to meet them. Difficult interface areas between different categories of personnel, different functional and regional departments, and different organizational levels will have been studied and programs and workgroups composed to improve the relevant contacts and to create a holistic, interfunctional, and interdepartmental understanding of business problems and operational procedures. Programs are uncompromisingly business-oriented, aiming to produce better service and productivity and having job satisfaction and motivation as intermediary variables.

Training programs sometimes have to be regarded in a *strategic* rather than primarily an operational light. A large innovative company in the insurance field, which has grown rapidly as a result of acquisitions and which has developed services that are far more advanced and complex than they were only a few years ago, has used an educational program as one of the main ways of "unfreezing" established structures, achieving interunit communication and a harmony of values and culture, and promoting new "role models" adapted to the radically altered business situation. Such new educational programs will also effectively create a new image of the company directed toward new groups of employees, thus making it easier to implement the new or modified personnel ideas necessary to a different business orientation.

Thus it is not only the operational issues that must be carefully analyzed before an educational program is launched. It is also necesssary to consider factors such as the current stage of development in the industry and in the specific company, as well as the overall service management system of the company. Educational programs are only one of the many tools with which management can make an impact on the organization, and the programs must be thoroughly understood within that total context.

FOLLOW-UP AND REINFORCEMENT

Providing people with education (which perhaps has an immensely exciting impact on them) and then simply forgetting about them may result in a serious backlash. Thus, another feature of the appropriate context for an educational program concerns what happens to the people who have gone through it. Obviously we could say that training should continue and that the programs should be renewed, but that may not be enough.

A crucial concept is *reinforcement*. Some companies and consultants who have specialized in running educational programs make a point of literally measuring at regular intervals the behavioral effect on the people who have taken the courses, in order to discover what kind of reinforcement will have to be applied: perhaps reward systems favoring the desired behavior patterns, or regular feedback on individual performance, group performance, and company performance (in terms of relevant variables such as growth, profit, and service quality). Other reinforcement mechanisms may involve the education of supervisors, meetings and "tours" by senior executives which include question-and-answer sessions, or frequent videotaped programs stressing the required values and behavior. One large company established a pattern whereby "dilemmas" were exposed and former course participants were asked to say what they would do. Or, after the course is over, participants might be given the chance to join interfunctional workgroups dealing with specific problems or with general issues such as "How can we improve the quality of our service to customer category X?" And there are many other possibilities.

JOB DESIGN AND ROLE DESIGN

Effective service delivery systems are characterized by a good "fit" between the special needs and motivations of particular employee target groups and the special features of the job in question. The relationship works in both directions, and the fit may be achieved either by changing recruitment strategies or by changing the role of the job, or both.

Where motivation is lacking and people are not developing, it is always worth investigating whether jobs and roles can be redesigned to make them more interesting and enriching to the employee. To be rewarding and attractive, jobs should contain the possibility of situations in which the employee can learn, for example interesting contact work with clients or the chance to work with knowledgeable seniors.

A related concept is that of role models. In good service companies there will almost always be a clear idea of "the model employee" for different types of jobs, the employee who lives up to the specified criteria necessary to do a good job and therefore to achieve success. In the case of the insurance company mentioned above, it proved very difficult to achieve any understanding of the new strategy throughout the company until an easily understood "new role model" evolved which could be communicated to people. In fact, it also had to be shown that people corresponding to the new role models did exist, or could be developed, before the strategy became credible.

CAREER DESIGN

The career problem in service organizations may not be very different in principle from the corresponding problem in other organizations, but it is usually accentuated. Service jobs are often intensive; they involve a lot of customer contact, which means that they may be very rewarding or very wearing for the employee and they are often both at the same time.

A special problem concerns the "beautiful exit." Something should be done about peo-ple who find themselves in a trap as regards their own personal development. We have come across many companies in which individual people or whole categories have become almost indispensable to the operation; they are thus kept in their jobs, although their personal development would really benefit from a change (and although in some cases the wellbeing of the company seems dangerously dependent on unmotivated but apparently indispensable employee groups).

The analysis of successful and unsuccessful internal recruitment policies and ensuing careers is usually a rewarding exercise, from which many conclusions can be drawn about career and role design.

PERSONNEL—SUMMARY

The most important thing that can be said about personnel in service companies is probably that personnel policy can never be regarded as an auxiliary or merely supportive function. For top management it is a crucial strategic issue. It is hard to conceive of a successful service business manager—much less an entrepreneur or innovator—who is uninterested in personnel matters. Even minor questions related to personnel policy are usually vital to the service business, and the way they are treated and the location of responsibility for human resources management in the organization should reflect their importance.

REFERENCES

ROSENBAUM, B. L., 1982, *How to Motivate Today's Worker*, New York: McGraw-Hill.

SCHNEIDER, BENJAMIN, 1980, *The Service Organization: Climate Is Crucial*, New York: AMACOM.

A Better Way to Select Service Employees: Video-Assisted Testing

CASEY JONES
THOMAS A. DECOTIIS

The famous hotelier Ellsworth Statler recognized the problem of finding guest-oriented employees decades ago, when he advised his managers to "hire only good-natured people." Indeed, one of the ways to ensure a service-oriented staff is to select people who are guest-oriented in the first place. This article tells of a new personnel-testing technique in which prospective employees are exposed to videotaped situations simulating job demands to which they might be exposed in real life.

Service quality in a hotel or restaurant depends absolutely on the ability of an operation's employees to deal graciously with guests in all situations. Topnotch employees have guest-contact skills—a complex mixture of courtesy, communication (particularly listening), response to guest needs, good judgment, and teamwork. The problem for managers is to select employees whose basic abilities can be developed into appropriate guest-contact skills. In this article, we will explain a video-based employee-selection technique to help hotel managers hire people suited to guest-contact positions.

Useless Tests

The traditional personnel-selection tests used by many hoteliers are essentially useless for determining which employees would be best for guest-contact positions. Such familiar techniques as interviews and reference checks lack validity for predicting job performance.[1] This is particularly true for such

[1]R.D. Arvey and J.E. Campion, "The Employment Interview: A Summary and Review of Recent Research," *Personnel Psychology*, **35** (1982), pp. 281–322.

"soft" aspects of a job as interpersonal or customer contact.[2] But customer skills are critical to successful job performance in the hospitality industry. What hotel and restaurant managers need is a way to identify job applicants who have the proper skills and aptitudes. Such a system must work even in the case of a soon-to-be-opened hotel, when management might screen hundreds or thousands of job applicants in a short time.

New Approach

Work sampling, a new approach to personnel selection, is one way to choose service-oriented employees. As the name implies, work sampling tests employees by presenting them with situations simulating the actual job. Work sampling is more likely to result in successful hiring decisions than such other selection techniques as the employment interview.[3] Moreover, work sampling conforms to current legal guidelines for employment tests. While work-sample testing is often expensive and time-consuming, the technique's accuracy in the selection of high-performance employees may well justify the effort and expense required.

Working with a major hotel company, we developed a *video-based* work-sample test for the selection of hotel guest-contact employees. The idea was to develop a valid test for selecting service-oriented employees that could be administered easily to large numbers of applicants and be scored quickly.

ADVANTAGES OF VIDEO

Video testing is a novel approach to employee selection in the hospitality industry, where interviews and reference checks are the most common methods used to screen job candidates. While the use of video for employee selection is new to the hotel industry, video has been used in other industries (e.g., communications, banking) to provide applicants with realistic job previews and to orient new employees.

The advantages of using video in hiring stem from its unique ability to expose a person quickly to a variety of verbal and visual cues. Such exposure is not possible with other employee-selection techniques, including written work-sampling tests, for the following reasons. First, video can expose job applicants to a broad range of guest-relations situations—for example, dealing with unreasonably demanding guests, handling angry or intoxicated guests, or responding to unwanted personal or sexual advances by guests. Second, the visual and auditory aspects of video depict a situation in a realistic fashion. The applicant hears the actual words exchanged by individuals, notes voice inflections, sees facial expressions, body language, and the physical environment, and observes nearby conversations and activities. In fact, by realistically presenting job demands, a video test not only allows the employer to evaluate prospective employees, but also serves as a "self-screening" device for applicants who may find they are not suited to the work. Third, applicants for whom English is a second language are less handicapped by video tests than by written tests, because they can both see and hear the test problem.

CLASSIC DEVELOPMENT

We followed the four classic steps of test development in designing the prototype video test—namely, job analysis, criterion development, test construction, and test validation. A management and technical review panel composed of company employees assisted us in the development of the video tests.[4] In addition to providing technical in-

[2]H.G. Heneman, D.P. Schwab, J.A. Fosum, and L.D. Dyer, *Personnel/Human Resource Management* (Homewood, IL: Richard D. Irwin, 1983).

[3]G.F. Dreher and P.R. Sackett, *Perspectives on Employee Staffing and Selection* (Homewood, IL: Richard D. Irwin, 1983).

[4]The panel comprised a corporate vice president, two general managers of hotel properties, the corporate director of human resources, the corporate director of rooms, and the corporate director of food and beverage.

put, panel members coordinated support from individual hotel properties.

Job Analysis

The first phase of the project involved analyzing guest-contact jobs to determine the relative importance of the elements of each job and to define in operational terms the dimensions constituting the job. For these purposes and for the subsequent pretesting and validation study, we studied three hotels operating in three major metropolitan areas. The selection of hotels was made primarily on the basis of differences in racial and ethnic representation among employees and the geographic location of the three properties.

We interviewed 61 employees at the three hotels and surveyed members of the management and technical review panel to gather job information. We asked everyone to list specific "critical incidents" that demonstrated job competence. In this way, we were able to identify the most typical and most difficult guest-service situations and the interpersonal skills required to perform appropriately and gracefully in each of the situations.

Based on the compilation of critical skills, we administered a job-analysis questionnaire to a sample of 318 guest-contact employees at the three hotels (32 percent of all guest-contact employees). The employees rated the relative importance of each job element on a six-point scale.

From this analysis, we identified 14 guest-contact jobs for which we would design the video-selection test: food and beverage server, cocktail server, front-office agent, reservation agent, garage attendant, banquet server, telephone operator, luggage attendant, bartender, guest-room server, room-service order taker, greeter, valet parker, and door attendant. We dropped from consideration one important job, housekeeper, because the job analysis showed that guest contact is a relatively minor part of that job.

Criterion

Not surprisingly, the job analysis determined that the most important performance criterion for all guest-contact jobs was guest relations. Based on the job analysis and the input of the review panel, we defined the guest-relations criterion as follows:

Ensuring the satisfaction and security of guests, believing in the integrity of guests, working cooperatively with others to serve guests, working for guests' pleasure and positive experiences (not the convenience of the hotel), and accepting responsibility for one's actions.

TABLE 1
Behavioral Definition of Responsiveness to Guest Needs

The employee:

1. Observes guests closely for "body language" that may indicate needs or problems.
2. Listens carefully to what the guest says and remembers essential information.
3. Asks questions courteously to identify or clarify guest needs.
4. Listens objectively to guest complaints.
5. Neutralizes irate guests without personalizing or worsening the conflict.
6. Assumes personal responsibility for meeting guests' needs or solving guests' problems and follows through promptly.
7. Offers alternative solutions to guests' problems.
8. Exhibits a positive, "can-do" attitude.
9. Accepts criticism constructively, apologizes, and takes immediate corrective action.
10. Responds readily to requests for service that are outside of the employee's department or area of responsibility.
11. Focuses on guest needs or problems and avoids offering excuses for poor service.
12. Responds negatively but diplomatically to requests for service that are clearly contrary to company policy.
13. Tries to make each guest feel that services are provided equitably and in a personalized manner.
14. Attempts to comply with unusual requests within the service capability and policy of the hotel.
15. Informs guests in advance if service is going to be delayed.
16. Assumes personal responsibility for correcting the hotel's mistakes.
17. Anticipates guest needs and offers to help before being asked.
18. Acquires familiarity with nonhotel facilities (e.g., tourist spots, night life, shopping, transportation, and cultural or recreational facilities) to respond informatively to guest questions.

The criterion would be measured along the following six dimensions of job performance:

- Courteousness to guests,
- Responsiveness to guests' needs,
- Sales of hotel services,
- Cooperation with other employees,
- Belief in guest integrity, and
- Display of good judgment.

The performance elements of each of these dimensions were defined in behavioral terms. As an example, the behavioral elements defining responsiveness to guests' needs are shown in Table 1.

The final step in developing the guest-relations criterion was to design an instrument supervisors could use to rate employees' performance in guest relations. This survey instrument was designed specifically for the development of the video tests. (It was not a formal performance appraisal.) The results of this survey showed no significant score differences when employees were sorted according to race or sex.

VIDEO PRODUCTION

The guest-relations criterion and performance dimensions formed the foundation for 40 simulated guest-service situations used in the video test. To begin with, employees' recollections of critical incidents were used as the basis of rough scripts for each of the test situations. The rough script consisted of written scenarios describing an employee's interaction with a guest in a given situation. Each script described guest and employee behavior, and then presented four possible employee reactions to the guest's behavior. After a detailed review by the management and technical review panel, each script was written in final form, fully setting the scene and specifying dialogue, actions, physical setting, props, and voice-over narration.

Lights, Camera, Action

Hotel employees played all parts in the video production. The workers also became on-location consultants whenever there was a question of realism in the setting or acting.

TABLE 2

Three Video Scenarios

Situation 1:

The scene is the front desk, where a single clerk is on duty, checking out a guest. Several other guests are waiting in line to check out. Suddenly another guest rushes to the desk and says, "Hey, I'm going to miss my plane. I need to check out right now, or I'm going to miss it." The frame freezes. The clerk should:

A: *Ask the people in line if it's okay to check the guest out ahead of them.*
B: *Say, "I'm sorry, sir, but I'll get to you as soon as I finish with Mr. Steinberg, here."*
C: *Say, "Yes, sir, right away."*
D: *Look for a supervisor.*

Action B is the best. It acknowledges the guest's special need, but allows the clerk to continue serving the guest who is already at the head of the line (and may also have a time problem). Action A would shift the problem to the other guests, and if one of them objected, an embarrassing situation would arise. Action C would be viewed as extremely inconsiderate to the guests in line and the guest being served. Action D is a last resort; supervisors should be called for help only in very difficult situations.

TABLE 2

(Continued)

Situation 2:

The scene is the front door, where a single door attendant is on duty. A guest approaches the attendant and says, "Hi. I'm looking for a good restaurant. Can you recommend one?" The frame freezes. The door attendant should:

A: *Give only the names of restaurants in the hotel.*

B: *Give the names of good restaurants nearby the hotel.*

C: *Ask the guest to check with the front desk.*

D: *Tell about the hotel's own restaurants, and then give names of other restaurants.*

Action D is the best. It helps to sell the hotel's services, while responding fully to the guest's specific request for a good restaurant. Action A is self-serving and is not responsive to the guest's needs. Action B fails to sell the hotel's services. Action C merely shunts the guest to another employee.

Situation 3:

The scene is the hotel valet-parking area, where two valet parkers are on duty. When a male guest approaches, one of the valet parkers says, "Good afternoon, sir, may we get your car for you?" The guest responds, "Yeah, get my car, boys." One parker leaves to get the car; the other exchanges small talk with the guest. During the conversation, the parker notices that the guest is intoxicated.

Valet parker: Staying in the hotel with us, sir?

Guest: Nope. Came for lunch, did a little business, and then did a little drinkin'.

VP: Did you come with anyone today, sir?

G: Nope. Came alone.

VP: Are you feeling all right, sir?

G (Resentfully): Of course I'm feeling fine. How are you feeling?

VP: I'm fine, too. It's just that I wonder if you should be driving today.

G: I don't care what you think. Just do your job and get my car.

At this point, the other valet parker has brought the car around. The guest is about to enter the car, as the frame freezes. The valet parker should:

A: Offer to drive the man.

B: Call hotel security.

C: Remove the keys from the car, and then call hotel security.

D: Let the man have his car.

Action C is best. The man is effectively and tactfully prevented from driving. This prevents a possible accident, the liability for which would fall upon the guest and ultimately upon the hotel. With the keys in hand, the valet parkers could suggest a taxi or offer a room. (It would have been better if they were more observant to begin with and never brought out the car.) Action B would probably take too long to prevent the man from driving. Action A is impractical, but it would be better than action D, which is the worst of all.

All the scenes were shot in a hotel during off-peak times, using a single camera (Sony BetaCam). The raw tape then required further studio editing on one-inch videotape that permitted top-quality reproduction onto cassettes.

In its final form, each test situation starts with an introduction by a narrator, who explains what the job candidate will see. After the enactment is presented, the prospective employee chooses among four possible responses, which appear on the screen while they are read by the narrator. Table 2 presents three test examples, together with the correct answers and the rationale for those answers.

A major concern in developing the test was that it be understood even by applicants with less than a high-school education, with poor reading skills, and for whom English is a second language. As the examples in Table 2 illustrate, the test enactments avoid situations requiring specific job experience, knowledge of policies and procedures, or situations that might be culturally or sexually biased. The test portrays minorities, for instance, in approximate proportion to their representation in the employee population, and acting in both positive and negative roles.

VALIDITY

The test's validity as a predictor of job performance was established through a concurrent validity study. The test was administered to representative samples of guest-contact employees, while their supervisors concurrently rated the employees' skills on the guest-relations criterion. The raters, who had no knowledge of the employees' test scores, used a rating instrument designed specifically for this test-development project. (The employees and their supervisors knew that neither the test nor the ratings would be made a part of the permanent record of the employee or affect his or her standing with the company.)

The resulting test score for each employee was correlated with his or her performance rating to determine the degree of association between the test and the guest-relations criterion. These correlations were statistically significant for most of the 14 jobs (see Table 3). Additional validity data are being collected for the other jobs. The jobs that involve the greatest degree of guest contact received the highest validity scores.

The overall validity of the test (0.38, $p<.001$) puts it in the top rank of personnel tests for guest-contact employees. The validity scores are uncorrected for measurement errors, and when this correction is made, the test validity increases greatly (to 0.55), far exceeding the validity of most tests used for personnel selection. Even uncorrected, the validity score of the video test exceeds that

TABLE 3
Guest-Contact Jobs Suited to Video Testing*

Job	Validity Coefficient
Recreation aide	.71
Door attendant	.60
Food and beverage server	.50
Cocktail server	.42
Bartender	.42
Front-office agent	.40
Reservation agent	.37
Garage attendant	.37
Banquet server	.34
Telephone operator	.25
Luggage attendant	.16
All hotel jobs (average)	.38

*The validity of video testing was found to be statistically significant for the above jobs, which are listed in descending order of validity. The validity coefficient indicates the extent of validity for the video test. A perfect score is 1.00; a score of 0 would indicate no validity at all. The maximum validity of most personnel tests is about .20.

of most personnel-selection devices, particularly tests designed to assess traits or behavioral tendencies (whose validity rarely exceeds 0.20).

TEST PATTERN

After this pretesting, the video test was first used to hire guest-contact employees for a new, 420-room, full-service hotel. The test took approximately one hour to administer. (A subsequent revision has reduced the time to less than 40 minutes.) To administer the test, three video monitors were hooked to a videotape player. As many as 120 applicants were tested and scored in one hour.

TEST EFFECTIVENESS

Clearly the video test is valuable. It is an efficient and effective means for screening and hiring a large number of employees. The test is easy to administer and score, and it has been well received by managers and job applicants alike.

While the test avoids sex stereotypes associated with particular jobs, we did observe a difference in test scores for different racial groups. To correct this problem, we adjusted the "cut" score on the test, so that approximately the same proportion of applicants of various racial or ethnic backgrounds passed the test as applied for jobs. This adjustment accounts for variations in test-taking ability arising from cultural differences among various ethnic and racial groups. The modifications were required to avoid unfairness in employee selection, as mandated by federal law.

The effectiveness of the test is also shown by its usefulness in hiring employees who are superior in guest-contact jobs. An ideal personnel-selection test should bring in employees who are strong performers. As personnel-selection techniques improve, so should staff performance. The results of our tests confirmed our belief that the video test would allow the employer to select topnotch employees.

The key indicator of the test's effectiveness in actual use is the proportion of employees who meet or exceed the guest-relations performance standards in ratings by their supervisors. As a yardstick of comparison, this proportion in the original validity study (the "base rate") was 57 percent. We have conducted followup effectiveness studies at three hotel properties, one each in Denver, Orlando, and Washington, D.C. Of the employees selected with the help of the video test, supervisors rated between 73 and 88 percent as meeting or exceeding guest-relations performance standards.

PRODUCING YOUR OWN VIDEO

The favorable results of the pilot video test should encourage hospitality managers to use video tests. Some firms may want to develop video tests to fit their own business approach and operations. The test developed by the authors also can be used by any hotel com-

pany, provided its guest-contact jobs are substantially the same as those covered by this test. Companies interested in so doing should first administer a job-analysis survey in representative properties. If the guest-contact duties are similar, the test will probably be appropriate, according to the principle of validity generalization.[5]

Considerations

It took about six months and $150,000 to develop this video test and confirm its validity. Large organizations with in-house industrial psychologists and video-production facilities can probably cut production costs by using their own staff as consultants and by doing their own video shooting and editing. For organizations that want to do it themselves, here are some suggestions:

- For a validity study, select operating units that are representative in terms of both service demands and employees' racial or ethnic backgrounds.
- Brief unit managers fully on both the project's demands and the resources required. One of those resources is time. The time contributed to our test-development project totaled 1,594 person-hours, as shown in Table 4.

  Our on-site shooting took about 100 hours. The production crew consisted of a director, camera person, lighting specialist, audio technician, two talent coordinators, and two production assistants.
- Train your supervisors in personnel-rating techniques to minimize errors. Supervisors' ratings took up 181 hours (one-half hour for each test) of the 543 person-hours consumed by the validity test. In their first try, the supervisors were likely either to rate everyone in the middle or to be too lenient. After the supervisors were trained in performance ap-

---

[5]Validity generalization is the process of determining whether a selection procedure used by one organization is valid for another. Validity generalization is an increasingly accepted approach to adapting tests for use by several organizations, where job content is determined to be substantially the same. See: F.L. Schmidt, J.E. Hunter, and K. Pearlman, "Further Tests of the Schmidt-Hunter Bayesian Validity-Generalization Procedure," *Personnel Psychology*, 32, p. 262.

TABLE 4
Videotape Production Time Requirements

Job-analysis interviews:	61 employees @ 2 hours	122 hours
Job-analysis survey:	318 employees @ 0.5 hour	159 hours
Videotaping tests:	40 employees @ 15 hours	600 hours
Pretesting videotape:	113 employees @ 1.5 hours	170 hours (rounded)
Validity testing:	362 employees @ 1.5 hours	543 hours

praisal, their errors dropped in the second ratings.

AWARD-WINNING PERFORMANCE

The goal of personnel selection is to hire good employees at a reasonable cost. The value of good employees is incalculable. They are a major factor in guest satisfaction, and proper hiring and training practices are one answer to the question of how we can encourage the guest to come back again and again. A hotel-industry axiom states that when a guest has a good experience he or she tells no one, but when the experience is a bad one, the guest tells at least ten others—all of whom might have been potential customers.

Once an employee is hired, of course, his or her basic talent should be reinforced by strong orientation and training programs and by consistent management. But a good guest experience *starts* with a hiring decision, so it is worth the effort to make well-founded personnel decisions. Video testing is one way to improve those decisions.

Packaging
the Service Provider

MICHAEL R. SOLOMON

Major service businesses are beginning to resemble regional or national product brands. Packaging will thus become a more crucial aspect of the service mix. Unlike products, however, the actual service rendered is intangible; its attributes are embodied in the person delivering the service. This person must be correctly "packaged." The symbolic power of service apparel should be harnessed to increase the consumer's preference for the service brand, bolster employee morale by facilitating group cohesion, and serve as a vehicle for brand positioning and promotional strategies.

INTRODUCTION

The product tangibility will be judged in part by who offers it—not just who the vendor corporation is but also who the corporation's representative is. The vendor and the vendor's representative are both inextricably and inevitably part of the "product" that prospects must judge before they buy. The less tangible the generic product, the more powerfully and persistently the judgment about it gets shaped by the packaging—how it's presented, who presents it, and a lot's implied by metaphor, simile, symbol, and other surrogates for reality [Levitt, 1981: 97].

Services are different. The growing emphasis on service marketing has brought with it a recognition that basic, inherent properties of service delivery may pose unique challenges compared to the problems and solutions of traditional product marketing [Berry, 1980].

While many specific differences have been proposed in recent years, a common denominator is that people are simply harder to manage than are things. In contrast to packaged goods, *people* are the *product* which service marketers must sell. As such, the manager is faced with the challenge of transforming

The author would like to thank officials of The National Association of Uniform Manufacturers and Distributors for provision of market data. Reprinted from the *Service Industries Journal*, July 1986, by permission of the publishers, Frank Cass & Co. Ltd.

a collection of idiosyncratic units into a cohesive, homogeneous offering.

Does this dilemma *really* make services different? The answer, it will be argued, is *no*. True, certain logistical issues, such as inventory control, are certainly more problematic for the service manager. Overall, though, it is proposed that several of the fundamental issues confronting evolving service industries are actually quite similar to the problems faced by marketers of packaged goods. These problems center on the goal of implanting a bundle of subjective product attributes in the mind of the consumer. Regardless of its physical form—whether tangible product or intangible service—the offering must communicate an image to the consumer which is: (1) favorable; (2) consistent; and (3) unique. The evolution of systematic and strategic packaging and branding may be viewed as a central route to achieving these goals for manufacturers.

Although a bank transaction, bus ride or blood test does not appear to have much in common with a shirt, breakfast cereal or industrial pipe, the provider of these services has the same *raison d'être* as the manufacturer of these products: to entice the consumer to make a purchase which satisfies a need, to convince the consumer that this particular solution satisfies this need better than that of a competitor's, and to assure the consumer that this need will be satisfied the same way the next time it arises.

People-intensive businesses must thus concentrate on achieving three basic goals to offer a successful service: tangibility, consistency, and differentiation. Product marketers have long known that a major step toward fulfilling these three demands—of creating and perpetuating a desired *image*—is developing a sound packaging and branding strategy.

The same reasoning can be applied to service delivery. The presentation of the product is crucial—the only difference is that since the product is largely people, it must be people who are correctly packaged. The success or failure of an elaborate product marketing strategy can often be determined by how well the product sells itself at the point of purchase. In the same way, a company's service offering can rise or fall on the consumer's impression of, and confidence in, the employee rendering the service. Service quality is commensurate with the person delivering it. The company's image is only as good as the image communicated by each person interacting with the public. For this reason, management must use all available means to ensure that the service provider, both verbally and non-verbally, accurately communicates the company's attributes.

Service Apparel and Service Delivery

Like brand packaging, it is proposed that service apparel (for example, company uniforms) performs several vital functions for service delivery. Apparel affects the determination of how service quality is assessed, it implies consistency of service, and it differentiates the service provider from its competitors.[1]

The growth of the career apparel industry and its expansion into some service markets is evidence that managers are beginning to grasp the implications of the packaging of service personnel for service delivery. Although the primary role of service apparel has historically been for protection and convenience, even early adopters also recognized its promotional power. For example, postal workers in sixteenth-century Scotland wore their town emblems on their sleeves, and firemen in seventeenth-century England wore uniforms to boost morale and generate publicity. Today, more than 23 million Americans wear some type of career apparel (including uniforms) and the industry projects an annual dollar volume in all categories of $3.8 billion by the end of the decade. In addition to such traditional users as

---

[1]For a review, see Rebecca H. Holman, 1981, "Apparel as Communication," in Elizabeth C. Hirschman and Morris B. Holbrook (eds.), *Symbolic Consumer Behavior,* Ann Arbor: Association for Consumer Research, pp. 7–15, or Lawrence G. Rosenfeld and Timothy G. Plax, 1977, "Clothing as Communication," *Journal of Communication,* Vol. 27, pp. 24–31.

nurses, police officers, and the airline industry, large companies such as Hertz, McDonald's, and Coca-Cola have initiated extensive career apparel programs. Other large companies do not employ the service apparel concept, but may possess either written or implicit dress codes which create similar effects. For example, IBM was long known as "the white shirt company."

In the following sections, the benefits of "people packaging" for customers, employees, and managers will be amplified.

THE POTENCY OF APPAREL SYMBOLISM

> Because a service customer will, in part, judge the quality and nature of the service he is to purchase on the basis of outward appearance, the service business must not only be good, it must look good [Bessom, 1973: 14].

Product packages are designed to evoke a particular sensory or emotional reaction in the consumer.[2] Hopefully, this reaction is consistent with the image desired by the marketer. In the product arena, color and shape are two of the most evocative dimensions. They allow the consumer an effortless way to identify a product and form an evaluation of it.

Uniforms as Service Packages

In the service arena, clothing may well be the single most potent medium to communicate desirable service attributes. Researchers in a variety of disciplines have documented the communicative power of clothing. Psychologists have long been aware of the role of appearance in forming assumptions about a person's political views, ethnicity, religious

---

[2]Some research suggests that mere repeated exposure to an object which is initially evaluated neutrally increases feelings of liking and familiarity for that object, cf. Robert B. Zajonc, 1968, "Attitudinal Effects of Mere Exposure," *Journal of Personality and Social Psychology*, Vol. 8, Monograph, pp. 1–29.

affiliation, income, etc. Numerous studies have demonstrated that people assume well-dressed people to be more intelligent, hardworking, and socially attractive [Rosencranz, 1972]. More important in the present case, even when a person's clothing is not an accurate indicator of what qualities lie within, others respond to the person *as if* these qualities were present. Thus, a self-fulfilling prophecy is created. The current media and retailing emphasis on "dressing for success" affirms the strategic value of clothing for making impressions and getting results in the business world.

The Need for Evidence. The reliance on clothing cues to communicate image is especially warranted in service industries, where intangible product attributes are dominant. Since customers cannot actually see, touch, or taste a service, they must look elsewhere for "evidence" of service quality [Shostack, 1977]. Thus, it has been proposed that the need to supply *tangible evidence* during market positioning increases as the concreteness of the offering decreases. The marketer must essentially create a physical surrogate for the product [Levitt, 1981].

Sending a Message. Service apparel does double duty in communicating to the consumer. In addition to the usual denotative function played by clothing, the uniform serves as an emblem as well. That is, service apparel assumes the properties of the group it represents; it embodies the group's ideals and attributes. The uniform allows its wearer to transmit the dominant values of the company or organization. When properly executed, the message sent out by service apparel goes a long way toward the establishment of a proper image: the hygienic nurse, the brave soldier, the responsible bank teller. The communicative power of the uniform is perhaps most apparent when it works at cross purposes with the desired image. An accountant wearing a loud suit, a *maître d'hôtel* in jeans, or a female executive in an alluring dress will rarely inspire the trust required to carry out his/her duties. The individual is trying to communicate a certain image; his/her clothing stands as a tangible contradiction. A person who is not dressed for the part will not be able to play that part effectively [Solomon, 1983: 319–29]. Thus, one function of service apparel is to communicate the selling point(s) of the company, whether it be cleanliness, professionalism, safety, or just plain good taste.

Reducing Risk. A second, more immediate function is to reduce perceived risk. Since the consumer in a service setting often cannot physically inspect the product before purchase (for example, an airline flight is not bought on approval), there is greater wariness and less inclination to take a chance on an unknown quantity. To counteract this hesitancy, the uniform supplies credibility. It is a known quantity—recognizable and familiar to the consumer.

Another factor contributing to credibility is that the very presence of a uniform implies a coherent group structure [Joseph and Alex, 1977: 719–30]. The consumer can infer the existence of at least a two-step hierarchy in the organization—the wearer and his or her superior. The superior has granted the employee the right to wear the uniform. In so doing, the company has authorized the employee to act as its representative. It must, therefore, assume responsibility for the employee's behavior. The uniform thus assures the consumer that recourse is available should the need arise.

Ensuring Consistency. Service apparel serves another function as a branding mechanism—it facilitates consistency of service. In dealing with a service business, there is a strong possibility that the customer will in fact be served by several people. Fluctuations in performance quality are severe annoyances to service managers. These variations are also a source of confusion to the customer, who is faced with the task of piecing together a coherent picture of the organization from the jigsaw pieces to which he or she is exposed.

The continuity of the uniform can smooth over variations in service quality by providing a consistent picture of the service provider role, regardless of the individual who happens to occupy that role at any given time. This process is not necessarily superficial, since uniforms may actually contribute to the productivity and morale of service employees. As will be seen, the donning of a uniform may lead to more "uniform" performance in that role.

THE UNIFORM AS A UNIFIER

The survival of a group rests on its ability to exert control over the members who are needed to carry out its goals. Service businesses which rely heavily upon consistent and enthusiastic employee performance need to ensure that service providers are loyal to the goals of the organization. Such devotion is not always commonplace, and the quality of service suffers as a result—with substantial ramifications for customer loyalty. In retailing, for example, poor service has been found to be a leading source of consumer dissatisfaction with a store [Westbrook, 1981: 68 –85]. Service apparel is instrumental in identifying group members and in building group cohesion. It serves a number of adaptive functions which are highlighted below.

Socialization and Standardization

Most companies recognize the importance of indoctrination. It is vital that service employees learn the rules of the organization and become team players. This is especially important because when the employee joins the organization she or he may not have a clearly defined *pre-existing* role [Mills and Chase, 1983]. When some standardization of output is required, all players must to some degree internalize the company philosophy and leave their idiosyncratic ways outside the company gate. Soldiers, nuns, and doctors understand the importance of group socialization; it is no coincidence that the apparel of new recruits in each case is immediately standardized upon induction. Admission to the group is indicated symbolically by permission to don a uniform. Initiation allows the new member to think in terms of "we" rather than "they."

Rewards of Membership. After initiation, the member begins the climb up the group hierarchy. Changes in status are accompanied by changes in self-concept as the member advances from novice to veteran. This movement is accompanied by increasing internalization of company goals and reliance on the group for rewards. The uniform can play a major role in facilitating the employee's satisfaction with his mobility by symbolizing the change in status. The designation of rank in the military is one obvious example. As another, promotion from probationary status in the New York City Police Department is accompanied by a change from a grey uniform to a blue one. This change in status is referred to by the recruits as "moving up to the blues" [Joseph and Alex, 1977]. The reward function of the uniform is recognized by Xerox, which gives a company blazer to employees upon their completion of certain technical classes.

Control of Deviant Members. Conversely, since group members are easily identified, deviations from desired performance standards are more conspicuous and hence less likely. The employee is clearly playing only one role; this eliminates the confusion and poorer performance which may result from role ambiguity. A telling illustration is the recent change in uniform policy for pregnant American soldiers. At one time, expectant soldiers were permitted to wear civilian clothes once pregnancy was well advanced. The military, however, began to encounter discipline and morale problems as these servicewomen began to lose their identification with their soldier roles. The temporary return to civilian symbolism interfered with commitments to the organization. Maternity uniforms are now standard issue in the Air Force, Army, and Navy, as well as at US Air, Eastern Airlines, Hertz, Safeway, McDonald's, and the National Park Service.

The uniform allows the employee to filter out "noise" in his environment as he identifies more closely with the organization of which he is a component. Goals are clarified, and behavior leading to the attainment of those goals is made salient.

Management of Tension and Conflict. The employee providing service often represents the organization to its external environments. Since the employee interacts with both insiders (co-workers) and outsiders (customers and vendors), stresses arise from the performance of boundary activities. Such *boundary role persons* [Adams, 1976] experience the role strain which arises from exposure to two parties whose goals are often contradictory. The direct involvement of the customer in the production function renders the zones of authority between the customer and the employee more nebulous, which leads to organizational strain. Thus, there is the constant possibility that a boundary role person will begin to identify more with the needs of the customer at the expense of the organization, and group cohesion will be diluted.

The uniform can help to delineate more precisely the appropriate role boundaries and serve as a tacit reminder to employees of their primary allegiance (during business hours). The interface between firm and customer is thus crystallized. For example, Corning Glass and Eastman Kodak have outfitted their receptionists and tour guides in company uniforms, as they realize that these employees are outsiders' first contact point with the organization. Thus, the uniform clarifies the employees' role in the organization and communicates consistent role expectations to both the employee and the customer.

Practical Issues

A second set of conflicts that faces the employee which can be resolved by uniforms is more mundane but, perhaps, is equally important. These issues concern the practical problems of what to wear to work. First, economic problems are reduced because the uniform cuts the costs of maintaining a work wardrobe. Second, the uniform eliminates dress competition among employees. In many contexts, much energy is expended in fashion one-upmanship. A preoccupation with preening and showing-off can be distracting and divisive. Recently, uniforms were introduced in a New Jersey inner-city high school for just this reason. Students claimed that the continual contest among students to be the best-dressed sapped concentration in the classroom and eroded discipline [*The Record*, 1983].

Third, service apparel can act as a class equalizer. Differences in employees' income levels, backgrounds, and tastes will be hidden during working hours. Again, this homogenizing influence will be beneficial when the consensus-building manager wishes to accentuate group commonalities and downplay differences. Morale may be improved when the individuals are forged into a cohesive team with a common clothing code. This galvanizing effect was illustrated in the recent movie *The Longest Yard*, where a ragtag group of prisoners is dramatically transformed into a powerful football *team* immediately after receiving uniforms. Lessons learned from athletics on the role of team clothing in communicating cohesiveness and pride among players and fans can perhaps be fruitfully applied to the company "team."

DIFFERENTIATING THE SERVICE TEAM

Because a service tends to be intangible, consumers may find it difficult to choose among competing offerings. Service apparel provides a way to package an abstract concept and thus employ brand positioning strategies. Distinctive apparel makes the service stand out for the consumer. He or she can identify the firm and thus identify *with* it. This strategy will help to build patronage and customer loyalty. For example, the gold blazers worn by real estate agents in the Century 21 organization enable this service to be positioned as a national "brand." A recent Burger King advertisement depicts an employee sitting next to a McDonald's worker. The identities of the two companies are communicated only by the distinctive uniforms worn by each representative.

Repositioning

An organization also needs a mechanism to promote repositioning strategies. The phasing-in of a "new look" is a powerful way to reinforce changes for employees and customers. A restaurant with three locations in the Washington, D.C., area recently employed this strategy. A fourth unit was opened with a new decor which was somewhat more elegant than the other locations. The company adopted elegant uniforms to boost its public image and communicate the upgrading of its image to consumers.

Promotion

Finally, service apparel possesses untapped promotional potential as a distinctive corporate symbol. Company logos, colors, and themes can be extended across delivery and promotional systems. Some banks which employ MasterCard sales representatives dress them in orange and yellow outfits to coordinate with the colors of the charge card. Perhaps the most outstanding example of this strategy is Texaco's classic assurance to the customer that "You can trust your car to the man who wears the star."

CONCLUSION

The service industry appears to be following an evolutionary pattern similar to that of packaged goods in that production systems are becoming broader in scope and more routine. Service retailers are increasingly likely to be members of a chain rather than single-unit operations. This growth and added sophistication brings with it a tendency for service offerings to be marketed much like product brands. Whether it be McDonald's, Kaiser Permanente, or H&R Block, consumers are now often buying a "brand" when they choose a service provider. As this tendency continues, greater emphasis must be placed on packaging of competing service alternatives. Consumers are looking for service brands which communicate the proper image, which deliver consistent quality, and which stand out from other choices. Service apparel is an inexpensive, practical, and powerful way to satisfy these needs.

REFERENCES

ADAMS, J. STACY, 1976, "The Structure and Dynamics of Behavior in Organization Boundary Roles," in M.D. Dunnette (ed.), *Handbook of Industrial and Organizational Psychology*, Chicago: Rand McNally.

BERRY, LEONARD L., 1980, "Services Marketing is Different," *Business*, May–June.

BESSOM, RICHARD M., 1973, "Unique Aspects of Marketing Services," *Arizona Business Bulletin*, No. 9, November.

JOSEPH, NATHAN, AND NICHOLAS ALEX, 1977, "The Uniform: A Sociological Perspective," *American Journal of Sociology*, Vol. 7.

LEVITT, THEODORE, 1981, "Marketing Intangible Products and Product Intangibles," *Harvard Business Review*, May–June.

MILLS, PETER K., AND RICHARD B. CHASE, 1983, "Motivating the Client/Employee System as a Service Production Strategy," *The Academy of Management Review*.

The Record, 1983, "Eastsiders Dress for Success," 22 September, Bergen County, NJ.

ROSENCRANZ, MARY LOU, 1962, "Clothing Symbolism," *Journal of Home Economics*, Vol. 54, 18–22.

SHOSTACK, G. LYNN, 1977, "Human Evidence: A New Part of the Marketing Mix," *Bank Marketing*, March, 32–34.

SOLOMON, MICHAEL R., 1983, "The Role of Products as Social Stimuli: A Symbolic Interactionist Perspective," *Journal of Consumer Research*, Vol. 10, December.

WESTBROOK, ROBERT A., 1981, "Sources of Consumer Satisfaction with Retail Outlets," *Journal of Retailing*, Vol. 57, Fall.

Fixing People
as Well as Machines

GREGORY L. SCHULTZ

As competition for valuable service accounts heats up, vendors of high technology equipment are developing new strategies to keep customers "thinking positive" about service, and expanding the role of the service technician.

When the customer is the most ticked off, the first person he sees is the field service person.

—Michael Costello,
Field Service Manager, Kontec Service

Field Service representative John Smith is a top technician with ABC Computers. John can diagnose a problem, devise a solution, and implement that solution while blindfolded. Usually John arrives on the scene and performs his magic without a hitch: John does his job and leaves, and the ABC customer is happy because he knows that John gets the job done. But when a customer becomes irate and blames John for everything from promises made by sales to his leaky radiator, John doesn't know what to do. It isn't fair that he should be blamed for what isn't his fault. Besides, John is a top-notch tech, and that's what counts—that's what he's paid for. He isn't responsible for anything but service. So what does John do?

Customers are demanding better relationships with service vendors, and as competition for the larger chunks of the growing service market becomes hot and heavy, vendors are designing customer relations strategies that will help them capture a lion's share of the market.

As business and industry become more

Reprinted by permission of *Service Management* magazine, Vol. 2, No. 3, July/August 1985, pp. 28–31.

dependent on high-tech equipment and equipment operations are integrated, down time becomes more costly. This puts a strain on tempers and customer relations. When this happens, the ability to handle a DMM or socket wrench becomes almost secondary to the ability to handle an irate customer. At this point, when something has already gone wrong in the customer's eyes, the relationship between the customer and the vendor is particularly vulnerable. And with the cos of getting new customers reaching dizzyir heights, why risk an established account?

So now the vendor-customer relations! is at a crossroads. Can the field service r resentative restore the product *and* rest tate vital customer confidence in organization?

You don't have to be a genius to appreciate the value of maintaining loyal customers and positive word of mouth referrals. Key findings in a TARP survey (Technical Assistance Research Programs) indicated that consumers whose complaints had not been satisfactorily resolved told an average of 9–10 people of their experience, while consumers who were completely satisfied with complaint response told an average of 4–5 people. A negative reaction generated nearly twice the word-of-mouth experience activity as the satisfactory experience.

So the effect of John's reaction to the irritated customer has a much greater breadth than John—or his boss—may perceive. After all, when you hear a negative comment about a product it tends to stick with you. But if you hear a complimentary remark, you aren't necessarily convinced.

For this reason it is critical that service industry people (and anyone who wants to succeed, for that matter) be people-oriented as well as tool-oriented. Management must bear in mind that the field service representative is usually the only contact the customer has with a company after the sale.

MOVING TOWARD THE MULTI-DIMENSIONAL TECH

"We expect our techs not only to be technically competent, but also competent in cus-

tomer relations," says Roger Mayer, director of customer assurance at Carrier Air Conditioning. "Techs go through extensive training programs that include consumer relations, replacement sales, and business philosophy.

"The service technician must be multidimensional. He must be able to restore confidence in the product. If for any reason he does not, the customer will usually call us up."

Carrier also publishes an in-house bimonthly service news magazine. "This helps us to compare experiences," says Mayer, "and promote a good attitude among our techs."

So the basic formula appears simple: training to make techs aware of the importance of good customer relations. But what if you have 20,000 techs, and on an average day you get about 37,000 calls for service? This is the domain of Jake Carlin, staff manager for the field service organization at AT&T.

AT&T has a "circle of service system." This places the customer and technician at the center of the "circle." Surrounding the circle are the elements that support these people—the "spokes."

"This is a new operation," says Carlin. "It creates an identity for the tech with the customer and represents an ongoing relationship. It applies to all types of maintenance.

"In this way the tech is not just reacting to a problem but being proactive. Customers have been extremely supportive of the program.

"We train the technician not to just 'put-it-in-and-fix-it,' but to act as a problem solver for the client," says Mike Quigley, who is the staff manager for AT&T's education services in Denver. "We try to turn the relationship from a customer to a client relationship. Along with the responsibility of fixing the equipment is to know the client, know the client's business, and be aware of and be prepared to discuss problems that relate to our business."

CUSTOMER VERSUS CLIENT

What's the difference between a customer and a client?

"A customer would come to us and buy strictly in terms of price," says AT&T's Quigley. "A client perceives the overall value of the purchase—and the technician becomes a part of that value. It's like your relationship with your doctor. You don't go in and tell him how to treat you. You go in and say: 'Here are my symptoms, what is my problem?' We hope techs can fill this function.

"The first course in the tech training program is Basic Contact Skills," says Quigley. "Basic contact skills means having a plan before going on the premises as to how you are going to diffuse what may begin as anger from the client.

"We teach them that their job as a tech is to uncover their client's needs—and they may be hidden, or the client may not understand them. Then the tech needs to make a commitment to try to alleviate the client's problem, either through his own action or by putting the client in touch with the right people."

Quigley emphasizes the importance of a face-to-face meeting with the client every time a tech goes on a call. The client must understand the nature of the work, and must be satisfied with it.

Ken Breece, Field Service Manager for Sentinel Computer Systems, agrees: "As a third party servicer we have to maintain the highest degree of visibility to the customer. Our product is our people, so our people have to encompass our philosophy of satisfying the customer.

"Our training program includes communications skills, dealing with difficult people, and role playing. We videotape the role playing, play it back, and critique it. That way an engineer can see how he looks to the customer.

"My job is to make sure techs can not only take care of problems relating to hardware, but also answer other questions on the account. Defining the customer's problem is usually the biggest challenge," says Breece. "The customer usually hasn't defined his own problem, or doesn't understand it completely. He just feels 'Something is broke.' That's why communication skills are so important. Just a slight oversight in communication can cause a relatively minor problem to be blown into a super-big thing.

THE SERVICE CONSULTANT

"We are looking at service in a broader sense, as opposed to just fixing machines," says John Puccini, vice president of operations at Serviceland, an independent chain of PC servicers. Serviceland has recently converted its technical force from hardware technicians to "service consultants," following the industry's movement toward personalized, all-around service. The conversion was basically an expansion of the role of the technician, according to Puccini, into more customer service type functions.

"There is a level of customer, and I'm not talking about the *Fortune* 500 guy, but the user who has the computer and who bought it from someone who may be knowledgeable to a certain extent, but doesn't provide for his continued needs. But because the service guy is so visible, he is always asked the questions about hardware and software applications.

"Someone may call us with a problem and it may not even be a hardware related problem. He may literally have just run out of machine, or it could be something else. So we have formalized our ability to help them out.

"The ingredients that we add to our people to make them service consultants are training and resources. Most guys out fixing machines are fully capable of recommending solutions to their customer's problems. We are just expanding on that concept."

To a certain extent, Serviceland's consultants have become salesmen/technicians. "We train the technicians not in brand names but in particular applications to need," said Puccini. "We are saying to our customers 'if you have a need let us know, and if we can help you we will.' The point is I'm here to take care of the customer and not to try to talk him into buying anything he doesn't need.

"They also learn basic communications or selling skills, they're really the same thing: how to turn a request into action. Service people on the whole have an aversion to being called salesmen, so the hardest part of the whole concept was to be very clear to the technicians that we weren't trying to turn them into salesmen, just expanding their customer relations role.

"What really matters is the customer. Machines will come and go, we don't know whose will and whose won't. But if we have a customer, no matter what comes and goes he'll stay with us if we satisfy his needs."

MANAGING FOR SATISFACTION

One alternative to training technicians to spend their valuable time soothing the frayed nerves of red-faced customers (or clients): Customer relations specialists who are part of a team approach involving the technician and the customer service function.

"If I were running a service organization," says Dick Munn of the Ledgeway Group, a research organization with expertise in computer service, "I would give techs basic training in customer relations but not spend a whole lot of time. These guys are in short supply and the customer will be pleased when something is fixed correctly. If a guy gets a little snarly or doesn't comb his hair right that's less of an issue."

But Munn's solution is not extensive tech training in customer relations, but rather a separate front man from the service organization who says: "I'm managing your satisfaction. I'm sending out a heavyweight tech to take care of your problem."

"We found that when users really felt good about a customer service program it was because they felt their particular customer service person acted as much like their employee as a vendor employee. He was their advocate within the organization," Munn said.

It has become apparent, then, that the days of put-it-in-and-fix-it are gone. The customer relations function of service is intrinsic to the success of effective technical support, and customer service must be looked at as a much more tangible element of service. Responsibility may lie with the technician, or a customer service specialist, but there must be a high degree of contact and clear-cut strategies for dialogue with the client. Only then can companies begin to untangle the web of customer satisfaction.

Ten Service Workers
and Their Jobs

CHRISTOPHER H. LOVELOCK ET AL.[1]

*Service workers in a variety of industries talk about their jobs,
their backgrounds, and their interactions with customers, managers, and fellow workers.*

How often do users of a service get a chance
to interact with senior managers? Unless they
are VIPs, the answer is: rarely. Except
in professional service firms, most personal contact takes place with low-level
employees—receptionists, flight attendants,
service engineers, bank tellers, restaurant
servers, letter carriers, bus drivers, customer
service reps, and gas pump attendants. To
succeed in a service business, as one executive wrote, "you have to turn the organization chart upside down."

Since service personnel at the bottom of
the totem pole are often the major points of
contact between customers and the organization, the performance and demeanor of
these individuals can have a powerful effect
on the quality of service delivered.

A few companies require executives from
the head office to spend a certain amount
of time each year in the field, observing—
or even working—in service positions. There's
probably no better way to get a feel for the
nature of the demands placed on employees,
the variety of customer situations encountered, or the problems entailed in trying to
deliver good service.

Managers who are really effective in get-

The ten profiles in this chapter were prepared under the direction of Christopher H. Lovelock by
the following members of the Harvard MBA Class of 1984: Elizabeth Gans, Douglas MacKinney,
Jane R. Borthwick, Stephen Harper, David Harmuth, Jeffrey Duke, Merideth Durden Dolan, Lisa
M. Rakov, John Fess, and Gordon Wilson. Their contributions follow in the same sequence as their
names.

ting the best possible performance out of their employees take time to understand each individual's personal background, needs, and career aspirations. This chapter provides brief profiles of ten service employees, working in a variety of different customer contact jobs, in an attempt to portray both the people behind the jobs and the environments within which they try to deliver service. The names of the individuals profiled have been changed and, in a few instances, so have the names of the organizations they work for.

SHERRY—RESTAURANT WAITRESS

Sherry, a 22-year-old Ivy League graduate, works as a "waitron" at a new, chic little restaurant while applying to medical school. She prepares the restaurant for opening, greets customers seated at one of her seven tables, offers them beverages and explains specials, memorizes orders, delivers food, watches a customer's progress through drinks/salad in order to time the cook's preparation of the entree, anticipates a customer's need for water refills, etc., checks on the customer two or three times during a meal, delivers the bill without rushing the customer, and collects payment.

As stated in the menu, the restaurant's service concept is to provide "a dining experience prepared with quality ingredients and attention to presentation that comes from truly caring." The basic structure of Sherry's job supports this concept. Sherry's low wage rate ($2.00/hour) induces her to provide good service in order to earn good tips. Also, the job allows her the discretion necessary to personalize service and present an attitude of "caring." For example, she suggests her own unusual drink combinations, such as hot cider and saki. She can request rush or special orders, as long as she stays in the good graces of the cook. Her skill at personalizing service comes from her own intelligence and intuition rather than from training at the restaurant.

Difficulties Sherry has in performing as a caring waitron stem from her interactions with management, not with customers. One problem is the way management has at-

tempted to alter her personal style. A restaurant consultant that the owner-manager brought in to make operations more efficient has instructed her to sound more "professional" (e.g., "Say 'house special soup,' not 'regular soup' "). Interpreting his definition of professional to mean "less friendly," Sherry disagrees with his approach. She also resents his efforts to make her "sell" rather than respond to customers' wishes (she quotes him: "I don't care if she says she's on a diet; tempt her with the dessert tray anyway"). She feels that the manager penalizes her for not "selling" by unfairly assigning her to less lucrative shifts. Because of this, her loyalty has dwindled. Management's failure to communicate new performance standards clearly and in a positive framework, and the resultant perception of unfair treatment, may well contribute to the 100 percent turnover Sherry has observed in the last four months.

Sherry's enthusiasm for performing the job has also declined because the consultant-manager has introduced a less benevolent management style, eliminating many job benefits that were important to Sherry and to maintaining her sense of dignity in a service position. He has cut back on the quality of staff meals, no longer allows staff to take home leftovers, makes waitrons feel that they are being "watched," assigns prep tasks to specific waitrons (which has reduced cooperation and increased blame-shifting among waitrons), and relays customer compliments only in a qualified manner. While he complains about the staff's "negative vibes" driving customers away, he may himself be responsible for creating a colder atmosphere.

JOHN—MAILMAN

John works as a substitute mail carrier at the Arlington, Massachusetts, branch of the United States Postal Service. John began working for the Postal Service nine years ago, shortly after graduation from Kent State University with a B.S. After seven years working as a postal clerk, John applied to become a mail carrier. He had three days of classroom and on the job training and then began work as a substitute carrier two years ago.

The typical mail carrier progression is to start as a substitute carrier, advance to utility carrier, and then to regular carrier. Further career movement depends upon the initiative of the individual to apply for posted opportunities in other areas of the Postal Service. The roles of the substitute, utility, and regular carrier are identical except for route assignment. The regular carrier has his own route and delivers mail on five of the six delivery days each week. The utility carrier delivers mail for regular carriers on their respective days off. The substitute carrier fills in on any route as needed. Despite his substitute status, John usually delivers mail five days a week.

John begins work at 7:00 A.M. For the first two to three hours he sorts the mail for his route, sequencing it by street and house number and putting it in bundles. If the route is a "Park and Loop" route John will load the bundles into a Postal Service Jeep or Pinto and be on his way. On a "Park and Loop" route John parks and delivers the mail by foot, usually doing a loop around the block. On a "Walking" route, the mail bundles are delivered by a parcel truck driver to strategically located transfer boxes (those mailboxes painted olive drab) along the carrier's route. The "Walking" route requires good timing between the carrier and the truck driver so that when a carrier has completed one neighborhood the mail for the next neighborhood will be waiting at the transfer box.

The degree of customer contact on a route varies. With businesses, the mail is often delivered in person. Residential customers sometimes wait for their mail and thus also receive it personally. This is more likely the case for regular carriers who often know most of their customers and deliver the mail at a specified time each day. For "signature" mail (certified, registered, insured, special delivery, and express mail) a signature is required from the customer. A final source for customer contact is complaints, which vary widely but often involve not getting mail.

Safety, security, and customer contact are key operating issues for mail carriers. Dog bites and vehicular safety are the most important safety concerns. Dog spray is issued to mail carriers to protect them from bites, and monitoring and training help promote driving safety. Security procedures include signing out mailbox keys and signature mail each morning. Courtesy and neat public appearance are strongly encouraged and monitored.

John likes his job, primarily for the job security, good fringe benefits, and ease of relocation. John complained, though, that as a substitute carrier he was shoved around a bit and given undesirable routes. He also noted that the relationship between supervisor and employee was often one of unquestioned authority, not unlike the military. He attributed this relationship to the vast number of Vietnam veterans hired and to their highly proceduralized work rules. John also noted that mailmen often took a lot of unwarranted criticism from disgruntled customers. He felt more public image advertising might help.

ANNE—FLIGHT ATTENDANT

"I don't think of myself as a sex symbol or a servant, I am someone who knows how to open the door of a 747 in the dark, upside down, and under 30 feet of water."

Anne has been a Delta flight attendant for five years and is convinced she works for the best airline in the industry.

Training

Initially, FAs are trained for one month in service techniques (serving meals, interacting with passengers) and in first-aid and emergency procedures. They annually attend an FAA-mandated "Jet recurrent" program which focuses on aircraft modifications and updated emergency procedures.

Supervision

An FA's actions are always subject to close scrutiny and evaluation. In fact, only when she/he is out of uniform are her/his actions considered private. Evaluation comes from three sources: Delta, the FAA, and passengers. Flight pursers and supervisors check to ensure that Delta service and safety procedures are met. The FAA monitors safety requirements and issues fines for noncompliance. For example, failure to collect glasses prior to landing results in a $1,000 fine which must be paid by the FA personally. In addition to these formal checks, passengers, who view FAs as The Airline, provide constant evaluation through their letters. For each positive letter, an FA receives a tax-free flight, while six negative letters trigger a review. Anne feels there is every incentive to resolve problems quickly and diplomatically. These evaluations, however, are not reflected in compensation. All FAs receive pay increases based solely on seniority.

Career Development

According to Anne, slower advancement is the biggest problem facing FAs today. With the recent down-turn in the industry, turnover is slower and it is taking everyone much longer to achieve the rewards of seniority. Previously, new recruits spent 1–2 years "on call" before they could bid for a regular schedule. Now they must wait up to six years. Seniority translates into a higher salary and fewer and better working hours. FAs are not typically considered for management positions. Because a career track does not exist, the reward of seniority is the freedom to pursue further education, family, and small independent businesses.

Analysis

While passengers may view an FA as a glamorous waitress, the airline and the FAA insist that safety comes above all else. In fact, much of the friction on-board results from a lack of appreciation of the reasons behind many safety procedures. For example, while passengers may feel instructions to "place luggage firmly under the seat in front of you" are annoying, the possibility of a need to evacuate the aircraft necessitates a clear exit-way.

The public stereotype is partly due to the inherent limits of the job, the essence of which is to follow an established routine. Anne characterizes her job as "mindless." The challenge and opportunity for an FA to "show her/his stuff" is in emergencies which thankfully are infrequent. To more fully utilize FAs' capabilities, Delta has increasingly involved them in other airline activities. For example, Delta encourages FAs to suggest specific design modifications for aircraft which will increase comfort and safety. For example, a Delta FA suggested that Boeing place "L" shaped bars under aisle seats to prevent luggage from sliding into the passageway.

While Anne feels less challenged, she is committed to Delta because of steps the airline has taken to "serve" its employees better. Delta is the only airline that has never laid off an FA. Further, it is the only airline that allows FAs unlimited schedule swapping ability. Management also holds annual meetings to solicit employee suggestions. For Delta this has translated into stronger employee loyalty. For example, Delta FAs are willing to tidy airplanes themselves to ensure rapid turnaround, while other airline FAs would insist on waiting for cleaning crews. At the height of the recent recession, three Delta FAs initiated a movement to purchase a Boeing 767 as an expression of their commitment to the airline.

JANE—HOTEL DESK CLERK

As a front desk clerk during the morning shift (7:00 A.M. to 3:30 P.M.) at a first-class hotel in Washington, D.C., Jane spends about 80 percent of her time "checking out" hotel guests. The checkout procedure requires retrieving the guest's file from the computer, pulling the bill out of a file box and presenting it to the guest for verification, accepting payment, and recording the transaction on the computer file. The remaining 20 percent of Jane's time is spent cashiering (cashing checks or exchanging currency), posting charges (telephone, valet, etc.) to guests' bills, checking in guests, and

SERVICE AS PART OF MKTG MIX

answering inquiries. These latter tasks, however, do not begin until later in the morning. From 7:00 until 9:30 A.M., the front desk clerks rush to keep up with the deluge of checkouts. As the tempo slows to a leisurely pace, the variety of tasks expands.

Like the other clerks, Jane is young (mid-twenties) and has a high school education. She enjoys her work because she likes the guest contact and the perks, particularly the free meals at work and the free accommodations at affiliated hotels in other cities. Also, the glamor of the hotel business is attractive ("Last week, I checked in Tom Selleck!"). Still, the turnover rate of clerks is high. One source of frustration is the uncertainty of shift schedules. Often, the clerks know only one week in advance which days they must work and which days they have off. Another frustration is that the front desk clerk must deal regularly with complaints or problems—typically five to ten per day. These problems frequently pertain to departments in the hotel with which the clerk is unfamiliar. Nevertheless, the guests expect—and deserve—first-class treatment, so that even a seemingly minor problem must be remedied swiftly to ensure that the guests' expectations are met.

The clerks are trained in front desk operations by their shift supervisor for two weeks before actually going behind the desk. The operating procedures are tightly prescribed and each clerk's work is checked closely. It appears that the operating system is designed to minimize errors by extracting as much discretion as possible from the clerk function. For example, if a guest disputes a charge on a bill or wishes to check out after the specified checkout time, the clerk must obtain the supervisor's approval before entering any change into the computer. Ironically, no supervisor ever refuses such requests because of the risk of offending a guest. Since this approval process consumes "real time" with the guest and unnecessarily amplifies the guest's request, the discretional control is questionable. The apparent consequence is that the clerks depend entirely on supervisors to solve even the most simple problems. In effect, the current operating system fails to offer the promptness and efficiency that guests demand from the front desk.

BILL—ANSWERPHONE SPECIALIST

Dial 1-800-626-2000 and a voice will answer, "General Electric AnswerCenter. May I help you?" 24 hours a day, seven days a week. The Center is staffed in Louisville, Kentucky, by both technical specialists and trained generalists who can answer questions on virtually all GE consumer products and services. From prepurchase and selection through follow-up service and repairs, the staff is available to describe, explain or make referrals. In addition to reference manuals, specialists use computer terminals to call up full parts listings, operating instructions or listings of service centers.

Bill, a 26-year-old graduate of St. Lawrence University, has been an AnswerCenter specialist for 1½ years. Prior to taking the AnswerCenter position, he had worked at GE's Appliance Park in Customer Service. Because of his prior work experience at GE's Major Appliance Division he felt comfortable about the promotion to the Answer-Center. Upon joining the AnswerCenter he participated in a training program which provided instruction on GE's consumer products, telephone etiquette, and computer terminal operation. In addition to the initial training they have regular meetings explaining new materials, new products, recalls, and general company information. When asked why he left Major Appliances, Bill stated that the Answer-Center provided him with much more exposure to the Company's other consumer businesses as well as their respective marketing and sales groups.

In response to my queries about his fellow workers and supervisors, Bill described the environment.

Many people think we are just telephone operators. Contrary to this we have a philosophy that we are a hybrid group. We are a cross-breed of a sales/information counselor and a service advisor. Many of the specialists hold advanced degrees and have had some customer relation experience, such as myself. As a result, the AnswerCenter pays significantly higher salaries than operators receive, to attract and retain qualified people. We receive individual evaluations annually as do other GE personnel. However, we receive immediate feedback from our superiors and consumers, particularly if the lines are busy or consumers are on hold for more than a couple of minutes. Supervisors also receive computerized reports detailing telephone efficiency rates and follow-up calls generated by each specialist. The quality of our telephone conversations is also randomly monitored by our supervisors. All these measurement systems and standard procedures frightened me at first, however there is still lots of room for creativity. Let me explain. I receive hundreds of calls daily, not one of them is the same. I find the creativity in talking with the different consumers. For example, if the computer is slow (particularly during busy periods), I will ask the customer more information about the product or his usage patterns. Sometimes we even engage in a conversation about the weather.

Mondays tend to be the busiest days when we handle upwards of 7,000 calls. We use some regular part-time specialists during these times as well as in the afternoons. There is particular pressure during these periods to answer customer questions more quickly so that the next call may be handled. During these peaks we have had as much as a ten minute wait on our switching system. These busy periods can get quite hectic, particularly if I am unable to locate the correct information or provide an answer. In such cases, I usually seek advice from a specialist next to me or from a supervisor. If it appears that it will take too long or that I am unable to answer the question I advise the caller that I will call him back (at a slower time within 24 hours) or that someone who is better qualified to answer his question will call him back (Division Marketing within 72 hours). I usually prefer to take an extra minute or so to locate the information needed to answer the question while the consumer is on the phone. I often have difficulty getting a hold of the consumer on return calls, thus it takes more time.

CRAIG—REGISTERED NURSE

Craig is a registered nurse. He has worked for eight months as an RN, twelve months as an LPN, and twelve months as an orderly. He currently works forty hours a week during the hospital graveyard shift. Craig is a bright, extremely outgoing, compassionate individual who is dedicated to his work. He loves working with people of all walks of life, and enjoys helping individuals, both healthy and ill, to feel good about themselves and the predicaments in which they find themselves.

There are a number of factors that contribute to a nurse's success, but according to Craig, the most important is comforting the patient. This is manifested in medicating, cleaning, and feeding the patient, examining lab reports, and carrying out the attending physician's demands. As a nurse, Craig is the liaison between the physician and his patient, which necessitates the ability to effectively communicate with the physician, the patient, and other hospital staff. Such communication not only takes the form of orders and words of comfort; the nurse is also expected to not only know how a patient feels but why. Because the physician is rarely attending his patients during the early morning hours, the nurse's ability to diagnose a patient's immediate problems is of critical importance.

Nursing is not unlike other medical disciplines in that it is governed by a myriad of rules, regulations, and operating procedures. A majority of these prescribed procedures are itemized in hospital manuals. One's ability to adhere to these rules and regulations is in large part the basis for a quarterly performance appraisal conducted by Craig's supervisor, the floor nurse, who reports to a floor coordinator, who in turn reports to the Director of Nursing. The successful completion of one's tasks coupled with the requisite experience will enable one to progress through the ranks of nursing. According to Craig, progression to supervisory roles in specialty areas is based primarily on skill, while advancement to the position of floor supervisor is based largely on seniority.

When asked what he enjoys most about being a nurse, Craig expressed the satisfaction he derives from making people feel well. He said he also views nursing as an opportunity to continually develop his knowledge and understanding of the human body, and to figure out what causes his patients to ail. He also said the remuneration is excellent for only two years of schooling, although the disparity between what a nurse and a physician make is often discouraging given the amount of time the nurse spends with the patient. On the other side of the ledger, Craig said that it is tough being in the minority as a male nurse. This means receiving many of the physically demanding jobs, as well as the less desirable jobs related to serving male patients. However, Craig was quick to recognize the preferential treatment he often receives when it comes time for layoffs and advancement. Craig said he also disliked working with physicians in many situations. As a nurse working the graveyard shift, Craig often finds himself in a prisoner's dilemma: if he wakes the physician in response to a patient's request, he usually gets yelled at for not waiting until the morning; if he doesn't serve the patient's needs (which usually requires doctor approval), he stands the risk of getting yelled at. This he finds very frustrating. He also finds the charting of patients and shift work to be generally undesirable, although he recognizes that these are necessary elements of the job.

If he could bring about change, Craig would chart less and give nurses more authority, perhaps in the form of standing orders from the physician. This would allow him to spend more time with the patient, which he sees as his primary responsibility. He said it's frustrating to have to call a physician regarding something as simple as the administration of an aspirin.

SARAH—HOSPITAL TRAYGIRL

"Traygirls" are the lowest status workers on the hospital cafeteria staff. But by talking to any one of the four at Mariemont Hospital, you'd think it was an exclusive club.

"We come in together, we get dressed together, we eat together, and then we work hard together," says Sarah, a two-year veteran. "Oh yeah, we also go to school together." Sarah is part of a strong high school clique that works part time at the hospital during the school year and full time during the summer. They come in right after school daily and work with the seven other full-time cafeteria workers. They work quickly, noisily, and enthusiastically.

The job requires "setting up" certain types of food on to individual patient trays (e.g. "Mr. Johnson—Room 311—Low Salt"). Traygirls can ask one of the two cooks or three other cafeteria workers about which food type is right for which diet, but most traygirls are experienced and knowledgeable enough to work quickly and correctly. At the end of the line the "boss," the dietician, checks each tray. Then traygirls load the trays onto a huge mobile cart and begin another tray. When the cart is full, a traygirl volunteers to push it around the wards and deliver trays. When the cart is empty, she returns to the cafeteria to fill trays.

The two different tasks a traygirl performs are very different; setting up trays requires speed and accuracy, while delivering trays demands a slower, empathetic style. Yet, no distinction is made of the different skills involved, and the crucial selection about which traygirl delivers the trays is very ad hoc. This is unfortunate; not only are some traygirls clearly more suited to one task or the other, many of them also have *strong*, yet unrecognized, preferences about which job they want. So the hospital could have both higher levels of patient *and* employee satisfaction by recognizing the different jobs and letting traygirls volunteer in advance to push carts.

Another big problem with the traygirl job is that speed and efficiency are encouraged when delivering trays, but that is exactly the *opposite* of what the patients want. Patients' only contact with the cafeteria is the traygirls, and they want lavish service and personal attention—actions that primarily involve the traygirls' *time*. But traygirls are encouraged to rush through tray deliveries so they can get back to where the "real" work is done—inside the cafeteria.

"I'm one of the slowest deliverers," Sarah says. She seems proud. If there is an error or omission on a tray, she tells the patient, "I'll come back with it." Yet it is hard to explain to her friends on the clean-up crew just why, as she returns the empty cart to the room where they are madly cleaning up, she must now take a very few food items and disappear for half an hour.

BONNIE—BANK TELLER

Bonnie has been a teller at Barclay's Bank at the Bronxville branch for five years. While she enjoys her job most days, to her it is still "just a job," and from the end of the lunch crunch onward, she looks forward to "proving out" and going home.

Bonnie's daily routine begins with her arrival at 8 A.M. to the branch. She gets out her money tray and puts her receipts in order. The day begins with a buzz as people stop by to do their banking transactions on their way to work. From about 9:30 to 11:30 is a rather quiet period, and she has specific tasks that she performs, such as counting out the money in the night bags and filing checks. Around 11:30 A.M. peak lunch hour traffic begins. Bonnie is kept constantly busy, and her main objective is to keep the line of customers moving and complete transactions as quickly and accurately as possible. The traffic slows around 1 P.M. and she spends the next few hours handling a slower stream of customers and completing half-started transactions from rush hour. After the window closes, she begins the nightly task of "proving out"—accounting for all her receipts and disbursements for the day. This is the part of the job Bonnie likes least, and she states that it is like a daily performance appraisal on how well she's done for the day. If she doesn't prove out, she can spend hours tracking a mistake. "I feel like there's a lot of pressure from my boss to keep customers happy and not make them wait, but if I don't prove out at night, I regret that I hurried so much."

Critical skills for this position are the ability to count money quickly and accurately, a pleasant customer manner, and working as a team with fellow tellers. Because the peak hours are so hectic, this team cooperation is necessary to keep things flowing smoothly. It is important that they help each other with handling phone calls, exchanging money or obtaining information quickly.

There seem to be two types of tellers: the "career teller," who may be promoted to head teller but is generally content to stay at the current level, and the "mobility teller," who aspires to move on to a position on "the platform." The platform job has much more status attached to it and has less frenzied customer contact. Bonnie states that there is definitely a "WE/THEY" relationship between the tellers and platform assistants, but that they must learn to work effectively together despite their differences to better serve the bank customers. Bonnie feels that she doesn't have either the training or motivation to become a platform teller.

The job is very structured, and procedures for each transaction are very specific. The hours are regular and Bonnie likes being able to arrive home at 5:45 each night. Her lunch hour is a structured half hour and her daily duties are tightly prescribed. Overall, she feels that she is lucky to have this job because it is a "clean and respectable" workplace and she likes her fellow tellers.

Like McDonald's, this job's biggest problem area is managing the uneven traffic flows during the day. Bonnie's greatest frustration is not having the time to be accurate during peak hours, and being bored during slack hours. Rescheduling the lunch breaks may be one solution, so that all four tellers work during that peak time instead of only three. While this may meet with some initial resistance, it would give the tellers slightly longer lunch hours either later or earlier. Another way to ease the traffic would be to install ATM's to handle the more routine transactions. It would also leave the more challenging transactions to the tellers, and would require managers to hire more qualified entry-level tellers.

Another problem is maintaining a teamwork spirit among the tellers. Bonnie feels that she often competes with her peers to be the quickest or most accurate. A more balanced team of old, new, career, and mobility tellers would keep the group dynamic and ease strict peer competition. Finally, training is currently on-the-job with little formal instruction on use of machines or special transactions. A longer training program would mean slower initial start-up, but would result in fewer mistakes longer term.

BETH—TRAVEL AGENT

Beth is a retail "walk-in" travel agent for Crimson Travel Service. Walk-in customers wait up to 30 minutes (average 15) for a free agent, and require from two to sixty minutes of service. Three-quarters of the walk-in customers require only simple ticketing and reservation services, while the other quarter want more elaborate vacation planning. Anomalous situations, such as irate customers, or those who are demanding a refund, are referred to a supervisor. Crimson receives a fixed percentage commission on ticket sales, thus Crimson's success hinges on volume and efficiency. The travel business is characterized by a huge variety of operational procedures required to make bookings and by a high rate of change in these procedures—between one and two each day.

Beth is in her sixth year at Crimson, making her one of the more senior agents. Her job mirrors the variety of the business: she must master a wide variety of tasks, draw on a wide variety of information resources, and interract with customers who can be in widely varying states of mind. Tasks range from simple ticketing to design and arrangement of around-the-world tours. Information resources include travel guides and brochures as well as an on-line information system. The customer's state of mind can range from a newlywed couple planning a honeymoon, to someone in need of an air reservation to attend a funeral. Beth must know how to handle each of these situations and know what questions to ask to most efficiently handle each particular travel request. Crimson's cost and volume focus leads to some very strict procedural rules, but personally developed style is also important in handling the wide variety of situations. Prior to becoming an agent, Beth received six months of training at night while she worked at Crimson as a receptionist. Periodic ongoing

training covers major procedural changes and new-product offerings.

There are two particularly positive elements of Crimson's setup which deserve comment. The first is the on-line computer system which includes, in addition to airline reservation information, an internal bulletin system called "Star." Star is used to communicate—companywide and on an instantaneous basis—the many procedural changes which occur in the business. The system is also used to leverage the agents' experience, making particular agents' expertise available to all. The second element is the "buddy" system, which pairs agents sitting next to one another, formalizing coverage when one or the other is out. Using this system, agents tend to learn each other's style and particular customer circumstances so that when one agent is out the other doesn't need to start out "cold" with repeat customers. This leverages the style and expertise of the more experienced agents and speeds up the training of new agents.

There are a number of conflicts caused by differences between Crimson's business focus and what Beth finds most rewarding about her job. Beth feels most rewarded by travel opportunities and benefits, positive feedback from satisfied customers, recognition of her value as gained through experience, and being able to operate with minimal supervision. Crimson's low-cost focus tends to value lower-paid (newer) agents higher than the more experienced and expensive agents. This leads to high turnover, reducing the experience base. Turnover increases Beth's seniority, thus reducing the level of supervision, but it also causes her to spend undue time helping out the newer agents. The volume and efficiency focus keeps agents unusually busy, which they resist by slowing down. A focus on strict procedures also makes Crimson tend toward staffing with agents who are "trained by the book" rather than those who have developed their own particular style. Crimson's strong desire for scheduling efficiency sometimes causes agents to lose travel opportunities and free trips. Also, it seems that most feedback the agents receive is negative, including angry customers and supervisors who have detected a ticketing error (via a computerized monitoring and control system). Agents' appraisals define "good" as the lack of "bad" occurrences—an emphasis which stimulates Beth to achieve only minimum standards and no more. Finally, the Office Manager seems to concentrate on taking care of special customers rather than taking care of the employees. According to Beth, this leaves agents feeling quite detached from the company.

RICHARD—ELEMENTARY SCHOOL TEACHER

Spring Hill Day School is located on a wooded hill in a wealthy community west of Boston. It is small, with approximately 160 children spread over eight grades. In admissions policy and educational style, the school emphasizes a supportive atmosphere that is conducive to learning. Its students are intellectually above average but not elite; they are chosen just as much for being socially well-adjusted as for being bright. Spring Hill enjoys a strong reputation: it regularly places its graduates into prestigious preparatory schools, and it has a comfortable admissions waiting list. Similarly, there is a heavy demand for teaching positions at Spring Hill.

Richard will be leaving the school at the end of this school year. He is currently the Science Teacher: he teaches fourth and sixth grade science along with fourth grade reading and sixth grade math. He has his own classroom, which is well stocked with pictures of fish, a diagram of the human anatomy, jars of "mystery powders," windows on two sides, squeaky stools, and the largest rabbit this interviewer had ever seen.

Richard has been at Spring Hill for three years. Until this year, he was the third grade homeroom teacher. Before coming to Spring Hill, he taught third grade for three years at Dillingham, Driggs, and Mickel (DD&M), another local private school. Richard left DD&M because it was an "unfriendly place, very competitive, both the parents and the student body. It's hard to serve people you don't like. . . . I think that at Spring Hill, kids

get trained as better thinkers, because they can develop more confidence. They don't just have stuff thrown at them."

Although Richard enjoys Spring Hill's educational approach, he feels that it is now time to move on. A recent divorce makes his teacher's salary insufficient, and "frankly I'm just burned out." Possibilities for the future include graduate school in educational administration, teaching in England, or law school.

Richard's evaluation of his job has two sides: Spring Hill as a place for teachers, and the teaching profession in general. On the balance, he thinks highly of Spring Hill as a place for teachers. He has flexibility with his curriculum and "a nice bunch of kids." Faculty members have a serious decision-making role in hiring teachers and admitting students. Communication among faculty is reasonably good. He also thinks that the hiring is "cautious—and that's good."

On the other hand, the close parental involvement courted by the school can be a nuisance. For example, every Friday afternoon the entire school puts on a "sharing assembly" for the benefit of the parents—or, in Richard's view, for the "1950's PTA mothers." Beside taking enormous amounts of time away from academic work, these assemblies strike Richard as "cutesy." In a similar vein, the headmaster functions less as an educational leader than as a parent-pleaser. He almost never visits the classroom, and Richard has "no idea how he evaluates us." Spring Hill's low salaries are a drawback. Richard's current salary of $15,000 is only a little more than half what he could make in the Boston Public Schools. Then again, "if I were out for money, I wouldn't be in this business. They couldn't pay me enough to teach in the Boston Public Schools."

The teaching profession in general has some strong advantages. First, "It's a noble job. You feel like you are contributing as much to society as anybody could."At least at first, it is "stimulating to learn how people think." At a school like Spring Hill, "you get to work with good people," and the summer vacation is a real plus.

Why, then, do teachers burn out? A principal reason is the emotional intensity of the job: "If you are doing a good job, you've got to be draining your batteries." Also, "the capable ones resent the lack of professional status. You have to be incredibly dedicated and have a strong independent streak" to ignore the opinions of the rest of the world. Money is not a reason by itself, but it fits in with other reasons, both in signalling a lack of respect and in making teaching practically unaffordable as a career. Richard also mentioned the lack of a career track: "The only way to rise in teaching is to rise out of it; to administration, or out of education altogether." More than the lack of externally visible career progress, Richard feels the lack of an internal sense of change and personal learning. "I'm still doing essentially the same job I was doing six years ago. After a while it gets to be so much of a muchness. . . . You are about as good after three years as you'll ever be."

First National Bank

CHRISTOPHER H. LOVELOCK

A bank has expanded the nature of the teller's job. It now expects its tellers to help sell bank products, either directly or by referral, in addition to performing their operational tasks. But one of the best tellers at a large branch declines to engage in active selling. The branch manager wonders what action to take when the employee applies for promotion to head teller.

"I'm concerned about Karen," said Margaret Constanzo to David Reeves. The two bank officers were seated in Constanzo's office at the First National Bank's branch in Federal Square.

Ms. Costanzo was a vice president of the bank and manager of the Federal Square branch, the third largest in First National's 92-branch network. She was having an employee appraisal meeting with Reeves, customer service director at the branch. Mr. Reeves was responsible for the customer service department, which coordinated the activities of the customer service representatives (formerly known as tellers) and the customer assistance representatives (formerly known as new accounts assistants).

Costanzo and Reeves were discussing Karen Mitchell, a 24-year-old customer service rep, who had applied for the soon-to-be vacant position of Head CSR. Mitchell had been with the bank since graduating from junior college with an associate in arts degree three and a half years earlier. She had applied for the position of what was then called "head teller" a year earlier, but the job had gone to a candidate with more seniority. Now, that individual was leaving—his wife had been transferred to a new job in another city—and the position was once again open.

Both Costanzo and Reeves were agreed that, against all criteria used in the past, Karen Mitchell would have been the obvious choice for head teller. She was both fast and accurate in her work, presented a smart and professional appearance, and was well liked by customers and her follow CSRs. However, the nature of the teller's job had been significantly revised within the past year to add a stronger marketing component. CSRs were now expected to offer polite suggestions that customers use automatic teller machines for simple transactions. They were also required to stimulate customer interest in the broadening array of financial services offered by the bank. "The problem with Karen," as Reeves put it, "is that she simply refuses to sell."

THE NEW FOCUS ON CUSTOMER SERVICE AT THE FIRST

Although it was the largest bank in the state, the "First" had historically focused on corporate business and its share of the retail consumer banking business had declined in the face of aggressive competition from other financial institutions. Three years earlier, the board of directors had appointed a new CEO and given him the mandate of developing a stronger consumer orientation at the retail level. The goal was to seize the initiative in marketing the ever increasing array of financial services now available to retail customers. The new CEO's strategy, after putting in place a new management team, was to begin by ordering an expansion and speed-up of the First's investment in electronic delivery systems. The bank had tripled the number of automatic teller machines in its branches and was engaged in an active branch renovation program. The First also joined a regional ATM network, which boasted free-standing 24-hour booths at shopping centers, airports, and other high-traffic locations.

New financial products had been introduced at a rapid rate. But the bank found that existing platform staff—known as new accounts assistants—were ill equipped to sell these services, because of lack of product knowledge and inadequate training in selling skills. "The problem," recalled Ms. Costanzo, "was that they were so used to waiting for a customer to approach them with a specific request, such as a mortgage or car loan, that it was hard to get them to take a more proactive approach that involved actively probing for customer needs. Their whole job seemed to revolve around filling out forms."

As the automation program proceeded, the mix of activities performed by the tellers started to change. A growing number of customers began to use automatic teller machines for cash withdrawals and deposits, as well as for requesting account balances. The ATMs at the Federal Square branch had the highest utilization of any of the First's branches, reflecting the large number of students and young professionals served at that location. Costanzo noted that customers who were older or less well-educated seemed to prefer being served by "a real person rather than a machine."

A year earlier, the head office had selected three branches, including Federal Square, as test sites for a new customer service program. As part of the branch renovation program, each of these three branches had previously been remodeled to include no less than four ATMs (Federal Square had five), a customer service desk near the entrance, and two electronic information terminals that customers could activate to obtain information on a variety of bank services. The teller stations were redesigned to provide two levels of service: an express station for simple deposits and for cashing of approved checks, and regular stations for the full array of services provided by tellers. The number of stations open at a given time was varied to reflect the volume of anticipated business. Finally, the platform area in each branch was reconstructed to create what the architect described as "a friendly yet professional appearance."

With the new environment came new training programs and new job titles: customer assistance representatives (for the platform staff) and customer service representatives (for the tellers). The training programs for each group included sessions designed to familiarize CARs and CSRs with new products (the former received more extensive training in this area). All staff members in customer service positions participated in sessions designed to improve their professional image: wardrobes, accessories, makeup for women, and interactions with customers were all discussed. Said the trainer: "Remember, people's money is too important to entrust to someone who doesn't look and act the part!" CARs were instructed to rise from their seats and shake hands with customers. All employees working where they could be seen by customers were ordered to refrain from smoking, drinking soda, and chewing gum on the job.

Although First National management anticipated that most of the increased emphasis on selling would fall to the CARs, they also foresaw a limited selling role for the customer service reps, who would be expected to mention various products and facilities offered by the bank as they served customers at the teller window.

For instance, if a customer happened to mention a vacation, the CSR was expected to offer travelers' checks; if the customer complained about bounced checks, the CSR should suggest speaking to a CAR about opening a personal line of credit that would provide an "automatic overdraft"; or if the customer mentioned investments, the CSR should refer him or her to a CAR who could provide information on money market accounts, certificates of deposit, or the First's discount brokerage service.

In an effort to motivate CSRs at the three test branches to sell specific financial products, the bank experimented with various incentive programs. The first involved cash bonuses for referrals to CARs that resulted in sale of specific products. During a one-month period CSRs were offered a $50 bonus for each referral leading to a customer's opening a personal line of credit account. Eight such bonuses were paid at Federal Square, with three each going to just two of the seven CSRs. However, this program was not renewed since it was felt that there were other, more cost-effective means of marketing this product.

Another promotion followed and was based upon allocating credits to the CSRs for successful referrals. The value of the credit varied according to the nature of the product—for instance, a cash machine card was worth 500 credits—and accumulated credits could be exchanged for merchandise gifts. This program was deemed ineffective and discontinued after three months. The basic problem seemed to be that the value of the gifts was too low in relation to the amount of effort required.

Other problems with these promotional schemes included lack of product knowledge on the part of the CSRs and time pressures when many customers were waiting in line to be served.

The bank had next turned to an approach which, in David Reeves's words, "used the stick rather than the carrot." All CSRs had traditionally been evaluated half-yearly on a variety of criteria, including accuracy, speed, quality of interactions with customers, punctuality of arrival for work, and appearance. The evaluation process assigned a maximum number of points to each criterion, with accuracy and speed being the most heavily weighted. The number of points scored by each CSR had a direct impact on merit pay raises and on selection for promotion to the head CSR position or to platform jobs.

To encourage improved product knowledge and "consultative selling" by CSRs, the evaluation process was revised to include points assigned for each individual's success in sales referrals. Under the new evaluation scheme, the maximum number of points assignable for effectiveness in making sales—directly or through referrals to CARs—amounted to 30 percent of the potential total score.

Karen Mitchell

Under the old scoring system, Karen Mitchell had been the highest scoring teller/CSR for four consecutive half-years. But under the new system, her ranking had dropped to fourth out of the seven full-time tellers.

She ranked first on all but one of the operationally-related criteria (interactions with customers, where she ranked second), but sixth on the selling effectiveness criterion.

Costanzo and Reeves had spoken to Mitchell about her performance and expressed disappointment. Mitchell had told them, respectfully but firmly, that she saw the most important aspect of her job as giving customers fast, accurate, and courteous service.

"I did try this selling thing," she told the two bank officers, "but it just seemed to annoy people. Some said they were in a hurry and couldn't talk now, others looked at me as if I were slightly crazy to bring up the subject of a different bank service than the one they were currently transacting. And then when you got the odd person who seemed interested, you could hear the other customers in the line grumbling about the slow service.

"Really, the last straw was when I noticed on the computer that this woman had several thousand in her savings account so I suggested to her, just as the trainer told us, that she could earn more interest if she opened a money market account. Well, she told me it was none of my business what she did with her money, and stomped off. Don't get me wrong, I love being able to help customers, and if they ask for my advice, I'll gladly tell them about what the bank has to offer."

Two weeks after this meeting, it was announced that the head CSR was leaving. The job entailed some supervision of the other CSRs (including allocation of work assignments and scheduling of part-time CSRs at busy periods or during employee vacations), consultation on—and, where possible, resolution of—any problems occurring at the teller stations, and handling of large cash deposits and withdrawals by local retailers.

The pay scale ranged from $7.00 to $12.00 per hour, depending on qualifications, seniority, and branch size, as compared to a range of $5.40 to $9.00 per hour for CSRs. Full-time employees (who were not unionized) worked a 40-hour week, including some Saturday mornings. Ms. Costanzo indicated that

the pay scales were typical for banks in the midwest, although the average CSR at the First was better qualified than those at smaller banks and therefore higher on the scale. Karen Mitchell was currently earning $7.80 per hour, reflecting her associate's degree, three-and-a-half years' experience, and significant past merit increases. If promoted to Head CSR, she would qualify for a rate of $9.50 an hour initially.

When applications for the position closed, Mitchell was one of three candidates. The other two candidates were Jean Warshawski (an older woman at the Federal Square branch who had worked there for two years) and the head CSR of one of First National's smaller suburban branches who was seeking more responsibility. Neither of these two candidates had received past evaluations as good as Karen Mitchell's, although in the most recent six months Warshawski had ranked ahead of Mitchell as a result of being very successful in consultative selling. Since the third candidate was not working in one of the three test branches, he had not been exposed to the consultative selling program and its corresponding evaluation scheme.

Costanzo and Reeves were troubled by the decision that faced them. Prior to the bank's shift in focus, Mitchell would have been the natural choice for the head CSR job which, in turn, could be a stepping stone to further promotions, including customer assistance representative, customer service director, and eventually assistant branch manager. Mitchell had told her superiors that she was interested in making a career in banking and that she was eager to take on further responsibilities.

Compounding the problem was the fact that the three branches testing the new customer service program had just completed a full year of the test. Costanzo knew that sales and profits were up significantly at all three branches, relative to the bank's performance as a whole. She anticipated that top management would want to extend the program systemwide after making any modifications that seemed desirable.

Turbulent Skies for TWA

CHRISTOPHER H. LOVELOCK

Determined to make TWA profitable again, the airline's new management has imposed wage cuts and new work rules on its flight attendants, thus provoking a strike. New attendants are hired to replace the strikers, but on-board service is poor and the union claims that TWA flights are unsafe. New talks are scheduled in an effort to settle the strike.

Carl Icahn, Chairman of Trans World Airlines (TWA), was meeting with senior executives of the airline to decide what posture the airline should take in new talks with striking flight attendants on wages and work rules. The Independent Federation of Flight Attendants (IFFA) had agreed to resume negotiations the following day, March 26, 1986, in New York City.

On March 7, 6,500 IFFA members—a union specific to TWA flight attendants—struck the airline after management had imposed new work rules boosting work by 12 hours a month, reducing wages by 22%, and establishing a two-tier wage scale. Management estimated that these changes would save TWA some $100 million per year. Mr. Icahn, who had taken control of the airline two months earlier, insisted that the proposed changes were essential to return the airline to profitability after an extended period of losses.

Negotiations with the union had broken down on February 5, after management rejected the IFFA's counterproposal of wage and benefit cuts amounting to $30 million a year. Both parties were then released from federal mediation for a 30-day cooling-off period, at the end of which the flight attendants went on strike and the company replaced them with 3,000 newly trained attendants working longer hours at lower

344

wages. Union members picketed the airports and distributed press releases claiming that it was unsafe to fly TWA.

CHANGING PRACTICES AND CHANGING FORTUNES IN THE AIRLINE INDUSTRY

From the end of World War II through the early 1970s, the United States airline industry enjoyed a remarkable era of growth and stability. Industry concentration increased as smaller carriers failed or—more commonly —merged into larger ones.

In addition to safety regulation by the Federal Aviation Administration (FAA), the industry was also regulated by the Civil Aeronautics Board (CAB). The latter agency's policies served to discourage entry of new interstate airlines and made it difficult for existing airlines to reshape their route networks. In addition, permission had to be obtained from the CAB if an airline wished to change its fares.

Transcontinental routes within the USA were dominated by three major carriers in the mid-70s: American Airlines, TWA, and United Air Lines. Other large carriers, such as Delta, Eastern, Western, and Continental, focused on route networks covering perhaps one-third to one-half of the United States. Pan American World Airways served international routes exclusively. Only three carriers had both a significant domestic and international presence. These airlines were Braniff International, which served South America; TWA, which had an extensive transatlantic network; and Northwest Orient, which flew to the Far East.

With the notable exception of Delta employees, most airline personnel were unionized. However, different categories of employee belonged to different unions, and the nature of their jobs created different cultures. Cockpit crews at that time were exclusively male, highly paid, and usually members of the Air Line Pilots Association. The cabin crews, by contrast, were almost exclusively female, with the exception of a few stewards or pursers on international routes. Although unionized, they were significantly less well paid than pilots and engineers on the flight deck.

Ground crews included machinists, who maintained the aircraft and belonged to the powerful International Association of Machinists (IAM), gate and ticket agents, and reservations staff.

Until the advent of equal opportunity legislation, many airlines were very restrictive in their hiring practices. They recruited only young single women, forbade them to marry, and terminated them if they did. Since stewardesses over the age of 35 were strongly encouraged—or even required—to take ground jobs, there was continual turnover of stewardesses and only limited seniority.

New Employment Practices

During the first half of the 1970s, the environment of the airline industry changed dramatically. Operations costs rose sharply, due to rising fuel prices. The industry was buffeted by recession in mid-decade. Airport and aircraft security was tightened sharply in response to domestic and international hijackings and terrorist bombings.

Significant changes also occurred in the area of personnel. Lawsuits brought by stewardesses successfully put a stop to a variety of management practices, including termination on marriage, prohibitions against wearing glasses on the job, forced grounding of women in their thirties, and even prohibitions against allowing stewardesses to continue working in the air while pregnant.

Meantime, equal opportunity legislation required the airlines to open cabin crew positions to qualified males and flight deck positions to qualified females. The terms steward and stewardess were eventually replaced by the new job title of flight attendant.

With growing seniority among their ranks, the various airline unions were able to negotiate increased salary scales and more restrictive work rules for their members. Critics alleged that senior flight crews were being paid more and more for less and less work. But lack of significant price competition in the industry enabled the airlines to pass through increased wage and fuel costs to passengers, in the form of higher ticket prices.

The Impact of Deregulation

With the advent of airline deregulation in 1978, the rules of the competitive game changed dramatically. Barriers to entry fell away, new routes became relatively easily available, and restrictions on pricing policy were eliminated. In the words of one observer, deregulation "turned the skies into an aerial free-for-all."

Fourteen new or intrastate carriers entered the interstate airline market within the following five years, including Air Florida, America West, Midway, People Express, Piedmont, Southwest Airlines, and New York Air. Their labor costs ranged from 19% to 27 percent of total operating costs, reflecting use of newly hired personnel working for lower wages on more flexible schedules than those permitted under many union work rules. At major unionized carriers, by contrast, labor costs ran between 33 percent and 37 percent of total costs.

In addition, several new entrants flew secondhand DC-9s or Boeing 727s and 737s purchased at huge savings; Midway, for instance, paid a total of $9.2 million for three used DC-9s that would have cost $12 million each if purchased new. These lower operating and capital costs enabled the newcomers to offer deeply discounted fares, resulting in a surge of new passengers. Older airlines saw reduced profits or larger deficits as they matched discount fares in an effort to protect their market shares.

Two major innovations sprang from the intensely competitive new environment. One was adoption by most airlines of the hub and spoke system of route structure. The second was frequent flyer programs.

Most airlines selected several airports as hub locations, with routes reaching out like the spokes of a wheel. Hub facilities required a significant capital investment to allow terminals to service more aircraft in a short time period. However, the operational payoff was that hubs enabled airlines to make more efficient use of aircraft and crews. From a competitive standpoint, hubs allowed air-

lines to offer passengers a much wider choice of connecting flights, since nearly all flights into a hub were scheduled to connect with departing flights to other destinations. This system also enabled carriers to retain passengers who might otherwise have used another airline for the continuing leg of the journey.

The first frequent flyer program was devised by American Airlines in May 1981 as a way of building brand loyalty. The airlines wanted to give regular business travelers a reason to fly American without resorting to promotional fares that simply eroded revenues. Other airlines quickly followed suit and within eighteen months, all major carriers and many regionals offered their own frequent flyer programs. Subsequent research showed that these programs had become a significant factor in consumers' airline choice decisions; one study showed that they ranked second only to safety as a criterion.

Several major domestic airlines expanded overseas, feeding their international flights with passengers arriving at their domestic hubs. In turn, Pan Am attempted to build domestic routes feeding its international services to defend itself. But some carriers overexpanded, and found themselves unable to achieve the high load factors required to break even at lower fares.

Braniff International became the first casualty of deregulation, filing for bankruptcy in 1982 after selling its South American routes to Eastern. Braniff was later resurrected as a much smaller discount airline, serving domestic routes only. Air Florida went bankrupt in 1984 and was liquidated.

A different style of bankruptcy took place in September 1983 at Continental Airlines, which had been taken over by Frank Lorenzo's Texas Air Corporation (owner of Texas International and New York Air). Unable to win agreement from its unions for $100 million in cost savings, Continental filed for bankruptcy and Lorenzo shut down the airline. Two days later, Continental resumed operations, flying a truncated schedule at sharply lower fares and employing 35 percent of its former workers at half their previous wages. Despite union resistance and court challenges, Continental survived, gradually rebuilt its schedules as a discount carrier, and absorbed Texas International.

Continental's actions sent shockwaves throughout the industry. Several established airlines, including Pan Am and Republic, had previously obtained temporary wage concessions from employees. But now the talk turned to permanent cost-saving measures, such as reduced wages and benefits and more flexible work-rules.

Many observers cited People Express as the model for a new style of airline operation and management. Headquartered in Newark, NJ, just across the Hudson River from Manhattan, People Express was a no-frills discount carrier which had expanded its operations with extraordinary speed during the 1980s. Almost all employees were known as "managers" and were required to own stock in the carrier. Customer service managers were cross-trained in several different jobs, including flight attendant, gate agent, and counter agent at the departure desk. The idea was to maximize their flexibility and give them exposure to as many areas of the operation as possible.

A notable feature of People Express service was that the ticket price did not include meals, beverages, or checked baggage: these services cost an additional fee, enabling People to keep its fares extremely low. Although immensely successful in its early years, People Express incurred a substantial loss in 1985. Critics claimed that the airline had expanded too fast and lost control of quality —disgruntled passengers called it "People Distress." By early 1986, some industry analysts were expressing concern about the carrier's future financial prospects.

American Airlines' response to low-cost carriers such as People was twofold. First it sought to become a low average cost carrier through an aggressive policy of expansion. This airline had long been rated each year as the business traveler's favorite, reflecting its high quality cabin service and wide choice of convenient schedules. The company expanded its routes and schedules to improve its coverage even further. Wishing to preserve good employee relations, American's management reached agreement with the unions to preserve existing salary structures but to create a two-tiered structure whereby new hires would be paid on a substantially lower scale.

A second element of American's strategy was a very selective policy of discounting— sufficient to attract passengers who might otherwise fly by a discount carrier but not to erode revenues from business travelers with expense accounts. In this way, American could promote itself as offering full-fare service at bargain prices. The airline saw good quality service as a major point of differentiation in an industry where complaints about poor service were becoming increasingly strident.

THE SITUATION AT TRANS WORLD AIRLINES

TWA's response to deregulation was one of cautious retrenchment on domestic routes. In the early 70s, Trans World had focused on increasing its market share, in order to maintain its Number 3 position among domestic carriers (behind United and American). This approach required maintaining competitive flight schedules, even when they were unprofitable. After a $132 million loss during the recession year of 1975, the airline's president and senior vice president-marketing were let go.

As president, the board appointed C. E. Meyer, previously the airline's vice president-finance. Meyer, an accountant by profession, began by getting rid of inefficient, unprofitable operations and sold off older aircraft (such as Boeing 707s) in TWA's aging fleet. In many instances, two 707 schedules were consolidated into one flight by a Boeing 747 or Lockheed TriStar jumbo jet. The airline also retreated from markets that were too competitive and profit-draining, such as Chicago. Instead it built up operations at its St Louis and New York hubs. More than 3,000 jobs were eliminated.

By 1983, however, TWA was finding itself in increasing difficulties. The previous year, it had lost $31 million on revenues of $3.3 billion. Increasing success overseas—an operating profit of $110 million—contrasted with increasing domestic losses.

TWA's declining domestic traffic led competitors to refer to it as "the incredible shrinking airline." Indeed, Eastern Airlines had displaced TWA as the nation's third largest carrier.

Severe capital constraints made it difficult for TWA to buy the new equipment needed for domestic expansion. Attempts to cut labor costs had met with limited success. In 1982, pilots and noncontract personnel accepted a 17-month pay freeze, but machinists and flight attendants rejected a similar freeze and won new contracts that provided for a 30 percent wage increase over three years with no productivity givebacks (in the form of more flexible work rules).

Part of TWA's problem in labor negotiations was that the airline was a subsidiary of TransWorld Corporation, a large holding company that also owned Hilton International Hotels, a car rental firm, and other subsidiaries. "There's always the perception that the parent will bail out a subsidiary," remarked one observer. This crutch was removed when the parent firm spun off the airline as an independent company in February 1983.

A New Owner

During the next two years, TWA was frequently in the news. In June 1985, TWA Flight 847 was hijacked by Shiite Moslems shortly after takeoff from Athens and forced to fly to several airports in Mediterranean countries during the next few days. One passenger was killed but the others and the crew (who were widely praised for their heroism) were eventually released. That same summer, TWA came close to being purchased by Texas Air Corporation. But the deal fell through and Frank Lorenzo turned his attention elsewhere. In late 1985, Carl Icahn, a so-called corporate raider, made a play for Trans World. After prolonged maneuverings, Icahn won control of the airline with 52 percent of the stock and became chairman on January 3, 1986.

However, Icahn's victory proved to be bittersweet. During the months that he had been pursuing his quarry, TWA's financial position had deteriorated significantly. Although 1985 traffic had increased by 13.3 percent to 32 billion passenger miles and the average load factor stood at 65.2 percent, the airline lost $193 million that year; during the fourth quarter alone, losses totalled $123 million.

Icahn moved quickly to cut costs, dismissing hundreds of office workers, and reaching agreements with pilots and machinists for pay cuts of about 15 percent. He then turned his attention to the flight attendants, whose contract was up for renegotiation.

TWA Flight Attendants

Trans World had some 6,500 flight attendants, who were represented by a union of their own called the Independent Federation of Flight Attendants (IFFA). According to the company, the average TWA flight attendant received wages and benefits worth $44,000 a year—up from $20,000 in 1978. The union noted that this period had included several years of rapid inflation and that since the airline had done little hiring in recent years, it employed a higher proportion of senior flight attendants than its competitors.

The great majority of TWA flight attendants were college educated. Some had been recruited directly from college, others had worked previously as teachers, nurses, social workers, or in office positions. Others had previously worked for the airline in reservations, on ticket counters, or as gate agents and saw a cabin position as a step up in pay and prestige.

Candidates were attracted to the job by the pay and benefits (which increased with seniority), the opportunity to travel, free flights for family members, and a working schedule that was limited to about 14-15 days per month. During their time off, many attendants worked at second jobs—some had small businesses of their own—or pursued their education. However, although salaries and benefits improved with seniority, the opportunities for further career progression were minimal. There were possibilities to work on the ground in supervisory or training positions, but the pay was no higher (and sometimes lower) than the earnings of a senior attendant. Also the hours were longer.

The FAA limited the number of hours that attendants could fly each month as well as setting minimum requirements for days off from flying assignments. The flight attendants' union had negotiated work rules that improved upon FAA requirements, so that a TWA attendant would normally fly about 75 hours a month. However, this excluded time spent waiting at airports and on call, as well as overnight stays in distant cities. On average, an attendant could expect to spend about 250 hours a month away from home.

Junior attendants served in the "Ready Reserves," on call for five hours at a time and ready to arrive at the airport within 50 minutes to fly wherever they were needed. Attendants resented the uncertainty and idle time. However, with seniority came priority in bidding on schedules for the following month.

TWA attendants worked in randomly selected teams of five to seven persons, which were changed monthly. Through this bidding system, attendants could ask to fly on their preferred schedules; because of the priority system, senior attendants had a better chance of avoiding weekend and holiday travel, flying on routes which were perceived as more glamorous, and picking schedules that would avoid the need to stay overnight in distant cities and allow them more time with their families, second jobs, or pursuing additional education.

Recruitment and training of flight attendants was strongly influenced by the requirements of the Federal Aviation Administration (FAA), which continued to regulate airline safety. The TWA training program had historically lasted about five weeks. Most of this period was spent in classroom instruction, with more than half the time being devoted to FAA-prescribed sections on safety procedures and medical first aid, including CPR. The course also covered passenger handling and on-board services, as well as personal grooming and familiarization with the company. There were approximately three dozen written tests.

Education in safety procedures included timed emergency exercises, resembling an obstacle course and designed to simulate real-world disaster situations. Trainees found themselves working in darkness, fire and smoke, and even underwater as they sought to help others and themselves escape from a simulated accident. Between 5 percent and 10 percent of trainees failed to complete the program satisfactorily. Training continued after "graduation," with attendants being required to attend short refresher and update courses in safety each year.

In spite of the emphasis on safety training, an attendant's day-to-day work focused on providing service to the passengers. She or he would greet passengers as they boarded, help them to find seating assignments or stow carry-on baggage, and give special assistance to young children traveling alone or to infirm and disabled passengers. Safety procedures were emphasized before take-off, but once the flight was airborne the focus of the job switched to food and beverage service or "glorified waitressing," as many of them described it.

The nature of the attendant's job was tightly prescribed and included strict dress codes and grooming requirements. Yet a flight attendant's work was not closely monitored in the air. One attendant on each flight was given the coordinating role of "flight service manager," and then assigned each attendant specific duties based upon passenger seating. However, the flight service manager did not evaluate her or his fellow attendants. Written complaints and commendations from crew members and passengers were placed in an attendant's employment file; too many negative complaints about poor service could lead to disciplinary action. Failures to observe safety requirements could be punished by fines or termination.

Many attendants expressed regret that there wasn't more time to give personal attention to passengers, since they recognized that the quality of personal service they provided was a significant factor in passenger satisfaction. Although TWA had a good reputation for service on its international flights, many observers felt that the company's food and cabin service on domestic flights could be improved.

THE STRIKE

Having reached agreement for new contracts with pilots and machinists amounting to a 15 percent cut in pay, Carl Icahn proposed even more significant cuts for TWA's flight attendants. A spokesman for the airline stated:

> We are essentially seeking a 22 percent pay reduction and work rule changes that would amount to being available for duty less than two more hours per week.

The spokesman stated that these cuts would save the airline $100 million annually.

The attendants countered with an offer to reduce wages and benefits by 15 percent, a move that they said would save TWA $30 million a year. They stated that a 22 percent cut, which would save the company some $45 million annually, was excessive, as were the work rule changes, which they claimed would be worth $35 to $65 million.

With neither side able to reach an agreement, the two parties entered a 30-day cooling-off period, which Icahn used to train 1,500 reservation agents and other TWA employees as flight attendants. He also recruited 1,500 new employees for attendants' jobs and began training them, too. However the airline gave no guarantee of permanent employment as flight attendants to any of these individuals. Under the proposed new work rules and assuming a continuation of current schedules, TWA would need only 3,500 attendants at the lowest point of the winter season and 5,000 during the summer "high" season.

On March 3, four days before the union would be free to strike, Icahn claimed that a strike that was successful in shutting down the airline for a considerable period might force him to break up TWA and sell off the pieces.

The day before the strike, the two parties were still talking and still trading charges. The airline claimed that the average flight attendant's pay was $35,000—double the starting price at many airlines. The union said the $35,000 figure was inflated. TWA offered to reduce its pay cut demand to 17 percent but refused to budge on work rule changes. The union rejected the offer. It was reported in the papers that personal antipathy between Carl Icahn and IFFA president Victoria Frankovich had not facilitated negotiations. Frankovich accused Icahn of "negotiating in a sexist fashion."

The Strike Begins

The Independent Federation of Flight Attendants struck TWA at 12:01am EDT on May 7th. The airline's newly hired flight attendants crossed picket lines to the jeers of picketing IFFA members. The pilots crossed the picket lines "regretfully," stating that their contract contained a no-strike agreement. And 85% of the company's machinists crossed picket lines, too. Industry observers were not surprised, pointing out that airline unions rarely displayed solidarity in a labor dispute that affected only one of them.

On the first day of the strike, TWA claimed that it had operated 52 percent of its schedule and said that it planned to restore all flights "within the next several days." Substantial fare cuts were offered through the end of the year to lure passengers. Union representatives disputed TWA schedule claims and stated that the newly hired flight attendants were not properly trained on safety procedures.

Three days into the strike, TWA announced that it was continuing to restore flights and that the figure was now up to 54% of the total flight schedule. That day, the airline took the International Association of Machinists to court to force them to stop honoring flight attendant picket lines.

On March 11, TWA announced that it would meet the union with a federal mediator in Philadelphia the following day. However, these talks broke off after four hours with no new meetings scheduled. That same day, striking machinists obeyed a court order to return to work and the airline announced that 62 percent of its flights were now operating.

The Strike Continues

During the next 12 days, TWA continued to rebuild its schedules and the strike continued to receive broad media coverage. Photos showed sign-carrying picketers shivering outside terminals at northern airports. Strikers spoke of their commitment to TWA and claimed that Icahn was just a corporate raider bent on making money by breaking up the airline.

The newspapers reported that although TWA passengers arriving at airports were mostly ignoring picket lines, a well known singer—Joan Baez—had switched to another airline when she learned that she had been booked on a TWA flight. It was also reported that the airline was losing over a million dollars a day.

Passengers confirmed union claims that on-board service was poor and that flight attendants were slow and inexperienced. Said one traveler after a transcontinental flight:

> It was just amateur hour on board! They took forever to serve the drinks and then forgot to come back and collect money from those who had had alcoholic drinks. The meal service was a shambles.

Many travelers also complained of delayed flights.

Both the union leadership and the rank and file continued to allege that flying on TWA was unsafe, since the new attendants lacked both experience and adequate training. TWA refuted the charge, stating that the FAA's stringent criteria had been fully met. Noting that "several hundred" IFFA members had defied their union and returned to work, TWA argued that the rank and file were not behind the strike and demanded that the leadership take a strike vote. Union leaders, however, scoffed at the claim and stated that the membership was "overwhelmingly" behind the strike.

The union's claim of safety problems received a significant boost a few days later when smoke filled the cabin of a TWA airliner descending for landing at Boston's Logan International Airport. Although the aircraft landed safely and there were no injuries, the shaken passengers told reporters that the flight attendants had panicked and that the situation in the cabin had been chaotic. The incident received wide publicity and the authorities announced that there would be an investigation.

On March 25, TWA and the union announced that they would resume negotiations the next day in New York.

PART VIII
Organization and Integration

Notes on Climate and Culture

BENJAMIN SCHNEIDER

Climate and culture are crucial in service organizations, since there is so much variability in jobs that require interactions with customers. If service employees are to provide a quality experience for their customers, then the organization must first create the right climate and culture to shape employee behavior.

CLIMATE AND CULTURE

Research on organizational climate has been conducted since about 1955 (Argyris, 1957) and there are now about a half dozen good reviews of the literature. In the 30 years of research on the topic, climate has generally referred to incumbent perceptions of what is important in the organization, be it service, creativity, and/or safety. Research has typically tried to specify organizational policies, practices, and procedures that through reward, support, and expectations "tell" incumbents what is important. The nest of policies, practices, procedures and reward, support and expectations, as a whole, are thought to create a sense of imperative and it is this sense of imperative that has been called "climate."

In the past five years the construct of culture has been put forth in the popular (e.g., Peters and Waterman, 1982) and scholarly (e.g., Schein, 1985) literatures. It is fair to say that culture has become a much more accepted term than climate ever was although the research literature on culture is very sparse. Culture seems to refer to a "deeper" issue than climate; it refers to:

- the values that lie beneath what the organization rewards, supports, and expects
- The norms that surround and/or underpin the policies, practices, and procedures of organizations
- the meaning incumbents share about what the norms and values of the organization are

My reading of the two literatures (Schneider, 1985) suggests they are both important issues for organizations and that what I call climate is, in fact, the manifestation of what others call culture. That is, organizations communicate their norms and values to incumbents through their policies, practices, and procedures and through what they actually reward, support, and expect.

I should note that people of the cultural persuasion would argue that myths and stories about founders and critical organizational events (fires, mergers, new buildings, etc.) are important sources of information about values and norms and I would agree. However, fires, mergers, new buildings, and founders, too, are also a source/cause of policies, practices, procedures, and what gets rewarded, supported, and expected—so, climate and culture are usefully conceptualized as supporting constructs.

WHY CLIMATE AND CULTURE ARE IMPORTANT

I'd like to quote from Katz and Kahn (1978, pp. 403–404) to show you why climate and culture are important:

> The organizational need for actions of an innovative, relatively spontaneous sort is inevitable and unending. No organizational plan can foresee all contingencies within its own operations, can anticipate with accuracy all environmental changes, or can control perfectly all human variability. . . . An organization that depends solely on its blueprints of prescribed behaviors is a very fragile system.

What Katz and Kahn are suggesting is that human systems need some glue, some central theme or themes around which behavior can coalesce. In the absence of such

a thematic, incumbents cannot know *when* to direct their energies, at *what* to direct their energies, and *how* to direct their energies. Climate and culture provide this thematic coherence to the behavior of organizational employees when the climate and culture are focussed on desired organizational behaviors.

HOW ORGANIZATIONS CAN CREATE THE DESIRED CLIMATE AND CULTURE

My reading of various anecdotal and research efforts clearly indicates that there are no quick fixes, no one or two buttons to push, to create a climate and culture. In what follows, I have tried to abstract six issues that every organization needs to attend to in order to create a strong climate and culture. Attention to these six issues will communicate to organizational members the desired message when all six are targeted at the same theme—in a service organization, the theme would be service to consumers.

Prior to outlining these issues requiring attention, I need to emphasize *why* in service organizations climate and culture are so critical. They are critical because the jobs of people who deal continuously with other people cannot be clearly specified. So, in a customer contact facility, the shape/form/type of the customer is not predetermined; what comes down the so-called "assembly line of customers" is not uniform and must be handled effectively even with its inherent variability. Further, given that the *process* by which service is delivered to customers in customer contact consumer service organizations can frequently *be* the service, the people who do the delivery become very important indeed.

So, my logic suggests that if employees are going to create the right kind of experience for consumers, create the right kind of ambiance if you will, then the right kind of experience needs to be created for employees themselves. And, just as organizations must do many things right and do the right things to create a quality service experience for consumers, organizations must do similarly for their employees. The issues requiring attention are these six:

1. Membership Issues
2. Socialization Issues
3. Identity Issues
4. Structural Issues
5. Interpersonal Issues
6. Environmental Issues

Membership Issues

All of what we address as climate and culture can ultimately be reduced to people because it is people behaving the way they do that communicates. Memos, directives, booklets, posters—all are trivial compared to what behavior communicates. Since people can differ dramatically in their predispositions to behave in certain ways, all organizations need to be concerned with the kinds of members they attract, select, and retain. Recently I've been accumulating evidence to show that different kinds of people tend to be attracted to, and selected and retained by, particular organizations (Schneider, 1983).

In general, people and organizations tend to make choices that are appropriate matches—assertive sales types tend to go to stock brokerage houses not YMCAs; socially and interpersonally oriented people tend to do the reverse (Campbell and Hansen, 1981). Occasionally, however, mistakes can be made and these mistakes can yield problems for both the individual and the organization.

On the one hand, organizations can give off the wrong kinds of signals and inappropriate people can be attracted as candidates for openings. This makes recruitment more important than we usually think it is because recruitment in my way of thinking starts the long chain that results in the kinds of personalities in an organization. Obviously, since it is the people in an organization that make it the way it looks and feels, the *source* of people from whom selections are made is very important. Service organizations need to attract service-oriented people.

As noted, however, people can make er-

rors so organizations need to have selection systems that weed out bad matches. Most selection systems have some kind of nondirective (read that as "loosey-goosey" or unfocussed) interview and, if they use some more formal procedures, paper and pencil tests of cognitive competency. What they need is formal procedures for assessing interpersonal competence and service orientation. The question is: When faced with problems requiring good service and the creation of a positive service experience, how do they respond? Techniques now exist for developing work simulations that can be used to find persons with service-oriented skills and competencies (Schneider and Schmitt, 1986).

Finally, a membership issue overlooked in service organizations is *who* is quitting. Most service organizations have high turnover and they worry about their "turnover" problem. Invariably, it is assumed that the turnover is due to poor pay, perhaps an appropriate conclusion. My point, however, is that *who* quits is more important than *how many* quit. If the persons leaving are your best service persons then you are in trouble. Research I have done with David Bowen (Schneider and Bowen, 1985) shows that bank tellers who feel they are not providing good service are most likely to quit! So, my message here is to find out why good service employees are quitting and to try and rectify that situation. It could go a long way to improving the quality of service consumers receive.

In summary, membership issues are critical for insuring a service climate and culture. This is true because it is people who transmit climate and cultures through their behavior. Both the popular and scholarly literatures on climate and culture have ignored these issues so I have spent considerable time on them. Since people are the capital assets of service firms, service firms should invest heavily in the kinds of members on which they build their organization.

Socialization Issues

Appropriate attraction (recruitment) and selection can provide organizations with the raw materials of a quality service firm. But when newcomers enter an organization, two kinds of socialization experiences are critical to "fix" the service perspective in their minds: informal and formal socialization.

Informal socialization refers to what newcomers are told and what they see happening to them and around them. We know that when people are new to a setting they are literally starved for information and try to make sense out of what they hear and see (Louis, 1980). This makes early experiences of newcomers potentially overdeterministic of their sense of what is important. If customers, for example, are denigrated and/or if supervisors emphasize speed over quality and/or if no training is provided to emphasize the delivery of quality service, then newcomers can only draw the conclusion that consumers and good service are unimportant.

Training is what I mean by formal socialization. Here, too, several points can be made: Who does the training and how good are they (is training and/or personnel a "dumping ground")? Are service skills as well as technical skills taught or is the emphasis only on the technical (operating the cash register, the telephone system, the computer)? When the newcomer comes to the job, do co-workers and supervisors reward, support, and expect what was trained or is the training denigrated with something like "forget everything they taught you—I'll show you how it's really done" (Goldstein, 1986)?

Clearly, the combination of formal and informal socialization is a powerful kind of communication. How well are these socialization processes managed in your organization to promote the centrality of service?

It is probably clear to you by now that what I'm going to continue to emphasize is how each of the six issues interact with and feed on each other. So, for example, how can you have a positive, service-oriented, socialization process for newcomers, or a service-oriented selection system, unless top management emphasizes service in many other ways? The point is, of course, that climate and culture are a *product of* a network of interacting systems—climate and culture are not any one thing to be easily manipulated.

Identity Issues

One other link in the climate and culture network concerns how people come to feel a part of their organization—how they come to identify with the organization's goals and values. In organizational behavior, the issue of identification and commitment has a rich theory and data base (cf. Mowday, Porter, and Steers, 1980). In general, we can show that increased sense of identity is correlated with improved job satisfaction, improved extra-role performance (going beyond the job description) and lower turnover. What is not so clear are the antecedents of identity.

I think, as you might suspect, that identity begins with a good match of persons to organizations. Now what is very important here is that organizations need to be as explicit as possible about what their goals and values are. If this is not done, then a good match is problematic; trying to match or fit an ambiguous goal is going to require a person who *also* is ambiguous about his or her goals and values.

After people are hired, trained, and informally socialized, however, organizations can still manage identity; they can still help promote a sense of belongingness. Some ways of doing this include:

- Involvement of employees in the design and development of new services (Schneider and Bowen, 1984).
- Using employees as models in advertisements of the company's products and services.
- Merely advertising quality service.
- Even the use of symbols of membership like buttons, coffee mugs, or even uniforms.

The message here is that organizations need to continuously reward and support the attachment of employees to the organization. In a service organization this may be particularly important because attachment is such an important *marketing* issue. We can show, I'm sure, that when employees identify with their organization because of its service values as revealed in its policies, practices, and procedures then *consumers* will have "brand loyalty" (Schneider and Bowen, 1985).

Structural Issues

What I mean by structural issues are all those policies, practices, and procedures that guide life in most organizations. The question is: Toward what end are organizational structures motivated?

We have done some research to show that when service organizations establish rules and procedures to promote bureaucratic efficiency, service employees tend to be dissatisfied, frustrated, and likely to leave (Parkington and Schneider, 1979). In addition, we've shown that when service organizations create an "efficiency ethic" compared to a "service ethic" (Schneider and Bowen, 1985) by their rules and procedures consumers experience poor service (Schneider and Bowen, 1985).

Do organizations need rules and procedures? Of course. The question is: To what end are they promulgated? Certainly all of the traditional functions of management (planning, organizing, controlling) can be thought of as structural issues and no one would argue that organizations can exist without these. The point is that service organizations need to ask themselves planning for *what*?, organizing for *what*?, controlling *what*? If the answers are superior service quality then the organization is on the way to creating a service climate. If the answers are (planning) to reduce costs, (organizing) to increase efficiency, and (controlling) human variability then high quality service is not a likely outcome (Bowen and Schneider, 1985).

Interpersonal Issues

High contact consumer and professional service organizations (CSOs and PSOs) are dominated by interpersonal interaction. To be effective, the organizations need to attract, select, and retain interpersonally oriented people, they need to be formally and informally socialized to be interpersonally sensitive and responsive, part of their organizational identity will be their attraction to other persons in the organization, and the organization's structures should facilitate interpersonal interaction.

In other words, a central management responsibility in PSOs and CSOs concerns the management of interpersonal relationships. The problem, as just noted, is that interpersonal relationships require effective management in every facet of organizational life—selection, training, planning, ad infinitum. I think that the extent to which interpersonal issues are at the forefront of management's concerns in a service organization, to that extent is the service organization likely to be effective.

Let me be more specific. At the boundary of service organizations, the relationship between server and served is an interpersonal transaction. The quality of that transaction will depend upon everything the organization does to reward, support, and expect an effective interpersonal relationship. The "messages" incumbents have about the importance of excellent service have all come to them via interpersonal interactions—with trainers, co-workers, and supervisors. So, you can see this unbroken chain of internal interpersonal relationships extending beyond the boundary to the consumer. It seems safe to hypothesize that the quality of the link to the consumer can be no stronger than the quality of the other interpersonal links.

Environmental Issues

Schein (1980, p. 233) asks the following questions regarding the larger environment of organizations:

How does an organization cope within its environment? How does it obtain information and process it validly? What mechanisms exist for translating information, particularly about alterations in the environment, into changed operations? Are the internal operations flexible enough to cope with change? How can the organization's capacity to cope be improved?

Service organizations, especially high contact CSOs and PSOs, are to be envied because they can capitalize on their boundary spanning employees as sources of information and ideas to help the organization cope. They can do this, but will they?

I have seen service organizations spend

hundreds of thousands of dollars to run focus groups of consumers to find out what they should be doing and how they should be doing it. Such a waste. Those same organizations could be gathering much if not all of the same information from customer-contact employees.

Think of it this way: Each employee has information from *hundreds* of consumers while each consumer has only his or her experiences. My point is that employees are a potentially *marvelous* source of critical information regarding long-term survival. Employees know at least the following:

- What makes consumers unhappy
- Why consumers are leaving
- What the competition is doing

They know this because consumers are not bashful!

So, my answer to Schein's questions is conduct periodic focus groups with your own employees. Think of the benefits:

- Accurate information based on hundreds if not thousands of encounters
- Creates a sense of employee identity with the organization and the value of service
- Dear to the heart of all, it is cheap.

If you do this, please remember to treat your employees as valuable consumers and provide the same ambience (nice room, snacks, and so forth) you would provide for your customers.

SUMMARY

I hope I have convinced you that a multi-pronged approach to climate and culture can yield an organization with a definite service thrust. If you leave with the idea that there is no quick way to create a service-oriented climate and culture, I'll be content. If you also leave with the idea that a service climate and culture *can* be created, I'll be happy. If you go away with six specific facets by which

you can make it happen, I'll be delirious. Please make me delirious.

REFERENCES

ARGYRIS, C. (1957). Some problems in conceptualizing organizational climate: A case study of a bank. *Administrative Science Quarterly, 2,* 501–520.

BOWEN, D. E., AND SCHNEIDER, B. (1985). Boundary-spanning-role employees and the service encounter: Some guidelines for management and research. In J. A. Czepiel, M. R. Solomon, and C. F. Suprenant (eds.), *The service encounter.* Lexington, MA: Lexington Books.

CAMPBELL, D. P., AND HANSEN (1981). *Manual for the SVIB-SCII.* Stanford, CA: Stanford University Press.

GOLDSTEIN, I. L. (1986). *Training: Program development and evaluation,* 2nd ed. Menlo Park, CA: Brooks-Cole.

KATZ, D., AND KAHN, R. L. (1978). *The social psychology of organizations,* 2nd ed. New York: Wiley.

LOUIS, M. R. (1980). Surprise and sense making: What newcomers experience in entering unfamiliar organizational settings. *Administrative Science Quarterly, 25,* 226–251.

MOWDAY, R. T., PORTER, L. W., and STEERS, R. M. (1980). *Employee-organization linkages: The psychology of commitment, absenteeism, and turnover.* New York: Academic Press.

PARKINGTON, J. J., and SCHNEIDER, B. (1979). Some correlates of experienced job stress: A boundary role study. *Academy of Management Journal,* **22,** 270–281.

PETERS, T. J., and WATERMAN, R. H. (1982). *In search of excellence.* New York: Harper & Row.

SCHEIN, E. H. (1980). *Organizational psychology,* 3rd ed. Englewood Cliffs, NJ: Prentice-Hall.

SCHEIN, E. H. (1985). *Organizational culture and leadership.* San Francisco: Jossey-Bass.

SCHNEIDER, B. (1975). Organizational climates: An essay. *Personnel Psychology,* **28,** 447–479.

SCHNEIDER, B., (1983). An interactionist perspective on organizational effectiveness. In K. S. Cameron and D. Whetten, eds., *Organizational effectiveness: A comparison of multiple models.* New York: Academic Press.

SCHNEIDER, B., (1985). Organizational behavior. *Annual Review of Psychology,* **36,** 573–611.

SCHNEIDER, B., and BOWEN, D. E. (1984). New services design, development, and implementation and the employee. In W. R. George and C. E. Marshall, eds., *Developing new services.* Chicago: American Marketing Association.

SCHNEIDER, B., and BOWEN, D. E. (1985). Employee and customer perceptions of service in banks: Replication and extension. *Journal of Applied Psychology.*

SCHNEIDER, B., and SCHMITT, N. (1986). *Staffing organizations*, 2nd ed. Glenview, IL: Scott, Foresman.

Some Organizational Problems Facing Marketing in the Service Sector

CHRISTOPHER H. LOVELOCK
ERIC LANGEARD
JOHN E. G. BATESON
PIERRE EIGLIER

Marketing in the service sector tends to require different relationships with other management functions than is the case in manufacturing firms. This paper reports the findings of a study of managers at four large service companies, exploring the interaction between marketing, operations, and personnel management at both the corporate and field levels.

INTRODUCTION

Marketing has not traditionally played a major role in the management of most service businesses. To be sure, service managers have often performed marketing tasks, including actions in such areas as development and introduction of new services, decisions on retail site location, pricing strategies, and the conduct of communication campaigns. But such actions were rarely planned, coordinated, and implemented by professional marketing managers with a strong orientation toward customer needs, market trends, and competitive analysis. As likely as not,

they were taken by managers with responsibilities in such areas as operations, finance, economic analysis, real estate, advertising, and public relations.

This situation stands in sharp contrast to the mode prevailing in manufacturing firms, especially those in the business of selling consumer goods. For the past quarter century or more, marketing has been a dominant management function in consumer goods firms, offering strategic direction as well as tactical expertise.

Both conceptually and in practice, professional marketing management is still relatively new to the service sector. However, the

Reprinted from *Marketing of Services*, edited by James H. Donnelly and William R. George. Copyright © 1981 American Marketing Association.

increasingly competitive nature of many service industries is serving to emphasize the
importance of a marketing orientation and
the link between good marketing practice
and profitable performance (Eiglier et al.,
1977).

Nature of the Research Study[1]

This paper reports the findings of a pilot
study of how marketing relates to other
management functions in large consumer
service businesses. Four large service firms
—three banks in different regions of the
United States and a national chain of quick
service restaurants—allowed themselves to
be used as sites for our research. While such
a convenience sample has its limitations, it
is worth mentioning that subsequent discussions with other types of service firms have
provided a validation of our basic conclusions.

We'll begin by briefly examining the nature of the interaction between marketing
and other management functions in both
manufacturing and service firms.

We'll then discuss the insights obtained
from in-depth personal interviews with 32
senior managers. These managers, who held
corporate or regional positions in general
management, operations, marketing, and
personnel, were asked about the role played
by each function, with special reference to
the evolution of marketing in recent years.

Next, we'll review the findings of a mail
survey of 162 field-level managers, employed by the same four companies. This
survey was designed to test our hypothesis
that managers at a specific service "site" had
responsibilities akin to general managers, in
that their job included and integrated marketing, personnel, and operations tasks. A
brief conclusion will identify five approaches
for ensuring that a marketing perspective is
present at both the corporate and service-
site levels.

---
[1]This research was conducted under the sponsor-
ship of the Marketing Science Institute, Cambridge,
Massachusetts. The authors gratefully acknowledge MSI's
support.

INTERACTION BETWEEN MARKETING AND OTHER FUNCTIONAL AREAS

A major problem facing marketers in the
service sector is the historical dominance of
the operations function. In a manufacturing
firm there is a clear separation between production and consumption. A physical good
can be produced in one location, sold in a
second, and consumed or used in a third.
Hence, there is normally no need for production to have any direct involvement with
customers. Marketing plays a linking role,
providing the manufacturing division with
customer-oriented guidelines for product
specifications, estimates of the extent and
timing of demand, and feedback on marketplace performance. Marketing is also responsible for developing distribution
strategies—through company-owned outlets or retail intermediaries—to deliver the
product to prospective purchasers.

In a service firm, however, where the finished service is consumed as it is produced,
there has to be direct contact between production (operations) and the consumer. No
inventories can be stockpiled to insulate productive capacity from the fluctuations of demand. Many service operations are literally
a "factory in the field" (Levitt, 1972) which
customers enter at the specific point in time
that they need a service.

The simultaneous nature of final production and consumption in a service business creates a major problem for marketing
management. Unlike their counterparts in
manufacturing firms, service marketers cannot take responsibility for the product as it
leaves the factory gate. Instead, the marketing function is closely interrelated with, and
dependent upon, personnel and operations.
Indeed, it might be hypothesized that a decision made by any one of the three, because
of the explicit link between production and
consumption, would automatically affect the
other two. This mutual dependence can be
depicted as a management triangle. (See Figure 1.)

Organizationally, therefore, service businesses cannot totally separate the marketing

FIGURE 1

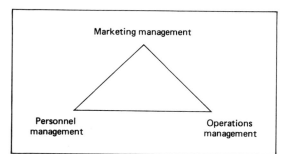

FIGURE 3

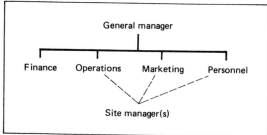

and production functions, as is typically done in consumer goods companies. This poses a need for general managers to coordinate different functional perspectives and resolve interfunctional conflicts. In developing our research project, we hypothesized that a general management role would exist not only in the upper echelons of the organization but also at (or near) the site level, where services are delivered to customers.

Figure 2 depicts a simple functional form of organization commonly found in manufacturing firms. But our hypothesis suggested that in a service firm the de facto organizational structure would appear more like that shown in Figure 3.

Figure 3 depicts the site managers as coordinating each of the elements with which the customer must interact. They control what has been called the "servuction" (service production) system, which is the visible part of the organization where services are produced, distributed, and consumed (Eigler et al., 1979). This suggests that site managers must take responsibility for making trade-offs between any conflicts that arise between marketing, operations, and personnel.

FIGURE 2

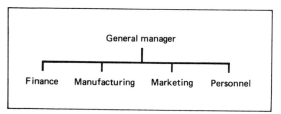

In the next two sections of this paper, we will summarize the findings of, first, a series of personal interviews with head office and regional managers in four large service firms, and second, a mail survey of field (or site) managers in these same four companies.

INTEGRATING DIFFERENT FUNCTIONAL PERSPECTIVES AT THE CORPORATE MANAGEMENT LEVEL

This portion of the study is best described as clinical research. It consisted of personal interviews with a total of 32 senior managers in four different service companies.

Methodology

With the assistance of a coordinator at each of the four participating firms, interviews were arranged with 18 executives at the head office of each firm (4 or 5 from each company). They were drawn from top management, and from the marketing/strategic planning, operations, and personnel departments. Another 14 executives were interviewed at the regional level, representing positions in general management, branch operations, and marketing.

The interviews were open-ended and conducted on location at company offices. The discussions emphasized: (1) relationships between different functional areas and between head office and regional offices; (2) changes in the organizational structure and in job definitions and responsibilities, particularly as these related to the evolution of marketing within the organization; (3) the nature of any interfunctional conflicts encountered in both day-to-day operations and during periods when new services were being introduced; and (4) procedures adopted for reducing, resolving, and avoiding such conflicts.

Role and Relative Importance of the Different Functions

These interviews generated qualitative insights into how respondents perceived the roles played by different functional areas within their firms. We'll look at the personnel, marketing, and operations departments in turn.

Personnel. We found that management of personnel in the four service organizations studied was divided into staff and line responsibilities. Those responsible for the *staff* personnel function had two major tasks. The first involved monitoring of the overall system and addressing such questions as: Are we managing people efficiently? What is the state of employee morale? (If not unionized) are we vulnerable to unionization? How closely do our hiring and promotional practices conform to government guidelines and legislation? The second task involved monitoring current compensation and hiring policies: Are we spending money wisely and getting value for money? Are we able to recruit the types of people needed by the firm? Is turnover excessive on account of noncompetitive compensation policies?

Those responsible for *line management* of personnel were managers who were responsible for getting the job done and were evaluated on the results obtained. The personnel staff function appeared to have little involvement with day-to-day decisions affecting customers, and to be more concerned with hiring and benefit policies, formulated at the corporate rather than the field level. We gained the impression that neither operations nor marketing actively sought the assistance of personnel specialists in introducing service innovations such as automatic teller machines, other new banking services, or major additions to the fast food menu.

To summarize: in the four companies studied, the personnel staff function had minimal short-term involvement in creation and delivery of services. Management of employees in those companies was the responsibility of operations, which had to orchestrate facilities, technology, and personnel and ensure that these three interacted satisfactorily with customers at the point of service delivery. The finding led us to emphasize the interaction between operations—with its responsibilities for managing both operating personnel and operating systems—and marketing.

Marketing. This function is still a relatively new one in service businesses. In each of the organizations studied, a formalized approach to marketing had first been developed during the 1970s. As one senior executive in a fast food firm remarked: "Marketing used to be a catch-all term. There was no philosophy of the role marketing should play in the organization. We started with quite a small group, focusing on copy, media, and promotion. Then we began to expand the role of the department, building in marketing research, operations liaison, and new product functions. We got into operations issues as they related to customer service, new product formulations, etc."

The marketing function in this company had clearly evolved over time. At the head office level, marketing was a staff function with an eye on the future of the business. "The critical aspect of the job," we were told, "is not advertising and media—that's fairly straightforward. It's identifying direction, competitive frame, where you want to be on a market basis, product line, definition of what the products are, what you should be doing to serve the customer now and five years from now." At the regional level in this firm, marketing was more concerned with shorter term issues, such as promotional activities and pricing strategy.

In banking, too, we found that marketing had been going through an evolutionary process. One bank marketing specialist who had been in the banking industry for ten years remarked: "This is really a transition period in banking, and I think marketing is going through all kinds of transitional stages. A lot of bank executives still don't look at marketing as much more than advertising and public relations."

Although marketing specialists at one of the banks we studied had all originally been based in the head office, a more decentralized marketing organization had evolved. "Four years ago," one banker commented:

> All our marketing talent was in our head office. Today, it's all over the organization. And that's by design, as those people were needed in other areas. Many of them have moved into line jobs. Marketing today in the head office is at a "second stage." A stage of respect has been achieved, and now we really need to develop the organization. There are two kinds of marketing organizations here—a central group of about ten people and, in the regions, a marketing person reporting to each regional manager and dealing with regional marketing problems.

In addition to the two regionalized organizations discussed above, we learned that the third company we studied had confined its marketing staff to head office, where they were organized primarily on a product management basis. The fourth company had recently reorganized its head office structure, instituting a new, marketing-oriented strategic planning group and also setting up marketing and systems staff groups which had only limited interaction with the rest of the organization. In short, we found no single approach to organizing the marketing function.

Operations. From our interviews, it became clear that, despite the advances made by marketing in recent years, the operations function still dominated line management in the four service firms studied.

In some respects, this should not come as a great surprise. Operations has traditionally been the dominant function in the service sector, and effective management of operations remains the most important require-

ment for success in a service business. As the regional vice president of a quick service restaurant company put it to us: "In fast foods, you're both a manufacturer and a retailer. You're taking in raw materials and processing them in thousands of individual plants, which then turn around and, as retail outlets, sell the finished product. So control of the variability of the product is critical, and I'd call that operations execution."

Summary and Discussion

The personnel function, as we have seen, can be split into a staff function responsible for setting policies and procedures, plus a line function that falls under operations and involves managing personnel as productive resources. Marketing is still a relatively new function in service firms and is only slowly gaining clout. Operations managers are not only likely to have been with the organization longer than their marketing colleagues, but also to understand it better. Inasmuch as a "management triangle" exists, it appears from our interviews to consist of three very unequal functions, two of which still emphasize staff rather than line tasks.

But as service organizations change and devote more emphasis to proactive marketing efforts, the potential for interfunctional conflict increases. Marketers are likely to see the operations perspective as narrow and one-sided; even if they recognize the dominance of operations, they may not accept it. Alternatively (and representing the opposite extreme), marketing may be content to accept a passive, staff role entailing no initiatives. The challenge for top management is to stimulate a two-way flow of communications in order to ensure that both marketing and operational perspectives are recognized and understood.

FIELD MANAGERS' PERCEPTIONS OF THEIR ROLES AND RESPONSIBILITIES

Based on an investigation of the same four service companies, we tried to assess the nature of the general management role at the

TABLE 1
Response Rates by Company to Field Manager Mail Survey

Company	Mailed	Returned	Response Rates
A	120	78	65%
B	75	48	64
C	26	18	70
D	45	18	40
Total	266	162	61

field level, as perceived by employees responsible for managing individual branches or subregional groupings of such service outlets.

Methodology

A questionnaire was developed, reviewed by representatives of the participating companies, and mailed to a total of 266 field managers in these four firms. Two slightly different versions were developed, adapted to the activities and terminology of the banking and fast food industries. This survey dealt with the following broad areas:

- The field managers' perception of their role
- The nature of their time commitment to the different management functions
- Their perceptions of the importance of these different functions

Questionnaires were distributed to the field managers by corporate headquarters, but returned by mail directly to the researchers. We developed guidelines for sample design at each of the four participating companies, but since actual selection of prospective survey respondents was in the hands of our contacts and there may also have been some nonresponse bias, we cannot be entirely sure that respondents constituted a truly representative cross section of field managers in each company.

As shown in Table 1, there were 162 usable responses in total, representing a response rate of 61 percent. In view of the low number of respondents in companies C and D we will report findings for the total sample, with individual breakouts for companies A and B (both of these being banking organizations).

Table 2 shows the percentage of managers reporting that responsibility for each of the three functions—marketing, operations, and personnel—was part of their job. Respondents evidently saw all three of the basic functions as part of their job as field managers.

Perceived Importance of the Different Functions

Respondents were asked to rate on a 5-point scale how important they considered the management of each functional activity to the success of their job. The scale ranged from 1 (not at all important) to 5 (extremely

TABLE 2
Percentage of Field Managers Responsible for Different Functional Tasks

	Total Sample	Company A	Company B
Management of Personnel	100%	100%	100%
Marketing/Customer Relations	98	100	98
Operations	93	94	92

TABLE 3
Perceived Importance of the Different Functions to the Field Manager's Job

	TOTAL SAMPLE MEAN	SD	COMPANY A Mean	SD	COMPANY B Mean	SD
Managing Personnel	4.4	0.7	4.3	0.7	4.3	0.8
Managing Procedures, and Practices	4.2	0.8	4.1	0.8	4.0	0.8
Dealing with Customer Matters	4.7	0.5	4.8	0.4	4.6	0.6

Note: All ratings based on five-point scale; SD = standard deviation.

important). The results for the combined sample and for Companies A and B are shown in Table 3. This shows that each of the functional tasks was perceived as quite important. (The differences in the importance ratings between banking and fast food, and between each of the three banks, proved to be relatively small.) Note that respondents tended to rate managing personnel and dealing with customer matters slightly above operations ("managing procedures and practices") in importance.

Allocation of Time Between the Functions

Another way to look at the relative importance attached to each activity is to ask how each manager divides his or her time between these functions. The results are shown in Table 4. We can see that respondents claimed to allocate slightly more time to dealing with customer matters than to the two other types of functions. Managing personnel took less than a quarter of these managers' time, on average.

TABLE 4
Allocation of Time Between the Functions by Field Managers

	Total Sample	Co. A	Co. B
Managing Procedures and Practices (operations)	37%	27%	44%
Managing Personnel	23	23	18
Dealing with Customer Matters	40	50	38
Total Allocated Time	100	100	100

A number of interesting insights emerge from this table, especially when it is studied in conjunction with Tables 2 and 3. In Companies A and B all of the site managers in both organizations perceive marketing/customer relations as part of their role, yet those in Company A are devoting a much larger proportion of their time to "customer matters," and much less to operations-related matters.

Summary and Discussion

The great majority of field managers we surveyed perceived themselves as being involved in each of the three functional areas composing the triangle. These findings tend to support our hypothesis concerning the interdependence of the three functions at the field level as well as at the top management level.

CONCLUSION

Service marketers must develop organizational structures and procedures that establish a better balance between marketing and other management functions—especially operations—than currently exists.

There are various approaches for ensuring that a marketing perspective exists at both the corporate and field general management levels. They include: (1) decentralization of revenue responsibility; (2) "internal marketing" that communicates and reinforces the need for different functional areas to work together; (3) adherence to quality control standards that reflect customer needs; (4)

use of matrix organizational structures; and (5) creation of interfunctional task forces. Future research should evaluate the contributions that such approaches can make to improving the effectiveness of service marketing under a variety of different conditions.

REFERENCES

EIGLIER, P., E. LANGEARD, C. H. LOVELOCK, J. E. G. BATESON, AND R. F. YOUNG (1977). *Marketing Consumer Services: New Insights*. Marketing Science Institute.

EIGLIER, P., E. LANGEARD, J. E. G. BATESON, AND C. H. LOVELOCK (1979). "Consumers' Participation in the Servuction System: Concept Definition and Measurement." *Proceedings*, 6th International Research Seminar in Marketing at Senanque, Aix-en-Provence, France: Institut d' Administration des Entreprises. (Note: original in French.)

LEVITT, T. (1972). "Production Line Approach to Service," *Harvard Business Review*, Sept.–Oct., 41.

Lessons in the Service Sector

JAMES L. HESKETT

The best service companies create a strategic service vision that integrates operations and marketing. Further, management recognizes that the health of the enterprise depends on the degree to which core groups of employees subscribe to and share a common set of values and are themselves served by the firm's activities.

- *A large food and lodging company creates and staffs more general management jobs than any ten manufacturers of comparable size. This company, like many others dispensing high customer-contact services, has eliminated functional lines of responsibility between operations and marketing. In its planning the company routinely combines operations and marketing with what I call a strategic service vision.*

- *The most profitable large American company assumes daily the task of managing a work force of window washers, cooks, and maintenance personnel. An almost single-minded concentration on people— their jobs, their equipment, their personal development—accounts for much of its success.*

- *The quality control process in a decentralized oil-field services business involves careful selection, development, assignment, and compensation of employees working under varying conditions and in widespread locations where close supervision is impossible. In this prosperous company, the process builds shared values and bonds people together.*

- *An international airline, by paying more attention to market economies than to production scale economies, reduces the average size of its aircraft and increases its net income.*

- *Products introduced since 1982 by a well-known financial service generated 10 percent of its revenues in 1985. The raw material for these products is data already existing in other forms in the company's vast data base.*

These examples give a glimpse of forward-looking management practice. When examined closely, they offer insights into the ideas on which successful competitive strategies have been fashioned in the much-maligned and little-understood service sector.

It's no coincidence that dominant industries have cutting-edge management practices. Some U.S. railroads in the nineteenth century pioneered in divisionalized management of their far-flung systems and in good procurement procedures to support their sizable construction and operational needs. At the turn of the century, basic industries led the way in experimenting with scientific management. Then the rise of the large consumer goods manufacturer, epitomized by the auto industry, spawned concepts of decentralization and a full product line aimed at carefully segmented markets.

Today service industries have assumed the mantle of economic leadership. These industries, encompassing trade, communications, transportation, food and lodging, financial and medical services, education, government, and technical services to industry, account for about 70 percent of the national income and three-fourths of the nonfarm jobs in the United States. In generating 44 million new jobs in the past 30 years, they have absorbed most of the influx of women and minorities into the work force, softened the effects of every post-World War II recession, and fueled every recent economic recovery.

In view of this leadership role, now is a good time to look at the exemplars in the service sector for insights into ways of boosting productivity and altering competitive strategies. Despite their diversity, leading companies in many service industries display some common themes and practices. And they yield lessons for managers in any sector of business. Let's look first at the way the best service companies are structured.

INTEGRATED FUNCTIONS

Most goods-producing businesses follow the traditional organizational pattern of separate and equally important marketing and manufacturing functions, with coordinating authority at high levels. Some service businesses do the same thing, but the pattern is much less common in service companies where contact with customers is close, as in retailing, passenger transport, and food and lodging. In these businesses, service is marketed and produced at the same place and time, and often by the same person. Naturally, close coordination between marketing and operations management in these cases, regardless of reporting relationships, is essential.

Integration of marketing and operations is often found at very low levels in these organizations. In fact, more than 90 percent of all field managers in four multisite service companies surveyed in one study claimed responsibility for operations, personnel, and marketing, could not say which was most important, and paid great attention to each.[1]

Even where operations are buffered from marketing activities in organizations offering little customer-contact service, there are ways to break down the traditional functional barriers. Several years ago, the Chase Manhattan Bank launched an effort to upgrade its nonloan products, improve its external communications and customer service, and make its back-office (production) operations more market based. A weak spot was Chase's international business. In the highly visible "product" of international money transfer, differences of viewpoint between marketing—embodied in the account relations manager in the field—and the back office in New York had frustrated communication. Errors were frequent, a large backlog of inquiries about balances and transactions had piled up, and morale in the operations group was poor.

A study ordered by the executive put in charge showed that headquarters accounted for operational errors in only about one-third of all the inquiries and that the marketing people had little idea what operations could offer the bank's customers. The executive traced the backlogged errors to their sources, often a correspondent bank, and resolved them. He launched a campaign to improve operations staff morale around the theme "We make it happen" and formed a new group, the customer mobile unit, consisting of the bank's most experienced international operations people. The unit visited Chase customers at their businesses to help resolve problems and smooth operations. The executive brought the marketing and back-office people together to talk about ways to improve the flow of information. Perhaps most important, the bank revised reporting relationships so that operations units serving specific market segments reported to both the customer relationship manager and the head of operations—a move that improved functional coordination.[2]

The product manager's job was created in many manufacturing organizations to address the problem of coordinating manufacturing and marketing. But in most cases, product managers have had profit responsibility without the authority to coordinate. Assignment to these positions has been regarded as temporary, which encourages decisions with a short-term orientation.

Because of their importance, the high-contact service company makes a point of developing numbers of marketing-operations managers, often carrying the title of store or branch manager. At hand, therefore, is a large cadre of talent from which the company can draw senior managers already trained for administrative responsibilities.

STRATEGIC SERVICE VISION

The need of most service organizations to plan as well as direct marketing and operations as one function has led to the formation in leading companies of what I call a strategic service vision. Its elements consist of identification of a target market segment, development of a service concept to address targeted customers' needs, codification of an operating strategy to support the service concept, and design of a service delivery system to support the operating strategy. These basic elements are shaded lighter in Table 1.

A company naturally tries to position it-self in relation to both the target market and the competition. The links between the service concept and the operating strategies are those policies and procedures by which the company seeks to maximize the difference between the value of the service to customers (the service concept) and the cost of providing it. This difference, of course, is a primary determinant of profit. And the link between the operating strategy and the service delivery system is the integration achieved in the design of both. These integrative links are shaded darker in Table 1.

To see how the strategic service vision works, examine the Hartford Steam Boiler Inspection & Insurance Company. For many years, HSB has been in the business of insuring industrial and institutional equipment. Its market targets are organizations using boilers and related pieces of equipment with high operating risk. It offers the same risk reduction as many other insurance companies but positions itself against the competition by emphasizing cost reduction as well.

HSB concentrates on a few types of equipment and has built a large data base on their operating and performance characteristics. (Manufacturers of the equipment often turn to HSB to get wear and maintenance data.) The information furnishes the actuarial base on which HSB prices its insurance. The company's engineers, who inspect customers' equipment before and after it is insured, are also qualified to give advice on preventing problems and improving utilization rates, and through many years of association they often get very close to their customers. As a service manager of one HSB client told me, "If I tried to replace that insurance contract, my operating people in the plant would let me know about it."

This practice enhances the perceived value of the service to the customer at little extra cost to HSB. Of course, by reducing the risk to the customer HSB can improve its own loss ratio.

HSB has a larger cadre of engineers than any of its competitors. These engineers, in tandem with the big data base, make up a service delivery system that capitalizes on the knowledge of marketing and operating

TABLE 1
Externally Oriented Strategic Service Vision

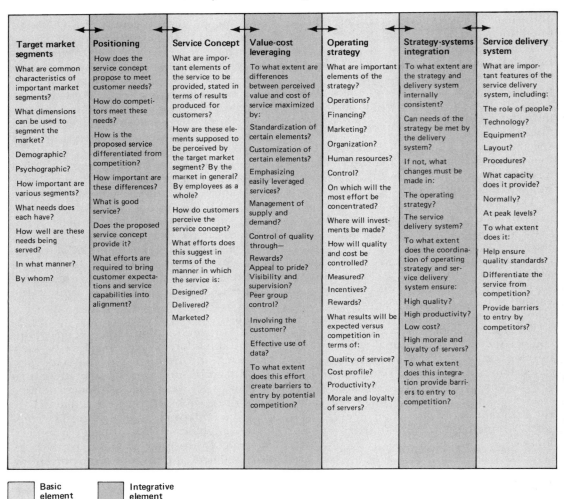

Target market segments	Positioning	Service Concept	Value-cost leveraging	Operating strategy	Strategy-systems integration	Service delivery system
What are common characteristics of important market segments?	How does the service concept propose to meet customer needs?	What are important elements of the service to be provided, stated in terms of results produced for customers?	To what extent are differences between perceived value and cost of service maximized by:	What are important elements of the strategy?	To what extent are the strategy and delivery system internally consistent?	What are important features of the service delivery system, including:
What dimensions can be used to segment the market?	How do competitors meet these needs?	How are these elements supposed to be perceived by the target market segment? By the	Standardization of certain elements?	Operations? Financing? Marketing?	Can needs of the strategy be met by the delivery system?	The role of people? Technology? Equipment?
Demographic? Psychographic?	How is the proposed service differentiated from competition?	market in general? By employees as a whole?	Customization of certain elements? Emphasizing easily leveraged	Organization? Human resources? Control?	If not, what changes must be made in:	Layout? Procedures? What capacity
How important are various segments?	How important are these differences?	How do customers perceive the service concept?	services? Management of supply and	On which will the most effort be concentrated?	The operating strategy? The service	does it provide? Normally? At peak levels?
What needs does each have?	What is good service?	What efforts does this suggest in	demand? Control of quality	Where will investments be made?	delivery system? To what extent	To what extent does it:
How well are these needs being served?	Does the proposed service concept provide it?	terms of the manner in which the service is:	through— Rewards?	How will quality and cost be controlled?	does the coordination of operating strategy and ser-	Help ensure quality standards?
In what manner? By whom?	What efforts are required to bring customer expectations and service capabilities into alignment?	Designed? Delivered? Marketed?	Appeal to pride? Visibility and supervision? Peer group control?	Measured? Incentives? Rewards?	vice delivery system ensure: High quality?	Differentiate the service from competition?
			Involving the customer? Effective use of data?	What results will be expected versus competition in terms of:	High productivity? Low cost? High morale and loyalty of servers?	Provide barriers to entry by competitors?
			To what extent does this effort create barriers to entry by potential competition?	Quality of service? Cost profile? Productivity? Morale and loyalty of servers?	To what extent does this integration provide barriers to entry to competition?	

☐ Basic element   ▨ Integrative element

managers at all levels of the organization.

The net result is a strategic service vision (though HSB doesn't use the term) that is highly valued by its customers and very profitable for its provider. It addresses implementation issues as part of the strategic plan, and it requires agreement and coordination among marketing and operating managers throughout the organization.

INNER-DIRECTED VISION

High-performance service companies have gained their status in large measure by turning the strategic service vision inward: by targeting important groups of employees as well as customers. In the head offices of these organizations, questions such as those listed in Table 2 are heard often. The questions parallel those in Table 1; but in asking them about employees, management shows it's aware that the health of the enterprise depends on the degree to which core groups of employees subscribe to and share a common set of values and are served by the company's activities.

The basic elements, shaded lighter as in Table 1, start with the service concept designed with employees' needs in mind. The operating strategy is set to meet these needs in a superior fashion at the lowest cost, a result often achieved through the design of the service delivery system. The integrative elements, shaded darker, include positioning of a service concept, which it is hoped will lead to low turnover, low training costs, and the opportunity to develop shared goals and values. High-performance service organizations invariably have operating strategies designed to maximize differences between operating costs and value perceived by employees in their relations with the company. And delivery systems designed with

TABLE 2
Internally Oriented Strategic Service Vision

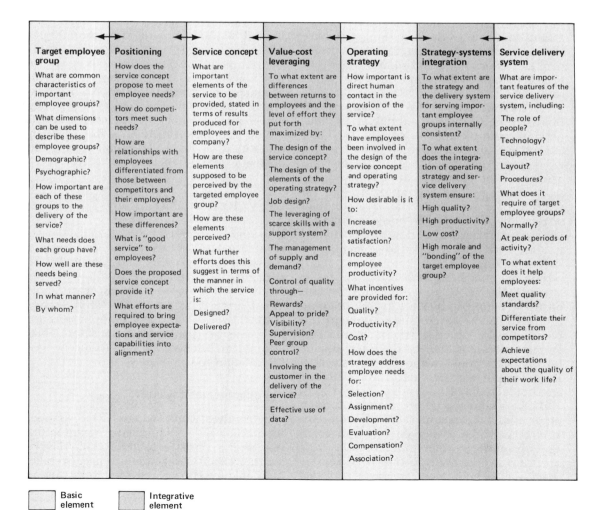

Target employee group	Positioning	Service concept	Value-cost leveraging	Operating strategy	Strategy-systems integration	Service delivery system
What are common characteristics of important employee groups?	How does the service concept propose to meet employee needs?	What are important elements of the service to be provided, stated in terms of results produced for employees and the company?	To what extent are differences between returns to employees and the level of effort they put forth maximized by:	How important is direct human contact in the provision of the service?	To what extent are the strategy and the delivery system for serving important employee groups internally consistent?	What are important features of the service delivery system, including:
What dimensions can be used to describe these employee groups?	How do competitors meet such needs?			To what extent have employees been involved in the design of the service concept and operating strategy?		The role of people?
Demographic?	How are relationships with employees differentiated from those between competitors and their employees?	How are these elements supposed to be perceived by the targeted employee group?	The design of the service concept? The design of the elements of the operating strategy? Job design? The leveraging of scarce skills with a support system? The management of supply and demand? Control of quality through— Rewards? Appeal to pride? Visibility? Supervision? Peer group control? Involving the customer in the delivery of the service? Effective use of data?		To what extent does the integration of operating strategy and service delivery system ensure: High quality? High productivity? Low cost? High morale and "bonding" of the target employee group?	Technology? Equipment?
Psychographic?				How desirable is it to: Increase employee satisfaction? Increase employee productivity? What incentives are provided for: Quality? Productivity? Cost? How does the strategy address employee needs for: Selection? Assignment? Development? Evaluation? Compensation? Association?		Layout? Procedures?
How important are each of these groups to the delivery of the service?	How important are these differences?	How are these elements perceived?				What does it require of target employee groups?
What needs does each group have?	What is "good service" to employees?	What further efforts does this suggest in terms of the manner in which the service is:				Normally? At peak periods of activity?
How well are these needs being served?	Does the proposed service concept provide it?	Designed? Delivered?				To what extent does it help employees:
In what manner?	What efforts are required to bring employee expectations and service capabilities into alignment?					Meet quality standards?
By whom?						Differentiate their service from competitors? Achieve expectations about the quality of their work life?

☐ Basic element   ☐ Integrative element

the operating strategy in mind can form the foundation for remarkable gains in productivity.

A case in point is the ServiceMaster Company, based in Downers Grove, Illinois, which manages support services for hospitals, schools, and industrial companies. It supervises the employees of customers' organizations engaged in housekeeping, food service, and equipment maintenance. These are services that are peripheral to the customers' businesses and therefore get little management attention.

Many of the people whom ServiceMaster oversees are functionally illiterate. To them, as well as its own managers, ServiceMaster directs a service concept centered around the philosophy stated by its CEO, "Before asking someone to do something you have to help them be something." ServiceMaster provides educational and motivational programs to help these employees "be something."

To its own supervisors the company offers training leading to an ambitious "master's" program taught in part by the chief executive. New responsibilities and opportunities present themselves via the rapid growth of the company, approximating 20 percent per year, nearly all of it from expansion of existing operations rather than acquisition. Elaborate training aids and a laboratory for developing new equipment and materials enhance the employee-managers' "be something" feeling.

For customers' employees ServiceMaster tries to build the "be something" attitude and improve their productivity by redesigning their jobs and by developing equipment and pictorial, color-coded instructional material. In most cases it is the first time that anyone has paid attention to the service of which these employees are a part. ServiceMaster also holds weekly sessions to exchange ideas and offers educational programs to, among other things, develop literacy. ServiceMaster also recruits up to 20 percent of its own managers from the ranks in jobs it handles. The service concept clearly is improved self-respect, self-development, personal satisfaction, and upward mobility.

Another company slogan, repeated often, is "to help people grow." When a hospital served by the company decided to hire a deaf person, ServiceMaster's local head didn't object. Instead he authorized three of his supervisors to take a course in sign language.

It should be no surprise that the turnover rate among ServiceMaster's 7,000 employees is low. Further, the turnover rate in organizations it services is much lower than the averages for their industries. And when ServiceMaster takes a job, the productivity achieved by supervised support workers invariably rises dramatically.

Now a billion-dollar company, ServiceMaster had a return on equity from 1973 through 1985 that was the highest of all the largest service or industrial companies in the United States, averaging more than 30 percent after taxes. It oversees the support service employees for 15 hospitals in Japan, which probably makes it the largest exporter of managerial talent to Japan. According to one ServiceMaster executive, "The Japanese immediately recognize and identify with what we do and how we do it." This company turns its strategic service vision inward with dramatic results.

THE VISION APPLIED

In addition to building a strategic service vision, the best service companies apply it to customers and to those who deliver the service and oversee its delivery—in new or different ways. From my study of organizations like Hartford Steam Boiler and ServiceMaster, I've gathered a series of lessons useful for service providers to consider. These lessons can furnish goods producers food for thought too.

Rethink Quality Control

Executives whose careers have spanned service as well as manufacturing agree that reaching a consistently high quality level is tougher in services. In high-contact (so-called high-encounter) services, the interaction between two people or more varies with each transaction. In low-contact services, people many miles from the customer have to rely on their own judgment in handling orders and other transactions and in fielding complaints.

Those who have tried to solve the quality control problem by adding more supervision have found that it limits effectiveness. A service transaction cannot be halted, examined, and recycled like a product.

The most effective approaches to the problem have included restructuring of incentives to emphasize quality, designing jobs to give service providers higher visibility in dealing with customers, and building a peer group to foster teamwork and instill a sense of pride.

One incentive that is often effective in organizations ranging from rapid transit companies to hotels is the employee-of-the-month award—especially if based on customer feedback. Both monetary and nonmonetary incentives have been used successfully. What's more, the cost is low.

Making the person who delivers the service more visible is another technique. In England, at the Lex Service Group's luxury auto dealerships, the customer is encouraged to go directly to the mechanic working on the car. The Shouldice Hospital near Toronto, Canada specializes in the repair of hernias using only local anesthetic—a practice that allows the doctor to talk with the patient during the operation. Defective work is referred to the doctor responsible. The remission rate for hernias performed at Shouldice is less than one-tenth that of the average North American hospital. At Benihana, the U.S. chain of Japanese-style steak houses, the chef cooks at a grill in front of the restaurant guests. The chef's visibility and proximity to customers promote a consistently high quality of service and a consistently high level of tips.

Incentives and visibility may be insufficient for those tasks performed without supervision and out of view of the customer. In these cases, some companies rely on careful selection and thorough training of employees and the development of programs to build both a sense of pride in the service

and a sense of identification with the company. This bonding process can be hard for rivals to emulate and can thereby contribute to competitive advantage.

Schlumberger's wire-line service has roughly 2,000 geological engineers, each responsible for a mobile rig equipped with more than $1 million worth of computers and electronic gear that helps predict the outcome of petroleum producers' drilling efforts. Each year the company recruits those it considers the brightest of the crop of college engineering graduates, spends months teaching them how to use the equipment, and goes to great lengths to make them feel a part of a special tradition. As one engineer put it recently, "Indoctrination is just as important as technical training." This is all in preparation for an assignment to represent Schlumberger in the field, without direct supervision, often in a remote part of the world. Two measures of the success of this program are Schlumberger's dominant share of the world's wire-line business and the profit-to-sales ratios for this company, which consistently exceed others in its industry in good times and bad.

Often effective in achieving and maintaining quality is peer group control, supported by incentives, training, job design, and service delivery system design. In cases where professional standards have been established for a task, they reinforce peer group control.

In an architectural firm, the mere existence of a policy requiring partners' review of every piece of work can keep partners and associates on their toes. Surgeons are sometimes assigned in teams to foster the learning process and encourage peer group control. A partner of a leading real estate development company told me, "There are three things I'm most concerned about in my work. In this order, they are not to embarrass my colleagues, not to cast a bad light on the company by inadequately serving my clients, and making money." It's not surprising that this company has a strong sense of shared values, reinforced by a policy of encouraging partners to invest in the projects that they propose and carry out.

Recent research suggests that the internal strategic service vision, quality control, and success are connected, especially in those providers of high-encounter service requiring judgment in delivery. I show it as the "quality wheel" in Figure 1. Studies directly link customer satisfaction and the resulting sales volume to the satisfaction derived by the person serving the customer.[3] Naturally, the more motivated the employee, the better the service.

The selection and development of employees, care in assignment, and the layout and equipment of the facility (in a high-contact environment) are all integral elements of the design of the service encounter, which in turn is based on the company's assessment of customer needs. Preconditioning of the customer may also be a part of the design of the service encounter. Review and redesign of the encounter go on continually as the organization assesses how well it is meeting those needs.

A part of the internal service vision is the design of policies and performance measures that further the fulfillment of customers' needs. For example, the server's well-being in the job apparently depends, at least

in part, on the extent to which his or her superiors emphasize the solution of problems for customers rather than strict adherence to a set of policies and procedures.[4]

Driving the self-reinforcing elements of the wheel of quality takes a great deal of executive time and requires an honest interest in people across the organization. The senior vice president for finance of Delta Airlines, an organization well regarded for its service and its employee programs, remarked recently, "I would guess that 25 percent of the time of the finance department officers is spent listening to people problems."

For most service companies, people obviously are more important than machines in the control of quality. But even where the machines employed carry an unusually high value, as in Schlumberger and Delta, developing and building the dedication of people takes precedence.

Reassess the Effects of Scale

In service organizations, scale economies are often much more important at the company level than at the operating unit level. This is particularly true for companies that have many units over wide areas connected by a common identity. Such scale gives McDonald's and Hertz great purchasing clout and General Cinema the advantage of selling soft drinks of its own manufacture.

Large scale at the company level is important for exploiting network effects, a phenomenon much more important in the service than in the manufacturing sector. To a point, the addition of new network links augments volume for those parts already in place, thus building average network capacity utilization. The addition of service to Las Vegas from its Memphis hub gave Federal Express more volume on the Memphis-New York link. When Visa adds a large retailer to its network of card-accepting establishments, it increases the attractiveness of its credit card to present and potential cardholders and the potential volume to be realized by retailers already accepting the card.

Bigger is not better in those service in-

FIGURE 1
How Success Builds High-Contact Services

dustries in which the factory must be taken into the marketplace to sell a more accessible, visible, and convenient product that meets customers' needs. Factories operated by the Hyatt and Marriott organizations (called hotels) have not, on average, grown in size for years. These companies have settled on a range of hotel dimensions that can be designed, located, and operated effectively to achieve the capacity utilization, quality of service, and financial performance they want. The range describes sizes at which diseconomies resulting from poor supervision and inflexibility tend to outweigh advantages of larger scale. In the design and siting of hotels, Hyatt and Marriott give the less quantifiable advantages of market flexibility weight equal to operating economies of scale.

At the unit operating level, many service companies have found that the loss of flexibility and greater difficulty in supervising those delivering the service far outweigh any savings realized in operating costs as unit size grows. In the rush to cut costs per seat-mile, for example, many of the world's airlines bought large, wide-bodied aircraft like the Airbus 300 and McDonnell DC-10. While these plans performed admirably, their effective utilization required funneling large numbers of passengers into the airline's hub. Moreover, because business travelers, who represent the most attractive market segment, are prone to choose an airline on the basis of times and frequency of flights, the load and schedule consolidation necessary for effective employment of wide-bodied aircraft worked against the goal of building traffic.

When Jon Carlzon became CEO of Scandinavian Airlines System in 1980, wide-bodied aircraft were used extensively between the airline's hub at Copenhagen and major cities like London and Paris. With smaller DC-9's, SAS funneled travelers between the hub and other Scandinavian cities. To reclaim the business travelers SAS had lost, Carlzon relegated most of the wide-bodies to charter work and offered nonstop flights using DC-9s between Scandinavian and principal European cities.

A size question confronts nearly every power utility in the United States today. For years it was industry gospel that the more power-generating capacity concentrated in one place, the greater the economies of scale. This was the case until the 1970s, when ever-larger units began encountering reliability problems. Furthermore, construction schedule stretchouts, at times fomented by environmental groups' agitation against big plants, caused the expected power-generating economies to vanish. Finally, an improved capability for transmitting excess energy from one market to another made it possible to buy energy for less than the big units could afford to charge. So many utilities today are meeting the needs of smaller markets' fluctuating demands more economically through new means.

Replace and Create Assets with Information

For decades, manufacturers have sought ways of substituting information for assets. Foremost among these are forecasting and inventory control techniques. For many service operations, information offers creative new ways to substitute for assets.

Heating oil dealers, by maintaining data on the capacity of their customers' tanks, on habitual consumption rates, and on weather, program fuel oil deliveries to provide 100 percent availability while reducing delivery times and the number of trucks and drivers. These companies substitute information for assets.

The Rural/Metro Fire Department extends effective fire protection at a fraction of the cost of most municipally run fire departments. This Scottsdale, Arizona-based company analyzes data on past fires and uses much smaller, less expensive trucks staffed with smaller crews and equipped with a large-diameter hose that can shoot a lot of water on a fire very fast. On the way to a fire, a truck crew can learn the floor plan of the building to which it is going. While speeding through the streets, the crew examines a microfiche of the layout on a screen. Rural/Metro substitutes information for assets.

Many service industries are information

driven, beginning with familiarity between the server and the served. In many (not all), assets have never been allowed to become dominant, perhaps because of limited capital. But with the development of new technologies for processing and communicating information, companies in these industries have advanced far beyond the use of information as a substitute for assets. They are instead using the information they have collected in one business as the basis for new services.

Companies servicing manufactured goods, for example, have built data bases on the types, wear rates, and failure rates of various parts of a furnace, appliance, or automobile. A company can use this information for sending timely service reminders to customers and also to manage parts inventories to reflect the age and condition of the particular machine serviced. In the process, the data have taken on great value for the producers of the goods—and they're willing to pay for the information.

A credit card service builds expenditure profiles for its customers; broken patterns may signal a problem like stolen cards. Theft is sometimes suspected when a large expenditure is made far from the cardholder's address. Instead of outright disallowance of a retailer's request for a big charge, one major travel card issuer tries to determine whether the cardholder indeed is traveling in the retailer's area. Information collected for this service yields person-specific data about travel patterns that often is valuable to airlines and hotel chains (to name two businesses). But the company limits the use of such information to ways that benefit its cardholders.

Dun & Bradstreet's $2.7 billion enterprise is centered on its data base, a file of credit information describing businesses in 30 countries. Through development and acquisition, the file steadily grows. D&B has consistently realized about 10 percent of its revenues from business that did not exist three years before. Nearly all of these services use the same data base but package the information in different ways. A potential competitor would have to spend an estimated $1 billion—nearly half D&B's net asset value—to duplicate the data base.

Though a data base may constitute a service provider's most important asset, it doesn't appear on the balance sheet and can't be depreciated. But the degree to which many such companies rely on an accumulation of knowledge as their chief competitive weapon and source of new business development suggests opportunities for their counterparts in the manufacturing sector.

Harlan Cleveland has pointed out that information, unlike most manufactured products, is often infinitely expandable (as it is used), compressible, substitutable (for capital, labor, or physical materials), transportable, diffusive (hard to keep secret), and sharable (as opposed to exchangeable).[5] If it is infinitely expandable, those who possess it are limited only by their imagination in creating new ideas, revenue sources, and job opportunities. As the demand for creative exploitation of information grows, so will job creation in the service sector.

The Service Economy

Many successful service providers have strategies in common that offer lessons to other companies. Among these are:

- Close coordination of the marketing-operations relationship.
- A strategy built around elements of a strategic service vision.
- An ability to redirect the strategic service inward to focus on vital employee groups.
- A stress on the control of quality based on a set of shared values, peer group status, generous incentives, and, where possible, a close relationship with the customer.
- A cool appraisal of the effects of scale on both efficiency and effectiveness.
- The substitution of information for other assets.
- The exploitation of information to generate new business.

Why these particular lessons among all I might cite? For one reason, they feature characteristics that distinguish many service industries from goods-producing industries. Notice the emphasis on people, ideas, and information instead of things. For another, they promise twin benefits as part of a business strategy. Each can further differentiation of the service product as well as lower costs.

These lessons have significance for the economy too. While the service economy has wrought a gigantic social restructuring of the United States, it has come in for unwarranted criticism for its low rate of productivity gains. Companies like those I have described, however, have created new jobs while raising productivity. If other companies learn these lessons, job opportunities in the service sector will continue to expand and productivity continue to rise. These developments will ease the pressures for the inflation of service prices, sharpen the already respected competitiveness abroad of U.S.-based services, and contribute to the partnership between services and manufacturing that is crucial to a healthy, balanced national business base.

NOTES

[1] Christopher H. Lovelock, Eric Langeard, John E. G. Bateson, and Pierre Eiglier, "Some Organizational Problems Facing Marketing in the Service Sector," in *Marketing of Services*, ed. James H. Donnelly and William R. George (Chicago, Ill.: American Marketing Association, 1981), p. 168.

[2] See James F. Loud, "Organizing for Customer Service," *The Bankers Magazine*, November-December 1980, p. 41.

[3] Benjamin Schneider and David E. Bowen, "New Services Design, Development, and Implementation and the Employee," in *New Services*, ed. William R. George and Claudia Marshall (Chicago, Ill.: American Marketing Association, 1985), p. 82; and Eugene M. Johnson and Daniel T. Seymour, "The Impact of Cross Selling on the Service Encounter in Retail Banking," in *The Service Encounter*, ed. John A. Czepiel, Michael R. Soloman, and Carol F. Surprenant (Lexington, Mass.: D. C. Heath, 1985), p. 243.

[4] This is the implication of John J. Parkington and Benjamin Schneider in "Some Correlates of Experienced Job Stress: A Boundary Role Study," *Academy of Management Journal*, June 1979, p. 270.

[5] Harlan Cleveland, "Information as a Resource," *The Futurist*, December 1982, p. 37.

Cunningham Inc.:
Industrial Service Group

PENNY PITTMAN MERLISS
CHRISTOPHER H. LOVELOCK

A major manufacturing firm has diversified into services. Its Industrial Service Group provides repair and maintenance services to a wide array of electrical and mechanical equipment. Management is evaluating the results of a regional experiment involving a new territorial organization of previously independent service centers, designed to improve planning, sales management, and service execution.

Adam Newman, director of strategic planning for Cunningham Inc.'s Industrial Service Group, felt a mixture of nervousness and suspense as he tapped on the open door of his general manager's office on a February day. We've finally got it, he thought—the territorial organizational blueprint that's going to carry this division through the eighties. But is Paul McDonald going to buy all these new ideas?

The answer was not long in coming. Glancing up from his paper-strewn desk, McDonald waved Newman to a chair, leaned forward, and declared:

Adam, I'm concerned about some of the implications in this latest plan to reorganize our field operations. There's no question that our marketing management in the field is weak, and with the prospect of 15 percent annual earnings growth, we've got to do a better job of training and directing our sales force. We've got a national network of 15 large service centers that can service just about any kind of mechanical or electrical equipment, and 50 smaller ones with more limited capabilities. And, of course, each center has its own salesmen.

McDonald tapped a thick binder on his desk.

This case was prepared by Penny Pittman Merliss, Research Assistant, under the direction of Associate Professor Christopher H. Lovelock. Copyright © 1981 by the President and Fellows of Harvard College. Harvard Business School Case 9-581-022. Reprinted by permission.

You've got a plan here that integrates the sales effort for both large and small service centers at the territorial level. I know Tom Simmons has had some success trying it out in his region, and you're telling me now that this is the way of the future for ISG.

Newman watched as the older man walked over to a corner window and surveyed the busy industrial scene four stories below. Finally, McDonald turned and continued:

What worries me about this reorganization is its effect on management development. Traditionally, our small-center managers have been one of our best sources of talent. We need better marketing, all right—but if you take control of the sales function away from a small-center manager, you're taking away a good chunk of his control over his own work flow. You're weakening his autonomy and cutting into his decision-making powers. And is that really going to help the group in the long run?

SERVICE BUSINESSES AT CUNNINGHAM INC.

Cunningham Inc. reported approximately $7 billion in annual sales and $430 million in net income. It offered a wide range of manufactured goods and services to its customers, including motors and generators and power delivery equipment, as well as a broad line of consumer and defense products. The company had entered the service business more than half a century earlier by providing after-sales equipment repair for its own products. As Cunningham's line of manufactured products had grown, so had the range and scope of services. Over time the company came to offer its repair and maintenance services to customers who operated equipment produced by other manufacturers.

Service businesses, including financial services, broadcasting, and industrial maintenance and repair made up an increasing share of the company's income. All the service operations, like those in manufacturing, were measured as independent profit centers, not as contributors to other divisions of the corporation, and all were managed with an aggressive invest-grow strategy. Cunningham's chairman drew attention to the success of the service groups in the company's latest annual report:

Today, the management and stockholders of Cunningham Inc. can take pride in an organization which has grown far beyond its original area of expertise—the manufacture of high-quality electrical equipment. This is still our key business, but earnings in our service businesses are growing too, at about 13% annually. Services now account for 25 percent of our revenues.

Industrial Service Group

The Industrial Service Group (ISG) was among the fastest-growing groups of the company; sales more than doubled in the previous five years (*Exhibit 1*). ISG was one of the leading domestic and international suppliers of high-quality repair and maintenance services for all manufacturers' electrical and mechanical equipment. Through its extensive geographic coverage—service centers existed within 100 miles of 83 percent of potential business—the group had established a strong position in a field where fast turnaround was considered extremely important. ISG had 65 domestic service centers; the national network included 15 large centers—capable of repairing the largest

EXHIBIT 1
ISG Sales and Earnings
($ millions)

Year	Sales	Net Income	Percent Return on Sales*
1974	148.3	10.1	6.8%
1975	200.5	15.6	7.8
1976	225.4	18.0	8.0
1977	251.9	19.9	7.9
1978	302.3	21.8	7.2
1979	356.7	25.7	7.2
1980	406.7	27.7	6.8

*Includes income going to international joint venture partners.

SOURCE: Company records.

transformers (20 feet high) and motors (20 tons)—and 50 smaller centers where technicians spent much of their time rewinding electric motors of less than 200 horsepower.

Structurally, the ISG organization was divided between five headquarters departments and three field regions. The headquarters organization consisted of directors of service programs, strategic planning, employee relations, and finance, plus a legal counsel, and their staffs. The field organization consisted of three regional general managers who had profit center responsibility for the service centers in their regions. Each of these eight individuals reported directly to the group general manager, Paul McDonald (*Exhibit 2*).

The key to the complex central organization was the service programs department, a matrix within which were located five program managers—each of whom had nationwide responsibility for marketing and technical direction (with measurements tied to the results of their segment sales and earnings in the service centers) and five functional managers specializing in sales, communications, pricing, manufacturing,[1] and training.

The five program managers and their supporting staffs each interacted with regional management and the service centers, as did the five functional managers and their staffs. Likewise, staff from the strategic planning, employee relations, finance, and legal departments also provided specialized assistance to the regions and the service centers.

ISG had no marketing manager. As Adam Newman explained from his vantage point as director of the strategic planning department:

> In this kind of matrix, what you've really got is a kind of double integration—both groups of managers within the headquarters staff, plus the field territories. The person charged with bringing together field marketing and head-

quarters sales, communication, and pricing people is our group general manager.

Market research was handled centrally by ISG's strategic planning department. The division's planners and program managers worked closely with field service center managers and ISG's general manager to review sales and performance data from the field and set each center's sales goals for the upcoming year.

The field operating group was composed of three geographically dispersed regions. Each region contained four to six large service centers—whose managers reported directly to the regional general manager—and 14–20 smaller centers, which were often clustered about the larger ones. The average annual sales volume for large centers, most of which occupied about 50,000 square feet in floor space, was approximately $10 million; small centers occupied 10–12,000 square feet and averaged about $4 million each year in sales. The seven sales reps assigned to each large center had an annual sales quota of $1.5 million per person. Small centers averaged three salesmen each, and their individual quotas were $1.3 million. Small-center managers reported to a manager of development and operations (MDO), who was responsible for opening new shops and expanding existing shops as well as overall supervision. The MDO, like the managers of the large centers, reported directly to the regional general manager. It was ISG's goal to make field management responsible for all service segments in a geographic area.

Service Segments

Equipment serviced by ISG was divided into five major categories or service segments: base electrical, large transformers, transit equipment, installation and field service, and mechanical apparatus (*Exhibit 3*). Each required different equipment and service skills and faced different kinds of competition. All ISG customers performed some of their own maintenance, but many lacked capacity for major overhauls or repair. Some firms operated their own maintenance fa-

---

[1] The manufacturing manager had staff responsibility for new repair technology, new plant construction, safety, and environmental programs.

EXHIBIT 2
Organization Chart

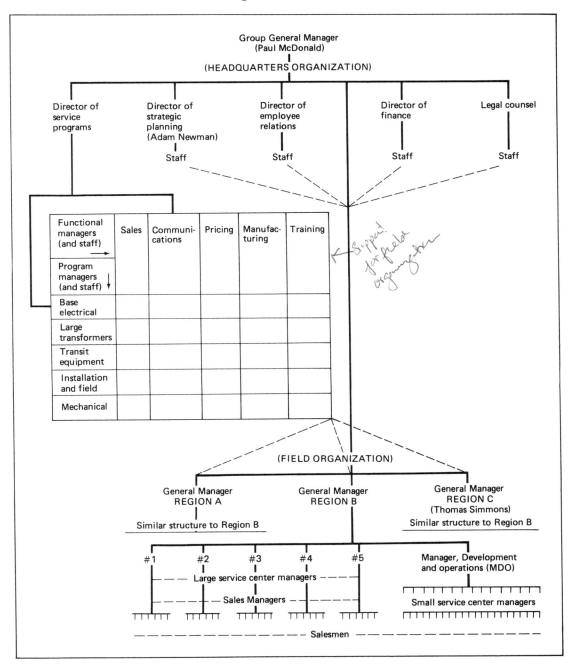

EXHIBIT 3
ISG Service Segments

Equipment Serviced	Major Competitors	SHARE OF ISG REVENUES	
		1976	1980
1. Base electrical (motors and generators, switch-gear, small transformers)	Independent service shops—6,000 in U.S.	46%	42%
2. Large transformers	Morison Electric	12%	11%
3. Transit equipment (traction motors, generators, electrical auxiliaries)	Captive shops	8%	8%
4. Installation and field services (electrical on-site service, management, inspection)	Captive shops, some specialized independents	14%	12%
5. Mechanical (pumps, fans, blowers, compressors, valves, centrifuges, mining equipment)	OEMs, independent machine shops	13%	21%
6. Other		7%	6%

SOURCE: Company records.

cilities, known as "captive shops." These could be huge; the Consolidated Edison shop in Astoria, N.Y., for example, had about 400,000 square feet of floor space (ISG's nearest large service center had about 80,000).

Yet the competitive threat posed by captive shops, ISG managers felt, was becoming less and less significant. Although unions often resisted sending out work, it was difficult for the captives to keep pace with technological developments. The division's sales reps stressed that since customers' work volumes often did not justify investment in specialized equipment and training, captive shops were inherently inefficient, misapplying resources that could be better spent elsewhere in the customer's company.

ISG's major competitors were Morison Electric, with a national network of 70 service centers, and Marlborough-Fuchs. Despite Morison's long-standing reputation as a major manufacturer of electrical equipment, ISG market research showed that Cunningham was preferred by slightly more customers than Morison in three of the five major service segments (*Exhibit 4*). Marlborough-Fuchs was potentially a more significant competitor. It owned Republic Electric Inc., with a substantial but smaller network of electrical centers, and had recently acquired the Katz-Hartley Corp., which controlled a national network of mechanical service centers.

Privately owned independent service shops could be substantial regional competitors in motor and generator repair. Many specialized in electric motors; because of their proximity to customers, they could frequently offer faster turnaround time than Cunningham.

Other customers might turn to an independent or to an OEM (original equipment manufacturer) for service because they were unaware that ISG serviced all brands of equipment, not just Cunningham's.

Prospects for Growth

Management considered ISG's growth prospects excellent. The market growth rate was expected to average 12 percent annually during the next five years. Sales growth had reached 12–15 percent annually. Appraising the future, Newman commented:

In a world of limited resources and continuing economic stress, ISG is going to thrive. We've been hit by the recession, of course, but not as much as the new equipment businesses. Our business has always lagged recessions by three to six months. The first thing that's shut off in a recession is capital investment—while repair is continued, although at a somewhat lower level. Also, inflation is pushing up the prices of new equipment right now faster than productivity improvements can offset costs. That's another reason why repair and moderniza-

EXHIBIT 4
Cunningham Survey of Major Supplier Standing

Fifty-five service centers were surveyed and classified by number of mentions as a preferred supplier. The following tabulation indicates how frequently Cunningham, Morison, or an independent was mentioned as the leading supplier. The mentions for preferred supplier of total electrical service have been weighted by size of the product markets.

| | PERCENT OF TOTAL CENTERS IN FIRST PLACE | | | |
	Cunningham	Morison	*Independent* *#1*	*Independent* *#2*
Base electrical	30%	28%	32%	10%
Large transformers	38	36	24	—
Transit equipment	40	45	15	—
Installation and field service	45	49	5	1
Mechanical	20	18	52	10

*Independent #1 refers to the leading independent in each geographic region surveyed. Independent #2 refers to the second most popular independent in that region. Many service organizations classified as independents were centers managed by OEMs such as Katz-Hartley.

SOURCE: Cunningham Inc. market research department.

tion, as compared to new purchase, will be more and more attractive to our customers.

Equally important to Newman and the division's other planners was ISG's favorable strategic environment. According to Newman's analysis of the market for industrial service—which included captive shops—ISG had only a 3.2 percent share of the domestic market, though it was among the market leaders worldwide. ISG sales were about 80 percent those of Morison, its nearest rival; corporate planners saw no serious roadblocks to expansion.

Customers and Markets

ISG's customers and markets varied widely from segment to segment. In recent years, the division had concentrated on diversification in those shops that were highly dependent on any single customer segment. Frank Mays, manager of ISG's large New Mutley center, recalled:

After the last oil crisis, it occurred to us that the utilities represented a very high percentage of all our revenues in New Mutley. We suddenly woke up and said, "Hey, maintenance is the only cost that they can control—

EXHIBIT 5
ISG Customers by Industry and Location

Industry	Percent of Customer Base	Primary Location
Steel and other metal producers	17%	Midwest
Refineries	6%	Southwest
Chemical manufacturers	7%	East and Gulf Coast
Pulp and paper	12%	Northwest, New England
Utilities	15%	National
Transportation	12%	National
Mining	11%	Midwest and Rocky Mountains
Other	20%	National

SOURCE: Company records.

and they could cut us off at any time." So I put together a plan stating that no segment was to represent more than 25 percent of the shop's business, and no single customer was to account for more than 10 percent. The point is not to cut back on our service to utilities, but to broaden our offerings as we expand and to concentrate on high-growth segments.

Nationally, ISG categorized its customers by industry, as indicated in *Exhibit 5*. ISG was required to match the delivery time, quality, and price offered by its competitors when it went after a Cunningham job, and internal accounts were treated much the same as any others, receiving regular calls from ISG salesmen. "If they get preferred service when they're down," one manager commented, "it's because they're big, regular customers, not because they're Cunningham."

A VISIT TO A SERVICE CENTER

The New Mutley service center was one of ISG's largest facilities, with annual sales exceeding $14 million. Like most of the other centers, it was located in a commercial and light-industrial area on a heavily traveled suburban road. Staff offices were small and functionally furnished; the heart of the operation was out on the floor.

"Don't forget your safety glasses," directed Steven Meyers, the center's assistant manager, as he led visitors into the first of the service areas, where motors were rewound. Electric motors of all shapes and sizes in various stages of cleaning and assembly were neatly ranked around the work space. Sunlight filtering through the service center's windows gleamed on bright copper wire as a 6-foot technician stepped out of a 30-foot-high cylindrical machine.

"Ever seen one of these before?" Meyers asked. "It's a ball mill drive motor. A ball mill is like a giant tin can rotating its side, with a number of large metal balls inside. You insert chunks of stone or cement and start to rotate the mill. As it revolves, the balls drop down and crush the stone into small pieces. The motor on this mill is about 6,000 horsepower—Bill's just finished rewinding it.

"We employ about 200 men here," Meyers continued, gesturing toward another area where a technician was welding a connection on a high-pressure descaling pump. "Our people work in two shifts. You're probably surprised to see how few technicians are out here on the floor—well, this is a job shop operation, not a production line, and a single group of employees will usually do the whole job on this piece of equipment."

Moving to the transformer repair area, Meyers pointed to an oven the size of a small garage: "We can bake just about anything in there. We usually use it for curing the transformer's insulation system, after the equipment is rewound and ready to go back in its tank. Maximum temperature is about 600°F. Over there," he continued, pointing to a tank twelve feet in diameter, "is the second-biggest vacuum pressure impregnation tank on the East Coast. The VPI tank is what we use to provide the new insulation to a motor or transformer like the one I just mentioned. It takes a lot of maintenance to keep this tank ready for use—we've got to keep 10,000 gallons of resin in a separate tank, chill it, and stir it off and on so it won't harden. The VPI tank is idle right now, and it may be idle for weeks. But when we need it, it'll be there."

Meyers's comment was overheard by Anthony DiGrazia, the center's sales manager, also making his way across the floor to check on a job. "That's true for a lot of our most important equipment," DiGrazia explained. "When we approach a customer, we emphasize that we're selling capability—the ability to help him when he's down, at any time of night or day. Our electric utility customers may need that large lathe over there only once a year—but when they do need it, they want it right away."

Stepping aside to make way for a trolley loaded with pump casings, DiGrazia led the way to a hydroturbine generator rotor approximately seven feet in diameter. "Take a look at this thing," he directed, and scraped it carefully with his fingernail, revealing over two inches of caked-on sludge. "This rotor was struck by lightning recently. We're repairing its burned-out stator coils and we're trying to talk the plant foreman into letting us clean the rest. It's costing $17,000 just to disassemble the thing and transport it to and from this shop; it'll cost $20,000 to repair it, and it would take another $25,000 to give the rotor the cleaning it needs. I doubt that it's been properly cleaned since it was first installed 60 years ago. On the other hand, without proper maintenance the rotor could fail, and fail catastrophically—ruining associated equipment and causing upward of $400,000 worth of damage."

The group continued to another work space, stopping to inspect a structure that resembled a square tent pitched on the shop floor. "Here you're looking at a little ingenuity," Meyers remarked, smiling. "We're doing a lot of fluorescent penetrant black-light work these days—testing components like turbine nozzle boxes for defects that are invisible in natural light." He turned to point to another technician across the floor. "That fellow working on the 50-ton crane over there is using a device similar to a Geiger counter to do magnetic particle testing, looking for surface cracks that could disable the equipment later. Nondestructive testing in general is becoming a very big area for us; it lets the customers know where trouble's developing *before* their equipment goes down."

Just before leading his visitors back to the front office, Meyers paused to point out a vertical file of job orders. Many had a photograph clipped to the front page. "That picture is for our protection, as well as the customer's," he explained. "The customer can show us just what he wants done—and we can prove to him that we're returning what he gave us. Makes it a little more difficult for a guy to point to a part that 'we' must have broken while it was here in the shop."

MARKETING

ISG's marketing function was decentralized. Headquarters program managers for sales planning, communications, pricing, and market research constituted a planning and teaching force, but the actual marketing was executed at the centers themselves.

ISG employed 255 salesmen, of whom 105 were associated with large centers and 150 with small centers. Those at the large centers reported to a sales manager based at the center; the others reported to the small center managers. Each facility was considered a profit center and encouraged to pursue all segments of business; each salesman, with only a few exceptions, called on accounts representing every segment the center serviced. It was a divisional policy that any small center, if aggressively managed and marketed, could become a large one.

Almost by definition, however, large centers could service more segments than small centers, which did not encounter enough business in some areas to justify investment in expensive specialized equipment. Yet even though the small centers frequently uncovered business too complex for their own facilities to handle, they did not go out of their way to send it along to their larger neighbors. As Mays, of the New Mutley center, put it:

> That small-center manager is measured for his center alone. The salesmen work on straight salary, no commission, and unless their center can do the job, they don't really have the incentive to go out there and represent everybody else.

Sales

ISG sales representatives were recruited from a variety of sources—colleges, other Cunningham operations, the service centers themselves. Although many had an engineering background, advanced technical expertise was not considered a requirement for the job. In Mays's opinion, recruitment had historically been less than selective: "Too many people felt that the Cunningham name alone would bring in 60–70 percent of our business." The group policy of individual performance measurement for all centers, added to the fact that small-center salesmen reported to small-center managers, created other problems. Small-center managers had been known to use salesmen as replacements for foremen, or as on-site job supervisors—taking them off the road for as long as six months.

On the other hand, the small-center manager's close involvement with the sales force could constitute a real advantage, according to Mark O'Hara, manager of one of ISG's small centers:

> My salesmen cover all the accounts except for one big customer, which I handle; I also cover all problems and questions coming into the office from customers. That way we've got salesmen out knocking on doors, and the manager in the office. I'm always on the phone with customers; the most important thing for them—in some ways even more important than the work itself—is feeling free to get back in touch with the center easily, knowing that someone's watching over the job.

The ISG sales force received little formal training, after a one-week course in salesmanship. Some follow-up training was available in the form of three-day courses introducing new services. Large-center salesmen could consult their sales manager when problems came up—although the manager also received relatively little training in sales direction and had only occasional contact with other sales managers in the division. Small-center salesmen rarely saw their colleagues in other centers and received sales direction from their center managers, whose sales experience varied widely.

Near the end of each calendar year, salesmen began planning for the next by filling out a budget sheet for each account, stating available and target business. These figures were checked and adjusted by the sales or center manager and given to the regional general manager, who compared them with projected figures drawn up at headquarters. If the regional figures appeared too low, they were increased, and the center was faced with the burden of deciding whether to spread the new quotas out, hire new sales representatives, or seek out new markets.

Newman and other ISG planners held strong opinions concerning the need for effective sales management within ISG. According to Newman:

> The job of time management is much more important here than it is in selling something like a steam turbine where you can work for three years on the same job before it closes. ISG selling means repetitive calls, often keen competition, a diligent effort to diversify services.

It was difficult to measure sales effectiveness, although each member of the sales force did make out a weekly call plan to be reviewed by the sales or center manager after calls were finished. Because calls were often made under emergency conditions, sales representatives were expected to use their own judgment in allocating their time. As Carl Hoffenberg, sales manager for a large service center, pointed out, this could be risky:

> Think of the case where you've sent out a salesman to cultivate a potential $100,000 maintenance contract—and he suddenly hears that a $1,000 motor has broken down somewhere else. We do have guys who will cancel the contract meeting to go look at the motor.

About 25–30 percent of sales calls were made under emergency conditions at customer request. To keep business growing, the ISG sales force knew it was necessary to schedule calls at other times also—when some of them found it difficult to know what to talk about.

Mark O'Hara, who had joined ISG as a service technician and spent six years in sales for the New Mutley center before moving up to management, felt that even a routine sales call required a carefully planned presentation tailored to a customer's specific needs. Sales brochures with color pictures were essential tools in introducing customers to ISG's capabilities; but even the brochures, O'Hara told his sales force, were not as effective as case histories and examples related to the customer's own equipment.

It was a group sales goal to move ISG along a continuum that ran from emergency repair to regular maintenance, toward "turnkey maintenance"—a contract to maintain equipment either during its scheduled maintenance shutdowns, or continuously all year long.

A Sales Manager's Comments

Tony DiGrazia, sales manager for the New Mutley service center, had come to ISG from new equipment sales and considered his current job a particular challenge. "You're really selling an intangible," he noted, "capability, manpower, yourself, your organization. It's a job that has real room for creative selling, because you can't demonstrate your product in place and working." He added:

> You're usually directing your selling effort to first-line supervision and middle management—the foreman, sometimes his superintendent or general foreman, or the manager of maintenance. Some of these people are very cautious—they've often worked their way up from the floor—and it can be extremely difficult to convince them to spend $25,000 on maintenance to keep a $500,000 generator from breaking down.

DiGrazia saw one of the hardest sales tasks as "selling away from the OEM"—convincing a satisfied user of Morison equipment, for example, to try Cunningham service. He described his approach as "flexible":

> On one hand, for Cunningham equipment we have all the drawings and the background and we know how it works and so forth, so we're the ideal service supplier. When we're competing for another manufacturer's equipment, we sell our Cunningham expertise. Also important is our centralized matrix support and ability to replicate what we learn at one center across many centers, which is a real strength in servicing virtually all manufacturers' electrical and mechanical equipment.

Hoffenberg saw even more challenging difficulties in the sales job:

> I think the hardest problem is getting work out of captive shops—fighting unions and getting public agencies to spend money. Depending on the segment we're talking about, captive shops do 25–70 percent of the total maintenance work available. It can also be extremely frustrating trying to persuade customers to order maintenance work that they can put off —even though their faulty equipment could malfunction, possibly causing extensive damage and downtime.

Advertising and Promotion

Advertising and promotion at ISG were divided between headquarters and the field. National media purchases were planned by the group's communications manager, who had budgeted $1.5 million for sales promotion of all kinds that year. Because most potential buyers were not thought to be print-oriented, ISG had traditionally spent little money on newspaper or magazine advertising, usually limiting ads to industrial magazines such as *Plant Engineering* rather than the general business press.

It was up to a center's sales manager to put together a local marketing strategy—in small centers, the center manager handled the job. Investments in promotion varied widely; some large centers spent several thousand dollars a year on local promotion, and some small ones spent $100. The most common promotional tool, outside personal selling and brochures, was direct mail addressed to a plant's maintenance superintendent, and sometimes composed by a local sales manager (*Exhibit 6*).

Pricing

The repair industry as a whole was characterized by wide price flexibility. Markets were local, with local competition; moreover, the cost of emergency repair for any customer was usually insignificant compared to downtime costs. Company research indicated that speed of delivery and quality of repair were valued most highly by customers in selecting service suppliers (*Exhibit 7*). Accordingly, ISG positioned itself as a price leader whose technical expertise and excellent facilities would ensure the speedy turnaround and high craftsmanship that customers valued over price.

EXHIBIT 6
Direct Mail Promotion

Cunningham Inc.

Industrial Service Group

Dear Customer:

A penny 🪙 for your thoughts—your maintenance thoughts that is! If you are like most organizations these days, you are trying to solve repair problems and maintain your equipment while staying within an ever-shrinking maintenance budget. As the penny in our letter illustrates, our money-buying power is getting smaller daily, especially in these times of high inflation.

The Cunningham Service Center can help you with this maintenance dilemma with sound advice and excellent service. Take a moment and ask yourself a few questions. Are you able to stretch your pennies to cover all your pressing maintenance needs? Are you really getting your money's worth on repair service? Is your present equipment service a good value for the money spent? What areas can be improved by new ideas?

As part of our standard capabilities, we have values that can help you with each of these questions and would like to share our ideas with you.

Our service capabilities include:

- Base electrical service for motors and switchgear
- Transit equipment repair and maintenance
- Transformer testing and repair
- Mechanical repair of all types
- Installation and field service

All of these capabilities can be performed within our center or on-site at your plant.

Send back the enclosed reply card and we'll share our maintenance ideas with you. You have nothing to lose, but you can gain more value for the money spent by your company.

It's as simple as a penny—we want to be your maintenance vendor.

We are ready to put our people in touch with your organization at a moment's notice—are you ready?

Best regards,

Anthony DiGrazia
Sales Manager

ARG:im
Enc.

EXHIBIT 7
Cunningham Profile of the Ideal Service Supplier

Respondents in each of the product categories were asked on an unprompted basis why their current supplier(s) were preferred. This table reflects the ideal service offering for each product category.

	PERCENT OF MENTIONS				
	Base Electrical (%)	Large Transformers (%)	Transit Equipment (%)	Installation and Field Service (%)	Mechanical (%)
Delivery-related comments: good, fast service, fast delivery, etc.	43	32	34	35	36
Quality and Competence comments such as quality of workmanship, reliability and dependability, past performance and experience	30	39	33	33	29
Cost comments	18	19	12	15	11
Location/Facilities	7	7	9	9	10
Preference for OEM	1	2	10	6	12
Other Factors	1	1	2	2	2
TOTAL	100%	100%	100%	100%	100%

SOURCE: Cunningham Inc. market research department.

Routine repairs such as the rewind of small motors were included in a pricing handbook published by headquarters; such jobs accounted for approximately 30 percent of ISG's sales. The field retained authority to change prices when it appeared advisable to do so—for instance, to meet competition. For less routine work, pricing calculations were facilitated by the use of an estimating sheet, which allowed sales representatives or service technicians to identify the operations required for a particular job, then estimate the cost of labor, materials, and equipment. To this, Cunningham added a target margin which took into account the nature of the job and the technical and scheduling risks it involved. "Each job is unique; each situation is different," observed one center manager.

Hoffenberg, discussing pricing at a meeting with DiGrazia, commented:

What this all comes down to is an opportunity to be fully paid for value given. We had a call last week from a ship with a broken pump shaft, and we were there within an hour and got the shaft right into the service center.

DiGrazia cautioned:

If you're smart, you darned well better give *some* kind of estimate to make sure the customer understands the magnitude of the job. During an emergency, price is not important, but later they can get irritated if you didn't give them some notion of what was coming. I look at a job and say, "You've got about a $10,000 job here on this shaft"—and try to estimate and anticipate all the work that will be required. It's a very delicate thing—you should give the guy a feel for the job, but not to the point where he latches onto the number and won't negotiate later. You've really got to know the value of your service, which is why face-to-face negotiation is one of my favorite parts of this job. Where's the challenge in carrying a price book around all the time?

Also important in pricing negotiations, as one service center manager put it, was the fact that "we have a total capability for service which many of our competitors don't have, and that costs us every day whether we use it or not." Hoffenberg amplified:

We've got a 350-ton wheel press in the Dorset center that nobody else has got. Now suppose a customer finds he has some expensive piece of large equipment with a bad wheel. Without a press of that tonnage, he can't separate the wheel from the shaft and save the shaft—he'll have to replace them both. What do we charge him? Well, he saved $5,000–$10,000 on a replacement shaft, if not more, so he ought to be willing to pay a few bucks.

The relative costs of repair versus new purchase, as Hoffenberg pointed out, were essential in pricing negotiations. A small coupling, for instance, might be repaired for less than half its replacement cost, in which case the customer's savings over replacement would affect pricing. When a replacement wouldn't be available for six months, the value of ISG's service was even greater. DiGrazia noted:

The whole situation is so totally up in the air that it really puts the onus on the salesman, and the sales manager and the center's organization, to be fair, because these are continuing relationships that we have with these customers.

Added Hoffenberg:

We try to get it through to customers that we're in the service business, not the business of selling machine time. Particularly in the mechanical area, a lot of work has traditionally been done on a machine-time basis, involving the replacement of a part rather than the overhaul of a whole piece of equipment. You can get into a fight with customers where they'll say, "Gee, that machine only took so many hours to work" and so forth and we keep telling them we're in the business of performing repairs and doing overhauls, not of selling a machine operator. We're selling capability, readiness to service, and expertise—and we're saving money and production time for our customers.

One of the sales force's most important duties was pointing out to customers the quality difference that lay beneath very different competitive estimates for the same job—the fact that, as Hoffenberg put it, "One guy's metallizing with platinum and the next is metallizing with lead." The key was to sense the customer's needs—"to find out whether he doesn't want the extra benefits, or just doesn't know about them." For a brand new account the center might do a "Cadillac job" at no extra charge, calling its quality to the customer's attention at intervals and trying to sell the same job next time.

Although much pricing was left to individual discretion, the group did place limits on the size of the jobs which each rank in the selling hierarchy could approve. Sales representatives were limited to $10,000; sales managers and small-center managers, to $25,000; and large-center managers, to $100,000. "It's important to keep in mind that competition and customer relations do keep pricing within reasonable limits," Newman commented. "The group's ratio of net income to sales is considerably less than 8 percent, which is typical of most industrial service industries."

PLANNING FOR GROWTH

Newman and a few other ISG planners and managers had come to feel that ISG's field organization needed improvement if it was to support continuing growth during the 1980s. They were concerned about ISG's failure to provide marketing direction to its sales force, as well as the group's lack of what Newman called "rationalized capacity between centers." Ideally, he felt, even salesmen working for a small center should be able to offer customers access to all ISG services. Others felt that fragmentation of the marketing effort was seriously affecting sales. Said Frank Mays: "We really aren't serving all the markets because of the boundaries we've set up."

Past Changes in Organizational Structure

ISG had gone through several reorganizations in the past as its potential became more widely recognized. For many years after Cunningham's founding, the service centers had handled only Cunningham products and had reported to regional selling organizations. In 1960 came the first major change, as the service centers were joined together into a national organization with a national general manager. Subsequent growth came from increased geographic penetration as well as the addition of new services. In 1975 the service centers were given corporate group status; soon afterward the three field service regions were set up and a manager of development and operations (MDO) appointed in each region to supervise managers of the smaller centers (*Exhibit 2*).

Because the backgrounds of small-center managers varied widely—some had degrees in engineering or business administration, others were foremen who had worked their way up from the floor—it was thought that these centers needed special senior management attention. ISG prided itself on the entrepreneurial spirit of the small-center managers, and gave them a chance early in their careers to handle almost all the functions of running a business. In Newman's words, "The concept was that the MDO would be a senior person (usually a former large-center manager) who really knew how to run service centers, and he could teach the small-center managers." But Mays believed that these expectations had not been fully realized:

> As we've continued to grow, the demands on the MDO's time have shifted from operations to business development. Almost 50 percent of his time is now devoted to acquiring new accounts and identifying new service offerings, and about 50 percent to operating the centers. The attention that the small-center managers are getting has been slipping and when that happens, growth in the small centers slows down.

Newman disagreed; he thought the MDOs devoted substantial time to the small centers. However, because they were measured on the success of the small centers, the MDOs tended to keep as much work there as possible, ignoring the resources of the larger centers. Yet Newman, like Mays and other ISG managers, felt the MDO concept was a step in the right direction. The problem was, what should come next? Several ISG managers urged that the group be broken up nationally by segments, rather than geographically. Newman had different ideas:

> If you look at market share performance, you'll see a great difference between the large and the small centers. The large centers are doing more large, specialized work, and relatively few smaller, repetitive jobs. The small centers are doing a lot of general service and repair, but fewer specialized projects. To take full advantage of both capabilities, the centers will have to work together—and that means we need an integrated geographic organization and a regional sales force.

The Regional Experiment

Thomas Simmons, who had been appointed regional general manager for one of ISG's three regions three years earlier, agreed with Newman's assessment. Simmons subsequently broke his region into four geographic sales territories, placing experienced, aggressive sales managers in his four biggest centers. As before, seven local sales representatives reported to the sales manager of each large center. Now, however, for the first time, all small-center salesmen also reported to a sales manager, located at a large center (*Exhibit 8*), receiving professional sales planning help and direction from this individual. Small-center managers reported to the MDO as before. Sales was the only function reorganized during this experiment.

The need for centralized, professional direction of the work of each center was one of the key motivators to the experiment, according to Newman. He felt it was very easy for ISG salesmen to become reactive, following current jobs through the center rather than developing new business:

> One of our centers, for instance, was inundated with work during the Vietnam war, doing ship conversions. Business surged and we really didn't pay enough attention to what the mix of that business was. When the war ended, the

EXHIBIT 8
Organization of Region "C" Sales Territory

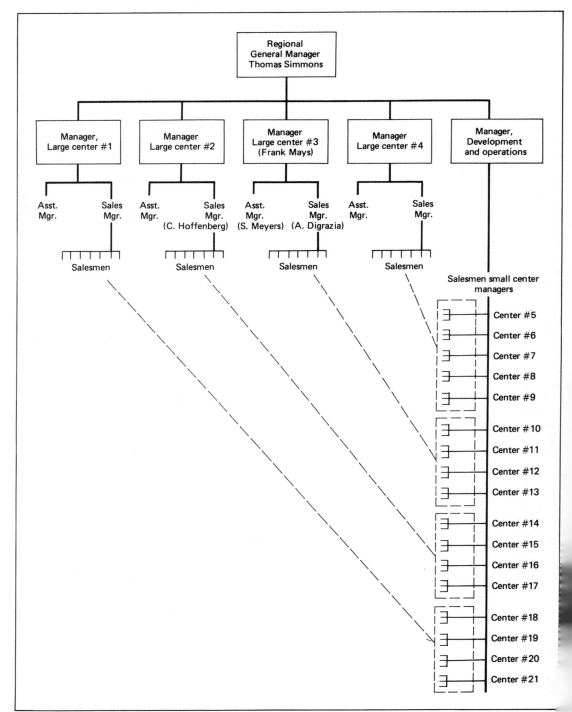

center manager found that he had lost the customers for the base service business in his territory.

When Newman and his colleagues analyzed Simmons's experiment after one year, they discovered mixed reactions. Many were enthusiastic. One sales manager noted that for the first time, sales managers were being encouraged to discuss their problems with other sales managers, and salesmen in small centers were getting coordinated, professional sales direction. Mays added:

Walls are definitely breaking down. Now the small-center manager is really interested in the New Mutley center because the salesmen are bringing some of his customers to us. Since the work flow is more directed, each center is beginning to develop an expertise. We're sending all the centrifuge work to Devonville, for example. It's still a local business, but it doesn't have to be as local for some services as for others. Customers are not reluctant to ship some major pieces of equipment a few hundred miles—for good work.

Throughout the experiment, however, MDOs continued to be compensated based on the profits of the centers reporting to them, and thus had a strong incentive to keep as many big jobs as possible in small centers. The fact that the large-center sales manager, who was now directing small-center sales, reported to the large-center manager, led to built-in conflict with the MDOs. Despite these constraints, sales figures supported Mays's optimistic impression of the territory concept; it was considered largely responsible for an annual rate of sales growth in Tom Simmons's region averaging 15 percent over the past three years, up from 12 percent for the six years prior to the reorganization.

The greatest opposition to the experiment came from small-center managers. Newman himself sympathized with their fears, commenting that, "You won't find anywhere else in Cunningham Inc. a situation where a young person can take on as much responsibility so early in his career." One small-center manager added:

You don't have to be a genius to look at this new type of organization and figure out that if we're not very careful down the road, my small center could be only a specialty arm of the territory and not a complete service organization. And what about the impact on customers? How can my salesmen prove to customers that they're keeping a close eye on a job several hundred miles away?

Mark O'Hara had even more misgivings. Although he favored more group help with time management, he felt his sales force had a greater need for down-to-earth personal assessment of the way they handled sales calls. Even under the territorial experiment, he believed, salesmen lacked the personal attention they needed; instead, they were invited to meetings and given general tips on how to sell technical service. Shaking his head, he added:

Under the territorial plan, my center will be in the New Mutley territory and Joe Green's center, which is only 100 miles away from mine, will be in a separate territory. Well, this means Joe is not supposed to send me any more of his business, and I'm supposed to send my overflow to New Mutley, where they have all kinds of guys running around—unit managers, foremen, project managers—who all have different interests. If I send a job to New Mutley, I've got to call the foreman myself and tell him. Mays and the unit manager aren't going to know about it. But when I sent my jobs to Joe, I knew he was going to be involved in them—and if he sent me one, I told my foreman and production people, it's Joe's job, let's get on it.

Internal Consultants' Study

It seemed logical to some planners that if the territorial concept were extended, service centers should no longer be measured as individual profit centers. Yet a corporate consulting team assigned to the problem detected much support for maintaining the small centers on an independent, full profit-and-loss basis. ISG did have excellent geographic coverage, as the consultants' report noted, and small centers were still capable of servicing a variety of customers; but because of their limited capability, small-center market share was not as large as it could be. Moreover, large centers tended to favor the bigger, more specialized jobs in their area and therefore had lower market share for smaller, more general service work. One consultant added privately to Newman:

> We're troubled by the parochial concerns of some small-center managers and salesmen. They have been seen to take business first, and worry later about how to do it. Small centers don't even have the capacity to handle large mechanical work, one of our biggest growth segments.

THE NEXT STEP

As he cleared his desk for the weekend, Newman was still brooding over McDonald's objections to the territorial reorganization. Maybe, he thought, the chief's fatherly feeling for the small-center managers is getting the best of his judgment. Or is it really impossible to implement this plan without hurting the small centers?

At that moment, the phone rang. "Any more ideas on what we talked about this morning, Adam?" McDonald asked.

"Well, nothing new right now," Newman replied. "As I see it, we have several choices. We can continue the territory experiment in Tom's region, maybe with some changes to keep small-center managers happy. We can extend the experiment to another region. We can drop the whole idea and run the group nationally, by service segments. Or maybe . . ."

McDonald interrupted:

> Or maybe we still haven't found the solution. Adam, I've directed this group for many years, and I've seen it grow very fast. As far as I'm concerned, we've grown because we've got a lot of service centers out there run by venturesome guys who'll take on any job they can get and somehow use their resources and ingenuity to get it done. I know our marketing and our field organization can be improved, but those entrepreneurial managers are the backbone of our business—and I'm not going to approve any change that lessens their enthusiasm for the job.

Dunfey Hotels Corporation

ROBERT J. KOPP
CHRISTOPHER H. LOVELOCK

The president of a chain of 22 rather dissimilar hotels has developed procedures for standardizing the strategic planning process employed by each hotel. A concerted internal training and educational effort is employed to get managers to understand and use this process.

"THE DUNFEY CHAIN: A SAVIOR OF DYING HOTELS" ran the headline above a half-page story in the financial section of the Sunday *New York Times* for June 22, 1980. The story began:

Suburban motor hotels. Sprawling convention hotels. Small and elegant city hotels. Foreign hotels. At first glance, the collection of properties under the Dunfey name seems an unmanageable mishmash.

Yet the Dunfey Hotels Corporation, which within the last year and a half has put together such a chain of unlikely properties, is getting to be known as a comer in the lodging indus-

try, with a knack for taking over aging hotels and returning them to profitability. In fact, Dunfey is a success story on top of a success story.

Success Story No. 1 goes back to the 1950s and features the Dunfeys, an Irish-American family of eight brothers from Hampton, N.H. The Dunfey boys, who started with a hot dog stand at Hampton Beach, built a multimillion-dollar New England hotel and restaurant chain.

Success Story No. 2 stars Jon Canas, brought in by the Dunfeys as chief operating officer and executive vice president in 1975. Mr. Canas . . . is a marketing man who is not afraid to step in to operate a hotel where others have

This case was prepared by Robert J. Kopp, Research Assistant, and Christopher H. Lovelock, Associate Professor. Copyright © 1981 by the President and Fellows of Harvard College. Harvard Business School Case 9-581-114. Reprinted by permission.

faltered. With Mr. Canas on board, Dunfey has become one of the nation's fastest growing hotel chains.

COMPANY HISTORY

After being discharged from military service shortly after World War II, John and William Dunfey opened a clam and hot dog stand on the boardwalk at Hampton Beach, New Hampshire. Soon John and William were joined in the business by four younger brothers. In 1954, the six brothers formed a partnership with their mother, and purchased Lamie's Tavern in Hampton, N.H., 3 miles from the original business in Hampton Beach.

In 1958, the family business headed in a new direction when a 32-room motor inn was constructed adjacent to Lamie's Tavern. Further acquisitions followed. By 1968, Dunfey Family Corporation, as the firm was then known, either owned or managed 18 hotels in the eastern U.S. Many of these properties, including the original Lamie's Motor Inn, were operated as franchises of Sheraton Hotels, the nation's largest hotel corporation.

In 1969, Dunfey Family Corporation made two new moves. First, Dunfey's Tavern Restaurants were opened in four of the company's New England properties. Second, the company acquired its first downtown hotel by purchasing the historic Parker House in Boston. The experience gained in succeeding years in renovating and repositioning the Parker House was to play an important role in shaping the future growth strategy for the Dunfey hotel business.

Injection of New Capital and Management

To finance further expansion following the purchase of the Parker House, the Dunfey family sold the company to the Aetna Life Insurance Co. in 1970. Six years later it was acquired from Aetna by Aer Lingus, the national airline of Ireland. But throughout these changes in ownership, the Dunfey family maintained managerial control over the business, with Jack Dunfey continuing on as the chief executive officer.

During the early 1970s, a number of professional managers were hired. They included Jon Canas, who joined the company in 1975 as vice president of sales and marketing. Canas, a Frenchman by birth, had been educated at the Cornell School for Hotel Administration and also held an MBA from Northeastern University; he had worked for six years with the Hotel Corporation of America and, subsequently, four years with the Sheraton Corporation, where his most recent position had been vice president of sales and marketing for Sheraton's two international divisions—Europe/Africa/Middle East and Hawaii/Far East/Pacific.

A New Approach to Planning

Canas recalled how his experience with Sheraton had led him to develop a planning approach based on market segmentation for marketing widely diverse hotels:

About four years before coming to Dunfey, I was assigned the position of sales director of Sheraton's Hawaii Division, consisting at that time of seven hotels. Since I had no previous experience in the day-to-day operation of the selling function as such, I decided to approach the job from a planning point of view. I began immediately to ask those questions, the answers to which would result in a better understanding of the market: Why do people come to Hawaii? What kind of hotel experience are they looking for? What does competition currently offer? Are there segments of consumers who differ in their needs for the level and quality of service? The more I worked on it, the more I could see practical solutions evolving out of this approach.

In Hawaii, at that time, virtually the only thing standardized about the Sheraton properties was the Sheraton name. The individual hotels varied widely in terms of size, age, location, rates, and types of customers. Faced with marketing such a diverse portfolio of properties, I was forced into understanding market segmentation. In the hotel business, this translates into offering different types of hotels for different types of customers . . . the idea really isn't revolutionary but you must remember that it ran against the tide of an industrywide move toward standardization of the "product"—a move which was clearly at the heart of the corporate strategies of most chains. . . . We were very successful in Hawaii. Not only did current properties perform well, but two years later our territory was expanded to include several new and existing hotels in the Far East and the Pacific.

When the Dunfey opportunity came up, a friend of mine in the industry told me that, as a group, the Dunfey properties were "a mixed bag" of hotels, widely diverse in location and service level. Several had generally reached the end of their life cycle. I could see some similarities with the Hawaii situation. I took the job partially to see whether the planning approach I had developed was really successful or whether I had just been lucky in Hawaii.

Dunfey Hotel Properties

Since purchasing the Parker House, the Dunfeys had continued to acquire additional properties and management contracts as the opportunities presented themselves.[1] In 1972, for instance, when Aetna Life Insurance acquired Royal Coach Motor Inns, Dunfey was hired to manage four units of this chain, each located on a major suburban highway in Atlanta, Dallas, Houston, and San Mateo, California, respectively. Each was built in an exterior style reminiscent of sixteenth century English Tudor, set off against a round, stonefaced, castellated tower, while the hotel interiors were decorated in a Scottish clan theme. The previous owners had gone bankrupt.

By mid-1980, Dunfey Hotels fully or partially owned, leased, or managed 22 properties in the United States and Europe, containing a total of 8,950 rooms (*Exhibit 1*). Fourteen of these properties had been part of the Dunfey organization for six years or more. Each hotel was managed by a general

[1]Between 1975 and 1980, the company had discontinued its relationship with twelve units. This turnover included properties that no longer fitted in with the Dunfey product line, either because of product, market, or owners' objectives. The properties replacing them tended to be larger and more important hotels.

manager who headed an executive operating committee (EOC) of department heads.

The Dunfey inns and hotels were divided into four groups, each directed by a group director of operations (*Exhibit 2* shows a corporate organization chart). These groups were as follows:

1. Dunfey Classic & Luxury Hotels (four properties: the Parker House, Boston: the Ambassador East, Chicago; the Berkshire Place, New York; and The Marquette, Minneapolis).
2. Dunfey Major Meeting & Convention Hotels (seven properties, located in Atlanta, Dallas, Houston, Cape Cod, San Mateo, New York, and Washington).
3. Dunfey Inns and Airport Hotels (nine properties; located in New England and Pennsylvania).
4. International Hotels (two properties, located in London and Paris).

Some of the airport hotels and motor inns were affiliated, for marketing purposes only, with another chain (Sheraton or Howard Johnson). Although this affiliation had the advantage of linking the inns to national advertising campaigns and toll-free telephone reservation numbers, it did nothing for the visibility of the Dunfey organization.

Between 1974 and 1979, average occupancy, systemwide, increased from 56 percent to 72 percent. A financial summary, showing total revenues and operating profits for all U.S. units in the Dunfey organization, both owned and managed, appears below:

Dunfey Hotels Corporation Financial Summary (U.S. units only)

Year	Total Revenues	Operating Profit
1976	$ 58 million	$ 7 million
1977	72 million	9 million
1978	88 million	16 million
1979	120 million	21 million
1980 (est.)	165 million	34 million

Jon Canas and the Dunfey "System"

When Canas joined Dunfey in May 1975, the company had a marketing staff, but not

EXHIBIT 1
Properties Owned or Managed by Dunfey Hotels, October 1980

Group	Type	Property	Location	Year Acquired	Status*	No. of Rooms
1	Classic Hotels	Ambassador East	Chicago, IL	1977	P	300
		Berkshire Place	New York, NY	1978	P	500
		Marquette	Minneapolis, MN	1979	M	270
		Parker House	Boston, MA	1969	F	550
2	Meeting and Convention Hotels	Dunfey Atlanta Hotel	Atlanta, GA	1971	F	400
		Dunfey Dallas Hotel	Dallas, TX	1971	F	650
		Dunfey Houston Hotel	Houston, TX	1971	L	450
		Dunfey San Mateo Hotel	San Mateo, CA	1971	F	300
		Dunfey Hyannis Resort & Conference Center	Cape Cod, MA	1972	F	250
	Other Metropolitan Hotels	New York Statler	New York, NY	1979	P	1,800
		The Shoreham	Washington, D.C.	1979	P	900
3	Inns	Howard Johnson's Motor Inn	Newton, MA	1970	L	275
		Sheraton Inn and Lamie's Tavern	Hampton, NH	1958	F	30
		Sheraton Lexington	Lexington, MA	1967	F	120
		Sheraton N.E. Philadelphia	Philadelphia, PA	1973	F	200
		Sheraton, Tobacco Valley	Windsor, CT	1968	F	130
		Sheraton Wayfarer	Manchester, NH	1962	F	200
	Airport Hotels	Sheraton Airport Inn	Philadelphia, PA	1974	M	350
		Sheraton Inn	South Portland, ME	1973	F	130
		Sheraton Airport Inn	Warwick, RI	1973	F	125
4	International Hotels	London Tara Hotel	London, England	1976	F	850
		Hotel Commodore	Paris, France	1979	L	170
	TOTAL: 22 Hotels					8,950 Rooms

*Key: F = Fully owned by Dunfey Hotels
P = Partially owned by Dunfey Hotels (joint venture with management contract)
L = Leased by Dunfey Hotels
M = Strictly management contract

SOURCE: Company records.

398

EXHIBIT 2
Corporate Organization Chart, December 1980

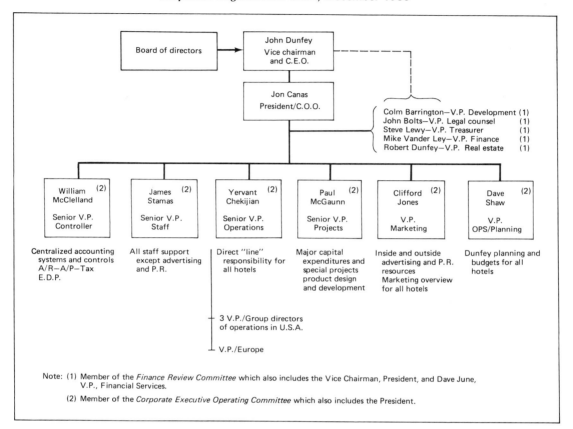

Note: (1) Member of the *Finance Review Committee* which also includes the Vice Chairman, President, and Dave June, V.P., Financial Services.

(2) Member of the *Corporate Executive Operating Committee* which also includes the President.

an organized marketing effort. Recalled Canas:

> The operation was characterized by extremely tight cost control, declining occupancy, and declining market share. Internally, many units were perceived to be at the end of their life cycle. We moved quickly to take some specific actions which paid off, and we were helped along by an improving economy beginning in 1976. Group sales doubled in three years and occupancy went from below the industry average to above.

In reviewing the specific areas of the business that the company had concentrated on, Canas divided the years 1975–80 into three distinct periods:

Our greatest need during 1975 and 1976 was to build occupancy. I don't have to tell you that profit in the hotel business comes from selling rooms, and we did everything possible to "keep the lights on," as they say in the industry. This meant going after any and all types of business, including lower rated (in terms of revenue-per-room night) market segments. As an example, we found early success in attracting what we call "training and destiny" business. This is primarily in-residence programs centered around training sessions, often lasting five to eight weeks. One example would be a flight attendant training program by an airline. Such programs are typically repeated many times over the course of a year by the same company, and effectively amount to an extended rental of space in the hotel. The meetings are planned far in advance and don't require elaborate arrangements such as banquet facilities; demand is fairly price sensitive. Of course, as occupancy began to improve, we instituted a policy of actively pursuing higher rated segments and gradually substituting this new business for the lower rated segments.

During 1977 and 1978, we embarked on a major program to improve the overall appearance of our properties. In most cases this involved renovating, restoring, repositioning, and remarketing individual properties. Basically, we made the decision to *reject* the life cycle assumptions which prevailed in the firm at the time. The Parker House in Boston is a good example of this philosophy. The Parker House was an old property which had a deteriorating and outdated physical plant, declining occupancy, and had been given up on by the previous management. We saw an opportunity in the hotel's heritage—and the fact that it occupied an excellent location in a metropolitan area where quality lodging was in short supply. The result of this renovation was dramatic increases in occupancy and profitability.

Now as room occupancy rates topped-out on a companywide basis, we sought revenue in other departments. We went into a very creative period where new restaurants and lounges were created. We didn't just open a room, we created a *concept*. A key product of our "creative period" is the Tingles lounge and discotheques located in several of our hotels; these discos were unique in that the sound, loud over the dance floor, but softer at surrounding tables, allowed people to sit, relax, and converse. As an example of the impact on revenue, the conversion of the lounge in the Atlanta Hotel to a Tingles took food and beverage revenue from $8–9,000 per week to over $25,000 weekly in that room.

In 1979 we entered a new phase. With both room and food and beverage (F&B) revenues peaking, we turned our attention to better cost management to maintain profit growth. We brought in an outside consulting firm to help us develop a rather sophisticated cost management/payroll efficiency system. The system was tested at the Parker House in 1977–78 and was expanded to our other units in 1978–79. In addition, we sought cost savings in centralized purchasing and in better heat, light, and power management.

So in looking back, I suppose you could say we concentrated our efforts on different areas of the business at different times. We were consciously trying to improve the "state of the art" in all areas of the hotel business, and I think the results show that we succeeded.

The situation facing Dunfey in 1975 was surprisingly similar to that of the Sheraton situation in Hawaii when I became sales manager: the mixed bag of food and lodging businesses grouped under the Dunfey corporate name ran the gamut from small, outlying motels to larger urban hotels. In fact, unlike Sheraton, the Dunfey group lacked a common name and identity—there were Sheratons, a Howard Johnson's, a group of four hotels purchased from Royal Coach renamed Dunfey Hotels, as well as several properties which stood alone in terms of identification. Thus, it was out of a need to simplify the management task that the Dunfey Planning Process and the Dunfey Management Approach evolved.

In essence, our approach to marketing planning is based on the belief that there exists a unique strategy or market position for each property which will maximize revenues in the long term. While other hoteliers were focusing on product efficiency and standardization, at Dunfey our commonality became the planning process. Of course, we've come a long way since 1975. In particular, we have grouped our hotels in a way where we can take advantage of some economies of scale in marketing. However, our basic approach is still at the individual hotel marketing level.

THE DUNFEY PLANNING PROCESS

DISCIPLINE BEING IMPOSED

As a first step toward development of a management system for all the Dunfey properties, Canas had drafted a series of internal documents. "The Dunfey Management Approach" and "The Way We Work" enunciated a management philosophy based on the conviction that each hotel had to recognize and satisfy certain needs from its customers, owners, and employees. The third document, titled "The Dunfey Planning Process," laid out a clearly defined system of annual and quadrimester (four-month) planning, dealing with objectives and strategies relating to customers, owners, and employees.

Canas believed that the planning system

for any given unit must begin with the needs of one or more clearly identified customer segments which, when related to the nature and extent of competition, served to determine the positioning the hotel would have in the marketplace. Time and again, remarked Canas, he had seen chains, which had standardized their offerings against certain market segments, expand unsuccessfully into geographic areas that already had an excess of hotel rooms serving those same segments.

He emphasized that profitability in the hotel business was primarily based on the revenue side and stressed the importance of good rooms merchandising through a specific planning process which was evaluated with the help of a performance measure he called Room Sales Efficiency (RSE).[2]

The key to good rooms merchandising and to good cost control, he said, was accurate forecasting of demand at all times of the week and all seasons of the year.

Every year, the management of each Dunfey hotel had to prepare both an annual plan and a series of three quadrimester (four-month) plans, referred to as Q-Plans. The planning process for each hotel proceeded through four basic steps, supported by appropriate documentation.

1. Assess supply-demand relationship—by examining the type (e.g., conventions, tourists, business travelers, etc.) and quantity of customers available in a given geographic market. A careful evaluation was made of the positioning of competitive hotels against each segment.

2. Determine where Dunfey *should be* in terms of the market position of the hotel as a whole, and of each food and beverage outlet within that hotel.

3. Identify the gap between the hotel's current position and the desired position.

4. Structure the measures required to move the hotel and F&B outlets toward the desired market position. Requests for capital expenditures—to add to or improve facilities—were a key element of Step 4.

The outcome of Steps 2, 3, and 4 was a "Mission Statement" for each hotel which had as its input the supply/demand relationship, and as its output a set of specific operating objectives for all members of the field operations team.

Exhibit 3 summarizes the planning process. In essence, broad strategic goals embodied in the Mission Statement were "stepped down" into key result areas (KRAs)—specific actions to be undertaken in support of unit or departmental objectives—via a series of annual planning forms referred to as Y1s (unit objectives and strategies), Y2s (departmental objectives and strategies), and Y3s (specific goals for each unit and department objective). These goals formed the basis for the employees' incentive plan. Similar planning efforts, with a shorter-term focus, were undertaken each quadrimester; these were referred to as "Q-Plans."

The planning process for each unit (hotel) was carried out by that unit's executive operating committee (EOC) with the participation of the corporate planning committee (CPC). The unit EOC usually consisted of the general manager (GM), assistant general manager or resident manager, sales director, rooms manager, food and beverage (F&B) manager, and personnel director. The CPC comprised Jon Canas, the controller and five vice presidents in charge of operations, staff support, product design, profit planning, and marketing. The CPC was assisted in its review of individual unit plans by the vice president-sales, the corporate F&B director, and the relevant group director of operations.

Each group director of operations was responsible for coordinating the preparation of key planning documents by each of the unit EOCs in his group of hotels. The various documents were submitted to the corporate planning committee for approval in a succession of steps carried out from July 1 to November 1 of each year. Units were required to submit an outline of their pre-

[2]RSE equals the total room sales revenue received during a period divided by the total revenues that could have been obtained if all available rooms had been sold at the maximum price.

EXHIBIT 3

Dunfey Hotels Unit Planning Process

OBJECTIVE: Corporate Planning Committee (CPC) to provide corporate input and direction for each unit's 1981 Mission and Annual Plan; the CPC includes the Corporate Executive Operating Committee (see *Exhibit 2*) plus, as appropriate, Vice President—Sales, Corporate Food and Beverage Director, and the relevant Group Director of Operations (GDO).

A. *For the CPC to do this, it needs:*

   1. *Marketing Assessment, which includes:*

      a. 1–3 page summary of supply/demand analysis.

      b. 1–page report to indicate if S/D calls for a significant change in strategies or product.

      c. Historical and Proposed (1981) Market Segmentation and F&B and total revenues.

   2. *Financial Assessment, which includes:*

      a. 1 page, outlining:

         1. Corporate Objectives for the Unit.

         2. Are we meeting Corporate objectives (if not, why)?

      b. Historical Financial Summary for 3–5 years showing financial results and key statistics.

   3. *Outside Owners' Assessment:**

      a. Page outlining outside owners' Objectives.

      b. Assessment of current results.

B. The CPC will review the above material resulting in a memorandum to the GDO and Unit EOC outlining:

   1. Unit is on track and should not change direction.

O.K. TO PROCEED
TO ITEMS C AND D

   2. Unit is on track except for certain items (outlined) which should be corrected (no major direction change).

NOT O.K. TO PROCEED
TO C AND D

   3. Unit is off track seriously—people will be assigned to assist in making major direction changes.

C. The Director of Marketing and GDO will then write the Unit Mission Statement and send it to the units (after CPC has approved the wording).

D. Unit EOC will then prepare Y-1, Y-2, and Y-3 (GDO and Corporate Staff must review and approve).

E. CPC will have final approval on Item D.

*For properties managed by Dunfey Hotels for outside owners.

---

liminary thinking in July in order that the CPC could provide early feedback on the appropriateness of tentative plans.

Based on these early submissions, the CPC had, by early August, classified individual hotel plans as:

- "green," signifying that the unit was on track and should not change direction;
- "yellow," signifying that the unit was on track except for certain items (outlined) which should be corrected (no major direction change);
- "red," indicating that the unit was seriously off

EXHIBIT 3 (continued)

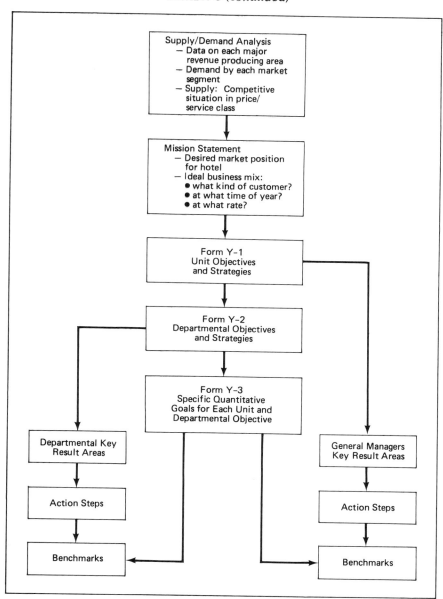

track—corporate staff would be assigned to assist in making major direction changes.

Each unit EOC, working with their group director, was required to prepare a Mission Statement addressing the following questions:

- What type of customer are we aiming for?
- Where do we stand versus the competition?
- What are we trying to be?
- Where should we focus our efforts to satisfy targeted customers, as well as dealing with owners/corporate needs and also employees' needs?

The hotel business, noted Canas, was operations oriented, involving a multitude of basic activities that were repeated again and again, yet could be done in a number of different ways. He continued:

We believe that people carry out functions in different ways depending on the purpose they have in mind. The GM may have one purpose, the F&B manager another—and neither may be in concert with the corporation. So, as simplistic as it sounds, the Mission Statement integrates the activity of unit and corporate management. Any management team that has succeeded in crystallizing and communicating the mission of the hotel will find the various departments pulling together, in the same direction, to create the sought-after hotel experience for the customer. It provides more fulfillment for the employees and better results for the owners and the corporation. Also, the process helps achieve agreement between corporate and unit management.

The Ideal Business Mix

"The most important part of the mission," Canas noted, "deals with what we call the IBM—ideal business mix. This defines the customer segments we will direct our sales efforts toward at various times of the year." He elaborated:

There are many ways to segment the market. The first, of course, is the way we categorize business on our control reports: for instance, pure transient, regular corporate group, bus tours, and so forth. In addition, we segment our marketing effort by geography and by industry, and we assign sales coverage to whatever groupings seem to make sense for a particular area.

The point is that, once we identify our desired segments, it becomes a simpler task to set objectives for the operating departments—such as sales, rooms, and food and beverage. We've found that certain segments of the market tend to have common needs—or "reason to buy." Very often the marketing challenge is to define these needs: is the customer primarily interested in price, in location, in facilities, in social status—or is he just looking for a hotel consistent with his personal tastes in furnishings and food?

The ideal business mix also carries implications for our capital spending and renovation and maintenance decisions. We often say, "We could reach this segment *if* we had certain facilities." The *if* here is important: we may have an intended market position, but we must have programs and facilities to reach it. The restoration and revitalization of the Parker House taught us a lot about repositioning—a lesson we have been able to apply to other properties in the chain.

After we have outlined our goals by type of customer, amount of room nights, period of year and rates, then we ask two further questions: (1) How do we market—how do we reach these customers? And (2) How do we deliver? (And deliver at a *profit*?)

Our Rooms Merchandising Plan and the supporting Account Coverage Program guide our sales efforts. As part of the Rooms Merchandising Plan, you have your ideal business mix prioritized by segments and by lead time in their respective buy decisions. If, for example, a convention cancels 9 months ahead of time, then you go after alternative segments. It's like starting all over again. But, at least you will have identified in advance where you are going to go to make up that business.

Most hotels hire a sales manager and tell him or her to "fill the rooms." This usually works in the short term, but is not a good business approach in the long term. Customers contribute to the atmosphere or hotel experience; you should choose your clientele selectively to match your market position. In our system we specify: (1) a certain kind of customer at (2) a certain time of year at (3) a certain rate.

With the Rooms Merchandising Plan you know what to ask sales and reservations people to do. In general, in the industry, salespeople often don't know who to see, they don't know how many rooms are available, and they don't know what rate to charge. At Dunfey we provide these guidelines as closely as possible in order to maximize our profitability and productivity.

In general, we find there is an inverse relationship in the lead time between the buy decision and consumption by various market segments and the rate we can get. In other words, the farther in advance groups book the cheaper the rate usually is. So, most hotels used to book business way in advance, without consideration of more desirable business which could be booked later on.

So, the moral for the periods of time where we anticipate strong demand—and since we have a limited supply of rooms—is that we shouldn't sell on a first-come, first-served basis. For better profits, we plan the IBM proportion which is set aside for long lead time groups and for shorter lead time groups, and then save some capacity for higher rated walk-in business.

When business for the future begins to pick up, we try to monitor whether we're attracting our target customers. We want to build our business with the correct market segments—not just fill rooms—because we're building an image for the future and the profile of customers we take in has a tremendous impact on the position of the hotel. Of course, when occupancy is very low, oftentimes we will sell rooms to less desirable segments, but as we build occupancy, we can become more selective in our marketing.

Now, talking about the Account Coverage Program, in a lot of cases we find that 20 percent of the accounts give us 80 percent of our business. Therefore, it is important to identify, qualify, and quantify all our accounts to set proper sales priorities. It also allows us to know what accounts we'll have to approach to get what business. Moreover, we identify what "buy decisions" exist for each individual account. For instance, for corporate groups it's usually either a "price buy," a "location buy," or a "facilities buy."

Also, our sales department provides a significant amount of information and feedback on our supply-demand studies. Through the direct salespeople we know what to sell, to whom, and at what rates. We truly use "need satisfaction" as a sales approach to sell and get repeat sales.

A MANAGEMENT ISOLATION MEETING

An isolation meeting—so designated because the participants were isolated from the interruptions of the home office—was held in the early fall of 1979 to discuss the status of the 1980 planning process and to reinforce understanding of Dunfey management philosophies among the top 15 corporate operations and marketing executives.

Jon Canas opened the meeting by reiterating some of the basic precepts of the Dunfey Management Approach:

The Dunfey Management Approach is companywide. It includes not only the concepts inherent in the way we look at our business, but also includes the process and the systems through which we operate. We must have agreement at top on our philosophies. That means amongst all of us. And then we must attempt to achieve concurrence at lower levels.

What we're saying is that the traditional "get results and we don't care how you do it" doesn't work at Dunfey. We *do care* how you do it! We're concerned with the manner in which results are obtained.

The mission becomes the point of reference for the selection of unit objectives and strategies. The process to be followed by the EOC is to ask: "If we were totally successful in reaching our mission, what are the desirable things that would happen, or desirable conditions that would prevail (positive indicators of success), and what are the undesirable conditions that should be eliminated (negative indicators of success)?"

It's here that we should use the scenario approach: That is, take any aspect of the operations—such as the guest experience at the front desk—and talk through what would happen if we were successful. Each department and facet of the business should be able to visualize what the operation would look like if fully successful. Out of this come the specific action steps that we can focus on as our key result areas—KRAs.

Each department must understand what was expected of it, continued Canas, and how it contributed to the whole. "Sometimes," he observed, "we move too fast from the mission to our planning structure without understanding the implications of what we're doing."

Pushing the Dunfey Approach Down the Organization

Following a brief discussion of the basic approach, Canas turned to his area of principal concern.

Overall, I think you will agree we have been successful in establishing the Dunfey business philosophy among members of the organization down through the level of the EOCs of each hotel. The challenge I want to discuss with you today is in modifying the behavior of people farther down in the organization. In order to convey our philosophy and our approach to the customer, we must push a commitment to our management style down to the very lowest levels of the organization. This is a particular problem when, like us, you take on many new people during the year.

Also, we have had some areas of confusion, such as in defining KRAs. When we talk about key result areas, we're talking about the 20 percent of items against which we can devote effort which will account for 80 percent of the success in reaching our goals. A good selection of KRAs requires a narrow focus and clear delineation of those few key areas which will make the biggest difference in our results at the end of the year.

Now, for instance, if the food and beverage manager gives us 36 things he wants to do, these are *not* KRAs. Most of these are just doing his job; after we get through those, there are probably one or two KRAs which we can identify which will really make a quantum improvement in his operations. If he works 14 hours a day and doesn't accomplish his KRAs, he has failed. But if a manager has a list of 17 KRAs, he just doesn't understand our planning process!

Yervant Chekijian, at the time group director of operations for the three Dunfey Classic Hotels, caught Canas's eye and offered an illustration:

I can point to an example of that at the Ambassador East. The engineers had many KRAs but I noticed the stoppers in the sinks weren't working. I asked them to get to the basic problems like stoppers in the sink before they submitted a bunch of lofty KRAs. And I mentioned to them that they shouldn't just say they're going to fix the stoppers, they should propose an action plan as follows:

1. Inspection.
2. Locate the problems.
3. Define the scope of work.
4. Allocate man-hours.

5. Commit to having the job completed by a specific date.

Canas nodded agreement and added:

What we need is a scenario documented for each member of the operating team. We need to describe a certain level of service, start setting some standards of guest expectations, and relate the scenarios to these. Otherwise, the people we are dealing with at the lower levels easily forget the basics that we are expecting from them.

Canas turned towards the group directors of operations. "I guess you could say that our planning process and programs have given Dunfey people a common language. It also means we can transfer people from property to property and they will know the system." He went on to say, "One of the things I need to know is how well this planning process is actually being implemented by the EOC in each of our hotels."

Yervant Chekijian answered:

At the Parker House, the EOC meets on a weekly basis to go through the Q-Plan and review benchmarks. At the Ambassador East, on the other hand, they work with it, but they have a tendency to be overwhelmed by what happens during the day—putting out fires, if you will. They usually "intend" to use the plan when things are "normal." One general manager did the plan three times—over and over again—threw up his hands, and asked me if he should get back to work. My answer was, "How can you work without a plan?"

A regional director of sales observed that in some ways the plan was "sophisticated—even scary—but it's very natural when you get into it." Chekijian responded that the plan would not get used if its content wasn't real. The group directors, he said, must be responsible for ensuring that individual hotels not only understood the plan but had also proposed realistic goals and action steps.

Canas then turned the discussion towards the question of contingency planning:

We didn't predict the slowdown in business resulting from the 1979 gasoline shortages until nine months into the year. Very frankly, the oil crisis just wasn't predicted, so we didn't have a "Plan B" in marketing. However, we had one in cost control, which is a lot easier to implement. Another question is, how do you build in sales flexibility when rooms merchandising calls for such advance bookings?

Jurgen Demisch, group director of operations for Dunfey's Inns division, offered a solution: "If sales aren't coming in, we can go to the sales force and ask them to use their account coverage program and get more business from the segments lower down the list."

"So, what you're saying," responded Canas, "is that we already have a system. We have sales action plans, pricing flexibility, ability to cut costs over a 30-day period, and an account coverage program. What we need now is to fully learn to use these things."

"Overall, I see our planning as an evolutionary process," remarked Demisch. "As people learn to work with the plan, they become Dunfeyized, and then when these people are promoted, they can get into the plan from day 1 at any new property."

"We must get the planning process down to the third level: to restaurant managers, engineers, etc.—down the organization," Canas emphasized. "What I think we need for your division, Jurgen, is a simplification of The Way We Work. All the ingredients must be there and we don't want to short-circuit it—but Jurgen, we must find a way to have a simplified planning process for a division like yours where you take in so many new people in a short period of time. After all, the basic objective is to be professional innkeepers."

Chuck Barren, group director of operations for several medium-sized hotels, entered the discussion:

At Hyannis we have a very structured, Dunfeyized team. They are using the planning process and they're moving on without looking back to where they were. We've had a new sales manager in there for 10 days and he already has an excellent plan for the first quarter. The planning system was readily applied here and worked very well.

Baltimore was initially a distress property, and we said, "Do we really want to work from a checklist?" After three months, we went into the planning process. The owners sat in at our planning meetings and it really helped *them* understand our side of the business and to set mutual objectives.

It's clear that the planning process tends to break down where we don't have Dunfeyized people. And where this occurs, we should have a checklist or a simplified version of the plan to use in situations like takeovers.

Conclusion of Meeting

In answer to a question from one participant, Canas conceded that Dunfey had indeed developed its own management language, which made it hard to acculturate new people, and especially to bring in top management people at the operations level. On the other hand, he felt that the Dunfey process still allowed individual styles to come through, and in fact, called on the creativity of each manager. "The process provides no solutions," he stated, "only managers do!"

Before the meeting adjourned Canas reiterated the essence of the corporate operating mission, which he read to participants:

To create and/or maintain the structure that provides for the appropriate satisfaction of specifically defined needs of targeted customers, owners, and employees.

He added:

The key here is that we're talking about a structure—and a structure has strength. It has durability. It's an entity which must be full and self-supporting. The structure is our management philosophy and our planning process which, when implemented properly, will provide for the needs of owners, employees, and customers.

INDEX